PASSPORT TO PARIS

and

LOS ANGELES POEMS

PASSPORT TO PARIS

and

LOS ANGELES POEMS

Vernon Duke

Poems translated
and Introduction by
Boris Dralyuk

PAUL DRY BOOKS
Philadelphia 2025

A number of the poetic translations in this volume originally appeared in the journals *Arc Poetry*, *World Literature Today*, and *Ocean State Review*, and one was read on *The Slowdown* by Major Jackson. The translator thanks Jackson, as well as the editors Luba Markovskaia, Chris Johnson, Daniel Simon, and Charles Kell, for their enthusiasm and support. He also thanks the generous support of the Tulsa Artist Fellowship, which allowed him to complete this project. Above all, he thanks Kay Duke Ingalls for her trust and her warmth.

First Paul Dry Books Edition, 2025

Paul Dry Books, Inc.
Philadelphia, Pennsylvania
www.pauldrybooks.com

Printed in the United States of America

Library of Congress Control Number: 2025932839

ISBN 978-1-58988-204-1

To the memory of my mother.

Contents

LOS ANGELES POEMS

Introduction

Boris Dralyuk

What can I say about Vernon Duke that he hasn't said himself, with greater charm than I could ever muster, in the memoir you now hold in your hands? A contemporary of his friend Sergei Prokofiev, his nemesis Igor Stravinsky, and his fellow polyglot Vladimir Nabokov, the Russian-American composer, songwriter, and poet was a cosmopolitan raconteur of the old school. I am tempted simply to get out of the way and let him cast his verbal spell, as he did one evening in the late 1950s in the company of music historian Arnold Shaw:

> After [Burt] Bacharach and David became hot in pop, show composer Vernon Duke asked me to arrange a meeting with lyricist Hal David. The three of us spent part of an afternoon together, during which Duke, who was a fast, bright, nervous talker, regaled David with anecdotes, analyzed music trends, discussed different lyricists with whom he had worked (an impressive list), and pitched for their collaborating. It was quite a performance and Hal, who is not chit-chat verbal, was overwhelmed by Duke's display of enthusiasm. Afterward, Duke exclaimed: "I had him mesmerized, didn't I?"[1]

Duke might as well have handed David a copy of *Passport to Paris*, the strangely mesmerizing pages of which overflow with his colorful anecdotes, acerbic comments on musical trends, and uniquely vivid accounts of collaboration with the giants of classical and popular music, from Sergei Diaghilev and George Balanchine to the Gershwin brothers. *Passport to Paris* appeared in 1955, when Duke was 52, and the book to which it

1. Arnold Shaw, *The Rockin' 50s: The Decade that Transformed the Pop Music Scene* (New York: Da Capo Press, 1987), 32.

begs to be compared is Nabokov's *Speak, Memory*, which first appeared four years earlier, when that émigré author was 52. The contours of Duke's and Nabokov's stories are strikingly similar.

Both were precocious children raised in opulence by noble families in the Russian Empire (Nabokov in and near St. Petersburg, Duke largely in Ukraine); both were forced to flee their homeland in the wake of the October Revolution of 1917 and the ensuing Civil War, along with as many as two million of their countrymen (Nabokov from Crimea, Duke from Odesa); and both established successful dual careers abroad (Nabokov as a bilingual author, Duke as a composer of classical and popular music). They even share a name; Vernon Duke was born Vladimir Dukelsky and continued to sign that name to his "serious" music. Yet the contrast between Duke's and Nabokov's approaches to autobiography is equally striking.

Duke's lightness of tone bordering on carelessness, his conversational looseness, would have made a sophisticated craftsman like Nabokov wince. But one of the great values of Duke's account lies precisely in this lightness and looseness: his irrepressible buoyancy counterbalances the well-worn image, still haunting our culture, of the morose, melancholy East European émigré, mourning irrecoverable losses. *Passport to Paris* is not without its wistful notes, but its author keeps his focus on what he's gained over the years—no small amount of success, no dearth of wisdom, a wide network of luminous friends and colleagues, a handful of hilarious grudges, and winning stories to beat the band.

There is another important difference between *Speak, Memory* and *Passport to Paris*. Their authors might have been the same age when their memoirs were published, but they were at different points in their respective careers. Nabokov's American masterpieces—*Lolita*, *Pnin*, and *Pale Fire*—still lay ahead of him, while Duke had already made his major contributions to music. Those contributions had come in a variety of genres, much to the chagrin—as Duke grumbles at the very start of this book—of musical critics in both the classical and popular camps. It must be said, however, that his classical compositions, though highly accomplished and enjoyable, would not in themselves have earned him eternal fame.[2] His claim to immortality rests on the irresistible tunes he managed to lodge in the Great American Songbook.

2. The best overview of Duke's career in classical music, from his early triumph with the ballet *Zèphire et Flore* (1925), which Sergei Diaghilev commissioned

Three of those tunes—"April in Paris" (1932, with lyrics by Yip Harburg), "I Can't Get Started" (1936, with lyrics by Ira Gershwin), and "Autumn in New York" (1934, with lyrics of his own)—are enshrined in Ted Gioia's definitive *The Jazz Standards* (2012), and a third, "Taking a Chance on Love" (with lyrics by John La Touche and Ted Fetter), has been a hit for many artists since Ethel Waters introduced it as part of the all-Black cast of Duke's musical *Cabin in the Sky* (1940).[3] The stories behind the music are best told by Duke himself in these very pages, but a number of critics have highlighted the qualities that make his standards stand out. Of "Autumn in New York," Gioia writes:

> [T]his piece, more than any of his other popular efforts, seems to straddle the divide between conservatory ambitions and commercial considerations, especially in its unusual harmonic movement. When the song eventually resolves into F minor, you can look back and contemplate the intricacy and misdirection of a structure that never states that chord at any point in its first 24 bars. The melody, with its alternation of downward-stepping and upward-sweeping phrases, perfectly matches the emotional arc of the words.[4]

And he is just as full of praise for the lyrics: "Duke gets kudos for the daring of his wordplay. How many tunesmiths, seeking a rhyme for 'invit-

---

for the Ballets Russes, to his nasty feud with Stravinsky in the early 1960s, is Scott Holden's "The 'Adventures and Battles' of Vladimir Dukelsky (a.k.a. Vernon Duke)," *American Music* 28, no. 3 (Fall 2010), pp. 297–319. The essay that sparked the feud, "The Deification of Stravinsky," is collected in Duke's combative, entertaining, and enlightening book *Listen Here! A Critical Essay on Music Depreciation* (New York: Ivan Obolensky, 1963), which, like *Passport to Paris*, has long been out of print.

3. See Ted Gioia, *The Jazz Standards: A Guide to the Repertoire* (Oxford: Oxford University Press, 2012), pp. 21–24, 156–58. "I Can't Get Started," which was recorded with unparalleled intelligence and emotional intensity by the short-lived trumpeter Bunny Berrigan in 1937, is the subject of an excellent monograph by George Harwood Phillips, *The Tunesmith & The Lyricist: Vernon Duke, Ira Gershwin, and the Making of a Standard* (Camano Island, WA: Coyote Hill Press, 2016).

4. Gioia, p. 23.

ing,' would settle on the syntactically challenged 'thrill of first-nighting'? Or, with New Yorkers in mind, envision 'dreamers with empty hands' sighing for 'exotic lands'?" Indeed, only an émigré—and not just any émigré, but one as witty and as comfortable in his bicultural skin as Duke.

It should come as no surprise that the man behind the lyrics to "Autumn in New York" also dabbled in poetry. The truth is that he did more than dabble. Duke had begun to write verse as a teenager in Ukraine, and he refined his skills in the early days of his exile, in Constantinople, where he formed a "Guild of Poetry" with one of the most original Russophone poets of his generation, the tragically short-lived Boris Poplavsky (1903–1935). Duke paints a colorful portrait of "Russian Constantinople" in his American memoir, but his touching memories of Poplavsky were, appropriately enough, committed to Russian verse. My translation of that elegy follows the text of the memoir, along with eighteen other poems Duke composed in the last happy decade of his life, which he spent in California with his late love, Kay McCracken Duke Ingalls.

A mezzo-soprano from Bozeman, Montana, who had come to Southern California to learn from Lotte Lehmann, Kay was less than half Duke's age when they met in the mid-1950s. The romance was a whirlwind, and the two tied the knot on October 29, 1957. Their wedding day is the subject of another of the translated poems at the end of this book, and I had the distinct pleasure of sharing my version with Kay over the phone a couple of years ago. Duke had told her that she'd inspired him to return to verse, and she vividly recalls picking up copies of the four collections he had printed by an émigré press in Munich in the 1960s—*The Sorrows of Elderly Werther* (1962), *Epistles* (1962), *Picture Gallery* (1965), and *A Trip Somewhere* (1968)—but their contents remained inaccessible to her, locked away in another language, for exactly six decades.

The poems these books contain range from Duke's earliest juvenilia to translations into Russian of everyone from Ezra Pound and Edna St. Vincent Millay to Ogden Nash and Lawrence Ferlinghetti. The best of his original poems, however, take in the new views and new experiences of life in the Southland, which also happens to be where I, another émigré from Ukraine, spent my youth and young adulthood. Much of the poetry by Duke's Russophone émigré peers is shot through with despair, but our man, though never blind to suffering, is dead set on enjoying himself. He infuses his portraits of faded starlets, frugal dowagers, gap-toothed beatniks, gyrating hippies, and short-order cooks with ironic humor and measured sympathy; however sad a state the world appears to be in now, the poet's tone suggests, he's seen worse. That tone is set by means of playful diction, jaunty rhythm, and clever rhyme—the specialties of songwriters. Lucky for me, Duke had left a template for what his verse would have sounded like had it been written in English. "Autumn in New York . . . It spells the thrill of first-nighting . . ." Lovingly attentive, sparklingly inventive, and enjoying every moment precisely because he knows it has to end.

Duke's journey ended suddenly on January 16, 1969, when he passed away while undergoing surgery for lung cancer. In his biography *Taking a Chance on Love: The Life and Music of Vernon Duke*, George Harwood Phillips quotes a letter the Russian-American musicologist and composer Nicolas Slonimsky sent to Kay upon learning of her husband's death:

> Dearest Kay—how can it be? Vernon, Vladimir, Dima—the most vital, the most imperishable, indestructible of my longtime friends, filling the world about him with wonderfully stimulating talk and action, marvelously gifted in so many different fields, full of intellectual and physical energy and inexhaustible vitality, establishing personal relationships in a vivid, lively, affectionate, assertive manner. . . . An enfilade of scenes passes before my mind. Fifty years! Kiev in 1919, Constantinople in 1920 and 1921, Paris, New York, Pacific Palisades. And Boston in between. I recall Vernon's sayings, his chuckles, his youthful triumphs in music, his amazing culture and eagerness for knowledge. There is no one like him in life, and I have a sense of loss that is a loss of a part of me that was related to Dima.[5]

That enfilade of scenes, that cosmopolitan culture, all captured in a vivid, lively, affectionate, assertive manner, are what await the first-time reader of *Passport to Paris*. Anyone with even a passing interest in the vanished worlds of Civil War-era Ukraine, of Russian Constantinople, of Montparnasse in the time of the Ballets Russes, and of Broadway and Tin Pan Alley during the golden age of popular song would be hard

5. Nicolas Slonimsky to Kay McCracken Duke, New York, January 18, 1969, Vernon Duke Collection, Music Division, Library of Congress, quoted in George Harwood Phillips, *Taking a Chance on Love: The Life and Music of Vernon Duke* (Norman: University of Oklahoma Press, 2019), p. 190.

pressed to find a more engaging tour guide than Vernon Duke. And once your tour is concluded, spread a blanket on the beach in Santa Monica, where

> [t]he smoke of time swirls like a curly cloud
> above the figure of a tanned old man,
> who lies with fingers laced behind his head.
> He smiles, recalling his unlikely story.
> America, Crimea—does it matter
> where I cross over into Purgatory?

Boris Dralyuk
University of Tulsa
June 2024

Passport to Paris

Illustrations

All illustrations will be found between pages 246 and 247.

CHAPTER I

I EMERGE

ACCORDING to *Who's Who,* I have spent my "entire career" (come, come, I'm still spending it) writing two kinds of music: the serious or unrewarding kind as Vladimir Dukelsky and the unserious but lucrative variety as Vernon Duke. Almost every interview I've ever had has brought forth some tired references to "the Jekyll and Hyde of Music," "the Two-Headed Janus of Music," etc. There have been quite a few cases of composers who successfully managed to write in both the high- and low-brow genre, but I am entirely unique in one respect. Gershwin always remained Gershwin whether he wrote *Porgy* or "I Got Rhythm"; Weill was easily recognizable as Weill whether he tackled *Mahagonny* or *One Touch of Venus;* and even Lennie Bernstein is his ingratiating self whether he tears into *Jeremiah* or *On the Town;* but Dukelsky in no way resembles Duke.

There isn't a note of jazz in my serious music, and there are no symphonic overtones to my musical-comedy output. I don't think that's anything to be proud of, and as a matter of fact, the wide gulf between the two styles has proven entirely too wide for most people's comfort, particularly for critics and fellow composers. It has often been said of George Gershwin that his Broadway enemies thought he belonged in Carnegie Hall, and his high-brow detractors kept repeating in print that he should never have left Broadway. This same attempt at pigeonholing has been applied even more severely in my case.

My versatility, far from being a boon, has in reality been infuriating to most musical people. Just why that is I have no way of knowing, but the critical boys seem to think there is something monstrous and unnatural about a composer writing two different kinds of music under two different names. It annoys them not to be able to say that I go slumming when writing jazz, and it annoys them still more not to be able to classify me as an ambitious peasant, gazing at the musical Olympus behind a Lindy's herring.

It is a matter of record that I have never been a critics' darling. In 1927, the era of "bright young people" and Oxford bags (trousers, not frumpy women), I, the slave of fashion, was never without a pair. Accordingly, when the late Serge Koussevitsky asked me to play a short and not very good piece of mine with his orchestra in Paris, I eagerly accepted, and crossed the Channel armed with the orchestra parts and my prize pair of striped trousers neatly tucked away in the week-end bag. The concert was to be on Saturday afternoon, and a morning jacket plus striped trousers were *de rigueur.*

Following two rehearsals came the concert. At the appointed time I made my appearance, mincing to the piano in the center of the stage as gracefully as I could. My entrance was greeted by an audible gasp and some spotty applause; the French never really took to Oxford bags and I presented a strange spectacle, clad as I was in a tight-fitting morning coat (I was very slim in those days) terminating in balloon-shaped trousers which, although cut by Anderson & Sheppard, would have been an excellent fit for the then-popular Fatty Arbuckle.

The piano part of my piece (it was called, somewhat pretentiously, a "sonata for piano and orchestra") was not spectacular and was very easy to play, as I, no virtuoso, took good care not to overburden myself with technical difficulties. We did finish together, Dr. Koussevitsky, the orchestra, and I. The applause was even spottier than at my entrance, and a few days later (the French critics never review anything the next day, bless 'em) the leading music critic wrote: "Mr. Dukelsky's music was barely visible behind his sumptuous trousers."

In the same year Poulenc, Auric, Rieti, and myself played the four pianos in the London *première* of Stravinsky's *Les Noces* by the Diaghilev ballet at His Majesty's Theatre. Ernest Newman lost no opportunity to tell his *Sunday Times* readers that: "There was a quarter of a composer at each piano."

At about the same time I began to function as Vernon Duke (a name invented by the late George Gershwin, whose quarters I then shared in London) and wrote my first musical comedy, for Daly's

Theatre; this opus was entitled *Yvonne,* and promptly retitled "Ivan the Terrible" by Noel Coward.

In 1935 the above-cited Ernest Newman, on reviewing a ballet of mine given by the de Basil Ballets Russes (it was called *Jardin Public* and had a scenario by André Gide) confessed that my music irritated him so profoundly that he couldn't make himself look at the stage because of the horrible sounds emanating from the pit. To this day it isn't clear to me just *where* Mr. Newman was looking, but I know darned well that he was listening and, after all, what more can a composer ask?

I was often overly fond of stinging letters, ill-timed righteous gestures, and experienced an exaggerated delight at putting a man in his place. These things do not make for popularity, and since quarrels are everyday fare in musical and theatrical circles, I have had more than my share of them. I never hesitated about speaking my mind when it would have been far wiser to remain blandly noncommittal. The not-so-green pastures of Broadway, 57th Street, and Hollywood are peopled with professional villains of all hues who go about their villainies with an air of such innocence that to remind them of their true nature is a rude, and to them undeserved, shock. These iniquitous souls, instead of becoming penitent, denounce their victims as trouble makers if they dare yell when kicked. It is a golden rule on Broadway never to sue a producer and never to argue with a critic — I've done both.

Prior to embarking on this job, I read a great many autobiographies, particularly those of my contemporaries. I have discovered that autobiographies can roughly be divided into two groups, those with emphasis on facts and those preoccupied with literary style. Sir Osbert Sitwell is a good sample of the second type, and Tallulah Bankhead and Agnes de Mille are typical of the first school. That doesn't mean that the two women don't go in for much editorializing and Marie Corellizing, although their lives seem hectic enough without such additional veneer. At least there is a minimum in their books of the "rich, beautiful prose" which makes Sir Osbert's pretty tough going.

As for me, I thought a great deal about a tongue-in-the-cheek approach, the poker-face approach, the Dali or sensational-at-all-costs approach, the Freud or turn-over-a-new-fig-leaf approach, and finally decided to stick to the facts and the hell with it. Just to record the facts is quite a job without indulging in the luxury of stylistic orgies.

I envy people pregnant with fruity memories of their childhood. Tolstoi did a wonderful job on his early youth, and it would seem that the older he got the further back he went and the more he remembered. A Russian composer now in his eighties writes about his childhood as if he were still in the first one. Facts, sights, smells follow one another in precise chronological order, whereas I have difficulty remembering what happened last year unless I go through files and files of letters and income-tax returns. Fortunately the really important incidents never desert my memory, and more fortunately still, I have recently found a touching and artless biographical essay written about my early years by my mother. This copybook, along with her personal belongings, was forwarded to me from New York, and for these recollections, as for everything she did for me, I must bless her. I will try to reconstruct my early days with the help of this little document written in July, 1930, in Arrochar, Staten Island.

There is something indicative of my subsequent dual role in music in the very manner in which I was born. Four months before this event took place, Mother went to see a famous St. Petersburg specialist significantly named Professor Phenomenov. While crossing the river Neva on a small Finnish ferryboat, she had a frightening experience: she unwittingly sat down under the siren, which suddenly sounded with such force that Mother instinctively seized her left ear and twisted it. On recovering from the shock, her first thought was a fleeting superstition that the left ear of her unborn child would be marked. This fear was substantiated when, on examining me at my first appearance, Mother perceived the irregularity of my left ear; the lobe was cleft. Possibly my left ear has never heard what the right ear heareth, and there you have the whole mystery of Duke and Dukelsky in an earshell. The question is, which of the two ears is attuned to jazz?

I emerged into being, irregular ears and all, on October 10, 1903, in an obscure railroad station called Parafianovo, in the government of Minsk. Mother gave birth to me in the railroad station because she happened to be traveling by train and I imagine the station facilities were superior to those of a railway carriage. There is some considerable irregularity, too, not only in the fact that I was born by accident as it were, but also because my citizenship papers and my passport would indicate that I was born in the historic town of Pskoff. The reason for this discrepancy lies in the fact that an English immigration officer back in 1925, on filling in the required data concerning my birth and nationality, began writing out Parafianovo and, not finding enough room in the allotted space, stopped at "Paraf." This was subsequently interpreted by various officials as Pskoff, and thereby that ancient city was elected as my birthplace.

Another factor that might have contributed to the warring influences in my musical nature lies in my mongrel-like antecedents. Although I am technically speaking a native Russian, there is exactly one quarter of Russian blood in my veins. That was supplied by my mother's father, Alexis Kopylov, a self-made man of, I believe, peasant origin. He made his money in sugar, as he was general manager for the famous Count Bobrinsky Refineries. Kopylov married a pretty and rather social young girl who was half Viennese and half Spanish and whose name was von Köestel. On my father's side I am half Lithuanian and half Georgian (Caucasian); my grandfather, Vladimir Apollonovitch Dukelsky, was a highly placed official in Tiflis, where he occupied the post of general administrator under the Grand Duke Michael, the lord lieutenant of Caucasus. Grandfather married the beauteous Georgian Princess Daria Toumanov, nicknamed Dariko and noted for her lavish parties, eccentricity of dress, and somewhat Catherine-the-Great-like self-assertiveness. Both grandmothers were extremely musical and played the piano quite well; the maternal one, according to the family legend, was Anton Rubinstein's favorite pupil and appeared in public playing her teacher's D-minor concerto with a provincial orchestra. Princess Toumanov was an amateur of conservative tendencies and I remember distinctly her taking me to a symphony concert in Pavlovsk (just before the First World War) and telling me to put my fingers in my ears while an "abomination by that scoundrel Debussy" was being performed by the orchestra. The conductor on that occasion was the very able Aslanov, who later settled in New York and made a reputation for himself as a vocal teacher.

Both grandfathers were more or less unmusical and would have probably been happier with Duke than with Dukelsky. Grandfather

Kopylov, having settled in Kiev, became partial to Ukrainian folk songs, but I suspect it was because of the strapping girls who interpreted them rather than for the music.

Father and Mother were addicted to music in the customary manner of Russian dilettantes in comfortable circumstances. Father, a handsome man of medium height, with brilliant black hair and a resplendent mustache, was a civil engineer specializing in railroad building and occasionally given to singing gypsy songs in a pleasant baritone. Mother studied the piano diligently while an inmate of the Institute for Maidens of Gentle Birth (the equivalent of an American finishing school) in Kiev, and her two great passions, which I never shared, were Beethoven and Wagner.

According to Mother's testimony, I was something of a sickeningly romantic child. Not only was my head adorned with curling brown locks, but my face perpetually wore a serious, not to say profound, expression, and of usual childish pranks I would have nothing. I cried only on the rarest occasions and then almost inaudibly, which perturbed the whole household, brought up in the belief that healthy children are also healthy vocalists. At the age of eleven months I apparently had quite a vocabulary of Russian and French and soon got used to being exhibited to the politely enthusiastic friends of the family. A few months later (Ah, here it comes now!) I developed a habit of getting under Mother's feet when she played the fine Bechstein concert grand, which was a wedding gift my grandmother brought from Vienna. I was even more fascinated by a huge Gramophone with an imposing metal horn which was made to play an eclectic assortment of musical bits and pieces ranging from Italian operas sung by Battistini, Anselmi, Caruso, and the Russian gallery gods Sobinov and Smirnov (tenors both), to gypsy songs. A ritual was established of lulling me to sleep each night with florid Italian airs.

My brother Alexis was born a year and a half after my advent, and we soon moved to Nikolaiev in the government of Kherson, where my father was engaged in laying out the Kherson–Nikolaiev Railroad. We remained in this colorful southern town for nearly three years. In Nikolaiev, I manifested considerable signs of precociousness. When taught the usual childish games by my parents, I reneged on the rules and insisted on inventing my own. I detested mechanical toys, anything machinelike in fact, but had a passion for stuffed animals, especially dogs and elephants. This penchant grew into a grandiose game (in which my brother shared enthusiastically) of an imaginary dog kingdom where certain dogs were assigned the roles of composers, novelists, and painters and sculptors. The crown prince of this kingdom was, for no particular reason, a small tin frog beloved by me because of its bright-green color. On learning to read and write between the ages of two and three, I began to cover page after page of fat copybooks with accounts of life in the dog kingdom (the name I coined for the kingdom, *Sobatchania,* meaning Dogland, stuck with my family for many years), hieroglyphics significant only to myself, and eventually dots and dashes that I imagined to be musical notes. All this was natural enough, but when I switched to writing reams of completely meaningless poetry, which I recited eloquently to the uncomprehending butler and cook, Mother and Grandmother called a halt and, greatly alarmed, took me to the local psychiatrist. On viewing some particularly fruity samples of my handiwork, that worthy proceeded to ask me searching questions which I answered not only satisfactorily, but so nonchalantly as to disconcert the man. He let me off easy, but recommended some more suitable sports and recreations (I was four at the time) rather than the pedantic pursuits in which I took such unseasonable pleasure.

My brother, one of the quietest and gentlest of men, was an insufferable brat in his early life. He didn't have much hair on his head until he was about five, but he certainly could scream that head off and did so with uncommon relish. None of my precocious nonsense for him; physical exploits and bodily harm inflicted on whoever came within his reach were his special delights. Of linguistic prowess he showed but little, and to make matters worse he seemed to be afflicted with various impediments of speech which I strongly suspected were imaginary. His attitude towards me was one of awe mingled with contempt and acute and ever-present jealousy. Fully realizing that I was a self-appointed genius, demanding and receiving rapturous attention at all times, he never failed to kick or bite me when least expected to do so. His jealousy, provoked by my cultural attainments, manifested itself in grudging but slavish imitation of my creative activities; for instance, he was furious at the speed with which I filled my diary with the daily trivia of our lives and insisted on being given a similar diary, although he could hardly write at all. He would then proceed to scribble at great speed and would ask me every few minutes how many pages I had completed. On hearing that I had completed my fourth, Alex would say that he had just finished his fifth, and if I registered some skepticism, would reward me with an extra-vicious kick accompanied by copious tears of rage.

Our collection of stuffed animals was soon augmented by the live addition of a large, sad-looking poodle, Caro by name. This ordinarily gentle dog developed a dislike for the assorted citizens of *Sobatchania* and took large chunks out of them when we were not present. By way of retaliation, I, abetted by my grudgingly admiring brother, fed the poor dog all sorts of unsavory concoctions liberally seasoned with pepper and mustard which I cooked up on a toy stove given me by my grandmother. Caro would obediently swallow the multicolored messes and then have fits of sneezing and coughing which ended in an unholy whine. This usually resulted in the stove's being locked up for a day or two. In spite of these poisonous experiments, Caro lived to be eighteen and died in Kiev at the height of the Bolshevik revolution. Outside of the psychiatrist, *Sobatchania,* Caro's banquets, and the epic diaries, my only other recollection of Nikolaiev is an outing with Father to a country fair where he regaled himself with pickled watermelon, which I insisted on tasting and found so vile that I maliciously passed a piece of it to my brother, who swallowed it heroically, delighted at the thought of sharing his elders' pleasures.

The next event recorded by Mother was our removal to the small city of Kungur in the Ural Mountains. Father, who reveled in this nomadic existence, was now heavily involved in the building of the Perm–Catherineburg Railroad. I still remember the open sleigh in which we traveled for eighty miles in the frosty Ural air from Perm to Kungur. The magnificent Ural forests, the smells of fresh snow and crisp apples and the tart flavor of the birch juice from the young trees were a far cry from the semitropical, indolent atmosphere of Nikolaiev, but we all thrived on the change. According to Mother's notes, it was during the three years spent in Kungur that she grew from a simple young matron to a poised hostess and an avid student of letters and arts. She began entertaining her husband's business associates and soon presided over a group interested in philosophy and two-piano playing. Mother was very fond of teaching her sons a large repertoire of Russian nursery rhymes set to music, and while I had the better ear, Alexis had the louder voice. However, since his r's, l's, and most sibilants were defective, he made a good deal of noise but very little sense, which gave me another opportunity to shine which I seldom failed to seize. Beginning with our sojourn in the Ural Mountains, we were never without governesses of assorted nationalities; one of these was a gay Czech, another a dog-faced German spinster, and a third, supposedly a Frenchwoman, turned out to be Swiss-Italian. Soon Alexis and I learned to express ourselves in a Franco-Russo-German patois with a generous admixture of the dog language understandable only to us children.

My first essay in composition somewhat resembled the meaningless poems that so frightened the womenfolk in our family, in that the notes looked like notes but were undecipherable to a musician. This essay, which was prophetic in a sense, was a ballet in fourteen acts, one page to each act, entitled *Cassiopea.*

Father, on completing his Ural job, was characteristically transferred many miles away, to Crimea. This time we, accompanied by the Czech governess, traveled by Volga steamboat all the way down to Nijny-Novgorod and thence by Pullman to Sebastopol.

It was at the time of our removal to Crimea that I was first able to see Mother as she really was, not as the legendary Good Fairy of one's chaotic beginnings. Mother was something of a Russian version of the Gibson Girl, although she was dark and Spanish-looking. She had a splendid carriage, a small waist and the traditionally ample hips of a good-looking female of the pre-War Number I vintage. In reality, Mother was not beautiful, but rather uncommonly handsome, as her features were irregular, her nose a bit too long, and her mouth too full, but she had huge luminous brown eyes with the longest-imaginable eyelashes and a truly Gibsonian head of hair. What made her immediately attractive, and this attraction she retained to the end, was the trusting, childlike appeal of her entire mien. She had a touching curiosity about every human being she came in contact with, and an insatiable quest for friendship in which she was invariably disappointed.

On arriving in Sebastopol, we boarded another steamer and finally reached our destination, the small and none-too-fashionable resort named Evpatoria. Apparently there was some miscalculation on Mother's part, as here it was July and the season was to end

August 15th. Russian vacationists were very strict about observing seasonal deadlines, and we arrived in the middle of the general exodus. The female servant who went with the villa turned out to be a chronic alcoholic and her drunken railleries alternated with the dismal howling of the numerous dogs abandoned by the departed vacationists. A short winter interlude in Kiev followed, remarkable only for my first taste of the theater; the first two spectacles I witnessed were Maeterlinck's *Blue Bird,* and Massenet's *Cinderella.* At the beginning of 1910, Father obtained the much-coveted job of construction engineer for the proposed south-shore Crimean Railroad. This was a private enterprise undertaken by the multimillionaire T. K. Ushkov, the brother of N. K. Koussevitsky, the second wife of the conductor who played so significant a role in my musical development. Ushkov's country estate, Foros, was the most-photographed showplace of Crimea.

That spring Mother and we two boys migrated to the Alexandrov-Dollnik "Pensione" situated next door to the celebrated Vorontzov Park in Alupka. Father lived in the mountains in a tent surrounded by engineers and students and joined us on holidays only.

The Crimean peninsula was the Russian Riviera, actually much smaller than its prototype, but considerably more lush as to its flora and fauna. The Black Sea is bluer than the bluest Mediterranean; the fish more varied and far tastier; the flowers larger and more fragrant; and above all, the fruit not to be compared with any obtainable elsewhere. My most vivid recollection of Crimea is the taste of the local grapes and the astonishing variety in their shape, size and flavor. I particularly remember three: the huge yellow-green Chaoosh, the subtly perfumed Isabella, and the common but infinitely juicy Shashla. The everyday drink of all tourists and residents of Crimea was a fresh grape juice squeezed before your eyes from a pound of Shashla; this drink, amber-green in color, in no way resembled commercial grape juice as we know it in the U.S.A. Crimea was famous as a health resort for tuberculosis patients, and fresh grape juice was their diet staple. Chekhov supposedly thrived on it.

After a heavenly summer and autumn in Alupka, we were to spend the nonexistent winter in Yalta. Mother rented a dilapidated villa belonging to one Usatov, Châliapin's first vocal teacher and an obscure operatic composer. The little fat man, something of a "card" by reputation, obligingly removed himself and his wife to a small annex nearby. They were a delightful couple. Usatov had given up a promising career as an opera singer for his wife, a sudden TB victim. They were both small, rotund and ever-smiling, just like the celebrated Old World landowners in Gogol's tale. Outside of having coached Chaliapin (who, in common with most overnight phenomena, proved forgetful of Usatov's valuable contribution to his success), the old man's new claims to fame, which I'm afraid never came off, were a new Chaliapin called Matveiev and a five-act opera entitled *Love Is Closer Than the Mountains*. I immediately told Usatov that I went him one better by writing a fourteen-act ballet, which announcement was greeted by thunderous laughter and a gift of a dozen apples, Usatov's favorite food.

Shortly afterwards, Father was sent to Europe by Ushkov for four months and Mother, with time on her hands, began giving me piano lessons. I was no *wunderkind,* but on Father's return, I knew enough to play easy piano duets with Mother or *Fräulein.*

My other two recollections of Crimea were the spectacularly handsome Tartar *provodniks* (guides) whose thriving trade was to teach well-heeled gentlewomen the art of horseback riding. Mother's sister-in-law, Aunt Genia, and numerous other young divorcées donned Godey-like riding habits with tall hats and starched jabots and disappeared into the mountains accompanied by these Tartar Valentinos with their girlishly narrow waistlines and flashing white teeth. The other recollection was a charming young lady tutor Mother found for me with whom I was secretly in love. My tender feelings for this deserving young woman caused me to prepare my lessons with uncommon zest, which was rewarded by the glowing accounts the girl gave to Mother. Alexis, true to form, was proceeding at a much slower pace, but he now grew into quite a sentimentalist; Mother records an episode when Alex, on hearing the first pages of *Uncle Tom's Cabin,* burst into tears and refused to hear more of the book.

In the spring of 1911, my piano studies were resumed in earnest, but Alexis now displayed a good deal of determination to have lessons also in spite of Mother's great doubts as to his readiness. He astonished us all, especially myself, with his ability and zeal and pretty soon was making such progress as to put me to shame. His formerly hairless dome was now resplendent with silken blond locks and he was definitely beginning to come into his own, to my consternation. While in Crimea we met the three sons of General Mdivani — good-looking lads owning a fleet of expensive toy battleships, but no princely titles at that time.

In March of 1912, Father, whose excessive mountain-climbing exploits began to take their toll, had a serious heart attack. He was not quite thirty-nine. Mother, greatly alarmed, took us children back to Kiev to the Kopylov town house, and on doctor's advice, started on a journey abroad with Father. He was ordered to Bad Nauheim, a German health resort, but apparently the doctor's diagnosis was faulty and, following a short sojourn in Switzerland, my parents returned to Kiev for further consultations with the family physician.

On their return, we were taken for a short summer holiday to the unusual beach resort of Mejigorye on the banks of the Dnieper. It was unusual because it was run by the nuns of the Mejigorye Convent for married gentlewomen and their offspring. The husbands were not allowed on the beach for the reason that all bathing was done in the nude, but quite unorthodox leniency was exercised insofar as the children were concerned; they were allowed to swim in the nude with their mothers regardless of their sex.

My only experience with sex up to then had been in my grandmother's quarters on the family estate when I was about six years old. Grandmother, a strict Catholic, allowed no men on the premises, and consequently the young peasant wenches whom she employed were somewhat starved for male company. One of them, a nineteen-year-old Polish amazon named Marylia took a great fancy to me, and I dimly recall certain liberties she took with me, to which I submitted rather sheepishly and for which I was rewarded by succulent sweets stolen from Grandmother's larder. This episode, redolent of the writings of Restif de la Bretonne, left a mark on me, as I became peculiarly addicted to Renoir-like women in later life.

I also recall that some years after this vaguely erotic interlude I became fascinated with the Scriptures and was engulfed by a wave of religiousness; on recapturing the odd sensations provoked by Marylia, I was driven to utter despair and started thinking seriously of suicide. This was at about the same time that we went to Mejigorye, and the spectacle of abundant feminine flesh on all sides made me cringe with terror and remorse. Some of my companions exhibited a premature interest in their surroundings, and I remember a little pug-nosed boy called Petya being chased off the beach by an enraged good sister completely naked except for a huge black umbrella with which she succeeded in getting the culprit off the sacred territory.

There was a small island in the middle of the Dnieper which was the favorite swimming haunt of men vacationers whose wives were entitled to the privileges of the nuns' beach; these men spent most of the day gazing rapturously at their friends' wives through powerful binoculars, which pastime the nuns were unable to suppress.

While luxuriating on the nuns' beach, I again demonstrated my capacity for bluff by wading to a sand bank located in apparently deep water and pretending to swim, inviting Mother and her friends to admire my prowess.

This all too short vacation was brought to an abrupt end by a series of family tragedies, beginning with the death of my maternal grandmother on September 8th, in Kiev, where we were summoned to her funeral.

With no chance to recover from her grief, Mother had further cause for increasing worry about Father's condition. He now walked with considerable difficulty, and in early December was ordered to his bed, which he was not to leave again. The whole household was busy preparing a true Russian Christmas, a ritual quite unlike that in any other place, and we children were reveling in the protracted bounties of the holiday, when on December 28th, Father had his second heart attack, which proved fatal. *Fräulein,* Alexis, and myself sneaked into the library next door to Father's bedroom and heard with horror his gasps of agony. At one point, he cried out with indescribable pathos: "I don't want to die!" and shortly afterwards was no more.

We ran to Mother, begging her to tell us what was happening, and Mother's strange look of spent resignation told us the truth. We both burst into uncontrollable tears, whereas Mother remained inexplicably silent. The next few days brought all the paraphernalia of the Greek Orthodox conception of human frailty and untimely demise: swarms of hastily arriving relatives and yellow-faced nuns with ikonlike burning eyes, who mumbled inaudible but strangely terrifying prayers, their monotonous chants at the bier, the singing of the large choir brought back speedily after performing a similar chore for Grandmother, the frightening smell of incense mingled with that of unnaturally beautiful flowers and the damp leather of the servants' freshly varnished boots, the black crepe over the mirrors, and the hordes of the usual curious onlookers — all of these many emblems of death contributing to an untimely awakening after the innocuous dreams of our pastoral childhood. All at once, *Sobatchania,* bulging diaries, and piano duets became like so much gilt on the gingerbread of our beginnings.

On July 16th of the following year, Mother's younger brother, Uncle Vassily, a six-foot-three Guard's officer in Her Majesty's celebrated Uhlan Regiment, put a bullet through his head. He was barely twenty-three at the time, but in true Russian fashion had led a sumptuously wild existence. I recall vividly a breakfast at Grandfather's table, with Uncle Vassily, arriving after a sleepless night spent in Kiev dives with gypsies of easy virtue, demanding champagne in the midst of our oatmeal. Grandfather, a choleric and uncompromising old man whose secretary Akivisson usually sat at his left at table, thought nothing of upbraiding Vassily with forceful invective; Grandmother had alone been able to remonstrate with Grandfather and stand up for her son, but now that she was dead, Vassily had no supporters except us children, who loved him for the sweets he brought us, but had no say in the matter. These breakfast scenes usually ended in Vassily's demanding one hundred rubles, which would start a violent row terminating in Grandfather's abrupt exit. He was followed by Akivisson, shaking his head ominously, and an enormous Saint Bernard named Satan, whose affections were divided between Grandfather and Vassily, but who knew in canny dog fashion where his next meal was coming from. Uncle Vassily's pranks were of such a nature that he was about to be demoted to the rank of sergeant. This dishonor, plus his unrequited love for a celebrated French operetta star and his chronic debts, apparently precipitated his untimely end. A thing I recall with some delight about Uncle Vassily was his insistence on dragging poor Satan, carefully washed and beribboned, to his rendezvous with the heartless Frenchwoman. Vassily apparently believed that no female could resist the huge, perpetually drooling dog, but Alexis and I had a sneaking suspicion that the Saint Bernard contributed but little to Uncle Vassily's amatory chances; the dog was more adept at staging one-sided battles with Caro, who sometimes attached himself to Satan's ear and was nonchalantly dragged the length of the court.

Thus, with Vassily's suicide, our family was thrice visited by death in the course of ten months. September came, and Mother, in spite of Grandfather's entreaties, refused to remain in his house, where so much grief had been endured by her. She was quite comfortably off and set up housekeeping in an attractive flat at Bolshaya-Podvalnaya Number 14, where we remained until the time of our exodus from Russia in the winter of 1919.

CHAPTER II

TO MUSIC

ONE OF the leading figures in Stepanov's popular novel *Port Arthur,* published in Moscow in 1945, is my paternal uncle George Dukelsky. On the first page of the novel he is described as: "Lieutenant Dukelsky, Admiral Stark's flag officer, a tall, handsome young man . . ." He was later made aide-de-camp to Admiral Makarov on board the battleship *Petropavlovsk,* the flagship of the Russian Pacific Fleet. This ship, under fire from the entire Japanese fleet, went out of Port Arthur to save sailors from the sinking Russian destroyer *Strashniy* on April 13, 1904.

The *Petropavlovsk* struck a nest of Japanese mines in the Yellow Sea, exploded and sank within one and a half minutes. Among the men lost were two admirals, Makarov and Molas, the famous Russian painter Vereschagin, twenty-seven officers and six hundred and fifty-two sailors. Only seven officers and fifty-two sailors were saved — among them Grand Duke Cyril and Lieutenant Dukelsky, mortally wounded, died the same day in Port Arthur Naval Hospital.

Uncle George, or Gigisha (his Caucasian nickname), was a great ladies' man, and even the Soviet novelist, while not without proletarian indignation at the young officer's foppishness and aristocratic pretensions, gives his charm and courage their just due. Gigisha married a lovely Nagasaki girl some few months before his tragic end and the result of this temporary marriage was a handsome Russo-Japanese boy who was later to send me postcards to New York addressing me as the "flower of his soul." It was probably at the instigation of Uncle George that I was enrolled in the St. Petersburg Naval Academy at birth, to the subsequent delight of Grandmother Dariko who, enchanted with my early flair for languages, saw me as a combination naval officer and diplomat.

Thus, shortly after our removal to the Bolshaya-Podvalnaya flat, Mother received a letter from Dariko outlining her plans for me and requesting that steps be taken to insure the proper sort of preparatory education, preferably in St. Petersburg.

So far, the only formal education I could boast of had been morning sessions at a glorified kindergarten of progressive tendencies presided over by a famous lady educator, Madame Jekulina; the Froebel and Pestalozzi systems then fashionable in Russia were employed in this institution, which was pleasantly co-educational and gave me a first taste of feminine company my own age. Madame Jekulina's school was paradise compared to what I feared might be in the offing educationally speaking.

Although fascinated by the sea, particularly the Black Sea, I was frightened by the harrowing tales of the midshipmen's rigorous training, which included diving from the top of the mast into the raging waves. I was too proud to admit my fear, but suddenly developed a devouring passion for composing music, writing longer and obscurer poems, and sketching whoever and whatever happened to be around, such as Alex, Caro, and our ugly cook, Pauline. These activities were indulged in to impress Mother with my artistry; I was taking no chances and practiced all the arts at once. Of the three, Mother preferred music, and after hearing a long "sonata" I had completed, saw fit to wire Grandmother that I was a composer of great promise and my naval career was not to be.

A long wrangle ensued, with the maternal relatives upholding Mother, and Father's brother's sticking by Grandmother Dariko. I kept my mouth diplomatically shut and opened it only to tell my uncles and aunts that I didn't see in what way Beethoven's sonatas were superior to mine. So astonishing a statement made it imperative for Mother to take me to a composition teacher, Lubomirsky, and seek his impartial verdict.

Lubomirsky was somewhat distressed on discovering that I did not boast perfect pitch, in those days regarded as a "must" for future composers. With my customary aplomb I told him that my pitch was indeed perfect; but it proved to be a hit-and-miss, one of my ears probably at variance with the other. Not giving Lubomirsky a chance to recover from his disappointment, I plunged into my latest sonata, which was so long and loud that the kind little fellow was taken aback and had no other way out but to accept me as a pupil. His summing up was rather on the guarded side; what he actually said was that he saw no reason why I should not become a composer, but this was optimistically interpreted by Mother and myself as a bona fide passport to greatness. Suitable telegrams were dispatched to all the members of the family and the "jumping off the mast" terror subsided somewhat.

The first intelligible piece of music I wrote was not the over-long sonata, but a little waltz composed at age seven. Mother testifies in her notes that I jumped out of bed in the morning and ran to the piano, seized by the kind of inspiration people love to read about; ah, those inspirations! Soon enough writing music becomes like signing checks, just as methodical and just as disseminated. My studies with Lubomirsky were to start in the autumn of 1914; that summer Mother discarded her mourning and felt the need of a change of scene to which she had become accustomed by her migrating husband and off we went to untrodden paths, this time to the so-called Riga Strand, which consists of a cluster of small watering places on the Baltic Sea. What a change from the warmer and darker waters of Crimea. The swimming was actually better as there were none of the rocks or pebbles characteristic of Crimean beaches; the sand was fine and lemon-yellow, the water steel-blue, and the surrounding smells were tarter and cleaner, but not as mellow as the subtropical scents of the balmy Black Sea.

We soon found a small pink villa in Bilderlingshof and joined the waxen-blond Latvians and Germans summering there. Alexis and I were elected to an amateur fire brigade of Russo-German boys, cannily managed by two German lads in their early teens. We were given fancy uniforms and made to pay large dues to purchase an almost full-scale fire engine, which the German boys craftily appropriated at the end of the season. Alexis was a much better fireman than I. We were both elected "spritzers," which gave us an opportunity to squirt large quantities of salt water on giggling little German girls in white dresses.

In the evenings, Mother played accompaniments for a young Polish violinist called Michalski and I became enamored of Kreisler's "Liebestraum" and "Liebesfreud."

One of Mother's closest friends, the stately Mrs. Dityatin, and her three children occupied a little house in Bilderlingshof. The husband,

Vitaly Fedorovitch, a polished Anglophile type, was a friend of Georg Schneevoigt, the Finnish-born conductor whose influence was then great in the Scandinavian countries. Dityatin offered to show a would-be orchestral piece of mine to the eminent Schneevoigt, then vacationing in Marienhof a few miles away. Although I was immensely flattered, I somehow was smart enough to decline.

On June 16th, war with Germany was declared; our German firemen suddenly disappeared, carrying off the splendid fire engine, and we Russians began a precipitate exodus to Riga. The hotels were packed to the roof, the prices rose alarmingly, but we let Mother worry about that and happily roamed the streets of the beautiful medieval town. One afternoon I wandered into a sixteenth-century square on the outskirts of Riga and heard a group of sad-looking Latvian children led by a girl not more than fifteen in a monotonous chant which, while it seemed to be a nursery rhyme, filled my heart with extraordinary sadness. I believe that they sang in Latvian; the odd music with incomprehensible words scared me off and I ran home in inexplicable terror.

There was more violin music in Riga, and quantities of delicious smoked fish (particularly one called *seeg,* the like of which I have never tasted since), but such luxuries soon came to a premature end as we finally booked train space home to Kiev.

Everybody was being mobilized all around us, but with Uncle Vassily's suicide, we had no immediate relatives of conscription age. Having graduated from Madame Jekulina's establishment with some distinction, I was now to experience the thrill of becoming a full-fledged gymnasiast, or high-school pupil. Russian high schools were much stricter than their American counterparts. They were not co-educational, and the boys were made to wear uniforms at all times; the government high-school students were decked out in black with silver buttons and in caps with silver insignia. Alexis and I were sent to a private high school run by a much-esteemed pedagogue named Naumenko, and our specially designed uniforms were of powder blue with golden buttons and cap insignia. This provoked great hostility on the part of the "plain" or government boys, who called us blue-breasted sissies, Mamma's boys, and offered to fight us at the drop of a hat. In school I was good in history, literature, languages, and geography, and rotten in all mathematical subjects. I was frail and reasonably aesthetic-looking, which went well with my proclivities for writing poetry and music, drawing caricatures of my classmates, and disdaining athletics.

By an uncanny coincidence, there was an attractive boy a year older than myself whose name, exactly like mine, was Vladimir Dukelsky. To make things more complicated, he too wrote poetry, but, unlike me, showed promise as a soccer player. One day we two got mixed up by the athletics coach, and I was ordered on the field to join the team. Not being able to run fast enough for a forward, I was entrusted with the responsible position of goal keeper. The coach didn't have much faith in me, but I somehow miraculously blocked a few assaults during practice periods and was allowed to play on the second squad in an interschool match. The score on this momentous occasion was four to nothing in favor of the opposing team, all four goals being scored due to my fatal fumbling; following the game I was severely beaten by my classmates and spent the next three days in bed.

While at Naumenko's I learned to play the domra, a round instrument of the mandolin family whose metallic strings are manipulated by a plectrum but whose sound is more nasal and twangy than that of a mandolin. The domras, of assorted sizes, were employed to take the "melody lead" in the balalaika bands always popular in Russia. Every school boasted one and so did Naumenko's. I was only a fair performer on the primitive Russian lute, but I did make some efforts at arranging, with indifferent results.

Meanwhile I was progressing satisfactorily with my piano lessons under the guidance of one Josephine Leskevitch, a pupil of Dombrovsky, who was later to become my teacher at the Conservatory. Lubomirsky was now instructing me in elementary theory and first harmony; he, too, was a minor case of musical schizophrenia, having written a textbook on theory and a "Danse Orientale" in great favor to this day with cooch dancers, oriental travelogues, and Caucasian knife throwers. These were Lubomirsky's only known accomplishments, and I began seriously to question his adequacy as a teacher of composition on so slender a record.

This was the era when the "Russian Decadence" school in poetry and painting was becoming all the rage. The first futurists, like the Burliuk brothers, Kruchenikh, Khlebnikov, and others of that ilk, true to the teachings of Marinetti, the Italian founder of the school, donned eccentric garb, wore carrots and radishes in their buttonholes, painted their faces blue or green and created disturbances in theaters and other gathering places, to attract publicity. The effete, *coiffeur*like ego-futurist Igor Severyanin made women swoon with his would-be chic poems, in which he glorified imported motor cars, Paris dress-makers, pineapples filled with champagne, and other attributes of High Life. Severyanin had his low-brow apostle in the person of Alexander Vertinsky (at this writing still flourishing in Moscow), who got himself up as Pierrot and mumbled Frenchified inanities to strangely gypsylike tunes — a weird but eminently successful combination. Russian women were, and often still are, captivated by these two home-grown catchpenny Baudelaires, and their influence was enormous everywhere. Vertinsky was responsible for the cult of the exotic-at-all-costs; one of his best-known songs was called "Purple Negro," another, "Your Fingers Smell of Incense," and there were tattooed sailors and super-virile cowboys galore in his *chansons*.

Poor Mother didn't escape this unhealthy fad; in common with her women friends she began smoking out of long amber cigarette holders, wore Mexican earrings, and studied the tango. This new word meant not only the latest dance craze, but also was the tag of flaming orange color. Alexis and I were badgered into learning the steps of the Argentine *pas de deux* and in a week or so could put on a fair exhibition, with Alexis the unwilling *danseuse*.

On reading Severyanin and Co. avidly, I perceived to my great exhilaration that their poems made even less sense than my own early ones. I began to consider myself a futurist, too, and even appeared in high school with a painted face on one occasion, to be ordered out of class immediately. My Beethoven-like "sonatas" were now discarded and gave way to more experimental essays which consternated Lubomirsky, who complained to Mother about my non-conformist tendencies.

I, at first a model student, was now beginning to sow my oats in school — contributed ego-futurist poems to the school magazine, played my "revolutionary" piano pieces at children's parties, and found less and less time to do my homework, particularly math and physics. The math teacher was an old friend of Mother's and let me off easy until he was shown a cruel caricature I had drawn of him; then he cracked the whip and failed me. Mother was greatly alarmed by this unpleasant change in my scholastic standing and began to cite Alex as an example of a not-too-imaginative but diligent student. This was the last straw, and instead of reforming I was determined to get out of the gymnasium, as I deemed it unworthy of my highly specialized talents.

Mother had a box at the opera and we boys soon began to anticipate every operatic outing. Although I loved opera, symphony concerts fascinated me even more, especially when conducted by the placid but thorough Reinhold Glière, then just made director of the newly created Kiev Conservatory. Glière, born in Kiev, was of Belgian origin, which could not be guessed from his conventionally Russian, Glazunov-like music. He was forty at the time, dressed well, and quite captivated Mother, who began to nurture the ambition of annexing him as a teacher for me. On one occasion, she took us to hear his interminable *Ilia Murometz Symphony,* a favorite warhorse of Stokowski's. Another time, we went to hear the piano concerto of a young St. Petersburg Gold Medalist, Serge Prokofiev by name. This last experience proved something of a turning point for me, but not in the obvious sense.

After a conventional overture, and sympathetic applause, Glière bowed and shortly reappeared with a tall young man of extraordinary appearance. He had white-blond hair, a small head with a large mouth and very thick lips (unlike the purple African of Vertinsky's imagination Prokofiev was then nicknamed the "White Negro") and very long, awkwardly dangling arms, terminating in a bruiser's powerful hands. Prokofiev wore dazzlingly elegant tails, a beautifully cut waistcoat, and flashing black pumps. The strangely gauche manner in which he traversed the stage was no indication of what was to follow; after sitting down and adjusting the piano stool with an abrupt jerk, Prokofiev let go with an unrelenting muscular exhibition of a completely novel kind of piano playing. The prevailing fashion in those days was the languorous hothouse manner of a Scriabin or the shimmering post-Debussy impressionist tinklings of harp and celesta. This young man's music and his performance of it reminded me of the onrushing forwards in my one unfortunate soccer experience; there was no sentiment, no sweetness there — nothing but unrelenting energy and athletic joy of living. No wonder the first four notes of the concerto, oft-repeated, were later nicknamed *"po cherepoo"* ("hit on the head"), which was Prokofiev's exact intention. I will not say that I was fascinated by the piece. Far from it,

Mother, Aunt Genia, Alexis and I were all horrified, all said that the so-called concerto was a disgrace and that there wasn't a tune in it. (How often was I to hear those words applied to me in my later career.) To our consternation, there was frenetic applause and no less than six flower horseshoes were handed to Prokofiev, who was now greeted with astonished laughter. He bowed clumsily, dropping his head almost to his knees and recovering with a yank.

"That's not music, Dima (my family nickname)," said my mother sternly. "Don't you start writing like that. Remember, my boy, melody first and last."

I grunted my approval. Little did Mother know the warring influences already rife in my breast.

My scholastic labors were interrupted by two bucolic episodes; the first, a short sojourn in Grusskoye in the government of Kursk. This was an estate belonging to one Kourdiumov, a rich epicurean totally paralyzed by the gay sins of his Hussar youth. He was still young, but had to wear yellow-black eyeglasses, which were supposed to strengthen his unseeing eyes; his face retained traces of the good looks typical of his regiment and had the faded color of a vellum binding. His limp and useless body was propelled in a wheel chair by an old servant with white side whiskers. Only his hands were eloquent and his palate active; Kourdiumov lived for food and was a true gourmet in the old Russian — not the finer French — tradition.

Every morning at breakfast, Kourdiumov summoned his chef and his two apprentices and held a long conversation, often interspersed with hectic arguments, on the subject of the day's menus. Varieties of game supplied by full-time hunters employed by our host, baskets of imported fruit, and cobweb-covered bottles from his vast cellars were exhibited, compared and critically sampled before the day's gastronomic program was decided upon. Menus in French with the family crest were then hectographed and deposited in all the guest rooms, including the children's.

Noontime marked the arrival of the hungry guests, consisting of neighboring landowners, a few generals, retired and active, and a horde of "Popes" as the members of the Greek Orthodox clergy were familiarly called. These Falstaffian clerics sported luxuriant beards, wore the somber black garments of their calling, and had a truly Byzantine capacity for eating and drinking. Long before mealtime they assembled in Kourdiumov's bedroom, where large carafes of herb-distilled vodka were consumed amid wall-shaking laughter and distinctly pagan jollity.

Alexis and I, accompanied by the Lvov children, a brother and sister of twelve and fourteen respectively, were ushered into the enormous dining hall chaperoned by our two governesses. Mother and Mrs. Lvov arrived in fresh *mousseline* dresses fragrant with Coty's L'Origan, the perfume then in vogue. Both women were somewhat apprehensive of extra poundage from the daily eating festivals, but the food was so good that they soon joined the noisily masticating throng.

The daily luncheon began with four tables of hors d'oeuvres wheeled in by as many white-gloved footmen; the first table covered with smoked and pickled fish of the rarest species, another with five or six kinds of caviar of all hues, the third with meats and fowl in aspic, and the fourth with hot sausages, veal patties, lobster and crab concoctions, and other savory dishes. On certain days there was a fifth table on which reposed two or three hundred heavenly pink-boiled *raki,* or large fresh-water prawns cooked with dill. As a grand finale to the entrances of these groaning boards, a perambulating bar of rainbow-hued vodkas appeared, the vodkas varying from the fresh green of the *zubrovka* to the clear pink of the *Ryabinovka,* distilled from a berry not unlike the U.S. cranberry. The idea was to wash down the hors d'oeuvres with these potent liquids, and there was quite a trick to use the right vodka with the right appetizer, although after a while it didn't particularly matter.

At table, the first course was usually the beloved *blini,* or light fluffy pancakes, which were, as brother Alexis was fond of saying, easy to eat. First the *blini* were smeared with hot melted butter, then with a thick layer of sour cream, and finally garnished with caviar, although some connoisseurs disdained that delicacy in favor of lightly smoked salmon *couleur de popo d'enfant* (color of a baby's behind). The *blini,* of which we children ate approximately a dozen and the grownups not less than three or four dozen, were washed down by bouillon, and then the real meal started.

The first course was some magnificent fish, preferably out of season, like cold sturgeon with *sauce verte;* then game traditionally cooked in sour cream with cranberry sauce; then the main meat course, either a boiled suckling pig accompanied by creamed horseradish or a baby lamb served whole with *kasha* (buckwheat groats);

then a fancy salad with wonderful Russian mayonnaise, the secret of which is irretrievably lost; then the pride of the chef — a huge *plombières,* an elaborate ice-cream mold with *glacé* fruits adorning it and Kourdiumov's initials for decoration. For those who were still hungry, a table decked with every imaginable cheese was trotted out, and finally a vast assortment of liqueurs, the particular delight of the clergy. Enormous vintage cigars and specially blended coffee terminated the feast.

The children and their governesses, as well as the ladies, were now allowed to leave the table while the men remained to regale one another with bawdy stories. Half an hour later, the assorted company adjourned to their respective bedrooms for a lengthy two or three hour siesta. An hour after waking, the vodkas reappeared, this time in the drawing room, where one of the ladies was called upon to tackle the piano, and then dinner was announced, always twice as elaborate as the luncheon. It was Kourdiumov's custom to kiss all the ladies, including young girls, the younger the better, after each meal, a ritual not at all to their taste.

We children never slept in the afternoon, but were provided with facilities of croquet, volleyball, and — to my alarm — horseback riding. The ringleader of the sports was a tall and prematurely worldly wise gymnasiast, Serge Golinevitch by name, who was to graduate that year and was therefore much admired and envied by all us small fry. The belle of the younger group, a dark-haired fourteen-year-old named Nina, looked rather like Judy Garland at her début. This girl, although secretly adored by Alexis and myself, was annexed by the enterprising Serge, who impressed her with his big-town airs and easy chatter. The three younger boys, her brother, Alexis, and I, saw the young couple mount the fine Cossack horses provided by Kourdiumov's grooms and disappear in a shower of golden dust. They were usually absent for not less than two hours, and there was much leering and whispering on the part of my companions as to the exact nature of these expeditions. I pretended to be above such unworthy speculations, but was in reality horribly envious of the suave city slicker.

I demanded from Mother that I be given riding lessons, to which she reluctantly acceded; I never liked or understood horses, and don't to this day, but was determined to make a nuisance of myself and to become a master equestrian. It took me quite some time to learn to post for the trot, my behind was increasingly sore, but I persevered. In a few days I bribed a groom with Mother's ruble and suddenly appeared on a small brown horse, bent on accompanying Serge and Nina on their outing. Nina, already a true representative of her sex, was of course gratified by my zeal, guessing the great effort it cost me, but Serge was not at all pleased and arrogantly galloped off with Nina, leaving me behind.

On a certain Sunday, hordes of juvenile visitors made their appearance, and each was provided with a nice tame horse; my favorite, Arabchik (Little Arab), was already engaged, and the only horse left available was a black brute of a stallion named Barbarian. This horse was reluctantly assigned to me, as I was determined to join the merry cavalcade, especially since Nina's horse had just been saddled. I gave Barbarian a dirty look and was hoisted into the saddle by ominously scowling grooms. Somehow I managed to sit up straight, and bestowed a triumphant smile on Nina, who smiled back admiringly, when Barbarian emitted a bloodcurdling whinny and lunged forward entirely on his own. In a furious gallop, my feet deserting the stirrups, and my would-be æsthetic hands clutching wildly at the brute's mane, we traveled at such a diabolical pace that the entire cavalcade was soon left behind, and I began to scream my heart out unheard by anyone. There was no hope except to hold on to the black mane for dear life, but the beast had a horrible habit of shaking his head, which made this safety device rather precarious. My terror increased when Barbarian swerved from the bridle path and headed for the main house, a marble-columned eighteenth-century edifice. Directly facing the porte-cochere was a formal garden, Kourdiumov's delight, planted with the rarest flowers, and this was apparently Barbarian's destination. In a flash, I saw Mother at an open window knitting, and Barbarian threw me at her feet in the prize-tulip bed with a disgusted snort. I wasn't hurt, but with my already pronounced flair for the theatrical, played dead. A whole Greek chorus of terrified women, led by Mother, surrounded me, suggesting fancy remedies for me and a bullet for Barbarian. Best of all, Nina appeared, flatteringly solicitous, and temporarily deserting the disgruntled Serge for me, the hero of the moment. Needless to say, I played the scene to the hilt; yet my happiness was but short-lived.

One day, we children heard a violent harangue emanating from Kourdiumov's bedroom, and a few minutes later the wily Serge emerged white and trembling, refusing us any explanation. Stifled cries in Nina's room in answer to her mother's shrill scolding were equally incomprehensible and disturbing. Alexis did some snooping around and came up with the astounding intelligence that Serge and Nina had been discovered in a most compromising position in the summerhouse by one of the governesses. Serge was sent home that same evening and Nina was confined to her room and put on a strict and no doubt antiaphrodisiac diet. I, of course, knew the exact location of Nina's window and spent the next morning playing detective under it. Nina, her splendid sunburned body meagerly hidden by a white nightgown, finally appeared at the window, opened it and stared unseeing ahead. I will never forget the girl's look of adolescent despair mingled with wanton longing and helpless rage at the absence of her lover; a large tear ran down her cheek and I could no longer be silent.

"Nina," I gulped, "what is the matter? Is there anything I can do?"

The look she gave me was witheringly contemptuous. "You? Why, you wouldn't know what to do, even if there was anything to be done. You're nothing but a child!"

With these words she closed the window and disappeared. There is nothing sadder than telling a boy just past ten that he is only a child, except, on passing forty, to hear "old man" for the first time.

The second episode involved my only trip to Moscow.

Moscow, something of a Paris to Russians (while there was a London-like austerity and aloofness about St. Petersburg), was the goal of every provincial Russian. The sing-song of the native Muscovite with his broad a's and o's was considered irresistible, although not quite as *comme il faut* as the crisper, less emotional St. Petersburg accent. Mother, still disconsolate over the loss of her husband, began to seek solace in the Moscow Art Theatre season then holding forth at the Solovtzov Theatre in Kiev; she much admired the versatile Kusnetzov, who tackled Gogol's *Revizor, Charley's Aunt* and *Hamlet* with equal ease. After the performance there were gay suppers with the *Moskvichi* (Muscovites) at the Praha, the lights of which we could see from our fifth-floor flat.

A gay Moscow couple, the Savostianovs, were ringleaders in these nocturnal outings of Mother's, whereas Alex and I were told to display our best table and play manners to the Savostianov children, Nata and Youra. This new friendship resulted in the Savostianovs' invitation to spend the Christmas holidays at their country place near Moscow, which Mother gratefully accepted.

The three things I recall best about Moscow are the broadbacked, bearded and vociferous *izvostchiks* (coachmen); the heady smell of the freshly baked Moscow *kalatch,* the tastiest bread known to man; and the famous department store Muir and Merrilies, the Scotch-owned Russian forerunner of the Macy's and Selfridge's of the occidental world — at least that's what the Russians are sure to claim, if they haven't already done so.

The Savostianov *datcha* was typically suburban; of Kourdiumov's feudal splendor there was none, but there were the simple country pleasures of snow games and tobogganing with the Savostianov children. The slim, Circassian-looking Nata got along famously with Alex, and they, with Youra, would disappear after the tobogganing for some mysterious sessions in the bushes, where I strongly suspect the three of them played an oriental version of the "doctor game." I, with my pious reputation, was never asked to participate and pretended no interest in their pastimes. One day I overheard a shockingly colorful description of these goings-on and melodramatically declared that, being a true Christian, I would have to report such sins to the two mothers. Nata, terrified, tried to buy me off with an offer to join me in the bushes, but I indignantly declined and burst into uncontrollable tears, which brought Mother and Mrs. Savostianov running. The three culprits glared threateningly while I was questioned as to the cause of my hysterics, but I am proud to say that I refused to play the informer.

After the holidays, the two families went their separate ways to Moscow, where Alex and I were fed *pirojki,* bought from Filippov, the caterer, and allowed to roam about the Kremlin.

We listened to the melancholy and elephantine waltzes played by a military band at the Moscow skating rink, where cocky gymnasiasts showed off in daredevil fashion for the watching schoolgirls, blushing and giggling into their handmuffs, the sharp Russian frost biting their little ears.

Mother took us back to uneventful Kiev to resume classes at Naumenko's Gymnasium, to Scarlatti with Miss Leskevitch, and for me to wrest from him the last of the now steadily dwindling stock of Lubomirsky's musical surprises.

The great day came when Mother felt that I was ready to beard

Kiev's musical lion in his den; she put on her caracul *manteau* over the orange "tango" dress with its matching fur border, and we headed for the Conservatory's inner sanctum — Glière's *cabinet de travail.*

In the *izvostchik* on the way to the Conservatory, Mother sighed over my snowballing reputation as a Peck's Bad Boy at Naumenko's, but I grandly reassured her that it was all part of a "plan."

Glière greeted us impeccably turned out, and after appraising Mother's ensemble and taking a whiff of her violet corsage backed up by the ever-present L'Origan, he bowed and kissed her hand with obvious pleasure. After Mother's excited explanations, he sized up my kneepants with some surprise.

"So young and already a composer," he observed sadly. "And when you compose, young man, do you actually write it down?"

I whipped out the orange-colored (the tango influence) cover of my "sonata" and asked Glière if he would care to follow the music while I played it. Thus cornered, Glière had no choice — he folded his arms and prepared to listen. I'm afraid his response was more or less the same as Lubomirsky's at my first audition. The longer I played, the more startled Glière became, until finally he asked me to stop and told my mother that I was indeed peculiarly talented; he suggested that I take some private lessons from him prior to entering the Conservatory. Glière considered my piano playing sufficiently advanced for the class of Professor Marian Dombrovsky, who was Miss Leskevitch's teacher. The interview was most satisfactory to Mother and me and we left Glière's office feeling that we had Euterpe by the tail.

The next morning I entered the Naumenko temple of learning in a particularly flip mood. When the geography teacher asked me to point out the Carpathian mountains on the map, I deliberately located the Crimean range. My brazenness brought a gasp from my classmates, but I topped this in the Russian literature class (my favorite subject) which followed. A handsome young Ukrainian named Galiun was the teacher and the idol of all the schoolgirls. Because of my overly advanced ego-futurist experiments, I was no longer allowed to write for the "serious" school publication *Our Thoughts,* and had enterprisingly retaliated with my own satirical journal, *The Ventilator.* No sooner had Galiun begun class than I circulated the newest hectographed copies of my rag, which featured his likeness on page one in a rapt embrace with the schoolgirl popularly considered his pet. There was ill-repressed mirth among the readers, and with a mock bow, Galiun appropriated one of my gay little sheets. He reddened up and stomped out of the schoolroom, *Ventilator* in hand, shortly returning with the school principal; I was then called out of class.

The next morning I was formally expelled from the gymnasium, which was exactly the result I desired. Mother was perturbed of course, but I set her right by claiming that my Pegasus was far more likely to be Glière than Naumenko, and that I would reach Olympus much faster in the Conservatory chariot.

CHAPTER III

KIEV CONSERVATORY

I WOULD give anything to take a long look at Kiev as it is now, thirty-four years after I left it, if I could avoid winding up in a Soviet torture chamber. Whatever the modern improvements, I don't believe it can be in any way more enticing than it was in the days of my musical beginnings. True, the railroad station was a horribly ugly edifice which was to be torn down and replaced, and surely has been by now; once through its gates, Kiev was a world half-occidental and half-medieval Russian. The modern and luxurious thoroughfares of Kreschatik (Kiev's main street) and the exclusive Lipki residential section, named for its abundant young linden trees, seemed highly kinetic next to the peaceful golden domes of the city's many sixteenth-century churches; of these the Lavra of Petchersk was the Saint Mark's of Russian Christendom. The city's parks included the Gorka (Hill) of St. Vladimir, the splendid Czarski Sad (Gardens), and the Merchant's Gardens, the home of the summer symphony concerts. Our street, the Bolshaya-Podvalnaya, was well paved, clean, and boasted a cinema where we saw the first super-colossal movie epic, *Cabiria;* the hilarious comedies of Max Linder, the monocled predecessor of Charlie Chaplin; the homemade sexy melodramas that starred the Russian favorites Vera Kholodnaya and Ivan Mozjoukin.

The Gromov sisters, two enchantresses in their early teens, lived nearby, and it was strongly rumored that they smoked cigarettes, drank their father's champagne, wore their mother's silk stockings, and had week-end adventures with young cavalry officers. We boys were no match for them, but we constantly spied on the demure sirens as they trotted in and out of their house, schoolbooks under arm.

The rich and glamorous Mouraviov and Ilyashenko families lived near us in expensive private houses and gave festive parties for young people to which Alex and I were often invited. I recall that some of the older boys, habitués there, urged us to visit a brothel to which they were already resorting; this premature invitation filled me with terror as it was commonly known that the Kiev venereologists were getting richer by the year attending to their patients. The best-known of these doctors, an ex-wrestler named Alphonse Schwartzer, had his office near our house and I always quickened my steps on passing his fearsome sign with its ominous 606-914 glaring at me. With the advent of penicillin, Schwartzer switched to general practice and became my physician in New York at the time of World War II.

Two blocks away was a puny little two-story edifice with a large sign in its window proclaiming its ownership by "A. Razilo-Olizar, Free Artist, Vocal Lessons, Italian Method." I was entranced by so unorthodox a monicker until it dawned on me that Olizar was Razilo spelled backwards.

Between our house and the teeming Kreschatik was the *pereulok* (mews) where the Conservatory was located; in the opposite direction was grimy and unfashionable Lvovskaia Street. Off Lvovskaia was another mews called Dionisovsky Pereulok, where Grandfather's townhouse stood, the scene of the three family tragedies; next door to him was a convent run by nuns in some way affiliated with those at Mejigorye, the sanctified nudist beach.

Grandfather had combated his gloomy solitude by taking his housekeeper for a mistress. Mother brought us to see him occasionally, but we didn't enjoy these trips very much; the food had deteriorated, Grandfather was increasingly irascible, and poor Satan, the Saint Bernard, was sinking into the hairless and toothless miseries of age. However, Grandfather expected attention from Mother and the other four offspring who would share in his estate. That is, excepting Mother's brilliant brother Alexis, who was *persona non grata* with Grandfather because of his involvement in a conspiracy during the 1905 revolution. Grandfather's politics were of a markedly monarchist variety; he and his friend Dobrynin were among the chief stockholders in the Tory sheet *Kievlyanin,* and their feudal views went Nicholas II one better. Paradoxically, Uncle Alexis married Dobrynin's daughter Liza and settled down to teaching political economy at Novotcherkask University, so Grandfather grudgingly received but never forgave him.

Uncle Alexis had a genuine feeling for music, among his many interests, and of all my maternal relatives did the most to encourage me. His tastes in music were those of a serious dilettante, worshipful of standard symphonic literature and fairly contemptuous of anything that smacked of the music hall.

Mother's Moscow friends tried to cheer her up by taking her to operetta performances. She sometimes brought home sheet music from such hits as *The Chocolate Soldier, Sylvia,* and *The Merry Widow* for which I, the future Vernon Duke of Broadway, roundly scolded her. On one occasion, an *avant garde* lounge lizard presented Mother with some hot platters of American imported ragtime; the raging two-steps had such detestable titles as "Automobile" and *"Très Moutarde"* (Very Mustard). Alexis and I watched aghast as the daring young man demonstrated, with Mother as his startled partner, the vigorous arm-pumping and jerky steps of these pre-Scott Fitzgerald favorites. Mother tactfully eschewed an opportunity for terpsichorean advancement and led our visitor into the familiar tango, which I magnanimously played on the piano; I wasn't fond of dance music or the pseudo-gypsy wailings of the early Russian crooners of prerevolution days.

Our apartment boasted a small but diversified library, which started me on the long and adventurous road I have traveled to Bibliophilia. Memories of *Sobatchania* probably accounted for Alex's and my love for the eight illustrated volumes of Braehm's *Life of the Animals.* The rarer and more repulsive the animal described, the better we liked him.

There were two books on the shelves forbidden to Alex and me: Forel's *Sexual Question* and a fat volume on atheism, *Bezverye.* In the Russian language *zver* means animal and *bez* means without; consequently Alex and I had deduced that this book wickedly championed the destruction of animals, a plan abhorrent to us. The title really should be translated *Without Faith,* since *vera* means faith in Russian.

One night Mother went to the theater and Alex and I sneaked out these two guilty volumes; I plunged into the mysteries of sex and Alex probed the animal-less world. After some furious reading, we looked at each other with puzzled disappointment. Alex had found no animals at all, only obscure pagan gods and obscurer Greek and Roman philosophers, and I felt the sex act as scientifically explained was unfeasible, the whole thing being preposterous. We replaced the books sadly, unable to find answers to our surreptitiously acquired questions.

The date had rolled around for my first lesson with Glière. I had an idea that so esteemed a member of the artistic community would occupy palatial quarters in the Lipki sector. Instead, Mother left me at the door of a small house next to a disreputable market place in Bessarabka. Glière opened the door for me in furry slippers, his face unshaven and Bohemian-looking, quite unlike his urbane polish on the symphony platform.

We plunged immediately into first harmony. I was waiting for his lead to describe my latest efforts at composition, but he hewed to the pedagogic line. Finally, as he was dismissing me, I ventured the information that I was starting my first symphony.

"A symphony?" queried Glière with a supercilious smile. "My dear boy, prove to me that you can write a thirty-two-bar prelude first and then we'll try a small piano study before we progress to the symphony."

He patted me on the back and turned me out into the cold air. On the tram trip home I tried to fit the acclaim he received at the concerts and the meager, shabby home he worked in together. I had thought that composers and artists of all kinds moved in a teratogenic and prodigal world, their most extravagant wishes the command of an adoring public. Glière was the lion of Kiev and he lived more humbly than its lambs.

Although I always took my music seriously, even at that remote period I had the unwise tendency to attempt media for which I had no proper equipment. Unbeknown to Glière I had written a piece purporting to be a string quartet, without the most rudimentary notion of the technique or limitations of stringed instruments. I brought my score to a sweet old drunk named Grigorovitch, who taught calligraphy for a living and played string quartets for amusement. At his request I copied the parts of my quartet, and to my delight the kindly Grigorovitch volunteered to give it a reading. I'm sure the opus must have been awful, but hearing four grownups execute sounds arranged by me filled me with exaltation. Whenever a particularly juicy chord made its appearance, I jumped for joy and asked the musicians to please play that bar again because "it sounded so good." The four good-natured Ukrainians were gluttons for punishment; they complied by repeating the work throughout the evening and Grigorovitch even offered to give it a semipublic hearing, from which fate my prudent mother saved me.

At that same time I was practicing conscientiously for my piano examination, which called for two taxing technical studies and in which I intended to include my most radical sonata, an addition not at all obligatory. I appeared before the assembled pedagogues, headed by Glière, who did not show me any favoritism and stopped me cold on the third page of my sonata. However, my general musicianship was pronounced excellent and my piano technique acceptable for Dombrovsky's advanced piano class.

I then became a full-fledged Conservatory pupil and since that institution ran gymnasium classes for its students, the matter of general education was not neglected either.

The students were mostly aspiring singers, pianists, and violinists; composers were a distinct minority and loftily aloof from the lowly interpreters. In later years I found that, ironically, it was the interpreters who made a good living out of music, while the creator often worried about his next meal. The sharpest of the students were the young violinists, as high-strung as their fiddles, who raced after the girls along the corridors, solfeggio-stuffed satchels in tow. The girl singers were always prettier than the girl pianists, and from the adolescent exchanges I overheard, the boys considered them far more rewarding partners in the emotional dramas that teemed among us.

I remember two of these inconstant nymphs of music, both ten years older than myself, whom I admired through their surrounding crowds of fiddlers; one was the Nordic Znamenska, who sang my songs two years later at a Conservatory recital, the other a luscious Scheherazade-like contralto with the odd name of Vera Character. Of the male pupils I recall sad-eyed and long faced Vladimir Horowitz, who studied then with Serge Tarnovsky and later with the celebrated Felix Blumenfeld; his piano playing was already dazzling, but most of us students championed Horowitz's friend and rival, Sasha Doubiansky, who tragically committed suicide in his early twenties. Horowitz specialized in Chopin and Liszt, whereas Doubiansky leaned toward the moderns, particularly the charming Polish composer

Szymanovski, who later became my friend. Another pianistic luminary at the Conservatory was Harry Neuhaus, a cousin of Szymanovski; he was considerably older than the other two virtuosi. Neuhaus was identified with all the latest musical fashions and was a close friend of Pierre Souvtchinsky, the rich and influential publisher of the *Musical Contemporary,* the most luxurious musical magazine ever printed.

In Glière's class were two young men in their twenties who were regarded as master craftsmen by us beginners; they were Liatoshinsky, now the leading composer of Ukraine, and Mischa Levin, presently a successful background-music composer in Hollywood, under the name of Michel Michelet. Liatoshinsky's music was a blend of the seemingly incompatible styles of the two prevailing Messiahs of every Russian conservatory, Scriabin and Glazunov. Levin was more of a "modernist," in that he was not averse to French influences and was rather cosmopolitan in his tastes, due to previous study with Max Reger in Leipzig.

Tall, awkward Liatoshinsky was married to an excellent coloratura, nee Tzarevitch, who affably sight-read the latest songs turned out by the Glière pupils; once a week we met at Liatoshinsky's large apartment and played and sang each other's music far into the night.

In the summer of 1915 Mother took us to Finland to visit my paternal great uncle, Nikolai Apollonovitch Dukelsky, who had a villa in Kuokkala, about forty miles north of St. Petersburg. We swam in the cold waters at the gloomy and forbidding seacoast. A Wuthering Heights brooding hovered over the place, and my cousin Vera would have made a good Brontë heroine had I been a little older.

We went to St. Petersburg, my only visit there and a pleasurable one; I saw the celebrated Tzarskoe Sielo, the name of which sings nostalgically to Russians who associate it with Pushkin's happiest years.

Moscow's scent can be likened to that of overripe passion fruit; St. Petersburg seemed to me redolent of lemon and verbena, emanating from the River Neva, and there was an acidy, lemonish pallor to the St. Petersburg faces.

It was here that I was awed by the phenomenon of the Nordic white night, which I translated many years later musically in my cantata *The End of St. Petersburg;* after one performance this work disappeared into a musical limbo as inexplicable as the polar lights which brought it into being.

Grandmother Dariko, the Princess Toumanov, received us in a magnificent Patou summer frock whiter than the night of her city, scrutinized us closely through her lorgnette, felt for my muscles and, on finding them nonexistent, told Mother I was probably better off as a composer than a naval officer after all. It would have given the thwarted lady pleasure to see me commissioned a lieutenant in the U.S. Coast Guard in 1944.

She ushered me to the piano and bade me display my latest musical attempts; I complied with zest, but it was obvious that Grandmother wasn't too smitten.

"You undoubtedly have talent," she conceded graciously, "but your musical style is already polluted with that horrible futuristic hogwash; all those Rebikovs, Scriabins, Debussys, and, God forbid, Schoenbergs. Ugh!"

To show there were no hard feelings, she took Alex and me on a round of the pastry shops. At the Confiserie Berrin we ate heavenly apricot ice cream; we swallowed éclairs and *petits fours* at several *pâtisseries,* and wound up in an arcade where pale, pretty St. Petersburg girls in white uniforms dispensed the latest concoction, raspberry ice drowned in seltzer, a Russian version of ice cream soda.

Father's younger brother, Colonel Ilya Dukelsky, lived in a luxurious flat in Basskov Pereulok, ostracized by the rest of the family because he belonged to the despised Corps de Gendarmes; he cynically asserted that he intended to indulge his expensive tastes, which included gold-digging cocottes. Mother took us on two visits to Uncle Ilya, who looked like a dissipated version of my late father, and Alex and I played big-game hunters with the bear and tiger skins stretched over the floor. I overheard Uncle Ilya's fascinating confession that his chief occupation in the Gendarme Corps was spying on Rasputin. Although the czar held the Siberian ex-monk in awe and had succumbed to his hypnotic influence, my uncle kept close tab on Rasputin's relationship with the czarina and her favorite lady in waiting, Anna Vyrubova. At his death in Nice during the German occupation, Uncle Ilya left a journal presumably full of the scandalous adventures of Rasputin in the hands of a friend who also died without bringing the memoirs to the light of day.

On another occasion Mother took us for a visit with young Prince

Irakly Toumanov and his pretty first wife, a Georgian, who lived not far from Tzarskoe Sielo. Uncle Irakly, who was Father's cousin, wore the beautiful uniform of a Czar's Strelok (the czar's crack rifle corps). While the young princess and Mother drank tea from a giant samovar, spiking it with quantities of choice cherry jam (an excellent recipe, by the way), Uncle Irakly took several rifles off the wall and proceeded to perform inspection of arms, to the terror of Alex and myself. His house was full of champion pointers, hunters, and beagles, as hunting was Irakly's favorite recreation.

The year immediately preceding the revolution was unremarkable musically speaking, as the World War made normal pursuits of learning more and more difficult. Mother and most of her female friends joined the Red Cross as volunteer nurses, and our apartment became the meeting place of young officers fresh from the front, quite a few of them wounded. Some of Glière's older pupils were mobilized, but on the other hand, there was an influx of aspiring composers from St. Petersburg and Moscow. Food was still plentiful in Kiev, and life was easy and carefree compared with the growing feeling of insecurity and unrest, as well as various economic restrictions, in the two Russian capitals.

Mother, who was a one-man woman if I ever saw one, dropped the frivolous Muscovites one by one and divided her time between the hospital and her new religion — theosophy, in which she was absorbed to the time of her death. Several St. Petersburg theosophists of note appeared in our midst; among them was the spruce Colonel Alexis Fedorovitch Lvov, grandson of the composer of the Russian national anthem, "God Save the Czar," written in 1833. Lvov was a vegetarian, spoke in a high-pitched and petulant voice, and in spite of his aestheticism relished the company of pretty women. He directed Mother to the writings of Blavatsky, Besant and Krishnamurti, whose ideas so entranced Mother that she spent several weeks in the prophet's camp after we came to America. Lvov was attached to a railroad battalion of the army, a connection which proved most useful to us a few years later. The colonel had just arrived from St. Petersburg, was devoted to the czarina, and had bitter misgivings about the mysterious conspiracy surrounding the czar's entourage.

Mother was a mild liberal in her political views and talked lightly about the desirability of a "change," the corruption of the court, the sufferings of an ill-equipped and ill-fed army, and the stifling St.

Petersburg censorship, which made clear thinking and frank talk an impossibility. It was a tradition in our household for Mother to tuck us into bed and bless us Greek Orthodox fashion every night; having performed this ritual lovingly, she would return to her guests — wounded officers and fanatical theosophists whose clamorous discussions in the drawing room kept us awake many an hour.

My piano studies with Dombrovsky were not progressing too satisfactorily. The business of practicing five or six hours a day was odious to me, and with my customary capacity for bluff, I tried a system of doing no piano work for several days and then spending all the day preceding the lesson practicing. The first few times I did tolerably well, but the exacting Dombrovsky soon caught up with my tricks.

"You don't want to be a pianist, you're a composer first and last," growled the big Pole. "I'm wasting your time, and you're wasting mine. You're gifted and facile, but you won't work; I suggest that you go to a teacher more interested in musical development than in pianistic pyrotechnics."

He gave me a note to a fellow Pole, Boleslav Javorsky, who had a reputation for eccentricity, radical tendencies, and fanatical disciples who did everything but study the piano. Obviously a man after my own heart.

CHAPTER IV

CAME THE REVOLUTION

TO THE non-Russian world all Russians are divided into two classes: Russians proper, that is the present inhabitants of my native country, and the White Russians, or emigrés. The arbitrary division of my former countrymen into resident procommunists and nonresident anti-Reds is erroneous. There are probably as many suppressed "Whites" inside Russia as there are underground "Reds" outside it. The term White Russian originated in the civil war following the Revolution, and we and our friends were of the bourgeois class from which this group was culled. To such people the great upheaval that came about in February, 1917, was a gratifying fulfillment of a roseate dream without which no supposedly clear-thinking bourgeois could call himself a member of the intelligentsia. Everybody was openly contemptuous and even patronizing about Nicholas II because of his mildness, lack of will power, and because he was dominated by unscrupulous and grafting cabinet members, who stifled the *Duma* (Parliament) and allowed Rasputin to become virtually a one-man Tammany Hall.

All that the February Revolution meant to the white-collar idealists was the dethronement of the unpopular czar, the humiliation of the still less popular czarina, and the vague beginnings of a mildly socialistic paradise in which the fast-talking and histrionically capable Alexander Kerensky played a self-appointed Archangel Gabriel with sex appeal.

Russian women gave the puny Severyanins, the Vertinskys, and the Sabinins the heave ho and became pioneer bobby soxers, with Kerensky as their political crooner. What he stood for, what he preached, and what he did with the enormous power given him seemed to be of no consequence. The whole country was in an unseeing and unthinking ecstasy, and the crew-haircutted, khaki-clad Kerensky with his Napoleonic attitudes and rhetorical flights kept it at its highest pitch.

The early days of revolution will always remain in my memory as elaborate flower parades put on in every street to the deafening *oompahs* of military bands; as throngs of wildly gesticulating women in their still Gibson-girlish dresses now mingling with fat-cheeked Ukrainian peasant girls; as occasional shootings and skirmishes with the rapidly dwindling loyal monarchists; as a never-ending recess from school, from the strict daily routine of a student, from obligations of any kind.

Spring was especially beautiful that year — the cataclysmic Russian spring with its islands of melting snow and tons of bluish-green ice suddenly cracking under the onslaught of the March sun, the streets inundated by rushing rivulets that were snow and ice only the night before. The swiftness of this spring and the welcome and clean-cut suddenness of the first Revolution seemed perfectly and violently mated. The sternest admonitions didn't prevent Alexis and myself from joining little groups of happily shouting collegians whose chief fun was tearing the Imperial eagles from their caps and adorning their sleeves with flaming-red bands.

Almost nightly there were symphonic concerts, everywhere hastily gotten up for some revolutionary-charity benefit and, at first, for the War Loan and Liberty Loan drives. Best of all were the Merchants' Gardens Concerts, where on one occasion a full-sized symphony orchestra consisting entirely of enlisted personnel played Tchaikovsky's *Pathétique* symphony, which inappropriate hymn to death was greeted by tumultuous shouts and frenzied cheering. At another concert a string intermezzo of mine, composed behind Glière's back, was publicly performed by the Moscow conductor Palitzin. This was a mournful little piece, inoffensive but pleasantly mellifluous, and it got a respectable enough hand for me to come forward and take my first bow before a paying audience. When the assembled other boys' mammas saw me, a thirteen-year-old in knee-pants, they cooed and twittered audibly: "Isn't he cute?" and, "Now you can see why you should practice the piano, Junior!" I was not concerned with my juvenile appeal, but only my (in my own eyes) indubitable greatness and didn't neglect telephoning Glière the next morning to tell him of my first triumph.

To achieve this "triumph," Mother secretly bribed a Conservatory graduate named Jasensky, a disgruntled musical pen pusher who wrote small orchestral pieces with little music in them but showily orchestrated; Jasensky was hired especially to clean up some unwieldy writing in my string piece, and got paid extra (unofficially) to palm off the music on Palitzin. Palitzin had no idea as to the identity of the composer and was just as amazed as the audience at my appearance.

Every concert given that spring mixed music with politics in that intermissions were taken up by fiery speeches — some by soldiers "just back from the front" (never the politically suspect officers, as they would have been roundly booed), some by influential civilians hastily appointed to government posts, and quite a few by unkempt and ferocious members of the dreaded Council (Soviet) of Workers and Soldiers Deputies. The soldiers "back from the front" were of the popular-hero variety, and their reassuring slogan was War to the Victorious End; these "heroes," some of whom had never seen battle, patterned themselves on Kerensky, copying his khaki trenchcoats and eaglelike attitudes. The "important" civilians were mostly rich and polished members of the Constitutional-Democratic Party (C.D., or Cadets as they were popularly called), landed gentry most of them, titled as often as not and sporting golden pince-nez, well-kept beards and bulky fur coats. These were the bourgeois intellectuals and would-be liberals so ruthlessly exterminated by the Soviets in the ensuing years; at the time they were enthusiastically received, as they spoke well if somewhat above their audience's heads (which is always impressive to Russians). The third group, the Soviet boys, were members of the extreme-left parties: the Bolshevik division of the Socialist-Democrat Party (then still a small minority) and even an anarchist or two. Their speeches consisted of shrill and impassioned screaming, with much invective and fist-shaking; "fraternize with the enemy and come home, soldiers" was their appeal. These violent rabble rousers meant no good, and every time they appeared a strange chill and premonition of the horrors to come seized their listeners.

Worse still, no concert was complete without a passport examination, a "security measure" for which the Soldiers and Workers Council was largely responsible and which was more in the nature of a raid on monarchists and other political undesirables. We children got off easy, of course, but we saw fashionably dressed bourgeois of both sexes, their teeth chattering, their eyes glassy with fear, being led away to pastures unknown by burly ex-soldiers with the dread red armbands. Sometimes suspects attempted to flee and to our horror distant shots would ring out, mingling with the thick harmonies of a Glazunov symphony.

Some subtle changes were taking place at home. Our ugly cook, Pauline, got herself a "returned hero" sweetheart who instructed her in the joys of stealing. Each day some trinket of Mother's would disappear, and when questioned Pauline laughed disdainfully and threatened that this was only the beginning and Mother could fire her if she didn't like it. It was impossible to get other servants as they were always in the street celebrating, and poor Mother was so used to the treacherous Pauline that she didn't have the heart to show her the door. New money in large denominations appeared everywhere, prices rose alarmingly, and food — particularly country produce — became scarce. Some of our young officer friends, desperate and disgusted, took off their uniforms, put on peasant garb, and went into the country with their wives' jewels to get drunk with the festive Ukrainians and to return with live chickens and geese, butter and eggs and milk.

Shortly after the February upheaval, I was admitted into Glière's Conservatory composition class. Outside of Liatoshinsky and Levin, there were several newcomers, mostly St. Petersburg and Moscow refugees. The eldest was the bankerlike Shatunovski, fortyish and dandified, his music so closely akin to that of Ravel that distinguishing between the two became an engrossing game for us students. In true St. Petersburg fashion, Shatunovski held himself somewhat aloof from us. Also from St. Petersburg was the now-prominent Soviet musicologist Alswang, a typical conservatory bore given to long speeches and enamored of technical terms.

Thanks to a blond Ukrainian named Nadenenko I discovered Debussy's *Pelléas,* and after much poring over its ethereal pages, my style switched from the recognized, respectable Glière-Glazunov manner (with a dash of Scriabin) to slavish imitations of Debussy and Ravel. I wrote a suite for piano duet fancifully entitled "Verlainiana," and shortly afterward the first act of an opera based on Maeterlinck's *Aladdine and Palomide* in which I cribbed from *Pelléas* to my heart's content.

These pretentious works made quite a bit of noise among the students and were exhibited to Glière. The good Reinhold Moritzovitch played them over searchingly and smiled at me benevolently through his pince-nez: "What have you and Nadenenko done, applied for French passports?" The class greeted this sally with students' inevitably overgenerous laughter. "What are we beginners to do, Reinhold Moritzovitch?" I retorted. "You and Glazunov have said all that could be said in Russian; we shall have to learn another language." Glière grinned, patted me on the back, and told me to get to work on a chamber piece for the student's concert which would abide by the rules, and put aside the mists of *Pelléas*.

Scriabin, as I have inferred, was the reigning influence in the two years preceding the 1917 revolution; he died in 1915 at the age of forty-four. This feverishly emotional but most limited composer was then the accepted model and the idol of Russian concert audiences. He provided effective piano vehicles for the virtuosi (a splendid pianist himself) and the ecstatic erotomania of his best inspirations moved and exhilarated the listeners. Not to write à la Scriabin was the mark of provincialism; his imitators were legion in every Russian city.

In our midst appeared a St. Petersburg pupil of Essipova, Markian Frolov, whose music was almost undistinguishable from that of Scriabin; it had the same agitated leaps, capricious rhythms, and erratic but opulent harmonies. Frolov, whom we called *starik* (old man) since he was nearly thirty, was a good pianist, and his rugged pipe-and-tweeds exterior belied his Scriabin worship. Briefly I succumbed to his tenets too, and produced some unconvincing Scriabinesque essays, but the style was entirely foreign to me and the influence proved inconsequential.

Revolution is always identified with youth, and the young — for the most part blissfully unconscious of the grave social changes and the accompanying crises — thrive on haphazard, come-what-may restlessness and pleasant chaos. We saw old and respectable conservatory professors inexplicably vanish, their places taken by aggressive young men in military-style "frenches" (as American and British officers' tunics were then called in Russia) and polished cavalry-issue boots. They talked music, but instead of using words like counterpoint, double fugue, recapitulation, main subject, etc., constantly referred to ideology, proletariat, class war, bourgeois tendencies and social significance. Their talk sounded strange to us, but these early "commissars" were there to enforce the New Order, and we liked to consider ourselves "progressive" and to be part of it.

The two capitals began sending us dozens of precocious music boys, among them ten-year-old Julian Scriabin, the late composer's son. His mother, Tatiana Fedorovna, was a tragically beautiful figure in deep mourning, which she affected long after her husband's death of blood poisoning. Julian had enormous deerlike eyes, and a rather distant air. I was slightly resentful of his extreme youth, which displaced me as the official *wunderkind* of Glière's class. One night at Liatoshinsky's, Julian played some promising piano preludes for us; his mother and two sisters were accompanied by a Puckish young man of quick eye and ready tongue named Nicolas Slonimsky, who is now an entertaining writer on music in America.

Apparently Scriabin *père,* in common with most composers, had little money to leave his wife and children, for Tatiana Fedorovna and her son lived in genteel poverty. There was no electricity in the house they occupied and poor Julian composed by candlelight. He was peculiarly choosy about various orchestral timbres: disliked strings but adored the clarinet, which he called the aristocrat of instruments.

The first revolutionary summer, a lazy Ukrainian summer, started the usual desertion from Kiev to the countryside; this was no longer easy, as the trains were jammed with soldiers celebrating their return from the front, revolutionary officials and their staffs transferring from place to place, and with the ever-present Workers and Soldiers Deputies always holding the priorities. Finally we managed to accept the invitation of Mother's new friends, the Lipofka-Polovinetzes. The son Stass played the violin and was one of Alex's buddies. His uncle, a rich and cynical sybarite named Wulfert was a cousin of Tchaikovsky's tragic friend Davidov. Wulfert owned the lovely eighteenth century house where we vacationed, in the government of Poltava not far from Mirgorod, immortalized by Gogol.

The house was on Gogol's beloved river Psiol, and when I first saw it I had a strange feeling that I'd been there before and that I was familiar with every corner of it. Wulfert had a superb Erard piano; at dusk as I played it, the open windows of the drawing room wafted in the rich scents of honeysuckle and roses from the garden outlined in tall poplars, with the village church spire in the background; I heard the peasant girls singing as they sauntered home from their work in the fields.

Even in that provincial hamlet there was a feeling of insecurity and unrest and the peasants had begun to assert themselves bit by bit. But food was still abundant, there were no ration cards, no people lining up before understocked grocers' shops, none of the other discomforts we had known in Kiev.

We drank in that last summer in the Russian countryside avidly. There were boating and swimming daily in the willow-sheltered waters of the Psiol, and Mrs. Wulfert, an extraordinarily handsome rose-skinned blonde, had a floating bathing barge built for herself and could be observed every afternoon, completely naked, indolently stretching herself in the sun. My recollections of church-sanctioned nudism came back strongly, as the numerous peasant wenches employed on the estate were also fond of swimming in the nude, singing, giggling, and splashing about like clumsy white seals.

On our return to Kiev we found great changes. The "french-coated" young men were on every street corner, gesturing and shouting threats and promises to hypnotized citizens. Large posters covered with exclamation points and promising death to the bourgeois and all enemies of the working class were now signed openly by the central committee of the Workers and Soldiers Soviet and the Presidium of the Socialist-Democrat Party (Bolsheviks).

The lines outside the food shops lengthened daily. All clothing was severely rationed, shots rang out constantly, and the populace was asked not to leave home after sundown on certain evenings because of spreading disturbances. Alex and I were still handed our daily lunches carefully wrapped by Mother and sent off to school, Alex to Naumenko's and I to the Conservatory, Mother warning us not to endanger ourselves in the crowded streets. Going to the opera or to concerts was now a perilous adventure as all bourgeois children and grownups were recognizable by their dress and manner and were automatically asked for their identification papers and often held for annoying and officious examinations.

The reports from St. Petersburg and Moscow were more and more disturbing. In April the authorities had permitted a sealed train bearing Lenin and his cohorts across the Russo-German border; a few weeks later these men were joined by Trotsky, who arrived from Canada, and their nefarious plotting began to be activated in Russia in earnest. Although their first attempt in July to seize power with the help of mutinous sailors from the Kronstadt naval base proved abortive, their imprisonment was only temporary.

The country and the war effort undeniably were going to the dogs. The officers who still paid furtive visits to our flat dressed as soldiers or peasants unanimously denounced the vacillating Kerensky, who deprived the popular General Kornilov of command while he was en route to St. Petersburg to protect the provisional government until a *zemski sobor* (people's voting assembly) could be held; this allowed the Bolshevik leaders to seize power, the Red masterminds were released from prison, Kerensky, for whom Lenin issued a warrant of arrest, fled the country disguised as a woman, and the Soviets moved virtually unopposed into the custody of Russia.

Kiev, being a provincial town, did not receive the news of these events until a few days later, but the repercussions were swift and terrifying.

One of the first men to be arrested, held for questioning, and finally returned to his domicile with all of his money and securities confiscated was Grandfather Kopylov. Mother's comfortable yearly income vanished with the inflation that swept Ukraine, and she was unable to sell her stocks and bonds. She began to dispose of her diamonds, of which she fortunately had quite a few, and managed to carry on for several years. The two leading newspapers, including of course the reactionary *Kievlyanin* of which Grandfather was an important stockholder, were abolished and replaced by Bolshevik sheets which were carbon copies of the all-powerful *Pravda* and *Izvestya.* The Red Terror carried off hundreds of victims to the Che-Ka cellars daily, and we couldn't sleep at night because of the racing motors of the huge army trucks employed to drown out the screams of the townspeople being shot or tortured by the Chekists.

Each apartment house had a "house committee," the head of which was responsible to the Soviet government for his tenants; this resulted in people spying on each other, making up stories about unpopular neighbors, and carrying on a private revolution in every courtyard.

The new plutocrats were the food-shop owners, who took to sporting furs and Paris dresses; enterprising youths pursued the lady shopkeepers, offering their manly charms in exchange for butter and milk.

The fact that clothes were rationed became meaningless, because even with a ration card clothes were unobtainable. Mother spent most of her time cutting trousers and making outlandish coats out of old skirts, bedroom-window curtains, and woolen rugs to clothe her growing sons. I remember traipsing off to the Conservatory in a golden-yellow coat of a most unorthodox cut, with green trousers made *galifé* (cavalry) fashion, the origin of which I suspected was Grandfather's billiard table.

The Bolsheviks, pie-eyed drunk with power, mobilized boys of sixteen and men over fifty to fight the volunteer patriotic troops assembling throughout Russia; it was a moot point with these unfortunates as to which was worse — to wear a Red star on one's cap or a Red bullet in one's heart.

One afternoon, Glière's counterpoint class was interrupted by the unheralded arrival of the notorious Che-Ka executioner Pereverzev, accompanied by two Red Army officers and two music commissars. Pereverzev was a splendid Slavic specimen, tall and blond, wearing an unfamiliar uniform with three or four guns jammed in his holster belt; he shook hands patronizingly with Glière and turned to speak to the students, who were all frozen with fear.

"Composer Comrades, the hour has struck, now that the great October Revolution has given humanity a new hope and pattern for life; you musicians have the chance to combat the Soviet's dastardly enemies — the degenerate capitalists and czarist lackeys who conspire to stab the Revolution in the back!" He went on like this, using roughly the clichés of today's Soviet newspapers, and wound up with: "We ask you, therefore, on behalf of our beloved Soviet government and our noble leader Comrade Trotsky, to do your bit to help the Universal Military Training Program (*Vsievobutch*). To popularize this more than timely measure, we of the Communist Party have decided to present a full-length opera which you will write within two weeks."

This brought an involuntary gasp from the assembled students, and a whispered conversation between Glière and the intruders ensued. Pereverzev resumed his talk to inform us that he was fully in accord with Glière's plan to have the opera created "collectively" by the best of Glière's composing talent. The libretto was the work of Lev Nikulin, a mediocre poet turned Red, Liatoshinsky was to write the overture and orchestrate the entire opera, Nadenenko and Frolov were to supply the ballets and choral ensembles, and I, because of my melodic gift, was entrusted with the job of writing three "revolutionary" arias. In spite of his extreme youth, Julian Scriabin, the late composer's son, then only ten, was assigned the words of a "patriotic" girls' chorus.

Pereverzev nodded approvingly as the truly communistic work division took place, repeated a few more official platitudes, and with an ecstatic "Death to the World's Bourgeoisie!" strode out of the classroom, patting one of his guns, followed obsequiously by the officers and commissars.

The silence that ensued was quite the gloomiest in my experience. There was no arguing with the new masters, we all knew that; but what if we shouldn't deliver "the goods" they wanted? It was not for us, the earliest birds, nor for any Soviet composer since, to question the validity or possible effectiveness of such an assignment. All we had to do was to set Nikulin's servile verses and be damned quick about it. The lesson over, we, the collective Soviet composers, were ordered home to our frozen pianos.

Mother, on hearing of my strange assignment, became terribly perturbed, but dejectedly realized there was no way out. "Don't make it too good, Son," she said with an attempt at humor.

I went to work immediately and astonished Glière two days later by bringing in all three arias neatly written out. Little Julian was there, too, as he was having considerable trouble with his girls' chorus, professing not to understand the words assigned to him. Glière played over my songs and apparently found them satisfactory, for he called in one of the commissars and asked him to play over Comrade Dukelsky's inspirations. The well-groomed young commissar, a conservatory-trained pianist, played the arias through and said he thought them "just right" and very stimulating indeed. I confess that although I was not in tune politically with my new boss, I was quite elated at his praise; I went home to tell Mother that my songs had been accepted and would go into rehearsal the next day. Mother was horrified, as she had secretly hoped I would be found incompetent for such an important task, and vowed that although I must help during rehearsals, she would never allow me to attend any performances of the devilish Soviet propaganda opera. "How can you prevent my attending?" I queried incredulously. "If I don't show up they are sure to throw me in the Che-Ka!" Mother shook her head determinedly. "You will be very ill, Dima, and I will be forced to keep you in bed. Do you understand?" This prospect was not to my liking, but Mother was adamant. The opera was completed on schedule; all its component parts fitted like a jig-saw puzzle and were orchestrated by the harried Liatoshinsky, who gave up all hope of sleeping for several nights. After I got through rehearsing a fat blond soprano in my revolutionary anthems, Mother appeared at the Conservatory with our family doctor, who felt my pulse, made a grave face, and speeded me home in an *izvostchik*.

I was put to bed and given a peculiar-tasting drug which made me very weak indeed; I suspect it was a potent sedative as I remember being in bed for three days and floating in celestial dreams. On the fourth day I was awakened by sounds uncomfortably familiar. I ran to the window in my nightshirt and saw my fat blond soprano propped against a truck-borne piano, her accompanist being one of my fellow composers. She was singing one of my revolutionary hymns through a large megaphone, and Nikulin's flashy words set off almost as flashily by my music rang out abrasively in the morning air. Mother ran into the room in the middle of the refrain and burst into bitter tears.

Back to bed I went. An hour or so later, there was a loud knock at the door, of the kind universally feared in Russia. Mother went white and crossed me hastily. "This is it, Dimotchka," she said, her eyes misty with tears. "Have courage. If we die, we die together." She walked to the door and opened it cautiously. Four Red Army soldiers wearing huge squeaking boots entered carrying two big burlap bags.

"Does Comrade Dukelsky live here?" the tallest of the four asked.

"Yes, gentlemen," Mother said falteringly. "He is my son. He's sick in bed. Is there anything I can do?"

The soldier grinned. "In bed, eh, the little Bourjooitchik? Very well, here is his pay for contributing to our opera. Good day to you, Comrade." With these words, the soldiers threw the bags on the floor and walked out, their boots squeaking reassuringly.

Mother ran to the bags and, on feeling the burlap with her needleworn hands, exclaimed joyfully, "It's flour, flour!" She brought a kitchen knife and, after making an insertion, ascertained to her even greater delight that my pay consisted of precious white flour.

One afternoon in the spring of 1918, Julian Scriabin and his sisters went swimming on the Dnieper. He hid himself in the rushes to undress; apparently had a sunstroke, fainted, fell into the swift river and drowned instantly. His terrified sisters, unable to find him, ran back to town and unburdened their grief to Nicolas Slonimsky, as their mother was away on pressing family business in Moscow. Slonimsky telephoned Levin and they instigated a search which lasted a week before Julian's body was recovered. The two young musicians were faced with the inhuman task of telling Madame Scriabin, on her return, of her new loss.

Music became my only life, the one meager illusion of immortality in a rapidly vanishing world. I came down, in swift succession, with one disease after another, so that my health added to Mother's mounting tribulations; we were chronically undernourished and going into the country in search of food was now punishable by death. There was little desire for such expeditions anyhow as Kiev was surrounded by bands of disorganized rebels, "Yellows" and "Greens," as they called themselves; these were highway robbers who tried to whitewash their plundering and mayhem with the labels of various assumed ideologies.

In Kiev, we drank tea distilled from carrots, coffee made from tree bark and soup cooked with a stock of the bones of a raw herring used again and again. The only bread available was made of stale, sickly green peas and had a musty, forbidding odor rather like that of a rattrap. Horse meat was the standard luxury, but some of our acquaintances even essayed cat and dog ragouts, which we boys, with memories of *Sobatchania* still fresh, refused to sample. Little wonder that our gums bled regularly and that Alex and I began to lose our teeth.

From the beginning of the Bolshevik Revolution in 1917 to the time of our flight in the winter of 1920, there were nineteen changes of government in our city. Each one of these changes was accompanied by a bloody battle in the streets, including Bolshaya-Podvalnaya, and by all-night bombardment and incessant machine-gun fire. During these tense struggles, the house-committee leader ordered all tenants into the basement shelters, where we huddled together in fear and hunger. During one bombing which occurred in the middle of the day, I got acutely fed up with the whole thing — the evil-smelling fellow tenants, the prayer-mumbling old women, the ceaselessly whining children, and, I'm ashamed to say, my own mother's exaggerated preoccupation with my welfare. I ran out of the shelter and up five flights to our apartment, where I stole to the piano. This sounds like an affected theatrical tour de force, but I truly began composing, oblivious of the crashing bombs outside. As I was picking out a Frenchified reverie, a bomb hit the top of our building and caved in the seventh floor, with the sixth floor above the only barrier between me and certain death. A heavy chandelier plunged to the floor, missing my head by inches, and I tore back to the shelter, panic-stricken. I entered to a concerted wail led by Mother; her relief was as great as my delicious feeling of enveloping safety.

In the spring of 1918 I completed a four-movement string sextet, and this Glazunov-like work, quite respectable as to technique and musicianship, permitted Glière to devote one half of a Conservatory concert to my compositions; also programmed were some of my rather flowery songs and a set of piano pieces. The soprano Znamenska acquitted herself well in the songs, the sextet made a favorable impression, and by the time I appeared in one of Mother's better sartorial creations, the audience gave me a warm reception. After the concert there were even some cheers, and pretty girls came back to the artists' room to shake my hand, which quite turned my head.

Although Javorsky, my piano teacher, played the instrument beautifully, he was far less concerned with technical proficiency than with the all-around conception and feel of a piece assigned to his student for preparation. Javorsky discarded all accepted academic tools and created his own modal system, to which he devoted most of his life. He lived with his favorite pupil, Serge Protopopov, a pudgy, good-looking youth who usually wore an apron, as he did all the cooking in the Javorsky ménage. There were some strange stories about these two and Javorsky's morals in general, but I was too eager to absorb Boleslav Leopoldovitch's revolutionary musical theories and his new slant on piano playing to worry about the excessive kisses he showered on the pupils after each lesson. Javorsky was a fascinating talker and never lost an opportunity to kick whatever academic backside happened to be close by. He was most unpopular with the rest of the Conservatory personnel and his piano pupils never won prizes, which was all right with me; Javorsky was far more interested in what I wrote than in what I played.

Chronologically speaking, it is hard and unnecessary to list Kiev's bloody government changes in the order of their appearance and disappearance. Regardless of one's political beliefs, it is only fair to say that food, clothing, and other necessities returned briefly under the German-appointed *Hetman* (leader), General Skoropadsky, and the short-lived triumph of the Volunteer Army in 1919. Otherwise, whether they temporarily seized power in street skirmishes or full-size bombings, these varied regimes brought nothing but misery and acute distress to the Kiev people.

What Ukrainian patriots didn't bargain for was that with the advent of the *Hetman* Kiev was virtually German-occupied, and the steel helmets of Prussian and Bavarian *Burschen* bristled everywhere. Shortly after the installation of the *Hetman* regime, the revolution in Germany took place and the troops deserted Kiev, with Skoropadsky escaping, Kerensky style. With him fled our hopes for order, as the Ukrainian Nationalists took over briefly in bandit fashion, and in their wake followed the notorious Ataman Petliura, whose troops indiscriminately slaughtered Bolsheviks and volunteers alike, not to mention a few *Hetman* supporters who couldn't get out in time. After fourteen days and nights of incessant bombing, during which we only awakened when the shock of a ten-minute lull occurred, the Soviets retook the city and the Red Terror again engulfed us. We had little energy to keep track of the political turnover, being too preoccupied with where the next meal was coming from.

Then on August 31, 1919, the Denikin Volunteer Army made a magnificent entrance patterned on the seventeenth-century Boyards processions. We had never seen so many imperial standards, golden epaulets, glittering decorations, never heard so many prerevolutionary songs and czarist army marches. This time the joyous schoolboys and hysterical parents were out in full force, not to welcome a revolution but what looked like a release from it; the same rose-tossing females who had pelted Kerensky now favored the fat, red-jowled General May-Maevsky. I remember standing on tiptoe behind two Madame LaFarge-like, scrawny hags in the Place of St. Sophia to hear the general's speech of victory; his sonorous voice resembled an aged bulldog's bark. No one understood what he said, but who cared? The white officers were back and so were white bread, milk, butter, and plump country chickens.

Our officer friends, the same ones who had crawled in and out of the apartment disguised as workers or peasants, blossomed out in their dress uniforms with Saint George crosses dangling triumphantly on their chests. Colonel Lvov put aside theosophy and busied himself with his railroad battalion. Miniature theaters mushroomed overnight. Restaurants with renowned Muscovite names opened. Hordes of currency speculators flourished. A renaissance of the good old ego- and cubo-futurists took place: the Vertinsky imitators, decked out as

Pierrots, the Acmeists, who were a Russian continuation of the Paris Parnasse, and out-and-out poetical anarchists like Zdanevitch, who cantered around a stage and made sounds like a horse as his contribution to the arts. I wavered between continuing as a composer or returning to poetry; on one or two occasions, I painted my face subtly and recited some of my poems at one of the dozens of the poets' cafés. The intoxicated patrons rewarded my youthful aplomb with assurances that I was at least as good as Mayakovsky, which appraisal of my gifts did not displease me. Mother was too busy selling her diamonds and buying dubious bargains to criticize my exploits.

By the end of November it was clear that the Denikin cause was rapidly disintegrating, there were reports of wholesale corruption, and the newspapers reporting the progress of "our valiant army" were full of blank spots, due to the increased censorship. The volunteer forces not only had not reached Moscow, but were now retreating toward Kiev at a vertiginous pace; in spite of censorship, battles and skirmishes were reported at various points too close to Kiev for comfort.

One morning early in December we were awakened by heavy cannon fire; Colonel Lvov, who was rooming with us, located it at fifteen miles from Kiev. He dressed rapidly, dashed out of the apartment scowling ominously, and returned for a family conference. Lvov's folded arms and compressed lips promised trouble.

"I have just returned from the railroad-battalion headquarters, Anna Alexevna, and I have it on excellent authority that the Communists will be here in three or four days at the latest. You have been kind enough to give me sanctuary and the least I can do is offer you and the boys the limited facilities available for transportation to Odessa. Since, however, space is most restricted, you will be forced to leave all your belongings here and take nothing but the barest necessities."

"Leave my husband's souvenirs, my mother's Bechstein and silver? That's unthinkable!" Mother exclaimed.

Lvov shrugged wearily. "Then we must stay here and face the music; we may all be killed, but then again we may not. Who knows? As a true theosophist —"

This was my cue. "Theosophy be hanged!" said I. "We are all doomed here. Every Soviet spy in the neighborhood saw you in your splendid uniform; every errand boy knows that you are rooming with us; our family has been identified with the White regime. Even if they don't kill us here, life anywhere else would be better. If we stay on, Alex and I will lose all our teeth, Mother will sell her last diamonds, and I won't have the strength to write my music and poetry. We must go, please, please!"

The colonel tugged his mustache, shrugged again, and said that the decision was up to Mother; that nothing so absurd as my artistic pursuits should influence this momentous decision in the lives of four people. This made me boil with indignation and I began painting our impending doom under the Soviet onslaught so eloquently that Mother arose somewhat theatrically, her mind made up.

"Lead on, Alexei Fedorovitch; your opinion as to my son's talents is immaterial to me, although I regret that you are not sufficiently musical to appreciate his promise as a composer. Since my husband's death I live only for my boys; although my possessions are dear to me, they are nothing weighed against my sons' future lives. I am grateful for your offer and I accept it." A third shrug from the colonel and we began to pack.

The next day, December 14th, the newspapers were reduced to half a page, the rest all whitened out by the censors, the rout of the volunteers obviously in full swing. Mother's decision to entrain to Odessa was strengthened by the knowledge that my father's brother, Colonel Ilya Dukelsky, the former shadow of Rasputin, was now in charge of evacuation in the seaport; the train on which Lvov arranged passage to Odessa for us was the last to leave Kiev, as it turned out. Mother packed a few essentials under the eagle eye of the colonel while I made a tidy bundle of my music manuscripts, collected poems, and a prized green toothbrush; when the colonel spied this he sniggered disdainfully and said that at times like this, such superfluous trivia should not consume space. A prolonged verbal battle ensued, with Mother and Alex (never a Lvov fan) as my impassioned seconds. My precious bundle finally was passed by the colonel and we closed up our home and stole out into the sickly, silent streets. After dragging our belongings for several blocks we were hoisted into a grimy truck, along with other would-be exiles, and driven to the deserted and blacked-out Kiev railroad station. On Lvov's promised train, our accommodation was a dirty red carriage with the legend "40 men, 8 horses" on the door; we were grudgingly given cramped space on its floor by the crowded occupants. Thank God, there were no horses.

CHAPTER V

ODESSA

THE TRAIN to Odessa started forward with a weary whine after three or four violent preliminary jerks, stealthily deserting Kiev's icy, blacked-out station. Mother, Colonel Lvov, Alex and I crouched together, surrounded by a suffocating mass of human bodies, whose combined warmth heightened the acrid smells reminiscent of the boxcar's former horse-tenants. Male and female, old and young, sturdy and disease-stricken, the fur-clad bodies crouched or stretched out about us in a sleepy stupor, some of the faces wrapped in *bashlyks* (hoodlike woolen scarves) vaguely familiar to us.

Mother tried to keep from crying for her abandoned home. Alex and I had some pangs about never again seeing the citizens of *Sobatchania,* who were now locked up in the 1880 cupboard in the hall, and we wondered what boys would be appropriating our animal books in the musty little library; but when you're sixteen, you are blissfully aware that your life is before you, and leaving the familiar for the unknown is a challenge to be relished.

The train was maddeningly slow, stopping not only at all stations, but countless times between stations; something always seemed to be going wrong — there was much signaling and shouting which was hard to make out through our one, high boxcar window. At stations, the train groaned and squeaked to a stop and we opened the doors to the frosty air, searched for the sign bearing the station's name, and were sometimes rewarded by the sight of a stationmaster swinging a welcoming lamp while a howling group of *babas* (peasant women), coifed in their traditional kerchiefs (peculiarly known to American women as "babushkas," which in Russian is grandmother), and their raggedy children engaged in lively trade with the hungry passengers. Their wares were none too appetizing — pickles, *bublicks* (bagels) and sometimes hard-boiled eggs, at outrageous prices; the crafty peasants contemptuously refused the *"Kerenka"* (Kerensky's rubles) and the Denikin banknotes in high denominations and clamored for articles of clothing or jewelry. As in Kiev, Alexis and I scouted for boiling water, which cost more at each succeeding station.

In the bandit-infested areas the train was completely blacked-out; Greens, Yellows and even Blacks (anarchists) prowled for rich *boorjoois* to loot, killing Denikin officers and raping their women. Our train was twice held up by those blood-curdling Eastern counterparts of the James brothers, but our car miraculously escaped, leaving us in a bad fright, trying to curb some typically high-powered Russian feminine hysterics. *Cauchemar* (nightmare) was one of my mother's favorite words in normal circumstances (she had even applied it to Pauline's cooking on occasion), and now the poor woman was quite beside herself with terror.

The trip became a *cauchemar* in earnest when an epidemic of typhus broke out. The entire car was kept awake one night by the cries and convulsions of a man lying next to me, who died in agony at dawn. There were no provisions or time for burial; four of us heaved him onto a snowbank when the train stopped between stations. The infection spread, and two former inhabitants of our apartment building in Kiev had to be left at a country hospital; we shuddered at leaving them without proper doctors or medicine, but it was their only hope. Although we were suspicious of Alex's condition for a while, none of our quartet caught the typhus.

The journey from Kiev to Odessa, which ordinarily took about twenty hours, lasted for fifteen days. We arrived unspeakably dirty and ridden with lice and other vermin and set out to find my paternal Uncle Ilya to put ourselves under his powerful protection. Colonel Ilya Vladimirovitch Dukelsky held the ominous title of Head of Evacuation of the City of Odessa; obviously the persons whom he was to evacuate were the Denikin Volunteers. These erstwhile "liberators" were being pushed back into the Black Sea by the other self-styled "liberators," the Bolsheviks; but my Uncle Ilya and his fellow White officers, in that last overconfident month of 1919, seemed bent only on evacuating boredom and pessimism.

We were shown to the portico of 8 Deribasovskaya Street, a splendid private house commandeered by the Denikin headquarters for Ilya's use, and were startled to hear the impassioned sounds of a gypsy chorus backed up by an apparently sizable balalaika orchestra, ample proof that Uncle Ilya had transplanted his lavish St. Petersburg bacchanalia to Odessa. Mother and Colonel Lvov exchanged outraged glances before ringing the bell. The door was flung open by a massive orderly, who examined our tattered quartet with surprised distaste. Mother, in a proud if tremulous voice, delivered the information that we were his master's relatives, and after scratching his head, the orderly went off to interrupt the festivities with the news of our arrival.

Ilya Vladimirovitch appeared, a little unsteady on his feet, his eyes bloodshot, but elegantly uniformed and full of good — perhaps a little too good — cheer. His dissipations had aged him terribly, his glossy mustache had given way to unbecoming Edwardian side whiskers and his hair was now shot with untidy gray. After kissing us with caution and shaking hands ceremoniously with Lvov, he scowled, "Good heavens, Niura!" (Mother's family nickname.) "You must be covered with lice and bugs, you poor things! Come now, I'll order hot baths for you all and find some clean clothing. I'll drop in later to be sure you are comfortable."

"Aren't you going to talk to us for a moment, Ilya?" Mother questioned indignantly. "We aren't untouchables, you know. You don't know what we have gone through, escaping from our Kiev hell!"

Ilya stammered embarrassedly, "Yes, yes, of course. Only you see — a few friends dropped in for supper, so I'm afraid I must . . ."

Mother sighed, "Very well, Ilya, don't worry about us. Hot water, soap, and a change of clothing will be heavenly. We'll talk when you are free."

Ilya smiled, patted me on the head, and went back to the "few friends," who were now dancing with the hard-working, hired gypsies. Upstairs, we four had luxurious baths with stinging-hot water, pungent yellow soap, and outsized turkish towels; then we slipped into clean robes and were served chicken bouillon, as well as precious white bread and fresh butter. We said our prayers and happily flopped into four separate beds without waiting for Uncle Ilya's promised visit. He apologized the next morning for not breaking away, but we learned that it had been a birthday celebration for his Siberian mistress and therefore a special occasion.

"Odessa Mama" as the popular ditty had it, was an enchanting town. Far less Russian than Kiev or Moscow (the French, the Greeks and the Italians played important roles in its history), the place had an almost Mediterranean indolence and subtropical languor.

Having soon discovered that Uncle Ilya's temporary palace was no suitable place for us — it was heavy with the colonel's amorous intrigues and almost nightly "celebrations" — Alex and I were sent into the streets on insignificant but, to us, most attractive errands. My passion for *flânerie* (a sort of inspired strolling dear to the literary Frenchman), already begun in Tzarskoe Sielo, St. Petersburg and Moscow, was now being indulged hourly and, since my sturdy brother was equally fond of walking, we soon explored the town very thoroughly indeed.

In the realm of music instruction, Glière was now replaced by Vitold Malishevsky, a good-looking youngish Pole, then director of the Odessa Conservatory. Like Glière of foreign origin, Malishevsky — also like Glière — adhered strictly to the Belaiev group and wrote (in Diaghilev's phrase) "samovar and red boots" music. This music was no better and no worse than the productions of the Belaiev minor gods. Malishevsky's fastidious taste, however, led him to tinker with a little Debussy-and-water on the side. In appearance and manner he somewhat resembled that great charmer Karol Szymanovski; they both had (if you'll forgive the too-easy gag) that irresistibly Polish polish, catlike suavity and softness of speech. They subsequently succeeded one another as director of the Warsaw Conservatory in the days prior to the Communist annexation of their country. To Malishevsky I brought some highly spiced songs which he professed to like. One of them (salvaged from Kiev and now adorning one of my walls) is perhaps the first really decent piece I wrote, and Malishevsky praised it unreservedly; another ("Like the White Swans" was the title) intrigued him chiefly because of its inhuman range. "Why do you insist on making the poor soprano hit high C's all the time?" Malishevsky asked me. My answer was typical of my early cockiness: "Because I only want *good* singers to sing my music and bad singers can't hit a C." Malishevsky burst out laughing and took me under his wing.

During the day, I studied the counterpoint problems set me by Malishevsky, and at night the bizarre human patterns of my Uncle Ilya's ménage, which my mother considered distressingly unorthodox. Ilya's two favorites of the moment were the Siberian beauty Olga Stepanovna and an ample seductress named Claudia Mikhailovna, who had a most melodious laugh, an irresistible habit of squinting sensuously and a laudable capacity for taking on all comers. One of these, the tiny but muscular dandyish Goulaiev, was the classical "life of the party" Russian, and prided himself on outsinging, outdancing, and outdrinking them all. After warbling "To the Darling Women," a cavalier's serenade I always thought insufferable, he drank champagne out of his chosen lady-of-the-evening's slipper, then led her to one of the cozy Persian divans for more concentrated gallantries.

Olga and Claudia detested one another and, to make things worse, Uncle Ilya was of extremely jealous nature and, with truly gendarme-like persistence, spied on Olga, occasionally even stooping to questioning us boys about her comings and goings. Alas, the Siberian siren considered poor Ilya an "old man," while availing herself of his generosity, and to irk him further, embarked on an energetic flirtation with a sixteen-year-old boy — myself. This was both flattering and terrifying to me; I was clearly no match for the athletic and amoral *bons vivants* of Ilya's entourage, so, to assert myself, I began showering the lady with amorous sonnets. On receiving these tokens of my adoration, the heartless Olga would read them aloud to her circle, punctuating her delivery with mocking laughter. Some of my rhyming proved surprisingly ingenious, which the younger men grudgingly admitted, but Ilya was not at all amused and complained to Mother; she, in turn, took my poetic offerings very seriously and even remonstrated with Olga, asking her to leave me alone.

In the evening, when the balalaika orchestra was unavailable, I would be pressed into service, rattling off polkas, tangos, and the increasingly popular American two-steps. The nearer the Reds came to Odessa, the more worried and despondent Ilya's group became, and the nightly orgies grew more frantic and noisy in our false oasis of pleasure.

An American enlisted man, Corporal Krouglov, who had been born in Russia, was one of the lions at these *soirées dansantes*. Krouglov was a huge bear of a man whose hands, big as Smithfield hams, could have crushed the puny poets who had long sung of "gentlemen cowboys" and now found themselves uncomfortably deserted by the ladies in favor of a living personification of their super-virile dream prince. With his colorful, broad-brimmed hat, cavalry boots, and Sam Browne belt, since discarded by the U.S. Army, his impressive position with the American Red Cross, and his exaggerated nasal twang, "Big Jim" Kroughlov succeeded in conquering all hearts in Ilya's harem.

Things soon assumed an unpleasantly familiar pattern. The News From the Front section in the Odessa newspapers began to resemble a chessboard with so many white quadrangles. Our "valiant allies," mostly in the shape of French sailors with their gay pompons, Senagalese infantry of the flashing white teeth and shining black faces, phlegmatic Britishers, were still about, but we began to suspect that they were there to protect their own interests rather than Denikin's.

Mother attempted to interrogate Uncle Ilya on this unhappy turn of events, but, beyond references to "our brilliant leader, General Denikin" and "our valiant allies" got nothing out of him. Poor Ilya was too preoccupied with Olga's perfidies to bother about the political scene. Mother's younger brother, Nicholas, a rising gynecologist, appeared at 8 Deribasovskaya and declared that he was desperately in love with one of his patients — the young wife of a rich manufacturer — and "wouldn't budge." Plenty of budging was quietly going on all around us, with journalists, doctors, businessmen and just plain speculators offering large bribes to captains and first mates of various commercial vessels stationed in Odessa port, for transportation for themselves and their families to the Crimea, where the courageous Baron Wrangel was still firmly entrenched, or far-off Constantinople, at the other end of our own Black Sea.

Krouglov was now too busy at the American Red Cross headquarters to bother further with Ilya's women. He needed a few English-speaking lads to help him guard his organization's warehouses in the port, and since I had a smattering of English and since among Krouglov's promises was space on a transport bound for Constantinople, I eagerly volunteered. When Krouglov, with a skeptical glance at my frail physique, asked whether I could handle a gun, I lied by replying in the affirmative. I was given a rusty Enfield rifle, an American khaki uniform, and a Red Cross armband. Every evening we young volunteers (there were seven or eight) were picked up by a Red Cross truck and taken to the port, there to stand watch, report possible disturbances and shoot at sight, if necessary. This last possibility was purely academic in my case, as I didn't know how to hold the rifle correctly, let alone fire it. However, what I missed in knowledge and experience, I made up in bluff — a formula I often relied upon with satisfactory results, and Krouglov soon told Mother that I was a willing worker and a model sentry. Luckily, outside of a sailors' brawl or two and some shots that occasionally rang out nearby but caused no damage, there was no trouble and I was never put to the test of using my Enfield.

A few days later, the city of Odessa awoke to the sounds of heavy bombing, and on rushing into the street, we beheld posters on which were printed a *prikaz* (order) calling for a general and immediate evacuation. The *prikaz* was signed by a general unknown to us, not by poor Ilya, who either resigned or was relieved of his duties. The flight to transports, barges, small passenger steamers and even private yachts, now requisitioned by the Denikin command, was on in earnest. Krouglov summoned "his boys" and told us that we were to guard the warehouses as usual that night and, in the early morning, round up a half-dozen senior officers and escort them to the small Spanish transport *Navaho,* a disreputable old tub already familiar to us. To my dismay, I read the name of Uncle Ilya on the list handed us by Krouglov. Did this mean that he was under some form of arrest? As Krouglov later explained, the senior officers on the list were heavily involved in anti-Bolshevik activities and ran the risk of being slaughtered by the Soviet underlings, even before the Red Army's entrance into Odessa, expected momentarily. We teen-age boys were thus entrusted with the task of protecting the lives of professional military men, veterans of many battles. When I told my uncle, already irked by my attentions to Olga, that we had orders to escort him and his fellow officers on board the *Navaho,* he shrugged wearily without looking at me. "It's a sad farce," he muttered. "It is also the end of everything for us all; good thing that Niura has a few diamonds left." These were the last three diamonds Mother still owned, and she was constantly inventing new and unusual methods of hiding them should we have to flee Russia.

That last long night on duty in the port was bitterly cold and there was a thick layer of ice on the bay. The ceaseless bombing reached closer and closer. Our sentry duty passed uneventfully, except for handing a few prowling drunks over to the port police. At dawn we were served steaming coffee in big mugs and coarse black-bread sandwiches with country bacon; thus fortified, we were started off with the detailed itinerary of our "round-up." We must have been a strange sight — seven or eight undersized boys, dressed in American uniforms far too large for us, stepping along the deserted streets of the besieged city brandishing useless rifles.

We learned at our first stop what an awkward errand we were discharging; the first to be picked up was a middle-aged general, who was dead drunk and furious when he learned our mission. He called us every name in the unwritten military dictionary, but followed meekly enough when threatened with arrest. Another man, a fat colonel, had to be forcibly parted from the blowzy mistress who was in bed with him. After a prolonged wrangle he dropped his demand that she be allowed to accompany him, and invoking hell's fire on Lenin, Trotsky, and the American Red Cross, walked out, ignoring the piercing screams of the deserted girl. None of the officers relished having to march, unshaven and unkempt, convoyed by scrawny youths, especially Uncle Ilya, who smoked furiously, stalking disdainfully ahead.

Krouglov had arranged that Mother, Alex, Colonel Lvov, and the "Ilya regulars" were to be driven to the port; when my procession reached there I was unable to search for them as we were under orders not to leave our officers until they were safely escorted on board the *Navaho.*

The port presented a spectacle worthy of Hogarth or Doré at their cruelest; literally thousands of frenzied citizens pushed and kicked madly, all codes of decency abandoned, with men fighting women, lost children howling in a maze of luggage, bundles, and even furniture, with no one to organize the unwieldy mob and hold it in check. Two larger transports were loaded to the point of danger, and the rest of the raging humanity apparently was to be squeezed into the rat-eaten entrails of the decrepit *Navaho.* Krouglov appeared at last, energetic and unruffled as ever, and ordered us boys with our charges "to wait until everyone else gets aboard."

Suddenly furious shooting started nearby, and we learned that the Soviet cavalry was entering the Port of Odessa. Ours would be the last ship to leave, and the crowd knew that the ship was their only hope of avoiding mass slaughter. The scene that ensued was unforgettable. The danger-obsessed crowd crushed itself on board the creaking ship, we boys followed and were ordered to remain on deck ready to shoot if necessary. The captain ordered full speed ahead; the rusty engines gave one tortured screech — and then stopped. The ice in the bay had us marooned, and the Soviet cavalry was bearing down upon us. Luckily, the ship next to us, the *St. Andrew,* an old Imperial Navy ice-breaker, pushed ahead, cracking the ice, with the *Navaho* following like a scared Eliza out of range of the Soviet's hounds.

We had a hellish trip, as the *Navaho* was built to hold cargo, not a crowd of human beings; without a proper balance in the hold, the ship rolled from side to side with each wave, tossing us and our belongings about like oranges in a sorter.

There was a blinding snowstorm (the first of its kind in twenty-three years) as we started across the Black Sea. The storm subsided, but an impenetrable fog reared and the captain was unable to see the proper course when we reached the Bosporus Straits. With the lives of all on board ship in his hands, the captain made three stabs at finding the opening, each time running into a blank wall of fog, the waves sky-high, and the ship barely recovering with its dangerous list. After the third failure, the man locked the door to his cabin and shot himself. He was replaced by a young sailor, who gambled on finding the gate as we were more likely to be bashed against the rocks if no positive move was made quickly.

The sailor took the wheel, closed his eyes, and ordered, "Full speed ahead!" Death never seemed closer to any of us. A slight lurch — the ship shuddered, and suddenly glided forward as smoothly as if it were on the surface of a Swiss lake. "We made it, we made it!" went up the cry, and most of us ran on deck to verify the miracle. We stood in the clear January air screaming our lungs out with joy — the blue Bosporus, soothing and serene, just as advertised.

CHAPTER VI

TURKISH DELIGHT

CONSTANTINOPLE decorated both shores of the canal-like Bosporus in Turkish-delight technicolor. The *Navaho* stopped dead in the middle of the anchored vessels—proud British battleships, glistening luxury steamers, weather-beaten tankers—none as unkempt as our old tub.

"What now? Why are we stopping?" The exhausted passengers stretched their necks inquisitively, like so many hungry turkeys. The word went around that we were halted until the immigration and health officials decided our fate. With the chronic inconsistence of the human race, the horrors of the trip from Odessa were forgotten, and the bourgeois dowagers, used to lording it over husbands, children and servants, started bitching at their new status as unwanted refugees as if it were the worst blow of all. We "Red Cross Boys" returned our rifles to the genial Krouglov, got into a hot huddle and began bitching, too. We demanded to know if his promises of sanctuary were to be broken, but Krouglov waved us away and went off to his shipboard flame, a pale young baroness who looked like a poodle in need of a haircut. She was munching dejectedly on oversalted canned corned beef, washing it down with sickly condensed milk, the two staples of the *Navaho* cuisine.

The only man on board who appeared unperturbed by our detention was the musician Oscar von Riesemann (his book on Mussorgsky is still widely read); I joined him to discover the source of his detachment from the all-Russian bedlam. A tall, Baltic baron in a lamb's-wool *papakha* (Cossack cap), von Riesemann drawled pleasantly: "I don't mind this a bit. The Bosporus is very decorative, and who knows what the Turks or our so-called allies have in store for us? Let's talk music."

He told me about his old friend Rachmaninov; how he played the whole series of Scriabin sonatas (ten of them) at a Moscow concert and at the conclusion slumped wearily on the piano, oblivious of the deafening applause; how young Prokofiev, in tails and monocle, had then dashed onstage and slapped Rachmaninov on the back, exclaiming: "Well played, old man!"

Oscar chuckled as he recalled the scathing review critic Leonide Sabaneiev published the morning after the announced *première* in Moscow of the *Scythian Suite* by Prokofiev (Sabaneiev's *bête noire*). The Prokofiev performance had been canceled as the orchestra parts failed to arrive in time.

Von Riesemann was extolling the composing talents of Issay Dobrowen, a Moscow name unfamiliar to me, who has since acquired a reputation as a conductor rather than as a composer. Meanwhile a snappy black-and-gold tugboat, with the red-and-white Turkish flag fluttering its star and crescent on the mast, secured itself alongside us, and discharged the long-awaited and dreaded officials. Two were doctors in red-and-green uniforms, a third was the immigration officer, and with them a bearded civilian who acted as interpreter.

The entire ship's company was ordered to line up for a medical examination and a searching inquiry into each individual's political, military, financial, and family status. This was old stuff to us, veterans of nineteen Kiev regimes.

The inspection lasted several hours and uncovered two typhus victims among the passengers. We were to be quarantined right in the middle of the Bosporus for three days, and then dispersed to one of the four islands in the straits known as the "Princes."

The three days went by swiftly enough. The American Red Cross supplied more corned beef and canned milk, a few crafty merchants from Constantinople sneaked on board and tempted us with *gazos* (bottled lemonade), halvah, *rahat-lokoum,* and genuine berry-red Turkish fezes with black tassles. The matrons went on with their verbal hair-pulling, Krouglov paid court to Olga, Claudia, and the baroness, Mother and Colonel Lvov talked theosophy, and Alex and I speculated as to whether I had been justified in tearing the family away from Kiev. There was wild talk that the Allies would ship all refugees back to Odessa; that the valiant General Wrangel had begun a major counteroffensive and was headed straight for Moscow; and that those of us who couldn't be accommodated on the Prince islands would be sent to the dreaded Dogs' Island, to be eaten alive by the thousands of wild dogs imprisoned there by Constantinople's governor.

Of the Prince islands, Prinkipo was the largest and most luxurious, Halki was the next best, and Proti the smallest, poorest and dirtiest. With the customary Dukelsky luck we were assigned to Proti. Our group, led by Krouglov, consisted of the four Dukelskys (including Uncle Ilya), Colonel Lvov, the rival crooners Dolinsky and Nyegin (Goulaiev's stage name), the rival courtesans Olga and Claudia, the ex-General Pestrikov, our uncle's crony, who was darkly plotting a diamond coup, the languid baroness with her fourteen-year-old, husky son, and a sociable couple, the Berestnevs (who later settled in Boston, Massachusetts).

A small American cutter transported us to the barren, torturously hilly island of Proti. An old Greek monastery on the hilltop, converted to a military hospital, was to be our new quarters. The rooms were all filled with officer patients, so we were stationed in a corridor, men at one end and women at the other. We were supplied with cots, linen and blankets, and individual clothes lockers. Men and women were issued drab semimilitary olive-green uniforms, particularly shocking on the formerly highly decorated general and Uncle Ilya. The corridor of our "Krouglov crowd," as we were becoming known, opened on a meager garden featuring olive trees which never absorbed enough vitality from the poor soil to produce olives.

As soon as we were settled, the usual Russian intrigues and squabbles began. Olga, Claudia, and the baroness gossiped behind each other's backs about their sex adventures, until they nobly decided to serve as hospital aides; Uncle Ilya and Pestrikov whispered about the diamond market in dark corners and found a way of sneaking into Constantinople daily; Dolinsky and Nyegin sighed over the loss of their "public" and the good old days; and Alex and I spent most of our time on Proti sick in bed, with Mother worrying over us.

Life on the wretched island was bleak enough, but viewed from a hospital cot, it was so desolate that I was inspired to write long pessimistic poems in the genre known to the French as *larmoyant*. One of them started with the fatalistic line: "I want to die as simply as possible," which was a poetic exaggeration as I had no intention of dying but was merely sick of being sick.

Mother met the director of the Constantinople YMCA through

some American theosophist friends and was asked to help out with the Russian Lighthouse, a club for refugees organized by the YMCA in Pera, the European quarter of Constantinople. I was finally cured of my nth disease and given a *laisser passer* so that we might leave humble Proti, unsung by any travelogue commentator for its barren hills, stubborn donkeys, undernourished trees, and the largest bedbugs known to man. We had learned there, though, that when an Oriental shook his head he meant "yes," and when he nodded energetically, often emphasizing the nod with a crisp "tsk," he was saying "no."

The white, villalike Lighthouse in Rue de Brousse became our headquarters. The ground floor contained the offices of the American director and lesser employees, along with a well-appointed gym. A wide marble staircase led to the dining hall and library, with an adjoining salon of considerable elegance. The salon boasted an excellent Steinway as it was sometimes used as a chamber-concert hall, and this became my personal haunt. The third floor was given over to a "progressive" kindergarten, and as Mother was good with children and they loved her, she was soon put in charge of the other nursery teachers. Our sojourn at the Lighthouse brought much-needed comfort and harmony into our lives and has left me with a high regard for the YMCA's kindly policies.

I was not so much attracted by the universally known landmarks of Constantinople — the Aya Sophia, the Golden Horn, the interminable staircase which was used as a street to lead into the mercantile Galata from our district of Pera; it was the mysterious zigzagging sidestreets which intrigued me, peopled with masked matriarchs stolidly sitting on the curbs, vendors hawking pungent foods and liquids in fiercely polytonal counterpoint while whipping their donkeys along, bearded philosophers in white-tiled cafés tugging at their waterpipes or sipping the vile *duziko,* the baby lambs being roasted on a spit right in the street and being eaten without benefit of cutlery, the terrifying fat whores in Galata, their faces immobile and grotesquely painted, their bodies like gallons of inferior vanilla ice cream, squatting in cages to be gaped at by pencil-slim American sailors.

Along the Galata staircase you could buy Siberian furs, trained fleas, pornographic postcards whose salesmen extolled their delights with coloraturalike commercials, violins played cello fashion, bleating clarinets and crazily cackling records of Turkish, Armenian and

Greek hits of the moment (the Greek ones always tangos, for no conceivable reason), the heavy buttocks of black-silk-clad Armenian belles and their heavy blacker-than-olive eyes — overweight women being a specialty of the Orient. These Levantine curios mingled happily with Longines watches and Walk-over shoes, dazzling one from behind their Pera *vitrines* — the Longines and Walk-overs tokens of their wearers' opulence and forever denied us insolvent refugees.

Mingling with the oriental *boulevardiers* were strutting, corseted French officers, bemonocled and faultlessly tailored British officers, hordes of overfed Greek and Armenian civilians — everyone seemingly armed with a Longines watch and shod with a pair of freshly shined Walk-over shoes — and the universally despised and impecunious Russian refugees like me. I cringed when I saw former heroes, proud earners of all four Saint George crosses, still bearing the now-obsolete insignia of no-longer existing regiments, in their faded and artlessly patched uniforms, ambling aimlessly and shamefacedly along; or worse, Russian women, many of them still pretty, still hopeful, with the bold flag of Parisian lipstick on parched lips, an overdose of mascara on their eyes, which had seen too much too soon, their dresses out of fashion — even in Turkey — their shoes pitifully disguised wrecks, who haunted the Grande Rue de Pera at all hours, window-shopping masochistically. There were grim stories of our women becoming desperate and essaying prostitution, clandestinely and otherwise; the worst one concerned the languid baroness, Krouglov's erstwhile protégée. Her son, having passed the turbulent stage of puberty, became urgently aware of his surging maleness, and went out in the Pera of an evening, in search of feminine company, his mother's five liras firmly in his pocket. After wandering back and forth along the nocturnally bright Pera, he ventured hesitantly into a dimly lit arcade where assorted *demoiselles de la nuit* plied their trade, armed with the universal trade-marks — outsize all-purpose handbags and beribboned umbrellas. He ducked several too-vividly painted harridans and smiled shyly at a fairly ladylike specimen, dressed in severest black, then approached the tart awkwardly and opened his mouth to make the usual overtures, when the girl let out a wild shriek and fled, sobbing — it was the boy's mother, the languid baroness. I quite realize that the anecdote sounds like poor Maupassant; it is, nevertheless, authentic.

Mother, Alex, and I had moved to a small flat just off Rue de

Brousse at No. 27 Rue Agha-Hamam. Uncle Ilya, up to his ears in diamonds, including the smallest of Mother's three stones (our entire fortune), shared a more opulent habitat with Pestrikov, and Colonel Lvov was quartered at the *Russky Mayak* (lighthouse). Mother spent most of the day in her kindergarten, Alex became a platoon leader in the Russian Boy Scout organization, and I wangled the job of music supervisor, concert manager and accompanist at the Saturday concerts of the *Mayak;* for performing these duties I received three meals a day and the use of the club facilities, but no money. My rather flexible position left me with a lot of time on my hands, and I used it for the purpose of doing nothing most agreeably, when not composing or arranging the club's programs, hiring the artists and rehearsing them. Of an evening, Mother and Alex would often have a meal at home, happy in the family warmth that only new poverty, intimately shared, gives people, and I occasionally joined them, sensing my mother's troubled and infinitely loving glance scanning my face — at which I'm ashamed to say, irritation welled within me. Mother knew I had plenty of free time to gad about, and she disapproved of most of my new friends. She was right, as mothers generally are, and I resented her rightness in the equally general fashion of recalcitrant sons.

Among my new friends was the son of the famed St. Petersburg baritone Tartakov; he later became a gypsy singer and *conférencier* in London, and was a "good-time Charlie" from way back. He struck up an acquaintance with the Sultan's chef and wangled an invitation to dinner at the chef's house in Beshiktash for four of us Russians. The host, a storybook Turk, portly and cordial, greeted us in a mixture of French and Russian. We sat down to a Babylonian banquet, the main feature of which was a whole lamb stuffed with turkey, the turkey with a chicken, the chicken with a quail. All manner of exotic side dishes and international wines and liquors accompanied this gastronomic surprise package, and as toasts in Turkish, French and Russian succeeded each other, each more effusive than the last, by the time coffee appeared we were all orgiastically drunk. The host and Tartakov kissed and embraced tearfully and followed declarations of undying devotion with a peculiarly choreographed and somewhat untidily executed dance, the rest of us contented with shouting and clapping our hands. The chief cook, who did *not* cook the dinner, now grew positively reckless and summoned his six wives from what I presume was an authentic old-fashioned harem. The coy young women, unused to such outlandish goings-on, duly appeared, clad in black and dark purple; at least two of them were extremely pretty.

I remember dimly, in the mists of my first major alcoholic bout, reciting one of my Russian poems to the youngest wife, who had the largest eyes and longest eyelashes I've ever seen; although she didn't understand a word I said, she nodded her approval. We were initiated into smoking hashish, and after the six wives honored us with a stately native dance, parted from our host, declaring our eternal friendship. I also remember that I was violently sick on leaving the cook's mansion and was supported by the three fellow gay blades, who immediately became sick too, and were then supported by me in turn, and that, finally, I was deposited at my doorstep at 7:30 A.M. and fell into the anxious arms of Mother, who was getting Alex's breakfast but had to set it aside to put me to bed.

There were other and similar diversions, but I took my musical duties at the *Mayak* very seriously and executed them ably enough. Constantinople was then rich in refugee talent — concert artists, ballet dancers and opera stars. I remember three of these whose names all ended with "etz," including Nina Koshetz, a great dramatic singer, Rachmaninov's protégée and later a success in the U.S.A., where she now lives. These and lesser stars were more than available — they were anxious to appear at the *Mayak,* because it meant desirable American contacts and a few Turkish liras.

My poetical pursuits were not abandoned either. Constantinople was crawling with poets, young and old, and the *Mayak* was as suitable a meeting place as any, although it was no *Closerie des Lilas* and I was far too young to be a new Jean Moreas. What I lacked in authority and renown, I made up in nerve, and soon persuaded the Americans to subsidize a poetic almanac in Russian, with me as editor. My new status made the poets unbend a little, and they began to gather in the *Mayak* salon, armed with poems, some of which were quite remarkable. Among the older poets was the Quasimodo-like Valentin Goryansky, a bitterly brilliant satirist, and the enigmatic Zavyalov, with the massive build of a professional athlete, a rich and domineering Polish wife, and reams of the most savagely destructive and violently defeatist poetry ever produced.

There was a significant aftermath to these poetic strivings. On sorting out the various contributions to our proposed almanac, I glimpsed an unopened blue envelope, addressed to me and marked "Personal." The arresting thing about the envelope was the startlingly recherché, baroque calligraphy with which my name was written — my name, not an especially pretty one, literally sang out from the fine blue paper on which it was so lovingly emblazoned. "A man of taste, obviously," I murmured smugly and opened the letter with the utmost care, so as not to cause damage to the handiwork of the artistic sender. The envelope contained three or four poems in the same unearthly handwriting, poems rather affected, although not uncharming, dealing mostly with angels and precious stones, and signed Boris Kochno. I liked one of these verses, something about an emerald or sapphire which "sang, nay screamed at me" in the poet's phrase, and decided to read them that evening to Goryansky, Zavyalov and company. My colleagues were more impressed with Mr. Kochno's calligraphic prowess than his poetic ability, but we decided to summon the man to one of our gatherings — there was something about that handwriting that made us all eager to see its owner.

The young man (he proved to be almost exactly my age) appeared at the appointed time and we had tea in the *Mayak* salon. I beheld, for the first time in my life, a faithful replica of a youthful man-of-fashion — an *incroyable;* Kochno was of good height and figure, wore a well-tailored sack suit with a great air, sported a Doucet bowtie and even smoked an English cigarette in a long jade holder. His face, felinely soft, was quite beautiful, and his voice, although undeniably affected, had an ingratiating ring to it. I, who intended to give Kochno a piece of our collective minds about his merely prettyish poetry, was so awed by all this magnificence that I couldn't go beyond a few urbane *politesses* in my best, hastily produced, drawing-room manner. Kochno was accompanied by a middle-aged actor whose heavy-lidded eyes gave him the look of a decadent Pompeian. He spoke a few words in provincial Russian, his eyes never leaving Kochno, and after we had exchanged a few urban nothings, and I had promised "to do something" about the Screaming Emerald, the pair left. I hardly could foresee that Boris Kochno would become the scenarist of my two ballets: the Dukelsky *Zephyr and Flora* (1925, Diaghilev Ballets Russes, Kochno-Braque-Chanel-Massine) and the Duke *Le Bal des Blanchisseuses* (1946, Ballets des Champs Elysées, Kochno-Stanislao Lepri-Roland Petit). In 1921

Boris stood out chiefly for his looks and clothes, which contrasted cruelly with the beggars' garb of so many of the others. Yet, I couldn't help liking and even envying young Boris — I, no social butterfly at that remote time, in my semimilitary olive-green getup; I kept my promise and did "something" about his Screaming Emerald — gave it to Nicky Slonimsky, who set it to music unhesitatingly and got Madame Voronetz to sing it at one of our concerts. Boris, impeccable in dark blue, reappeared with his actor friend, smiled contentedly and left after thanking Slonimsky and the singer. A week or so later he went off to Paris, where he met Serge Soudeikine, the painter, and his wife (now Mrs. Igor Stravinsky); they in turn introduced him to Diaghilev, whose secretary, confidant and librettist he became.

It was here in Constantinople, too, that I met Pierre Souvtchinsky, the musicologist, magazine publisher and, later, head of the Eurasian movement (they believed that Russia wasn't either Europe or Asia, but a continent in itself — Eurasia). He listened to some songs of mine (one of which, "The Wooden Church," is still, I think, an arresting piece of music) and displayed considerable enthusiasm, which was to increase in 1924 with the birth of *Zephyr and Flora* and give me a new lease on musical life in 1947, when I reappeared in Paris with *Le Bal des Blanchisseuses* and the Third Symphony. Together Souvtchinsky and I listened to a score by Theodore de Hartmann, a man with a huge skull and the high-cheekboned face of a Tartar, who was shortly to form a symphony orchestra in Constantinople and give a series of quite respectable concerts.

Nina Koshetz's accompanist, Nicolas Stember, the nephew of Nicolas Medtner, was playing Medtner's effective, if derivative, piano sonatas and "Fairy Tales" all over town, and I was overjoyed when he approved of my one-movement G-minor piano sonata, begun in November, 1920, and completed in April, 1921.

Not all of my musical activities were on so elevated a plane. Mother was doing her best to keep Alex and me well fed and clothed, but the proceeds from the diamond sale were quickly gone, and her salary from the kindergarten was barely sufficient for a Spartan existence. I cast about desperately for a paying job and became a pianist in a "salon trio" in one of the better Pera restaurants. Slonimsky was already directing a similar group at Tokatlian's, Constantinople's most fashionable café. We were both fed up with "O Sole Mio," Toselli's "Serenade," the "Berceuse" from *Jocelyn,* "Otchi Tchornya" and other such stand-bys, without which proper digestion is an impossibility. For an evening's work, my pay was three liras; the job lasted about two weeks, and then I transferred to a cinema, where I had to supply suitable accompaniments to "silent" films.

A English colonel visited the restaurant where I held forth with my violin and cello partners, and engaged me on the spot for a concert in his barracks. The pay was good but I had no notion of what was expected of me. On arriving, I found masses of enlisted men, roaring drunk on Turkish beer, who greeted my entrance with hoarse shouts and demands for songs like "K-K-K-Katy," "Tipperary" and "For Me and My Gal," which I knew by heart; after a successful start, I was urged to play various English folk ballads totally unknown to me. Here I was seated at the rickety piano, bewildered by the singing, shouting Tommies, who demanded encore after encore. God alone knows what I played and how the Tommies were able to follow me, or I them, but at the end of the evening, the tall cockney sergeant shook his head and handed me five liras, adding, " 'Ere's yer money, chum, even if you ain't much good as a pianoforte player."

I always had the enviable ability to talk about a flop as though it were a hit (it proved most helpful in later years), and told awed friends of having conquered the British. A young Greek decided that I was ripe for the British Embassy and arranged for a recital there with a portly Russian baritone. For this I was to collect ten liras, and of course we joyously accepted; on the day of the concert it was pointed out to me that we were to dress, meaning white tie. I don't think I owned a necktie in 1920, white or colored, and as for tails, they were associated in my mind with the Russian Imperial Court or the films. The possibility of my getting into one of those things never entered my mind. Yet here it was — tails or no ten liras. In despair, I ran to the kind little Greek, who was short and somewhat crippled and produced a morning coat and striped trousers from his own wardrobe. His tails were at the tailor's, but the morning coat was certainly formal as hell, so no one could say I was not "correct."

I played my accompaniments looking as if my clothes had been shrunk in a rainstorm, and at the end of the concert, after warmly congratulating the baritone, the ambassador dismissed me with a cool nod. I did get the ten liras, for which I would happily have dressed in a barrel.

That first winter out of Russia I began to function (unofficially and unprofitably) as Dukelsky and Duke. I disliked popular songs, owing, no doubt, to such exponents as Nyegin, and I loathed the "arty" sex-serenades of the industrious Vertinsky, who was always popping up unexpectedly. One afternoon after lunch, I saw the original Moscow Pierrot lolling dandiacally in the *Mayak* salon, all the "well-born" waitresses (ex-gentlewomen, naturally) worshipping at his impeccably shod feet. The master was at his most affable and was reciting his latest sexotic, as Walter Winchell would have it, roundelay. He then distributed engraved cards bearing the legend *The Black Rose, Cabaret Artistique.* The Moscow Pierrot had found himself some well-heeled Armenian Harlequins, and they had provided him with his own *boîte.* I was too young and too poor to frequent such dens, but I heard a few months later that the authorities staged a raid in the place and unearthed quantities of cocaine and 100 per cent syphilis among the lady servants and entertainers. No more Black Rose.

But the Rose of Jazz, healthy and blooming, was by now firmly planted on the European shore of the Bosphorus. *Mayak* patrons began to request "Hindustan," "Tell Me" and "Till We Meet Again." I promptly purchased all three, also Irving Berlin's earlier successes and a thing mysteriously entitled "Swanee" by a man improbably styled Geo. Gershwin. The Berlins were good in their way, but the Gershwin sent me into ecstacies. The bold sweep of the tune, its rhythmic freshness and, especially, its syncopated gait, hit me hard and I became an "early-jazz" fiend. That's not quite what I mean, because (shudder, ye New Orleans purists!) the "real" New Orleans jazz and the true-blue blues impressed me considerably less. "What can you expect from a long hair" did I hear you say? Perhaps I can explain it best by admitting my admiration for the "musicality" and a composer's inventiveness in young Gershwin, which was (and is) missing from the "real" thing, largely a collectively produced mood, anonymous and crude.

Daily I was glued to the piano, wrestling with the new medium. This was like playing golf, after reading too much Schopenhauer. I wanted to acquire the knack of writing popular tunes in the American idiom. The purist will tell you haughtily that it's not jazz at all — so be it; but if "Tea for Two," "The Man I Love," "Night and Day" and — forgive the plug — my own "I Can't Get Started With You" aren't jazz, you can have all the "Tiger Rags" in the world, and welcome.

My tunes of the Constantinople vintage, 1920–1922, sounded as if they were in the authentic American jazz idiom, but harmonically they weren't. Those first pop songs without lyrics, imitative of Gershwin and early Jerome Kern, weren't signed Duke or Dukelsky: I coined the phony-sounding "Ivan Ivin," later replaced by the Americanese "Alan Lane." Slonimsky, pounding away at the Tokatlian, composed a Turkish-American fox trot called "Yok, yok, effendi" ("No, No, Sir"), the lyric concerning a Turkish girl spurning an "ally." The tune wasn't bad but jerky and a bit "crowded," just as my tunes were.

After my job playing at the Turkish cinema evaporated, I donned a fez and went off for a holiday in Istanbul with some young Mussulman highbrows. We visited Eyoub, a celestially restful retreat of white mosques, white-bearded monks, and whiter doves, Boyouk-Dere, a sumptuous summer resort, and humbler villages where Turks played wailing jeremiads and snappy, although minor-keyed, two-quarter-time dance tunes. The native bands included the already-mentioned violins played cello fashion, the *oud* (like a mandolin), the *kanoun* (a forty-stringed instrument played with two picks), and the *zourna* (a clarinetlike reed thing).

The outcome of these agreeable wanderings was three Turkish songs, which I harmonized, and which my Turkish friends succeeded in having published by Pera's Maison André. One of the three songs was "Telgirafin Tellerine," a song about the beginnings of the telegraph in Turkey, with which I can still liven up any Moslem gathering.

New faces appeared at the Lighthouse; Pavlik Tchelitchev for one, now a distinguished painter, then an apple-cheeked Adonis fond of exuberant laughter and good-natured practical jokes. He was a few years older than I and easily sold me some cock-and-bull stories about vicious Orientals lying in wait for me, 300-pound Galata belles plotting to seduce me, etc. I met the dancers Zimin and Kniasev (Kniasev was later choreographer for de Basil and married to the great Spessivizeva), who were both dancing at Constantinople cafés at that time. Zimin partnered Italian ballerina Bianca Fosca and asked me to create an oriental ballet for him. The title was *Conte d'une Nuit*

Syrienne (*Tale of a Syrian Night*) and the music minor-league *Scheherazade-cum-Glazunov*. Tchelitchev designed Bakst-like sets and costumes, I wrote out parts for the eight- or nine-piece orchestra, and the *première* at the Theatre des Petits-Champs (in 1921) was fairly well received. Soon after, Tchelitchev left for Germany, where he wound up designing sets for the Berlin Opera House.

Things seemed to be humming on all fronts, except the lowly, but important, carnal domain. My adolescent technique of reciting verse to the belle of the moment and then progressing to sentimental kisses was a signal flop, because girls who liked poetry usually stopped right there and those who had designs on me (a distinct minority) didn't see any point in poetry prior to going to bed. Alas, it was the going to bed that I dreaded, because, having adopted the pose of a jaded rake, I was ashamed of my anatomical status, which was certain to betray me. One uninhibited female, daughter of a naval officer, cut me short in the middle of a fancy ode, and proceeded to take off her clothes, complying realistically with the urgent entreaties of my verses. After a perfunctory caress or two, I invented some cockeyed excuse and fled, cursing my ode, the cause of my predicament.

More of our relatives arrived with the supporters of Baron Wrangel, who had finally been beaten out of Crimea. Uncle Irakly (Prince Toumanov), with a new wife and two infant sons, Uncle Nicholas's divorced wife, Aunt Genia and her son Yura, a handsome naval cadet, and my mother's brother Professor Alexis Kopylov, all appeared in Constantinople on their way elsewhere. Yura died of consumption at sixteen, in Gallipoli, where his naval academy was transplanted. Uncle Alexis and his wife, Aunt Liza, went to Poland, where they owned land. Prince Toumanov began to talk rhapsodically of the United States.

My artist friends such as Kochno, Tchelitchev, and others, were already in Belgrade, Sophia, or Paris. Constantinople began to seem like an outmoded health resort, peopled with dull patients.

A benevolent YMCA official offered to help Alex get a scholarship in a good New England prep school (Cushing Academy in Ashburnham, Massachusetts, made famous by its alumna Bette Davis). No one offered me an education, as I was reasonably if sketchily educated, but I was convinced that the United States couldn't get along without me. Mother began losing her favorite pupils as their parents deserted Turkey, Colonel Lvov was directed to American theosophist contacts, and Uncle Irakly threw his princely weight around with the caste-conscious officials at the U.S.-sponsored Robert College, where he lectured.

Our collective merits were weighed, the hard-earned immigration visas supplied, and we sailed for New York on the not-so-good Greek ship *King Alexander* in the autumn of 1921.

CHAPTER VII

THE BAD OLD DAYS

THE *KING ALEXANDER,* of German origin, was a ship of about 22,000 tons displacement, cleanly scrubbed and reeking of disinfectants — the genteel refugee smell. Here again were squealing children, the anxious eyes of their mothers bent on delivering their offspring into the bountiful arms of the legendary Statue of Liberty, unwashed journalists, pseudo-poets and gloomy bourgeois, peering unhappily at their companions of the voyage, who at least had their youth, and therefore no recollections of former comforts and riches. We traveled third class, bunk fashion, and the trip from Piraeus to New York took exactly one month.

Life aboard the *King Alexander* wasn't very different from the one we had led on Proti; but the food was plentiful and devoid of corned beef and condensed milk, and the faces around us were good old faces. Colonel Lvov went on meditating merrily in the best Blavatsky fashion; the Berestnevs danced the one-step without musical accompaniment; and Mother, when not suffering from seasickness, watched us tirelessly, as if to make sure that we were there intact, with no new dangers confronting us. There were no dangers to speak of, except a huge Armenian diamond merchant, a San Franciscan of recent vintage, who endeavored to initiate me into the joys of homosexuality after ensnaring me into a Turkish bath. His entreaties had an unforeseen result — I laughed myself sick at his amorous antics, which so disconcerted him that he cursed me in Armenian and returned to his ablutions.

Our delight at the first appearance of the yellowish-green Jersey shore and the bluish-green Rubensian lady, identified with the freedom and self-respect so long denied us, was as vociferous and spontaneous as that of so many previous generations of immigrants. There was one difference — Russians used to flee from the czar, we fled from the czar's murderers. Ellis Island was Proti on a miniature scale, with fewer trees and darker inmates, rather like a rehearsal of *Scheherazade* in a hospital. The immigration officials were surprisingly kind, everybody talked like Krouglov and, the usual formalities over, we were released into the New York streets, Mother proudly clasping her hard-won first papers, which were issued automatically to each legally entered immigrant. Alexis and I were too young to have separate papers, so we were included in Mother's.

The Manhattan skyline in 1921 was not as impressive as the 1955 one, but we spent most of the first three days craning our necks and just gaping. Mother, who had passed her fortieth birthday, would not part with her favorite hat — an odd straw number with artificial flowers and a dark-green velvet ribbon tied under her chin shepherdess style. This hat had been purchased from a Kiev modiste just after the revolution, and I suffered agonies encountering ironic glances and even sneers from uninhibited passers-by, startled by such ludicrous headgear. Mother was unaware of this silent censure, so busy was she watching us protectively as if afraid that we would be crushed by the granite towers around us.

New York seemed even dirtier than Constantinople, but there was electricity and feverish promise in the air. The town was new, ungainly and cockily, awkwardly young, rather like a wolfhound pup with legs too long for the rest of his body — not only the town's legs, but also the girls' were interminable, straight and perfect, like so many miniature skyscrapers. The girls' small, birdlike heads under the absurdly close-fitting cloches, the vogue of the day, were lit up by shining eyes and teeth, exactly like so many electric signs suddenly flashing up on Broadway at night. Like all wonders of the world, the skyscrapers, along with the Paris Eiffel Tower and the Tower of London, completely lost their fascination after a few days, but Broadway at night was an awesome sight, nowhere equaled on earth.

On the suggestion of our YMCA protectors, we put up at a smallish (by New York standards), though comfortable, businessmen's hotel on Madison Avenue near 31st Street. Alex and I, left to our own devices on the first afternoon, amused ourselves by examining the big, fat, telephone book with a red cover. We chanced on the letter "M" and discovered, to our consternation, that there was a separate listing for "milliners," which we, with our imperfect knowledge of English, took to mean "millionaires." "God, there are so many of them!" exclaimed Alex. "And they all seem to have foreign names," I chimed in incredulously. "But where are the Rockefellers and the Vanderbilts?"

The next morning Alex and I went off to Central Park, a rather disappointing place, the trees poor and anemic-looking — the surrounding tall buildings seemed to squeeze all the juice from the joyless oasis. The park's meager charms failed to dampen my spirits. Seized by a strange fervor, I pranced about the hilly slopes, singing one of my Constantinople refrains at the top of my lungs. "What's that?" Alex queried skeptically. "I like Irving Berlin." Whereupon he whistled Berlin's newest air, then all the rage. "Oh, you do! Well, I'll outdo Berlin, just you wait and see," I retorted. I'm afraid this prophecy is still unfulfilled, and Mr. Berlin, whom I met many years later, was never in danger of competition from this source.

There are several New Yorks. There's the amiable pre-Pickwickian New York of Washington Irving; the elegant, Lady Blessington-conscious metropolis of the unjustly forgotten Nathaniel Parker Willis; the shopgirl's Manhattan of O. Henry; the immigrant's New York of Gorky and Korolenko; the merciless monster of a city sung by John Dos Passos; the hip-flask-flashing, girlish-thigh-revealing, bathtub-gin-happy, debutante-studded New York of Scott Fitzgerald; the stately, urbane literateur's club world of Henry James; Maxwell Bodenheim's Greenwich Villagey daisy-chain conception of the big town; the phony nobleman's favorite haunt as depicted by Ben Hecht; the Harlem-cum-Montparnasse paradise of Carl Van Vechten; the garment-center slicker's city of Jerome Weidman. We saw, smelled and tasted a bit of each, but the refined Upper West Side brownstone singing teachers' New York, the town of aging ex-prima donnas of the dyed hair and the drooping gardenia, decked out in Klein's best, of deadly "musicales" featuring Town Hall ballads and music-loving Elks and Shriners, of tired chicken salad and tepid Manhattans, remains unsung, and it's a pity, because it was quite a place in the twenties, the place to which we were removed from our Madison Avenue hotel.

Colonel Lvov and Mother sold the last Dukelsky diamond, scanned the newspaper advertisements and triumphantly came up (or rather down) with an inexpensive basement in the West Sixties. The proceeds from the diamond sale constituted our capital; Mother and the colonel soon became factory workers (the match factory then considered the thing by refugees), Alexis was busily absorbing various sciences, as he was about to enter the Cushing Academy, and I volunteered to earn my keep by putting music to practical use.

That wasn't an easy task. I was seventeen, no longer spoiled (the Revolution took care of that), but unaccustomed to the dubious ways of the world, and quite unknown. Making music pay for one's keep is no cinch, even now that I have a name — or, rather, two names. How to be a composer without being a conductor or a virtuoso instrumentalist is a tough proposition — either get yourself a rich wife or write music for music consumers, *not* music lovers.

The catalogue of my would-be "commercial" activities in the 1921–1923 period denotes an uncommon versatility, if nothing else. I played accompaniments for ersatz gypsies in Second Avenue restaurants; wrote "incidental" music for vaudeville performers, which they commissioned and then declined to buy, declaring it unsuitable; played piano on the stage for Alexander Oumansky's ballet vaudeville act on the Keith circuit; played piano for a small-time adagio team content with any old circuit as long as they got paid, which wasn't often; wrote music for Horace Goldin, the famed magician, who gave me two hundred dollars for labor involving a lullaby for a trick rabbit, a tango for vanishing handkerchiefs and suddenly appearing bouquets of roses, a languorous waltz for card tricks and a diabolic *galop* to denote the time-honored feat of sawing a woman in half; conducted an orchestra of five musicians for a burlesque show, an exploit that deserves a little digression.

I never could conduct, and the art of coordinating one's arm and body movements with sounds emanating from a large group of instrumentalists still seems inhumanly difficult to me. How I ever got the job of conducting the pit band for *Jazz Babies* (the title of the burlesque piece entrusted to me) is not clear, except that I remember playing piano in a hired room at Leo Feist's for a bouncy blonde, her hair the color of a ripe banana, who was the jazziest of the gum-chewing Jazz Babies and who took a fancy to me. I remember, too, the horror and the excitement of our first stage rehearsal: ten meaty females — this was the pre-Gayelord Hauser era — in baby rompers or tight bathing suits, wearily undulating and kicking their outsize legs to my meticulously, but "cornily" executed accompaniments. "Stick to the rhythm, Kid, stick to the rhythm," admonished the bowlegged dance director, a half-chewed White Owl dangling from his mouth. "This is Amurrica." At least one of that country's citizens — the banana-haired bombshell — always rose to my defense by stroking my hair and giving me a hug.

Thanks to my benefactress, I was promoted from pianist to conductor, although, in reality, I was both, thereby saving some money for the producers. My nightly task, after the show's opening, was elementary and not very tiring, but the spectacle of all that unsavory flesh pounding the runway over my head, twenty bare legs strutting lasciviously in a heady cloud of cheap talcum powder and sweat, proved too unnerving. I mixed up my music, missed my cues and was invariably and rightly upbraided for this by the White Owl-loving dance director. He also resented the unmistakable advances made to me by the banana-haired Jazz Baby, and consequently I turned in my notice at the end of the week, or was fired — I forget which happened first.

Living as we did in the singing teachers' quarter, I soon began meeting some of the clan. I was rather good at sightreading and so began to pick up a few odd dollars helping out ex-prima donnas by coaching the would-be prima donnas, their pupils. Through Koka Stember, I met Isolde von Bernhardt, a good Wagnerian mezzo-soprano, who provided me with occasional jobs. Koka mastered my Constantinople piano sonata and especially praised the passages that sounded like Medtner, of which there were not a few. Stember was then serving as accompanist to Nina Koshetz, who moved her enormous bulk, her slim water-color-painting husband, and her small daughter, to a big, sprawling flat on Riverside Drive. It was a delicious refuge for lost young souls like myself, who often repaired to Nina's after an overdose of poor jazz or synthetic gypsy wailing. We drank oceans of tea and devoured innumerable *pirojki* and other Russian goodies; we talked of Rachmaninov and Scriabin and that impertinent young coxcomb Prokofiev, who had locked himself up in an abandoned Bavarian castle and was busily scribbling a new piano concerto (this turned out to be his best — the sparkling and ever-fresh No. 3) as well as an opera based on Dostoievsky. One evening Nina sat down at the piano, wrapped in a red Spanish shawl, and accompanied herself in Prokofiev's songs on Akhmatova's poems and one of his five "Vocalises" — songs without words. The eerie, uncannily simple and uninhibited, uncerebral music filled me with sudden ecstasy; I drank in every note, and the Jazz Babies became utterly unreal, as if they had never, never happened.

At Nina's I met Lazare Saminsky, the composer, and Aaron Baron, the critic, a benign and fussy little man who wrote for Jewish and German newspapers and was fond of old ladies who gave musical teas. Baron loved to act as escort and confidant of visiting musical celebrities. I was no celebrity and I was not visiting, but nevertheless little Baron took me in hand and introduced me around as a promising one hundred to one longshot. It was Baron who caused me to swallow innumerable *petits fours* and lettuce and cucumber sandwiches in settings of mangy potted palms, aspidistras, keepsakes of McKinley's era, where vocalists — hopeless and hopeful — regaled the bespatted attorneys and dentists with anything from Nevin's "Narcissus" to Wagner's "Brünnhilde." "The boy is a composer," Baron would whisper in the hostess's ear. A polite smirk would ensue, followed by a Medtnerian prelude by myself, a little indulgent applause, a few more *petits fours*.

But I'll ever be grateful to little Aaron Baron, for it was through him that I met Karol Szymanovski, Chopin the Second of Polish music, and it was through Szymanovski that I knew the Kochanskis — Paul, the great violin stylist, and Zosia, his bright and warm-hearted wife; and, had I not met the Kochanskis, my composer's career would never have happened.

Mother gave up her exhausting match-factory labors and turned to designing children's clothes for a Fourth Avenue establishment. Alex was accumulating scholastic honors at the Cushing Academy. The colonel was diligently punching the clock somewhere; thus, everybody was honorably and regularly employed, except myself. I led a fascinating but oddly unproductive life and earned nothing to speak of. Lvov began muttering something about aesthetic "ne'er-do-wells," and there were heated arguments with Mother, who defended me stoically behind closed doors. It was no use denying that Mother and the colonel were the only providers in our family of four (the colonel's position was somewhat unorthodox, as he was neither a relative nor Mother's lover), and whatever they succeeded in saving was given to Alex and myself as pocket money. I was, however, determined to make music pay and began turning over new leaves every morning.

We were now "installed" in Washington Heights on West 172nd

Street, our basement in the Sixties having proven something of a hellhole during the first murderous heat wave we experienced. This was a pleasantly nondescript neighborhood, too new to be redolent of anything except fresh paint; the kind of place that was described as "steadily growing," "making rapid strides," etc., by the municipal authorities in 1922. The air was purer here because of the proximity of the Hudson, and the rents were cheaper.

It was fun to take the subway at 168th Street every morning and be surrounded by cleanly scrubbed young people hurrying to their downtown jobs. I invariably alighted at 50th Street and would wander into the heart of Tin-Pan Alley, which was much noisier then than it is now; every publisher of renown had at least a half-dozen song pluggers thumping battered uprights and bent on selling material to recognized vaudevillians. With the aid of a kindly song writer named Lee David, I managed to get a hearing now and then, but my songs were not in the idiom of the street and were instantly rejected. They were not good songs, and the lyrics, concocted by myself with the aid of a Russian–English dictionary, were deplorable. I remember two — one was called "Spooning on a Crowded Bus" and featured the startlingly rhymed climax: "Underneath the bridge our paradise we *cross,* spooning on a crowded *bus*"; the other was ingeniously titled "Don't Waste Your Time Wasting Your Time on Me." The publishers didn't.

On one especially humid afternoon, I wandered into a cheap barber shop, several rejected manuscripts under my arm. The barber was a small Sicilian named Baretti and, prior to cutting my hair, he pointed at my piano copies and desired to know whether I was a song writer. "No, I'm a composer," said I with dignity. "Same thing," was Baretti's rejoinder. He began cutting my hair, then suddenly stopped, the glistening scissors high in the air. "Say, Kid, I have an idea. I'm a great composer myself, only I can't write down the notes — my parents always wanted me to be a barber, not a musician. How would you like to write down some of my stuff? I'll cut you in on the royalties or else it's five bucks per." (I thought this over quickly and settled for five bucks per. This turned out to be a smart decision, as I discovered that Baretti published his music himself and was in the habit of presenting it to steady customers with a suitable autograph. I don't think he ever sold a copy.) Baretti sang in a loud and intensely nasal voice, but he sang in tune and writing down his ditties was no problem at all — that's how simple they were. His favorite was a waltz entitled "Pay More Attention To Me, Dearie," which I suspected was swiped from an old Irish air, but I pocketed my five bucks and said nothing. I harmonized three or four of these songs and was ready for more when Baretti suddenly decided that I was too expensive and made me an offer of ten dollars for three new ones, which I haughtily declined. Baretti became indignant and I had to switch to a Washington Heights barber who had no musical leanings.

Lee David introduced me to Leo Edwards, Gus's brother, who was then producing a night-club revue for Murray's Roman Gardens on West 42nd Street. This was *Jazz Babies* on a higher and more refined level; the girls were slimmer and cleaner, most of them had garment-center "boy friends" (a term I always detested) who gave them Guerlain scents, fur coats and (very occasionally) diamonds. In the time-honored chorine tradition, these girls always fell for the trombone player or the drummer — they still do — and thought the piano-playing foreign kid (myself) too skinny and too young. I, in turn, thought Murray's girls too brassy, their faces too blatantly painted, their bodies too extravagantly scented. Thus we worked in comparative harmony, but not for long; although the revue's theme song proudly asserted that "in Murray's Roman Gardens there's never a lull," pretty soon there never was a customer there either.

Without realizing it, I was already leading the dual musical existence which became my trade-mark in the thirties. Out of an odd sort of self-defense, I began to torture and complicate the musical dialectics in my "serious" output; thus, the simpler and more down-to-earth my tunes, the more cerebral and *voulu* my "good" music became, until it was practically indistinguishable from that of the twelve-tone boys. I sounded off with ten songs on *avant garde* Russian poems, including one by myself. These were exhibited to Nina Koshetz, who attempted to decipher them, couldn't, and worked herself into a violent diatribe against young men who are born old and would rather die than be caught red-handed with a melody. She was right. Poor melody became (unwittingly) a tawdry 32-bar refrain by Alan Lane or Ivan Ivin (Vernon Duke was yet to make his initial appearance), whereas Dukelsky, thus robbed — by himself — was in danger of sinking in a harmonic marsh. The songs, disdained by Nina, were then taken to Eva Gautier, that remarkable and cruelly unrewarded exponent of new music. Madame Gautier, looking not unlike an amiable Siamese cat, liked two of the songs and proposed to perform them at an International Composers' Guild concert. The reader is not likely to remember that there were two new-music citadels in the twenties in New York: the I.C. Guild and the League of Composers. The former was a militantly aggressive organization headed by the admirable Edgar Varèse, one of the few authentic new voices in music, and his less radical but most able colleague, Carlos Salzedo, who revolutionized the harp. The Guild's concerts were packed with explosive excitement, as some highly debatable and indigestible music was always played; it was a joy to see the hall jammed to the doors with extroverted young people who made rude sounds at the slightest provocation, reacting violently and noisily to whatever novelties were served up by the Guild. The hissing and booing in counterpoint with shouts of approval that accompanied the *première* of one of Carl Ruggles's harsher pieces was as thrilling to me as was the occasion when Stokowski had to repeat Stravinsky's "Renard," so great was the audience's insistence! Such things do not happen today, and a living composer is lucky if he manages to duck into the wings *before* the patronizing applause dies down.

The League of Composers was another matter. It had more solid financial support and there was a reassuring aura of nice bureaucratic tedium about the goings-on. A lot of middle-of-the-road music was being played and it was as if the sponsors were bent on selling the customers the idea that new music could be conformist and respectable. Ditto for my reception by the two groups; the League, in response to my timid inquiry, became frigidly noncommital on hearing my "no-name" name and rattled off something about membership fees, etc. On the other hand, the fact that I was totally unknown served as a password to the Guild, and I was instantly invited to a Greenwich Village gathering where my hand was shaken by Varèse, an imposing hunk of a man with superbly chiseled strong features and a bomb-thrower's manner, the feline, impeccably mannered Salzedo and an odd, birdlike pipe-smoking creature in shabby tweeds who turned out to be the blood-curdling eardrum smasher — Carl Ruggles. They liked my two songs well enough to accord them a place on one of their programs and fed me cheese and Chianti.

Madame Gautier mastered my songs — even provided English translations — and sang them at the next Guild concert. The audience reception was indicative of other such receptions traditionally accorded new, but not *too* new, music — the sort of reception where the hopeful composer asks his best friend, "Well, how did it go?" and gets this answer: "Pretty well, I thought, how did *you* think it went?" The critics said nothing much and nobody "hailed" me — except a swarthy young man named George Gershwin, whom I first knew as *Geo*. Gershwin, the creator of "Swanee," the copy of which was by now gathering dust on the big piano in the Russian *Mayak* in far-off Constantinople.

Gershwin impressed me as a superbly equipped and highly skilled composer — not just a concocter of commercial jingles. His extraordinary left hand performed miracles in counter-rhythms, shrewd canonic devices, and unexpected harmonic shifts. "Where did you study?" I asked, after listening to him play. George laughed, a cigar stuck between his white teeth. "Oh, I didn't study much — some piano and harmony with a man called Charlie Hambitzer, some lessons from Rubin Goldmark — but on the whole I guess I'm just a natural-born composer."

When I informed him of my years with Reinhold Glière, the difficulty I had had mastering counterpoint and orchestration at fifteen, he was vaguely impressed. "Gee, it must be great to know so much," he said, eyeing me with curiosity. "But now that you've learned it all — what are you doing with it?" By way of reply I played an extremely cerebral piano sonata. Gershwin listened, rather impatiently, I thought, and then shook his head. "There's no money in that kind of stuff," he said, "no heart in it, either. Try to write some real popular tunes — and don't be scared about going low-brow. They will open you up!"

This rather startling remark of George's — "they will open you up" — stayed with me through all the years that we were friends. Too many people have climbed on the bandwagon of George's posthumous glory. Yet, together with two or three others, I was as close to him as a friend can be. This friendship lasted until his last trip to Hollywood, which brought about his tragic and untimely death at the age of thirty-eight.

I doubt that Gershwin, then just beginning to "hit it," liked the strange little songs I wrote. As he expressed it to me later, he was surprised by the fact that so young a man (I was five years his junior) should write such dry and intellectual stuff. Eva Gautier sang three of George's songs at her own recital (composer at the piano) and the audience literally shouted the place down with approval. A few months later, Marguerite d'Alvarez, then at the height of her fame, "stopped the show" with more composer-accompanied Gershwin. Odd that some of our present-day recitalists don't hire Duke Ellington (or the other Duke — Vernon — for that matter) to inject a little much-needed life into their Town Hall appearances.

I was now branching out in all directions. Greta Torpadie, the Norwegian, sang three more songs of mine. Marie Kiekhoefer, then an executive of the Wolfsohn Musical Bureau, took me in hand following the Guild initiation and suggested I write an orchestral piece. I had always wanted to write an overture to the Russian acmeist-poet Gumilev's "Gondla" — a high-flown post-romantic tale of Iceland in beautiful marblelike verse. I went to work happily and completed the job in little over a week. The overture, which I orchestrated hesitantly, was shown to Dirk Foch (the father of film actress Nina Foch), the colorful Dutch musician who had just formed the short-lived New York City Symphony, and that courageous man accepted it for performance. This was quite a jump from the intermezzo of my short-pants debut, and I sat in a blissful haze through the two rehearsals, and bowed from a box after the Carnegie Hall performance just before the more than meager applause died down. H. E. Krehbiel, the then all-powerful *New York Tribune* critic, called my "Gondla" a "farrago of atrocious noises," and most of the others dismissed it facetiously, but it was a start, and playing the misunderstood genius at so early an age was good fun.

The Foch, Gautier and Torpadie "breaks" gave me my first taste of the contemporary composer's plight; he gets a performance — then, perhaps, another performance — then a seemingly interminable lull. Thirty years ago most of us had the same trouble — performances led to *nothing* because the new-music market, as today, was extremely limited and there was far too much supply and far too little demand.

I remember sitting idly on a Central Park bench after the first and last performance of "Gondla," pondering my fate. There wasn't much pondering to do, really. It all amounted to the same thing: I must make music pay — but how? The pudgy little man with a glistening checkbook who runs up to you after a brilliant *première,* wrings your hand and shouts, "Great! You've got what it takes — I'll give you ten thousand a year and here's five on account; just sit tight and write music," doesn't pop up these days, and I suspect he wasn't accessible in the days gone by — not unless his name was Ludwig of Bavaria and yours Wagner. So, back to synthetic gypsies I went, as accompanist to one of the tribe in a pseudo-Russian midtown night spot.

The first clash between the embryo Duke, the wage earner, and Dukelsky, would-be composer, occurred there and then: one evening when I was about to charge into the obnoxious "Otchi Tchornya," who should walk in but the impeccably clad Karol Szymanovski, a half-dozen composers in tow. This, as I presently learned, was to be a banquet tendered the Pole by his admiring colleagues — Alfredo Casella, Emerson Whithorne, Aaron Baron, Lazare Saminsky and several others. Words cannot describe my despair and mortification. Here were my senior contemporaries, proudly practicing their craft — nay, *my* craft! — and here was I, a young fellow composer, about to prostitute myself publicly. I closed my eyes, raced through the hateful "Otchi" at breakneck speed, causing the gypsy diva intense discomfort and annoyance, then excused myself and buttonholed Saminsky. "I'm so sorry," I stammered miserably. "Try and understand why I'm doing this." Saminsky shrugged his shoulders philosophically. "Don't worry, I understand perfectly. One must eat, mustn't one?" Nothing was more obvious than this truth, but Oh! how it hurt at the time.

The next morning, I had a long talk with Mother. I told her that the hellish humiliation of my lower-than-lowbrow jobs was not justifiable in view of the pittances I received for them, that I would seek and obtain something more remunerative and that I would forever renounce the métier of an eatery piano player. Dear Mother agreed completely, as she always did when my music and my musical progress were at stake. The "Otchi Tchornya" interlude proved to be an epilogue, and never again did I have to don a red silk blouse and black dress trousers (part of a dinner suit, purchased on Eighth Avenue for seven dollars) to entertain hiccuping customers. I called up Gershwin and asked him whether he would listen to some freshly written tunes of mine. George said he sure would and I was off to West 103rd Street, a new hope in my heart.

When not playing ping-pong on the ground floor with brothers Ira or Arthur, George could be found at his piano, playing tirelessly for hours, never practicing in the Czerny sense, just racing through new tunes, adding new tricks, harmonies, "first and second endings" and changing keys after each chorus. He was a born *improvisatore* yet never changed tempo, nor played rubato, the relentless 4/4 beat carrying him along—it was physically difficult for him to stop. This was just what he was doing when I walked in and sat down to listen. George's sister, Frankie, a chubby chestnut-haired flapper, ran in, and after singing a chorus in a husky little voice, with "gestures," ran out again. George then switched to a blues, closed his eyes and, pushing out his lips in an oddly Negroid manner, began intoning Ira's lyrics. There was the "feel" of an incantation in George's "vocals," and no subsequent performer of his songs has ever invested them with such arresting fervor. Chorus No. 3 became a duet with mild, bespectacled Ira, who sang "harmony" to George's lead and provoked his brother's ire by screwing up an especially juicy passage. The music stopped, a heated argument ensued; this was my chance and, by breaking up the argument, I hastily slid onto the piano stool.

"O.K., Dukie, let's have it," said George, baring his teeth and lighting a pipe. The Brothers Gershwin called me Dukie long before George baptized me Duke. The first two tunes were shrugged off politely, but on hearing the third, George's attitude changed. He took the pipe out of his mouth and ordered me to repeat the chorus. "That's a funny chord you got in the second bar," George said reflectively. "It's good, though. It's so good that I'll tell you what I'll do — take you to Max Dreyfus." Max Dreyfus, as most everybody knew, was the musical-comedy potentate publisher. This was the real article at last.

Harms, Inc., Dreyfus's firm, was then located on West 45th Street and consisted of an old-fashioned suite of offices. In the waiting room sat members of the Dreyfus "stable" — Vincent Youmans ("Tea for Two"), Joe Meyer ("California, Here I Come"), Phil Charig ("Sunny Disposish"), Harry Ruby ("Thinking of You"), Oscar Levant ("Lady, Play Your Mandolin") and a few others. The place was like a political hell, with Boss Dreyfus dispensing patronage to the Faithful and selling producers on commissioning entire musical-comedy scores to the older and better-established "boys," or interpolated numbers to promising beginners. Most of these privilege characters were drawing small weekly advances against future royalties on a yearly basis—and that's what I was after.

Dreyfus, looking not unlike a well-groomed Mahatma Gandhi, sat at his huge mahogany desk, puffing on a long cigar. He handed a similar one to George and managed a thinnish smile. George was definitely a comer and a special favorite, but mine was a new face, young and unfamiliar. After some jocular shop talk concerning the new Kern musical (*Sitting Pretty*) and the eccentricity of Youmans, an unpredictable creature, Gershwin lit the Dreyfus cigar and said, "Max, Dukie is a Russian and writes classical stuff. I want you to hear a tune he wrote that I like." Dreyfus looked me over, this time unsmilingly, and waved me to the Steinway with his cigar. "Go ahead, young man," he said shortly. I attacked the Gershwin-approved chorus, but was stopped at the tenth bar when the "funny" chord reappeared. "Just a minute," said Dreyfus. "What kind of a chord is that?" I carefully translated the Russian conservatory term for the chord. "Oh . . . all right, continue," was the new order. I modulated into a brighter key and stole a look at mighty Max. His eyes were closed, his face set—he was listening attentively. I managed to go through the prescribed 32 bars. Long silence. "Why do you like that tune, George?" Dreyfus queried calmly. I don't remember George's answer, but I do remember taking leave of the potentate a few minutes later—his hand was cold and so was the nod I received, signifying dismissal. "Funny," mused George as we left Harms, Inc., "if I were Max, I would have signed you up on the spot."

It was Nina Koshetz who restored my rapidly vanishing faith in myself. She needed someone to coach her for a forthcoming concert with Leopold Stokowski and gave me the job. Nina took a house in Monmouth Hills, New Jersey, and invited me to spend a month as her guest and collaborator; outside of playing accompaniments I was engaged to orchestrate Rachmaninov's "Vocalise" and Moussorgsky's "Gopak," the two pieces Nina was to sing with Stokowski's orchestra. My knowledge of orchestration was distinctly sketchy, but I was grateful for the invitation. There is no greater satisfaction for a composer—young or old—than to have a performer turn to him and say: "I need you. Come and help me." Unfortunately, they usually reserve such pleadings for their managers or lovers.

I was given a comfortable room and an old Chickering piano,

which suited me fine. Armed with Gevaert's and Widor's orchestration manuals I did the job reasonably well, and working with Nina was fun because she was not only a musician, but also had a sense of humor—the two seldom go together. There were always young people around the house, including Salima, a florid blonde of nineteen who was vaguely reported to be Nina's niece; we had romantic designs on one another that came to naught. The younger element went in for tennis, swimming, some typically Fitzgeraldian petting in Stutz rumble seats and Saturday outings to the Monmouth Country Club, which was reputed to be the last word. I wasn't good at sports and couldn't drive a car; as for the country club, I never had enough cash and was too proud to sponge off of visiting Princeton and Yale men. When not flirting with Salima, I composed or orchestrated and was happy to be able to work away from sleazy rehearsal rooms and Second Avenue samovars.

Then it was back to New York, the relentless heat strangling the big town, its pavement strewn with the discarded festoons of the summer. I saw Arrow-collar-type young men in their Wanamaker or Brooks Bros. suits, according to the social strata, returning home from vacations—the younger ones soon to be off to college, the older back to Daddy's bank or Uncle's soda fountain. They seemed to have a purpose in life and a well-planned future, as did their "dates," pert, slim-limbed city sirens, complete with the new boyish bob, oriental earrings and a long cigarette holder, bent on marriage or a "career"; they all had fresh memories of energetic necking at Princeton house parties or on the less recherché sands of Coney Island. I again felt suspended in thin air as I returned to my daily pursuits of Euterpe and greenbacks.

Through Alan Tanner, a wistfully handsome youth much in demand as accompanist, I had met Vadim Uraneff, whose claims to fame were a Moscow Art Theatre apprenticeship and a small part in John Barrymore's *Hamlet*. Uraneff, who had distinct directorial talents and some (not enough) ambition, thought of putting together a double bill of an abridged "Song of Songs" in pantomime and a one-act playlet by Alexander Blok, the Russian poet of pre-Revolution despair. I looked dreamy and arty enough—as did Uraneff—and composed what was then regarded as "modern music," so I was introduced to the regal Edna James, actress-backer of the proposed venture, and asked to write incidental music for what proved to be a mild amalgam of Meyerhold eroticism and the Bible. I wrote my score, not an unpleasant one, for seven instruments, with a piano part for myself; there was nothing incidental about the music, which flowed copiously from the overture to the curtain without a single break. Our bill was put on at the Lyric Theater, 42nd Street, for a "limited" engagement of three weeks, which had to be further limited to two because of lack of patronage. One of the critics wearily mentioned the music and printed my name.

Eva Gautier took me to a gay party given by Adolph Bolm, the ex-Diaghilev *premier danseur de caractère,* who then had his own "intimate" ballet company, with Ruth Page as the *prima* ballerina. Bolm had successfully choreographed Carpenter's *Krazy Kat* and had a ballet synopsis, a rather stilted harlequinade, which he handed me after some concerted sales talk by Eva, Alan Tanner and Aaron Baron. I composed industriously, and the results were not altogether wasted, as I used some pages in Boreas's variation in *Zephyr et Flora* two years later. Bolm never produced the little ballet, as he soon disbanded his small company and went on to more lucrative things. At about the same time, my new friend and youthful sponsor, Gershwin, was "arriving" at a tremendous pace. Outside of the long runs of George White's *Scandals* (of which he wrote several editions), there was *Sweet Little Devil,* with songs like "Virginia" and "Innocent Ingenue Baby" of sassy, full-blodded freshness, at which he banged away at all the best parties, the guests clamoring for more. On top of all this came the evergreen *Rhapsody in Blue.*

I am still young enough to sigh for the Bad Old Days, and not old enough to long for the Good Old ones. "I wanna be Bad" was the sophomoric motto of my New York companions, and how they loved achieving badness, not the involved post-Freudian aberrations, just drink and lechery in very large doses. My composing career was not panning out right; the nearest thing to a "break" I got was the Koshetz performance of the two Russian pieces I orchestrated. This took place in Detroit; no one needed me there, so I didn't go and consequently didn't hear my versions. With the sweeping abandon of youth, I decided to go bad in a big way. This proved simpler than chasing the Muse and the Moola at the same time. I was under twenty, not unattractive and wore my secondhand or borrowed clothes with an air, though without a cent. Obliging mentors turned up on all sides; there were gay Englishmen like Oswald Balfour, certainly the most diligent diner-out of his day, Lord "Naps" Alington, and their American cronies, Johnny McMullin and Lester Donahue, the "social" pianist. These men were fashion dictators (McMullin wrote on men's clothes for *Vanity Fair*), salon habitués — for salons thrived in New York in 1923 — and occasional slummers in Harlem, then on the crest of a gigantic wave, and in Greenwich Village, which combined Montparnasse and Montmartre with a touch of Rue de Lappe. I'm not sure just why I was taken up by such established dandies but, thanks to the Kochanskis, I frequented musical Fifth Avenue — and dined at Hoytie Wiborg's, or Dorothy Monroe Robinson's, or Mrs. Otto Kahn's, three somewhat "intellectual" hostesses who entertained splendidly and liked to mix Gershwin's airs with Burke's Peerage's graces.

Theirs was a Bohemia on a grand scale, complete with butlers and white tie *de rigueur*. The *doyen,* the real *animateur* of Bedlam-in-Gotham was none other than Robert Winthrop Chanler, six feet eight inches of massive man, screen painter, one of the Astors and *bon vivant* extraordinary. Chanler's high priestess and mistress of ceremonies was Louise Hellstrom, widow of the Swedish novelist, who possessed the rare knack of raising Cain imaginatively and at all times. Bob Chanler had a brother named Willie, generally supposed to be potty; when Bob married the tempestuous and highly publicized beauty Lina Cavalieri, Willie cabled him: "Who's loony now?" Willie had something there, because the Chanlers were soon divorced in a manner that brought about a major disaster in Bob's life. He painted a large screen on which he depicted a white deer being bitten to death by a black panther; he would often take new friends to the cellar, where the screen was displayed, and, shedding drunken tears, would beat his breast and hint at the symbolic nature of the screen — the deer was himself, the panther Cavalieri.

Louise was of medium size, sparingly put together. Her hair was red of a striking redness, made still redder by the bluish-whiteness of her skin; she had oddly shaped green eyes, her best feature, talked in a hoarse baritone, pausing just long enough to inhale the smoke of her cigarette or gulp down her highball; unless you knew her well and were used to her mannerisms, her speech was extremely difficult to follow, as she was fond of interspersing her narrative with unintelligible mumbling. Here's a sample: she'd say, "My dear, how can you possibly like that pot-bellied bastard, he's so mzz, bzz, mzz, bzz." This accompanied by violent grimaces and much shoulder-shrugging. Or, "I saw Kitty and Johnny last night at T. R.'s and we had one hell of a good dinner, then T. R. and I went into the library and had some of his scotch and when we came back to the living room Kitty and Johnny vzz vzz vzz on the sofa." Louise would now animate her pretty legs, attempt a lascivious leer and then burst out laughing delightedly. I later learned that the mumbling was an imitation of Bob Chanler's speech. You knew eventually that with both of them "mzz bzz" signified things boring and unworthwhile, whereas "vzz vzz" indicated epicurean and priapean delights, also anything cozy and *gemütlich*. To Louise all people — and she met hundreds daily — were either "mzz bzz" or "vzz vzz" (caressingly intoned) and were immediately and ruthlessly screened: The "mzz bzzers" never went farther than Louise's Village flat, from which they were often forcibly ejected; the "vzzers" were reinvited, this time to mix with some established members of the Hellstrom group, and if met with general approval, accorded the supreme honor of being taken to Bob Chanler's of an evening.

Chanler's house was the goal of all pleasure seekers, because life there consisted of one continuous party — nightly, after sundown into the not so small hours. I don't remember the servants, although they must have been remarkable characters too, but whoever opened the door to admit a new arrival, was invariably followed by Louise or Carlotta, Louise's big Spanish rival in Bob's affections. A "mzz bzzer" daring to crash the sacred gates would find the door shut tight in his face — even if brought by friends of the family — a "vzz vzzer" would be greeted with piercing shrieks of joy in which Bob, suddenly emerging from nowhere, would join, roaring like a demented lion. The guest would then be literally carried upstairs to the third floor, where uninterrupted revelry reigned. The second floor was known as "respectable" (strictly "mzz bzz") and given over to Chanler's debutante daughters, who'd occasionally appear on the staircase, white-gloved and disdainful, to greet a white-tie eligible creature and make sure that he didn't make a mistake and wind up on the wrong floor. Because of my youth, non-Chanlerian looks and correct clothes, I was once ushered into the daughters' sanctum and, after dancing rapturously with a tall dark divinity, her Coty-scented arms locked around my neck, upon being asked the name of my fraternity, gave an answer so unorthodox that I was thrown out instantly. I cannot say that I felt very much at home where I belonged — on the third floor — not being good at either drinking or lechery; but Bob and Louise took to me, rather like one takes to an absurd yet somehow endearing trinket or piece of furniture, and made me feel that no party was complete without my presence. They nicknamed me "Dodo," I was pronounced strictly "vzz vzz" and I will always have a soft spot for the strange and lovable "bad" couple, whose badness artfully disguised that very rare commodity — a big heart.

I suspect Louise was something of a snob — in her own way, the way in which I, also, am a snob. She cared very little for titles, fat bank accounts or social-register listings, but collected people of talent — literary, theatrical, painting or musical — preferably, but not necessarily, touched by recognition and accompanying publicity. To her great credit she helped and mothered many so-called "struggling" artists, making sure first that they had some *art with which to struggle;* Bohemian hangers-on and career charlatans she detested. The inmates of "Chez Chanler" were an astonishingly motley crew. The "regulars" consisted of T. R. Smith, the publisher and anthologist of erotic poetry, a small belligerent-looking man wearing pince-nez; Joseph Stella, the Italian Brooklyn painter, whose 14-year-old daughter danced bare-breasted for the guests on one occasion; Marcel Duchamps, the celebrated abstract painter; E. E. Cummings; Carl Van Vechten; the Russians Ivan Narodny and David Burliuk; and many others. Two other Russians, Bobritsky and Alajalov, who did well in the ensuing years, were then making a living as batik painters and dwelt in Fourth Avenue in daytime, at Chanler's at night. Louise's own circle — determinedly *dernier cri* — was no less colorful, but rather out of Chanler's orbit, finding his coterie too mixed for comfort. The circle was made up of women like Jane Heap and Margaret Anderson, the *Little Review* masterminds; Djuna Barnes, the novelist (both Margaret and Djuna great beauties); Georgette Leblanc, Maeterlinck's ex-wife; and Yvonne George, the Edith Piaf of her day, who died young. Yvonne, much feted all over New York, lived at the Brevoort, undermining her robust good looks by a steady diet of morphine. She once took a slight shine to me but, on finding little cooperation from this source, said, *"Tiens, tu aimes les garçons. Il fallait me le dire."* It was useless to tell her that the *garçons* meant nothing in my young life — and that neither did the whole sex business, which still filled me with uncomprehending terror.

The above enumerated stalwarts, when at Chanler's, were soon joined by assorted visitors of note or reasonable promise. In the course of a few months, I saw Somerset Maugham, Jack Buchanan, Bea Lillie and Gertrude Lawrence (who had just taken New York by storm in *Charlot's Revue;* Gertie's singing of "Limehouse Blues" is still one of my most poignant memories), Arnold Bennett, Jane Cowl, Dorothy Parker, Judith Anderson, John Murray Anderson, Augustus John, Alexander Woollcott, Arthur Bliss, Noel Coward (then broke and fighting for recognition), Marguerite d'Alvarez, Sam Hoffenstein, H. L. Mencken, Burton Rascoe, Arthur Guiterman, John Dos Passos, etc., etc., as well as the young actresses Blythe Daly and Tallulah Bankhead.

John Murray Anderson, looking like an amiable cockatoo, was always surrounded by young boys and girls who adored him. He had the gift of curt and deliberately cruel repartee, and I never knew whether to be insulted or enchanted by his cryptic and very personal remarks. Murray was then producing *Jack and Jill,* with music by Augustus Barratt, who was better known for his monocle than any particular talent. Elizabeth North and Barbara Bennett, later Mrs. Morton Downey, were in the chorus and smuggled me into the show's rehearsals, held at a Third Avenue German *Bierstube* which reeked of hops and sawdust. It was wonderful to watch the labor pains of a musical comedy — even from the sidelines; Murray paid not the slightest attention to me and would not listen to my songs, for which I did not blame him — they were simply not good enough. I remember Barbara Bennett, who was the heaviest and, I thought, the prettiest girl in the show (the two usually went together with me), developing acute hysteria in the middle of an intricate dance routine, and being carried out by two husky chorus men. There was a big party at Murray's penthouse — on top of an early-vintage skyscraper in East 34th Street — following the opening; but the notices were grim and *Jack and Jill* folded shortly afterwards. Murray was then chiefly known for his imaginative *Greenwich Village Follies,* which usually employed my pantomimic friend Jimmy Watts. The two — Murray and Jimmy — were in the habit of dropping in at Bob Chanler's and having a heated argument with Louise, who loved arguments more than anything else in this world.

Chanler's celebrated third floor consisted mainly of a long and narrow living room with a well-stocked bar at the end; this led to two mysteriously partitioned-off beds, hidden by Chanler-painted screens. As often as not the guests, after copious libations and much noisy talk, would pair off and disappear behind the screens; they never escaped the eye of their host who, towering over his screens, would delightedly watch the proceedings, vzz vzz vzzing under his breath.

These Peeping Tom activities of Chanler's sometimes led to trouble, as on the occasion when he discovered an especially virile young man in the screened-off bed, with the wrong girl; the young man's official girl friend, also present, was indignantly notified of this by the host, who then obligingly helped her pull the offender out of bed. Another bit of pulling quickly followed when the girls went at each other's hair, with the entire entourage forming a semicircle around the contestants, Bob beating his breast and guffawing ecstatically. This was a typical climax to an evening which started most innocuously with Ivor Novello, then an entirely too beautiful youth, playing "And Her Mother Came, Too," an agreeable little tune which pleased Gershwin, also present. Following the hair-pulling act, two Chinese servants appeared with champagne to celebrate Virtue's victory, the girls kissed and made up and we all repaired to Harlem to hear Florence Mills. Everybody was mad for *Shuffle Along* and *Liza,* the two reigning Negro musicals, shortly to be followed by the "immortal" *Blackbirds.* At 6. A.M., a group of intimates was driven at breakneck speed to a Long Island spot where we were fed a breakfast of steamed clams and coffee.

Notwithstanding all this depravity, I managed to compose a piano concerto for Artur Rubinstein. He was not the success then that he is now, and was more receptive to new music, playing Szymanovski and Stravinsky superbly. On hearing some piano pieces of mine at Zosia Kochanski's, he suggested that I write a one-movement concerto, pianistically grateful and "not too cerebral." Were it not for Artur, I would have probably gone back to "Otchi Tchornya," although he never played the concerto, through no fault of his or lack of willingness — but I'm anticipating. It is sufficient to say that in a life made up of turning points as well as of "points of no return" the concerto proved a turning point of major proportions. Mother was seriously worried about the frenzied existence I led and in her many letters, made available to me by the addressees after her death in 1942, spoke feelingly about "poor luckless Dima, who never seems to get started." Yes, the title of my subsequent song hit, "I Can't Get Started," could well be applied to this early chapter of my life. Mother and I knew that the Hellstrom and Chanler parties, the fancy waistcoats artlessly copied from Oswald Balfour's, the occasional sorties into the great, glittering world of well-heeled art patrons were not for me — not yet — that I had no right to think myself a part of fashionable Manhattan; that this was merely a desperate cover-up and that, when stripped of my secondhand finery, I was a badly frightened young man.

The concerto, my first well-knit and technically adroit piece, was finished by Christmas 1923. I tried it on Koka Stember, who liked it instantly and volunteered to learn it, then on Gershwin, who became enamored of the lyrical second subject and made me play it at parties as an aftermath to his "Do It Again" and "Stairway to Paradise." Thus encouraged, I took it to my new mentor, Rubinstein, who received me dressed in a brocaded silk dressing gown, with a large pearl stick-pin in his tie, affable and courtly as is his wont. The one thing I dreaded was a polite brush off: I had learned the concerto painstakingly, but, having given up practicing long ago, was barely equal to my task. I gave a fairly good account of my work, nevertheless, and Artur, bless him, was quite transported. He grabbed the manuscript and began looking it over page by page, his large bulging eyes shining. "It's amazingly good, far, far better than I expected. Forgive me, but I expect very little from new composers," he said. "They all have two faults which make their work hopeless for a pianist who must earn his bread; firstly, they have no melodic gift or are ashamed to display it and secondly, they don't know how to write for the instrument. They think the piano is a kettledrum. Thank God, you don't. Also, the concerto is full of tunes." He sat down at the piano and essayed the first solo, then added: "Yes, I'll play this music — only not here; the managers won't let me play what I like — they're always complaining about poor Karol's [Szymanovski's] things, which I love. As for concerti — they don't hire me too often to play with orchestras, and when they do, it's always Tchaikovsky, Beethoven or Liszt. No, the place for you and your concerto is Europe. Go to Paris, where I'll be this summer." I was speechless with excitement and gratitude. I knew, of course, that Paris was ever the Mecca of young composers. Having learned all about New York the hard way, I hoped I might have something to offer this big, hard-boiled city, but my time hadn't come; I needed a Parisian passport first.

The decision having come so swiftly, so irrevocably, I was not worried about the main requisite for a trip to Europe — money. I just knew I'd get it somehow. I sprang the plan on Mother that evening and pleaded my cause with such infectious eloquence that she became persuaded I should go. The colonel thought anything better than my Sybaritic way of life and even gave me a theosophical blessing.

The next morning I was on the telephone to Gershwin; told him of my decision, assured him that I didn't want to borrow money but simply had to make some and would he have ideas on the subject. George, with his customary generosity and big-brother kindness to me, told me to come right over. When I did so, he was arguing violently with his father, the legendary New York Micawber, who is yet to find a Dickens to immortalize him. Pa Gershwin liked me and I always felt at home with him. "Well, young man, and how are you? Still writing those long symphonies?" he enquired facetiously. "O.K., Pop, see you later," George countered; he was habitually rather snappy with his father, but they loved each other and the arguments were the food of their love. Pa exited, whistling a non-Gershwin tune.

My hunch was good. Things began to work out at a swift pace. It transpired that George, overburdened with work, needed a "ghost" writer for a black-and-white ballet — a simple bit of ragtime for a high-kicking precision routine — for the Tiller girls, who were to appear in the 1924 edition of George White's *Scandals*. I turned out the thing in a few hours and was paid $100 by George. Deeming the job satisfactory, George then desired to have me try my hand at "piano copies," publishable voice and piano versions of songs to be used in the revue. I arranged six of these and was paid twenty dollars a piece by Harms, Inc. The songs I "arranged" were the ever-popular "Somebody Loves Me," "In Araby," "Kongo Kate," "Tune in on Station J-O-Y," "Year After Year," and a rhythm song, the name of which escapes me. I was quite proud of the "fill-ins," I provided for "Somebody Loves Me" and was amused to find that they were also used in the stock orchestration — obviously, the arranger thought them eminently Gershwinesque, which indeed they were. That was another $120.

Last, but certainly not least, George entrusted me with the piano solo version of the "Rhapsody," for which I was paid $100, the personal check signed by Mighty Max. My pockets suddenly bulging with money, I next invited Zosia Kochanski to lunch and started selling her on my European venture. I didn't have to oversell, because Rubinstein had already told Zosia of the good impression my concerto made on him and she was ready to do her darndest to help. We compared our listings of rich and influential people and Zosia picked Dorothy Monroe Robinson as the most likely and willing victim. Mrs. M. Robinson (now Mrs. Elbridge Gerry Chadwick) came of a prosperous and cultured Boston family, was pretty in the New England way — than which there is nothing more seductive — and was an amateur ballet dancer. A séance at the lady's house followed: I played, Rubinstein and the Kochanskis lent weighty support, and a day later I was richer by $500. My luck changed literally overnight.

In 1924, the sum of $800 was more than enough for a young musician's needs for a six months' sojourn in Paris. Mother was elated at my good fortune and even the stern colonel began referring to me as a "composer of promise." It wasn't altogether clear to anyone, including myself, just what Paris would do for me, but, supremely confident, I was determined to do something for Paris.

I felt I needed some letters of introduction. From my social mentors I obtained three — to Princesse de Polignac, Baron de Meyer (then the *Vogue* photographer) and Misia Sert. Szymanovsky gave me a letter to Henry Prunières, the editor of the *Revue Musicale*. Now that Max Dreyfus paid me for Harms-published arrangements, I felt free to ask him for a letter to Salabert, the top Paris publisher of light music. The customary interview was obtained, complete with the thin, long cigar, a thinner smile and few, very few words. The secretary appeared, was told to type the "usual" letter, then a curt nod, a vague circular gesture with the cigar, indicating, I hoped, *bon voyage* and good luck — and back to the waiting room I went to hear Joe Meyer's latest joke and Harry Ruby's newest baseball story.

The ship I sailed on was the *Rochambeau,* a small, rickety vessel, but the passengers — wide-eyed students, for the most part — were young and in search of happiness, the food excellent. Before sailing Mother gave me a small Greek Orthodox icon, that had been in the family for generations, a little theosophical pamphlet and a thick wool sweater, knitted by herself. "It is significant," said she, "that Mother was Anton Rubinstein's favorite pupil, and that you are now going to Europe sponsored by another Rubinstein — Artur!"

CHAPTER VIII

PASSPORT TO PARIS

EVERY great city — and there aren't many deserving that adjective — has an immediate and special effect on one exposed to it for the first time. New York hits you between the teeth, London makes you straighten your tie and roll up your umbrella, Venice soothes and saddens you, Rome turns you into an actor, Berlin forces you to dislike the human race, Copenhagen causes you to like it again, Constantinople lulls you into a sweet sleep, Vienna . . . forgive me, I've never been there . . . Paris enchants and exhilarates you as no other place can. From the moment I was ushered into my room at the Hotel Majestic and made up for the poverty of my luggage by the excessiveness of my tip to the bellhop, from the second I opened the window and looked down on the busy street scene, catching that first unforgettable whiff of crushed lilacs and gasoline — the nowhere to be equaled Paris smell — I knew that I loved Paris and would love her until my dying day.

The Majestic was, of course, a big mistake, as the Kochanskis, whom I met in the lobby, told me concernedly. They knew my finances to a franc and remonstrated with me, pointing out that I was no spleen-killing tourist, merely a poor aspirant to recognition and a Paris endorsement, and had better try the Left Bank. My finances may have been low, but my spirits never higher. I agreed with my benefactors thoroughly, assured them that I would move that afternoon, but stayed one whole week. "Stayed" is certainly the wrong word, as I was in a state of perpetual motion from the time I landed, bent on discovering Paris for myself without anyone's help, unarmed with Baedekers or Michelins. By walking about ceaselessly, lounging in cafés, riding in the Métro, buses, horse carriages and *bateaux mouches*, by chatting, arguing and exchanging pleasantries with natives, I learned to my delight that the Left Bank was more Parisian than the Right; that ordinary *oeufs sur le plat* and *salade de tomates* were ambrosiacal and assuredly more than just eggs and tomatoes; that the subway was more attractive and comfortable than the New York variety, but that you needed a gas mask if traveling second class; that the French girls often had mustaches under their noses as well as under their arms; that their often chunky bodies and voluminous busts were supported by bony toothpicklike legs, usually too short; that the men were smallish and exceedingly badly dressed — even dandies had an oddly overdressed "wrong" look; that the "flics" (cops) were corpulent, untidy and bewhiskered and spent most of their time arguing with even untidier taxi drivers, when the latter weren't too busy insulting one another; that the lady concierges were addicted to beards and glared at you until you gave them *un petit franc,* at which point they displayed the most exquisite manners; that the *urinoirs* on street corners were none too safe as they were the habitual haunts of pederasts on the prowl; that the wine was incomparable and the beer deplorable; that the French didn't like foreigners but were intrigued by them; that Paris was a most virtuous city (this is even more true today) because, unlike New York or London, where sex is indulged in for health or athletic reasons, it's very hard to get a woman to sleep with you; that it's either *le grand amour,* in which case the girl moves her belongings into your flat, whether invited to do so or not and starts darning your socks — or you've got to pay up; that the method of paying varies from so much per hour in a "house" to so much per dress at a good couturier's or so much per jewel; that for a modest sum you could indulge every known and unknown vice from *massage sous l'eau* to necrophilia; that Bois de Boulogne at night wasn't a healthy place, unless you wished to participate in a *partouse* or become prey to elderly voyeurs; that there is no pastime more delicious than bookhunting on the *quais* (that's where my bibliomania began, trivially enough); that kissing a girl in a café in full view of curious strangers was most agreeable; that bathrooms were scarce but with practice you could perform wonders with a *bidet* (which always looks like a *cello made of marble* to me); that some people eat to live, others live to eat, but the French *eat to eat,* and no nonsense; that a Frenchman shakes a friend's hand by lifting it up in the air and then pulling it downward with a sudden jerk;

that Paris dogs are the best front men and mixers of their kind — they sit outside their owners' cafés, make with the charm and lure the customers in; that Paris children are the best-looking in the world, which argues well for the city's future; that when eating his excellent bread, a Frenchman places a piece of it directly against his navel, holding on to it firmly with both hands, then breaks it noiselessly and proceeds to wipe his plate clean with it in order not to miss any of the sauce; that no one can smoke a cigarette as artfully as a Frenchman, who sticks it in a corner of his mouth, lights it, purses up his lips (this is very difficult) and then proceeds to talk rapidly, the dangling cigarette and the pursed-up lips giving him the desired "tough" look — try it the next time you smoke; that the prettiest American girls hung out in Rumpelmayer's tearoom or the Ritz and, galvanized by "Gay Pay-ree," were chronically on the make; that music was everywhere, from Salle Pleyel to Le Jockey in Montparnasse; that everybody gave parties and most everybody who knew how to kiss a lady's hand was invited; that taxis were cheap and unsafe and telephones bewildering and unreliable; that snobs read Proust and Claudel, not the *Almanach de Gotha* or the social register, and went to concerts, not just dinners, weddings and horse races; that everyone gave and took, and no one *gave a damn* — in short, that Paris was Paradise.

Educationally speaking, I was doing fine, but I was spending too much money and not progressing along the self-prescribed lines. The initial fever over, I took myself to 150 Boulevard Montparnasse and descended on Pavlik Tchelitchev and Alan Tanner, then sharing a big, untidy flat which by a stretch of the imagination could have been called a "studio." The living room had the right kind of light in it and all the painter's paraphernalia. It also housed an upright for Alan to practice on — which he did but seldom, as he was lazy and preferred to linger in bed pushing the keys of a tiny *piano muet* (soundless), while Pavlik painted diligently. They were an odd pair; Alan pale and willowy, his small mouth in a perpetual pout, while Pavlik was healthier than ever, all golden hair and plump rosy cheeks, shouting and gesticulating out of sheer exuberance. Their painter friends were always in and out — pugnosed Tereshkovitch with a shrewd peasant's face; small, silent Pougny (both recognized "masters" now); Count Lanskoy, who later switched to abstract painting and gained a reputation by so doing; and Boris Shatzman, with the head of a minor prophet, his fine eyes glaring at Tchelitchev's prospective customers, forever dropping in but seldom buying anything. Among the "non-customers" was Nicolas Nabokov, a tall youth a year older than myself, who had studied composition with Rebikov, the now forgotten "whole-tone scale" champion, prior to coming to Paris. He played some music of his — Omar Khayyam songs and an overture in the Satie manner; we liked neither, but Nabokov himself was an engaging young man with an open Russian face and the disarming clumsiness of adolescence.

Tchelitchev, as I soon found out, had made a name for himself in Berlin, where he painted sets for the opera house. He was entrusted mainly with Russian operas and, since "Russian" was synonymous with "garish" in those days, adopted a flowery Bakst-Soudeikine-Rabinovitch manner which delighted the Berliners. It didn't satisfy the painter who, in spite of his youth, had a genuine capacity for self-discipline; he, therefore, gave the *echte russische Kunst* a swift kick in the behind and retreated to Montparnasse to learn painting from scratch.

We dined that night, my first in Montparnasse, at Rosalie's, which is around the corner on Rue Campagne Première, still full of memories of Modigliani, whom the good woman fed when the painter was ill or broke or both. The tiny place was crowded with tousled Swedes and awkward Texans with cornfed grins and big feet; the ample-bosomed Kiki sat in a corner with Foujita — on another night I saw Helene Perdriat, Juan Gris and Kisling, but not together. The food was not bad and very cheap. Pavlik picked a quarrel with one of the painters present and, when the shouting and fist-shaking died down, we paid the modest bill and returned to 150 Montparnasse.

"Well, let's hear this music that you came to conquer Paris with," Tchelitchev said, winking good-naturedly at Tanner. I sailed into the concerto with gusto and was rewarded by the astonished faces of my two listeners. "What's gotten into you, Dima?" Alan queried, pouting no longer. "This is a really good concerto — a little too much Prokofiev, a bit of undigested Rachmaninov here and there, but you can write music — of that there is no doubt." Pavlik roared with pleasure, then sat down, suddenly pensive: "Yes, you might do . . . for Beaumont, not for Diaghilev. Diaghilev is too great a snob and wants names. However, the Count de Beaumont is launching a ballet season with Picasso, Massine and Satie, is calling it Soirées de Paris, and we all know him. He *may* commission a score from you." Alan made a face. "What about Valitchka?" he asked Pavlik. "Not Valitchka Bolm, surely?" I cut in. They both laughed. "No, silly — Nouvel, Valitchka Nouvel; Diaghilev's business manager and administrator — a man, not a girl. He's crazy about Alan and — who can tell — may take a fancy to you," went on Tchelitchev. "He knows a lot about music, having founded the Contemporary Music Group with Nourok in Russia. Valitchka is a crotchety old boy, but he means well."

I expressed my delight at the prospect of meeting the male Valitchka and Alan promised to telephone him in the morning. My two friends then helped me move to the small and smelly Hotel de Nice, practically across the street from their home, where the prices were right and the company wrong, principally whores and traveling salesmen. I don't know just what the salesmen sold, but they seemed to travel mostly from one whore's room to another's.

While waiting for Valitchka to materialize, I decided to put my letters of introduction to good use and began with Salabert, then sitting on top of the world with Maurice Yvain's gay and unrefined musicals like *Ta Bouche, Pas sur la Bouche* and others. I told the receptionist I had a letter from the great Dreyfus and was immediately ushered into Salabert's office. The publisher shook my hand cordially, waved me to a chair, and opened Dreyfus's letter. His face fell. "Haven't you played your music for Max?" he asked icily. "Yes, Mr. Salabert, I have indeed. . . . Why?" I faltered. "Well, read this." I glanced at the letter, which was very short. "Dear Mr. Salabert," it said. "The bearer of this letter is Mr. Dukelsky, a young man who composes music. Any courtesies shown Mr. Dukelsky will be greatly appreciated. Faithfully [etc.]." Needless to say, the door was the only courtesy shown me; on returning to my hotel, I gave myself to a fit of rage and tore up all the other letters. From now on, my music alone was going to make or unmake me.

Nouvel showed up that same evening — a pint-size, natty man with an old-fashioned pince-nez under bushy eyebrows, a clipped mustache and a fierce scowl, a little too fierce to be authentic. Dear Valitchka was, in reality, one of the sweetest of God's creatures, but also a frustrated composer (like his friend Diaghilev), frustrated lover, frustrated sybarite — he loved luxury and could not afford it — and I think was genuinely angry at himself for possessing so kind a heart. He was fond of cutting and artfully insulting remarks, which he made often between puffs on his eternal cigarette, and would follow them with a snakelike sound — a cross between a hiss and a chuckle — winding up with an asthmatic cough, which would make him angrier still. In a perpetual rage at himself, he covered it up by being ingeniously unpleasant to people — especially if he liked them.

After kissing Pavlik on both cheeks and pinching Alan, Valitchka clucked contentedly and turned to me: "I hear you write music — *must* you?" This sally was accompanied by the hissing-snake act, followed by violent coughing. No answer was expected, obviously, and Nouvel went on: "Don't be scared by me; nobody is scared by Valitchka any longer; they took out my fangs and they won't let me talk. Seriozha [Diaghilev] occasionally listens to me, but never agrees with me. What kind of music do you write?" This very abruptly. I was somewhat taken aback. "Good music, I hope," I replied. More clucking from Valitchka and then: "They all say that. I once said that about *my* music — I was the only one who said it. Let me see if Aliousha's piano is in tune." He hobbled over to the upright, struck a few disjointed chords and let out a yell. "How can you play on this casserole? I'm prejudiced against your music already." There was some violent shouting on the part of the hosts, which permitted me my habitual sneaking maneuver of taking possession of the "casserole."

The concerto was again rattled off, and this time greeted by thoughtful and (to me) ominous silence. "I don't know whether Seriozha will like your piece," Nouvel said finally. "I don't think he will, but you never know with him. There is too much Prokofiev in this music and Diaghilev now hates Prokofiev. I keep telling him that he is a better composer than Stravinsky, but what's the use? *Chout* was a failure, so Prokofiev is out. Play something else — not as longwinded as the concerto, khe, khe, khe. . . ." I played part of the second sonata and, to my surprise, Valitchka liked that better. He asked me to repeat a certain passage, cocked his head amusedly and then rose, glancing at his watch: "I must go now and sup with Serge at the Cabaret [Diaghilev's favorite restaurant]. I promise nothing, but I'll tell Diaghilev all about you and maybe get him to listen to you. I understand you know Boris Kochno?" "I met him in Constantinople." "Does *he* like your music?" "He's never heard it.

He didn't like my poems too well and, frankly, I wasn't insane about his." "Good, very good. Khe, khe, khe . . ." A long hiss this time, kisses all around and Valitchka took his departure.

The next day I was offered a diminutive, but cheerful, room next to Alan's and, gratefully accepting it, said good-by to the smelly, small hotel and the whoring salesmen. I was fast becoming a real Montparnos, nursed "bocks" at the Dome or the Rotonde for hours, danced with American girls, who thought me terribly foreign and "so different" at the Jockey, and with French painters' models at a students' ball, a pale replica of the famous Quatz Arts; apparently, not ten minutes after I left the ball (at 3 A.M.) everybody took their clothes off. My timing was bad — and still is.

A few days later Valitchka telephoned and in a slightly pompous voice announced that I was invited to Diaghilev's box that night and should I pass the inspection, would most likely be taken to a supper party for Stravinsky after the performance. I was to wear tails or, at least, a dinner jacket. Did I own one? I most certainly did. "All's well, then," Valitchka said. "Oh, youth, youth! khe, khe, khe . . ." and rang off.

Could this be happening to me? I was to meet the great man, the aesthetic dictator of the century, in his own lair — and so easily, so painlessly — only within a few weeks of my arrival in Paris. Life was good and so was Valitchka Nouvel. "Just you wait, Pavlik," I said gaily to Tchelitchev. "I'll get a ballet commission and you'll do the sets." "No, I won't," Tchelitchev replied. "I hate the theater."

I, for one, loved the theater that evening. It was a Stravinsky gala and featured *Les Noces,* with the music of which I was only vaguely familiar. In the box sat Misia Sert, covered with glittering jewels, a square-headed important-looking woman with a massive jaw and rather a mean mouth; a young-old man in tails with an Italian accent; and Koribut-Kubitovitch (nicknamed "Pavka"), a benign sexagenarian of the type known as "venerable"; he had the whitest of white beards, the pinkest of pink lips, an expression of infinite benevolence and turned out to be Diaghilev's cousin. Diaghilev was busy backstage, settling a quarrel between two dancers, as I overheard Koribut say. Decked out in my inoffensive Eighth Avenue dinner jacket, I was overwhelmed by the distinguished company, who paid not the slightest attention to me, and, modestly tucked away in a corner, became absorbed in the proceedings on the stage. Gontcharova's black-and-white décor for *Les Noces,* the choreography, shrewdly mixing paganism and geometry, and best of all, the luminous "undressed" uncannily persuasive music, the four pianos clashing and clicking their teeth, the constantly changing rhythms chasing each other without stopping for breath, fired my whole being. At the final curtain I screamed "Bravos" with the rest of the Stravinskyites, with such undisguised abandon that even the majestic Misia rewarded me with a smile and studied me with mild interest through her tortoise-shell lorgnette.

Shortly afterwards the door behind me opened and in walked a man of an appearance so remarkable that it will be hard to give the reader a faithful pen portrait of him. Sergei Pavlovitch Diaghilev was a big man — slightly over six feet tall — broad and big-limbed, but not corpulent; his head was enormous, and the face — a world in itself; you hardly noticed the rest of his body. The still-abundant graying hair was parted meticulously on the side and displayed the oft-described silver-white patch in the middle — no crafty coiffeur's trick but, from all accounts, something of a birthmark. When I first gazed at Diaghilev's face, I thought instantly of a decadent Roman emperor — Caligula, perhaps — although Diaghilev was allergic to horses among other things, then the Tartar in him — possibly Genghis Khan — or even a barbarous Scythian, became visible — and lastly, what he really was: a Russian *grand seigneur* of Alexander III vintage. The eyes had a piercing, mocking intensity about them, softened by unusually heavy eyelids, and he was fond of closing them slowly, as if persuaded by some unseen Morpheus, but only for a moment; they were soon peering at you again, not missing a thing. The mouth was cruel and soft at the same time, the mustache even more close-clipped than Valitchka's, the smile irresistible and oddly feminine. Sergei Pavlovitch carried monocles in all his pockets and had a habit of dropping one into his left hand, producing another with the right and screwing it into his eye languidly, making a lazy chewing motion with his mouth the while, as if munching spinach. He was well, although not conspicuously well, dressed and wore his Davis dinner jacket as if it were a dressing gown. His voice seemed monstrously affected at first — the Imperial Page's voice of aristocratic St. Petersburg — but you soon knew that he must have, too, been born with it. Diaghilev spoke French superbly, and English adequately.

He walked straight up to Misia, took her head in his hands and kissed her on both cheeks. "*Mon Serge! Mon ange!*" cooed Misia, and started an excited and unpunctuated monologue. She had the rare knack of talking to one person in a room full of people in a loud and even booming voice, but with intonations so intimate and a vocabulary so special, that the monologue was unintelligible to all but the person addressed. That was an essentially Paris-snob stunt and I was being treated to it for the first time. Little Valitchka soon appeared, emerging from the dark of the *avant-loge,* with Boris Kochno on his heels, handsomer than the dancers on the stage and smiling at no one in particular. Boris patted me on the back, somewhat tentatively, and then ran up to Mme. Sert, bowing low to kiss her bejeweled hand; Misia went right on talking, with barely a nod to Boris. Diaghilev soon turned to Nouvel, exclaiming: "Heavens, hadn't we better go off to supper? Stravinsky is in a good enough mood, but he must be starving." Valitchka adjusted his pince-nez, obviously nervous, and muttered: "Seriozha, this is Vladimir Dukelsky, the young composer I told you about." Diaghilev then noticed me, dropped his monocle, adjusted another in its place and did the spinach-munching routine, the three actions permitting him to examine me minutely. "Ah, a good-looking boy," he drawled. "That in itself is most unusual. Composers are seldom good-looking; neither Stravinsky nor Prokofiev ever won any beauty prizes. How old are you?" I told him I was twenty. "That's encouraging, too. I don't like young men over twenty-five; they lose their adolescent charm and sleep with any woman who gives them the nod. I fire most of my male dancers when they reach that age." More spinach-munching, then an amused smile. "This is all very simple. If your music is bad I can always hire you as a dancer. *N'est-ce pas, Misia?*" Misia smiled thinly, wrinkling up her small nose, and surveyed me again through the lorgnette. I was embarrassed by this initiation, well aware of the fact that I'd never do as a dancer — my body was too thin and unmuscular. "Oh, so you still can blush," Diaghilev went on. "Valitchka, I think him a very pleasant young man and I want him to come to supper with us. Come with Boris — I believe you two already know one another. *Viens, Misia.*" The regal Mme. Sert nodded, permitted herself to be enveloped in her evening cloak by the taciturn old-young man, whose name I never learned, and they went out, followed by Diaghilev, Valitchka traipsing daintily behind him, Boris and I the last to leave.

Supper at Pré Catalan in the Bois was a very Parisian affair. I recall the crimson-and-gold décor of the room, the excellent champagne and the superlative food — Diaghilev was an accomplished gourmet, but his palate was so jaded that he had to pour virtually a whole shaker of salt and another of pepper on whatever he ate, and then cover the dish with a thick layer of Savora, his favorite condiment, in order to taste anything at all. Five or six *élégantes* were present — including Misia, Daisy Fellowes, Daisy de Segonzac, Lady Abdy and one of the d'Erlangers; Stravinsky, in tails, was not unlike an emaciated Pickwick, accompanied by the faithful Winkle and Snodgrass — George Auric and Francis Poulenc, two husky and amiable youths, one fair, the other dark — and the amorous Tupman — Valitchka Nouvel. To continue with the possibly far-fetched analogy, these gentlemen were soon joined by an overdressed Jingle — Jean Cocteau of the fallen-angel face, sleeve-cuffs unbuttoned to permit the bourgeoisie to feast their eyes on the fireman-red lining (a sartorial must with him) and the fanciful, if not always intelligible, line of gab. These people, including Stravinsky, talked of Stravinsky and I drank in every eloquent word.

I wasn't asked, but managed to tell Igor Fedorovitch how transported I was by *Les Noces,* which effusion was graciously received. Coco Chanel walked in, looking like a jockey in drag, and demanded to know who the new young man (me) was, and whether, by chance, I wasn't a new dancer. When told that I wrote music, she looked at me without interest, and turned an appreciative ear to Cocteau's newest epigram. I was too happy to care. My departure was as unspectacular as was my entrance and I went back to Montparnasse in a cab and in a daze.

Two days later the ever-punctual Valitchka telephoned again and told me that Diaghilev desired me to play my concerto for him; and would I come to the Baron de Meyer's house that afternoon, as the baron had an especially good piano *and* it was in tune?

So the big moment had come, though, in the anticipation of it, my new self-assurance vanished. It was all working out too well; to a young man already used to the bitterness of bad breaks, such persistent good fortune appeared suspicious. "What does he want with my concerto?" I thought sadly. "Nouvel doesn't really like it and I myself think it reminiscent in spots." I made up my mind to at least play it well and, pushing the indignant Alan off the piano stool, went on a four-hour practice jag.

The de Meyers lived in *un hôtel,* which, in this instance, meant a private dwelling (*hôtel particulier*), not an inn. The house and its owners were typical of the all-powerful *tout Paris* set — Louis XV and Marie Laurencin with *Vogue* trimmings. There was a faint tinge of violet in the beautiful white hair of both de Meyers — a decorative pair, aggressively agreeable, as people of their class are, when receiving; the class that labels everything that comes their way as either *divin* or *d'un ennui mortel* — be it music, a new novel, a new restaurant or a new concubine. I was brought by Diaghilev, the magician and explorer, therefore there was a good chance of my being *divin.* I don't think they knew that the frail youth with jet-black hair was in their home "on approval" and that his fate hung perilously in the balance.

I was the first to enter the de Meyer drawing room — a regrettable mistake, as no one *divin* is ever punctual. My embarrassment was somewhat relieved by the cordiality of my hosts and the perfection of the dry Martini I was offered, a drink still misunderstood by Parisians, who call it *un dry* — pronounced "dree" — and make it almost entirely of vermouth, using gin as sparingly as if it were Fernet Branca. Some small talk followed, very small indeed on my part, and then Sergei Pavlovitch entered with Boris in tow, both splendidly shaven and eau-de-cologned.

I was much too nervous to listen to the gossip that made up the general conversation. I drank two more Martinis and, just as I emptied the second, was asked by Diaghilev to show him the concerto I had brought with me. After carefully wiping and then adjusting one of his monocles, he began perusing the manuscript, humming to himself in a strange catlike voice and conducting with a pudgy index finger. I watched the performance with awe and astonishment. Diaghilev, who never missed anything, smiled indulgently and put down my music. "Few people know it, but I'm a *compositeur manqué,*" he remarked. "I was always behind in my harmony lessons with Rimsky-Korsakov, but once managed to write a piano piece, which I showed him. It was very bad and he said so." Sergei Pavlovitch then rose brusquely and led me to the piano. "Let me hear your concerto: I'll turn the pages for you."

With the determination of despair and, encouraged by the excellence of the instrument, I gave a creditable account of my "Passport to Paris." I remember vividly thinking as I played on: "I don't care, here it is. It's the best I can do, take it or leave it." When I hit the last crashing C-major chord, there was a moment of dreadful, complete silence — I didn't turn around but knew that the two de Meyers and Boris were looking at Diaghilev, awaiting his verdict. To my astonishment, the great man began clapping his hands thunderously and with such determination that the others soon joined in the applause. "*Bravo, jeune homme,* and congratulations. Best new music I've heard in years. Now — what shall we call your ballet?" he inquired suddenly. I was completely taken aback. "*What* ballet, Sergei Pavlovitch?" I queried. "The one you will write for me, of course. You *will* write one, won't you?" Kochno now intervened. He got up, embraced me and, smiling knowingly, declared that he already had an idea for "my" ballet and that the idea was certain to please Sergei Pavlovitch. I dimly remember that I was then made much of by the de Meyers and that a bottle of champagne appeared mysteriously and toasts to the new Diaghilev composer were drunk by all, including the toastee.

I was taken home to 150 by Diaghilev himself — Kochno stayed on to dinner at the de Meyers' — in a large chauffered limousine. My discoverer had his arm around me and talked softly and earnestly about my talent, the future before me, the task he was entrusting me with and his hope that I would fulfill his expectations; I was so dazed and drunk with the Martinis, the champagne and my crashing, complete success, that I only understood half of what Sergei Pavlovitch said, but loved every word of it. He deposited me in Boulevard Montparnasse, kissed me heartily on both cheeks Russian fashion, and departed. Both Alan and Pavlik were out; I dined alone extravagantly on a corner terrace, paying eleven francs for a copious meal, and, exhausted by the events of the day, went off to bed. That night I cried my first, and probably last, tears of happiness and realized that Victorian novelists had something there, for never did tears taste so sweet to me.

What ensued was equally dreamlike. The next morning, my recital to Tchelitchev and Tanner, to which they listened with eyes popping and mouths ajar, was interrupted by Valitchka, who dashed in without bothering to telephone this time. He declared himself delighted with my success, there was more embracing all around, and then

I was let in on the newest developments; apparently Diaghilev, Boris and Valitchka had supper late the night before and Boris talked a great deal about the proposed ballet. All I could learn about it was that two leading male dancers' roles were envisaged — one for Dolin, the other for Serge Lifar, the remarkable new Russian boy for whom Diaghilev entertained the highest hopes; that a girl called Alice Nikitina with the "most beautiful legs in the world" was a hot candidate for the female lead, and that I had better drop everything and concentrate on my job as if my life depended on it. This was easy, because there was nothing for me to drop and I had no other life than the one that was so miraculously opening before me.

The news of a new Diaghilev protégé emerging from out of nowhere — Russia via the United States was an unheard-of beginning — spread rapidly through the Paris salons. Diaghilev nicknamed me Karsavina, as he claimed that I bore a striking resemblance to that dancer, and this led to obvious speculations as to the nature of our relationship; idle ones, I must add, because, quite outside my own "normal" leanings, I just wasn't Sergei Pavlovitch's "type." I quickly formed lasting friendships with both Auric and Poulenc, whose gay, lilting music was a relief after the strenuous Varèse and Ruggles diet. I liked Auric's *Les Fâcheux* with Braque's décor even better than the universally popular *Les Biches* (Marie Laurencin — Nijinska) by Poulenc. There was a splendid ruggedness, a bittersweet savor about the former, an uncouth but very personal harmonic language, and the rough-edged, graceless orchestration fitted the music perfectly; the ballet (produced in 1923) was only a moderate success, perhaps because of the rather pedestrian choreography. *Les Biches*, on the contrary, was (and still is, wherever revived) an emphatic hit, and rightly so because it is the perfect period piece and typified the twenties as did no other ballet. The morbid prettiness of Laurencin's décor was happily underlined by Poulenc's ingratiating music, slyly frivolous or voluptuously romantic by turn; he had a rather coy trick of perversely harmonizing the simplest Schubert-*cum*-Chaminade tunes, which alternately caressed and intrigued the ear. Nemtchinova's entrance, with her sleek black hair, tiny blue jacket and long, dreamy legs in white tights, to Poulenc's best tune in the score was a great and unforgettable *coup de théâtre.* Auric also liked to pepper his pseudo-seventeenth-century airs with "wrong notes" artfully distributed — and I much preferred this somewhat naïve device to the out-and-out vulgarity of Milhaud's *Le Train Bleu,* whose unashamedly cheap strains would have probably gained by a little shrewd mutilation.

Auric and Poulenc were wonderful company; Poulenc much more of a *mondain* than his friend. Auric was a big, unwieldly creature, a *megot* always dangling from his lips, the smile childishly good-hearted, the small Balzacian eyes malevolent and crafty. Francis, on the contrary, although fairly portly, too, spoke and moved with the easy assurance of a salon habitué; his voice lazy and nasal, his clothes unobtrusively right, his light hair cut *en brosse,* somewhat in the Prussian military manner, Poulenc was at his best when playing the piano, which he did with an impish nonchalance immediately attractive to the listener.

Auric and Poulenc returned favorable verdicts on my gifts and I was now maneuvered into a pilgrimage to Stravinsky's quarters, in the Pleyel building. The master, surrounded by multi-colored inks, erasers, pens, pencils and music paper of every conceivable variety, all in meticulous order, sat in an ultra-modern chair behind an even more aggressively modern writing desk. As he got up to greet me with the rather fussy politeness so typical of him, I became conscious of the enormous goggles he wore, propped up *above* his eyes, the chin, in its turn, propped up by an elegantly tied ascot emerging from a monogrammed sport shirt. Stravinsky's body was small, taut and compact, but in common with small men, he was fashion crazy, not unlike Ravel, who spent a young fortune on a light-blue tailcoat once, "launched" it, at one of the Princesse de Polignac's bigger soirees and then, to his mortification, heard a marquis ask a count: "Who is the little fellow who didn't bother to dress?"

Igor Fedorovitch was on the whole very nice about my concerto. "What pleases me particularly," he said, gently puffing on a cigarette in an extra-long holder, "is your technical proficiency; you are already a professional. There is nothing like Russian conservatory training and your young French friends would have been better off had they studied with Taneiev, Glazunov or their pupils. As to the music itself — well, it's good honest conservatory music, too, and how can it be otherwise?" Since the concerto, which I had had to perform daily for several weeks now, had begun to bore me, I didn't disagree. "Play something else — something not quite so formal and correct," Stravinsky asked. I don't know why, but I plunged into the allegro from my prematurely frozen Icelandic overture. Stravinsky smiled engagingly and patted me on the back. "That's the kind of music I expect from young men — it has meat in it, and it's musical meat, not fancy little ornaments." I remember him saying, "You should be able to write a good ballet — Diaghilev is seldom wrong."

I was most anxious to meet Prokofiev, whose third concerto was a model for my first — and so far only — one. Diaghilev warned me against seeing his "second son." "Serjosha is certainly very talented and full of melody — which Igor is not — but Igor is intelligent whereas Prokofiev is an utter imbecile. He always can be counted on doing the wrong thing — fancy calling a symphony 'Classical'; it's almost as bad as Scriabin — we detested one another — labeling his orchestral poem 'Divine.' " I was no longer afraid of Diaghilev and protested violently. "How can an imbecile write a piece as well constructed as the third piano concerto?" I wanted to know. "And those fresh, lyrical themes — what charm that music has!" Diaghilev winced a bit, then grew thoughtful. "Yes, charm . . . " he said quietly. "That's something impossible to acquire. *Stravinsky est le seul musicien slave qui n'a pas du charme slave.*"

If Stravinsky was reputed to be politely indifferent to everyone except himself, Prokofiev was feared by many for his bluntness, not to say boorishness. He carried this attitude to somewhat childish extremes, as when Siloti, the old pianist and Liszt's last living pupil, introduced him to pert and pleasant Lady Dean Paul, who, under the name of Poldovski, wrote Debussyan salon music. Prokofiev declined to shake hands with the woman, who was thrilled by his presence at her concert, because "she wrote bad music," as he put it. I was luckier than the unfortunate Lady Dean Paul, because Serge the Second (I often think the twenties the Era of the Three Serges — Diaghilev, Prokofiev and Koussevitzky) received me most cordially; I was brought to his flat by Souvtchinsky on June 17, 1924 — a significant date in my life, as a great and durable friendship began on that day. Souvtchinsky, spouting enthusiasm on the way, declared that I had nothing to fear from this new "test" as I had the makings of a "grand style" (in the French sense) and was already "completely autonomous." Prokofiev, looking like a cross between a Scandinavian minister and a soccer player, didn't go to quite such giddy heights, but, with some reservations, thought the concerto a good, solid job, convincingly melodious. His lips were unusually thick, explaining to some degree the "white Negro" sobriquet, and they gave his face an oddly naughty look, rather like that of a boy about to embark on some punishable and therefore tempting prank. His pretty wife, Lina Ivanovna, was part Spanish, sang well, and was a good housekeeper and mother (they had two sons), which didn't prevent Serge from picking fights with her hourly and throwing her out of the room at the slightest provocation. Prokofiev pumped my hand energetically, asked me whether I played chess (I did, badly) and suggested I write him in Brittany, where he was going for the summer, to report my progress or lack of same.

Summer was upon us and Diaghilev had made up all my plans for it. He told me that he wanted a ballet combining classicism with Russian overtones — tutus with *kokoshniks,* as he put it. Sergei Pavlovitch, who began his career as a sponsor of painting, adored Venezianov, Borovikovsky and Levitzki — Russian "classical" painters of late eighteenth and early nineteenth centuries — and was especially fond of Venezianov's peasants — clean, graceful creatures in white, their dress a fanciful amalgam of peasant headgear and a Russian landowner's conception of Olympian fashions. These landowners had their own theaters on their country estates, and it enchanted them to see their latest favorite — a Douniasha or Parasha — endowing her rustic charms with godlike attributes of a Flora or Psyche. Diaghilev was a *barin* of the old school; one of his ancestors had owned such a theater and this perverse conception of theatrical mythology was understandably dear to him.

The story selected and "rearranged" by Kochno was that of Zephyr and Flora, already "balletized" by Didelot, and also caricatured by Thackeray in 1836, but these antecedents only added spice to the idea. Zephyr was to be impersonated by Anton Dolin, Boreas by young Lifar and Flora by Nikitina of the perfect limbs. Diaghilev admonished me to stick to Glinka and Dargomijsky as models and to steer clear of Prokofiev; this I promised to do, meekly volunteering to add a dash of Dukelsky. The plan was for Boris and myself to go off to a small retreat in the country, near Paris, and go to work without delay. Boris became most industrious and businesslike, and a few days later we were in the Chevreuse Valley, sharing the second floor of a tiny house owned by one Veuve Gicquel, who ran a small village bistro underneath our quarters. The honest bourgeois who patronized her establishment must have been bewildered by the distinctly un-French sounds emanating from upstairs, but no one seemed to mind. The bourgeois drank, I composed, and Boris went about the fragrant countryside faternizing with the villagers, a favorite pastime of his in those days.

Kochno's synopsis was craftily made and gave a composer a free hand with his material. A word of advice in passing here may not be amiss — keep your ballet story to five or six lines and stay away from literature or editorializing of any kind; the simpler and more direct the scenario the happier the composer and choreographer, the more pleased the audience. Boris had (and still has) a rare knack for presenting his ideas with the utmost clarity — yet with great poetic feeling — and when you had so good an initial "peg" and an atmosphere as unmatchable as that provided by Diaghilev's presence, his enthusiasm, his quiet eloquence, his uncanny intuition — it wasn't easy to go wrong.

I began with the joyful Concert des Muses and the Nouvel-approved scherzolike episode from the second sonata for Lifar's first entrance. After this start, the next three "numbers" wrote themselves; never before and certainly never since (except perhaps in the 1946 *Bal des Blanchisseuses,* written in three weeks *also* on a Boris Kochno "argument") have I experienced such delicious freedom in composing. I played what I wrote to Boris of an evening, the smell of freshly mown hay mingling with other assorted odors of the French countryside. There were a few roughly clad customers of Mme. Gicquel's drinking *vin blanc au citron* below — they got used to the mad foreigners upstairs and were not above offering us *un pinard.* Boris loved what he heard, made detailed notes for the choreographer (not yet chosen), and then we trotted downstairs to join the pastoral drinking, happy and young and full of music. A few days later the result of our labors was exhibited to Diaghilev, who never came to see us in our Chevreuse retreat, but remained in Paris raising money for his next season. On this occasion I had my first glimpse of Lifar, a coltish youth with an unusually dark complexion and Ukrainian features. Lifar wore a perpetually ecstatic expression and talked mostly in excited monosyllables, like a young savage savoring the fruits of European civilization for the first time. His ecstasy at what he heard of *Zephyr* was so noisy that I couldn't hear Diaghilev, who was whispering animatedly in a corner with Kochno. But there was no need to worry. If Sergei Pavlovitch liked the concerto enough to commission a ballet from me, a total nonentity, he was enormously gratified by my new effort, particularly because, as he put it, "he was not sorry he had had faith in me." He thought the style exactly right, melodious and Russian but "minus samovars." That night Boris and I were driven back to Chevreuse in someone's town car, faintly Guerlain-scented and with a chauffeur of excessively good looks. I began to feel important, a dangerous feeling when one is twenty.

Valitchka turned up in our Chevreuse working quarters one evening, drank a great deal of red wine, listened to the new music, liked it and then produced a contract for me to sign. I'm a little hazy as to what was in the contract, but recall that the royalties were to be paid me through the French Performing Rights Society (of which I became a member through Boris's good offices) and that Diaghilev agreed to give me 1000 francs a month while I was working with him, "and maybe more later," said Valitchka darkly, "if your ballet is a success and you're asked to write another. I wouldn't count on it if I were you, khe, khe, khe. . . ." In 1924 you could live in France on 1000 francs a month about as well as you can in 1954 on 100,000 — just enough for a decent existence *sans faire des folies*. This arrangement was most welcome; my tastes were modest but Mrs. Monroe Robinson's money was dwindling rapidly.

Three more weeks *chez* Mme. Gicquel, who had got used to her strange tenants and was loth to see us go; about 40 per cent of *Zephyr and Flora* was written and approved by Sergei Pavlovitch, who declared that I would finish the score in Monte Carlo.

On August 4th, I wrote Gershwin:

My dear George,

Your letter was forwarded to me about two weeks ago, but, being extremely busy and lazy, I didn't manage to write you at once.

The thing is that Diaghilev ordered me (sic) a large ballet score on a rather difficult book for the coming 18th season of the "Ballets Russes"; this is to be produced next Fall, first in Monte Carlo, then in Paris. Of course, you understand that nothing better could have happened to me, and, although speed is not required in this particular case, I'm writing and writing. In two weeks I'm going to Monte Carlo to join Diaghilev, finish the score and start rehearsals. My concerto is to be played in U. S. A. in January; I also received an offer to play it myself in Paris next Spring. [Nothing came of these two projects.]

Your letter was adorable in its unselfish simplicity, but one thing makes me sad: you don't even mention the rhapsody — that is — the Real Thing. Now this is most important. I spoke about you to Diaghilev and played nearly all your tunes to his secretary, who finds them amazing. I also have a most interesting proposition for you (Diaghilev's). Do come to Paris before I leave.

Love,

On August 31st, Diaghilev wrote Lifar:

Dukelsky came yesterday and played me the music for Flore et Zephyre, which I liked enormously. I made such comments as I thought fit, and he very nicely said he would take note of it all, and go on working at it in Monte Carlo, under my eye, all of which pleases me greatly. For his twenty years he's extremely gifted and developed.

To Monte Carlo we then journeyed — by a slow and rather nasty train; my head chronically in the clouds and my heart wonderfully light. The company was soon to go on another tour and Diaghilev and Kochno were going along — they now trusted me to complete the job alone and assured me that I was on the right track. Diaghilev warned me to keep away from women, whom he professed to abhor, not merely as useless (to him) sexually but because of their colossal stupidity and greed. Sergei Pavlovitch was, I'm afraid, overfond of such generalizations; along with women, his pet peeves were homosexuals and balletomanes. This intelligence might appear startling in view of his being both of these things himself. However, he explained the paradox by insisting that he only liked manly and virile youths, afraid or suspicious of women, and thus falling into the able hands of the likes of him. Simpering and mincing *tantes* he detested and thought worse than women, whom they aped unsuccessfully. He was most sympathetic when I confessed to not being homosexual. "A pity in a way of course," he mused. "Poor Piotr Ilytch Tchaikovsky was always on the verge of suicide, so afraid was he that people might discover that he was a pederast; today, if you're a composer and *not* a pederast you had better put a bullet through your head." When I protested and cited the names of three especially successful living composers of old-fashioned habits (that is, heterosexual), Diaghilev retorted: "Nonsense. Two of them are *des tantes ratées* (would-be pederasts who failed to make the grade) and the third is impotent." He laughed uproariously, then shook a well-manicured finger at me. "Don't get mixed up with women, Dima . . . not now, anyway, while you're working for me. All they are good for is gold-digging or venereal disease — ghastly things both." I assured him that women played no part in my life and, to give weight to this statement, reluctantly admitted my still virginal status.

"A virgin at twenty — most interesting," drawled Diaghilev, dropping his monocle. "That reminds me of an uncommonly beautiful young man who was in the Horse Guards; about your age he was, too. I wined and dined him nightly with not the slightest success. He didn't seem to care for girls and, strange to relate, in spite of his superb physique was entirely allergic to sex, in his own admission. This began to nettle me, so I took him to the famous old Dr. Botkin, the inventor of the Botkin drops [a staple drug in prerevolutionary Russia]. Botkin was an irritable old party and fit to be tied after examining my frigid Horse Guard. 'What's your diagnosis, Doctor?' I asked him anxiously. 'Diagnosis? Hell, the young man is beyond all hope,' Botkin growled. 'I asked him whether he liked women. "I do not, Doctor," said he. "Do you like boys?" "No, indeed." "Do you indulge in solitary pleasures?" "Certainly not, sir." "Perhaps a slight affinity to canines or young sheep, then?" "What a horrible idea!" I was fast becoming exasperated. "Well, damn it, do you have dreams?" "Oh, yes, I dream occasionally." "Ah, now we're getting somewhere. Kindly describe a typical dream!" The young man concentrated for a minute. "It's really quite silly, but I often dream of waiting for a train at the Tzarskoe Sielo station. I wait and wait . . . and then I hear the chugging of the approaching train in the distance . . . chug . . . chug . . . chug . . . chug . . . nearer and nearer . . . it's practically upon me . . . and then . . . " "Yes, yes, go on!" "And then I have an orgasm!" Naturally, I threw the idiot out of my office.' "

Diaghilev's aversion to balletomanes was more justifiable than his contempt for women — his truest friends and admirers as well as financial backers were women after all, and he loved them and was touchingly grateful to them. Sergei Pavlovitch considered the musical score the *axis* of every ballet, sets and costumes came next in order of importance, then choreography and lastly a good or at least an adequate performance by the dancers, who, to him, were choreographers' tools — no more. "A balletomane — I was one myself in the Marinsky-theater days — has a fixation: the dancer's legs and feet. To him a ballet is a jewel box with his idol — be it a he or a she — the jewel. They have no ears for the music, no eyes for the decor — they are nothing but fetishists," he told me. "God help us if they ever become critics!" Alas, most ballet critics today are balletomanes; one has only to read a typical account of a ballet *première* in a London or New York newspaper or magazine and see the music dismissed with "poor" or "brilliant," the décor barely touched upon, the choreographer given plenty of space, but most of the space devoted to the interpreters. That was not so in my Diaghilev days, as music critics (and sometimes composers), both in Paris and London, wrote ballet criticism. It is still possible to get a non-amateurish notice for one's ballet score in Paris — but not in London or New York.

Sergei Pavlovitch and Boris alighted at the Hôtel de Paris — their habitual quarters in Monte Carlo — whereas I, my first ballet pay envelope in my pocket, went off in search of a cheap and "amusing" hotel. The establishment I selected in Monaco — which I thought had more character than Monte — was sensationally cheap, all right, but it proved anything but amusing. It was run by a pale and perpetually scowling *Auvergnate* with watery eyes and a distrust of foreigners, in which category she included every out-of-towner. She couldn't for the life of her see why a young *étranger* like myself should want to stay at her inn, inhabited mainly by croupiers and professional ballroom dancers; and when she took a look at my Nansen (League of Nations) passport — I had no separate American first papers at the time, being merely "written in" on Mother's — her displeasure became complete. She eyed me up and down, asked interminable tricky questions and, I'm sure, would have frisked me had she had the right to do so, but, the moment I produced a month's rent in advance, a benign smile appeared on her squeezed-out lips and I was admitted. The reader will wonder why I made so great an effort to secure so sorry a lodging — that's easy: the view was magnificent and the room clean.

There was a horrible harridan of a chambermaid at the place, a

Jill-of-all-trades and second in command to the *patronne*. She was all caky make-up and gold teeth and, in her own confession, liked two things — *pastis* (the anisy drink of the Midi) and young boys. The creature herself must have been somewhere around fifty, but her latest acquisition was a seventeen-year-old Marseillais named Honoré, a fervent *sportif* but none too agile as bellhop; Honoré was all muscles and pimples and the harridan promptly took him in hand. Her room was right next to mine, the walls were very thin, as is usual in French hotels, and I was often treated — punctually at 6 P.M., when I returned to my room to shave and, occasionally, change — to an erotic duet that filled me with terror; the duet consisted of a *cantus firmus* performed by the rickety bed squeaking rhythmically, a highly involved aria by the harridan, full of ecstatic roulades and well-executed tremolos, the whole punctuated by double-basslike grunts and snorts by the athletic Honoré. It made for fascinating, if gruesome, listening, and I once cut myself badly with the razor, shocked by a sudden tumultuous crescendo by the overvocal lovers.

The food at the hotel was unfortunate — it was bad and there wasn't enough of it, as the well-worn story has it. My appetite was ravenous and I would often gulp down the unpalatable dinner and then dine for the second time with Diaghilev and Boris at their excellent *brasserie*; they seldom took their meals at the highly gastronomic and costly Hôtel de Paris, and then mostly on festive or important business occasions. My first impression of Monte Carlo — and of the Riviera in general — was decidedly mixed and still is. I never could see why such astonishing natural beauty should be ruined by dingy and pretentious villas and, above all, the ever-present dirty-orange of the Riviera rooftops. The three colors which predominate in that land are orange, blue (the Mediterranean) and green (the flora) — a poor blend. I don't know why the roofs weren't painted pink, crimson or even pale blue in the first place.

The hideousness of the Monte Carlo casino is too well-realized without any further vilification on these pages. The whole square, with the birthday-cakelike Hôtel de Paris, the rotonda in the middle with benches occupied by has-beens — ex-*lorettes* of the Felix Faure day and retired British colonels living off a roulette "system" by which, if you possess inhuman restraint and self-discipline, you are "guaranteed" 2000 francs daily — and the casino in washed-out pink, is one of the saddest sights in the world, second only to a foggy afternoon in Manchester, England. I hated the casino because I lost the last few thousands of non-Diaghilev money there at roulette in slightly under ten minutes; yet Fate decreed that I should complete my *Zephyr* within its dreaded walls. There was no piano at my hotel in Monaco and anything more advanced than "*O Sole Mio*" or "*La Violeterra*" was unsuitable for the Hôtel de Paris and its clients, so Diaghilev made arrangements with the administrator of the casino, who obligingly moved to other quarters, to lend me his *cabinet de travail,* which boasted a good Erard and thus became a composer's workshop. It was wondrous strange to compose ballet music right under the gambling hell; by opening the windows I could occasionally catch the bored *rien ne va plus* of the croupiers over my head and wince remembering my shameful loss. However, the Théâtre de Monte Carlo — one of the most attractive of its kind in Europe — was next door, my good genius Diaghilev was across the street and all was well with *Zephyr and Flora* and the world in general.

Shortly before Sergei Pavlovitch and Boris went off with the company, I decided I had had enough of my Monaco rattrap and, by walking in the streets of hilly Beausoleil, found a "vacancy" sign in the window of a pleasant little house grandly styled Villa des Genêts. I rang the bell and soon beheld an unusually thin dark Italian lady with huge Giottoesque eyes, whom I instantly liked and who turned out to be Veuve Marcellin, the villa's owner. She greeted me in warm Italian fashion and was soon joined by a Mlle. Doucet, who was as fat as Mme. Marcellin was thin and whose hair was the reddest red known to nature or science. Mlle. Doucet was, technically speaking, an old maid, but there was nothing old or maidenly about her; she was amiable and coquettish in the extreme.

After showing me an agreeable room on the second floor and learning that it suited me perfectly, the two ladies offered me a Cinzano and we all sat down. "May I ask, sir, the nature of your business?" the widow said gently. "I write music." *"Ah, c'est beau, la musique!"* sighed Mlle. Doucet, adding, "So cultural and it aids the digestion." "The voice of the heart," Mme. Marcellin offered, clutching hers. "*And* of the soul, too. It's very dignified to be a *maestro compositore* and we are honored to receive you." "But we have no piano here," Mlle. Doucet suddenly remembered and looked at me with anxiety. On learning that I had my working quarters elsewhere and that I wrote for the Ballets Russes (next to gambling, Monte

Carlo's greatest magnet in those days) the two women expressed sincere delight at renting their prize bed-sitting room to so accomplished a young man and my health was drunk in another Cinzano. There was a smaller room, next to mine, occupied by various transients at uncertain times, but deemed unsuitable for a prolonged sojourn — otherwise, but for the owner and her *dame de compagnie,* the Villa des Genêts was empty.

With the departure of my collaborators, my Monte Carlo life assumed a duller but more regular pattern. I'd get up early, breakfast with the two ladies, walk over to the casino, compose for two or three hours and then take a bus to the Larvotto beach, which in 1924 was an unpretentious *petite plage de famille.* After a short immersion in the Mediterranean — I swam very badly — I'd lie in the sun for an hour and return to Beausoleil to lunch in one of the many small restaurants in that area. I would buy fruit or sweets for my worthy landladies and spend an inspiring half hour discussing the uplifting qualities of Art, music especially, and partaking of refreshments; then return to my casino quarters and work until six, when one of my new friends — among them the Comte de Segonzac, Daisy's husband, and Henri Gautier-Vignal, witty and gracious people both — would fetch me and we'd go on a motor trip to Eze, or la Turbie, or St. Paul de Vence. Dinner was at somebody's villa, as a rule, then more talk over brandy and cigars, occasionally a bad fox trot played by me somewhat disdainfully (I was now a *maestro compositore*) for the delectation of my hosts who, initiated by the *Boeuf sur le toit,* already had a distinct "penchant" for American jazz, and so to Beausoleil and bed.

Cocteau was summering in Villefranche at the Hotel Welcome and I was taken there a few times by Gautier-Vignal. Jean, in good form, was surrounded by admiring disciples, mostly the youths in search of Beauty and Truth (or Fun, at the very least) so aptly described by Maurice Sachs in *Sabbat.* He ran around the room, talking incessantly, the disciples just sat and worshipped. Somehow I could never fall under the man's spell, which, I fear, annoyed him not a little — it's always embarrassing to a hypnotist to try to lull to sleep a man who stubbornly stays awake. In spite of the marked and flattering interest Cocteau displayed in me, in spite of an enjoyable cruise in his famous boat *Ange Heurtebise* and the fact that he nicknamed me "*Le Duc Exquis*" (Dukelsky), I didn't very much care for these Villefranche outings. They were rather like drinking verveine tea with a snake charmer in a hothouse.

I much preferred my sunbathing sessions at Larvotto's beach. There were attractive young people about, disporting themselves on the sand or splashing in the incredibly blue water. Their meeting place seemed to be a small raft not quite a quarter of a mile away from the shore, and I gazed enviously at the gay group of American and English teenagers whose chief occupation seemed to be diving off the raft and then climbing back on again. One of the best swimmers of the group was a Nordic nymph with green-grey eyes, sunflower-colored bobbed hair, sugar-white teeth and a body so brown that the color seemed painted on her lithe but solid frame. She'd only linger on the beach for a minute or so and then would swim out to the raft, using a powerful and faultlessly executed crawl. I soon learned from one of the guards that the nymph's name was Karen, that her friends nicknamed her "Khaki" and that she was half-Danish, half-English. Watching the girl disappear in this manner every morning was torture to me as I was eager to get to talk to her; in order to win her attention I signed up for a course of swimming lessons with a big, stalwart Monégasque and told him that my aim was to swim well enough to be able to reach the raft. The Monégasque nodded knowingly and we began our lessons the next morning at an hour early enough not to be heckled by watchers.

I was in no way an exceptional pupil but, after six or seven lessons, mastered the common breast stroke and could even float on my back with some difficulty. Two more lessons and the Monégasque told me to go ahead and swim out to the raft, solemnly promising to come to my rescue, at no extra charge, should I fail to make it. Filled with romance and courage I waited for Karen to reach the raft, then started out, acutely conscious of the inadequacy of my "sissy" stroke, but determined to get to her. I was pretty tired by the time I reached the enchanted spot, but reach it I did, and who should help me climb aboard, my teeth chattering and breath heavy, but Karen herself! She gave me a beatific smile and looked me over with mocking curiosity. "That was quite a feat," she said encouragingly. "You're not much of a swimmer, are you?" I swallowed that and managed a smile myself. "If you must know the truth, I learned swimming to get to this raft and meet you," I said. Khaki broke out in a gay laugh, then shook my hand with some warmth. "I like that.

. . . It's flattering and it's sincere. I hope we'll be friends." This was a very healthy beginning and I inwardly blessed my Monégasque and reminded myself to give him a fat tip. After a few wonderful minutes on the raft, the assorted Anglo-Americans wondering who the intruder was, Khaki and I swam back together, which was much easier, the girl slowing down her progress not to embarrass me, breast-stroking diligently alongside her.

Following this somewhat *Saturday Evening Post*-like kickoff, we became inseparable. Khaki's father was a manufacturer, in fairly comfortable circumstances, and he was expected momentarily from London; meanwhile she was staying alone at a typically English *pension,* patronized either by young vacationists or the already noted retired colonels with unbeatable systems at roulette. Karen was nineteen and more or less engaged to a rising Cardiff football player known simply as Biddy. I thought myself in love, although it was probably autosuggestion; no matter, for it came at the right time and I wouldn't let any Biddies or British manufacturers stand in my way.

I was glad of this new development because, with the departure of Diaghilev and Kochno, I learned something about loneliness. I like loneliness now and have learned to live with it quietly and harmoniously for the most part. There is no getting away from it, you are lonely alone and you die alone — and so being lonely at intervals is like a series of leisurely rehearsals for death. You create alone, too, but almost everything else you do in a crowd; a crowd of two if you're lucky and have a lover, a larger crowd depending on the number of friends you have — worst of all, a kaleidoscopic procession of fellow mortals, totally indifferent to you and not especially pleased at finding you still alive. Theirs are the faces you see around you most often, theirs are the unwelcome telephone voices, theirs the letters destined for the wastebasket before you open them; but, as long as your business is a communal enterprise, a mass effort — and what business isn't? — you will go on seeing these phantoms more often than you'll see friends or lovers.

I didn't know all this when I was left alone in Monte Carlo to complete my *Zephyr and Flora* music — a clever move of Diaghilev's, because he knew that I'd have more time on my hands, and would have to use it to compose. When not composing, I'd turn to letter writing (still a favorite recreation of mine, bewildering and annoying to my friends, because I foolishly expect replies and just as foolishly become indignant when I don't get them; nobody writes anymore) and send Mother and Alex long and detailed reports of my miraculous progress. Alex was doing fine at Cushing and Mother had now switched to Russian embroidery and cross-stitching, much in demand at the time, to keep her younger son properly clothed and fed. She soon moved to Boston, to be near Alex, and stayed with the Irakly Toumanovs in Jamaica Plain. Both Mother and the indestructible colonel were now enamored of Krishnamuti, and the colonel, formerly hostile to my Muse, took to writing me theosophical treatises on the Cosmic Significance of my Art.

All this was dear and reassuring to me, but there already was a strange unrealness about the New World I left behind to recapture the Old. Khaki was, on the contrary, extraordinarily real and close to me; I never experienced anything more sensuously vital than the simple pleasures of dining *à deux,* oblivious to the surroundings but grateful for them being there, slowly walking down to the beach, my arm around Khaki's waist, and then lying on the cool sand close to the girl, kissing her lips, hair and bare shoulders smelling of salt water.

It seemed clear to me that Fate decreed that, to become a man, I should also become a husband. Forgetting Diaghilev's advice, I proposed to Khaki about ten days after we first met. My proposal was received with a somewhat evasive but encouraging counterproposal to "wait a few days." On returning to the Villa des Genêts, I wrote Mother the first of a long series of letters announcing the first of my several forthcoming marriages, none of which took place.

CHAPTER IX

FAME DID NOT DELAY

DIAGHILEV soon returned from his travels, and with him Boris, Lifar, Valitchka and Serge Grigoriev, the tall and somewhat military-looking *régisseur* of the company. My newly written music — I completed the score slightly ahead of the deadline — was noisily approved (except for a very complicated variation for three Muses, subsequently cut) and there was a lot of even noisier kissing. When I mustered enough courage to spill the news of my impending marriage, the kisses gave way to agonized screams. Then came another venomous antifeminine monologue by Diaghilev, with a stern warning not to mix matrimony with ballet composing. Torn between what I imagined to be love and what I knew to be my life's work, I suggested that Diaghilev meet Karen and have it out with her; I naturally hoped that Diaghilev, woman-hater though he was, would be unable to resist the girl. "I'll be glad to see the creature," Serge said more calmly. "But beware; I'll tell her that you're homosexual and penniless." "How horrible of you!" I exclaimed. "You know it's not true — I'm not homosexual and I'm earning a living." "You're earning just enough for one, and I'll see to it that you don't earn more. As for truth, the only thing that's true is that you've written good music for me and I always lie in the interests of the truth." This Machiavellian twist brought the discussion to an effective close and Diaghilev turned to other matters.

Fortunately for the fate of my ballet, Karen became more and more engrossed in Biddy, who arrived, sensing the danger; she reserved every evening for the big, powerfully built, football player. I was eaten up by jealousy, but Karen's perfidy prevented an ill-timed showdown, which might have resulted in a fatal rupture with Diaghilev.

After the *Zephyr* was completed, there remained the task of orchestrating the music, choreographing it and having sets and costumes designed. Choreography and scenery were Diaghilev's province, orchestration mine alone, and I plunged into it, unaided and frankly, unprepared. The sum total of my orchestrating experience amounted to three or four half-hearted stabs. Did I confess my almost complete ignorance to Diaghilev? I did not. With the wondrous impudence of youth, I went to work, the two Rimsky-Korsakov volumes on orchestration and a score of *Petrushka* by my side. Meanwhile, Auric, fortified by his *Les Fâcheux* experience, was scoring *Les Matelots,* the other ballet commissioned by Sergei Pavlovitch for the 1924–1925 season. When Auric fell ill, I grandly offered to orchestrate his colorful finale; luckily, the Frenchman was smart enough to decline my services with thanks.

The matter of the choreographer came up next. Lifar tells the story in his biography of Diaghilev: "The arrangement was that 'Zephyr' should be produced by Nijinska but, having for some reason taken offense because Diaghilev had entrusted me with the part of Boreas, she left the company. I vividly recall how astonished, how shaken I was when Diaghilev . . . said I was to be responsible for the choreography of this ballet, for I knew well the importance attached to it by Diaghilev; knew too, how much he admired the music of the young Dukelsky, whom he had recently discovered. Enthusiastically, and with immense zeal, I took on the task of producing the new ballet. Nevertheless, in the early days of the New Year 1925, I began more and more to feel irresolute and somewhat doubtful of the whole thing . . . because I feared that, by wholly devoting myself to a new art, I should fall behind as a dancer, just when I was beginning to succeed. Strongly influenced by this motive, I did my best to persuade Sergei Pavlovitch to be reconciled with Massine, in order that the latter might return as choreographer to the Ballet. A period of long and painful indecision followed, but finally . . . he yielded, and Massine began to work on 'Flore et Zephyre.'" I'm sure there was more to it than the "persuasion" by a young and untried dancer that resulted in Diaghilev's choice.

Arnold Haskell and Valitchka Nouvel, whose biography of Diaghilev appeared in 1935, gave an entirely different account of Massine's return to the fold: "For some time Massine had been seeking to rejoin the Ballet, and Diaghilev found that it would now be wise to make the peace. Nouvel and Wollheim (the London ballet agent) were entrusted with the negotiations, and they proved almost interminable, for Massine had learned the value of independence. Finally a contract was signed by which he was engaged as choreographer only, and entrusted with the novelties for the next Paris season." Whatever the facts, Massine arrived in Monte Carlo and, as the current phrase has it, we were in business.

I well remember the audition, in the course of which Massine heard both *Zephyr* and *Les Matelots* played piano-duet fashion by Auric and myself. Leonide Massine, although of small stature, was an arresting figure; his head was of extraordinary beauty, the eyes flashing and hypnotic, the smile rare and therefore all the more beguiling. His movements were brusque and oddly, determinedly virile, with none of the unmasculine grace and softness too often typical of male dancers. Massine's legs were a mystery, as he always wore loose, Spanish-type pantaloons at rehearsal and it was maliciously whispered that his legs were not the best part of the spruce, springy body of the man. His manner was distant, inaccessible and reserved in the extreme, possibly because of Diaghilev's aloof and barely civil politeness to his former favorite and Nijinsky's successor. Although nicknames and diminutives reigned in the company, Massine always addressed Diaghilev as Sergei Pavlovitch and Diaghilev stuck to Leonide Fedorovitch when speaking to the Beautiful Joseph of his past (Massine made his debut in Richard Strauss's ballet of that name). To my delighted surprise, this forbidding and admittedly difficult master, certainly the top choreographer of his time, took to me and my music almost immediately. He smiled repeatedly, nodded his head (he sat directly opposite me while I played) and then went into a long huddle with Sergei Pavlovitch and Boris, the only account of which, made by the latter, was, "Funny. Leonide likes nobody, but he liked you. I hope it's a good sign."

At about the same time I was introduced to the ballet company by Diaghilev, an incomparable showman, in the theater as well as the reheasal room. I was ill at ease in the long, low-ceilinged *salle* with its heady body smells and an occasional welcome whiff of resin or powder; ill at ease especially because of the two or three dozen young — and not so young — ballerinas, disappointingly unfeminine in their ugly black or gray tights, breathing noisily and perspiring copiously all over the place. They were in the middle of a class, conducted by one of the older ballerinas, who shrilled: "ee-raz, ee-dva" (and one, and two) as the dancers went through the prescribed "manual of legs," to paraphrase the army term. Diaghilev stopped the class and made a short introductory address in which I was presented to the company as the composer of one of the two new ballets. The dancers were obviously astonished by my youth and there was some barely audible snickering from the male dancers and agitated whispering among the girls. I was horribly embarrassed when three of the younger ones curtsied with mock reverence and intoned: *"Bonjour, Maître,"* in chorus, which brought a satanic laugh from Sergei Pavlovitch.

I soon got to know them all — girls and boys — and even became quite popular with them; I was their age and I was Russian — also, too much of a new face to be a "Diaghilev spy." There were two or three such informers in the company, who, knowing the great man's unmanly passion for gossip and scandal, kept him well advised about the members' ambitions, jealousies, deeds, misdeeds and sleeping arrangements. Diaghilev himself was always feared as an incomprehensible superman, detested for his stinginess (poor S.P. wasn't stingy, just perpetually, grandly broke, having to live in princely fashion as a necessary "front") and secretly adored by most. Grigoriev and Tchernicheva represented the "administration" and were unpopular; Woizikovsky, a Pole, and Sokolova, English in spite of her stage name, the next "ranking" couple were among the "rebels" and universally liked. Nemtchinova, exquisite on the stage, was not even pretty in private life, but replete with charm; the beauties of the company were Maikerska, a languid Polish Venus, chic Doubrovska of the mile-long legs, dark and well-rounded Nina Nikitina (Nikitina II as Diaghilev billed her), piquantly seductive Dorothy Coxon of Kensington and statuesque Ninette (then Nina) de Valois of the quick Irish wit and a friendly, direct manner (now Dame Ninette, the female Diaghilev of Sadler's Wells).

Zephyr's sets were entrusted to Georges Braque, who had done so beautifully by *Les Fâcheux* a season before and whose deep browns and greens in that décor were promptly styled "Braque colors." Coco Chanel attended to the costumes. An odd and utterly Parisian coupling; only Diaghilev could have hit on such a combination, which worked out surprisingly well. Coco was then in "residence" aboard the Duke of Westminister's yacht lying in the Monaco harbor, and often came to lunch with Diaghilev and his satellites. Misia Sert appeared out of nowhere one afternoon, all jewels and furs, and demanded to hear the music of my ballet. Misia's gruff speech and despotic air always intimidated me, but she knew and "felt" music, and having heard glowing — and certainly exaggerated — reports of my score, was excited by the prospect of hearing it. There is no greater incentive to a performer-composer than a rich and influential patron, thrilled *in advance* by his work, and I played like one demented. Misia was wild about *Zephyr,* clapped her plump hands transportedly, and declared that *"ce cher Serge* and especially his dancers must be so grateful for such music — it would make a corpse dance." She then took me to dinner with Picasso of the crafty peasant's face (as was Braque's on a larger and cruder scale) and his pretty red-haired Russian wife. Picasso was very pleasant and asked me to sit for a portrait, which I did a few days later (in Antibes). I don't believe the portrait was ever completed, although there were four or five sittings.

Most of my evenings were spent in the company of Massine, which annoyed Diaghilev, who insisted that Leonide had no soul, no heart and no taste and was only interested in money; from what I heard, Massine drove a hard bargain with Sergei Pavlovitch and the two new ballets were costing him plenty. Diaghilev grudgingly admitted that Massine was a capable choreographer — "but only in my hands," he added significantly. I, for one, found Leonide a stimulating companion, although he detested crowds, organized gaiety, disorganized drinking, and was the world's worst ballroom dancer; it is strange but true that most ballet luminaries are helpless on the dance floor. I clung to Massine also because Khaki made up her mind — not for long, it soon transpired — to take on a football-playing fiancé rather than a piano-playing one and went off to London, following the customary bittersweet scene, complete with imaginary heartbreak and mutual reproaches. The much-married Leonide (he and Balanchine are alike in this respect, if in no other) laughed at my sorrow and suggested that I had better make my mark in this world first and then marry, if marry I must.

I was too engrossed in the activity around my *Zephyr* to suffer from this separation too long. Massine staged a pretty *pas seul* for the poetic-legged Alice Nikitina as a first essay in his new choreographic assignment, and Diaghilev, adoring it in spite of himself, decided to give a foretaste of our work to the potentates of Monaco. These were an attractive young couple — the hereditary Princess Charlotte, a striking slim brunette, married to the blond soft-spoken Prince Pierre (né de Polignac), lovers and supporters of ballet both. I accompanied Nikitina at the piano and our little duet was extremely well received, as was the rest of the bill (the program of which, emblazoned with a golden crown and the date — January 31, 1925 — is before me); it consisted of excerpts from *Les Sylphides* (Nemtchinova, Tchernicheva and Dolin), others from *Carnaval* and *Les Femmes de Bonne Humeur,* the beautiful "Nocturne" from Auric's *Les Fâcheux* (danced by "Antoine Doline," as he was then styled) and — for a triumphant coda — dances by Alicia Markova, then fourteen years old, with music by Delibes and Rubinstein.

The "royal" approbation of my three-minute "variation de Flore" brought a flock of invitations to various social gatherings, such as dinners with the Dukes of Connaught and Sutherland, where I was made much of, but felt ill at ease in the presence of so many faultlessly dressed lions; my secondhand dinner jacket was by now dilapidated and shone brilliantly in the wrong places.

On the day my new dinner jacket arrived, flashily cut by a very bad Monégasque tailor, Massine suggested we celebrate both the new clothes and the forthcoming ballet by going to the Carlton, a none-too-respectable *boîte* in Monte Carlo. Dressed to kill, we dined elaborately *en ville* and then, filled with champagne and fancy food, ventured to the Carlton, where a ringside table was reserved for us. A spuriously American band, called something like Karol's Karlton Kids was holding forth, and wasp-waisted playboys were piloting short-skirted and heavily perfumed hussies through transatlantic gyrations.

Leonide and I were content to sip champagne and take in the festivities. Directly across from us sat three maharajahlike young men, sulky and intense-looking, playing host to three flashy demimondaines, obviously English, judging from their stodgily cut evening frocks. The tallest and prettiest of the three was a well-built blonde, her extra-short skirt provocatively accentuating shapely silk-stockinged legs. With the aid of my monocle, to which I clung in spite of the shoulder shrugs, I perceived that the luscious creature stole repeated flirtatious looks at me, pursed up her lips in my direction, winked outrageously and even waved once — all this while dancing with one of the sulky pseudo-maharajahs. Massine, too, noticed her behavior and laughed encouragingly: "You've made a conquest, Dima. Go to it." "What do you mean?" I queried nervously. "She is flirting with me, I can see that; but she is not alone. What about the three Indians?" "Oh, nonsense," retaliated Leonide. "Go over to their table and ask her to dance. Your hair is brilliantined gigolo fashion, your dinner jacket is the tightest I've ever seen and they'll take you for a professional — there are dozens of them around to make the women dance. Don't be a fool, up with you." As if hypnotized, I did as I was bid, made my way "across the crowded room," alighted at the Indian table, bowed from the waist — without losing the monocle, which is hard — and secured the blonde for a fox trot.

I noticed at once that the girl's mind was not on dancing. She clung to me as if in danger of falling flat on her face, although stone sober; her legs seemed to be glued to mine and her belly performed such sinuous undulations that dancing — unless you were a *danse du ventre* expert, which I was not — became difficult. This was new, exciting and bewildering. The blonde's laughing eyes scrutinized every bit of me, including the telltale blush which I knew was spreading rapidly — the blush that plagued my entire youth. "You are nothing but a silly child, and yet you wear that absurd monocle. Why?" the girl whispered. Completely abashed, I tried to think of a properly worldly rejoinder and, failing, muttered something like, "The better to see you." The blonde gave me an unmaternal squeeze for this clumsy compliment and then, her face suddenly serious, her lips practically enveloping my ear, said: "You're a funny monkey, but I like you. If you really want to see me, give me a key to your place, go there now and I'll soon join you. Be quick." As if in a trance, I reached in my pocket, produced the key and even managed to furnish the proper directions to my room at Mme. Marcellin's. "Room, eh? Young and poor, I see. But then, so am I — and so au revoir and ah tahn-tot, as the Frogs say. Are you a Frog?" "No." "Foreign, anyway — that suits me. Not queer, are you?" "No." "Good. Now take me to my table." I did so, bowed from the waist again to the gloomy potentates, and returned to Massine, who was enjoying himself hugely.

He congratulated me on my good work and suggested that I return home quickly and wait for the girl. Retreat was impossible this time, so I assumed a rakish air and took leave of Leonide, my heart beating furiously. I woke up poor Mme. Marcellin as I had no duplicate key, played drunk convincingly, causing the good widow to shake her head and say the proper thing about my mother not being there to see her son in this state, etc.; once in my room, I selected my best pair of pajamas, undressed in a great hurry, and hopped into bed.

The next hour was exceedingly trying: I listened eagerly for unfamiliar footsteps, torn between the necessity of playing the impatient lover and the prosaic yet acutely realistic desire to sleep. I finally succumbed to the latter; no sooner was I in the middle of a fairly interesting dream, than I was instantly awakened by a piercing electric light, which made me jump and sit up straight. Facing me was the blonde, stark naked — which was most becoming after all that Shaftesbury Avenue finery — grinning invitingly at me. "Asleep, little boy?" she intoned teasingly. "Well, if this doesn't wake you up, nothing will."

When I got up in the morning, there was no girl by my side. I had slept so soundly that I hadn't heard her dress and leave; had she stayed beside me, my vanity might have been pricked again by another brutal remark about my now lost virginal status. And then I made the deflating discovery that my watch had departed with Sally. (Some weeks later, the girl was deported for playing a similar trick on someone bolder than I was.) Dressing in a hurry, I sauntered out in the limpid Riviera air and headed straight for the morning rehearsal of my ballet. Three of the Muses were already there, wrestling with the "undanceable" variation, and Massine, in his wide black pantaloons, a big black book in his hands, was inventing a step, his eyes never leaving the opened book while his feet shuffled tentatively to my oddly rhythmed music. Massine's black book was the object of much excited speculation in the company; no one had any idea of its contents and no one was bold enough to steal or borrow it and make sure. Some said that it was a seventeenth-century treatise on choreography, a priceless rarity; others, that it consisted of perfectly blank pages and was used to intimidate dancers. Whatever the contents of his book, I never saw Massine choreograph anything without the huge volume before him.

So absorbed was Leonide in his work that he didn't even know I was in the room. A few minutes later, however, he stopped the pianist, diligently struggling with my variation, walked up to me and said: "Dima, this music seems to end before my dance design can possibly be brought to a close. I have an idea and I'm going to try it. Watch!" He gave a sign to the pianist and the three Muses were set in motion again. To my astonishment, when the music stopped — the way I wrote it —

the girls went on hopping unconcernedly. "What are they doing? The variation is over," I whispered. "Sh-h," hissed Massine, scowling. "That's the idea. They dance on *without music*. That's it. Felia — down — up — *plié* — hands so — together — together — finish. How do you like it?" I didn't and said so. Leonide didn't like my not liking it and said so. A quarrel was prevented by the welcome arrival of Tamara Gevergeva, the new beauty of the company; Gevergeva was the first wife of Georgi Melitonovitch Balanchivadze — George Balanchine to you. The four of them — Gevergeva, Alexandra Danilova (still flourishing as *ballerina assoluta*), Efimov (a good character dancer now at the Paris Opéra) and Balanchine fled from Russia in 1924 and were annexed by Diaghilev, who saw them dance at Missia Sert's Paris house in November of that year.

Tamara, part Tartar, was the standard Nordic beauty — pale and fair-haired, with cool blue eyes and a perfectly proportioned body. I first caught a glimpse of her at a rehearsal of the hateful *Scheherazade,* already outmoded then, but ever popular with the audiences, especially English ones. She startled Grigoriev, the stern disciplinarian, by wearing pink Russian boots to rehearsal; since *Scheherazade* is a character, not a classical, ballet, he let it pass. She also wore a pink ribbon in her lemon-blond hair and had seductive little wrinkles at the corners of her mouth when she smiled — I never saw a prettier girl. I paid little attention to George, a slender slight man with Georgian (Georgia, Caucasus, not U.S.A.) features and a barely perceptible facial twitch, which caused that irrepressible name-inventor John Murray Anderson to tag him "Mr. Tick" in later years. Unaware of George's prodigious gifts as choreographer I thought he was merely an inevitable nuisance in his lucky role as Tamara's husband. Gevergeva was one of the nine Muses, and I loved watching her as she easily mastered Massine's complicated dance patterns.

I wasn't allowed to linger long and exchange Russian badinage with the quick-tongued Tamara, as Nouvel arrived to whisk me away for a press interview. Diaghilev had a genius for well-timed publicity, and various French and English scribblers, paid and unpaid, always swarmed about at the advent of a new production; now that a new composer was about to be launched, they were dined and wined by Sergei Pavlovitch with a complete disregard for expense — someone would foot the bill eventually, nothing except wild drumbeating mattered now.

The next day I lunched with Poulenc, who, too, had been summoned by Diaghilev for an *avant-propos* on his new musical discovery. I played the entire score of *Zephyr* for my already-famous young confrère (only five years my senior). The talented and wealthy composer (Poulenc Brothers is one of France's biggest chemical products firms), a far better pianist than I, was a wonderful audience and wrote his impressions for a Paris music journal, titling his article "Dukelsky — A New Russian Musician." In it he said:

> I cannot adequately express my joy at our meeting, away from musical groups, and their sinister concerts. Dukelsky is not one of those laughable creatures, more concerned with systems than with music, that one meets in avant-garde magazine offices, always on the scent of an article or a first performance. Too strong and too conscious of his strength to stoop to musical politics, freedom alone suits him.
>
> Although only twenty-one, Dukelsky already knows all music and both continents. Leaving Russia at seventeen, he spends three [sic] years in America before coming here. As music, alas, does not feed her man, he composed varius Blues [sic] in an astonishing melodic style akin to that of Gershvin [sic]; but, too intelligent not to realize the danger assimilating such music to his, this musician who knows the technique of jazz profoundly gave it a kick in the pants ["punch in the nose" in the original] after helping himself to it, in such a way that no trace of Negro exoticism is discernible in his symphonic production. Isn't it the most beautiful lesson to those who believe that jazz is destined to renovate music? I know few works as heavy with music as "Zephyr and Flora." Dukelsky, without archness or affectations, touches the heart by the freshness of his melody. The harmony, always direct, and the boldness of the development give his charm the framework indispensable in living music. A desire for pigeonholing will make the public attempt to place this new arrival in a neatly defined category. His art, rather remote from the great Stravinsky, is perhaps closer to that of Prokofiev, but, if there exists a spiritual relationship, the realization differs profoundly in one and the other. Truly, Dukelsky is already himself. Listen, without prejudice, to this new voice, and I wager that you'll be conquered by its poetry.

Such a testimony from so representative a young musician carried considerable weight, and the atmosphere of feverish expectancy that surrounded me was, as I now see, unhealthy, though undeniably satisfying. I was fast becoming famous by virtue of so much favorable hearsay, without a note of my music performed to substantiate my premature fame. Easily persuading myself that I could do no wrong, because my contemporaries thought me right, I went on orchestrating serenely in the naïve belief that, since the music was right, the orchestral coat of paint was bound to be right, too.

The conductor for the Monte Carlo Ballet season was a native of Monaco — Marc-Cesar Scotto by name, a capable, well-routined musician, but no Nikisch; just the man to suit Diaghilev, who despised primadonna conductors. "There's nothing worse than a 'titan of the podium,' " he told me. "If it weren't for the composer who put little black notes on white paper, the titan couldn't wave his stick, strike leonine poses, thrill women and earn lots of money. What does the composer get? Take yourself — you have nothing and I pay you very little — but even that little is more, far more, than most of them receive. No, the only conductor for me is the kind that does what he is told by the composer, and never talks back."

This was logical and laudable, but like nearly every dictum of Diaghilev's, paradoxically at variance with his oft-expressed contempt for most composers; he thought there were far too many around — hardly a half dozen of them writing worthwhile music. It is well known that he rejected Ravel's "La Valse," which prompted a complete break with the composer; hated Delius (he pronounced it Dehlius) and Sibelius; despised Schoenberg and all the atonalists, although vaguely interested in Alban Berg and, later, Hindemith. He asked John Alden Carpenter for a ballet score, had it read to him by myself and, although the work was entitled "Skyscrapers" renamed it *"Massacre du Printemps"* and rejected it after one unsatisfactory hearing. With so many offered and so few chosen, becoming a Diaghilev composer in the twenties was quite a feat. Like Prokofiev, the big man could be cruel to those whose music he didn't care for. Boris and I once persuaded him to go to Benedetti's cello recital in Monte Carlo. On the program was a cello sonata by Alexandre Tcherepnine, who accompanied Benedetti in his own work; and, although you could tell by Sergei Pavlovitch's signs and grunts that the sonata was not his dish, he bore it patiently and good-naturedly. But when, right in the middle of the proceedings, the tall, awkward-looking composer got up suddenly and executed a few raps on the piano lid with his knuckles, certainly a novel effect, Diaghilev decided he had had enough. He rose in the middle of the movement, pushed his big body past the startled ticket holders and said in an audible whisper: "They are heading for a knockout — let's leave before blood is drawn." With this we three staggered out, turning a deaf ear to indignant shushes and hisses.

I, the pampered and tenderly nursed Benjamin of the troupe, had no complaints. Orchestral rehearsals had begun and I sat alone in the empty hall, enjoying myself unreservedly. There were many mistakes in the orchestral parts to be weeded out (there always are) and, with the orchestra constantly stopping, like a faulty motor, it was hard to tell whether the orchestration was good, adequate or downright poor. In all fairness, it must be admitted that it was no more than adequate for the most part. At times, what seemed like a lofty musical conception became muddled and distorted almost beyond recognition; the harmony seemed too thick, the basses that boomed so splendidly on the piano were hardly discernible and the inner voices stuck out for no good reason. The orchestration was, in the main, correct — academically speaking; in other words, heavy and flat. The music managed to overcome this self-imposed handicap to some extent; Prokofiev on hearing *Zephyr* in Paris dismissed the orchestration with: "Too much Glazunov and not enough Dukelsky."

These faults were not immediately apparent to me nor, luckily, to Diaghilev, Kochno or Massine, who blamed whatever defects were easily detected on the perspiring Scotto and the orchestra. I even wrote Mother that *Zephyr* sounded beautiful in its orchestral dress — and Francis Poulenc seconded this opinion.

Lifar had this to say in his *Sergei Diaghilev* about *Zephyr*: "The work was by no means easy, for though Dukelsky's music proved very refreshing, its rhythmic design was somewhat difficult and but little helped by the manner of its scoring."

Lifar nearly caused a catastrophe by falling heavily at reheasal, dislocating both ankles. Diaghilev was almost forced to give the part to Thaddeus Slavinsky, one of the better dancers in his company, because the doctor averred that fully six weeks must elapse before Lifar "could dream of dancing." Yet, owing to Lifar's determination and effective treatment, he danced at the opening on April 28, 1925, and "nobody in the audience had the least idea of the state of his feet."

Diaghilev was kindness itself — he gave me an autographed program inscribed: "To Dear Dima, in memory of a significant day," and a portrait of himself with the legend: "To my dear Third Son to commemorate his baptism." The *première,* before a bejeweled and befurred audience, went off without a hitch; the ballet obtained a sizable success, all three principals — the ethereal Alice Nikitina, bouncy Dolin and fervent Lifar — were applauded and cheered to a faretheewell, although the latter had one of his ankles "dislocated three times during the performance and it had to be reset on each occasion." Ailing Lifar's program was inscribed thus by Diaghilev: "To dear Boreas, the young and irresistible wind, on the day when he first swept through Monte Carlo." At the final curtain, following the bows of the three principals, Braque, Massine and myself appeared on the stage and I was presented with a laurel wreath of such gigantic proportions that, on accepting it, I almost fell under its tremendous weight. I didn't know what to do with the unwieldy thing (another Diaghilev offering) until either Dolin or Lifar put it over my head, making another bow an impossibility.

There was a gala supper for *Zephyr's* creators and dozens of staunch Diaghilevites after the *première*. Sergei Pavlovitch insisted on my drinking champagne, and since many toasts were made, several of them to me and my music, I threw all discretion to the winds and drank glass after glass, winding up in such a haze that I had to be escorted home by two male dancers, as I couldn't have found the Villa des Genêts without their help.

The *Daily Mail* correspondent's was the first comment on *Zephyr*: "The music is by a new Russian composer, Dukelsky. It successfully blends classic idiom with a moderate jazz influence in a close-woven texture and was warmly appreciated. The Duke of Connaught attended both the dress rehearsal and the public performance and warmly congratulated M. Diaghilev. The Prince and Princess of Monaco were also delighted." The royal approval was fine in its way, but I was far happier when the faithful Poulenc lent me his competent hand once again. Writing in *Figaro* on May 5th, Poulenc had this to add to his previously expressed views: "Dukelsky, whose name is as yet unknown in Paris, will be famous before long. At a time when young musicians hesitate between most arbitrary harmonic systems and a false simplicity, smacking of plain foolishness, Dukelsky, armed with a strong technique (the secret of all success) offers us a perfectly rounded work, always well-integrated — yet spontaneous. The score of 'Zephyr,' consisting of separate numbers, owing to the demands of the story, is never loose or disconnected. It is as if created in one breath; one cannot resist so much fresh invention and especially such authentic youth. When, at the insistence of the audience, the author appeared on the stage, holding a huge laurel crown [sic], one thought of a young athlete playing hoops."

The local papers were all complimentary, but they didn't matter. The word got around that *Zephyr* was a success and Diaghilev, without waiting for the Paris verdict, started talking to me about another ballet, which made me as proud as a peacock. There were a few discordant notes, such as the anonymous violinist who scribbled at the bottom of his part: "Do we have to play such utter nonsense?" and an unprintable epigram, circulated by certain members of the cast, which, freely and politely translated, went something like: "Music by Dukelsky, story by Kochno — lo, it's a new hit and it hit a new low." I happily attributed such stabs to jealousy or ignorance and went from party to party convinced of my greatness and making not a few converts to that idea.

Diaghilev now began active preparations for the all-important Paris season, for which the Gaîté Lyrique Théâtre, which he disliked, was booked. Massine was busy rehearsing *Les Matelots,* to be unveiled in Paris as it was too late for a Monte Carlo tryout. Lifar's leg was so badly swollen that *Zephyr,* in spite of its success, was given only once in Monte Carlo; there was some further talk about replacing Lifar by Slavinsky, but the new Diaghilev favorite was surer and surer of his ground and wouldn't hear of it. I used my well-earned "siesta" to flirt with Nina Payne, the American tap dancer, then the rage of the Riviera. We once sat in a night club in Cannes, deserted except for a fortyish tart, a regular at the establishment. The woman's evening was a fiasco as she had no clients; she sprawled in a corner, a Felicien Rops-like ferociously painted *lorette,* sipping her *fine à l'eau.* Nina and I, both young, well-dressed and playing at love, kissed rapturously throughout the evening, oblivious of the sleepy barman and the brandy-guzzling woman. After watching us sullenly for an hour, the tart sprang up and delivered a shrill and inflammatory speech about dirty foreigners corrupting *la belle France* with their lewd behavior. Although the help knew the woman to be no better than what she was, her arguments, brought about by her failure to secure a client and her loneliness, were so strident and impassioned, stressing the patriotic note with such fervor, that the bewildered barman asked us to stop kissing or leave. We left.

On May 11th, I was back in Paris, and on the 16th, a month before *Zephyr's première,* wrote Mother from the Hôtel d'Antin (where Valitchka always stayed): "I'm doing nothing at present, except trying to clarify my affairs; contacting publishers, authors' societies, etc. — anything to make a little money, of which I'm in dire need. I can't expect any further income from Diaghilev until July, when I'm to start work on a new ballet, and then we'll be back together on the usual terms. As for now, Diaghilev is willing to help but he owes me nothing for *Zephyr.* All my hopes are in jazz, which is well paid in London and in great demand everywhere." Thus, Duke was already stirring in Dukelsky's breast, ready to come to his rescue.

On entering the Hôtel d'Antin, I found Valitchka in his room, coatless, stretched out on his narrow bed, his short arms behind his head (his favorite posture), smoking energetically and gazing at the ceiling, rapture and boredom in his gaze. "Welcome, welcome, *jeune homme,*" he greeted me absent-mindedly. "How is the young genius today?" The young genius was down to his last three francs, otherwise pretty well. Valitchka was a generous man, but he was poor, and lending his friends money (which he did often) made him both angry and strangely elated. I suspect that one's indebtedness to him puffed up his badly shrunken ego and also gave him the coveted opportunity for a sternly administered lecture on the subject of idleness, women, drink and other ruinous excesses. The lecture was duly delivered along with some fascinating gossip about Beaumont, anti-Diaghilev intrigues, Satie's *Mercure,* in which Picasso featured three brawny men representing nymphs (seductive in bright green, with large melons simulating breasts) — Valitchka couldn't get over that, although *Mercure* was no longer news — and Prokofiev's Second Symphony about to be *premièred* by Koussevitzky. "Do you know him?" Nouvel queried. "No — I would certainly like to." "Get Prokofiev to introduce you. Koussevitzky, too, likes young men, but not for Diaghilev's reasons — khe . . . khe . . . khe . . ." Valitchka, now delighted with himself and the sly dig at his boss, produced a well-worn wallet, sighed tragically, and made me richer by a hundred francs.

My next visit was to the Parfenovs, he a busy lawyer whose sister

Sophie was my uncle Prince Irakly Toumanov's second wife, she, born Vera Vajevska, an excellent lyric soprano (one of Opéra Comique's best Melisandes) and a very handsome girl. I, vaguely related to Parfenov, and a fellow musician to his wife, was received in cordial Russian fashion and fed superb food, in return for which I displayed my new songs to words by Bogdanovitch, the amiable eighteenth-century poet; he was the best exponent of the peasant girl-turned-Greek-goddess-school so dear to Diaghilev. Under Sergei Pavlovitch's influence, I produced three works in that manner — *Zephyr and Flora,* the three Bogdanovitch songs and "Dushenka," a duet for women's voices on excerpts from that poet's delicious long poem of that name. The three songs were Stravinsky's special favorites (as I reported to Mother at the time) and Mme. Parfenov's was just the right voice for them — clear and limpid and truly lyrical.

I was impatient to acquaint Prokofiev with the music of *Zephyr.* Sergei Sergeivitch had a rigorous working schedule, which was self-imposed shortly after his graduation from the St. Petersburg Conservatory; any interference with this schedule was instantly checked by Lina Ivanovna or the housemaid, who under no circumstances would admit visitors before lunchtime. Mornings from nine to one were devoted to composing, an hour was allowed for lunch, another hour for disposing of people and routine errands, then two or three hours for orchestrating, proofreading and polishing the results of the morning's toil. This made reaching Prokofiev quite difficult, as he wouldn't come to the telephone in the morning, disliked being disturbed at lunch and was usually attending to business, bills, etc., prior to the "orchestrating period." I soon learned the trick of catching him immediately before he sat down to lunch, at which time he was in reasonably good spirits, especially if the composing had gone well that morning.

It hadn't gone well that particular morning, and Prokofiev's voice was even more gruff than usual. "What do you want?" he boomed. "This is Dukelsky. . . ." "I know it's Dukelsky — and I'm Prokofiev, and Prokofiev is very busy even if Dukelsky isn't." "But, Sergei Sergeivitch . . . I want you to hear my *Zephyr*. . . . You told me . . ." "I know what I told you — probably even told you that you're a composer — I may have been wrong. What do you mean by calling me in the morning?" "Sorry, S.S., but it's ten to one." Silence for cooling-off purposes. "Why didn't you say so? All right then, come to lunch and bring your ballet." Quickly I taxied to Prokofiev's house, was admitted by the master himself, whose face wore a scowl and a smile simultaneously and whose, this time friendly, greeting sounded as if he were giving me more hell. Such was Prokofiev, one of the most lovable and rudest men that ever lived.

Lina Ivanovna, her eyes red from weeping, was grateful for my entrance as she and her husband were not on speaking terms that day. She, too, volunteered to sing the Bogdanovitch songs, about which she had heard from the omniscient Souvtchinsky. Prokofiev snorted, "Don't try to ingratiate yourself with him. Learn how to sing a scale before you get to new music." Lina Ivanovna let out an agonized shriek, burst into tears and ran from the room, slamming the door with all her strength. "Good," said Prokofiev with another half-scowl, half-smile. "We can talk now." I was to witness many such scenes, and never knew how to act under such circumstances, so took refuge in polite silence. Sergei Sergeivitch mellowed rapidly, finished his wine and leapt from the table with startling suddenness, making me swallow my dessert in one gulp.

Prokofiev's working quarters were unlike Stravinsky's; the room was tidy and sunny, but presented rather a Spartan appearance, and, besides a concert grand, a pile of manuscript paper, a ruler and some pens and pencils, had no luxurious modern improvements or fancy gimcracks like the great Igor's. Sergei Sergeivitch threw himself into a chair, grabbed my orchestral score and ordered me to play. In the middle of the Muses' variations, Prokofiev jumped up and walked to the piano, puffing out his cheeks, his arms on his hips, his stomach pushed out to the limit; when I reached the final chord of the coda, he most unexpectedly kissed me full on the lips and blurted out: *"Zdorovo!"* (*Zdorovy* means healthy in Russian, but *Zdorovo* is oddly untranslatable when used as a term of approval — "swell" would be the nearest to it in Americanese.) Elated by this ejaculation, unexpected, as were most of Prokofiev's actions, I played on to the end with new confidence — of all my listeners, including Stravinsky, I valued Sergei's opinion most. After all, I always *loved* Prokofiev's music — I only *admired* Stravinsky's.

When I finished, Prokofiev banged the score shut and summed up thus: "The music's fine, the scoring only fair; too bad you couldn't show me the orchestration before giving it out to be copied. It's too late now, also it would cost Diaghilev too much money to have it redone. Don't tell Sergei Pavlovitch you played your *Zephyr* for me — it won't do you any good. Come on, come on, Lina, never mind the tragedy — Dima passed his exams." Lina Ivanovna emerged from the bedroom, still dabbing at her heavily powdered eyelids, but smiling a martyr's courageous smile. "Ah? Lina, ah?" went on Prokofiev, accompanying his pleasure with a sizable smack on my backside. "Here, for once, is singing music — melody and more melody. I'm very pleased with you — and now for a game of chess." He then smacked his wife's buttocks, which token of affection brought on another pout, a very mild one. "I heard it all from my room and I must say I agree with Seriozha, although he is not a bit nice to me. I hope you beat him at chess," said Lina Ivanovna, smiling more roguishly now. No such luck; I was checkmated on the tenth move, as Prokofiev was the best of all chess-playing composers and used to boast of trimming Alekhine, the chess champion, on one occasion.

To further indicate his satisfaction with *Zephyr,* which he thought a great step forward after the piano concerto, Prokofiev took me to the Samoilenkos, his best Paris friends, in Champ de Mars, one of the loveliest parts of Paris. Boris Samoilenko, a hearty, perennially happy-go-lucky sort of man, delighted in having people in his spacious flat, particularly Russians "who did things." His Mussulman wife, Fatima-Hanoum, a woman of infinite candor, zest and spirit, had a rare talent for living fully and richly without being rich; the warmth of her welcome, the carefree wit of her observations and the springlike, easy feeling she gave everyone who came to see her, made the Samoilenko ground-floor flat with its tiny, immaculately kept garden the most unusual salon in the city. Every Russian of note, and several of charm and nothing else, flocked to Avenue Emile Deschanel, where a continuous performance by the guests, regardless of the hour, and entirely unrehearsed, took place; the performance consisted simply of the guests being themselves, and since all of them were either amusing or worthwhile, or both, no one was ever bored at the Samoilenkos and everybody adored them. One usually saw one of the three celebrated Russian painters there — Shukhaiev, Grigoriev, and Jacovlev. Jacovlev's beauteous niece Tatiana, subsequently Countess du Plessis, and now Mrs. Alex Liberman, the wife of the New York *Vogue's* able art director, broke a good many hearts, including that of Vladimir Mayakovski, Soviet Russia's greatest poet, who managed to obtain a permission to visit Europe in the twenties, and promptly fell in love with intrepid Tanya. I remember him well, a big bruiser of a fellow, fond of billiards and Turkish baths, peculiarly handsome in his way, with an outsize lower jaw and a look of great determination and forcefulness which didn't prevent him from taking his life, at the age of thirty-seven, in 1930, because of an unhappy, and, likely, trivial love affair. Of the musicians, Stravinsky and Koussevitzky were frequent guests, but only Prokofiev was an everyday "dropper-in," and as indispensable to the Samoilenkos as they were to him. I was taken home in Sergei's big Ballot, a French car now obsolete, with which he was always tinkering and whose unpredictable behavior mystified and fascinated him. "I'll tell Koussevitzky and Eberg, my publisher, what I think of your music," Prokofiev shouted over the tremendous noise of the Ballot. "Your chess is no good." And off he went in a dirty-blue cloud of gasoline. I hadn't seen much of Diaghilev of late; he spent most of the time at the Gaîté Lyrique, where rehearsals of *Les Matelots* were progressing feverishly, or lunching with his patrons and patronesses, who were invariably mobilized by Sergei Pavlovitch at the beginning of the ballet season, to talk nothing but ballet, to give balls for the ballet and to keep *tout Paris,* the most capricious and unreliable snob aggregation in the world, ballet-conscious at all costs. Kochno delighted in this sort of thing and his help was priceless to Sergei Pavlovitch.

Zephyr's Paris *première* took place on June 15th; my ballet was flanked by Stravinsky's adaptation of Pergolesi's *Pulcinella* and that peerless bravura display, *La Boutique Fantasque* — an all-Massine bill. *Zephyr* obtained a good success with the audience, but nothing like the frenzied, ecstatic ovation granted *Les Matelots* two nights later. I was, however, recalled several times and garnered several new addicts, notably Milhaud and Sauguet. The first, declared himself delighted with my melodic invention, whereas Henri Sauguet, a droll and cuttingly witty little man wearing huge glasses, waved his arms excitedly and said that he especially liked that "big tune" from *Zephyr*; then he proceeded to sing something that bore not the slightest resemblance to it.

Most of the notices accorded my work were favorable, and some too much so. Emile Vuillermoz, for instance, praised my score to the sky the more to belittle Auric's; he was violently anti-*Les Six* and I was picked as a suitable pawn in his journalistic machinations.

I never knew the real "inside" of the Vuillermoz-Auric feud, but in a place like Paris such feuds are everyday fare and are seldom of any lasting importance. At the time I was quite startled by the amount of fist-shaking and name-calling around me, but very little of it involved me, not as yet a Parisian figure, so I wisely let well enough alone.

Vuillermoz wrote: "We are in the presence of a vigorous, living and muscular work of music [Zephyr]. One senses that happy spontaneity, that superior ease that sweep away all objections. A musician like Dukelsky, armed with an excellent technique, discovers in one fell swoop a liberated style for which we, in our country, are searching in vain. The score of "Zephire" offers a richness and an abundance of rhythms and a savor of sounds that make it a perpetual treat for the ear."

That splendid all-around musician and delectable operetta composer André Messager, who, among his many accomplishments, conducted the legendary *première* of *Pelléas* with Mary Garden as Mélisande, wrote in *Figaro* and made me very proud and, perhaps, justifiably so: " 'Zephyr' is a copious work, filled, I would almost say *stuffed* with music, which reveals qualities of the first order. The extreme youth of the author explains his abundance and his indecision. He is at the age where one doesn't know yet how to curb one's language, where one accepts with a little too much complacency all the ideas, without having the courage to choose. But can you think of a more praiseworthy defect? So many composers have nothing to choose from, since they have nothing to say! With Dukelsky, the mixture of sureness and inexperience is almost continuous. The style is irresolute, yet the ideas are personal; the orchestration is brilliant, not without heaviness and, at times, a bit empty. However, certain parts are developed with uncommon mastery and numbers like the 'theme and variations' show rare ingenuity where studied elegance does not shut out the natural. It seems to me that, since Stravinsky, we have not assisted at a manifestation so characteristic of what appears to be the new tendency of Russian musical art. This is a debut that contains more than merely promises and Mr. Dukelsky can be proud of a most merited success."

The Paris *Herald Tribune* chimed in with: "Dukelsky's cleverness is disconcerting. His 'Zephyr et Flore' is an excellent ballet in the first manner of Stravinsky." Poulenc threw all discretion to the winds and in a *third* article on my ballet summed up his impressions by saying: "This score, so new and so alive, seems to me, next to the gigantic production of Stravinsky's, one of the most significant works of modern music, and Russian music in particular."

All this must have incensed my detractors who, luckily, were none too numerous. They were led by the acid-tongued André Coeuroy, who wrote: "The musician's friends committed the great imprudence to announce the arrival of a new Messiah . . . who could possibly doubt that for a musician of twenty-one years, this is a beautiful achievement. No uncertainty in the disposition of this quasi-classical suite in separate numbers, not a blemish of taste in the orchestral sensibility, no shocking surprises in the rhythmic monotony; a precious ensemble of virtues — NEGATIVE ONES. Here's an occasion to reflect, yawning a little, on the dangers and the merits of abstract art." The other detractors extolled George Auric at my expense, but their comments were more on the line of: "Well, the greenhorn doesn't know his business, but has some talent — will do better one day." On the whole, neither Diaghilev nor I could have dreamt of a better press. I got quite a few dirty looks in the foyer of the theater on the evening of the second performance as I paraded up and down with Souvtchinsky, complete with tails, monocle and the usual outlandish flower in my buttonhole — with age I switched to carnations, but this was the rose and orchid period. I perceived a fine-looking man in a splendid fur-lined overcoat — he was about to leave the theater — who looked at me with amusement and interest; he was standing next to Nicolas Slonimsky, that indefatigable Boswell of so many musical Dr. Johnsons. Nicolas was then secretary to Koussevitzky, and I knew that the remaining Serge of the Three Great Serges was before me. Slonimsky introduced us and Koussevitzky said without any preamble: "I just missed your ballet but I already know about it from Seriozha Prokofiev and our friend Nicolas here. I want your ballet, both as conductor and publisher, and I want you to write a symphony for me." (Koussevitzky was the founder and owner of the Editions Russes de Musique, which published nearly all Scriabin, Stravinsky and Prokofiev.) Before I had a chance to stammer a word of thanks, Koussevitzky shook my hand and concluded: "I must be off. If you have time tomorrow, go to 22 rue d'Anjou and see Mr. Eberg, the director of my publishing house — I'm sure we'll agree as to terms. Good night and good luck." Slonimsky added a *sotto voce* postscript about telephoning me in the morning and they vanished.

The next day I received a check for 6000 francs for *Zephyr* from the very pleasant Mr. Eberg, who told me that Koussevitzky wanted to sign me to a *life contract,* whereby he'd be obligated to print everything I wrote in return for the exclusivity of my services as composer. I said, very nervously, that I'd be delighted to accept, if I hadn't already promised the piano concerto to Heugel, a prominent French publisher. Eberg smiled indulgently and suggested that "his firm might consider overlooking this little slip," and we made arrangements for a business meeting the following week. I knew I had three people to thank for this wonderful turn of events: Prokofiev, Slonimsky — and Diaghilev, who issued my passport to Paris, which was now miraculously turning into a passport to fame.

CHAPTER X

BRIGHT YOUNG PEOPLE

HEUGEL bought my piano concerto, for which I received 5000 francs, and it proved a poor investment for the publishers, because the work which caused Diaghilev to commission *Zephyr* was never orchestrated and, consequently, never performed. Diaghilev wanted me to play it in Monte Carlo, the two Rubinsteins — Artur and Beryl — made half-hearted inquiries as to its availability, but I was no longer sure of the piece, too transparent a mixture of several ill-digested styles; in *Zephyr* the influences were slight and the score had an unmistakable "presence" — not so with the concerto, in spite of its pianistic effectiveness.

A week after the last (fourth) performance of my ballet, I experienced my first Channel crossing, accompanying Diaghilev, Boris and Nouvel, who were London-bound four months ahead of the ballet season; this time the company was to appear at the huge Coliseum, a place even less suited for ballet performances than the hateful Gaîté Lyrique. To travel by sea with Sergei Pavlovitch was a trying experience as the man suffered from chronic hypdrophobia, and the mere sight of a ship's interior threw him into a helpless panic. The weather couldn't have been better or balmier; nevertheless, Diaghilev was carefully wrapped in a heavy woolen blanket on top of a beaver-fur coat, a cashmere muffler around his neck, his large face barely visible, encased as it was in the thick fur collar, the too-small Lock hat over his eyes, to prevent even the tiniest glimpse of the "raging" Channel, which was as still as a Swiss lake. He fingered a small icon of Saint Nicholas with his left hand and crossed himself repeatedly with his right, his lips moving noiselessly in prayer. Boris and I, entranced by the bracing sea air, ran about the ship, the high summer sun beating upon us, and would occasionally, for manners' sake, come down to the first-class "saloon" where Sergei Pavlovitch sat all a-tremble, his powerful back turned to the offending water, his eyes closed. "Sergei Pavlovitch, come out on deck — it's beautiful outside and so calm!" I exclaimed thoughtlessly. Diaghilev gave me a withering look and shrilled in a high falsetto, a sure sign of great displeasure, addressing himself to Kochno, ever the diplomat, "Boris, tell this impudent young hooligan to go drown himself!" He then pulled the fur collar over his face so that it practically joined the hat, sighed tragically and went back to his prayers. For once, he did resemble "a bear wrapped in Russian gloom," in Harold Acton's phrase.

A half hour later Diaghilev got bored with so passive a resistance to the spheres, and gave vent to his feelings by a violent diatribe against England and the English, as if they were responsible for the dangers and discomforts of the English Channel. He began by denouncing the language, which he likened to the barking of a bulldog; then switched to women, claiming that Englishwomen were even worse than the French or Russian variety. Eric Wollheim, the agent and a subject of the unfortunate kingdom, winced but remained silent until, provoked by an especially vicious dart of Diaghilev's, he attempted to check his boss by reminding him that he would be interviewed on arrival and that it would be smart to be pleasant and obliging. "Obliging?" snarled Diaghilev, crossing himself at the advent of an imaginary wave. "I assure you that I'll be most considerate of the poor beggars, the reporters. On one condition — that it will be *I* who will ask all the questions." "Whatever do you mean, Mr. Diaghilev?" inquired the agent nervously. "Just that — I don't want the reporters to wear themselves out by interviewing me — I'll interview *them*. I ask the questions — or no interview." The unhappy Wollheim shrugged his shoulders and gave up.

Diaghilev was as good as his word; on arrival at Victoria, he graciously received the press and requested permission to ask his questions "to save you trouble, gentlemen," as he put it suavely. The nonplussed reporters exchanged worried glances, then nodded acquiescence. "Thank you," Diaghilev went on in honeyed tones. "And now for the questions: Why aren't Englishwomen the prettiest in the world?" Astonished silence. "Why is English food inedible?" Silence. "Why are there no good English composers?" More silence. More questions, some of which were frankly unprintable —

there were a few titters, hastily scribbled notes and the baffled newspapermen, loyal British subjects all, were greatly relieved by the final "Good day, gentlemen" and a hearty handshake from their tormentor.

Once comfortably installed at his beloved Savoy, Diaghilev changed his belligerent tune and talked of *Zephyr and Flora* to the representative of *The Observer* in great detail. "Though there were four performances in Paris," he said, "I regard it as scarcely having been done at all, for it has been completely reshaped. The music has been revised, and instead of one scene, there are now three, so that the work of Georges Braque has become the most important he has yet done for the theater.

"Braque is the only wise — shall we say? — and settled personality in the whole combination, for he alone has reached years of discretion, whereas the combined ages of the composer, the author of the scenario and the principal artists, Nikitina, Lifar and Tcherkas (who replaced Dolin, no longer with the company) come only to ninety-nine years. It is truly a ballet of youth. The composer, Dukelsky, is the third I have discovered. His two elder 'brothers,' Stravinsky and Prokofiev, are too well-known to need discussion. If you ask me by whom Dukelsky is influenced, I should say that he has nothing in common with Stravinsky; that you could perhaps detect his admiration for Prokofiev, though in any case he is more classical; and that he is inclined rather to trace his heredity from his 'Grandfather' Glinka." Following the *Observer* interview, Diaghilev and Boris started unpacking and suggested Bloomsbury as a locale more commensurate with my finances than the opulent Savoy. I stumbled into the Brighton Hall Hotel, near Russell Square, a somewhat depressing neighborhood; the sunless room with the big, creaky bed, a cracked washbasin, overstarched towels and a slatternly maid in black cotton stockings, who asked me whether I would care for "a cup o' tzea" in the gloomiest tones imaginable, made me inexpressibly sad. I'm always sad during the first few hours in a place I've never seen before — Paris the exception. Strange sights and smells give me a horrible, sinking feeling of being detached from the busy life around me, of "not belonging." The first London meal only intensified my unhappiness; never did I imagine that harmless Brussels sprouts and a thin sliver of middle-aged mutton could taste like boiled toilet paper. When I ordered coffee and liquid boot polish appeared in a thick, badly chipped white cup, on the heels of something called "suet pudding" and a fishy-smelling "savory" for a final discord, I was ready to weep. The maid returned with offers of a hot-water bottle, although the evening was exceedingly warm; I laughed grimly, scaring the wits out of the poor thing, and fell asleep instantly.

The next morning, after a decent breakfast — not even the English can ruin eggs and bacon, and I wisely ordered tea instead of so-called coffee — I sauntered into the street and bought several newspapers. Finding my name in most of them in the drama and music sections, I immediately felt better. Funny what the sight of one's own name in print can do to one's sagging spirits. I marched on jauntily, through the dreary squares of Bloomsbury, past the squalid Greek and Italian grocery stores and supposedly French restaurants of Soho into the more animated but strangely shabby Shaftesbury Avenue. Things were getting livelier by the minute; big red buses, antique Daimler taxicabs, policemen twice the size of the French "flics," signs lauding Bovril, Guinness and Players' cigarettes, unfamiliar products all, had a cozy, comfortable look about them — naïve and outdated, perhaps, but oddly resassuring. If Paris smelled of lilacs and gasoline, the prevailing London odor was that of rotting apples. Theatrical posters were everywhere and the names of the plays as well as quotes from critics in English were good to see after too much French, crammed too quickly into one's brain.

As I reached Piccadilly, I was ready, nay eager, to be converted to things English — except, certainly, food. Never have I encountered so many faultlessly turned out men, bowlers and Homburgs at just the right angle, suits beautifully yet unobtrusively cut, ties a model of sobriety, umbrellas, like trained black eels, dangling effortlessly from the left arm, in spite of the blazing sun; the whole effect one of studied expensive simplicity with just a dash of amiable complacency and condescension. I caught a glimpse of myself in a mirror and was horrified: ill-fitting suit, trousers too short, tie too loud, shirt too French, hat beneath contempt — an outsider, obviously. Quickly I slipped into the nearest pub — a fascinatingly moldy yet clean establishment — and asked the buxom barmaid for a "glass of beer." With a knowing glance at my "wrong" clothes (maddening thought!), she bared her upper plate and demanded to know whether I desired bitter, ale or lager. The bitter sounded unpromising and I had never heard of lager, so settled for a tankard of warm, potent ale. Thus fortified, I next visited the Burlington Arcade and spent half my money on shirts, ties, a hat and the thinnest, most eel-like umbrella obtainable. "I'll show them!" I thought elatedly.

In contrast with the magnificent male, the London women struck me as peculiarly frumpy and ill-kempt. A good many of the girls were pretty, in the fresh Anglo-Saxon way, with the well-advertised glowing skin and sturdy, substantial legs, but the clothes were for the most part deplorable — ill-fitting, cheap "suits," sleazy prints and shapeless "utility" shoes; the color schemes, too, looked vile, unmatchable shades clashing willy-nilly and destroying the wearers' natural good looks. I spied a few impressively and rather severely clad *mondaines,* uptilted noses high in the air, teeth and feet a shade too large but solid and obviously built to last — as most things were in the old Empire.

At noon I telephoned Boris to find out whether my presence was needed for one reason or another. Boris sounded a bit irritated. "Where on earth are you keeping yourself?" he asked. "Come to the Savoy at once; Edwin Evans is lunching with us and you are to tell him all about your music — he knows a great deal and writes well. Hurry, Seriozha is very angry with you." But when I got to the hotel, Sergei Pavlovitch was beaming and cracking jokes with Evans, a bearded Bohemian looking not unlike Pissaro, with a soft cultivated speech and rather a diffident manner. Evans spoke good French, which endeared him to Diaghilev, who didn't like to speak English, although he knew the language tolerably well. After some unavoidable blasts at Ernest Newman (with whom he was always scrapping), the pro-Germanic stolidity of the British musical mind, and the long-suffering "Dehlius" and Sibelius, Sergei Pavlovitch ordered *steaks minute* all around, patted me on the back and said to Evans: "This boy is good, so be good to him." Evans smiled carefully and began interrogating me in English, while Diaghilev and Boris turned to business matters. I gave the bearded sage a suitably colorful account of my beginnings, confessed that my love for jazz was never platonic, due to my friendship with George Gershwin, admitted also that a fashionable New York lady reporter had told her readers that my early "Gondla" was "barbaric in its harmonies, Icelandic in its frozen remoteness, and decidedly hunchback [Gumilev's hero was a cripple] in its form." Asked about my ideas on music, I made a few reasonably snappy remarks, subsequently printed and reprinted in so staid a publication as the *Boston Symphony Program Notes:* "I hate all 'modernism' and I love being modern. I believe only in construction in the truly classical sense, knowing that it is more difficult to construct a fox trot than to write a thousand 'poems' on golden fishes, bald Chinamen, or oyster shells as the so-called 'modernists' do. I find that jazz is 'classicism for minors' and, therefore, very useful. We must and will, undress music; it doesn't need the heavy coat of harmonies and more — winter is gone."

So impudent a pronouncement from a young man not quite twenty-two was, doubtless, dismissed by the older British musicians as bloody cheek, but it exhilarated the struggling young and filled them with curiosity. This was 1925 and English music was in a sad state; today England can boast any number of gifted composers, but thirty years ago, with the exception of Vaughan Williams and little-known Philip Heseltine, who used the pseudonym Peter Warlock, and who killed himself in 1930 when he was thirty-six, the picture was dreary indeed. The great men of English music were such purely local figures as Elgar (whose "Dream of Gerontius" was dismissed by George Moore — an Irishman, I hasten to add — as "holy water in a German Beer-barrel") and Diaghilev's *bête noire,* Delius. Of the younger men, Arthur Bliss and Eugene Goossens were the only ones with any spunk at all and I was pleased when told by Diaghilev that the latter was engaged as conductor for the Ballets Russes season.

The next day Goossens himself telephoned me and invited me to dine with him *en famille*. The *famille* that evening was composed of Boonie, his tall Renoiresque wife, and a painfully thin, sandy-haired young man whose name was William Walton. Unlike Eugène Goossens, a consummate dandy, Walton was almost shabbily dressed and had a downtrodden, yet eager, look, bringing to mind a Chekhov hero. The dinner was very good and so were Boonie's looks and the music talk. Both men were familiar with *Zephyr and Flora* and professed to admire it unreservedly. Walton, eighteen months older than myself, with an engagingly modest mien told me of his beginnings as an organist, his discovery by the Sitwells and his struggle to obtain a hearing; so far only a string quartet, given at Salzburg at an I.S.C.M. concert, and the first (1923) version of Edith Sitwell's "Façade" were played in public. He wanted to show me his new "Dr. Syntax" overture and have me meet his friends the Sitwell brothers; Walton then stayed with Osbert in 2 Carlyle Square, Chelsea. We parted friends.

Pedro Pruna, the Spanish painter whose scenery and costumes contributed not a little to the universal success of *Les Matelots,* did a rather mannered drawing of Kochno and myself; on it I'm represented seated, one foot bare, the other beslippered, while Boris, standing, is holding a mongrel pup with his left arm (the pup, who must have been uncomfortable, appears to be legless) and a large peasant straw hat in his right hand. We are both wearing white toweling robes and manage to look beautiful and effete at the same time — Pruna's trick, not ours. This drawing, executed in Barcelona from memory, appeared in the October 1925 issue of the London *Vogue* on the "We Nominate for the Hall of Fame" page. The caption read, in part: "Dukelsky went to America where, like his friend Gershwin, he became interested in the serious potentialities of jazz. Diaghilev, with his flair for new talent, suggested his writing the music for 'Zephyr and Flora,' which we hope to see in London. He had also written a musical comedy which is soon to be produced here."

This was inaccurate, as the "musical comedy" was far from written, but had reached merely the talking stage. It all began with Massine, again on the outs with Diaghilev, signing a pact with C. B. Cochran, who can with some justice be called the Diaghilev of the light-musical stage, to put on ballets for a forthcoming revue as well as for the Trocadero cabaret. My friendship with Leonide continued unabated and I lent a willing ear to indignant words against Sergei Pavlovitch, his tyrannical unconcern for his collaborators and the lucrative vistas that would open before me were I to enter the commercial field under his, Massine's, and Cochran's auspices. My money earned in France was fast disappearing, also I had grandly ordered two suits and a tailcoat from the best Savile Row tailor and although almost anybody's credit was good in London in the twenties, I hated being in debt and fully intended to pay the man. While fascinated by Massine's proposals, I decided to defer all active steps in the "lowbrow" direction until after *Zephyr's* opening, for fear of antagonizing Diaghilev, my sponsor and benefactor, although my banker no longer.

Diaghilev left for Italy with Lifar in early August and this gave me an opportunity to tinker with a few tentative jazz tunes. London musical shows were of much better quality then than they are now, and the best of them was *Primrose* at the Winter Garden, with Gershwin's music and Desmond Carter's pithy and well-turned lyrics. This was George's second London musical, written especially for the English stage and never reproduced in America. The first was an unsuccessful revue by A. de Courville, Edgar Wallace (later my collaborator) and Noel Scott called *The Rainbow*, produced in 1923.

George often told me that he considered *The Rainbow* his poorest score, and it certainly couldn't compare with the exhilarating *Scandals* music or such gems as the unjustly neglected "Innocent Ingenue Baby" and the striking "I'll Build a Stairway to Paradise," which Carl Van Vechten considered "the most perfect piece of jazz yet written." Yet, at least two numbers could bear a revival — the shrewdly Englished "Sunday in London Town" and the Kern-like ballad "In the Rain" — both with good lyrics by Clifford Grey — the latter with five-bar phrases in the verse, which would be considered daring in 1954.

On the whole it must be admitted that *The Rainbow* score wasn't much; *Primrose* was another matter. The star of that show was the tantalizing Heather Thatcher, who, like myself, belonged to the monocle-wearing brigade, but was certainly pretty enough without that unfeminine appurtenance. The music and lyrics of *Primrose* were consistently delightful and I'll never know why "Wait a Bit, Susie," its best song, was never transplanted across the ocean. I was greatly influenced in my light-music exercises at the time by both *Primrose* and *Tell Me More,* Winter Garden's next tenant, with Gershwin tunes, and Heather Thatcher again; the new musical, a failure in the States, achieved a sizable run in London and contained the lilting "Why Do I Love You?" — this title reappearing many years later in the more celebrated Kern-Hammerstein ballad.

I wrote several fair-to-middling songs with Beverley Nichols, ex-secretary to Dame Melba, busy journalist, generous host and author of *25,* his autobiography — and still his best book. He lived in a very small and very pretty house — this was before his infatuation with gardens — and wrote facile and deft profiles of his celebrated guests, who were always in and out of Beverley's living room, drinking his excellent liquor and joining in the polite merriment. Our songs were not as good as the dry Martinis, the house's specialty. I remember demonstrating four or five pieces to P. G. Wodehouse, an old friend of Nichols's and one of the best lyricists in his day. Well-mannered P.G. smiled broadly when we started, thinly as we sang and played and not at all when we finished.

This, of course, was the heyday of the Bright Young People, ably recorded by Beverley, Lord Donegal and, especially, Patrick Balfour, whose book *Society Racket* was published in the early thirties. Patrick summed up the London twenties as "an age, in the course of which . . . actors and actresses tried to be ladies and gentlemen and ladies and gentlemen behaved like actors and actresses, novelists were men-about-town and men-about-town wrote novels, persons of rank became shopkeepers and shopkeepers drew persons of rank to their houses, the speed king supplanted the Guards officer as the beau ideal of modern woman and modern woman herself grew each day slimmer and slimmer — and slimmer." To this summation I must add that it was also the age wherein Armenians and Russians (Michael Arlen and myself, to name two) tried to be Englishmen and arty Englishmen would give their back teeth if someone thought them Russian, normal men and women carried on as if they were homosexuals, and homosexuals just carried on.

But let Patrick Balfour tell you about carryings-on: "What parties they gave! Parties for the Blackbirds; an unforgettable Russian party in Gerald Road, with a Negro band . . . the swimming party in the St. George's baths; David Tennant Mozart party, where the eighteenth century was recaptured for a night; Tallulah parties; Guinness parties; impromptu wild parties, in fancy undress, in the Royal Hospital Road. Between parties we went to the Café Anglais, to hear Rex Evans singing about white mice and snowballs and the wrong end of his horse . . . above all, there was Chez Victor, where Hutch, in his prime, would sing. . . ." Hutch was Leslie Hutchinson, a light-skinned Negro, svelte and dashing, who played a "lot of piano," as the phrase has it, and made a lot of love to a lot of wellborn hostesses, who worshipped at his feet — or was it his fingers? One of Hutch's most ardent champions was snub-nosed and energetic Zena Naylor, vaguely related to Lord Alfred Douglas and a great friend of Willie Walton's, who was a habitué of Zena's house in Hill Street, where a party was always on. I went to them all — wasn't my portrait in *Vogue,* my ballet announced and extolled by Almighty God Diaghilev himself, weren't my clothes Anderson & Sheppard's best? The people one always saw at these mad bacchanals were Lady Eleanor Smith, the Guinness girls (Tanis later became Mrs. Howard Dietz), the Jungman sisters, Elizabeth Ponsonby, the David Tennants, Brian Howard, David Plunkett-Greene, Hermione Baddeley, Madge Garland and such accomplished fun lovers as Oliver Messell, Cecil Beaton, Noel Coward and Boonie Goossens. I well remember one of Boonie's twins saying to Lloyd Mitchell of the "Blackbirds" (having been briefed): "Are you colored?" Lloyd Mitchell: "Yes, I am." Twin: "I am colored, too; my color's white."

Noel, the talk of London and the most sought-after playwright-actor in Mayfair — his dream, which he achieved at an early age — was invited everywhere and charmed peeresses to his and their hearts' content. He had a knack (by screwing up his face and looking deliciously impish) of making them feel as if he were about to let them in on a jealously guarded secret of the Paris underworld — had he not written *Parisian Pierrot?* — when, in reality, a conventionally sprightly exchange of well-turned trivialities was taking place. His manner, build and general demeanor were wickedly, endearingly "right" — and although no one could touch Jack Buchanan for sublime tails, it was impossible to approach Noel's perfection when attired in a gray flannel suit and brown suède shoes. I often wondered whether his success would have been quite the same had he the physique of, say, Arnold Bennett.

Noel was then appearing in his own *Vortex* at the Royalty Theatre and held court nightly in his dressing room. Massine, never good at social small talk, but determined to bring us together, took me to Noel's pleasant abode in Ebury Street, where we could talk business. Coward received us in a resplendent dressing gown (I made a mental note to get its duplicate regardless of cost), listened to my little tunes with every evidence of pleasure, played a few of his own and wound up with a first (for me) performance of "Tea for Two," then the rage of the United States. Noel didn't play well and his voice was curiously flat and unmusical; I thought "Tea for Two" dull in the extreme and said so. I love the song now — as who doesn't? — but still marvel at the nonsensical lyric which never gets back to the title; no one does any tea-drinking in the song, which is probably understandable as the song was not meant for English audiences, but then why call it "Tea for Two"?

At that time Noel wasn't too sure of his ground as songwriter; in *Present Indicative* he tells how: "Cochran's armour of evasive politeness cracked, and he was forced to say that he frankly did not consider my music good enough to carry a whole show." It was Massine's thought that Coward and I could collaborate on music and lyrics, with me attending to ballet music as well. I remember playing a very Gershwinesque refrain, which Noel liked enough to try writing a lyric to then and there. Nothing came of the proposed collaboration, because "Cockie" finally gave in and let Noel compose the entire score for the revue. He, too, went to too many parties and met too many people; he, too, "indulged a long-suppressed desire for silk-shirts, pyjamas and underclothes," but Noel was prodigiously industrious and never let pleasure interfere with business. At twenty-two, I never let business spoil my pleasure and had a childish and unreasonable conviction that Lady Luck had singled me out as her own particular pet and all I had to do was let her operate.

After Diaghilev's departure, Willie Walton and I became close friends. He lived on the top floor of Osbert's Chelsea house and I was taken there shortly after the Goossens dinner. Two Carlyle Square could perhaps be described as an exclusive annex to such meccas of "Smartistic" London (the word is Patrick Balfour's) as Lady Colefax's — the Lions Corner House, as the envious had it — Emerald Cunard's and Christabel McLaran's establishments. Osbert's house was small and appeared even smaller as you entered it, owing to the great number of precious objects and knickknacks, all of which reflected the special tastes of the owner. The painter whose work prevailed on Osbert's walls was Severini, who, in spite of his early reputation as "Futurist," always seemed a bit saccharine to me. Italian and Persian art mingled freely in the Sitwell house; in a letter to Mother, I recorded with some astonishment that even the john boasted a number of Persian miniatures. There are people who aspire solely to wit, others to chic, still others to money — Osbert Sitwell's niche was majesty. His looks, speech, walk and the ponderous graciousness with which he received his guests made you feel that you were in the presence of royalty and that your host's literary activities were rather like the present King of Denmark's penchant for orchestra conducting. Since I am not easily awed, Sir Osbert's awesome manner failed to intimidate me, which was doubtless wrong of me; I soon noticed a marked reserve in the Sitwellian remarks addressed to me in the course of the excellent luncheon Willie and I were offered, and even more marked remoteness about the cold steely eyes of my host, and was much relieved when the time came to rise from the table.

Willie and I always enjoyed ourselves hugely in his attic and I did much to veer him away from the pitfalls of atonality. I was brutal in my denunciation of the Schoenbergian string quartet and other like efforts, warmly welcoming the fresh water-color quality of "Portsmouth Point," the overture then being written and orchestrated. This ingenious piece was first dedicated to me, and I well remember my hurt feelings when "To Siegfried Sassoon" appeared on the printed score.

On November 12th *Zephyr* had its Coliseum opening with Braque's beautiful additional sets and a good orchestra, well-rehearsed and spiritedly conducted. If the Paris *première* had but a moderate success, there were no such reservations to be made of the London one. In the pet phrase of society columnists, it was rapturously received. No laurel wreath this time, but I wore a large white chrysanthemum in my buttonhole to match the floral tributes bestowed on Alice Nikitina by Lord Rothermere. Except for the outrageous chrysanthemum, reported by the tabloids the next day, my clothes were those of a gentleman at long last, thanks to Messrs. Anderson & Sheppard, and, like Noel in *Present Indicative,* I "savoured to the full the sensation of being well-dressed for the first time."

Two wonderful, fairytalelike things happened to me that evening. C. B. Cochran came to see me backstage during the intermission, his perpetually red, friendly little face beaming, his hand outstretched to grasp mine. Cockie looked more like a Surtees squire than a theatrical producer, but a shrewder appraiser of theatrical wares never lived. He told me that he thought the music of *Zephyr* extraordinarily exhilarating, fresh and young, and would I write a musical-comedy score for him? There is really no relation between the two media, and Cochran's proposal was, in the conventional sense, just as unusual, as if Ziegfeld had asked T. S. Eliot to write him a "Follies" score on the strength of "The Love Song of J. Alfred Prufrock." One must also bear in mind that Cockie had never heard any of my jazz pieces (probably it was just as well), though he might have had some comments by Coward or Massine. I accepted the offer with dispatch and promised to show up at Cochran's office for further discussion on the next afternoon.

No sooner did Cochran leave than he was succeeded by the arrival of Willie Walton, breathless and slightly disheveled; he told me in a dramatic whisper that Frances Doble, "the most beautiful girl in London," wanted to meet me, that she was entranced with the ballet, my music and, apparently, my looks. Miss Doble asked Willie to take her backstage after the last ballet and bring me to supper with her at somebody-or-other's house. No party was planned for that evening — Diaghilev, Boris and I were to sup quietly with Goossens, Evans and Wollheim in the Savoy Grill; I asked Willie to wait and ran up to Sergei Pavlovitch, who was standing in the wings with Lifar, to ask his permission to join Mr. Walton for supper. Although I purposely omitted Miss Doble's name in my request, Diaghilev's mocking glance told me at once that he knew the truth: "A girl again. What a perfect young ass you are; *Zephyr* is a real London victory. I'm proud of you as a composer; as a man, you're incurable. Run along now!" I thanked Sergei Pavlovitch warmly, feeling a bit remorseful — here I was plotting to "sell my soul" to Cochran and my heart to an unknown enchantress — both actions certain to displease Diaghilev.

Frances ("Bunny," as everyone called her) Doble, the daughter of a Toronto banker, was a gifted young actress and a great Mayfair favorite. I knew that her sister Georgia ("Baby") was about to marry Sacheverell Sitwell, Osbert's younger brother, with whom I was on the friendliest terms. I knew too that Bunny was celebrated for her beauty in a town noted for professional pulchritude (the term "glamour girl" was not yet invented), but I was not prepared for the celestial vision that appeared out of nowhere on the huge Coliseum stage, which was peopled with madly chattering ballerinas, stagehands scurrying about and young guardees not above a little post-Victorian stage-door-Johnnying, their mustaches all a-twirl, their "I say's" and "ripping's" straight out of Wodehouse. Yes, Bunny Doble was indeed rarely beautiful with her shining, almond-shaped eyes, voluptuous yet shy mouth, dark-brown hair, the natural sheen of which set off the cool, even pallor of her skin, almost free of cosmetics; her figure didn't quite match the perfection of her face, but it was a dressmaker's figure and Bunny's frock showed it off seductively. Our first meeting was an exact duplicate of countless such meetings in countless third-rate films, where the hero and heroine, speechless and dumbfounded by each other's charms, utter unbearable banalities, while the audience's collective heart palpitates wildly and enviously. I plead guilty to a scene which in cold print must look very cold indeed, and assuredly inane, but we were both galvanized by one another and went through the motions of that legendary cataclysm — love at first sight — with utmost sincerity. I hope the reader doesn't become nauseated by my narcissism, which never extended to my looks, only to my clothes, but I must report that Bunny's opening gem-bit was: "Oh, but you are beautiful!" I gasped and retaliated with: "You are the most beautiful thing I ever saw . . ."; thus having assured ourselves that we were the two most beautiful people on earth, we walked off arm in arm, gazing at one another with unbelieving eyes. Willie, astonished and amused, following us at a respectful distance. I don't remember a thing about the supper that followed.

The London notices were fully as good as the Paris ones; in some instances, even better. In the light of my subsequent strange and nonconformist career as composer, I feel I should again submit a few quotes. Luckily for me Ernest Newman didn't cover my opening for the *London Sunday Times,* but Dyneley Hussey did. "As for the music," said he, "it is a pleasure to welcome a work which not only avoids mere silliness but shows that the young composer really has something to say. It is not all on a level but some of the movements, such as the slow solo for Flora after Zephyr has been wounded, were beautiful. The ballet was received with great enthusiasm." The accomplished and erudite Francis Toye (who wrote the splendid biographies of Rossini and Verdi) was very complimentary: "It would hardly be true to write that Dukelsky's music had, except for a certain elegance, even a remote flavor of the 18th century, but it struck us as by far the most interesting of all the compositions associated with Mr. Diaghilev's most recent ballets. . . . Here is a young man who, despite the discordant idiom of the times, knows how to shape a musical phrase and conceive a musical idea. Strange though it may appear to many people in the audience, M. Dukelsky has a real gift of tune, and some of his contrapuntal writing is extremely happy." Hubert Griffith added another bouquet: "Dukelsky's music is a relief for sore ears after too much musical comedy. Dukelsky may or may not be a great composer. His music last night was a delight." *Vogue* thought it "spirited and stimulating, possessing a pleasant acidity somewhat reminiscent of Prokofiev." Lastly, my erstwhile interviewer, Edwin Evans told his readers: "It is a rich score — possibly even a little too rich, for there are things in it which scarcely come through — and does not need any of the indulgence that one accords to an early effort, for, apart from a certain youthful exuberance, its style is unusually settled and consistent." Clearly, I got off on the right foot.

Looking back at my London debut, which took place almost thirty years ago, it becomes clear to me that I missed my big chance and made the unpardonable mistake of dissipating the excellent first impression my music made, by not taking myself at all seriously. Had I but the stick-to-itiveness of, say, a Prokofiev (I am not comparing his gift with mine), I would have followed *Zephyr* with a yet better work, would have orchestrated the early concerto — a sure applause-getter whatever its faults — and, first and foremost, gotten back to study, especially study of orchestration. I had Diaghilev and Koussevitzky where I wanted them, my meteoric rise gave me an entree to almost any conductor you could name, and, on top of it all, Cochran, the greatest showman of his time, was commissioning a musical comedy from me — me, who had not a single printed song to his credit! Yet, with all these wondrous opportunities, I let all these birds in my hand fly away — and did little of consequence for the next three years — except, in the current colorful phrase, have myself a ball.

I went to see Cochran at the appointed time, was told that Arthur Wimperis, then one of the top author-lyricists in the game, would write the book for my score, signed a very pretty-looking contract and pocketed a check for £300 — a sum of money that would not be called inconsiderable even today. I doubt that Cockie paid out such large advances as a rule, but I was a "young man of the moment" and bagging Diaghilev's newest composer must have given the enterprising showman a real kick — especially because he was aware of Diaghilev's savage and vociferous disapproval of any theatrical entrepreneur who dared lure "his people" away from him — as was the case with Massine. Had I asked Sergei Pavlovitch's permission to work for Cochran, he would have first thrown a fit and then thrown me out of his room and his life. What was I to do? The new ballet, although seemingly a certainty, wouldn't bring me enough to live on and there were Mother and Alex to think about.

On graduation from Cushing in 1924 as salutatorian, Alex passed the college entrance examination and was admitted as a freshman at M.I.T. His first scholarship was granted by the Russian Relief in 1926, Alex beginning to show promise as an architect. By this time Mother had moved to Boston to save Alex from alcoholic excesses, as the Berestnevs began brewing their own bathtub vodka. Mother then obtained a scholarship for Alex through Koussevitzky.

She worked in Mme. Ouspensky's dress shop, specializing in Russian cross-stitching; everything Russian was then very popular. In 1928 Alex graduated with a bachelor of science degree with top honors, was granted the Fontainebleau Scholarship and went back to Tech to get his master's degree, which he received in 1929, with a traveling scholarship for a year's study abroad. While these distinctions were being achieved, Alex subsisted solely on what Mother was able to earn by hard work, and the two of them needed help urgently. I was determined to do everything in my power to provide that help.

Prior to meeting Bunny Doble, I met and liked Sacheverell Sitwell, as "easy to be with" a man as Osbert was difficult. Sachie, as he was known to his friends, had none of Osbert's glassy perfection; his clothes were baggy, his shirts rumpled, so was his unruly blond hair. Although some likened him to Bacchus, he looked more like an overgrown urchin with his odd, shy giggle and awkwardly angular gestures. There was something touchingly gauche about the man's appearance; you would hardly suspect that he was a master of colorful, yet meticulous prose and warmly sensitive poetry, that he was by far the best author of the three writing Sitwells — which estimate will not please him. The Sitwell trio's mutual devotion is too well-known to need discussion on these pages; to criticize one in the presence of the others is to invite a verbal explosion and a permanent ouster from the exalted Sitwellian spheres. There is a priceless paragraph in Cecil Beaton's *Photobiography* in which the author, with artful naïveté, tells of how he "as each week passed, became more panicstricken lest I should fail completely in adult life. Then one day a delightful and wise friend said to me, 'Don't worry so much about becoming anything very definite. Take it easy for a bit more and become a friend of the Sitwells.' " Cecil took the advice and things worked out beautifully for him. As for me, having "become very definite" indeed, I had the impudence to tell Sacheverell that I thought Osbert's *Before the Bombardment* a boring and almost unreadable book — the strident scene that ensued is not one of my happier recollections. Vernon Fane, reviewing Sir Osbert's *The Scarlet Tree* spoke of the author's "intense egocentricity" and "none too elastic view of life." Egocentricity not being one of my many faults — I sincerely dislike talking about myself for the unusual reason that I know all there is to know about me and would rather hear about others — and elasticity not being one of my few virtues, I was regrettably unmoved by the trio of Sitwells, who have always made it clear that they regard themselves as being *apart* and endowed with exceptional gifts. They have succeeded in securing an almost general acceptance of this belief by an unflinching and at times belligerent insistence.

My attentions to Bunny were, in reality, of the most inoffensive sort. We saw each other every day, held hands, walked through Chelsea or Hyde Park, kissed a great deal and talked all manner of childishly romantic nonsense — but that was all. Through my entire life I was cursed, or possibly blessed, with a dual personality as lover as well as composer. I have desired and I have loved, certainly, but with two exceptions I never desired those I loved, never loved those I desired. To further entertain members and disciples of the psychoanalytical cult, I will admit that I was never capable of sublimating sex, nor degrading love, with elaborate variations of the sexual act. I have read all about "love and sex being one and the same" or "going hand in hand" — so should music and money — but Duke and Dukelsky know better. I've never been married and my stock answer when asked why not is, "Because, should I be married to one woman, I'd be unfaithful to all the 'others.' " The real reason is not as pat and snappy as that, but it is a more valid one.

To save money in order to help Mother and Alex, not forgetting my own expensive outings and clothes, I moved to cheap digs in Torrington Square in the heart of Bloomsbury. The room, as I remember it now, had that very special London squalor about it, but the rent was infinitesimal and Mrs. Dupont, my sad-eyed Belgian landlady, had a way with beef and mutton, which was an added advantage on lean days when I wasn't asked out to dine. I composed — what little I did compose — on an antiquated upright, perpetually and fascinatingly out-of-tune — no piano tuner could help the prehistoric beast, which would be on its good behavior for a week, and then get back to complete acoustic anarchy.

It is a sad and probably little-known fact that composers are usually jealous of one another and inclined to speak disparagingly of their contemporaries' work. There is no jealousy in my make-up either in love or in music. I always liked all good music — good to my way of thinking, that is — and was always ready to give it a hand, exactly as if it were my own; I, too, felt, and still feel, that a really worthwhile new composer is so rare a bird that he should be caged at once and that the cage should be gold, not merely gilt, as is too often the case. Thus, on hearing Vittorio Rieti's "Noah's Ark" (1925) I became entranced with the man's talent and began "selling" him to Diaghilev; there might have been other salesmen too — at any rate, Diaghilev lent a willing ear and Rieti's *Barabau,* a hilarious "folk" ballet with inventive and dazzlingly fresh choreography by Balanchine, was put on at the Coliseum on December 11th and applauded to the echo.

In 1925–1926 I acted as a sort of an unofficial "musical secretary" to Sergei Pavlovitch and performed my duties with great zeal. Always a facile sightreader, it became my job to play new works submitted to Diaghilev, and, on occasion, to write composers and their publishers. Willie Walton's great ambition was to compose a ballet for Diaghilev, and I suggested that he play "Portsmouth Point" for him. Willie had a young friend named Constant Lambert, a product of the Royal College of Music, who had similar ambitions; while Walton pursued his goal through me as a go-between, "Kid" (as he was known to his intimates) Lambert had other ideas. He used to haunt the corridor outside Diaghilev's door at the Savoy Hotel and sit on the floor with the determination to waylay the great man and obtain a hearing. Diaghilev, who had an efficient bodyguard in Boris, was used to ducking composers and creditors alike, and outsmarted poor Lambert daily by sneaking into his suite before the boy had a chance to open his mouth. Kid Lambert was rather typical of arty Chelsea and insisted on wearing an unusually loud bright-orange shirt with a black tie. This trade-mark infuriated Diaghilev, who called me in to complain about the "infernal nuisance — that Chelsea *tapette* [fairy] who haunts me." I laughed heartily, knowing Lambert to be quite a ladies' man; I knew him slightly and thought his manner curt and disagreeable, but certainly not effeminate. Willie, with his habitual kindness, suggested that Lambert join him for the Diaghilev audition, which I succeeded in obtaining. I heard Lambert's newly composed "Adam and Eve" ballet, and thought it very mild fare, but promised to try and smuggle the Kid in. In this I succeeded, although Diaghilev grumbled unpleasantly at the sight of the orange-shirted prowler; Willie played first — he was no pianist, and got an icy reception from Sergei Pavlovitch, who then told me what he thought of "Portsmouth Point" in Russian, and it wasn't much. Lambert, a self-assured and efficient performer, went on next, gave an excellent account of his skimpy piece and — miracle of miracles — was rewarded by a beatific smile by the listener.

"Are you English?" he queried. "Yes, I am, why?" countered Lambert. "That's most surprising. I don't like English music, yet I like your little ballet. I'm going to produce it, but not with that silly title," Diaghilev went on. He took a big red pencil, crossed out "Adam and Eve" and wrote "Romeo and Juliet" over it. Constant burst into uncontrollable tears.

I was very upset by this turn of events, as I considered Willie's music immeasurably superior to that of Lambert's. At my insistence, and with some help from Goossens, "Portsmouth Point" was given as an interlude at His Majesty's Theatre in the summer of 1926. Arnold Haskell reported the Lambert "christening" thus: "Through London friends, he [Diaghilev] had discovered a young English composer, Constant Lambert." The London friends were Willie and myself. I have before me a clipping from either the *Times* or the *Telegraph* which reads: "The composer, Constant Lambert, is still a student and is not yet twenty-one. His music was brought to the notice of Mr. Diaghilev by Vladimir Dukelsky, the composer of 'Zephyr and Flora,' and Diaghilev, liking it, thought he could fit no more thoroughly British story to it than Shakespeare's 'Romeo and Juliet.' "

Kid Lambert was wretchedly poor at the time and Willie asked me whether I couldn't find some remunerative work for the young man, who not only didn't thank me for the Diaghilev audition but seemed to resent my role in bringing it about. Massine gave me five Albeniz piano pieces to orchestrate and I was glad to share the assignment with Lambert, whose orchestrating skill was superior to mine. Eight years later Lambert favored me with a single mention in his scrappy *Music Ho!* subtitled "A Study of Music in Decline": "Diaghilev was far more than a mere impresario. Though not, strictly speaking, a creative artist, he had very much more genius than many of the artists who worked for him, and it hardly seems worth while examining the work of such minor composers as Dukelsky, Sauguet, Nabokov, and others, apart from their connection with Diaghilev. They were merely the gunmen executing the commands of their Capone, who, like all great gangsters, never touched firearms himself."

In mid-December on moving to Torrington Square, I fell victim to a form of gastric fever and spent two depressing days in bed, drinking tea, reading Stendhal and playing chess with Indian students, fellow inmates of Mme. Dupont's establishment. On the second night of my illness, Walton stormed in to tell me that Viva and Willie Booth, of the St. John's Wood Branch of the Bright Young People, were giving a party for Bunny after her opening in a new comedy and that Bunny announced that she wouldn't come unless I came too. I felt wretched, but, my protests and excuses proving of no avail, allowed myself to be persuaded by faithful Willie, dressed hurriedly and, bundled up securely, ventured into the icy December air. On arriving at the Booths', I was received with mingled gaiety and solicitude and given a double brandy, on downing which I promptly fainted. I came to just in time for Bunny's triumphant arrival; she was radiant in shiny silver lamé, grateful for the plaudits she received at the theater and happy to see me among her welcoming friends. The crackling fire, Hutch's soothing singing and piano playing and Bunny's tenderness should have cured me instantly, but I felt gradually more and more ill and had to be taken to bed, Bunny playing nurse. The next morning, instead of recovering, I got steadily worse and, thanks to Willie's kind offices, was removed to 2 Carlyle Square — Osbert was vacationing in Italy.

I will always be grateful to Willie Walton for the friendship and concern he showed me during the next week, which caused me actually to enjoy my illness. Bunny came to see me and we had an emotional scene which started with the girl kneeling at my bed and crying, as she imagined herself responsible for my condition, having insisted at my turning up at her party. There was talk of marriage, of never leaving each other — Bunny in tears, I in bed with a high temperature which, according to the girl, gave me a magnificent color. Bunny then left and, I fear, Love left us shortly afterwards. What a relief it must have been to all our ill-wishers.

At Christmas time, I wrote Mother a long letter in which I said that my main and basic desire was to see her as soon as possible and, most important of all, to provide her even temporarily with some semblance of security. I continued: "Diaghilev is very much satisfied with my ballet and myself. As a token of his appreciation, he plans three exclusively *Russian* novelties for the 20th, *i.e.,* Jubilee season of his ballet. The three composers are to be Glinka (*Russlan and Ludmila* in an unusual scenic presentation), Stravinsky and myself. I keep good company, don't I? My new ballet will be, apparently, in two acts and the libretto is being developed by Boris. A large number of theatrical 'tricks' is being planned, but no musical ones; on the contrary, I'm plunging deeper and deeper into the purest lyricism. . . . So far I have no competitors; young Russian composers have failed to put in an appearance in Europe."

Prior to leaving for Berlin with the company (*Zephyr* scored another emphatic success in the German capital), Diaghilev had but two meetings with me. On one occasion he came to lunch at Osbert's, accompanied by Boris; he sat at the table wrapped in his beaver-fur coat (fear of catching a cold) and refused to sample the excellent oysters (fear of ptomaine poisoning). Following lunch, I played my Bogdanovitch songs, which he praised immoderately; Diaghilev then told several wildly improbable stories and departed majestically. Osbert's own majesty paled somewhat next to that of Czar Sergei's — no one could touch Diaghilev when he chose to be regal.

The other meeting was less pleasant. I composed some insignificant "arrangements" for Massine, who was then staging cabaret shows for Cochran at the Trocadero, and promptly forgot all about it. One night Sergei Pavlovitch, Boris and I went there for supper and, to my intense discomfort, one of the dancers performed a *pas seul* to the strains arranged by me. Following the dance, one of Cockie's henchmen came over to the table to congratulate me on the success of "my" music. Diaghilev went blue with rage, said nothing, drummed on the table with his knuckles and demanded the bill. I was handed my coat, ebony walking stick and brand-new top hat by the hat-check girl; no sooner were we out in the street than Diaghilev knocked my top hat off my head with my own stick, trampled upon it savagely, reducing it to a messy pulp, and with a one-syllable parting shot, "Whore!" disappeared in the dark.

Following my recovery from my illness, Willie went off to Amalfi to join Osbert, Sacheverell married Baby Doble and Bunny was reported to be in love with her leading man. Cockie was in the hospital about to be operated on for gall-stones, while I went back to partying in an attempt to combat a serious attack of London loneliness. My outlandishly elegant clothes, eighteenth-century walking sticks and botanical arrangements, far from attracting English females, usually convinced them of my "queerness." This I didn't bargain for and was torn between a passion for sartorial effects and a new and more natural craving for carnal conquests. While I was asked about a great deal and made much of by women at parties and opening nights, I'm afraid they regarded me more as a decorative object and, if not a full-grown lion, at least an acceptable lion cub, rather than a normally functioning male.

There was a lovely Nordic-looking dancer, whom we shall call Lita Maine, who had a part in Cochran's revue at the Pavillon and I decided to "give her a whirl." She whirled willingly enough — when it came to the Embassy or the Café de Paris, where on one occasion I stepped on the then Prince of Wales's foot while he was earnestly mastering the Charleston with an American partner, and was charming company at dinner — but that's as far as it went. What I didn't know was that Miss Maine was Cockie's special favorite and that it would have been far smarter to leave her in peace; my rivals, detractors and just plain busybodies apparently reported my friendship with Lita to the ailing producer, painting it in vastly exaggerated colors. I doubt that clever Cockie let such a puny matter interfere with his theatrical projects, but he dropped my musical comedy on his recovery and sent me a most polite note of regrets. He, however, retained my services as arranger and orchestrator (!) to Massine, then staging another ballet for the Trocadero.

Arthur Wimperis and I wrote two or three songs for the projected musical, an adaptation of a French farce, the procedure much in vogue in those days. Prior to going to the hospital, Cockie introduced me to William Allen, head of Asherberg, Hopwood & Crew, the old music firm, then a rival of Chappell's in the operetta field; Bill Allen, a sweet old Cockney with a walrus mustache, signed me to a contract at £250 per annum against royalties to be accrued from the sale of my music. Although my contract with Koussevitsky stipulated an exclusive lifetime partnership, I was permitted to prostitute my muse and publish such unworthy outpourings elsewhere, on condition that I find a suitable nom de plume. On my discussing this with Gershwin, he suggested that the family name was easily enough truncated to "Duke," but the Christian name presented some difficulty.

There was nothing resembling "Vladimir" in English, and all the Anglo-Saxon names beginning with "V" already had Russian counterparts—except Vernon. The name "Vernon Duke" had a somewhat purple-fiction ring to it, but since musical comedy was not an especially elevated form of art, that did not seem to constitute an obstacle. Thus my first published song, "Try a Little Kiss," was signed with the Gershwin-invented handle, which stuck through all these years until it became my official name and relegated the Slavic "Dukelsky" to the status of a pseudonym.

Through Allen, who was bewildered but somewhat impressed by me — I'm sure he had never feasted his eyes on so exotic a creature — I met redoubtable Jimmy White, the self-made Croesus and operetta lover extraordinary. The operettas he loved were all Viennese, crammed with luscious waltzes, skittish primadonnas with parasols and choruses of young men in white flannel trousers — stilted and intensely British versions of the *Mittel-Europa* originals. White's love for these imports was so great that he rented old Daly's Theatre for the purpose of installing an all-Viennese regime there; his calculations proved wrong eventually as the regime was already tottering and "bloody Yanks" were brazenly competing with Lehar, Oskar Straus and Emmerich Kalman by forcing "lewd and obscene jazz" down honest Londoners' throats. At the time of our meeting, Jimmy White was still sitting on top of the world, lording it at the Stock Exchange and czaring it at Daly's with a successful production of *Katja, the Dancer,* with Jean Gilbert's music and regal Lilian Davies in the title role.

If Bill Allen spoke the purest Cockney, Jimmy's speech was impure Lancashire; he couldn't finish a sentence without spicing it with a bad word, usually so comically mispronounced as to take the sting out of it. He took me on to "pep up" *Katja,* then in its second year, reasoning that a few "saucy" interpolations would further prolong the show's life. "You're a young man, Dulazy [which is how he pronounced my name], and I want young ideas for the old girl; give me that bloody Yankee monkey music — I hate the stuff myself — but I'll try it." It is a mystery that White should have applied to me, a Parisian Russian, according to the London press, for Yankee monkey music, but he handed me a very welcome contract and I started a career of "doctoring" ailing Viennese operettas and "jazzing 'em up" to suit the changing tastes of Daly's audience.

I began by interpolating "Try a Little Kiss" (with a Wimperis lyric) and "Back to My Heart" into *Katja,* and got a big thrill from hearing my first "jazz" tunes sung by "name" actors on a West End stage. Fred Leslie, the dance director, although not an American, did his best to create an American-style dance routine to "Kiss," the genteel Maida Vale chorus maids traipsing daintily through brazen Yankee steps. I hardly think the box-office receipts skyrocketed as a result of my interpolations, but Jimmy was pleased and hired me on a yearly basis to tinker with his forthcoming productions, of which the first one was to be *Yvonne,* also with a Jean Gilbert score. "I think the old man came a cropper with this one," said Jimmy. "You'll bloody well start from scratch, Dulazy." "Right you are, guv'nor," I said smartly and went back to Bloomsbury, new contract in my pocket.

Balanchine was then practically my neighbor, and I really got to know him. George, probably the most lovable creature that ever lived, was already his well-known unpredictable self — mixing sheer lunacy with phlegmatic *laissez aller,* carried to unheard-of lengths. Ever a diligent and inspired worker, he lived in a cozy little world of his own, disorganized and ill-assembled to the naked eye, but very dear to him. Untranslatable Armenian jokes and good Russian food were enough to make him happy; money meant (and means) nothing to him, and I'll wager that he is the poorest of all choreographers, although certainly the best. In the many years that I've known him, George turned down job after job in order to create ballets for his beloved New York City Ballet Company.

In his early London days, George spoke very little English and just enough French to make himself understood; he was fond of playing the guitar and, since non-Russian-speaking guests were always in and out of his place, learned a song or two in English and sang them in a peculiarly mournful voice. His after-dinner favorite was a Balanchinesque version of the then popular refrain: "Everybohdy lohves my bohdy, but my bohdy lohves nobohdy but me." George's constant companion was a middle-aged character dancer named Kremnev, a sly tow-headed Russian jack-of-all-trades whose supposedly perfect English was the object of Balanchine's great envy and admiration. In reality, Kremnev knew scarcely a hundred English words and mispronounced them atrociously, but to George, Kremnev's English was the purest Oxford and he was fond of saying:

"Ah, Kremnev, if I could only speak English like you!" The wily little Russian would then shrug his shoulders self-deprecatingly and reply with mock modesty: "It's not difficult with *my* talent for languages." This finally got George's goat and, unbeknown even to his wife, he began sneaking off to Berlitz's of an evening in an effort to prove to his friend that he too was a talented linguist. It must be added that Balanchine and Kremnev habitually breakfasted together on Sundays at Lyons' Corner House (*not* Lady Colefax's). As a rule, Kremnev ordered breakfast in loud, imperious tones, with Balanchine gazing at his friend reverently. On a certain Sunday, having acquired a bit of workable Berlitz English, George took his polyglot friend to Lyons' and, as they sat down, waited poker-faced for Kremnev to start operations. "Veitresss!" yelled the dancer with authority born out of practice. The Nippy duly arrived and awaited orders. "Veitress — ekky-bekky, plizz," said Kremnev; the girl, obviously new in her job, looked at the polyglot with consternation. "I beg your pardon, sir?" she stammered apprehensively. "You breeng ekky-bekky, veitress. . . ." went on Kremnev, frowning. This was Balanchine's opportunity. "No-o, veitress, no-o-o . . ." said George soothingly. "No ekky-bekky . . . Yeggs and beycon!"

Balanchine was fond of my *Zephyr* music and Diaghilev promised him, on the strength of *Barabau's* tumultuous success, that he would be entrusted with the choreography of the *Three Seasons,* Diaghilev's name for my projected new ballet. The three seasons were winter, spring and summer — with autumn omitted, as Sergei Pavlovitch detested that time of the year.

CHAPTER XI

AFTER THE BALLET IS OVER

MY FINANCIAL situation having become stabilized, I gave up my Torrington Square "digs" and took an attractive service flat in Pall Mall, under a similar one rented by Gershwin, who arrived in London early in 1926 and soon became the darling of Mayfair. He was showered with invitations, including those of Prince George and the Mountbattens. (Prince George gave him a photograph of himself inscribed: "From George to George.") When not busy with a London production of *Lady Be Good,* the Astaires' showpiece, then in preparation, Gershwin accepted these invitations with joy, because he loved to play piano for people who loved to hear him. George's superb piano playing took London completely by storm; clubmen, guardees and debutantes surrounded the American Liszt, architect of musical skyscrapers and the first transatlantic composer with a voice of his own. Europe was just discovering jazz and its musicians hastened to climb aboard the strange new bandwagon; Milhaud led the pack with the curiously prophetic *Création du Monde,* Krenek bowdlerized jazz mercilessly in his *Jonny Spielt Auf,* Stravinsky toyed with it unconvincingly in the early *Ragtime,* and even the young Englishmen helped themselves to its formulas, as witness Walton in some portions of *Façade* and, later, Lambert in his vulgarly garrulous *Rio Grande.* Florence Mills was the chic diva of the period and no Mayfair shindig was complete without a flock of "Blackbirds," imported by Cochran with enormous success. Most of the Blackbirds were sincere and talented performers and it was good to hear them at parties and in the theater; but things got out of control when their orchestra drummer's wife slashed a London matron with a razor, on finding her husband in the lady's boudoir. The drummer was duly deported and the lady repaired to Paris and temporary oblivion. It was at one of the Blackbirds' parties that Noel Coward performed a solo Charleston in virtuoso fashion — another token of his amazing versatility.

The lyric for Gershwin's "I'd Rather Charleston," interpolated into the Astaire show, was written by gentle, sloe-eyed Desmond Carter, a wonderful lyric writer who died young and who was to supply words to my *Yellow Mask* tunes in 1928. George and Carter were major kingpins in the House of Chappell, the London branch of Harms (or was it the other way around?), run by Max Dreyfus's brother Louis. Still smarting under Max's nonappreciation of my talents, I became determined to achieve success without the omnipotent Brothers Dreyfus. I knew, however, that kindly old Percy Greenbank, who wrote the lyrics to my music for *Yvonne,* was no match for Carter, whose verse was always smartly turned, and I was fascinated as Desmond, a model of tact and reticence, sat in an armchair, pencil in hand, while George, a big cigar in his mouth and eyes shining, played "I'd Rather Charleston" over and over in every existing key.

In late March I went to Monte Carlo with Walton, having concluded arrangements with Daly's to return in the end of April for rehearsals of *Yvonne,* starring Ivy Tresmand, who had made a hit as a soubrette in *Katja, the Dancer*. We first alighted in Paris, and I introduced Willie to Prokofiev, just back from the States. While on his American tour, Serge had stopped off in Boston and visited Mother and Alex, for which I was most grateful to him. Walton and I played our new music for Prokofiev, who puffed out his cheeks, made jokingly rude remarks and insisted on a game of chess with me. When I feebly remonstrated, knowing myself to be no match for him, Serge said that it delighted him to see me walk into every trap he laid for me, which pleasure was denied him by better opponents. He claimed that my game was hopeless, but my mistakes fascinating and "not devoid of genius."

Walton and I put up at the Hôtel Côte d'Azur in Monaco, a big and almost empty place whose only clients seemed to be a group of *petites mains* from a dress designer's establishment, cheerful and sparrowlike little Paris gamines, intoxicated by the Riviera sun and the blue Mediterranean. Unlike most such places, our hotel had no rules about noisemaking; the *petites mains* ran about and laughed delightedly, Willie and I banged away on the piano and everybody was happy. One of the girls, a small mischievous brunette named Monique, happened to live across the corridor from my room, was always dashing in and out, humming the latest "java" or "beguine" (these are always in ¾ time, notwithstanding Cole Porter's classic), bumping into me and running off with, *"Oh! Je vous demande pardon, monsieur . . . comme je suis maladroite."* This led to the inevitable *"nuit d'amour"* and the *nuit d'amour* to Monique's luggage being transferred to my room in the morning, without the small matter of consulting me about the desirability of such an arrangement. This one-sided idyll lasted about a week, at the end of which I presented Monique with a dress and a pair of shoes, went through the motions of a sentimental farewell and saw her to the station in a Victoria. At the time of this not very romantic escapade, Willie was completing his *Siesta* for chamber orchestra, a pretty lyrical piece which I called "very remarkable" in a letter to Mother.

But it was time to return to London and the new Duke-Dukelsky partnership. The book for *Yvonne* proved to be unusually inane, and Percy Greenbank, an amiable and easygoing man, found my American-style tunes rather difficult to lyricize. Some of Gilbert's melodies were retained, but the bulk of the score was mine (nine or ten numbers) and, on the average, the music was mildly pleasant, comfortably Kern-like in spots, uncomfortably Leslie Stuartish in others. Ivy Tresmand's first song was prefaced by this sort of dialogue:

IVY: Would you like a spot of tea, men?

CHORUS MEN (*in blue blazers and white flannels*): Jolly good idea!

IVY: I always find it rather nicer to be naughty with a few handsome young men to be naughty with — ha, ha! (*Business of pinching chorus men's cheeks.*) (*Song:* "It's Rather Nicer to Be Naughty [than to be always quite good]")

The orchestra was large, very brassy and conducted by Arthur Wood, a benign, rotund Victorian type of musician, a great pet of White's. It was at one of *Yvonne's* rehearsals that the famous timpani episode occurred, since erroneously reported in joke books and other people's reminiscences. At the final orchestra rehearsal,

White sat in an upper-tier box, reveling in the deafening noise made by the Wood-led men; he didn't know much about music and liked only two kinds — brassy marches and dreamy waltzes. All of a sudden, Jimmy noticed the timpani player, his arms folded on his chest, standing idly by at the back of the band. " 'Ere, 'ere, Arthur," White bellowed. "Who is that barstid with the three drums?" "He's the timpani player, guv'nor," said the startled conductor, stopping the orchestra with difficulty. "Now, then, why isn't this timbly fella playin'?" "Beggin' your pardon, sir, he's *tacet,* sir." "Well, you tell that bludy tacet to jolly well play, or I give 'im the sack!"

When told that the Charleston was all the rage, and given a demonstration of that pagan dance by Fred Leslie, Percy Greenbank, still living in his *Our Miss Gibbs* memories and visibly shocked, said hesitantly: "Don't you think Daly's patrons might resent so immoral an exhibition?" He offered to take the sting out of the number by calling the Anglicized version of it the "Dainty Charleston."

Thus I went into Jekyll-and-Hyding. But my "secret" was immediately discovered by the *Daily Sketch* snooper, who reported while we were still in rehearsal: "By the way, composers of ultra-modern ballets are not above picking up quite an honest penny or two by being a trifle lower in the brow for the nonce. Dukelsky, for instance, has written some songs, duly approved by Mr. James White, for 'Yvonne' at Daly's under the name of 'Vernon Dukes' [*sic*]."

Yvonne opened at Daly's on May 22nd after a "tryout" in Manchester, where the dirty-green fog is so thick it shuts you off from the rest of the world, whose leading hotel is a cross between a catacomb and a house of detention, but whose inhabitants love the theater. I had never been to an *un*chic musical opening before — Cochran's or Coward's first nights were always the peak of fashion — and the atmosphere of upper-middle-class respectability at Daly's, the thicknecked stockbrokers and Midlands' financiers — White's friends for the most part — with their blowsy wives in Regent Street's best, made me feel like a goldfish out of Diaghilev's pure water. *No* aesthetes were present — the Croesuses sat in the stalls and vociferous Cockney "theayter" lovers in the gallery. The galleryites thought little of the piece, and when the *jeune premier,* a plump and self-satisfied Public School boy, executed some awkward *entrechats* while singing the title song, not a happy idea of Fred

Leslie's, there were some audible titters and a rude remark or two. I saw Hoytie Wiborg, who didn't know what to make of the Viennese-Russo-American hodgepodge, leave in the intermission and felt an urgent need for a double brandy. The supper afterwards, at the "wrong" place, was substantial but dull, as was the show, and the notices the next morning ranged from lukewarm to downright insulting. The only hit in *Yvonne* was made by Hal Sherman, the "eccentric" little American dancer, who did a Chaplinesque routine to another tune of mine called "Don't Forget the Waiter," and brought down the house. My best songs were "Magic of the Moon" (a fair mixture of Kern and corn) and "Daydreams," agreeably sung and danced by Ivy Tresmand.

Jimmy White thought highly of Miss Tresmand's talents and kept the show going, which, considering that he had a lot of money, was not difficult. The show achieved a respectable run of 280 performances and could, by stretching a point a bit, be put down as a moderate success. I was anxious to keep Diaghilev and Kochno out of Daly's, but I believe they went there on the sly, because neither spoke to me for three days.

Nevertheless, money was now coming in from several sources. I was able to send some of it home fairly regularly, and Dukelsky, in return, was doing all he could to help Duke and his "*Yvonne* the Terrible." Kindly Eberg, the head of Koussevitzky's publishing house, died and was replaced by Gabriel Paitchadze, a Georgian like my grandmother, and a man of infinite tact and wisdom; he soon got to be close friends with both Stravinsky and Prokofiev — a miraculous feat. *Zephyr and Flora* finally appeared in print, and so did the stillborn piano concerto. The 1926 summer ballet season was exceptionally brilliant and the Bright Young People never shone so brightly. *Zephyr* was revived, with two additional sets, and again almost unanimously approved. My old Icelandic overture, "Gondla," was dusted off by Goossens and played as a "symphonic interlude" between ballets (a laudable practice of Diaghilev's that should be revived), leaving the listeners nonplussed. Koussevitzky announced the suite from *Zephyr* for Boston's next season and offered me an appearance with the Boston Symphony Orchestra as soloist in my concerto; aware of my rusty piano technique, I was compelled to decline regretfully.

Best of all, from the point of view of sheer excitement, I was engaged to play one of the four pianos (Auric, Poulenc and Rieti tackled the other three) in Stravinsky's *Les Noces,* about to have its London *première.* We learned our parts diligently, Goossens conducted cannily as usual, but every time we rehearsed the inhumanly difficult work, terror seized us, helpless terror mingled with an odd, elemental sort of ecstasy — rather like one's first airplane flight. The opening could best be described as a scandalous triumph, unique in London's theatrical annals and, according to the people who witnessed both, second only to the famous *Sacre du Printemps* battle in Paris. The noise was deafening — boos, hisses and catcalls mingling with cheers and thunderous applause. Diaghilev was delighted, but his delight turned to fury after he'd read the ghastly and, frankly, idiotic press reviews. The music was denounced as "barbarous, not even barbaric," consisting of "sounds, which the nursery knows as 'chopsticks,' " "amorphous," "hideous," etc. We four came in for some unexpected backhanded compliments and a good deal of pity and commiseration. The mysterious "Crescendo," after making short work of the "barbarous" ballet, stopped in his tracks suddenly to say, "I must be mistaken; if I am right, how could four men like Auric, Poulenc, Rieti and Dukelsky be induced to take part in 'Noces'?" "What they played," commented Philip Page, "was probably very difficult, for these accomplished young men cast glances of agony at the conductor; but if they had played not a note the composer had written and if they had come in consistently at the wrong moment, the effect would have been the same." H. G. Wells, our one "vigorous champion from an unlikely quarter" (C. W. Beaumont), wrote an indignant letter to *The Times* in which he stated: "I do not know of any other ballet as interesting, so amusing, so fresh or nearly so exciting as 'Les Noces.' I want to see it again and again."

But Wells's letter wasn't published until June 18th, four days after the *première,* and the damage was already done. The chief culprit was that arch enemy of Diaghilev's, England's Beckmesser-in-Chief, Mr. Ernest Newman. Not content with "quartering" us performing composers, he went after Stravinsky and exclaimed that "the world was tired of the *moujik* and his half-baked brain." It wasn't clear whether Newman was referring to a Russian peasant, to Diaghilev or the composer, but Sergei Pavlovitch was beside himself with rage. He called the "four quarters of a composer" into the manager's office at His Majesty's Theatre a half hour before the second performance of *Les Noces* and said with studied Olympian calm: "Gentlemen, I have it on good authority that Mr. Ernest Newman is in my theater again tonight. In his dastardly review he has insulted Russia, Igor Stravinsky, myself and you, my collaborators. Mr. Newman should be punished and I have evolved a most efficient plan for such punishment." He scribbled something on a small bit of paper, rolled it up, then rolled up three more bits of paper, leaving them completely blank and continued: "You see here four bits of paper, one of which contains Newman's name. You will draw lots and whoever draws the Newman-marked lot, will don white gloves, approach Newman's orchestra seat just before curtain time, ask him, 'Are you Ernest Newman?' and on receiving a reply in the affirmative, will pull his nose, in full view of the audience."

We did as we were told. As luck would have it, I drew the slip of paper with Newman's name. White-gloved and strengthened by whisky, my heart beating, I advanced to the location of the critic's stall, indicated to me by the theater's press agent. To my complete consternation, on arriving at the place, I found the seat empty. Whether Newman was tipped off by one of my colleagues (who alone knew of the conspiracy) and fled, or whether the prospect of seeing and hearing the *moujik* saga again proved too much for his Wagner-trained eyes and ears, is not for me to say. Whatever the reasons for Newman's disappearance, he was barred from the Russian Ballet's performances by Diaghilev and in later years never lost an opportunity to make critical mincemeat of the Man Who Almost Pulled His Nose.

Les Noces achieved seven performances and drew full houses. Londoners never got to like that remarkable ballet, but it was "the thing to see" and no dinner conversation was complete without some reference to Stravinsky's masterpiece — flattering or otherwise. I moved to a very sporty flat in Hanover Square and got my tailors to have some unusual cloth specially woven for me — the latest wrinkle in masculine fashion. The enterprising tailor came up with a spectacular number in gun-metal cloth — the only suit of that material ever worn by a male, I'll wager — and the shocked expression of staid dowagers on their first encounter with that creation was a joy to behold. I don't remember what prompted me to choose so outlandish a color, but it's possible that my subconscious helped select gun-metal as a discreet warning to Diaghilev's detractors. Wasn't I a gunman according to my protégé Mr. Lambert?

My life had now assumed a fascinating new pattern. My comparative financial solvency permitted me to travel, and I adopted the habit of shuttling between London and Paris, taking in a few undiscovered spots as well. In this I was often helped by Prokofiev, a passionate traveler himself and an ardent motorist, although the big, clumsy Ballot seemed always to be suffering from some "temporary" disorder.

On my return to Paris, I visited Stravinsky, who told me he thought the Bogdanovitch songs "my best music," talked of his new ballet for Diaghilev (their collaboration was of the "on again-off again" variety) and left for Nice a few days later, inviting me to come spend a week end.

Prokofiev was on vacation in Fontainebleau and wrote me a funny letter in which he congratulated me on becoming a "full-fledged cocotte" (he must have heard of the Diaghilev Trocadero incident), but nevertheless extended a pressing invitation to the cocotte to join him — an "honest composer," as he put it — in his humble retreat. The temptation was great, as no one's company exhilarated me as much as Serge's, but with my two celebrated seniors composing like mad, I realized that I had better get to work myself.

I found just the place for productive solitude in Villennes-sur-Seine, some thirty miles away from Paris, a tiny *pavillon* with what the French coquettishly call *une terrasse fleurie* and a lovely view. Boris came to see me and brought me some notes and notions for the *Three Seasons,* adding that I had better get busy as Diaghilev expected me in Italy in early autumn, with the score at least half completed. Kochno was in good humor, embraced me expansively and set off to Venice to join Sergei Pavlovitch. I spent a restful, bucolic month in Villennes, writing a little music, rowing on the Seine, swimming with occasional visitors and awaiting the Italian visa. With four or five numbers of the ballet completed, I left Villennes for Paris on September 8th, picked up Balanchine, who was to stage not only the *Three Seasons* but also Sacheverell Sitwell's and Lord Berners's *Triumph of Neptune:* the last two were already in Florence, where Diaghilev had established his working headquarters after the annual holiday in his beloved Venice.

Balanchine and I, delighted with the exciting prospect of a collaboration, boarded the train for Turin; disliking the food on the dining car, we got off at Dijon to buy various succulent goodies, ran back and nearly, but not quite, missed the train. On regaining our compartment we ate a whole roasted chicken and drank two bottles of red *ordinaire,* then fell asleep, exhausted and slightly tipsy. On awakening we found ourselves in Turin, where we were to change for Florence, of which fact we were not cognizant. Consequently, we remained in our seats until a tall, bewhiskered Piemontese demanded to see our tickets; on examining them, he informed us in tolerable French (most North Italians speak it) that we had just missed the Florence train and that the train we were on was bound for Milan — that is, in the opposite direction. He sat down, had a drink with us and, becoming very friendly, suggested an escorted tour of Turin — his native city. Since there was no decent train for Florence until night, we happily agreed to the proposal and spent a most edifying afternoon visiting points of interest and not forgetting occasional libations in local bars — our Piemontese seemed to be related to most of the bartenders. Properly fortified, he suggested a visit to the leading brothel.

That establishment proved an ornate, pointedly respectable sort of dwelling with a smiling maid in a starched apron and the sedate, discreetly mannered Madame with aristocratic pretensions. Our conductor-cicerone placed himself modestly in a dark corner, while Balanchine and I discussed the weather in French with Madame. This went on for quite a while, when, like hellish bolts from the blue, two young maids, dark and plump and entirely naked except for jade earrings and necklaces, burst into the "salon" and jumped on our knees without the slightest preamble. Madame smiled and muttered something about youth being *soo-o* impetuous, but George and I were panic-stricken as the bold hussies proceeded covering us with noisy kisses between shouts of: "*Ah, che belli ragazzi.*" We finally shook them off with great difficulty and started a whispered consultation with the conductor, assuring him that we would be happy to pay the girls "for their trouble" but had no intention of partaking of their charms. The Italian, perplexed, stroked his mustache and remarked that such conduct was "out of order" and might offend the good Madame; he then grandly volunteered to take care of both charmers and let us compensate them for their services only because of his own slight pecuniary embarrassment. We thanked him profusely for his manly offer and went on chatting with Madame while our new friend was "in retirement" with the girls. He emerged from the inner sanctum a few minutes later, stroking his mustache with a bit less of a flourish and, as we paid up and took our leave ceremoniously, was heard to confess rather haltingly that he was "not quite as young as he used to be."

On arrival in Florence, we put up at a noisy *albergo* in the commercial part of the city, and then reported to Diaghilev, installed in grand style in the old Hotel Palace on the opposite bank of the Arno. Boris, Lifar, Sacheverell and witty and gifted Gerald Berners (a frequent visitor of Beverley Nichols's, where I first met him) were in the lobby and we all had tea together. After the Englishmen took their leave, Sergei Pavlovitch suggested that I move to the Palace, so that he could "watch over me," also because "you are rich now," he drawled slyly, "so rich, that I won't give you any money for the *Three Seasons* until you finish it." "But, Sergei Pavlovitch . . ." "It's useless to insist. If you need money, you can always get it from Cochran or that mad bricklayer friend of yours." (He was referring to Jimmy White.) "And now we'll all go for a walk. Come along, Serge, Boris, and you, Mr. Balanchivadze." Balanchine was still a little uneasy with Diaghilev, the last of the *grands seigneurs,* an extinct race in Soviet Russia, where George's youth was spent, and there was a touch of courteous coolness in their relationship, although Sergei Pavlovitch thought highly of his new choreographer after *Barabau* and George always admired Diaghilev unreservedly. We went out into the warm evening street and walked in silence, drinking in the incomparable beauty of Florence.

Mother preserved a record of my initial impressions in a letter I wrote her on September 14th from a café in the Piazza Vittorio Emanuele glorying in the name of Bar Sportmen and described by the proprietor as "*L'elegante Ritrovo della Firenze sportiva.*" "This is the most miraculous city of all cities," I wrote (I was later to think that of Venice). "One feels like remaining idle permanently here; it's impossible to do anything except look, think and absorb."

My happiness was intensified by daily walks with Diaghilev, who knew Florence better than any Florentine and who enjoyed our wide-eyed wonder and Lifar's expansive shrieks at discovering more and more beauty wherever we went. In Boboli Gardens Sergei Pavlovitch stopped suddenly, his eyes misty with uncontrollable tears. "To think that one day I must die and not be able to see all this again — ever." We returned to the hotel in silence, our hearts heavy, our youth subdued as it always is when a mortal contemplates immortality.

Diaghilev and Boris were too busy with *Neptune* to worry about me and my lagging ballet, which wasn't progressing too well in spite of all the optimistic things I said about it to Mother. I was just as happy, as Sergei Pavlovitch's preoccupation with the English work enabled me to explore Florence in the company of Harold Acton, whose memoirs succeed in being both witty and petulant, and Violet, Lady Trefusis, who also published a gay record of her comings and goings. We dined at Acton's villa, La Pietra, one of the show spots of Florence, and in Fiesole with Vittorio Rieti, good composer and good companion. On one occasion, I dined *à deux* with Balanchine, whose Italian was as bad as mine — that is, nonexistent — and who, desiring milk and, not finding it on the menu, attempted to describe it to the perplexed waiter in pantomime. On all fours, he made a stupid face and uttered several heart-rending "moos"; the waiter smiled, snapped his fingers, nodded repeatedly and, a few minutes later, triumphantly produced a large steak.

By October 1st, I was back in Paris, although my original plan for the Italian voyage included visits to Rome and Venice. I don't remember the exact reasons for the change in my plans but, in a letter home, I admitted that "traveling alone — even in Italy — can be unbearable." Balanchine was no longer with me, while Diaghilev was too busy raising money for another ballet season; apparently the Berlin venture, although an artistic success, was something of a financial disaster. In Paris, I renewed my friendship with Valitchka Nouvel and Auric, who wrote a musical sketch for Spinelly, the French star, culminating in a rather tentative "fox trot" — a far cry from his 1953 best-selling song from *Moulin Rouge!* Prokofiev was back from Fontainebleau and played me the recently completed fifth sonata, which I found dry and excessively complicated and lost no time in letting it be known to the composer. He blurted out: "You're a fool. Listen again," but before he had a chance to turn the first page, two fashionably dressed American women slipped into the room, led by smiling Lina Ivanovna — all three daintily on tiptoe, but unasked and unwelcome. I knew that Serge, already irritated by my dislike of the sonata, would not stand on ceremony with the intruders, but what ensued was a bit strong even for Prokofiev. He rose from the piano abruptly, crossed his arms on his chest, pursed up his thick lips, puffed out his cheeks and uttered: "Get out!" in English and without raising his voice. The women smiled sheepishly, essayed a cordial greeting, then, realizing the absolute futility of their advances, turned on their heels and meekly trotted out. Prokofiev resumed the sonata and on discovering that I didn't like it any better, threw me out, too, with a short speech in which "lazy London tarts" and "lousy chess players" figured prominently.

It was high time to resume my London chores and try to replenish my wallet, which had shrunken visibly as a result of my continental junket. I played a few excerpts from the *Three Seasons* to Diaghilev before leaving Paris and got a qualifiedly favorable reaction, but not the immediate enthusiasm that had greeted a similar amount of *Zephyr* music. Sergei Pavlovitch said, however, that he'd work on my ballet as soon as he got the *Triumph of Neptune* out of the way.

Owing to economic difficulties, I returned to 55 Torrington Square, a practice which soon became a barometer of my finances. When in funds, I invaded Mayfair — or, at least, Knightsbridge and Chelsea — when broke, returned to Bloomsbury; Mme. Dupont knew me and understood me well — and I was always allowed to stay in her house without paying a penny for food or lodging until the month was up — a most welcome arrangement when one is forced to give up Boulestin's or the Savoy Grill for bread and margarine and fish and chips at a dingy tearoom.

Yvonne, kept alive by Jimmy White, was celebrating its 250th performance, but I had drawn my share of the royalties in advance and my future at Daly's didn't look too rosy. There was an American bandleader in London, Jay Whidden by name, who had replaced me in White's affections while I was luxuriating on the Continent; he was hired by Jimmy to lead a jazz aggregation in a melange of *Yvonne's* tunes and engage in a "Battle of Jazz vs. Music" (as the advertisements read), "music" on this occasion being represented by the amiable Arthur Wood and his pit orchestra. This was done to bolster the box-office receipts, but although the adversaries made a great noise, as did their respective followers, I don't recall any marked improvement in Daly's business. Arthur claimed to have won; nevertheless, Whidden was hired to "Americanize" White's next production, Lehar's *Blue Mazurka* — with only one song of mine added to that score.

This was a blow, as I fully expected to be commissioned to write an original musical for Daly's. Diaghilev's new season did not include *Zephyr and Flora,* and I began to suspect that all wasn't well with the new *Three Seasons.* Asherberg, Hopwood and Crew were still paying me four guineas a week, but even in Torrington Square you couldn't do much with so paltry a sum. The only hope seemed to be Koussevitzky, who asked me to write a symphony for his Paris concerts, was printing the songs and agreeing with Prokofiev that I was the most promising of the new Russians. It would have been a depressing winter were it not for the stacks of engraved invitations reposing grandly on Mme. Dupont's grimy mantelpiece. I now dined out every night and, owing to the easily soiled stiff shirts and backless waistcoats, spent most of my meager earnings on laundry bills. One of my favorite recollections of that winter is the time when I donned a morning coat and striped trousers to lunch at Mrs. Benjamin Guinness's only because all my other clothes were being pressed and I didn't have enough money to redeem them from the tailor's. On starting for Mrs. Guinness's, I debated with myself over the choice between a dark-red carnation for my buttonhole or a ride in the Underground — all I had left in the world was sixpence. Vanity won; I grandly gave up my last coin for a fresh flower, and walked two miles to Mrs. Guinness's, topper, morning coat, tightly rolled umbrella and all — all, that is, except a single penny in my pocket. On arriving at my hostess's fashionably late, I was rewarded by a dowager who appraised my superb attire with great interest and asked coyly: "You're a diplomat, of course. Which South American power, may I ask?"

When not partying, I concentrated on writing salable songs. *Blue Mazurka* opened and, although not without merit, flopped sadly. Three weeks after its opening, I was summoned by Jimmy White — whom I hadn't seen in months — and, on entering his office at Daly's, found that every songwriter in London was there too. White didn't look well and was in one of his "moods." "Gentlemen, I asked you to come here to help me," he started with outward calm. "I have a grand play on my stage, but the people won't come to see it. Why, you may well ask? I'll tell you why, gentlemen . . . because there isn't a good waltz in the whole bludy show!" White now glared at the assembled writers, as though they were responsible for *Blue Mazurka's* deficiency, banged the desk with his fist and came to the point: "Now, I want you, lads, to write me the *greatest* waltz in history — and I pay one thousand pounds to whoever writes it. Arthur Wood, Idris Lewis [his Welsh musical assistant] and I will be the judges — I give you one week. I wish you good day and don't come back without the bludy waltz." We trotted out unhappily, like a horde of backward school children given an overdose of homework by too exacting a teacher.

Nevertheless, most of us, including myself, were back in a week, waltzes in hand, spurred on by that thousand-pound prize. As White listened to each new waltz, he grew gloomier and gloomier, until after a particularly feeble sample by one of the older "boys," he jumped up and roared like a wounded tiger. "No, no, no, dammit — they're no good. The whole bludy lot of 'em. Idris, bring us a mirror." "A mirror, guv'nor?" stammered poor Idris, uncomprehendingly. "That's the idea — a ruddy mirror — I'll show you distinguished barstids a new waltz, since you can't write worth a damn. Now, *get it*." The mirror was produced speedily and Jimmy placed a copy of the "Merry Widow Waltz" on the piano, pushed Idris to the piano stool and shrieked: "Go on — play what you see in the mirror!" A horrified gasp came from those present, but Idris, gritting his teeth, struck up a chord and played the "Merry Widow Waltz" backwards. "That's it — that's what I want. Arthur, have it orchestrated at once — and let that be a lesson to you, gents. Come again!"

The "Mirror Waltz" was never added to the *Blue Mazurka* score, and the show expired after 140 performances. A month after its closing on June 29, 1927, Jimmy White, having failed to bring off a gigantic coup on the stock exchange, committed suicide.

In the early spring of '27 I was again asked by Koussevitzky to play my concerto with him at one of the four Paris concerts he was planning that season. Having lost my faith in that work and knowing it to be too difficult for me, I suggested writing a short piece for piano and orchestra instead. The idea appealed to Koussevitzky and I began work, helping myself to some odds and ends, such as discarded *Zephyr* material and an andantino from the *Three Seasons* which Diaghilev thought too pretty. A letter to Gershwin, dated May 24, 1927, tells of my efforts on both fronts, prior to again invading Paris as composer:

Dear old George:

How is your precious self? I'm dying to see you and to hear the very latest "Georgeousness" as Mrs. Aarons [Producer Alex Aarons' wife] puts it. I congratulate you on "Someone to Watch Over Me" which is excellent — how is "Strike Up the Band"? As to me, I had rather a dreary winter in London — went to fairly boring parties and wrote a lot of music. "Yvonne" ran for 34 weeks but otherwise was the worst show I've ever seen. I sold about ten songs to different managers — two of which are in "Two Little Girls in Blue" [Vincent Youmans's early success with Ira Gershwin's lyrics]. What do you think of "Somebody's Sunday" which Eastman has sent you [a song interpolated into "Little Girls" with lyrics by myself]? I write all my lyrics myself now and find it great fun. [The fun didn't last long.] Jackson [Frederick Jackson, American playwright] and I are working on a show called "Half a Wife." On June 4th I am playing the piano part in my "Sonata" for orchestra which Koussevitzky is doing in Paris. "Zephyr" was played recently by the Boston Symphony and was very well received [a distinct exaggeration.]

Since *Two Little Girls in Blue* was a Chappell publication, I had to be "loaned" to the Dreyfus firm by Billy Allen, who wasn't any too pleased. Neither were the backers of the musical, but for a different reason: the show, in spite of a lilting score ("Oh Me, Oh My" was in it) and a willing, youthful cast headed by the American Barry Oliver, touted as a "Second Astaire," expired on the road. "Half a Wife" was not even half a show, as we stopped working in the middle of Act I. The suite from *Zephyr* gave Bostonians the first taste of my music and, from all accounts, they found it but mildly palatable. Philip Hale, the "Boston Terror," thought more of Boreas than of the amiable Muses. More than once "the hearer was tempted to cry out in the words of the old song: 'Cease, rude Boreas, blustering railer.' "

Sergei Pavlovitch, although giving me the well-known runaround with the projected ballet, was again on the best of terms with me and even flattered me by stating that, although my conduct was "deplorable," my taste in music — *other* people's music — was well-nigh "impeccable." I was by now a little tired of the tra-la-la *musiquette* of the twenties, the salon romps with deliberately banal tunes garnished with spicy "wrong notes" for flavor, and so was Diaghilev, who felt the need for powerful, "muscular" music after too many frivolous confections. I seized the opportunity to resell him on Prokofiev and was helped in this by Nouvel, who couldn't abide the "Chaminade lemonade," as he called the then prevailing Paris musical tendency. I am proud of the part I played in the subsequent *rapprochement* of the two Serges, although it resulted in the commissioning of *Le Pas d'Acier,* a pseudo-Soviet epic. Diaghilev flirted with the Soviets at intervals, intensely interested in Russia's artistic and theatrical life, and was not above shocking his capitalistic listeners by maliciously praising the Communist regime — a pure bit of perverse bravado, as he was mortally afraid of the idea of returning to his native land while the Bolsheviks were still in power. According to Jacques Emile Blanche, "Lenin offered Diaghilev the post of People's commissar for Soviet Stage Production, but in spite of the overpowering curiosity which Serge confessed and the sway which he could exert artistically at Moscow, the fear possessed him that life would be unendurable under the eye of the 'Red Tzar.' "

Whatever the worth of the political aspects of *Le Pas d'Acier* — and Diaghilev was undoubtedly "leading with his chin" with so equivocal a theme: "a hymn to the Soviet Workers" — whatever the merit of the "constructivism" of Yakoulov, the Russian painter and set designer, specially brought over for the production, there was no denying the tremendous vitality and power of Serge's music, startling and invigorating after an overdose of syrup. *Pas d'Acier's* opening night caused another fracas — as did Lambert's jejune *Romeo and Juliet,* not because of the harmless music, but because the Leftists disapproved of painters Ernst and Miró, fellow radicals working for that staunch capitalist Diaghilev! — and Diaghilev was in a state of extreme anxiety, since he felt certain that there would be a terrific uproar, and that "the Russian *émigrés* would stage a mass protest," in Lifar's words. There was no mass protest but plenty of noise, deafening cheers and piercing catcalls; Lifar is, certainly, wrong in recording that "the performance was received calmly, even tepidly."

I sat in Diaghilev's box with Prokofiev, and, when he returned from backstage, flushed with his success and bewildered by the anti-Russian outbreaks in the audience, I asked him to come out for a smoke and talk things out. Once in the corridor, I told Serge of my great admiration for the massive, sinewy music of his ballet, which, in my opinion, would deliver a crushing blow to the decadent Parisian *musiquette*. No sooner had I uttered that last word, the only French word in the entire speech, when Cocteau appeared from out of nowhere, screamed out: "*Dima, les Parisiens t'envoyent de la merde!*" and slapped me, then vanished just as suddenly as he came, before I had a chance of retaliating. Prokofiev opened his mouth in astonishment, but was immediately whisked away, as he was urgently needed backstage; I ran down the corridor in pursuit of Cocteau, who must have ducked into his box as I couldn't find him. A minute later I ran into Diaghilev, white as a sheet, who grabbed me by the lapel and whispered: "I know all about Jean. Whatever you do, don't start a fight here in the theater; I'm having enough trouble with the authorities already . . . we could all be deported. No fight, understand?" I understood, but at this point began seething with uncomprehending rage, because, outside of the words "Paris" and "*musiquette*" Cocteau couldn't possibly have grasped the meaning of my tirade since he spoke no Russian; I therefore shook Diaghilev off, assuring him that I wouldn't do anything rash, and raced on, hoping to get the elusive Cocteau. Soon he appeared, several "disciples" in tow, waving his arms, and cried out hysterically as he saw me: "*Rends-moi ma gifle, Dima, rends-moi ma gifle. . . . Battons-nous.*" Remembering Diaghilev's orders, I composed myself, as best I could and said in measured tones, "You're wearing a summer suit, Jean, whereas I have my best tailcoat on; I have no intention of ruining it . . . therefore, I won't fight you here, but hereby challenge you to a duel." "A duel?" Cocteau shrieked, taken aback momentarily. "I have never used firearms in my life. Slap me, slap me back at once, coward!" I was about to throw myself at the man when some members of the Diaghilev entourage pulled me back and admonished me to stick to my promise to Sergei Pavlovitch.

I then arranged with two ex-officers of the Wrangel army who were in the audience to act as my seconds and told Prokofiev of my challenge to Cocteau. I was about to leave the theater when Mrs. Paitchadze, the publisher's wife, appeared in our box, greatly agitated, and implored me not to leave by the stage door as Cocteau was making an inflammatory anti-Russian, anti-Dukelsky speech to a large crowd of "admirers" and I would, doubtless, be torn to shreds were I to show myself. This so incensed me that I pushed the good woman aside and went backstage at such a clip that she had to run fast to catch up with me. There was a sizable crowd outside the stage entrance, with Jean, somewhat Hyde Park-oracle fashion in his light-tan gabardine suit with shocking-pink lining displayed by artfully unbuttoned sleeves, leaning on Desbordes, his newest "literary" discovery, addressing *les Parisiens* and shaking his bony fists. The moment he saw me, out went a long oracular finger, and stopping in the middle of a grandiose sentence, he cried menacingly: "Beware, Dima!" The effect of this cry was somewhat doubtful as no one in the group of *les Parisiens* knew who in hell "Dima" was; Dima contented himself with promising to send his seconds to 10 rue d'Anjou (where Cocteau lived) in the morning and was quickly whisked away in a taxi by Mme. Paitchadze.

My "seconds" ruefully admitting that they couldn't get past Cocteau's servant the next morning, I donned my morning coat with striped trousers and drove to Cocteau's house. Jean's servant opened the door, and perceiving so splendid a visitor, admitted me with a hesitant bow and bade me wait. I heard an agitated whispered conversation behind doors and a few minutes later the master emerged, pale and visibly nervous. "So you want to be slapped back?" I said steadily. "Here you are," and slapped him without awaiting a reply. "*Now* — will you accept my challenge?" The effect of my action was most unexpected: Cocteau grabbed me in his arms, embraced me and sang out: *"Embrassons-nous, Dima, embrassons-nous!"* I disengaged myself with some difficulty and left, utterly nonplussed. A day later Diaghilev received a letter from Cocteau explaining his reasons for declining a duel with me and describing my "cowardly" visit to him. We haven't spoken since.

I now had other things to worry about. My hastily contrived sonata for piano and orchestra (I didn't dare call it concertino) was announced by Koussevitzky and rehearsals were about to start. Sergei Alexandrovitch Koussevitzky then lived in Auteuil and held court daily. Most of his visitors were composers — good and bad, young and old; they sat around, scores in hand, drinking tea poured by inscrutable Natalya Konstantinovna (his second wife) and smiling politely at one another. In contrast with Diaghilev, "partisan of a chosen few," who closed his eyes and ears to everything that he instinctively felt was "not for him," Koussevitzky's tastes were determinedly eclectic. It was not, however, the usual eclecticism of an unprincipled conductor, not a mere passion for "first performances" (the conductors' occupational disease) but an unflagging curiosity about all genuinely "new" music. "Write it — and I'll play it." This typically direct approach gave many a struggling and disappointed composer an incentive to work. Starting with a championship of Russians — Scriabin, Stravinsky and Prokofiev, whose music he not only performed whenever and wherever possible, but also published *in toto,* Koussevitzky lent an untiring hand to Schoenberg, Berg, Bartók and Hindemith — at the time when such "shockers" spelled certain death at the box office — unwieldy and unpopular French "lone wolves" like Albert Roussel, and little-known Russian refugees like Obouhov, Vogel, Lourié, Berezowsky and Lopatnikov. Most of these men were constant visitors; I remember particularly courteous and self-effacing Albert Roussel, who liked my music and wrote flatteringly about it; also Ravel, with his fine face and elaborately elegant clothes, who didn't care for my *Zephyr* and told Prokofiev that "Diaghilev made a mistake by sponsoring the young man." Some composers arrived with their wives, always warmly welcomed by Koussevitzky, particularly when they were pretty like Mesdames Tansman, Lazar and Ferroud. The husband of the last-named was an extraordinarily active man, always busy with running music societies, making valuable "contacts," writing articles, going off on mysterious music missions in the remotest corners of Europe, a man full of good learning, good ideas and good will but, unfortunately, a dry and dull composer. Ferroud formed the important Triton, a modern chamber music society, and saw a great deal of Prokofiev, whose brusque manner he imitated, and whose services he enlisted on behalf of the organization; he died tragically, at the age of thirty-six, in a horrible motor accident. Poor Filip Lazar, a handsome Roumanian, his devoted friend, couldn't endure life without Ferroud and died a few months later.

Koussevitzky's Paris concerts, financed by Natalya Konstantinovna, were not too well attended, and caused her to grumble a bit about the determinedly "uncommercial" programs, but her adoration for her husband was such that she never dared to protest openly, preferring to voice her discontent when he wasn't present. I recall sitting in her box when a particularly insipid concoction of Ferroud's was being performed; the applause was meager, but Ferroud, his face shining, kissed the lady's hand, and exclaimed, "Beautifully played!" Whereupon she whispered in my ear: " . . . and wretchedly composed."

My so-called sonata was well-enough liked by musicians; Souvtchinsky ran up to me after the performance shouting: "The purest champagne!" But it was, in reality, distinctly small beer. In style it was not unlike *Zephyr,* but my repertoire of Russo-classical tricks was now exhausted and this kind of amiable music was no step forward, dangerously akin as it was to the selfsame *musiquette.* As to the notorious Oxford bags previously described, I should have remembered the remark made to foppish Whistler by Degas: "You dress as if you had no talent." Koussevitzky thought the sonata meritorious, the critics were kind and I was told to complete the symphony, for which I stored away some rather promising thematic material.

Following my shaky debut as piano soloist, the Prokofievs and I went on a long motor trip to the Haute Savoie mountains — Sofronitzky, the pianist, and his wife, Scriabin's daughter, were also with us. The trip, in spite of the unsurpassable food we ate (it was because of these early gastronomic trips with Prokofiev that I began to put on weight and lose my Karsavinesque looks) proved something of a sore trial, because of the constant quarrels between the Prokofievs, terminating in Jupiter-like shouts from Serge and copious tears from Lina. On my return to Paris, I wrote an article for Souvtchinsky's Eurasian magazine *Versty* (Miles) on Diaghilev and his work. In it was my first, as yet indirect, criticism of Stravinsky's "neo-classical" period, which has since ceased to be merely a period (in the Picasso sense) but has become the composer's settled and only manner.

My disillusion in Stravinsky, man and musician both, began a year earlier, when I dined at his house in Nice and listened to him talk. A day or two prior to this dinner, the invitation to which flattered and excited me, I ran into Nika Nabokov, who, on learning of my good luck, asked me to show Igor Fedorovitch his piano sonata; I said that I would be happy to do so and took the manuscript along. Stravinsky received me with the utmost cordiality; we drank vodka, talked music and sat down to a copious family dinner with Mrs. Stravinsky and the children. What astonished me was the passionate anti-Diaghilev monologue into which the composer plunged almost immediately on my arrival. Omitting the more personal barbs, I can recall Stravinsky's ire at the "execrable" orchestral performances, the cynicism with which his music was mutilated, the disgracefully inadequate rehearsals, etc., etc. Worshipping Diaghilev as I did and knowing full well the shaky finances of his organization (it was a miracle that it existed at all, as money had to be raised at the eleventh hour every season), realizing that before me sat a Diaghilev-made composer, who owed Diaghilev his entire career, I became intensely uncomfortable. It was not for me, a hopeful beginner, to contradict the master, but, profoundly grateful as I was for being "put on my feet" by Sergei Pavlovitch, by the touching care with which he prepared *Zephyr* for production, I restrained myself with difficulty from what would have been an unpleasant argument and kept silent. I showed Stravinsky the Nabokov sonata, and, after perusing it carefully, he pronounced it "not stupid."

The after-dinner conversation centered mainly around my host and his recent appearance as pianist at the Venice festival of the International Society for Contemporary Music. It seems that Stravinsky had been contracted to play his piano sonata at the festival for a five-hundred-dollar fee. A short while before leaving for Venice, he got an infected finger and was seized by fear of being unable to appear at the concert; on the eve of that event he visited a church and prayed fervently for his finger's recovery. Stravinsky appeared on the concert platform, his finger bandaged, and made a short speech of apology, pointing to the bandage and begging the audience's indulgence. Just before attacking the sonata, he removed the bandage and, Eureka! — the infection had subsided and the finger functioned normally. All this was told with pontifical, profound seriousness — the manner always adopted by Stravinsky when talking about himself. Four years later I glanced at the score of the *Symphony of Psalms* (1930), in my opinion the last of Stravinsky's important works — and, probably, his best — and was not startled to read on the back of the title page: "This symphony composed to the *Glory of God,* is dedicated to the Boston Symphony Orchestra on the occasion of its fiftieth anniversary."

No sooner did I return to London than the shocking news of Jimmy White's suicide rocked the town. The future of Daly's now appeared uncertain and I had to seek employment elsewhere. My sonata's half failure and Koussevitsky's generous readiness to perform my symphony — should I write it — made me feel like doing serious work again, particularly since Billy Allen was no Dreyfus and couldn't hand me a new show on a platter. I was overjoyed when Sir David and Lady Baird asked me to spend a month or two with them in their place at Newbyth in southern Scotland. I brought reams of manuscript paper and very fancy golf clothes, since the Bairds and their friends golfed daily at North Berwick. I had never wielded a golf club before, and the dour old professional at the club said I had "no golfing ability whatsoever" after two lessons. This didn't faze me unduly, as just to inhale the extraordinary air of Scotland, go sight-seeing in Edinburgh with Jean, Sir David's redheaded daughter, and flirt strenuously with Rosemary Hope-Vere, another deservedly well-advertised beauty of the period, were enough to make me forget my Paris tribulations and London debts, which were accumulating fast, the reminders and bills causing the Bairds' letter box to swell suspiciously.

The symphony "wrote itself" in such ideal surroundings, but was unusually short — only sixteen minutes of music; the first and last movements had a lot of Prokofiev about them, the slow lusciously Italianate cantilena of the middle one was yanked bodily out of the dormant *Three Seasons.*

Lady Baird, a kind and worldly woman of the Victorian-matriarch variety, occasionally entertained Americans, and I always marveled at the highly "special" manner in which they were treated. U. S. visitors she considered quaint, colorful, oddly provincial and not altogether civilized. "One must never forget that they are really cowboys and Indians in Savile Row clothes. I like all colonials, mind you," she said to me, "but they *are* quaint, aren't they? The other day a rich woman from Chicago, or some such place, came to tea; I thought her rather attractive and asked her to dine. 'Is it going to be *formal?*' the woman wanted to know. 'Formal? No, indeed; gay and spontaneous, I hope.' " Lady Baird was maternally fond of me, but I, too, baffled her. I wasn't a bona fide White Russian as I had no title and wrote music for a living. I came from America without being American, and looked and talked not unlike her daughter's "aesthetic" English friends, without being English. "I suspect you are what's known as 'cosmopolitan' nowadays, my dear," Lady Baird sighed. "I'm not sure it's a good thing to be. Cosmopolitans have no roots, you know — neither have Americans. I think you'd do well to marry an American girl." I'm afraid the good woman suggested such a step because she was aware of the attentions I lavished on some of her daughter's friends. She needn't have worried — English and Scottish girls are just as good as any other at spotting the "right" man, and there was nothing "right" about me, except my clothes.

On my return to London, I teamed up with Jimmy Dyrenforth for a song, "For Goodness' Sake," which we sold to the producers of a typically British "intimate" revue, entitled *Bow-Wows;* the ditty, sung by Elsie Gregory, was perhaps my first respectable effort in the idiom and had an unusual rhythmic pattern, which attracted some attention. Among the attentive ones was Julian Wylie, the pantomime producer, who had West End ambitions. I was broke again and getting discouraged; my spirits rose instantly when Wylie, a large, bilious, warm-hearted man, began sounding me out as to "terms." I had no agent and would have accepted anything within reason, but Wylie was not ungenerous and offered me 1 per cent of the gross receipts as well as £150 advance to compose the music for the *Yellow Mask,* Edgar Wallace's heterodox attempt to wed a "mystery thriller" to a musical comedy. Prior to signing me up, Wylie insisted on hearing a few tunes from my pen, and when I obliged, complained about the lack of rhythm in my performance. "The only thing those American chaps have is rhythm — can't say much for their melody. Your chunes are catchy but where's the rhythm?" He swallowed his tea and sighed. "Have you ever heard Maisie ply?" I didn't know any Maisie and apologized. "Smith, send Maisie in," Wylie said lugubriously to his secretary. "She is a wizard on the pianoforte, that she is." Maisie, a tall, bony peroxide blonde with teeth large enough to serve as piano keys, entered, beaming. "Maisie, ply us a chorus of 'Dardanella,' there's a love," Wylie asked. The blonde rattled off the chorus, 14th Street player-piano fashion, stomping her foot and lifting the pinky refinedly at the end of each flourish. Wylie and I drank more tea and applauded. I got my contract. Laddie Cliff was to direct and co-produce, Desmond Carter (he was being "lent" by Dreyfus — hallelujah!) to write the lyrics, Aubrey Hammond — then top man in his field — to design the scenery and Bobbie Howes, West End's most promising young comic, to get his big chance in the play.

I lived again. Poor Mme. Dupont read the papers and knew all the symptoms; four times I had achieved temporary solvency and four times, having achieved it, hastened to leave her hospitable but depressingly ugly oasis in Torrington Square. This time, I knew I'd not return, and so did Mme. Dupont, who invited me to a "farewell tea," her still-handsome wrinkle-ridden face even sadder than usual. She also asked the other "distinguished" but evasive tenant, one F. A. K. Dale, a mammoth of a man in his seventies, a solicitor by profession and a wretched bassoon player in his spare moments. F.A.K. had a rich and mysterious past in which peers of the realm, Gaiety girls, and polo players in India played a significant part; I always suspected that Dale spent some years in prison for I know not what offense, as his reminiscences (often startlingly purple-shaded) went only so far as the turn of the century — then he'd sigh deeply, imbibe some cheap port, light a pipe and mumble something about, "Fortune, that faithless jade." The faithless jade had not been treating the old boy right for quite some time, as he barely eked out a living in an unspeakably dingy office in the City, bereft of a telephone or secretary, and was hopelessly behind in his rent. On Mme. Dupont's suggestion, I took him on as a C.P.A., or whatever the English term for that office is; at this Dale proved surprisingly successful, as he had his own vastly effective methods of dealing with the income-tax people. He'd write them interminable and scarcely legible epistles about his clients' predicaments, their ailing aunts and unemployed brothers, their "essential" expenses far exceeding their income and so on. The Crown would reply impatiently, admonishing Dale to stick to the facts and send a check pronto; another twelve-page letter would follow, another still more impatient rejoinder, and so the matter would drag on for months until the Government representatives would give in and settle for one tenth of what was coming to them. I doubt that Dale's method would have had much success in this country.

The *Yellow Mask* rehearsals started on October 20th, and with the help of Wylie's advance, I was able to send Mother some much needed funds. It was gratifying to be surrounded by experts — people like busy, ferretlike Laddie Cliff; Leslie Henson, the English Bobby Clark, at whom I had laughed in the Gershwin musicals and who was lending "valuable assistance"; huge, gloomy-faced Aubrey Hammond; and the Master of Mystery himself, Edgar Wallace, a bland, impassive individual with an extra-long cigarette holder and the precise manner of a successful stockbroker. Volatile Bobby Howes was bent on a "killing" (which he accomplished, as the *Yellow Mask* catapulted him into stardom); Malcolm Keen strutted and ranted as the villainous Li-San, governor of the province of Chi-Fu; and London's favorite, Phyllis Dare was archly genteel as Mary Bannister, the heroine, complete with the parasol without which where would British musical comedy be?

Wallace, almost as good a drumbeater as C. B. Cochran, called Julian Wylie The Rajah of Revue and wrote an amusing "close-up" of the producer for the London *Tit-bits* in connection with our rehearsals: " 'The trouble with this piece,' Wylie said gloomily, surveying the empty stage, 'is that it's British. All the artists are British; you're more or less British.' 'I am a Wallace,' I said, coldly. 'Haven't you seen my tartan? Vernon Duke isn't British, his name is Dukelsky and he's a Russian; so how can you say —' 'For the purpose of his play, he's British,' said Julian, stolidly. 'Anyway, he's not American. Don't tell me he was with George Gershwin for two years, because I know it. We haven't a single American number or a single American comedian — that's going to ruin us!' " The non-American musical show was already a drug on the London market in 1927, but the *Yellow Mask* did not ruin Wylie — far from it, as it achieved quite a success, although not of gold-mine proportions. We opened in Birmingham to unanimously excellent notices and crowded houses.

I returned from the provinces encouraged by the show's reception and, especially, by the royalty checks that began to come in regularly, once the advance money was deducted. Prokofiev arrived in London to play a recital and it was good to get back to "music talk" after English theatrical slang, which is a queer mixture of Cockney and Broadway. Serge listened to "Dushenka," a prettily melodious effusion in the Russo-Italianate manner, and was especially curious about the symphony, which I had completed while rehearsing the *Yellow Mask*. He liked both, made some insulting remarks about "Dushenka's" orchestration and demanded that I score the symphony without delay, offering to help me should "prostitution" interfere. Prokofiev brought me a program sent on to him from Kiev on which my Bogdanovitch songs figured surprisingly; the singer's name was unfamiliar to me, but I had quite a pang on seeing B. Yavorsky (my Kiev teacher) listed as accompanist. While considered a "decadent bourgeois" and a "lackey of bloodthirsty capitalists," Serge somehow managed to get performances in Soviet Russia and even appear in concert in larger cities there. Since he never talked politics, I thought it best not to question him too closely about conditions in Russia. He jokingly offered to become my musical salesman and said that he was engineering a production of *Zephyr* in Moscow, "to annoy Diaghilev," he added, exploding with laughter. I was wise enough to refrain from exhibiting the luckless *Three Seasons,* except for the andantino, now the middle movement of the symphony, the movement he particularly liked. We dined at Simpson's in the Strand, drank a great deal of lager and wound up in a gaudy night club called the Silver Slipper. A loudly dressed tart brushed past us and suddenly stopped with a wide-eyed stare at me. I wanted to duck but it was too late — Sally, my Monte Carlo nemesis, stood before me. "Blimey, if it isn't the Monte boy wonder. . . . You're getting fat, me lad," she screeched familiarly. "I wouldn't dare to talk to a man you treated so shabbily, if I were you," I retorted stiffly, and motioned to Prokofiev, inviting him to leave the place. "On our 'igh 'orse, ain't we, your 'ighness?" Sally rattled on scornfully. We hastened out into the fresh air; I remained stubbornly silent and wouldn't explain anything to Prokofiev. He left in the morning with a promise to write Koussevitzky about the symphony and with an invitation to join him on a gastronomic tour of the South of France, which I accepted ecstatically.

I had abandoned Bloomsbury for Chelsea — 14 Church Street, to be exact — to be near the Embankment, which I loved. Carlyle Square didn't mean much to me any longer as I was on the outs with the Sitwells and saw less and less of Walton, who was always either in Rome or Amalfi; but Tony Gandarillas, art-loving South American diplomat, was nearby in Cheyne Walk, where I often dined with him and Christopher Wood, the promising painter who died before fulfilling his promise, or, occasionally, George Auric, who always put up at Tony's when in London; the Beaufort-Palmers, Francis and Sylvia, were practically across the street, and Ewart Garland in Paultons Gardens, a few blocks away. Ewart, who was good to be with because his brow was neither too high nor too low and his heart very much in the right place, became my everyday companion and we delighted in roaming London and the countryside in his trusty little Lea Francis. Through Ewart I acquired Gibbs, a non-Jeevesian manservant with a talent for cooking, answering the telephone glibly, and evasively when necessary, drinking my liquor unnoticeably and, as I found out later, padding my bills outrageously. He was pious and patriarchal-looking, somewhat on the lines of Dickens's Rev. Stiggins, with a nose of lush, tropical redness and a manner that went beautifully with my Jacobean furniture, Staffordshire dogs on the mantelpiece (no self-respecting

Londoner would live without them) and the soft candlelight which was my only illumination — the flat had no electrictiy and I was allergic to gas, except in Victorian novels.

On February 8, 1928, the *Yellow Mask* opened at the Carlton Theater in London with every evidence of lasting success — not the "biggest home-bred musical comedy success for years and years," as the *Daily Mail* put it, but a sizable one nevertheless. Alan Parsons, whom I saw at all the better parties, gave me this pat on the back: "Not so long ago I had the pleasure of congratulating M. Vladimir Dukelsky on the score of the ballet 'Zephyr and Flora.' I have the same pleasure in congratulating Mr. Vernon Duke on the music of the 'Yellow Mask.'" The first-night audience had almost a Russian Ballet-opening elegance and shouted its approval when Wallace, complete with a yard-long cigarette holder, made a deft little speech of thanks. I spotted Willie Walton in the intermission; his greeting was of the coolish variety, which rather upset me, but not for long — there was a party at Wallace's after the show and I was to fetch my girl of the moment backstage.

All we needed now was full houses; they were full for three or four months, then business began tapering off, for reasons that were not quite clear to anybody — they never are in the theater.

Whatever side of the ledger the *Yellow Mask* finished on, it did well enough for the rest of the year (1928) to enable me to take a deep breath, followed by a long pleasure trip. Gershwin wrote to congratulate me on the success of my "first complete score" and announced his impending arrival in Europe — this time family fashion, with sister Frances, brother Ira, and Ira's good-looking wife, Leonore, known to all Gershwinites as Lee. After a flying visit to London (where I barely missed them, having just left for France) the Gershwins alighted at the selfsame Hotel Majestic where I had first set up residence in Paris. True to my 1928 form, I paid them a call attired in the already-described gunmetal creation (now a little tight for me), a pale-yellow Sulka shirt, an orchid in my buttonhole, the whole structure supported by a magnificent eighteenth-century walking stick, a Christmas present from myself, purchased in Bath. So staggering a façade didn't fail to render the Gershwins speechless; they stared at me, then at one another, then back at me, and had good enough manners not to laugh out loud.

Ira Gershwin describes that memorable meeting in his diary:

"Paris, April 6th Friday (Weather — sunshine at last). Letter from Selwyn to George saying 'Strike Up the Band' would be done next season. All of us happy about it. Dukelsky came in for an hour or so. Argued with George about parts of 'American in Paris' saying that George was 1928 in his musical comedies and in most of his concert music but that in 'A.I.P.' he allowed himself to become somewhat saccharine in spots. When he left, Walton, an English composer friend of George's and Dukelsky's in London came in. Played us a parody waltz, a tune and part of his symphony which had been done recently by Koussevitzky. All pretty bad. Walton told George to disregard Dukelsky's advice as Duke was influenced by Prokofiev and thought anyone who wrote in another style old-fashioned; also, that nothing of Duke's had become popular, etc., etc., Most interesting what they all think of one another."

I was then ignorant of Willie's reappraisal of myself and was delighted to run into him in Koussevitzky's music shop. We chatted gaily and arranged to display our recent work to one another. I played my three-movement piano sonata, written that spring for Borovsky (who never learned it), which Willie seemed to like; he did make a remark which, in the light of the recently unearthed Ira Gershwin testimony, appears understandable — it rather stung me at the time. "Very good, Vladimir," Willie said. "I'm really amazed because I was told in London that you didn't write *music* any longer."

I then went to see Prokofiev, who knew I still wrote music and was doing everything in his power to get it played. Armed with gastronomic guides, cook books and treatises on the wine industry, we drove in the Ballot — just the two of us — with the minimum of luggage and a huge chess set in the trunk of the car. Our schedule was simplicity itself — we'd spend the night at an inn in the country, get up early, breakfast on coffee and *croissants,* and push off to the nearest gastronomic citadel. Proudly flashing our gourmets' manuals, we'd be escorted to the best table, given the best service and regaled with the best that the house could offer. We never hesitated ordering another *specialité* if the first proved to be up to snuff. It was at the Hôtel Commerce et Poste in Perigueux that I made an utter pig of myself; having fallen in love with the extravagantly caloried *pâté de foie gras* for which the region is noted, I bought a pound of it from the *maître d'hôtel* when Serge wasn't looking. On awakening the next morning, I ordered the usual frugal breakfast and, when it arrived, unpacked the delicacy and began gulping it down, smearing it on the hot *croissants* and taking great care not to masticate so vigorously as to awaken Prokofiev, who snored peacefully in the adjoining room. Small wonder that I was ill the rest of the day, to Prokofiev's intense annoyance; no sooner was he rid of women, he complained, than here he was stuck with an invalid. I paid the penalty of not being served the best *bouillabaisse* in Toulon the next day at lunch, and watched Prokofiev devour two huge helpings of it. In the evening we arrived in Monte Carlo to pay a visit to Diaghilev, then preparing the new ballets — Stravinsky's *Apollon* and Nabokov's *Ode*. It was Serge's idea; he wanted me to play the symphony to Sergei Pavlovitch and get him to reconsider the abandoned *Three Seasons*. On entering the administrator's quarters, I saw Sergei Pavlovitch, Boris and Nabokov, whose greeting was cordial and worried — it was now his turn to earn his place in the sun.

I don't think Nabokov's music ever really excited Diaghilev, although there were several good things in *Ode*, a badly integrated ballet whose abstract scenery had no connection whatever with the ultra-Russian Glinkaesque music. In Lifar's testimony: "The *Ode* frankly bewildered Diaghilev, both in its music and choreography, and he could hardly decide to allow us to put it on. It did not interest him at all."

I wasn't pleased at having to play my symphony with another prospective Diaghilev child in the room (although Nabokov never got to be the "fourth" son, Markevitch earning that distinction in 1929), but Sergei Pavlovitch was most encouraging and so I tore into the opening *energico*. On getting to the end of the slow movement, I suddenly realized to my horror that I had just played the big *pas de deux* from the *Three Seasons*, the piece Diaghilev had already heard. I didn't dare to look at the man and charged into the bustling finale at breakneck speed. When it was all over, Nabokov and Kochno looked at each other enigmatically. Diaghilev was on his best diplomatic behavior and all he said was: "A very good symphony, but I like *Zephyr* better." How often was I to hear similar, maddening observations in later years! Eugene Goossens, whom I'd meet every five years or so, when shown a new work of mine would exclaim dreamily: "Ah, *Zephyr and Flora* — *there* was a score!" In the commercial field, all I have to do is demonstrate a song to the head of a recording company for him to moan: "Gee, that 'April in Paris' — *there* was a song!" I often wonder why Leoncavallo, who never wrote anything decent outside of *Pagliacci,* or Charpentier, who couldn't top *Louise,* didn't put bullets through their heads. Prokofiev tried to console me by remarking dryly that Diaghilev had a "better taste in boys than he has in music," but I couldn't help feeling depressed, until the next gastronomic *étape* restored my spirits somewhat.

At the end of our three-week trip I was at least fifteen pounds heavier and couldn't get into my clothes. Without a doctor's advice I put myself on a murderous diet of lemon-and-orange juice and pickled fish virtually soaked in vinegar, and black coffee; such is the resistance of youth that I experienced no dangerous aftereffects and lost a lot of weight, only to regain it on eating normally for one week. These ups and downs became a regular and most troublesome part of my life after that trip with Prokofiev; when encountering a friend I haven't seen for a month, I'm always greeted with, "Putting on weight, aren't you?" or, "You don't look so good to me — getting too skinny." I've been on every imaginable diet through these twenty-five years and found them all excellent and most efficient *if* you become a recluse and stick to them. What happens if you dine out four times a week? Try and ask your hostess to serve you a half a carrot and two cups of shredded black figs with a teaspoon of lemon juice and a glass of soybean milk.

On May 29th, I took both Diaghilev and Prokofiev to hear Gershwin's piano concerto played by Dimitri Tiomkin at a concert in the Paris Opéra conducted by Vladimir Golschmann. Whether the fault lay with the French musicians, notoriously allergic to jazz, or with Mr. Tiomkin, an able pianist, but certainly no Gershwin, I cannot say. Diaghilev shook his head and muttered something about "good jazz and bad Liszt," whereas Prokofiev, intrigued by some of the pianistic invention, asked me to bring George to his apartment the next day. George came and played his head off; Prokofiev liked the tunes and the flavorsome embellishments, but thought little of the concerto (repeated by Gershwin), which, he said later, consisted of 32-bar choruses ineptly bridged together. He thought highly of Gershwin's gifts, both as composer and pianist, however, and predicted that he'd go far should he leave "dollars and dinners" alone.

One afternoon at Koussevitzky's I met a tall, stooping, hawk-faced young man who, Sergei Alexandrovitch told me in Russian, was the new "white hope" of American music and who answered to the name of Aaron Copland. A short piece of his had been conducted by Golschmann at the Tiomkin concert and didn't give me enough of an idea of the man's talent. Copland seemed intelligent and was flatteringly impressed by my dandiacal air and radical views on music, aired with complete disdain of established values and reputations; I bought him a drink at Fouquet's and we spent an agreeable hour talking music.

My first symphony was by now orchestrated (with Prokofiev's help), copied and accepted for performance by Koussevitzky, who was preparing for his annual invasion of Paris concert life. Meanwhile, I was elated to hear of my brother Alex's successful graduation from M.I.T.; he had received a Fontainebleau Scholarship and was about to sail for Europe.

The program of Koussevitzky's concert, which took place on June 14th, contained the first performance of Prokofiev's *Angel of Fire* (fragments of his opera of that name) as well as that of my symphony. I sat with the Prokofievs and the Paitchadzes and it was thrilling to bow from the box from which Serge also took his bow. In spite of so formidable a companion piece, my music apparently held its own. Koussevitzky was much gratified by the symphony's reception and programed it for his next Boston season. He wired Mother: "Dima's symphony dedicated to you. Wonderful piece. Great success at my concert, Paris. Congratulations."

Alex arrived a few days later, bronzed and happy and very collegiate. I met his train at the Gare St. Lazare and he had difficulty in recognizing me — that's how much I had changed in the four years since we had seen each other. He was surrounded by rah-rah boys and girls bent on raising a little traditional Franco-American hell. I wound up my Paris affairs and, accompanied by Ewart Garland, joined Alex in Fontainebleau a week later. My brother's enthusiasm for everything French, especially food and scenery, was contagious, and I loved impersonating a true Parisian and showing him the sights.

Then Garland and I ventured to Germany, for the excellent reason that we had never been there. I don't think anyone ever disliked Berlin as much as I did. For sheer ugliness you couldn't beat the misshapen Berliners with their robotlike, ill-fitting clothes and evil-smelling cigars, porcine necks and triple chins; or the ludicrous and pathetic make-up on Kurfurstendamm fairies. The two musical *Schlagers* of the season (1928) were crude exercises in Americanomania. One was *Jonny Spielt Auf,* Krenek's tuneless and jazzless jazz opera; the other was *Evelyne,* an elephantine operetta by Bruno Von Granichstadten, fully as unpalatable and Teutonic as the composer's name. The badly lipsticked and atrociously garbed chorus girls kicked sausagelike legs and shrilled, "Yes," "Okay," and "Get hot," at the top of their beer-greased lungs, to the accompaniment of three trombones, a tuba and the inevitable celeste and xylophone, all played in unison, which, to anyone familiar with German musical comedy, is an orchestrator's "must."

I didn't exactly expect a Welcome Home demonstration on my return to London, but thought that with *Zephyr,* a show running in the West End, and a successfully *premièred* symphony, I would instantly go on to bigger and better things. To my dismay, I soon realized that my three accomplishments were not of triumphant, definitive caliber — that *Zephyr* was already forgotten, the *Yellow Mask* on the skids and the symphony unknown to London. I learned, too, that ballet composers, while perfectly acceptable in their frivolous sphere, were not easily transplantable into the loftier symphonic regions of England. Ballet was bad enough in the eyes of the saturnine satraps who ruled that country's musical opinion, but all that "Vernon Duke" nonsense was really inexcusable; to this day, the august B.B.C. hasn't touched a note of my music.

In the realm of the commercial theater I could have said with Denry in Arnold Bennett's *The Card* that "I had committed the sin of not being a native of England." Although the *Yellow Mask* was no box-office smash and producers were in no hurry to sign me up, a regular hue and cry began in the London press on the subject of "alien" composers taking the bread out of their native colleagues' mouths and coining fortunes in the West End. Especially noisy was Hannen Swaffer, who resorted to editorials denouncing American and other "alien" influences in musical comedy and leading the pack of the "England for the English" journalists. Swaffer's taste in music was nil and in his patriotic zeal he always backed the wrong horse — his first all-British musical "must" was a fiasco named *Lumber Love* (there's a title for you) with music by Emmett Adams, celebrated for the "Bells of Saint Mary's" and nothing else, and *Eldorado* (1930), another total flop, composed by one Rutland Clapham, according to Hannen, "worth six of these ordinary musical comedies." Not that all English musicals were that bad — Cochran's revues were way ahead of their time, as in addition to first-rate composers and lyricists he engaged important painters (not glorified interior decorators) to do his scenery and bona-fide choreographers (not ex-tap dancers); but Cockie was no chauvinist and had a distinct penchant for foreign imports — Delysia (a Frenchwoman) was his favorite star in the twenties, Massine and later Balanchine his favorite choreographers, and he commissioned entire scores to suspicious aliens like Rodgers and Hart and Cole Porter.

I didn't at once perceive the noose that was slowly tightening around my neck. Fourteen Church Street was still old Chelsea at its best, Gibbs's cooking was still impeccable, the Staffordshire dogs grinned at me just as encouragingly, the candles shone as brightly of an evening and so did the eyes of my rapidly changing female companions. Among the new "bucks" were two colorful and rich giants — the Honorable Richard Wyndham, painter and writer, and Sir Anthony (Tony) Lindsay-Hogg, the last of the true dandies, daredevil driver, flyer and lover, who married Bunny Doble in 1930, divorced her a year later, then became and remained a warm and generous friend and fellow adventurer. We all lived within walking distance of one another and it was correct Chelsea behavior to drop in at a friend's place at an ungodly hour, drink his liquor and walk away with his girl if she and the host were agreeable, which they often were. At times, such exchanges were difficult, as when one of us paid a visit to a friend, a notorious sadist, and found their mutual inamorata strapped to the garage door, while his "friendly" rival was whipping her furiously and with evident relish. The visitor threw himself on the "villain" and was about to knock the whip out of his hand and the teeth out of his head when he was startled by the piercing cry of the girl, a delectable young German: "Stohp, stohp, you're spoiling my fohn!"

Came autumn and I began to think seriously of invading the United States; after all, I was a nonentity no longer, having amassed a number of "credits," as they say in Hollywood. Alex was still on his transcontinental tour, but he'd be returning to the States soon and nothing appealed to me more than a prospect of home-coming, although I still considered London my official home. My wretched Nansen passport was a big obstacle — although included in Mother's first papers, I had failed to take the necessary steps at the consulate to insure and prolong my immigrant's status; the best I could hope for was a visitor's visa, which wasn't granted too easily to expatriates like myself. I began hinting to Mother at the possibility of a Boston reunion. Living determinedly above my income, I was again in debt and began looking around for musical-comedy work. With some difficulty, I sold a song to Cochran (which he never used), another to the firm of Daniel Mayer, and descended on poor Billy Allen with would-be "world beaters" — which he reluctantly printed, advising the buyer that they were "Broadway Hits." Shrewd old Billy was not above "hand across the ocean" gestures for commercial reasons, Swaffer or no Swaffer, but I'm afraid I let him down shamefully. Thus 1928 came to a rather uncertain end, the new year a big, fat question mark.

Musically speaking, I was quite happy, because productive, that winter. Long a Pushkin devotee, I found just the right libretto for a two-act opera among the *Tales of Belkin,* that unique cluster of short stories that are, in reality, capsule novels. By an odd coincidence, my choice, "Mistress into Maid," is preceded by an epigraph from "Dushenka" by Bogdanovitch, whose poetry Pushkin greatly admired — the same "Dushenka" excerpts which I had set to music a year earlier. Having given up poetry almost entirely (except for some epigrams on Diaghilev, Kochno, Nikitina, Danilova and others, widely circulated in Russian-ballet circles) it was exciting to create one's own libretto, using big hunks of Pushkin's delectable prose — the kind that sings without music — and writing love poems in the Bogdanovitch manner for arias and concerted numbers. By January 1929, I completed the first act and, on playing it over a few days ago (1954) I felt exhilarated by the freshness of this young music and its theatrical effectiveness. I was also working on my Second Symphony.

Fred and Adele Astaire again had London at their nimble feet, this time in Gershwin's *Funny Face.* In the pit were two young and good-looking pianists — Jacques Fray and Mario Braggiotti — who played tricky and showily contrived two-piano versions of the sparkling Gershwin songs — " 'S Wonderful" and "My One and Only" among them. Mario, half Italian and half American, was very tall, spectacularly handsome and spent his free time chasing women, when not chased by them; such is the nature of the man that even the most irresistible ones prefer to pursue rather than be pursued.

Prodigiously facile as an *improvvisatore* Mario seldom practiced the piano, but played with great dash and éclat, making extravagant gestures and even growling melodically to strengthen the crashing climaxes; all of this was carefully calculated to render the girls limp with excitement and admiration. Then came an impassioned speech, three parts "confession magazine" and one part Gabriele d'Annunzio, in which red Chianti, Braggiotti-cooked spaghetti and nude-bathing among the rocks of the Italian Riviera invariably figured; another dash to the piano — to execute a Neapolitan song with Mario supplying a sex-laden vocal — and the selectee of the evening was ready, nay eager, for a kill.

Fray probably did nearly as well as his tempestuous partner, but he played the suave and polished "continental" game — soft lights, soft music (his pianism was of the self-effacing persuasion) and soft French-accented compliments. Thus the bobby soxers of early vintage (many of them wore silk stockings and furs) who swarmed at the Prince's Theatre stage door had their choice of push or polish. Both Gershwin and Astaire were amused by the piano-playing Casanovas and liked going to parties with them. I met Mario and Jacques in Fred's dressing room while he was taking his make-up off and ribbing the pair mercilessly. After a night of gallivanting about London (minus Astaire, who, prudently, went to bed) we found we had so much in common that a decision was made then and there to take a house together. This was accomplished a few days later, coinciding with my discovery of Gibbs's thefts when we took our belongings to rather ramshackle quarters in Soho; on discovering an unusual number of mice and bedbugs in the place, we paid off the landlord with an indignant speech, and established residence in a most attractive and eminently "correct" little house in Pont Street, Knightsbridge.

Having concluded these arrangements I went to Paris once again to take part in Vera Vajevska's recital on January 8th at the Salle du Conservatoire. She devoted nearly one half of her program to my music, singing not only the Bogdanovitch and Pushkin songs, but also an aria from *Mistress into Maid,* in all of which I played her accompaniments. There weren't too many people in the hall but we had a good success and pleasant notices, although *Le Monde Musical* harped chiefly on my great talent as . . . pianist. A day before, in faraway Boston's Jordan Hall, Gertrude Earhart *premièred* the

Bogdanovitch songs (thus obtaining first hearings in Paris, Boston and Kiev almost simultaneously).

I don't think my Stravinsky-endorsed songs created any stir in Boston, but Koussevitzky made the haughty patrons of Symphony Hall Dukelsky-conscious with somewhat better results than those occasioned by the *Zephyr and Flora* suite. The symphony was played on March 15th and the industrious Slonimsky (no longer Koussevitzky's secretary but trouble shooter for the one-and-only H. T. Parker) was again mobilized into propaganda on my behalf, this time for the pages of the *Boston Evening Transcript,* whose approach to music and music makers was the most unique and nonconformist in the world, thanks to H.T.P.

A photograph of me wearing a pronouncedly early-Dukelskian sartorial creation graced the music page, a day before the concert, with this italicized caption: *The Crime of Being Young.* Directly under the photograph there appeared a long, laudatory appraisal of the criminal in which he was described as "a composer of power and imagination."

Alas, the London-dwelling Dukelsky was weakening by the minute. Other people's music was applauded at the ballet and discussed at dinner tables, Gershwin reigned supreme as Musical Comedy King, and many other writers with the U.S.A. stamp had their fling. There was no getting away from it — America ruled the musical theater and I was neither American, nor British, nor Russian for that matter, with my aptly named League of Nations passport contemptuously thumbed and reluctantly stamped by immigration officials everywhere — especially in England, where I had constantly to report to Bow Street. "Why should I languish in London, up to my neck in debt, where they don't pay you half as much as they do on Broadway and resent your writing for their theater into the bargain?" I wrote Mother, not unreasonably. "I can't wait to get back to the States, where people of worth are properly remunerated, not just lionized. Alex Aarons wants me to write a score for him."

If the Bright Young People spent their short lives shuttling from party to party, my bright young housemates, Fray and Braggiotti, too lazy to move about, far surpassed them by making their Pont Street existence one continuous non-stop party, with themselves as generous hosts. Outside of such figures as the Astaires, Claire Luce (the actress), Benita Hume (now Mrs. Ronald Colman), Grand Duke Dimitri and Prince George of Russia, a never ending procession of young females was constantly on the premises, drinking, dancing, telephoning other females to come to the "most divine place — One Pont Street," staging fights and being made love to. Not in vain did Zena Naylor call us The Three Beddies. This was fairly amusing for a week or so, then I decided I had had enough and that such shenanigans were no remedy for the profound gloom in which I lived. I removed myself to the third (top) floor of our house and had a special lock made which could successfully shut me off from the wild doings below. Such a stand earned me the nickname of "the Monk" and annoyed the volcanic Braggiotti, who retaliated by making me the butt of violent practical jokes, painful to me in my melancholy frame of mind and uproariously funny to their perpetrator and his then faithful henchman, Fray.

My longing for America became intensified by the arrival of Boston notices for the symphony, which, while far from sensational, were distinctly encouraging.

I was much touched by Mrs. Koussevitzky's invitation to Mother to join her in her box on the night of the concert, and the kind letter she wrote her before the occasion; also by the artless interview published a few days after the concert, from which I gathered that Mother met Koussevitzky at a tea given by Mrs. Ralph Adams Cram. The conductor "looked at her quickly, hesitated and asked if possibly she were related to Dimir [*sic*]. He had known Dimir in Paris. Saturday night she graced the seat reserved for the guest composer on the program. . . . When she heard his Symphony Saturday, of which Dimir wrote her, 'It is the first piece I feel I have a right to dedicate to you,' she sat so concentrated that she never moved. 'I felt such a contact with my son; I was very deeply happy,' she answered when she was asked about listening there in the dark alone." On reading these lines, my heart went out to Mother, for I, too, was in the dark, alone.

That summer I visited Paris for what proved to be the last time until 1936 — went to the Fair with the Prokofievs, dined at the Samoilenkos, complained to Paitchadze about the slowness with which he was printing my music (I was a wretched proofreader and my early publications are full of mistakes) and, finally, ventured to the music hall where the "Blackbirds," again headed by the incomparable Florence Mills, were bewitching blasé Parisians. The performance was sold out, so I bought a *promenoir* and elbowed my way through the crowd to the back of the stalls; before getting to my destination I bumped into a large man in an unseasonable beaver-fur coat. He turned around to reprimand me haughtily for "pushing him about" when we both stopped dead in our tracks — the large man was Diaghilev. His mustache was carefully trimmed, the monocle shone as disdainfully as ever, the necktie was Hilditch & Key's best (Diaghilev always went there for his shirts and ties) but, in spite of the determinedly youthful pose, there was something about Sergei Pavlovitch's face, something new, hollow and haggard that I didn't recognize and that tightened my throat. Diaghilev was accompanied by a slim, wolf-faced youth who disappeared before I had a chance of being introduced; he was Igor Markevitch, Diaghilev's official "fourth son" and my successor in his musical affections. Sergei Pavlovitch greeted me with the old, warm friendliness, which was especially gratifying because so unexpected. "It's good to see you, Dima," he said. "You, at least, didn't desert me for that ogress Ida Rubinstein — she has already annexed Sauguet, Auric and Stravinsky. Shocking, isn't it? Rieti tells me that you played your *Mistress into Maid* for him; he liked it enormously. I'm so glad. I always adored the tale. What are your plans, Dima?" I told Diaghilev that I was to sail for the States a week later on the S.S. *Laconia.* "Not for long, I hope; I want you to come to Venice in September and play your opera for me — if I staged it, I'd have arias, duets and trios sung and danced at the same time — what fun!" I stammered something about being thrilled by such a project, vague though it was, and took my departure, after the traditional Diaghilev kiss on both cheeks.

While in Paris I met Igor Glebov (Assafiev), the celebrated Russian critic and musicologist and ambitious, but untalented, composer of conventional ballet music. In 1929, Prokofiev was his god; twenty years later, he, with Khrennikov and others, savagely denounced him for his "bourgeois formalism," causing Serge to be ostracized, reprimanded and banished to a provincial hamlet, all of which horrors doubtless precipitated the composer's death. Glebov was in Paris on I don't know what Soviet mission and in appearance was like a post-office clerk — small, mousy and oddly diffident. He professed to like my music — and so did Miaskovsky, according to him; in those days, liking music written by the "enemies of the working class" was comparatively safe, as long as honest Soviet composers were uncontaminated by such contacts. However, what interested Glebov most was my "jazz" music and my friendship with Gershwin, already a legendary figure even in Russia. "I have an unofficial proposition for you, Dukelsky," said the critic with an uneasy glance at Prokofiev, who, he knew, was above such frivolity. "I understand you write poetry and speak English. Why not translate the book and lyrics of Gershwin operettas — say *Lady Be Good* and *Funny Face?* You could then send them to me in Moscow and, who knows, you may be instrumental in revolutionizing our entire light-music production. I promise nothing, but I'd like you to try." So uncommon a proposition greatly intrigued me, as I felt that no better anti-Soviet propaganda could be imagined than a big, healthy dose of Gershwin music, and all the good American things it stands for. That night after dinner I tinkered with "Fascinating Rhythm" and "Lady Be Good," succeeded in Russianizing them quite expertly, and demonstrated them the next day to Prokofiev and Glebov, who applauded frantically. Glebov took the lyrics and the piano copies with him to Russia and promised to write; that was the last I heard from him.

As to my American trip, it had happened not at all according to plan. In Pont Street I met a little man with a very large head and the powerful hands of a pianist, whose name was Herman Wasserman and who was sent to Europe from New York by Otto Kahn, that art-loving banker, to "perfect himself" (he was a Josef Hofmann student) and give some recitals; Wasserman was as good at playing cards as he was at playing the piano and I don't believe the recitals materialized. Nevertheless, he knew good music, be it jazz or nonjazz, and thought mine good on hearing it. "You're wasting your time here in London," he said reflectively. (I already knew that.) "I'm sailing for home in July and if you come with me, will manage you and find you the right producers — Arch Selwyn is a great friend of mine." Parallel with this conversation, I sold a round dozen songs (no lyrics, just tunes) to Fred Jackson's newly found backer, for £300; these were to form the basis of the *Make Hay* score, soon renamed *Open Your Eyes.* Thanks to F. A. K. Dale I got away with a mere fraction of what I really owed in British tax, settled a few pressing debts, talked the American consul into granting me a visitor's visa, presented Fray and Braggiotti with a key to the "Monk's Quarters," and boarded the *Laconia* on June 22nd with the firm intention of giving America a second chance to discover me.

CHAPTER XII

BACK TO THE NEW COUNTRY

A DAY before sailing I was suddenly told by the new producers that my presence would be required for *Make Hay* rehearsals in late August. I cabled Mother that I was coming for a two weeks' visit and little dreamed that I would stay on and eventually become a full-fledged American.

On reaching New York, I presented my Nansen passport to the immigration officials and received my first serious setback. One of the officials took a long look at the one-page document, stared at me, then examined the paper again with a puzzled look and finally turned to his colleague. "Take a look at this," he said. "Would you pass him?" The colleague went through the same nerve-racking performance, gave the paper back to examiner No. 1, and shook his head. "I would not," he concluded firmly. The first officer pointed to a bench and bade me wait. I sat and sat, seemingly for hours, then was told that I'd have to spend the night in Ellis Island until my papers were straightened out.

I remembered Ellis Island unfavorably from my first trip to the States and liked it even less now. Black-haired, oily-skinned children and their jabbering mothers were present in full force, as were the sickening smells of chlorine and iodoform. "This is where I came in," I thought miserably; except that while I came in the first time, it now looked as if I might have to get out! After a meal which I hardly touched, I struck up an acquaintance with a Dutch missionary who was "passing through" on the way to some remote islands, where he was to convert cannibals to Christianity. Landing on a non-cannibal island must have been quite a shock. Together, we succeeded in proving to the overseer that, being first-class passengers, we were entitled to separate quarters, and were marched off to a barren but clean cell, where we spent a fairly comfortable night.

Alex arrived in the early morning, unshaven and worried, accompanied by an amiable and capable lawyer. Between them, they arranged matters and I was permitted to board the ferry and set foot on Manhattan soil.

Alex had to get back to his job; Mother was anxiously awaiting my arrival in Natick, Massachusetts. I had enough to carry me through the two weeks and expected another advance from England to pay for my passage back. I put up at the Times Square Hotel in a room so small that, when my huge trunk was brought in, I could barely move. I assured Alex that I'd join Mother in Natick as soon as I made the "necessary contacts" in New York, embraced him and was left alone to ponder my fate and my prospects. How much could I accomplish in two weeks? The brush with Ellis Island notwithstanding, I felt oddly at home in this overpopulated overadvertised city — inhumanly beautiful when viewed at a distance, inhumanly ugly and wretched at close quarters. Yet it was part of America, the country to which we Dukelskys owed everything — our exodus from enslaved Russia, our subsistence in Constantinople, Alex's brilliant scholastic career, made possible by Americans who had faith in him. Outside of Diaghilev and a chance of my *Mistress into Maid* being produced by him, there was really nothing for me in Europe — not in England (I had little faith in *Make Hay*) and not in France, as Koussevitzky was abandoning his summer concerts there and concentrating on the Boston job, which, from all accounts, was not easy. I resolved then and there to return to England for a month or two, if really necessary, and then make the States my permanent home. I felt I belonged here; I knew I wanted to be close to Mother and Alex and their adopted country, not the countries I had left behind — wonderful countries with scenery like stage sets; the theater is a splendid place to work in, not to live in, I reasoned.

New York was in its summer doldrums, the heat getting worse daily, and there was "no one" in town — certainly no one I knew. Bob Chanler and Louise Hellstrom were in Woodstock, New York, their summer habitat; Nina Koshetz and Koka Stember were vacationing, and so was Wasserman. New York not being a *flaneur's* happy hunting ground, I rode to Washington Square, on top of a bus — there was no one to spoon with there, a pastime rhapsodized by me in the 1923 waltz — and dined alone at the Brevoort. The next morning I telephoned Mother in Natick and our happiness at hearing each other's voice was such that I boarded a Boston train that same afternoon, stopped in Boston just long enough to learn that the Koussevitzkys, too, were away, and reached Natick late in the evening. Mother, overjoyed at seeing me unscathed after my Ellis Island imprisonment, although rather perplexed by the new "English" accent and London clothes, wanted to know everything left unsaid in my letters and we talked and talked late into the night. She looked rested and well, but was, as always, inclined to minimize all the trials and privations she had undergone while I was riding high in Europe.

New England, which I had never seen before, was like a cool drink of water after too much champagne. The landscape was no match for the scenic marvels of Italy or Switzerland, but its austerity and sober lyricism reminded me of central Russia and made the home-coming feeling even stronger. The food, devoid of frills and culinary refinements, was wonderfully good, with "regional" characteristics unsuspected by me; clam chowder, codfish cakes and even the scoffed-at "boiled dinner" were interesting creations all. I was also fascinated by the provocative dowdiness of New England's girls, dressed practically and economically in "no nonsense" clothes, their feet looking enormous in the clumsily made Boston shoes of best-quality durable leather. That about sums up my first impression of New England — unspectacular but of the best quality and, certainly, durable. It was a relief not to pour oneself into a dinner jacket every evening, to go for strolls with local belles, who were not averse to flirting in spite of their puritanical airs; they talked well in flat but not unmusical accents, and seemed to know more and pose less than their Manhattan sisters. There were Russian evenings with the Berestnevs, the Ouspenskys and, of course, Colonel Lvov, bombarding me with questions, arguing, giving advice and carrying on as if they had never left the good island of Proti — which, I dimly recalled, was just another Ellis Island, but with olive trees.

While in Natick, I received a £50 publisher's advance for *Make Hay*, now *Open Your Eyes,* and the news that rehearsals were postponed for at least a month and I could remain in the States until further notice. After a ten days' "breather" in Natick, I returned to New York and another tiny cage at the Times Square Hotel, which had the advantage of being around the corner from Shubert Alley and only a few blocks from Harms, Inc. My first business visit was to Max Dreyfus, whom I no longer dreaded. He received me quite cordially, told me that Alex Aarons (the producer) spoke well of my music and even hinted at signing me up should my Broadway activities warrant it. I was introduced to Morrie Ryskind, a promising member of the Harms "stable," a small, bespectacled man of blunt speech and a restless manner. Morrie and I went to work and produced several tolerably good songs — he wrote lyrics before finding his true vocation as librettist.

Gershwin returned to New York after the Boston trials of *Show Girl,* his new musical, with Al Jolson and Ruby Keeler, which Ziegfeld produced. This was one of those enterprises that look great on paper (the book was by J. P. McEvoy, the lyrics by Gus Kahn and Ira), "can't miss" and somehow do. In it, according to John Mason Brown, Gershwin's "American in Paris" broke out with an Albertina Rasch. Clayton, Jackson and the one-and-only Jimmy Durante supplied the comedy; Duke Ellington and his band were on the stage — all to no avail, for the piece was a failure. The music was not George's best, although it contained the provocative "Do What You Do," which Frankie Gershwin sang at parties with convincing abandon. George took the flop in his stride; other and more exciting projects were looming, such as his Stadium debut as conductor on August 26th and the new version of *Strike Up the Band* being prepared for a Christmas-night opening in Boston.

The Gershwins then lived at 33 Riverside Drive in adjoining penthouse apartments. George's was breath-takingly modern, with all the latest mechanical refinements and a fully equipped gymnasium. His *cabinet de travail* boasted a huge Steinway and a spectacular view of the Hudson, also a collection of modern paintings, to which some of his own (he painted remarkably well) were periodically added. Parties, again, were the order of the night and I, already a veteran party boy, attended regularly. The parties and the guests have been colorfully described elsewhere, especially by Isaac Goldberg in his *George Gershwin, a Study in American Music,* presented to me by George with a touching inscription in 1931, shortly after its publication. Among the regulars were Bill Daly, Gershwin's favorite pit conductor, elfin Kay Swift, whose "Can't We Be Friends" and "Fine and Dandy" promised a bright Broadway career, and the professional sourpuss Oscar Levant, a good-hearted neurotic. Oscar played Gershwin brilliantly, although with a certain caustic dryness, robbing George's tunes and piano pieces of their romantic lushness. I always thought Oscar an all-around musician of great resourcefulness, a maddeningly provoking conversationalist, but I never thought him funny — either in a room or, many years later, on the screen; I don't think sheer agony funny, even when accompanied by a wisecrack.

Of the nonprofessionals I recall kindly Condé Nast, exuberant Jules Glaenzer, vice president of Cartier's and organizer of musical parties where all the current Broadway gods were exhibited and lionized; I had first met him in Paris with Aarons and Gershwin when Poulenc and Jean Wiener were also present. There was always a contingent of pretty girls at 33 Riverside Drive — young actresses and show girls mostly, with an admixture of what's now known as café society. These enchanting damsels had a habit of sharing the piano stool with George when he would finally install himself there — not to leave it again for two or three hours; we all knew that George was enamored of the piano, but since we were enamored of George's music and his exhilarating performance of it, no one seemed to mind his almost continuous usurpation of the instrument. What some of us did mind — I, for one — was the fact that the sirens present never volunteered to share the piano stool with anyone but their host. "The longer they let him sing and play, the better he likes it," reported Goldberg. (The better the girls liked it, too.)

Ira and Lee, only a few steps away (via the terrace), led a quieter sort of life. Their own visitors were of a more intellectual persuasion — people like S. N. Behrman or George Kaufman or the lovable versifier-turned-schoolteacher Lou Paley, married to Lee's beautiful sister, Emily. It was at Ira's that I met stocky, aggressive E. Y. ("Yip") Harburg, then writing with Jay Gorney, who started him off on his lyric-writing career. I was shown a song the two had written for the Earl Carrol *Sketch Book* entitled "Kinda Cute" — it was just that — and returned the compliment by playing a half-dozen tunes, one of which struck Ira and Harburg as a possible hit. They began "writing it up" then and there and the ultimate result was "I'm Only Human After All," which resulted in my signing a Harms contract a few months later.

I felt I was back in my element, but didn't seem to make any sizable progress. A former Diaghilev rehearsal pianist, Nicolas Kopeikine, subsequently employed as the celebrated Major Bowes's music director (for the Amateur Hour), a huge, easygoing Russian, suggested I move into his rooming house in West 66th Street — the New York replica of my Bloomsbury digs, minus the charm, also minus my Belgian fairy godmother, Mme. Dupont. Sick of living, if not in a trunk, then certainly on top of one, I agreed gladly, but discovered that I was to share a small-sized bedroom with a pugnacious and ill-tempered Russian male dancer. I was really too broke again to afford to kick, and moved in with the fellow, who had the greatest contempt for me because I was practically penniless; he sneered at my European "successes" and assured me that I'd be a flop in America. The ensuing two weeks were pretty ghastly, not only because of the persistent nagging I had to endure from my roommate, but also because of Arkadina, an aging Russian prima donna who employed me as coach and occasional accompanist, and also because of the heat. In a former chapter I said some mean things about Manchester, England; I take them all back — that city isn't bad, compared to New York's West Sixties at any time of the year, but especially during a late summer's heat wave. Madame Arkadina, a kindly but insufferably pretentious and stagey sort of woman, beady-eyed and rosebud-mouthed, given to the well-known Russian tantrums, soulful glances and meaningful asides, thought of herself as Traviata, although in robust health; she was demanding, humble, domineering and submissive all at once and delighted in playing a highly complicated romantic game which bored me stiff. Desperately in need of the five dollars per session I received for my services, I didn't dare to offend the lady, for fear of losing my only job, and carried on fairly convincingly as a respectful but, to her consternation, uncomfortably platonic admirer. Commuting on foot between Arkadina's hotel and the Kopeikine establishment in brutal heat, unseasonably overdressed (I had no tropical clothes) and having to play the role of an attentive swain à la Samuel Richardson in one place and that of a misunderstood genius from a page of Turgenev's in the other was no fun at all.

Mornings were spent in Lee Shubert's waiting room; there was talk of the Shuberts buying *The Yellow Mask* for Broadway, but that project failed to materialize. There were usually four or five callers — actors and writers waiting to see the all-powerful Lee, whose technique in dealing with them was simplicity itself: he would appear briefly in the doorway, following a completed interview, gaze imperturbably at the bench warmers, his Egyptian pharaoh's face perpetually sunburned and expressionless, then suddenly point to one of us with a curt, "You," and retreat to his office, into which you were to follow him at breakneck speed. I found Shubert tractable and certainly approachable in spite of his seemingly discourteous manner. He listened to the recital of my achievements with laudable patience, listened to the tunes somewhat more perfunctorily (they sounded awful in the dark, heavily draped and carpeted room, with the piano lid down) and said that he'd give me a job, if I'd give him a book (libretto, not novel). Things haven't changed much, as getting a good musical book is even tougher now than it was then; the current standards are higher. Mr. Lee, as he was always called, said amiably that I should pop in often as he might eventually stumble on a good book himself; he introduced me to Agnes Morgan, the lyricist of the 1927 *Grand Street Follies*, and we worked on some songs. With the Ryskind and the Morgan lyrics, some Desmond Carter leftovers and "I'm Only Human After All" I was building quite a catalogue.

Most unwisely, I picked a quarrel with Arkadina, who dramatically accused me of loving her money and not her looks or her art — which was very true. She then indignantly refused to provide me any more with the thing I loved so much — the five-dollar bill for a "coaching" session — and there I was with my immaculately tailored pockets empty again. This catastrophe occurred at the most inopportune time (catastrophes always do), as I had just persuaded Mr. Lee to grant my entire "catalogue" a hearing; my rift with Arkadina took place late at night, Kopeikine was asleep, and all I owned was a bright shiny dime. Waking up the lazy Russian was out of the question — he always slept until late in the afternoon; so, with no one to borrow from, I skipped breakfast the next morning and started out on foot for Mr. Lee's office in Shubert Alley — a considerable enterprise on a full stomach, far more considerable on an empty one. I played my "catalogue" to Mr. Lee with the same semi-negative I'd-give-you-a-job-but-where's-the-book results; I thanked him and ran out to keep an appointment with Tom Weatherly, who, in partnership with Dwight Wiman, had just revolutionized the

American revue with the *First Little Show*. Weatherly, the dapper producer type, received me unenthusiastically, and when I got through, snapped, "Not for me. I'm producing a topical revue, not a musical comedy." "Don't you even like 'I'm Only Human After All'?" I queried lamely. "It's not for me, as I just told you. Good day, sir," was my dismissal. Alone with my shiny dime, hungry and discouraged, I ventured into an Eighth Avenue hash joint with a sign proclaiming it "A Good Place To Eat" ("Do they *eat* places here?" I thought savagely) and blew the dime on a nickel hamburger and a cup of coffee. On walking back to 66th Street, I recalled a similar episode in London where the walk was longer, but at least I was served a succulent meal at Mrs. Guinness's and taken for a South American diplomat. There was no mistaking me now for what I was — a jobless songwriter.

However, that classical prop of songwriters — the coveted silver lining — shone for me briefly on August 20th when, as I triumphantly wrote Mother, Lee Shubert, having decided on a suitable book (an Agnes Morgan adaptation of a Wodehouse story), was to sign me to a contract the next morning — which also meant a modest advance; an advance that would enable me not only to pay my rent and replenish my shrunken stomach, but also provide Mother with money for a return to Philadelphia, where Alex was working. My happiness was short-lived. The contract was duly signed, Shubert's check cashed and my dinner jacket pressed, as I was to dine that night at Gladys Barber's with Clifton Webb, whom I had met at parties in Paris. In the middle of dinner Webb told the assembled guests that Sergei Diaghilev had died in Venice on August 19th — one day before my apparent change of fortunes. My heart almost stopped beating. I remember crying out, as if in pain, then dropping my head in stunned silence and crossing myself. I asked my hostess's forgiveness and mumbled something about being taken ill, then stumbled out of Mrs. Barber's house, clutching the newspaper clipping Clifton gave me with the terrible news, and taxied home. I stayed in bed for two days, unable to touch food, and talked only to Kopeikine who, too, knew Diaghilev and all that Diaghilev stood for.

The three published accounts of Diaghilev's death — Haskell's and Nouvel's, Lifar's and Misia Sert's (in her posthumous memoirs, printed in 1952) — differ considerably in detail. Lifar claims that

Diaghilev took Markevitch to Salzburg to hear *Tristan,* his favorite opera. Misia insists that they went to Bayreuth as Diaghilev didn't want young Igor to hear *Tristan* "anywhere but in Bayreuth," Wagner's *terre sainte*. Haskell and Nouvel omit any mention of the German trip. But all three agree on something I already knew — that Diaghilev was grooming Markevitch, his fourth "son," for greatness, and endangered his own rapidly failing health by undertaking the pilgrimage especially forbidden by his physician. Sergei Pavlovitch had the highest hopes for the sixteen-year-old prodigy. "The Stravinskys, the Prokofievs meant nothing to 'little Igor,' possibly because he knew little of their music, his only allegiances being J. S. Bach and himself, Igor Markevitch," as Lifar testified. Diaghilev didn't wait for Markevitch to compose a ballet score, but decided to launch him with a piano and orchestra piece (a piano concerto, according to Lifar, a partita according to Misia), to be played as an interlude in the course of the Covent Garden season, with the composer as pianist. This event took place on July 15th — while I was acting out my own version of *le fils prodigue* in Natick, Mass. — and was followed by a series of parties for Markevitch, which brought back memories of my own London debut four years earlier. By the end of July Diaghilev and Markevitch were in Baden Baden, whence they proceeded to Munich for talks with Hindemith, whose viola concerto, heard at a Koussevitzky concert, so impressed Sergei Pavlovitch that a ballet commission followed. On August 8th, Diaghilev reached Venice, alone, to die there eleven days later. According to the Countess de Noailles: "A fortune-teller had once told him that he would meet death by the sea." Lovers of the macabre are directed to Misia's memoirs for the details of the great man's end. It is incomprehensible and somewhat monstrous to me that Lifar and Misia should disagree even on the manner in which Diaghilev died. Misia reported that the "fat priest," who was summoned to perform the last rites, on learning that the dying man was a Russian, became "red with anger" and declared that he'd do "nothing to assist a Greek Orthodox." Lifar, on the contrary, writes of "Father Irenius of the Greek Orthodox church," who, summoned by him (Lifar), "appeared in the room, and began to read the prayers for the dying in church Slavonic." In Lifar's defense, I must state that he speaks with respect and gratitude of Misia's role in the tragedy, whereas the scene described by Misia of Lifar and Kochno, whose "mutual hate" prompted them to fight "like furious dogs" at their master's deathbed, is really too ghoulish to be credible.

However he died, Diaghilev was no more and Europe — *his* Europe — died with him, I kept repeating to myself. I now hoped fervently that I wouldn't have to go there at all — and my hope was fulfilled, as the *Open Your Eyes* management, short of cash, forgot all about me, rehearsed the opus in 16 days *à la sourdine* and rang up the curtain at the Empire Theatre, Edinburgh, on August 26th. No one chose to inform me of the opening and no one sent me the lyrics of my songs (written by facile Collie Knox after my departure), a printed set of which arrived in New York three weeks *after* the show's opening. *Open Your Eyes,* while no eye opener, got off to a brisk start and respectable notices, due, I'm sure, to a fifteen-year-old newcomer named Ella Logan. This "wee Scottish lass" had to pass herself off as an American in order to land the part and was mercilessly snubbed by the "principals" — Marie Burke and Geoffrey Gwyther, the latter described by *The Era* as a "singer of culture." Joe Coyne and Robert Hale, seasoned comedians, were also in the cast, but it was little Ella who stopped the show, and, by so doing, enabled it to live on. My best song in the score was "I'd Do For You" (there's a British song-title for you!), and the music, in general surmounting the unusual handicap of noncollaborating collaborators, was better and fresher than that of *The Yellow Mask.* The lyrics were in the polite, gentlemanly idiom of the period. Two samples of the humor (quoted by the *Sunday Post*) will suffice: *"Je t'adore, je t'adore!"* "Now, now, keep the party clean"; and "He's just like a rabbit — born to be skinned." Jackson had found Ella singing at the Piccadilly Hotel in London. The year before, she was in a pierrot show in Portobello. The *Sunday Post* appraiser, an intelligent man, obviously, for he complained of the story being "on conventional lines" and expressed a hope that "some day musical comedy authors will get away from Countesses and swell crooks and comic detectives and so-and-so's house in the country," delivered himself of the by then shopworn complaint: "She [Ella] speaks with an American accent, and my admiration for her was tinged with a little regret that once more we had to yield to someone from across the Atlantic. I was relieved when she told me afterwards that although she was brought up in the States, she was born in Glasgow in Dennistoun."

It was just as well that I was 3000 miles away. Notwithstanding all these hopeful signs, the show, a "shoestring" project, was skating on extremely thin ice financially speaking and closed on September 14th "for lack of money." It subsequently reopened in London, where it had a two or three months' run, but by that time I had lost interest, since the producers were not interested in me and kept revamping and reshuffling my "score," adding numbers written by new backers and their relatives. Ella zoomed into stardom (at fifteen!) soon afterwards and saw her name in great, big lights in *Darling, I Love You* (a Laddie Cliff production); Hannen Swaffer, who campaigned so savagely against me and other foreigners robbing the English theatrical till, was the only critic to lambast the delicious Ella, convinced of her American origin.

The very minor royalties from my third (and last) English show were left unpaid by the insolvent producers; I borrowed a hundred and twenty dollars from the ever-generous Gershwin and took a month's "breather," this time in the quiet and refreshingly unspectacular city of Philadelphia. American family life can be observed at its best in that town, but it is death on the tourist or sight-seer. The hotels have neither the Swiss-watch efficiency of New York's palaces, nor the endearing quaintness of Boston's inns; the food is superlatively good — I know of no better dish than snapper soup — but the restaurants are depressing and accentless. The best theater — the Forrest — is situated in an excessively gloomy and dimly lighted street, and boasts the architectural oddity of having its stage door located *across* the street from the theater building, although the backstage quarters are in the theater building; I'm not an architect and could never fathom this bizarre arrangement. Market Street runs Times Square a close second for unsavory tawdriness, and a burlesque performance I witnessed in a sordid side street was quite the most obscene imaginable, with strippers straight out of George Grosz's city nightmares going through the cruder variations of the sex act with imaginary partners, every member of the audience a goggle-eyed and frustrated candidate. On the credit side were Rittenhouse Square, some old houses with the pleasantly American "homey" and "lived-in" look, spacious parks and Bookbinders' downtown.

Mother and Alex lived in a little flat in Pine Street, uptown in a modest residential section. Alex had learned to "conform" head-of-family style — which meant office until six, dinner with Mother, an excellent Russian cook (her Pojarsky cutlets were Balanchine's joy), a little reading, a neighborhood movie perhaps, and so to bed. This sort of existence had the charm of novelty for me. While Alex worked in his architectural firm in Broad Street, I orchestrated my Second Symphony, under Mother's watchful eye, wrote letters to Paris and London friends and rejoiced in the telephone's silence.

Mother's best Philadelphia friends were the Polevitzkys, a large Russian family — the father an engineer for General Electric, his wife an intelligent and gracious woman, an assistant professor of bacteriology at the University of Pennsylvania, their son Igor a budding architect (now a successful designer of the better Miami skyscrapers-by-the-sea), and their two daughters, Ksenia and Irene, pretty and carefree blondes in love with the good simple things around them.

Huge Russian gatherings at the Polevitzkys (who lived in Yeadon) were an almost nightly occurrence, and the lighthearted, undisguisedly provincial carryings-on right out of the pages of early Tolstoy were another welcome novelty. Ksenia was engaged to Stokowski's first cellist, Willie Van der Bergh, whom she subsequently married and divorced; therefore I concentrated on Irene.

My pose was that of a disillusioned globe-trotter, Eugene Onegin style — hardly convincing in a young man not quite twenty-six, and a Pushkin creation into the bargain, ill at ease in the early Tolstoy *ambiance*. Irene was not overly impressed, although she rather fancied herself in the role of Tatiana, the amorous dreamer. I made the tactical mistake of being too eager: my prototype, Onegin, was a genuinely cold fish. Cold or eager, I was no match — with my symphonies and ballets — for the brawny Tarkingtonian college youths, who dashed in and out of the hospitable Polevitzky house, were good at driving cars (which art I didn't master until 1951) and sweeping girls off their feet with adolescent horseplay, a "must" in America, an enigma to Europeans. My vanity was hurt, my heart (luckily) unbroken.

Seeing Prokofiev's Second Symphony announced on the posters, I ventured to the Academy of Music (a better place for concerts than the hideous Carnegie Hall of New York) and witnessed a Stokowski rehearsal. The symphony is one of Serge's lesser-known works, and perhaps deservedly so; it is unwieldy, overorchestrated and extremely difficult to play. Stokowski greeted me cordially during the rest period and complained of the piece's difficulty. I suggested, with forced playfulness, that he take a rest after its *première* and tackle an easy symphony — my First, for example; this brought a smile but no results.

Armed with the completed Second Symphony I took off for Boston with the plan of conquering Koussevitzky with the symphony and, on thus breaking his resistance, borrowing some money from him. I put up at Slonimsky's, then stormed Sergei Alexandrovitch's bucolic retreat. After the initial: "Oh's!" and "Ah's" and much sonorous kissing *à la russe,* the atmosphere cooled perceptibly, because I (always a mediocre diplomat) blurted out the real reason for my mission on the strength of so friendly a reception. It took an hour for me to explain why I needed so much money, that my income from England had suddenly stopped; then, Natalya Konstantinovna, ever the business brain and treasurer of the ménage, reluctantly agreed to give me a check on the receipt of a signed promise that I'd repay her by April, 1950. Underlining my deplorable gift of bad timing, I innocently embarked on this transaction on the very day of the epochal October 1929 market crash!

In order to dispell the considerable chill in the air caused by my ill-timed request, I quickly produced the score of the symphony and was led to the piano by Sergei Alexandrovitch. The subsequent audition saved the day for me; Koussevitzky literally suffocated me with a bear hug and declared that the Second Symphony was "ten times better than the first." This was a special characteristic of the man — he always proclaimed a composer's last effort immeasurably his best, until after the performance, the audience's reaction and the next day's notices. Few, very few, of us shone as brightly after that fire and water test. Momentarily, I was again the reigning favorite; Natalya Konstantinovna (or, as she always signed her letters to me, "Tante Natalie") beamed, left the room and returned with the check. "You've been a good boy and we are pleased with you," she said magnanimously. "Thank your symphony for this money," handing me the lifesaving slip of paper. This scene, reported in a letter to Mother on October 30th, ended with a sumptuous lunch and a firm promise to launch the new symphony in Boston and New York.

The report, understandably, ended with "Hooray!" in capitals. My letter was dispatched from the Wall Street station, hardly the place for rejoicing in October 1929.

With a breath of relief, I parted company with the boorish dancer, my unwilling roommate, and moved in with Jacques Fray, a recent arrival in New York. He was teeming with ambitious projects, such as a concert tour with Maurice Chevalier and the importation of his friend René Clair. Not three minutes after I left Kopeikine's rooming house, the Russian was held up by masked bandits who tied him to a chair, robbed him of eleven dollars (all he had) and left, brandishing guns presumably loaded. All these histrionics for eleven dollars — the bandits had probably been wiped out in the crash. The crash had no visible effect on me: I was broke before it and just as broke after it.

Claire Reis, probably influenced by Slonimsky's industrious drum-beating on my behalf, asked for "something" from my pen for her League of Composers (which survived, while the more progressive International Composers' Guild was no more); I accompanied a singer in two inconsequential songs at one of the league's concerts. A few months later both Nina Koshetz and Valentina Aksarova sang my Bogdanovitch songs at their recitals. *Good Morning, Bill,* my projected Shubert venture, entered the ominous stalling period, and while a few other possibilities loomed, they never seemed to leave the looming stage. Among such possibilities was the *9:15* revue being assembled by Ruth Selwyn under Don Voorhees's musical guidance; Fray and Braggiotti were to serve as duo-pianists, and played two songs of mine, "Funny Little Home" (with words by Morrie Ryskind) and "I'm Only Human After All." Almost every songwriter in town had a song in the show, which was the fashion of the day (composite scores are now comparatively rare), but most of the songs didn't even reach the rehearsal stage. My two were among their number; nevertheless, I was taken to Boston (or was it New Haven?) by Edgar Selwyn, Ruth's husband, who was then preparing *Strike Up the Band* and whom I met with the Gershwins. I remember being aghast at the terrible confusion that reigned backstage and the almost equally confused performance; *9:15* was a patchwork of good and bad, with the bad predominating. Among the good things were a Kay Swift song, "High Above the Chimney Pots" (unjustly forgotten), and "Get Happy," which made Broadway Harold Arlen-conscious. The revue was a quick flop and all I learned from my contact with it was that a revue can be fixed (this one wasn't) whereas a book show with a bad book cannot.

Prokofiev arrived in December and went directly to Cleveland to conduct a concert of his music; I never saw Serge conduct but, from all accounts, he was a far better composer and pianist than conductor. At a Koussevitzky concert in Carnegie Hall (I had a "permanent" invitation to the conductor's box) I sat between Lina Prokofiev and huge, hulking Alexander Glazunov, former director of the Petersburg Conservatory, sole remaining survivor of the Belaieff group of composers (which stemmed from the Mighty Five) and once a powerful enemy of Prokofiev's music. (When Serge appeared as gold medalist of Mme. Essipoff's class in St. Petersburg with his own first concerto, instead of the prescribed Beethoven or Liszt, Glazunov stalked out of the hall after the first few measures.) On the following Sunday, Prokofiev himself came to New York; I met his train and we went off to a dull performance of Cherubini's *Requiem,* followed by supper *à deux*. Serge talked of Diaghilev's last days, of Stravinsky's piano pieces, which he disliked, and of Nabokov's "lyrical" symphony, just *premièred* in Brussels, which he liked better than that composer's earlier efforts. Of Russia he said only that things were "very bad indeed" there — a startling statement from Prokofiev, then already a recipient of insistent Soviet offers.

The Koussevitzkys, the Prokofievs and I were invited to the Greek Orthodox New Year's party at the very rich Mrs. Loomis's house. This turned out to be a full-size ball with Kuban cossacks, gypsies, oceans of vodka and other Russian trimmings. At least five genuine grand dukes were present, not counting a minor Duke, not genuine and not grand — myself. Germanova, the Russian actress, read Pushkin's poems, pretty Marianne Gonitch (with whom I flirted energetically) sang and Natalya Konstantinovna, half mockingly, presented me with a huge orchid from her corsage — and insisted on inserting it in my buttonhole, probably as a souvenir of my Beau Duke Paris youth. On the following Tuesday, Prokofiev and I went to the *Strike Up the Band* opening and later to a midnight party in Gershwin's honor at the Warburgs, where there was no room for nostalgia but where the music was better: George didn't leave the piano until the notices — all excellent — arrived, then resumed his recital with renewed vigor. At the party Pop Gershwin distinguished himself twice: when Russel Crouse asked him how he liked the show, he parried with: "What you mean how I like it? I *have* to like it." And again, when George introduced him to Roger Pryor, the leading man, Pop remarked benignly: "Oh yes, you were on the American side." (*Strike Up the Band* had to do with an imaginary war between the U. S. and Switzerland.)

The year 1930 began uneventfully, although there was no lack of high jinks; George took me to a Lambs' Gambol, where he conducted one of his songs. I watched goggle-eyed as all the top male stars — Fred Stone, Jack Donahue, Fred Astaire, Victor Moore, Charles Butterworth and many others — had the assembled professionals in stitches by their improvised antics. The hilarity was contagious, but I couldn't help thinking of how much gayer I'd be with just one little job for one of those big men, so friendly and seemingly accessible on the small Lambs' stage. George and Robert Russell Bennett, whom I met in Paris, where he showed me an interesting organ sonata of his, promised every assistance — but they were not producers or stars, merely fellow musicians.

The ensuing four months were tough sledding, made tougher by Mother's extreme anxiety and worry; I wrote deliberately sprightly, optimistic letters, assuring her that I was just about to strike it rich — if not this week, then certainly the next. True, I was getting performances (of Dukelsky's music) and writing articles, three of which H. T. Parker, whom I was yet to meet but who was already championing me in Boston, commissioned for the *Boston Evening Transscript* at fifteen dollars per article. The articles were on Diaghilev, Prokofiev and Nabokov. As for performances, it costs money to write serious music and get it in performable shape.

Aaron Copland and Roger Sessions gave three concerts of their series "designed to meet the interests of the younger generation of American and European composers." Kopeikine played my piano sonata on their first program on February 9th — the first and (so far as I know) last public performance of this published and perhaps not unworthy work. On February 24th, the Boston Flute Players' Club presented a typical "occasion" piece of mine, styled "Canzonetta" and written for flute, oboe, viola, French horn, bass clarinet and bassoon.

By the end of March, Duke, jealous of Dukelsky's progress, began functioning at last. Harburg and I had a series of discussions with the bigwigs of Paramount Publix Corp., which had established Eastern studios in Astoria, L. I. It all began with a phone call from Frank Tours, the English conductor, whom I had known in London in the *Yellow Mask* days; Tours was made general music director for Paramount in the East and was completing his staff. Philip Cohan, later a radio executive at CBS, was mainly responsible for the Paramount interest; he was employed there in a business capacity and knew Tours well. Harburg and I were apparently wanted for the film version of Rodgers's and Hart's *Heads Up* — one of Aarons's and Freedley's lesser successes; according to the time-honored but hardly laudable movieland custom, original scores were seldom retained in filmizations of Broadway musicals. By mid-April I had a Paramount contract which called for seventy-five dollars a week plus one hundred and fifty dollars for each number accepted by the company. I sent a sizable sum to Mother in Philadelphia and I was able to go to Boston and attend my Second Symphony rehearsals in peace and with the rare feeling of comparative security.

At first the symphony seemed distinctly shaky, and I wrote Gershwin after the third rehearsal: "The first movement is very satisfactory; it sounds well throughout and Koussevitzky's tempi are right. The Menuetto I didn't quite get — there may be one or two things in the orchestration that I should change. The finale seems all right until the 'Coda,' which, through a misunderstanding, was taken *twice* too fast; this will be corrected at tomorrow's rehearsal (the last one). I'm dying for you to hear the work and to know your opinion. *Please* do all you can to be here on Saturday." But George had an important engagement that week end, Prokofiev sailed for Paris on the *Ile de France* on March 28th, and thus the two men closest to me and whose opinions I valued most were not present at the symphony's birth.

While in Boston I stayed with the Koussevitzkys in Jamaica Plain, and was again struck by the uncanny resemblance of New England's scenery to that of Russia; the Koussevitzky place had the feeling of a Russian *oussadba* (small country dwelling) as painted by Somov or Soudeikine. It had the same unostentatious comfort, harmonious simplicity and the well-measured, unhurried daily routine. The Russian note was further accentuated by the high-cheekboned, Mongolian-faced manservant and his typically Slav, nunlike wife;

by the simple Russian cooking hygienically and plainly prepared (Koussevitzky was a health addict and never began a meal without partaking of a pill or powder or both), washed down with the best tea procurable — Natalya Konstantinovna being a tea heiress — and vintage wine for European guests. Although indifferent to wine and liquor in general, Koussevitzky had the odd habit of downing a glass of straight whisky before eating. The midday meal was always preceded by a leisurely walk on the *Oussadba* grounds with Drollka, a disagreeable-looking but affectionate French bulldog, Koussevitzky's great favorite. These walks were an all-male institution, as Natalya Konstantinovna never joined us, and Sergei Alexandrovitch particularly savored such outings, which gave him an opportunity for exchanging musical gossip, hearing the latest New York or Paris scandal and listening to the newest "off-color" anecdote, unthinkable in the stern presence of his wife. After a half hour's walk we'd return to the house, flushed by the stinging New England air and ravenously hungry, Natalya Konstantinovna awaiting us on the terrace with the invariable amiably gruff "Well, talked your fill?" greeting; this meant that hands were now to be washed and that lunch was about to be served. After the meal Sergei Alexandrovitch retired for his afternoon nap; the guest was left free to rummage through the gigantic music library or be driven to Boston in the Koussevitzky family car. I once caught hell from N. K. for directing her chauffeur to take me to Slonimsky's (they were not on speaking terms), which dastardly act was reported to her on our return. On Koussevitzky's awakening we'd drink more tea, accompanied by sweets and pastries; then came a two-hour working period, during which a visiting composer was requested to play his about-to-be-performed piece on the piano, with Koussevitzky comfortably installed in a deep armchair, conducting an imaginary orchestra the while. I don't believe the nasty legend, circulated in some quarters, of Koussevitzky's inability to read an orchestral score, but it is true that he much preferred to study a new work by the above-described method.

At dinner, Koussevitzky, relaxed and jovial, would unbend considerably and voice various nonconformist opinions, some of them calculated to startle Natalya Konstantinovna, who would then frown and purse her lips in disapproval. Occasionally, there was a free discussion of Koussevitzky's conducting contemporaries; he had little use for most of them, particularly John (now Sir John) Barbirolli, whom he always called "Barbirolla" and even "Barcarolla." "No-o, nooo," he would say, smiling wickedly and winking at me, "and what is your Barcarolla up to now, eh?" I never met the conductor, but the mere fact that he conducted in New York, where I lived, made him "mine" in Koussevitzky's eyes.

Rehearsals in Symphony Hall were closely guarded secrets with only special appointees permitted to attend — Sergei Alexandrovitch didn't wish to have his work disturbed and Natalya Konstantinovna, ever the vigilante, provided her husband with a virtual iron curtain, as a security measure. Composers, troublesome and nosy creatures, were relegated to the first balcony and tolerated on condition that they remained silent and respectful. To correct a glaring mistake in the orchestra parts, or an erroneous tempo by the conductor, meant standing up and shouting — a daring feat, attempted by few. I remember leaping to my feet when the coda of the finale was tackled *twice* too fast, and screaming: "No, no! slower, please." Koussevitzky stopped the orchestra, turned to me with a terrifying scowl, screamed back: "If too slow, I play faster!" and did. I screamed louder this time, in genuine anguish. Sergei Alexandrovitch rapped the stand with his baton and hissed: *"Personne* play!" (which was his way of saying: "Nobody plays."), then added in tragic tones, addressing me: "You conduct," and crossed his arms on his chest. "But I cannot conduct, Sergei Alexandrovitch," I wailed. "Then you compose and I conduct and you — SILENCE!" Koussevitzky summed up grandiosely and resumed the offending coda. It was now taken at the correct tempo, but the episode looked like a Koussevitzky victory.

I was frankly apprehensive about the symphony's Boston fate, owing to my inability to make suggestions or last-minute alterations in the score. For once my fears were groundless; Koussevitzky straightened out the sore spots or glossed them over and the symphony scored an emphatic success. When Boaz Piller, the colorful contra-bassoon player (who looked exactly like his unwieldy instrument) and doubled as a sort of an unofficial Grover Whalen to the Boston orchestra, walked up to me after the applause died down and pushed his autograph book in my face, I knew I had "arrived." "You bowed three times — good, very good," boomed Piller in his thick Dutch voice. "I didn't think much of your first two pieces, but you can now sign my autograph book — here, right next to Richard Strauss." I was overwhelmed and thanked Boaz profusely for the rare distinction bestowed upon me. At supper after the performance Koussevitzky was all smiles and Natalya Konstantinovna shook her finger at me playfully, as if to reproach me for my bad behavior at the rehearsal, then drank a toast to me and the symphony in hastily produced champagne.

Transported by my Boston success, I began to compose a double-bass concerto for Sergei Alexandrovitch (a double-bass virtuoso prior to becoming a conductor); on my return to New York I sent ten pages of it to Prokofiev in Paris, to get his opinion on my writing for so "antimusical" an instrument. Prokofiev sent the pages back with "unplayable" scribbled in pencil on page one. The pages were destroyed instantly.

My job at Paramount was awaiting me in Astoria and I began punching the clock daily and liking it. At twenty-six I was regularly employed for the first time and found American efficiency, thoroughness and fairness unexpectedly refreshing and stimulating. Gone were the days of idle *flânerie,* of long consultations with my tailor, of gastronomic orgies — the leisurely pursuits of a bright young rake. I invested in an alarm clock and a stop watch, bought a business suit, ready-made but comfortable, and learned enough slang to exchange pleasantries with stagehands and orchestra musicians and not be thought pompous. I was given a freshly scrubbed cubbyhole of an office, with my name in modest-size letters on the door, a tinny upright, a writing desk, a music cabinet and a telephone, and told to write whatever music Paramount needed. I enjoyed turning out a song with Harburg for a two-reel short in the morning and a few pages of "emotional" background music for a dramatic feature in the afternoon. The music cabinet contained hundreds of stock compositions, neatly catalogued and labeled to facilitate my task. Should Claudette Colbert be upbraiding Fredric March for spending too much money, all I had to do was to pull out the drawer labeled Anger and help myself to officially endorsed angry music. Tallulah Bankhead's screaming would call for music tagged Hysteria; Maurice Chevalier sweeping a chick off her feet necessitated consulting the Seduction file; Nancy Carroll's breast-heaving was easy — help yourself to the Passion drawer — and so on. There were also Religious drawers, a Manhattan file — that city to this day is musically represented by hustle-and-bustle one steps with xylophone solo — Far East and Western musical documentation and, of course, Greed, Lust, Murder, Chase, and other suitable tools for mixing crime and music realistically. Once the material was chosen, you were advised to "trace it" — an inaccurate term — which meant changing the melody around and modifying the harmonic structure, yet remaining as close to the original as possible; this was necessary in order to prevent accusations of plagiarism and costly lawsuits. I haven't written film-background music in many years and I doubt that these music cabinets still exist, but they were a great boon in my Paramount days, when I was in a hurry and had to turn out music by the yard.

Among my co-workers was Johnny Green, an attractive dark youth with a Harvard background, now the able head of MGM's music department. Johnny, an intensely ambitious and well-schooled musician, was the first to greet me on my arrival in Astoria; he breathlessly told me of his pleasure at meeting so distinguished a colleague and apparently knew some of my "serious" music. "Mr. Dukelsky, do you mind if I ask you how old you are?" he asked. "Twenty-six," said I. "Oh, I have a chance then — I'm only twenty-one," Johnny said with a sigh of relief and ran out of my office. The big excitement in Johnny's young life then was his "Body and Soul," which was soon to repeat its London click in the States and become one of the truly great "standards." Johnny was originally hired as rehearsal pianist and soon promoted to "arranger."

Harburg and I didn't get the *Heads Up* assignment after all. Victor Scherzinger, the director, was also a songwriter, and supplied additional numbers himself, retaining most of the Rodgers and Hart score. We turned out a quantity of musical "shorts" instead, and these were far easier and more rewarding work than the machine-like "tracing." A young brunette with a raucous speaking voice and a million-dollar song delivery was hired for one of the shorts; she was just beginning to throw her not inconsiderable weight around and was obviously going places. Her name was Ethel Merman, and the Duke-Harburg song she sang was called "Old Devil Sea."

On completing the Merman assignment, we were introduced to an apple-cheeked, wholesome lass, who rejoiced in the quaint monicker of Ginger Rogers. I thought Ginger, then scarcely nineteen, fascinating and bought her lunch in the commissary, expressed polite wonder at her strange Christian name and was told that it stemmed from the girl's abruptly terminated vaudeville and marriage career, during which she and her dancer-husband were billed as "Ginger and Pepper," the ex-husband's legitimate name being Jack Pepper. Ginger was a better dancer than she was a singer, so Harburg and I wrote her one of those tinkly jingles of no consequence. Ginger was always accompanied by her youthful and ever-energetic mother; however, I talked her into a dinner or two, and we went through Central Park in a hansom at night on one occasion. Ginger was anxious to learn French — she undoubtedly speaks it well now that she has a French husband — and I taught her all manner of amorous nonsense during the hansom ride — of verbal variety only, I hasten to add.

Edmund Goulding was another director with songwriting ambitions. A well-turned-out Englishman with a unique gift of unconventional gab, Eddie had had a colorful career as actor, director, soldier, pugilist, professional man about town, first-nighter and lady-killer. There were talent and imagination in everything he touched, but his songwriting habits were baffling and somewhat uncomfortable. He played no musical instrument and couldn't sing, but would compose his songs by whistling them for hours on end. After whistling a passage he would stop for breath and to point out the extraordinary beauty of his "composition," then go right on without indicating whether he was starting all over again or continuing. He took a liking to me and insisted on my joining him for breakfast daily at the Ritz, where he then lived in a spacious suite over the barbershop. Breakfast *à la* Goulding consisted of quantities of the best beluga caviar, dry toast and champagne. I was happy with the astronomically priced caviar, but drew the line at champagne and insisted on coffee instead, to Goulding's displeasure. The princely repast over, I'd be led to the piano and asked to harmonize and develop Eddie's whistled inspirations, some of them recognizable as pop songs, others merely as Hungarian-restaurant music. I couldn't detect anything English about Goulding's refrains — they were all in a minor key and brought visions of a bushy-haired violinist shedding rhapsodic tears right in your soup. At least two of them became worldwide hits — "Love, Your Magic Spell is Everywhere," and "Mam'selle" (with Mack Gordon's lyric).

The picture he and I worked on was a would-be Czechoslovakian melodrama named *Night Angel,* with Freddie March and Nancy Carroll — a strange choice for a Prague romance. Walter Wanger, then Paramount's head in the East, had high hopes for this opus, but it proved a colossal fiasco. The story was excessively gloomy and the settings heavily "atmospheric"; colorfully garbed girls all over the place — Eddie insisted on a beauty chorus, although *Night Angel* was not a musical — caviar and champagne at intervals, enthusiastic whistling, faithfully taken down by me and blown up to symphonic proportions and frequent parties at night with Eddie and Helen Morgan, with whom he was in love at the time.

The best picture I was connected with when employed by Paramount was *Laughter,* a gay and deftly directed comedy in which the hero, also played by March, was a romantic composer. During one scene he was required to play a three-minute "rhapsody" (composed by me) on the piano; I also performed this piece in the film, with March going manfully through correct pianistics — in this I had to coach him. *Laughter,* as I recall, was voted one of the twelve best pictures of the year, and the stock of those involved went up immediately.

I was now much in demand and my salary was upped to ninety dollars a week. When not busy scoring my company's pictures, I'd be lent to other companies (Warner Bros. among them) to "musicalize" trailers, those idiotic few-minute previews of a coming attraction. They usually began with an ear-splitting drum roll, a fanfare and a few bars of "hurry" music — violins in unison rushing up to a big, crashing chord designed to emphasize a question suddenly flashed on the screen — something like: "Did you live, love and die?" then, before you could recover, another crashing chord and a triumphant: "Well, Cornelius Corn did!!!" Followed by a few entirely unconnected scenes, erotic and violent by turn. Writing music to these abortions was a bore fully as crashing as the so-called "modern" chords with which I was requested to underline the provocative captions.

While at Paramount I often saw Maurice Chevalier, whose irresistible charm was second only to his thriftiness, unusual even for a citizen of France — a country not noted for largesse. Chevalier disdained the reasonably priced commissary in favor of the still cheaper cafeteria, frequented mostly by carpenters and stagehands, and held the record for never picking up anyone's check — except his own. I had met Tallulah Bankhead in the Bob Chanler days and had seen her at London gatherings, but was never in her entourage of "dahlings"; I don't think I exchanged two words with her the entire time I worked on *Tarnished Lady,* one of her two flop pictures — an unusual record for two such extroverts as Miss Bankhead and myself.

Other jobs included something called *Sap from Syracuse* and an utter horror entitled *Secrets of a Secretary,* in which the late George Metaxa made his screen debut. Metaxa was one of the first authentic "glamor boys," a personable singing juvenile and a good friend; he lived too well, had too many wives and died too young. I knew him in the Fray and Braggiotti Pont Street days and first met him in the cast of *Bow Wows,* where he sang a reprise of my early "For Goodness' Sake" without understanding the words — not because the lyric was that poor, but because he spoke no English. After the two Tallulah turkeys and *Night Angel* Paramount's Eastern organization began to fall apart with ruthless rapidity.

Parallel with the Paramount engagement I finally got my Broadway entree, via the Theatre Guild, then putting its third (and last) *Garrick Gaieties* together. As the whole theatrical world knows, the first two editions of that impish and impudent revue launched Rodgers and Hart, the third was to launch me — with considerably less éclat; after all, Rodgers and Hart wrote both scores entirely unaided, whereas I made only four contributions to the free-for-all score of the third edition. You'd never guess it, but the man who first spoke to Theresa Helburn of my lowbrow talents was that arch highbrow Aaron Copland. I then met Miss Helburn at a Gershwin party, played "I'm Only Human After All" — which became my passport to Broadway — and was asked to join the assorted songwriters invited by the Guild to help write the *Gaieties* score.

I was not prepared for the spectacle which greeted my eyes, when I reached the Theatre Guild's rehearsal hall. Not less than thirty tunesmiths and lyricists — youthful eager beavers for the most part — were present, piano copies, lead sheets and typewritten slips of paper in hand. They displayed no animosity towards one another, but each one boasted a greater number of "accepted" contributions than the next fellow. "How many numbers you got in the show, Charlie?" an eager beaver would ask. "Five," Charlie would shout back. "How many you got?" "Seven," was the triumphant reply. "Eighth one coming up." Since an "intimate" revue seldom accommodates more than twenty musical entries and, judging from the number of prospective contributors and the size of their contributions, the third *Garrick Gaieties* would have an unusually generous score of some one-hundred-fifty items — what chance did I have with my *one* song, even with Ira as part author of the lyric?

There was no furniture in the rehearsal hall except a table and a chair occupied by a dark, intense-looking man with glasses who turned out to be Philip Loeb, the revue's director. When I entered the place, he was engaged in the difficult task of reading two lyrics at once, listening to a chorus sung by one of the eagerer beavers, and looking speculatively at a tasty dish of eighteen in a clinging practice dress, who was being considered for a secondary role. Loeb was too busy to pay any attention to me and after ten minutes of languishing impatiently, I decided to play an unusual trump card: I dove into my waistcoat pocket and produced my trusty monocle, a cherished relic of the Diaghilev days. It had been many months since I had used it last, as the monocle went unappreciated at Gershwin soirees, and cut no ice in Philadelphia; but drastic measures were in order and so, monocle brazenly glistening, I performed a sort of London strut and coughed significantly. That did it. "Hey, you!" Loeb shouted, nonplussed. "The bourgeois with the monocle — what can I do for you?" "That's easy, Mr. Loeb," I ventured playfully. "I want you to hear a song." "*A* song? Good Heavens, man, we have enough music for five shows," Loeb protested. "I don't doubt it — but mine has a lyric by Ira Gershwin *and* E. Y. Harburg." Phil's troubled face broke out in smiles. "Oh, Yip and Ira, eh? O.K. Let's hear it." I banged out "Human After All" triumphantly and noticed to my intense satisfaction that Loeb was soon joined by Terry Helburn and well-fed, capitalistic-looking Lawrence Langner, who listened to the song with every evidence of pleasure. There was a lot of whispering, some annoyed stares from the eager beavers — but the song was in — to be put in rehearsal at once. The next day, on reappearing in the Guild rehearsal quarters, I was buttonholed by Charlie of the five entries. "You with the dude clothes," he boomed. "How many songs ya got in the show?" "One," I confessed, blushing modestly. "Funny — I got four left; had five yestiddy. You wouldn't be hornin' in, would ya?" I smiled cryptically and retreated. That afternoon another song of mine, "Too, Too, Divine," from the short-lived *Open Your Eyes,* was sneaked into the *Gaieties;* the producers needed a lively one-step for their G. B. Shaw burlesque and Harburg was promptly ordered to rewrite the lyric, which now became "Shavian Shivers." A few days later Albert Carroll, an old friend, cast as Mei Lan-Fang in one of the sketches, needed an atmospheric background and I was pressed into service again, reducing Charlie's contributions to three. I got the Mei Lan-Fang job by producing my *Yellow Mask* notices, thereby proving my predilection for things Chinese. Then in the grand finale of Act I a Gilbertian lyric needed a Sullivanish tune — and who could do one better than the would-be Englishman with the monocle? In went a fourth number from my pen, with Charlie now down to two. Another reshuffling, another two last-minute additions by new composers, and poor Charlie was out in the cold. He took it like the fine sportsman he was. "S'long, dude," he said cheerfully. "I guess you're the better man — no hard feelin's. Wish me luck." I never learned Charlie's last name.

Alex had left on his M.I.T. traveling scholarship, and Mother came to New York to share a flat with me and to set up housekeeping. This was now feasible, owing to my improved finances; besides the weekly income from Paramount, I had the *Garrick Gaieties* and some hackwork (anonymous) for Earl Carroll's *Vanities* — mostly ballet music and odds and ends. Prokofiev wrote from the Palace Hotel in Brussels to tell me that my "Dushenka" and the Pushkin songs had been engraved by Paitchadze; of the festival of his music in Brussels, in the course of which Ansermet conducted Serge's Third Symphony, a Divertimento, a suite from *Chout* and the ever-popular Third Piano Concerto. He was also giving a piano recital — a task he seldom relished. Meanwhile, Koussevitzky, the initial wave of enthusiasm over, went back on his promise and didn't bring my Second Symphony to New York — which vexed me considerably. I was now all the more determined to make my mark on Broadway, Dukelsky needing Duke's help badly.

Garrick Gaieties opened "cold" (no out-of-town tryout) on June 4th and pleased the critics. "Lively and amusing," said Winchell. "A show you'd better see. It's fresh, fast and not too incurably collegiate," said Garland. "A lot of revue at $3 top," said Mantle. Business was helped, too, by gratuitous publicity by Grover Whalen, then police commissioner, and the John Wanamaker department store. They threatened suit because of the "They Always Come Back" finale, by Levy, Kay Swift and Duke, which satirized Whalen's return to Wanamaker's and the store itself. The "Johnny Wanamaker" song, the store's officials alleged, desecrated the memory of the founder. Whalen objected to my "I'm Grover" aria, wherein the spruce commissioner was described as the "Gardenia of the Law." "Human After All" received favorable mention, the *New Yorker* coming out boldly with the statement that it was the "best of the new show numbers." To top it all, in *Variety's* July Music Survey the three leading phonograph companies reported six best sellers, and Brunswick's list had "Human After All" (played by the Colonial Club orchestra) as *number one*. Shortly after the revue's opening I was summoned to the Harms' offices and signed to a composer's contract on the strength of my first Broadway showing.

Helburn and Langner were so pleased with Harburg and myself that when, after a four months' profitable summer run (yes, the shows could run for four months in 1930 *and* show a profit!), they decided to send the revue on tour, we were commissioned with augmenting and rounding out the score for provincial consumption; some of the original material was judged to be entirely too New Yorkish and la-de-dah for the "sticks."

The Guild people, ever the pioneers, had yet another new wrinkle in this venture: having disdained the customary procedure of a hinterland tour followed by a New York opening, they now "toured" the new version in Manhattan to whip it into shape for "out of town." "The selfsame responsible parties," the *Daily News* reported, "have decided not to teach the inhabitants of the prairies too much about the facts of life. Hence, the sketches retained in the new edition are practically blushless." Five new songs by Harburg and Duke were added to the score (mostly replacing the weaker entries), of which "Unaccustomed As I Am" and "A Little Privacy" were thought best by the critics, who gave the "traveling" edition their unreserved blessings.

It was altogether a most productive summer; a summer of hard work and a little play on week ends. At the Nina Koshetz recital I met Serge Soudeikine, the Russian painter, once too a Diaghilev protégé; Sergei Pavlovitch sponsored him in his Exposition of Russian Art days but never entrusted him with a ballet commission. Soudeikine's real contribution to Diaghilev's ballet reign was Boris Kochno, whom he introduced to Diaghilev in 1922 in Paris. His former wife, the statuesque Vera, subsequently became the present Mrs. Igor Stravinsky. Soudeikine bore a slight resemblance to Diaghilev, of which fact he was exceedingly proud; with a few facial characteristics and a difficult, domineering nature the resemblance ended. True, Soudeikine was also an inspired *causeur* and seemed to have a considerable knowledge of the arts and literature, but one soon became aware that this knowledge was no more than a handy bag of tricks with which to dazzle the listener. At the time he was doing sets for the Metropolitan Opera House and living at the Ansonia, then the opera singers' favorite, in a large, sunny studio, with his American wife, Jean, of the big Wagnerian voice and equally big physical proportions. Whatever Soudeikine's faults as painter, he was a warm and accommodating host and a welcome link with my colorful European "past"; like Vouvray, a hastily acquired Paris and London reputation does not "travel," as I learned only too soon. Even the Boston success of my symphony under Koussevitzky had no sizable repercussions in New York. "If it's that good, why didn't Koussevitzky bring it to Carnegie Hall?" was the usual query.

Soudeikine had a barn, for painting and living purposes, in Woodstock, New York, and we spent several week ends there. Bob Chanler and his faithful Louise had us to dinner; neither had changed much although the "vzz vzzing" was by now practically unintelligible and there was a previously absent bitter note, caused by the disintegration of the Chanler Circus, with only a few of the old faces still intact. Among the new friends were the De Liagres, neighboring landowners, a hospitable couple, and their handsome children — Alfred, just out of Yale, tall and "aesthetic," and his glowingly fresh-faced and healthy-limbed sister.

As if all these multihued activities were not enough, I managed to write a little "serious" music, but noticed, to my horror, that the more free and outspoken, the more "opened up" (in Gershwin's phrase) my commercial music sounded, the drier and more cerebral were my "serious" essays. I sent some of them to Prokofiev in Paris, and with them a half-boastful, half-apologetic letter describing my "slumming" or "whoring" (musically speaking) activities in New York. Prokofiev retaliated with a severe and, probably, not undeserved verbal castigation which really shook me at the time. Serge said: "The touching story of young maids who become prostitutes in order

Mother, Kiev, 1917

Myself, Monmouth Hills, N. J., 1921

Myself, Monte Carlo, 1924

Myself, London, 1928

Serge Prokofiev, Paris, *circa* 1932

Sergei Diaghilev talking to the chief machinist of the Monte Carlo theater

Paul Kochanski and Prokofiev, Paris (in the thirties)

George Gershwin, Beverly Hills, 1936

Ira Gershwin and Vernon Duke writing the *Goldwyn Follies*, Beverly Hills, 1937

Vernon Duke being congratulated on *Tars and Spars* by Admiral R. Waesche, Commandant, USCG, Washington.

George Balanchine, Vernon Duke and friend after the *Cabin in the Sky* opening, Havana, Cuba, 1940

Alexis, Mona and Natasha Dukelski (that's *his* spelling — Dukel*ski*), Los Angeles, 1954

Mr. and Mrs. Serge Koussevitzky, 1947

Jack Robbins, Ogden Nash — friends — and Vernon Duke, old Knickerbocker Music Hall, Second Avenue, New York, 1948

Lehman Engel, Vernon Duke, Mimi Cabanné and prospective backers at the *He and She* audition. March 1949

Vernon Duke, New York, 1945

Vernon Duke, New York, 1936

to feed their mothers isn't new. In the days of Karamzine [a sentimental Russian writer of the early nineteenth century] the story made people cry. However, they soon understood that, if the young maid secretly *likes* lying down, she is only too glad to find a respectable excuse for so doing; should she *not* like it, she'd find other means to help Mama. I doubt that mothers particularly relish their daily bread when secured by whoring daughters. No matter what the excuse, you simply love your half-respectable bread and cannot hide your ecstatic joy at the fact that your rotten little record [Serge was referring to "Human After All"] is Number One in sales. And, should I ask you what you've accomplished in the sphere of *real* music, you have nothing to show except two pretty dry piano pieces. Their dryness is characteristically typical of your case: when, after a long delay, you tackle 'serious' music again, you're terribly afraid of the taint of operetta, which has become your flesh and blood, without your noticing it. Russian music already had such a precedent, strange though it may seem, in Rachmaninov's case. In his day, he, too, was thrice as talented as most, and although he never stooped to cancans, unbosomed himself in several much too flowery songs. To appease the musicians' protests, Rachmaninov tried to assume a 'serious' mien, but resorted to such dry rot that he soon vanished from the scene altogether and remained in history as a composer of said flowery songs for the 'Greater public's' consumption. Let's hope that by 1931 you'll succeed in rehabilitating your name, already half-forgotten in Europe. I will be happy to do what I can for your Second Symphony. I persuaded Paitchadze to have your score copied, so it can travel from conductor to conductor." He went on to enumerate his efforts to "place" the symphony in Berlin (with Seidler-Winkler of the Radio), Brussels, and Paris (Ansermet or Monteux). A new Prokofiev festival was announced in Paris to take place on December 18th under Monteux's direction (Fourth Symphony and Second Piano Concerto), and I was profoundly moved by the fact that, notwithstanding his own frantic preoccupation with it, Serge found time to think of me and add . . . "that [the festival] will be an opportune moment to high-pressure Monteux with your symphony." Prokofiev went on to inform me of the impending publication of both the Pushkin songs (adding that he liked the Bogdanovitch ones better) and the "dry" piano pieces and then complained about "Dushenka" having just been printed *without* the promised dedication to him — which, incidentally, was Paitchadze's slip, not mine.

Prokofiev himself — without realizing it — was traversing his "extra-dry" period; he followed the overwritten Second Symphony, with third and fourth so-called symphonies — I say "so-called" because they were in reality suites culled from his Diaghilev ballet *Le Fils Prodigue* and the opera *Flaming Angel*. Aroused by Prokofiev's bitter denunciation of my selling my musical soul to the Almighty Dollar, I derided him for the dubious practice of thus "symphonizing" theatrical music. Also in his lengthy letter was the announcement of the forthcoming ballet *Sur le Boristhéne,* with Lifar's choreography, Larionov's décor, Gontcharova's costumes and Serge's decidedly inferior — for him — score. However, in the sad smile-provoking custom of all composers, Prokofiev cheerfully reported that Nouvel, Souvtchinsky and Lifar praised the music and rated it a step forward after the *Prodigal Son.* When the ballet was mounted at the Paris Opéra in May 1931 and resulted in a near catastrophe, with threats of lawsuits by all parties concerned, I shrugged my prematurely weary shoulders and thought of my own "step forward" — the *Three Seasons,* so wisely buried by Diaghilev.

Serge wound up his epistle by gloating over his American-type extension desk, recently purchased with money earned by concert tours. That, too, was a form of prostitution — which Prokofiev admitted to me in 1938 when I last saw him; having to play a piano to make a living disturbed his composing schedule, brought about a comparative lull in his creative work and finally resulted in his return to his Mother Country. In the letter, the implication was that he earned his comforts by legitimate means, I by illegitimate ones — and coming from Prokofiev, it hurt. In self-defense, I pointed out to Serge that I couldn't make a living playing piano or conducting, as he did, having no particular ability in either, although I subsequently became a good jazz pianist, and began to make records as early as 1934.

As a result of my first Broadway click, my stock started climbing. I met the urbane, mild-mannered S. N. Behrman at the Gershwins', played a lot of music for him and was handed the stage version of *Serena Blandish,* which he had adapted for Jed Harris a few seasons back. Berry, as everyone called him, said that I was the one right man for the job, speaking two musical languages as I did and possessing the necessary "cosmopolitan" outlook. I devoured both versions — the original by a "Lady of Quality" (Enid Bagnold) and Berry's smooth and canny theatrical adaptation — in one evening and resolved that there was the perfect book for me at last. I spouted enthusiasm over the telephone the next morning and received a letter from Berry authorizing me to write the score should a production be arranged. *Serena* turned out to be the first of my long list of unproduced musicals, and will recur periodically in this narrative as a persistent yet strangely stillborn leitmotif.

Among the contributors to the *Gaieties* was Edward Eliscu, an able lyricist who collaborated on some of Vincent Youmans's greatest songs. He liked my contributions and I liked his, so we talked things over and discovered that we were both "under consideration" by Tom Weatherly for the score of a Dwight Taylor musical named *The Gay Divorcee*. With gratifying ease, we were signed by Weatherly as a team and began turning out songs for his property.

On the classical front, I still wasn't composing enough, but thanks to Prokofiev (who, paradoxically, redoubled his efforts on my behalf while I was still smarting under the effects of his lecture) began getting important performances. Three weeks after the lecture, Serge wrote briefly to tell me that Seidler-Winkler had definitely programed the Second Symphony and that "on arrival in Warsaw, I attempted to persuade Gregor Fitelberg that you were Poland's greatest composer. He promised a performance with the Warsaw Philharmonic." Lina Ivanovna's postscript read: "Greetings, Dukie dear, am preparing some of your songs."

Thanksgiving, a heartwarming American institution, new to me, and Christmas were entirely family affairs that year — the small family consisting of only Mother and myself, since Alex was in Europe on his architectural pilgrimage. On New Year's Eve, in our two-room flat in the East Eighties, we drank toasts to Prokofiev, my European guardian angel, and to George Gershwin, my American one; to the Theatre Guild and the Paramount Studios in the lowbrow division; to Koussevitzky and Slonimsky in the highbrow ditto; to the absent Alex and to ourselves, happily present; and, lastly, to the United States of America, where I hoped to make my permanent home.

CHAPTER XIII

SETTLING DOWN

SHORTLY after my arrival in America, I began a thorough investigation of the local musical scene. My meteoric, though inconclusive, rise in Europe, the five excitement-packed years I spent there and the encouragement and interest shown me and my music in France and England led me to expect important reverberations here, a continuation, as it were, of a career begun with a resounding bang. In this I was grievously disappointed; it took me little more than a year to come to the painful realization that the composer, the man who supplies the very stuff without which music-making would be a physical impossibility, was indeed the Forgotten Man, the pariah of the music world which he alone created. The *Maître* of France, the *Maestro Compositore* of Italy became little more than a woefully underpaid handy errand boy of the Almighty Interpreter, the virtuoso, the prima donna, the star — the trusty meal tickets of thriving concert managers. The nonperforming, nonteaching composer is to this day — in spite of all the optimistic propaganda and publicity-seeking publishers' claims — a penniless lunatic in the richest country in the world.

Used to earning my pennies by lowlier pursuits, I hoped at least for a beneficial musical climate conducive to serious work; I found no such thing. It was taken for granted in Paris that composers of similar ages and tendencies were also friends. In some instances they even collaborated — as witness numerous ballets, suites, and sundry occasional pieces jointly composed. Our life in Paris was inconceivable without almost daily communion, playing one's newest work for the others, with the resulting helpful interchange of pros and cons. A similar condition existed with the Russian Five, the Schoenberg School and the Miaskovsky Group in Moscow, and I do not think any harm was done by the undoubted cliquishness of these groups. They had fun, even though they were often made fun of.

No such Arcady existed in the States, as I discovered. Fun among composers was unheard of or frowned upon. The composers themselves were sad, somber fellows in quest of jobs and performances, and distrustful not only of me, a European pretender, but particularly of one another. There was much talent among them, and also much genuine suffering. Every composer I met boasted a long record of inhuman trials and tribulations, of sums spent and none earned, of eternal promises by publishers, performers and conductors, never fulfilled. My curiosity soon gave way to indignation — indignation not entirely unselfish as I began to have somewhat similar experiences myself. Most of the composers I'd met were young if not exactly hopeful. A few were past middle age and apparently past all hope. Among these were at least two whose music had extraordinary merit: one of them asked me whether I could give him a copying job.

In the twenties and thirties, the currently oft-performed native "boys" were no more than beginners. Groping for recognition, stylistically insecure, these young men were understandably hostile to invaders with impressive European debuts behind them, and commercial jazz practitioners, worst of all those who operated under the cloak of Carnegie Hall respectability. "American music is not jazz. Jazz is not music" — that's how Paul Rosenfeld began his *An Hour With American Music,* which made its appearance in the year of my arrival in the U.S. After so pontifical a statement, Rosenfeld, a passionate champion of native talent, when free of the jazz taint, went on to assert just as pontifically: "We have an American music: there exists a body of sonorous work, *not jazz,* made by persons associated with the American community, to be grouped without impertinence with classic European works"; and further, "Some of the most important living composers are Americans by nationality and by culture." In 1929? Who were they? According to Rosenfeld they were Roger Sessions, Carl Ruggles, Roy Harris, Aaron Copland, the Mexican Carlos Chavez, the French-born Dane Rudhyar and Edgar Varèse, and the Russian-born Leo Ornstein. Adolph Weiss and Virgil Thomson got "favorable mention." The one man who rightly or wrongly has put the U.S. on the map, musically speaking, the real Voice of America, known and loved by millions the world over — George Gershwin was accorded little more than a page by

Rosenfeld, the Pure Music Apostle (to Ornstein's 10, Rudhyar's 7, Sessions's 13 and Copland's 15), and what a page! After blasting (rightly) Krenek's *Jonny* and dismissing Milhaud's jazz efforts with "soft and timid," Paul the Pathbreaker went after George with venomous relish. "The American parallels of these jazz experiments are equally indifferent," said he. "Gershwin's Rhapsody, Piano Concerto and 'An American in Paris' have found a good deal of popular favor; and Gershwin himself is assuredly a gifted composer of the *lower, unpretentious order;* yet there is some question whether his vision permits him an *association with the artists* [italics are mine. V.D.] The Rhapsody is circus music . . . not so much music, as jazz dolled up. The Concerto . . . is utterly bare of the impulsion towards a style which every living thing exhibits . . . we seem to hear Gershwin's instrument, like Balaam's ass, reproving the false prophet; directing him to the sphere congenial to his gift." As for the "artists," with whom an association of a puny circus musician was questioned by Rosenfeld, they fared extraordinarily well. Rosenfeld's method was to compare them with their European model (the existence of which he had to admit, however grudgingly) and find the native son immeasurably superior. Ornstein is "not as naïve as Franck [César] or Weber [Carl Maria von]." Rudhyar's sonorities are "harder and more intricate than Scriabin's"; Sessions, "even where he is closest to Stravinsky, has more robustness than *ever* comes the way of the somewhat chlorotic Russian." Thomson's tangos "were much better than Milhaud's"; and so on. Only dear old Horatio Parker's *Mona* does not surpass, but merely ranks with, *Salome, Pelléas,* etc.

These views, absurd though they may seem today, were echoed by most "highbrow" writers of the period, with the signal exception of Carl Van Vechten, who wrote well (Rosenfeld's writing was baroque in the extreme) and made sense. He also made the music world Gershwin-conscious, having predicted — *before* the advent of the Rhapsody — that jazz would be utilized in a musicianly manner by "The Great American Composer to create just the effect that Liszt got into his rhapsodies by the use of Hungarian tunes, or Albeniz into his Iberia suite." Four years before Rosenfeld's defiant assertion, refusing jazz the right to be classified as music, or George Gershwin as artist, Van Vechten wrote: "Jazz may not be the last hope of American music, nor yet the best hope, but at present, I am convinced, it is its only hope." A mighty armada of antijazz Columbuses must have sailed into the muddy musical waters four years later, to hear Paul tell.

Thus, a newcomer could take his pick; Ornstein, "the spring as it comes up through the pavements, the aching green sap. . . . Lazarus emerging in his grave clothes into the new world . . . sure of reaching the high heaven of art for which he seemed and still seems bound" (what became of the man, incidentally?); the "uncompromisingly and idealistically lofty" Copland; Roy Harris, "the rhapsode of the American migrations and pioneer existences"; or the well-heeled Cinderella of U.S. music — George Gershwin, the rhapsode of "splendiferous hotel foyers crowded with important people and gorgeous women," who, according to Rosenfeld, couldn't even "qualify as a *vulgar* composer." Our critic had a better definition — he called George the "laureate of musical advertisers."

I refused to take sides and listened avidly to the music around me, hoping for new sounds and new directions and disregarding the source whence they came. It's no idle boast when I say that I never let personalities or musical politics interfere with my appraisal of music, nor when I claim to be able to listen to a new work without checking with the program to make sure that it is musically "respectable" or having my enjoyment colored by the presence or lack of such respectability. When Prokofiev wrote what I thought a poor work, I said so; and when Copland, whose music I fail to admire, writes a Vitebsk trio or *Second Hurricane,* a moving and thoroughly theatrical children's opera, I'm ready to split my palms applauding; but I have the greatest contempt for those pitiful hangers-on of music whose misplaced partisanship compels them to lie prostrate in orgiastic ecstasy while listening to a few bars from their idol's pen. I had nothing but admiration for Varèse, the magician of acoustical invention, nothing but respect for Sessions, a solid craftsman and a true idealist; in short, I liked — and still like — all *living* music, the spontaneous utterance of every talented musician, every fresh, "reachable," nonsterile, noncalculated, unprefaced, unapologized-for musical realization.

Europe soon got the opportunity to acquaint itself with American fashions in music — the Rosenfeld party was to be represented by Sessions's Piano Sonata, the Van Vechten party by George's *American in Paris* — both works chosen for performances at the ninth meeting of the I.S.C.M. in Oxford and London in July 1931. Ever fair and impartial H. T. Parker reported on the American contributions and stated typically in the *Transcript:* "It is good to find so distinguished a body giving ear to the side of American music that Mr. Gershwin represents." The "distinguished" body had also chosen my Second Symphony — through the good offices of Prokofiev, who cabled me on January 21st from Paris: "Your Symphony accepted international Festival *Cambridge,*" the mistake causing me great consternation, as I imagined that the fair city of Cambridge, not to be outdone by its ancient rival, was staging its own festival. Walter Winchell announced to his readers that " 'Duke,' whose score will embellish Tom Weatherly's 'The Gay Divorcee,' is Dukelsky, whose Second Symphony, etc." The purists began to shake their heads — they never stopped shaking them; here, clearly, was another candidate for the "musical advertisers' " laureateship. Times have changed. Versatile Lennie Bernstein writes the *Jeremiah* Symphony with one hand, *Wonderful Town* with the other — and no one gives a hoot. A friend of Bernstein's was heard to exclaim at the Winter Garden: "Best score since Satie!" Adroit, if inaccurate, remark. So farfetched an appraisal gives a Broadway score a musically "correct" cachet and takes the sting out of the telltale box-office royalties. In reality the only resemblance between Satie and Bernstein lies in the fact that neither wrote song hits, but that is of no importance. Pity, no one was chic enough to say of *Strike Up the Band* that it was the "best score since Chabrier," which might have helped George in certain circles.

The English are noted for their phlegm and good manners. Perversely, these characteristics are not present in that nation's gentlemen of the press. No one can be more savagely abusive than an English critic when aroused — be it in the field of literature or art. No one could top such men as John Wilson ("Christopher North") or J. G. Lockhart, Walter Scott's biographer and son-in-law, when it came to neatly filigreed invective; in music, America's Krehbiels and Rosenfelds couldn't hold a candle to England's Davidsons and Newmans, whose pens were truly dipped in nitroglycerin. Yet I, piloted as I was by Diaghilev in my London debut days, had little idea of the English critical fraternity's destructive methods. I don't recall how Roger Sessions fared at their hands, but Gershwin and I were really massacred. The man on the *Daily Mail* called "American in Paris . . . innocent but tiresome babble" and confessed that Gershwin's "banal and silly piece drove me from the Hall." He then complained about "a shockingly noisy, tasteless symphony by the Americanized Russian Dukelsky." Another critic, signing himself R. C., called my symphony "the worst music of the evening" and George's piece "pretty bad music; not clever enough for the occasion." The *Telegraph* and the *Morning Post* were not quite as brutal, but brutal enough. Truly, a rude awakening after the honeyed epithets bestowed on me for *Zephyr and Flora* and the selfsame symphony at the time of its Boston *première*. However, Gregor Fitelberg, who conducted my work, nothing daunted, repeated it in Warsaw (at a regular concert of the Warsaw Philharmonic), where it was well received and favorably reviewed.

Meanwhile, I continued my labors on the *Gay Divorcee* and contributed numbers to various revues, among them Heywood Broun's *Shoot the Works;* so active did I become on Broadway that the *Billboard* in its September 5th issue listed Arthur Schwartz and myself as Broadway's "Most Prolific" composers, "with four shows apiece," although Sir Arthur Sullivan, of course, had his seven revivals. One of the four shows to which I contributed was that splendid revue *Three's a Crowd,* which also housed Johnny Green's "Body and Soul," sung by smoky-voiced Libby Holman. My contribution was an effective song and dance for my old flame Tamara Geva, a Diaghilev discovery like myself. Dashingly outfitted with a glistening topper and tight-fitting tails, Tamara sang and strutted my "Talkative Toes" to a smooth lyric by Howard Dietz.

I was still in my twenties, knew a lot of people and, depression or no depression, went about a good deal. My peregrinations in Mayfair's better drawing rooms were known to some of Long Island's and Westchester's Anglo-American hostesses, and invitations to coming-out parties and *soirées dansantes* soon made their appearance. It must be noted that I was invariably invited in the role of an agreeably cosmopolitan young man, "ineligible" certainly but "acceptable" perhaps, never as a composer of not inconsiderable attainments. I will dwell on American Society's attitude towards their creative contemporaries later; in 1931, I was just as happy to be asked to gay gatherings simply because I dressed correctly, danced adequately and said deliberately wrong things at the right time — not because of my status as two composers inexplicably rolled into one.

Girls, delectable New York girls, were in huge quantities everywhere; they went to bed with me willingly enough, but drew the line at marriage, realizing, with a woman's unerring instinct, that I simply wasn't "marriage material." The main difference between local sex habits and those of France lay in the female's widely divergent philosophy in the two countries; the American girl of the so-called "privileged" class is given to gay and lighthearted experiments with sex *prior* to her marriage, which in this country is synonymous with "settling down" to a one-man deal. The French girl is, as often as not, a virgin prior to marriage; the marital rites over, she achieves her freedom from family and prejudice ties, and acquires lovers — of either sex, if so inclined. The only difference between the young French bride and her husband is that he's led a turbulent sex life before his marriage and reaches still dizzier heights after it. The American husband tries hard to "stay put."

On the termination of my Paramount job, I went back to "serious" composing with renewed vigor, spurred on by Prokofiev's tongue-lashing and anxious to justify his faith in me and his untiring propaganda for my music. I wrote a difficult piano piece called "Spring 1931," which Paitchadze published in Paris, and began tampering with *Mistress into Maid* again, adding a prologue and two choruses.

Mistress into Maid (dedicated to Diaghilev's memory), based on a slender Russian anecdote not in itself original, having no production prospects, I decided on a more appropriate and realizable tribute to my discoverer's and benefactor's memory; I cast about for a poem which should in some way express a suitable idea. I did not wish to commission a poem, preferring to find something which had not been written on order. After a three months' search, I found exactly what I wanted in a poem by the Russian Ossip Mandelstamm, like Gumilev (who inspired the early "Gondla") a St. Petersburg "acmeist."

The poem blended the spirit of the North, Diaghilev's home, with the warmth of Italy, of which he was so fond and in which he died. "It depicts a theatre of Italian opera at St. Petersburg as it is being emptied after an evening's performance in winter," I said in a *Boston Transcript* interview. "I give the description of the scene to the chorus which acts as narrator. Lyric utterances go to a solo soprano, who evokes the spirit of 'Melpomene,' relates how Melpomene is strangely at ease in this old Russian land; how the native music is closely akin to Italian song. The poem ends with the Italian swallow dying on the 'hot snows' of Russia. I believed this idea an appropriate one for my purpose, since, by inversion, it mirrors the life of Diaghilev: he, the great artist born in Russia, died on Italian soil."

The *Epitaph* for Diaghilev was written in April and May of 1931 and scored in the fall of that year. In addition to the soprano and the mixed chorus, it assembled an orchestra with a large woodwind choir, scant brass, *two* guitars (to provide the wistful echoes of gypsy music in pre-World War I St. Petersburg), piano and the usual strings. This was my fourth work to be played by the Boston Symphony and I was fast acquiring a tolerable Back Bay reputation — as composer, *never* as man. The *Epitaph,* which very nearly turned out to be my own, as the reader will see, added nothing to that reputation and, although my intentions were laudable, did even less for Sergei Pavlovitch's memory. It was a diffuse, delicate piece with some lyrical high spots and an interesting bit of vocal writing for the soloist, but the orchestration was muddy and colorless, in spite of the two guitarists, who diligently strummed away, uncomfortable and bewildered in the fashionable austerity of Boston's Symphony Hall.

Prior to invading Boston again, I made friends with Mrs. Eugene Meyer, art patron and wife of the powerful Washington publisher and financier. Mrs. Meyer had a Westchester château and two decorative daughters, Katherine and Florence — not the least of the château's attractions. Mrs. Meyers's interests were education and modern art, Katherine was a budding writer, Florence, after a brief bout with a ballet career, became Mrs. Oscar Homolka. It was a good change to breathe the brittle Westchester air, roam about the immaculately kept grounds and talk with three intelligent and attractive women on subjects other than those usually discussed in the homes of the leisure class. I held forth on the composer's tribulations with Mrs. Meyer and found in her an attentive and sympathetic listener.

Late in 1931, little Aaron Baron popped up again, easygoing and ebullient as of yore, and took me to Courtney Burr's flat on Park Avenue, for a demonstration of my songwriting gifts. Courtney, a man of great charm, a social-registered boulevardier, listened with evident pleasure and, in common with Sam Behrman, liked the songs with a Franco-American flavor best. The bright-yellow canary sang loudly and remarkably out of tune throughout my recital, which, according to its owner, was an excellent omen; Burr, one of the instigators of Cole Porter's *Fifty Million Frenchmen,* was bent on producing a "smart" revue and thought me a smart enough writer to attend to the music. Courtney wanted Dorothy Parker, a friend of his and his crony Bob Benchley's at the time, to supply me with lyrics — but I insisted on Harburg, whose name was unknown to Burr; Miss Parker was not keen on writing lyrics, anyway, so the producer lent a willing ear to my hymns in Harburg's praise. The revue was tentatively "penciled in" for "sometime in 1932" and was also to launch Boris Aronson, the sensitive and resourceful scenic designer, just back from Paris and previously a worker in the Jewish Theater — another Baron suggestion. And in January 1932, the League of Composers accepted a second piece from my pen for performance; my short opus — an étude for violin and bassoon — was universally liked and critically endorsed.

Preparations for the *Epitaph* had meanwhile begun in Boston under the guidance of Arthur Fiedler, entrusted with the direction of the chorus. Adele Alberts was selected by Koussevitzky for the soloist's exacting part. She had a magnificent soprano voice, of enormous range and flexibility, and was a fine, self-effacing musician — qualities seldom encountered in the same artist. She was fond of me and fond of my *Epitaph,* which was an unlucky piece for both of us: poor Adele died shortly after singing in my work — of childbirth, in her early thirties — and I nearly died immediately after the performance.

Florence Meyer, intrigued by the *Epitaph,* came to Boston to hear it, and there was a youthful, festive atmosphere about the rehearsals, with no foreboding of the tragedy and the near-tragedy that my ominously titled piece brought in its wake. The chorus sang valiantly, Mrs. Alberts seraphically, Florence was all smiles and the two guitars were all arpeggios and St. Petersburg homesickness.

On the day of the performance, I suddenly fell ill; I thought it at first a common cold, as my throat was sore, but, on consulting the mirror, was horrified by the dark-crimson flush of fever with which my face was covered. I dressed quickly and went down to breakfast with Natalya Konstantinovna, cursing fate for such ill-timed pranks and determined to camouflage my illness until after the concert. But Tante Natalie was too sharp an observer: "Great Heavens, Dima!" she exclaimed. "Your face is flaming red — you must be feverish. Let me feel your forehead." After so doing and ascertaining that the said forehead felt like a red-hot iron, Tante Natalie said that I needed a doctor, but that it would be best not to call the family physician, "so as not to alarm Sergei Alexandrovitch before the concert." Koussevitzky, in addition to being a health addict, was mortally afraid of contagion and I, suspecting that my illness might well have been contagious, suggested removing myself to a hotel, but Natalya Konstantinovna wouldn't hear of it. "You stay right here," she said firmly. "I'll give you three aspirins and quantities of hot tea with rum — that will see you through the concert; more rum and more aspirin before bedtime and in the morning back to New York and *your* doctor you go." I readily fell in with this plan, thanked my hostess and airily assured her that I'd be "as good as new" in the morning.

However, I felt progressively worse and was on the verge of calling off my rendezvous with Florence at the Ritz. I pity those who are unfamiliar with that leisurely yet agreeably animated retreat; the Paris Ritz may be the haunt of international coxcombry and the best-preserved clotheshorses in the world, but its Boston replica offered a rare mixture of pert-faced Back Bay debutantes, serenely secure in their — to them — impeccable backgrounds, their inoffensively "arty" escorts with Richard Harding Davis strong-man profiles, Brooks Brothers clothes and an occasional deliciously daring *art moderne* waistcoat (the said arty inclinations suitably and safely tempered by cannily invested family fortunes and "must" memberships in genteel Boston clubs, impenetrable to unprivileged souls whose birth did not occur within a fifty-mile radius of Louisburg Square) and intruders from another square (Times), who too patronized Boston's Ritz-Carlton. The Broadway contingent, which often invaded the sacred premises, consisted of an occasional star or two, a brooding playwright or a beefy, bespectacled agent complete with cigar (wrong kind) and overly tailored clothes (wrong cut). The outsiders paid no attention to the strutting young Bostonians, yet were not above unceremoniously ogling their plainly, but expensively, dressed girls; the Bostonians, in their turn, were utterly oblivious of the outsiders' presence, so enveloped were they in their own cozy exploits and endless Back Bay gossip concerning mostly their cousins and aunts, fellow clubmen, sister debs, subdebs and postdebs. Thus invisibly segregated, everybody was happy — except, possibly, me — who fell between two stools as usual; I wasn't quite "Broadway" nor, certainly, "Boston," but appeared with tiresome regularity at eminently *comme il faut* dinner parties at the homes of the Boston Symphony's trustees and other musically inclined social luminaries. My hostesses, I may add, thought me disturbingly spectacular and regrettably colorful — "Not at all for you, my dear," they'd say firmly to their daughters. "He would never do in Boston."

Determined to brave fate, I drank double whisky sours with Florence, wouldn't look at food, and, in drunken stupor and high fever, took her to Symphony Hall, nearly missing the first number on the program, Mabel Daniels's "Exultate Deo." My head was swimming and it was with some difficulty that I could distinguish my own piece from Miss Daniels's; someone pushed me out at the *Epitaph's* conclusion, and I knew just enough to find the door leading to the hall's stage, kiss Mrs. Alberts's hand, shake Koussevitzky's and Richard Burgin's (the concertmaster) hands and bow to acknowledge the polite applause. The rest of the day is extremely vague in my memory, except that there was a party somewhere and that, exhausted and delirious, I took Miss Meyer to her hotel, which seemed hundreds of miles away, and was then taken back to Brookline by Koussevitzky's Russian chauffeur, to swallow more aspirin and flop into bed.

The awakening next morning was truly frightful. My throat seemed to be getting a thorough working over by zealous creatures of Satan, I couldn't swallow at all, my head was heavier than a church bell, and, bell-like, rang discordantly. Somehow I managed to dress and creep downstairs to join Sergei Alexandrovitch, frowning upon examination of the notices, which were anything but good — fortunately, I didn't bother to read them until later. "I feel terrible, Sergei Alexandrovitch," I blurted out in a voice that sounded like a rusty seesaw. "So do I," Koussevitzky rejoined. "Who wouldn't — with notices like these? Listen . . ." But I wouldn't listen and, hastily requesting that my bag be packed, ran out in the cold air, there to await the car that was to take me to Back Bay Station. Sergei Alexandrovitch stole a look at me, and what he saw upset him visibly; he became all solicitude and paternal anxiety, wrapped me up in a big woolen shawl (I still have it) and sent me on my way, suggesting a private bedroom on the train and "liquids, oceans of liquids."

The journey home was something of a protracted torture, further aggravated by the reading of the notices. Alone in my foolishly expensive private bedroom, I thought of death with considerable pleasure. Should I die at twenty-eight, I would join such young men as Mozart, Chopin, Bellini, Weber and that incredible Spaniard Arriaga y

Balzola, who died at nineteen having delivered himself of three wonderful string quartets. Why not? The obituary notices would be suitably romantic and might dwell on my orchid buttonholes and eighteenth-century walking sticks; on *Zephyr and Flora* and "I'm Only Human After All"; on the Duke-Dukelsky partnership so promisingly begun; and lastly, on the *Epitaph* which, like Mozart's *Requiem,* proved my own death warrant. The idea had charm and publicity value — only I wouldn't be there to read the notices, I quickly reflected. I then thought of Mother, alone in our small East Side flat, whose love was an indestructible shield, guarding me from all danger, and of reams of unwritten music that I knew was in me — and decided that I would try hard not to die — not just yet.

On arrival home, I tried to speak and couldn't; Mother knew at once how very sick I was. She forced me to open my mouth and let out a scream; the inside of it was the color of a newly hatched baby alligator's skin. A doctor was immediately summoned and Mother and I were told that I was a victim of diphtheria — a children's disease, unusual in a man pushing twenty-nine. Apparently I had a very severe case as my temperature was climbing swiftly to untold heights; I was given a serum injection — and another, a still stronger one, the next day. The house we lived in was immediately placed in quarantine and I began a long and obstinate bout with the unseasonable malady, which appeared mulishly persistent and wouldn't let go of me for several weeks.

To take my mind off my boring confinement, I wrote a set of languorous, magnolia-scented songs to Michail Kuzmin's "Voyage in Italy" — a pleasantly purposeless pastime, as setting Russian texts is about as practical as setting Latin ones; both Russian and Latin being dead languages today — unless you recognize the ghastly Marxist gibberish printed in Moscow as Russian.

Having been denied a further extension of my visitor's visa, I was told that, should I voluntarily leave for an adjoining country and there be able to secure a quota number, I would then be eligible to re-enter the U.S. as an immigrant and become a candidate for citizenship. Mother did all she could to help secure a quota number for me through friends in Riga, Latvia. Mexico was the "adjoining country" elected for my "voluntary" exit.

I sailed in May on the *Morro Castle,* which went up in smoke off the Jersey shore three or four trips later with most of her passengers burned alive. The ship itself was modern and clean, the service execrable and practically none of the stewards spoke English or any other known language. We arrived in Vera Cruz — an ugly, barren town — on an especially hot day; you felt as if you were a violin put back in your case and left there, the case shut tight. Breathing was out of question and I spent most of the time swigging crystal-cool Carta Blanca beer in a low-ceilinged bar bereft of windows or ventilation. That night I went to Mexico City by train — an experience I cannot recommend because it scared me out of my wits. I had to content myself with an upper berth (all the lowers had been sold) and couldn't sleep all night, having peered out of my window a few times to discover that we were traveling in the sky, taking sharp curves in order not to hit the moon and the stars, over an abyss of what looked like 100,000 feet. This didn't prevent some two hundred soldiers from cluttering up the vestibules and even hanging on to the hand railings for dear life, making the whole trip on the slippery steps of the railroad cars. They were fully armed and when I asked the porter the reason for all that ammunition, he grinned knowingly and said something about bandits lurking behind every cactus plant.

I loved Mexico City, even the crazily rare air due to the excessively high altitude, which nearly caused me to faint at first; even the strange food, exotic with a vengeance and smelling not unlike highly spiced fresh paint. It is customary for a foreigner to develop a violent stomach ailment after a few Mexican *commida corridas* (complete dinners), and I bowed to custom. It is also customary *not* to admire the Mexican-baroque (churrigueresque) architecture of the city's churches and edifices — there I refused to conform, and admired the elaborately ornamental façades and windows unreservedly. I explored the Zocalo, lounged in a Mexican gondola as I was rowed through the floating gardens of Xochimilco, climbed atop the cathedral to "take in" the celebrated view of the city, and drank pulque (horrible), tequila (take it or leave it) and nanche, a liquor distilled from honey (sheer ambrosia).

I was well received by Carlos Chavez, then director of the conservatory, conductor of the Mexico City Symphony and the leading musical figure of his country. Crouched at his office desk in the old *conservatorio* building, Chavez looked pretty much the way his music sounded: wiry, angular, nervous and aggressively functional. He was a small, keen-looking man of jerky, agitated gestures and what writers of mediocre fiction describe as "dark, dynamic looks." He listened to my *Zephyr and Flora,* called it "fresh, young music" and volunteered to give it a performance (which never took place); I was introduced to Frances Poor, the city's top "contact" woman, and Carolina Amor, Chavez's secretary, a girl as troublesomely pretty as her name (to whom I later dedicated my "Capriccio Mexicano," a wild violin piece) and taken to Carlos Obregon's for cocktails.

Obregon, the architect *en vogue* in Mexico, had built himself a roofless house which was one of the wonders of the city. I still don't know what he did when it rained, but can testify to the total absence of a roof. We drank unusually potent cocktails and were offered plates of unfamiliar-looking appetizers, brown little ovals that tasted like dehydrated peanuts. They were quite palatable and, after devouring a half dozen, I asked the hostess what they were. She looked around furtively, as if to make sure that the other foreigners present weren't listening, and then hissed dramatically: "They are dried and processed desert bugs. Delicious, no?" "Delicious, yes," I answered, and ran to the bathroom.

I also met copper-skinned, wild-eyed Silvestre Revueltas, the half-Indian composer, who died young. Revueltas was an impulsive, warmhearted man, and his excitement-charged, volcanic music was Mexico-hewn, perhaps more genuinely so than the sharper, wittier, better-made music of Chavez. Revueltas had a small, delicately featured Indian wife who had the beautifully shaped slim legs of the women of her race and a sad, melodious speaking voice. We drank and ate, and talked and made music — it was a little like Paris, the Paris of composers.

A Mexican friend took me to a mediocre bullfight (it was the wrong time of the year for that sport) and three unforgettable performances at the Teatro Garibaldi, which no longer exists. The Garibaldi was a species of American burlesque and the three performances all took place the same evening; the first of these, at 6 P.M., was a "family" affair, the girls appeared fully garbed and the comedians made mild jokes of an inoffensive nature. The second show, starting at 8. P.M., was considerably bolder; the girls, now in partial undress, displayed small firm breasts that looked like pale-pink oranges from where I sat, and the comedians indulged in energetic horseplay and scatological allusions, while the audience was "mixed," young couples predominating; at 10 P.M. the theater quickly filled with daredevil-type *aficionados* and in a few minutes there was not a woman in the cigar-scented place. What went on on the stage defied description. The women were either entirely nude or wore nothing under transparent short skirts. There was a runway in the center of the orchestra, U.S. burlesque style, and the women paraded up and down on it, strutting lasciviously, their faces strangely impassive and remote. Those who sat in the middle aisle were regaled by an anatomical display leaving nothing whatever to the imagination; the dress circle was occupied exclusively by Indians, and the runway was so situated that, by leaning forward, the Indians could touch the girls without difficulty. This was considered a cardinal offense and the police, strategically placed in the doorways, were on a sharp lookout for molesters; while I was in the audience, two such molesters were picked up immediately and marched off to jail. Trips to jail, my informer assured me, were part of the Indian's everyday life, and you could often see a high-cheekboned, stolid and serene-looking citizen being escorted by elegant Mexican cops, for who-knows-what offense, smoking a fat cigarette unconcernedly the while. The comedians — of either sex — who participated in performance No. 3 carried on in a manner that would make Restif de la Bretonne blush.

Chavez and I dined together frequently and I developed a great admiration for the man's energy and oneness of purpose, the second of these qualities being regrettably absent from my character. His "Pan-American" conception of the music of this hemisphere and his realistically democratic regard for all "toilers in music," however humble, coincided with my own ideas; we were both bursting with a righteous desire to make these ideas universally accepted and put in work. Chavez's pet project was a huge music festival of new music, sponsored and run by composers, not interpreters or prima donna-loving patrons; I thought of Mrs. Meyer and her magnificent Westchester County Center, an ideal place for such an undertaking. Mexico is the hotbed of romantic plots and counterplots; of upheavals and bloodshed. We would have gladly bled some of music's more affluent parasites, but, for the time being, contented ourselves with verbal violence in the shape of a first draft of a "Composers' Manifesto" — a time bomb which exploded in 1933.

A quota number was finally secured and I was enabled to sail for the States on the S.S. *Orizaba* on July 10th, an immigrant once again. This time everything went off without a hitch on my arrival, and I was admitted, never again, I hoped, to cast my eyes on the dreaded Island of Ellis; I couldn't foresee, of course, that I would receive my U.S.C.G. "boot" training on the island ten years later. I could have kissed the "sidewalks of New York," so great was my joy at walking them again, and even thought of writing a modern version of the affecting old ballad.

On landing, I bought the New York *Sun* and read, to my horror, of the *Gay Divorcee* going into rehearsal with a score by . . . Mr. Cole Porter. Thinking this a newspaperman's error, I telephoned the Weatherly office; Mr. Weatherly was out, but I thought of an ingenious trick — assuming the hesitant manner of a stage applicant, I asked the receptionist whether I could audition for Mr. Weatherly's show? "The *Little Show* or the Cole Porter musical?" the receptionist shot back innocently. I slammed the receiver, seething with rage, and ran to the offices of Harms, Inc. The whole of Broadway knew that Eliscu and I were engaged to write music and lyrics for Dwight Taylor's book, that we were paid advances and given contracts and that we even played "money" auditions for possible investors. All these facts had been duly trumpeted by Tom Weatherly, ever the energetic publicist. The question now was "To sue, or not to sue?" Wise old Max Dreyfus took a long puff on his cigar, pondered for a while, then opined that although Eliscu and I "had a case," it wouldn't pay to sue a producer. It didn't pay to work on a score for months, only to have it replaced by another writer's, without even the simple courtesy of a written explanation, either — but I swallowed my righteous indignation and learned the true meaning of "you can't fight City Hall," an expression that had always baffled me theretofore.

After lunch with Mother — that is, I lunched while she cried and thanked God for my safe return — I telephoned Courtney Burr and was told that he was having trouble raising money for the revue, but that Boris Aronson was doing a "great job" and inventing new scenic devices daily. Courtney didn't sound very encouraging, and with the Weatherly show out of my hands, it looked like a jobless autumn coming on. Dejectedly, I walked up and down Broadway, frowzy and evil-smelling in the glaring sun, like an unbathed cocotte after a night with too many customers. Broadway is still a Babylonian spectacle after dark, but were I the mayor of New York, I'd keep the visitors away in the daytime, or revoke the licenses of fruit-drink and popcorn sellers (incidentally, I'd forbid the hellish-sounding popcorn mastication in cinemas), hot-dog and hamburger stands, Bowery-style bars — all the tinseled trash that succeeded in utterly defacing the once great and stately theater street.

A few steps from Lindy's I ran into a small, pudgy man whose voice had a curiously strident nasal quality — a cross between a purr and a twang — and who answered to the name of Billy Rose. Mr. Rose looked me over, beginning with the shoes — they were fine, thank goodness, and did not betray the unenviable financial status of their wearer — then worked his way up to my face, tanned by the hot Mexican sun. "Doin' anything?" he asked playfully. "Well, not too much of anything," I answered, right to the point — which is one of my sterling characteristics. "I'm just back from Mexico." "Takin' it easy, huh?" Mr. Rose continued. "I understand you're a kinda thorough music man; may be able to do something with you. Come over to Lindy's and we'll talk." To Lindy's we journeyed and talked — or, rather, Billy did the talking and I listened, fascinated. Apparently, Rose was bent on producing a revue with sketches by Ben Hecht and Charles MacArthur, and he wanted an assembled score studded with nothing but hits. He felt that were he to entrust the job to one composer, he might come up with one world beater or two on the outside, whereas, by getting all the top writers to submit their best songs, one could, by weeding out the "dogs" (songs with no future) wind up with a 100 per cent commercial score. My job, Billy continued, would entail the examination of such material, a detailed report on the chances of songs submitted — both as music and as hit possibilities, and the writing of "incidental," ballet and "furniture" music and, possibly, a few songs as well. This, while not overly attractive, was a job, and I, mulling it over quickly, asked what my royalties would be. "Royalty?" Billy intoned, more nasally than before. "I'm not gonna pay you any royalty. Tell you what I'll do — I'll give you fifty bucks a week: fifty every week while you work on the show, fifty every week while it runs. Is it a deal?" My indignant protests proving of no avail, I asked Rose's permission to telephone Dreyfus and get his appraisal of such an offer. Permission granted, I reported our conversation to Mighty Max, who said wearily: "You have nothing else. Take it — we may get a hit song out of it." I took it.

For almost two months, my work was cut out for me by Billy, a severe taskmaster. Every night at around nine I had to report at Fanny Brice's flat (Rose was then married to her), and was handed a big batch of manuscripts, most of them unharmonized lead sheets — the voice part alone. I was then led to the piano, given a brisk pep talk and left to submit the songs to a ruthless screening process — hit-parade "maybes" to be placed to the right of the keyboard, doghouse candidates to the left. At about midnight Billy would reappear, listen to the evening's harvest and then take me to a Broadway delicatessen for a cup of coffee and a corned-beef sandwich; I didn't care for corned beef, but the show was tentatively titled *Corned Beef and Roses,* so I munched the symbolically styled sandwich in silence. Fanny, for whom I was to write two revues eventually, appeared once or twice as I labored; I was grateful for these interruptions, as she was friendly and immediately likable.

My evenings thus monopolized by the corned-beef musical, I found afternoon sessions on *Walk a Little Faster* with Burr and Boris Aronson a welcome relief. Boris, who looked as if he had just stepped from an Assyrian frieze and wore twentieth-century coat and trousers under protest, was then struggling manfully and performing miracles of revolutionary stagecraft in his dingy Central Park West studio. Evelyn Hoey, honey-haired and honey-voiced, Courtney, Monty Woolley (engaged to direct the sketches) and I sat for hours, hypnotized by Boris's excited guttural explanations and the beautifully made little models of sets — the ones intended for "April in Paris" and "That's Life" (a Clark and McCullough "special" with a bright and biting Harburg lyric) were especially striking. Another song superbly "imagined" by Boris was the atmospherically titled "Manhattan's the Loneliest Isle Without You," eventually dropped from the score. Money was slow in coming, but it *was* coming, Courtney said, both Jock Whitney and Vincent Astor having promised to invest.

"April in Paris" was written in April 1932, in New York, at Tony Soma's still-famous establishment, known to New Yorkers as the "West Side Tony's," as opposed to the plushier East Side bistro of that name. After auditioning some particularly untalented girls, we all repaired to Tony's; the "we" consisting of Dorothy Parker, Evelyn Hoey, Robert Benchley, Monty Woolley, Johnny McClain, Burr and myself.

Evelyn, whom I had first heard singing a pseudo-Scottish air of Cole Porter's in the American revue at the Ambassadeurs in Paris in '28 or '29 (Cole put her in his *Fifty Million Frenchmen* a year later and she scored a notable success), was to be entrusted with the singing chores in the new musical. After several double Scotches, we all got pretty sentimental, the Scotch reminding us of Miss Hoey's tartan skirt in her Paris number, and the mention of the number inevitably leading to Paris, how wonderful it was in the spring and how vile was Manhattan at that time of year. I can't think whether it was Benchley or Woolley who cried out: "Oh, to be in Paris now that April's here!" The rest went off in true Class B musical-picture fashion. "April in Paris . . ." said I, melodramatically. "What a title! My kingdom for a piano!" No sooner were these words uttered than the ever-obliging Tony ventured the information that an old and wretched upright was at my disposal on the second floor. The piano was wretched indeed, but it made appropriate sounds when persuaded and, using the title "April in Paris" for what they call the "front phrase" in the trade, I soon completed the reasonably immortal refrain. I then proceeded to "ham it up," telling all and sundry that I had just given birth to a masterpiece that was certain to "make the show." The lyrics were written a week later by Harburg.

On June 3, 1932, Prokofiev wrote from Paris:

> Thanks for the puffed-up letter. Nineteen pages is something of a record. Most of all I was touched by a certain youthful freshness of your style, a quality lost long ago by the various Markevitches and Nabokovs in their Paris struggle for survival. You somehow manage to preserve that freshness in spite of your constant peregrinations in the slums of New York music. — I held the manuscript of your "Epitaph" in my hands for a few moments some months back when you sent it to Paris to have the orchestral parts extracted; but on seeing that the work was written on "Jazz" manuscript paper, I felt an upsurge of squeamishness and put it aside. Since both you and Koussevitzky speak well of that work, I will take a better look at it. What a decadent idea to write a monumental work with dying St. Petersburg as the theme! Say what you will, that is the stamp placed upon you by your hobnobbing with the drying-up emigrants, these branches severed from the tree trunk, that dream of past splendid Springs while withering away. If you must write that kind of a piece, call it "Leningrad" or "Dnieprostroy."
>
> . . . it will not be difficult for me to place your chamber works either with the Serenade or Cortot concerts, or the new chamber society for contemporary music, which is being formed;

> I'll be on its jury. [The last-named organization was the Triton, of which P. O. Ferroud was the leading spirit.] I was happy to read that you liked my Third Symphony. I, too, feel that it contained a lot of "real stuff" and I don't understand why it is so slow in getting going. The suite from the "Prodigal Son" was put together with bits and pieces that didn't get into the Fourth Symphony — the one that was so unjustly buried in Boston by our precious representative of the Kous-Kous tribe.

The rest of Serge's long letter consisted of highly technical "music talk," and ended thus:

> Lina Ivanovna sang your music on the London radio and will soon do so on the Paris one. You have your Soudeikines, we have our Souvtchinskys and Tansmans — but they all vanished from the horizon.

Alex was back in New York and the Dukelsky trio gave up the excitements of our "uptown" existence for the relative quiet of Greenwich Village. We found a second-floor walk-up flat on West Fourth Street, right next to the Pepper Pot, just off Washington Square. Lower Fifth Avenue and Washington Square are still "real New York" to me, together with the Battery and what's left of Murray Hill. Our two years on Fourth Street would have been replete with peace and contentment were it not for the burglars. All our neighbors reported burglaries at one time or another, and then our time came — twice. The first visit of the looting boys resulted in the disappearance of my entire wardrobe; the second visit's toll consisted of every article of clothing Mother owned. When I telephoned the police after the first burglary, a bored voice answered: "Mister, there's nothing we can do — we get dozens of calls every day. It's the Village — get a better lock." We didn't call the police after Mother's things were stolen — we moved out.

Life on West Fourth Street was full and rich, despite our comparative poverty. Mother kept house, Alex worked for a fellow architect in Jersey City, and I wrote my two kinds of music, toiled for Burr and Rose, and entertained fellow composers in my leisure moments. Wallingford Riegger and Harold Morris, two of the best talents of the older generation, ever-young Percy Grainger and a trio of "cubs" — Bernard Herrmann, Jerome Moross and Irwin Heilner — could always be counted on to drop in of an afternoon; the younger group often came to breakfast, to Mother's delight. Of the three, Benny Herrmann was the most remarkable; still a Juilliard student, he lived for, with, and in music. Oblivious of his appearance, unruly hair, shirt ill-fitting and clothes unpressed, Benny was an aggressive, torrential talker, making up in sincerity and violence for the lack of superficial polish in his speech or any aptitude for felicitous phrase-making. His great honesty and overflowing love of music, his dogged determination to serve it as composer and conductor — in contrast to conductors' traditional tendency to make music serve *them* — were touching and disarming and worthy of respect. Benny Herrmann and Billy Rose had the same East Side background of poverty and privation; the difference lay in the fact that one was on the friendliest terms with Mammon, the other with Melpomene.

Jerry Moross, a talented all-around musician, was what's known in New Yorkese as a fresh guy. One morning, after downing a hearty breakfast, he demanded to hear my "Spring 1931." I played it for him. "That's a very bad piece, Vladi," Moross commented when I came to a stop, then exploded in a delighted cackle. Gradually other composers, New York residents all, found their way to West Fourth Street and together we plotted and argued excitedly. What emerged was a concrete plan for an annual composers' festival — based on the blueprint Chavez and I dreamed up in Mexico; this plan was presented to Mrs. Meyer, who thought it workable; she agreed to underwrite the project to the tune of $50,000 and to house it in the handsome and spacious Westchester County Center.

Our next job was to find a suitable conductor with a special flair for contemporary music, who would fall in with our revolutionary conspiracy — restoring the composer to his rightful place in the musical sun. I then made a cardinal, but understandable, mistake; aware of Koussevitzky's fearless and generous championship of new music, I thought him the logical choice for our undertaking. What I didn't realize was the fact that Sergei Alexandrovitch, aided and abetted by his rich and worshiping wife, was a despot — an amiable one, certainly, but a despot, nevertheless. I proposed his name at the next composers' meeting — attended, incidentally, by Aaron Copland and Nicolai Berezowsky, both of whom owed their careers to Koussevitzky — and Sergei Alexandrovitch was unanimously nominated as the Festival's musical director.

I went to Boston and consulted that human barometer of musical weather, Nicolas Slonimsky, who knew Koussevitzky as few people did. Nicolas told me with his habitual directness that we were climbing the wrong tree, that Koussevitzky had never consulted anyone about his programs and wouldn't take dictation under any circumstances — especially from composers, to whom *he* had dictated all his life. It was too late to retreat, so I manfully descended on the Koussevitzkys, was asked to supper and went into my song and dance about the Festival, the New Era in American Music, etc., etc. Sergei Alexandrovitch's initial reaction was one of boundless ecstasy — he jumped up from his seat at the table, embraced me impulsively, and said that an annual Festival of New Music was his pet dream and that, should it materialize, he'd give up the Boston Symphony and devote himself exclusively to working on the Festival's programs. "But that will be *our* work, Sergei Alexandrovitch," I said quickly. *"Whose* work, Dima?" Koussevitzky asked in astonishment. "Why, the composers', certainly. You see, the whole idea is that the composers' jury — you'll be on it of course — will be responsible for the programs," I went on. The Koussevitzkys exchanged troubled glances. "Surely you don't mean that your young people will pick the scores and Sergei Alexandrovitch will just stand by until called upon to conduct the orchestra?" Natalya Konstantinovna queried acidly. I had to admit that that was almost exactly what we meant. Koussevitzky began suggesting agitatedly that were *he* to attend to the music, and *I* to organization details, we'd do away with confusion and get better results, but Natalya Konstantinovna rose, cutting short our debate, and suggested drily that I spend the night and that we resume our talks in the morning.

In the morning, the atmosphere became chillier still. The couple had obviously "compared notes" and evolved a plan of strategy, which they would not divulge to me. Sergei Alexandrovitch simply said that he was interested "in principle," Natalya Konstantinovna adding that they'd let me know "in due time." A few days later, however, Koussevitzky accepted our proposal and we so informed Mrs. Meyer.

On my return, I had to busy myself with other things. Billy Rose took an office in the Wurlitzer Building and regaled the press with typically roseate announcements concerning his forthcoming revue. One of these announcements read: "Most of the tunes will come from the music stand of Vernon Duke." Alas, my music stand proved more of a standstill in the Wurlitzer Building, as Billy, busy with his stable of stars, his coffers bulging with "hit material" I helped select, somehow lost interest in me; when his revue got produced (under a new name and with a new cast) I was not among its composers. Not so with Courtney Burr, who stuck with me through thick and thin. The Astors and the Whitneys heeded his call; at long last, splendid offices at St. James Theatre were given over to Burr and his retinue, and a fully equipped bar was put within easy reach of the producer's desk — a great luxury in those sad speakeasy days.

Beatrice Lillie, always referred to as "incomparable," and rightly so, and Clark and McCullough were signed by Burr, as well as Boris Aronson for sets and costumes, Albertina Rasch for the dances, S. J. Perelman for the sketches and Monty Woolley to direct the dialogue. Perelman, whom I first met in Burr's office, looked like a bespectacled black panther in a Brooks Bros. suit.

Harburg flew into a rage very easily. Upon demonstrating a song of ours called "Speaking of Love," he wound up with the last lines: "Speaking of love, I'll be your *nin*compoop, just be my *in*compoop, speaking of love." When Dorothy Parker, listening with her deceptively demure air, asked sweetly: "Pray, dear Mr. Harburg, *what* is an *in*compoop?" Harburg let out an agonized yell, delivered a poignant address on the subject of Park Avenue Parasites and stormed out of the room. He was a busy man in the autumn of 1932 and could well afford to take such verbal duels in his stride. J. P. McEvoy's *Americana,* which opened in October at the Shubert Theatre, had several composers, but Harburg was billed as its only lyricist (although three songs were written in collaboration with Johnny Mercer). *Americana* was well liked by the critics and boasted two highlights — "Brother, Can You Spare a Dime" (Gorney-Harburg), that stirring saga of depression, and the lightly satirical "Let Me Match My Private Life With Yours," for which I supplied the tune; nearly every newspaper quoted the punchline: "You can have your City Hall — I'll take A. C. Blumenthal. Let me match my private life with yours," sung by Albert Carroll in a realistic take-off on Jimmy Walker.

The Boston opening of *Walk a Little Faster* coincided with the Chicago *première* of my Second Symphony, which was programed thanks to Prokofiev, who succeeded in selling Frederick Stock, the orchestra's conductor, on the virtues of my score, prior to returning to Europe. I couldn't break away from the revue's rehearsals, and thus had to miss the symphony's; from all accounts it was well played — the late Mr. Stock was a topnotch musician — and noisily received, "bravos" clashing with less complimentary exclamations. The notices were of the "in and out" variety. *Walk a Little Faster* rehearsals were not particularly memorable, except that Bobby Clark, one of the musical stage's greatest comedians, surprised me by seeming a mournful, pedantic little fellow, who kept complaining about "tricky lyrics" and "too many choruses," which were fed him by faithful Paul McCullough, who made up in efficiency for what he lacked in talent. The pair had a hilarious opening number in "That's Life" ("Just when you're getting ahead, bingo! You're dead — That's life."), a kind of a two-four strut, and I recall Bobby running across the stage arm in arm with McCullough, singing through his cigar and taking it out of his mouth every so often to bark at Harburg and myself: "You're making it tough for me, boys."

On several occasions we were within a hairsbreadth of not opening at all, because, among the backers of nearly every show, there's always at least one doubting Thomas who gets cold feet just before signing his check — and his withdrawal causes the show's future to hang perilously in the balance. We, the authors, were too busy with our own troubles to believe the wild tales we heard from some of the snooping members of the cast — and it was just as well; the tales were all based on truth, but that didn't prevent the revue from opening — shows having a habit of opening and — alas! — closing when least expected to do so.

Courtney invited the Koussevitzkys to the *première* and they accepted with pleasure; we didn't have time to discuss the proposed festival — Sergei Alexandrovitch wasn't any too anxious to do so, anyway, and as I led the couple to my box, they were all smiles and eager anticipation, quite like children with a multicolored, oversized toy. The Boston *Walk a Little Faster* opening night was one of the roughest in history. Two or three of the more massive settings were not shown because of first-night handicaps backstage: two or three of the less agile stagehands unintentionally appeared with the actors, and some of the actors didn't appear at all, unable to find their way to the stage. To paraphrase the report of an eyewitness, it was a splendid performance, contributed both by the invisible actors and the visible stage crew, but the show easily rose above such trifles. The wonderful Boston audience — there is no better, as any showman will testify — ate it all up good-naturedly, overlooking such items as the crash of a drop and its removal from the scene *for good.*

Again to the credit of Boston, it must be admitted that "April in Paris" clicked during our tryout in that city, while it definitely "laid a bomb" (in the current phrase) two weeks later in New York; and I must again pay a tribute to my unflinching supporter, Boston's own H. T. Parker by crediting him with the first out-and-out "rave" for the song. His notice for the entire score was of the sort that no one writes anymore and it lifted me right up to the sky. "Modernisms abound in Mr. Duke's music. He has confided it and Mr. Salinger has scored it [Conrad Salinger, who with Russell Bennett orchestrated the music] for a jazz, rather than a theatre orchestra. Being a modernist, Mr. Duke makes bold with rhythms. . . . Nor does Mr. Duke hesitate at modulations that might grate on the more innocent Berlin or Kern. Yet when need is, he can write a nostalgic, quasi-sentimental melody that touches most that hear. 'April in Paris' is worthy, in place and kind, of that city in spring. There is a catch in the throat from it — if one has too many memories. 'Loneliest Isle,' which is Manhattan, keeps it fit company. *Distinctly, Mr. Duke has gone several steps forward with our music for revue.*" Despite good notices, *Walk a Little Faster,* like most big, lavish revues, needed a lot of work in order to achieve the hit status prophesied for it by Boston's reviewers — and, rather unexpectedly, by Koussevitzky, who thought it the best show he'd ever seen; I doubt that he'd seen many.

Ray Goetz, Courtney's producer friend, arrived over the week end to lend a helping hand, and the two men were closeted together in Courtney's suite at the Ritz the whole of Sunday making drastic changes, without the assistance of the authors, who were not summoned, at Goetz's suggestion. On Monday morning we were told that a brand new "routine" was to be tried that night, that it was to be sprung as a "surprise" and would we please forego "looking in" at rehearsals, but attend the performance and make notes. Aronson, Perelman, Harburg and I spent the whole day resting in the lovely New England countryside, and, after a copious dinner at Locke-Ober's showed up at the Majestic Theatre. The performance was a surprise, all right; all the best sketches and songs were now in Act One, the audience was brought to its feet and we to the nearest exit.

Out in the fresh air we stared at one another, Aronson shaking his head unbelievingly, Perelman's bespectacled black-panther face wearing a typically savage scowl. Knowing that all the "weak sisters" were dumped into Act Two, no doubt with the assumption that the audience, shattered by the first act's magnificence, would, by then, swallow anything, we couldn't face the actors about to be slaughtered in the line of duty and betook ourselves to a neighboring bar. At 10 P.M. we emerged, unable to stand the suspense any longer, and were equally unable to re-enter the theater; masses of people were pouring out of the Majestic, looking sulky and dejected, and blocking all the entrances. Our first guess was that the paying customers, crushed by the horrors of the second act, left in protest; but that was not the case. Goetz's strategy was simply to cut out five of the more offensive items, without replacing them; thus the curtain went down at 9:50 P.M. (instead of the 11:45 of the opening night's performance) and the audience saw the shortest revue in theatrical history. The original routine was restored on the next evening, Mr. Goetz leaving Boston by an early train.

The receipts for the second week dropped quite a bit, but we rolled up our sleeves and worked doggedly, finally whipping the revue into acceptable shape. Another financial near-catastrophe was narrowly averted, and a hilarious party was given by Courtney and his backers on the Saturday preceding our exodus from Boston and the staid Ritz Hotel treated to the unusual spectacle of chorus girls performing audacious "grinds" in the hotel lobby at 6 A.M. and doing uncensored "bumps" against the columns adorning the establishment's interior. Courtney and Evelyn sailed into an uninhibited polka for the benefit of the wide-eyed bellhops, and even Monty Woolley essayed a species of a jig, but cut it short, probably to uphold his beard's dignity.

We opened in New York with considerable éclat, La Lillie's faithful admirers and the entire Astor and Whitney clans present in full force. The show was much smoother than in Boston, yet its smoothness exposed faults — a certain would-be recherché self-consciousness, a striving for originality at all costs and the sketches' tendency to peter out without reaching the hoped-for hilarious climax. Consequently, the notices were only fair — or, in hopeful theatrical parlance, they were "good box-office notices." My share of the notices was almost nonexistent, which was hard to take after the

Boston raves. Winchell's appraisal of my score was a far cry from Parker's colorful adjectives; he singled out "Where Have We Met Before," "So Nonchalant" and "Speaking of Love" as the best of the tunes, but thought the music for the most part "nothing to set your tootsies tapping." Walter proved a good friend in later years; I just didn't "slay" him in 1932. Nobody mentioned "April in Paris," except Bob Garland, who thought it "an unnecessary item." The first columnist to embrace my best-known and most durable song was amiable little Louis Sobol, who invited his readers to "clap calloused mitts for his favorite next to 'Melancholy Baby' — Vernon Duke's soft 'April in Paris.' "

The truth of the matter was that poor Evelyn Hoey was suffering from laryngitis and her rendering of my ballad seldom rose above a hoarse whisper; the lovely Aronson set — an imaginary Paris Left Bank café behind a transparent gauze curtain — and the waltz interlude by the young and supple Fitzgibbonses, well-choreographed by Albertina Rasch — weren't enough to put the song over. After the second performance, Alex and I, dejected and resentful of the critics' indifference, sat in the Times Square Childs' restaurant, Alex consoling me to the best of his ability, when in stormed Harburg, disheveled and obviously in a rage. "Ah, so you liked your Boston notices, my fine friend," he exclaimed, coming right to the point. "I hope you're satisfied with the New York ones. I told you 'April in Paris' might be all right for decadent Europeans, but not for this country — yet you wouldn't listen. Read this." With a dramatic gesture he threw Bob Garland's notice on my table. My shy, soft-spoken brother came to my defense and upbraided Harburg for his untimely and unfriendly onslaught on his collaborator, who, after all, got him the job. The scene was not pretty and my lyricist left in a huff, claiming that "April in Paris" should have been a saucy "jingle" in the first place.

While in Boston, through Slonimsky I had met and become a friend and admirer of Gershwin's and Gilbert's and Sullivan's vivid and erudite biographer Isaac Goldberg, a gentle, retiring soul, capable of unexpected flights of fancy and still more unexpected flashes of steel-edged wit. Goldberg was especially appreciative of the Duke side of me, rather than the Dukelsky one; as I suspected, most of the "serious" new music left him cold — mine, possibly, included. In the years that I knew Ike Goldberg (he is another tragic entry in my ever-growing list of those who died too soon), he did as much for me in the realm of musical comedy as H. T. Parker in the symphonic division. The music of *Walk a Little Faster* fascinated him, and some of the pleasanter Boston rituals were nightly gatherings, after the show, either at Ike's or Slonimsky's for a little modest eating and drinking, a few ribald stories and limericks (Ike reminded me of Philip Heseltine in that respect) and a capsule recital of my "catalogue of dogs," in Jack Robbins's immortal phrase, with myself at the piano.

Goldberg was indignant at the New York critics' treatment of my score for the Bea Lillie show and wrote me on December 13th: "From scraps that I read here and there in the Gotham (Goddamn) press, I gathered that they had been stupid — that is the 'mot juste' — with your music. It is nothing new. I shall be glad, as a public service, and not alone as a service to you, to write to one of the newspapers. The question is, which paper shall it be?" There was more in this vein, then an amusing reference to Gershwin's unsuccessful *Pardon My English,* which was shut up for repairs: "Maybe the English was unpardonable! I'm sure the music was O.K." Most gratifying was the P.S.: " 'April in Paris' is one of the finest musical compositions that has ever graced an American production. If I had my way, I'd make the study of it compulsory in all harmony courses." The paper for which Ike wrote his article, calling it "Dukelsky into Duke," turned out to be the *New York Evening Post,* which printed the article in January 1933. While Goldberg didn't quite "take the stump to pronounce Vernon Duke the greatest of composers — putting his work above Kern, Gershwin et al.," as the ubiquitous Winchell announced to his *Mirror* readers, Ike did very handsomely by me: "I consider it important for our lighter musical stage that a talent such as Duke's should not, at this point in his development, pass insufficiently appreciated. The man has an individual gift that makes him stand out in company of those who have made of our musical comedy something more than the dull routine it once used to be. In fact, I do not hesitate to say that he is the most important personality to come to our stage since Kern and Gershwin and Porter were followed by Rodgers, Youmans and their fellows, and that, if he is not allowed to find his place in contemporary revues, musical comedies and even comic opera, the loss will be, to us and to him, artistically considerable."

Such pronouncements were fine and soul-satisfying, but they didn't help sell copies or records, of which there were very few made, none whatever of "April in Paris." Dreyfus was not pleased and intimated that it was fine to be a "class" composer, but that turning out song hits was infinitely healthier. The "boys" in the Harms waiting room were thunderstruck when, on my way out of the "inner sanctum," I was stopped by a white-haired, birdlike little fellow who said in a high-pitched voice: "You're Vernon Duke, aren't you? Let me shake your hand — I'm Jerome Kern." We shook hands and I murmured something indicative of my profound respect for the dean of America's show composers, who interrupted me to say: "You may think it odd and I'm not in the habit of saying such things, but I'm crazy about your music — it's new and it's fresh. Believe it or not, I'm under your influence. Good day to you." And off he went to keep an appointment with Max Dreyfus.

Walk a Little Faster had a run of four or five months, was rated a moderate success and lost money. A representative of one of the backers, oblivious of the management's protests, hit on an effective idea; he would appear at the box office after the Saturday matinee and collect his principal's share of the week's take. This was fine for the principal, but ruinous to us authors — as, by the time the cast and the orchestra were paid, there was no money whatever left for us. Thus I, a busy Broadway tunesmith represented by two shows (*Americana* was in for a run), received no royalties — my microscopic share of the McEvoy show's intake excepted — and had difficulty paying rent and buying food for the house. It was no fault of Burr's, who did what he could to help and made a cash settlement with me — and the other writers — some months later.

Composers' meetings in Washington Square were now resumed and a vast dossier of composers' grievances, complaints and aspirations assembled and indexed — for the whole music world, which was in no hurry, to see. Shortly after the revue's opening, I was summoned to Brookline by Koussevitzky for what I knew was to be a final "showdown." Natalya Konstantinovna was not present at our conversation before supper, but she was the real power behind the conductor's throne and I knew at once that Koussevitzky's stand was influenced and, probably, insisted upon by his wife, who would never allow anyone to question Sergei Alexandrovitch's supremacy in matters musical. His main point was that a festival, to be lastingly successful, must be run and guided by one man and that letting composers run things without an authoritative leader spelled suicide for our project. A heated argument ensued, Koussevitzky bent on winning, I holding ground obstinately. Exasperated by my stubbornness, the conductor suddenly let the cat out of the bag: "This is all a waste of time. Mrs. Meyer agrees with *me,* anyway," he shrieked.

I went back perplexed and worried; something was radically wrong with the festival plans — the composers on one side of the fence, Koussevitzky on the other, with me in the middle, to which position I was fast getting used. On whose side was Mrs. Meyer? There would be the clue to the whole mystery, as all of our plotting was just so much idle talk without that gracious and energetic woman, her pet County Center and — let's admit it — her money. I went to see Mrs. Meyer on arrival; in answer to my question concerning Koussevitzky's statement, she readily admitted having corresponded with the conductor, who proposed *his* plan for the festival, severely criticizing ours. Worse still, Mrs. Meyer seemed to be convinced by Koussevitzky's arguments and now thought our original idea — of a festival run by and for composers — impractical and unbusinesslike. It appeared that Sergei Alexandrovitch was greatly vexed by "unknown amateurs" who wrote him offering program suggestions, and — in parenthesis — asking him to listen to their music. When I asked the identity of so bold an amateur, Mrs. Meyer checked with Koussevitzky's letter and said it was "somebody called Wallingford Riegger." I gasped. Riegger, born in 1885, studied at the Berlin *Hochschule* and conducted the Bluthner Orchestra; received the Paderewski award and the Elizabeth Coolidge Prize, and was one of America's outstanding composers. All of this was conveyed to Mrs. Meyer, together with a request to receive a composers' delegation and hear their side of the story before making a decision that might destroy the very *raison d'être* of the festival. To this the lady agreed; and after listening to my fellow conspirators, came to the realization that we meant business and that — musically speaking — there was only one lead to follow — that of the plan's instigators.

Another exchange of letters — and Koussevitzky sent Mrs. Meyer a telegram announcing his resignation as the proposed festival's music director. This was read at a hastily summoned meeting, and — with Mrs. Meyer's consent — a telegram sent to Eugene Goossens, a composing conductor, therefore better attuned to our problems, asking him to take over. On Koussevitzky's resignation, two members of the composers' committee resigned also; they were Aaron Copland and Nicolai Berezowsky.

The remaining members prepared a "composers' manifesto," based on the original suggestions of Carlos Chavez and myself, and sent it to Olin Downes, the music critic of the *N.Y. Times,* where it was published on May 31, 1933.*

* The manifesto began: "We, the undersigned, have united to form a Composers' Protective Society, to reinstate the composer to his rightful place in the world of music." After listing our "common difficulties," we stated our objectives, of which there were so many that it would be impractical to reprint them here in full. The objectives contained a plea to enable composers to "gain a livelihood from their work." We made a good point when we stated that the "yearly salaries for the conductors of but six of our major orchestras aggregate over $250,000, to say nothing of soloists' fees. Is it too much to propose that each of the orchestras budget a minimum of $1000 to commission a work from a representative American composer annually, and that their budget include fees for new works, which at the present time the average composer is generally forced to waive in order to have his work played at all?" Objective No. 9 was "to give an annual festival of modern music, the programs to be selected by a *composers'* board." The concluding paragraph read: "In the unity we propose lies the hope of a better day for the composer in America." There followed twenty-nine signatures: Joseph Achron, John J. Becker, Russell Bennett, Marc Blitzstein, Henry Brant, Israel Citkowitz, Henry Cowell, Fannie C. Dillon, Richard Donovan, Vladimir Dukelsky, A. Lehman Engel, Vivian Fine, George Gershwin, Aurelio Giorni, Percy Grainger, Charles Haubiel, Irwin Heilner, Bernard Herrmann, Philip James, Douglas Moore, Jerome Moross, Harold Morris, Wallingford Riegger, Carlos Salzédo, Lazare Saminsky, Joseph Schillinger, Elie Siegmeister, William Grant Still, Bernard Wagenaar.

CHAPTER XIV

THE GOOD YEARS

EXCEPT for the terrible blow of George Gershwin's death on July 11, 1937, the decade 1932–1942 was for me in general happy and productive on both fronts — serious and light — resulting in a chain of successes, although not the resounding, gilt-edged kind that befall Broadway's favorite sons. As a matter of statistics, my first real flop did not make its appearance until 1942 (*Lady Comes Across* with Jessie Matthews, who certainly didn't).

I had my share of small setbacks, but what success is complete without them? Take the composers' manifesto, for instance; it didn't start the desired fireworks and never brought about the festival, its sole realistic trump card. Yet it stirred up a little much-needed agitation and — who knows? — might have had some bearing on certain half-hearted moves made by music's rulers in the direction of music's creators. There were quite a few "letters to the editor" — for and against — the "fors" mostly from composers, the "againsts" from interpreters. I was saddened by the pitiless dissection of the manifesto by the man I thought would embrace it unreservedly — H. T. Parker, who called our *profession de foi* " . . . an American document that does not much help a good cause." His comments, I felt, seldom went to the core of the matter and were often highly debatable. Parker thus whitewashed the conductors' autocracy: "In organization someone must have authority, and the final word. There is no other way at present in human affairs. The whole world pines for dictatorship." The *American* world, too? More serious than Parker's severe criticism was Mrs. Meyer's abandoning the Westchester Festival idea, not because of her lack of faith in it but because her husband resigned as governor of the Federal Reserve Board, after a disagreement with Roosevelt, and gave his money and energy to the *Wash-*

ington Post, which he had purchased. This was hardly the time for either one of the Meyers to back music festivals.

What promised to be an epoch-making departure turned out to be yet another false alarm, and the composers went back to their composing and their struggles with the Masterminds of Music bent on transforming the entire music business into a species of gigantic Master Classes of Appreciation of Masterworks by the Masters of the Past. After a Koussevitzky concert in Carnegie Hall, I went backstage to congratulate Sergei Alexandrovitch and bumped into Tante Natalie, who gave me the Catherine-the-Great-dismissing-yesterday's-favorite look, meant as a warning signal. Tactlessly, I ignored the signal, and said something about the composers being left high and dry by Koussevitzky's abrupt resignation as musical director of their project. Natalya Konstantinovna, now furious, stomped her foot and shouted in Russian: *"Poteeshe ss vashimi kompositorami!"* (You be quiet with your composers.) I instantly rejoined that not being Milady's lackey, I would not be shouted at — and stalked out of the room.

Other conductors, probably unaware of my anticonductor campaign, began to interest themselves in my music. Leon Barzin dusted off my 1927 First Symphony and gave it a good reading for the subscribers to the American Orchestral Society, in April 1933; audience and critics were surprisingly kind to that youthful piece. Benny Herrmann launched a series of three concerts in the Twelfth Street New School auditorium and conducted his New Chamber Orchestra in provocatively unhackneyed programs. My Ballade for Piano and Strings was revised for Benny's concerts and got a "rousing reception" at the one on May 10th. This was probably due to Benny's savage-rite type of conducting (he's toned it down considerably since) and my having studied the piano part with Isabella Vengerova, Slonimsky's aunt and one of the greatest piano pedagogues living. I played my solos with dash and assurance (as the musicians told me later, not a single "clinker"), Benny and I made frantic faces at one another and perspired impressively.

That spring I busied myself with putting my musical house in order — with Prokofiev's usual unselfish help. When one realizes that most men who've made their mark in the Arts are hopelessly unreliable correspondents, the amazing punctuality of Serge's letter-writing habits was next to incomprehensible. The man seemed to live in airports and railroad stations — no two letters ever came from the same address — yet he managed to attend to his mail with clockwork regularity. His letters were typed in Russian as a rule, although quite a few were in his characteristic, peculiarly attractive longhand. Not all of them were pleasant — for Serge, as I have already noted, could be brutally, uncompromisingly frank, and cared nothing about one's feelings, although himself not insensitive to criticism.

Harassed by too many recitals, Prokofiev was traversing his least-productive years, "formalist" years as Soviet scribes had it, owing to the nomad existence, which interfered with his writing. While the mellifluous "Lieutenant Kije" film music was written in 1933, during one of his short visits to Russia, Paris (to which he returned) was the birthplace of the barren and overwritten "Symphonic Song," the first sketch of the cello concerto (of which only the first movement is good Prokofiev) and some excessively "cerebral" piano pieces. We neither of us minced words, and, on receipt of these pieces, I wrote Serge a detailed criticism of them, stressing (not without malice) the music's "dryness" — the same identical fault for which Prokofiev belabored me in the long letter already cited.

To make his answer understandable, it must be told that there was a critic in New York who disapproved of most contemporary music, excepting that of Gershwin; Prokofiev cited his articles as models of biased and cranky writing and nicknamed him Mr. Hotenough (which was close enough). Serge suddenly popped up in the States again and wrote me from Chicago:

> My dear Mr. Hotenough!
>
> It was with suitable respect that I read your report on my modest opus. It pains me to have to say that, since they threw you out of the N. Y. *World* [not me, but my prototype, apparently] you haven't made much progress nor acquired any new keenness of perception. Such is the characteristic trait of all Hotenoughs — not to discern real value, but pick on unimportant and often infinitesimal faults. Dear Mr. Hotenough! I know that in your spare time you too scribble notes and rests. On sounding out Stock [Frederick Stock, the Chicago conductor] I gathered that he regards you with some coolness; at any rate when I made inquiries about your Second Symphony, he wanted to know who Markevitch was. You understand that with my usual zeal I

attempted to explain "who is who." [English, in Russian letters, in the text]. The results were pleasant. Stock would like to see another score of yours, which we'll discuss on our meeting. *Au revoir,* dear Mr. Hotenough! Try and develop yourself, dear Mr. Hotenough! Your very trueny [a Prokofiev-invented Russo-American adjective],

S.P.

The letter was typical of Serge, who, obviously nettled by my comments on his piano pieces, and replying in the vein of bristling sarcasm, yet tells his detractor in the next breath of spreading the gospel of the detractor's music. Yes, Prokofiev's friendship was a rare and wondrous thing. A few days after returning to Moscow he sent me the following post card, with a view of the Kremlin on it. It was dated May 8, 1933, and read:

My dear Duke,

Your 2nd Symphony was performed in Warsaw a few days ago, broadcasted [*sic*], and approved by a group of young composers in Moscow. Greetings from us both.

S. & L. Prokofiev

That spring Harburg and I were summoned by Lee Shubert to help with the score of his proposed new edition of the *Ziegfeld Follies,* the title of which, evocative of so many memories, he purchased from Billie Burke, Ziegfeld's widow. This was again to be an "assembled" score, although originally most of the songs were by Lou Alter and Arthur Swanstrom. Then the portly frame of the late Sam Pokrass, one of the gypsy-songwriting Pokrasses (a brother was Russia's top tunesmith), a lovable jester and sentimentalist, emerged from out of nowhere; then Duke and Harburg muscled in — I was by now used to such athletic entrances — so that, by the time the *Follies* opened at the Winter Garden, only Pokrass and myself were listed as production composers.

Harburg and I had three good songs left over from the original Billy Rose revue, and since Fanny Brice was to star in the *Follies,* thought that there'd be no trouble transplanting the songs from a dead score into a live one. We didn't know Broadway's own

Billy; one would have thought that, having failed to produce the corned-beef extravaganza, Rose would have been big enough to let us use our material, intended for it and now reduced to an inactive status. Not on your life! Rose was going to make the Shuberts pay through the nose for *his* songs, which made our own negotiations with the producers extremely difficult. Rose's name was on one of the songs anyway — "Suddenly," which we had written in Billy's apartment — and so his claim was that of an author as well as producer. I firmly believe that the man ended by getting more for the three songs than Harburg and I together for the lion's share of the *Follies* score.

The show was being staged by Bobby Connolly, the easygoing, chunky dance director, who had had his taste of producing with *Sons O' Guns* and, less successfully, *Princess Charming*. Bobby lived high, cracked jokes and couldn't refuse a drink, but was no disciplinarian. He was no choreographer either, in the contemporary sense, but a dance director, which is another thing entirely. Dance routines in the thirties consisted of "hoofing" or "tapping," and ballets, when incorporated into a show's fabric, were usually staged by an outside specialist; Albertina Rasch was, I think, the first stager who was adept at both chores. The cast of the *Follies* was, certainly, heterogeneous, but it contained enough talented principals to make the fortunes of three revues.

Most revues are disorganized in the early stages, before the unnecessary material gets weeded out and the whole vehicle starts taking shape, but in the *Follies of 1933–34* sheer chaos reigned triumphantly. After weeks of quarrels, tantrums, firings, hirings, Connolly's disappearances, Lee Shubert's dreaded entrances, money and tears flowing, stagehands fleeing, we got off to an unpromising start in Boston. "Only God can make a knee — and that's where we come in," sang the girls. Not only a hen can lay an egg — we did; not one, but several. True, Fanny stopped the show, as was her habit, but faulty cues and backstage mishaps stopped it too — often. We expected a real lambasting from the critics, but to everyone's surprise they loved the show; scratch a Bostonian and find a theater fan.

Nobody was fooled; the consensus was that we had a big flop on our hands. Frantic reshuffling and rehashing of the show, wholesale dropping of skits and songs, exiting principals didn't seem to help.

Philadelphia (our next stop) wasn't taken in by the show's name, nor the star-studded cast, and the critics this time really gave it "the business" — but not the kind that brings lines to the box office.

We then went to Washington. I don't know whether the fact is well-known, but whenever a show is in trouble, the first one to be blamed is the composer. Songs that caused producers, stars and chorus girls to swoon in rehearsal rooms, theatrical offices and — as often as not — composers' bedrooms, are suddenly condemned for being tuneless, derivative, undistinguished and downright "dog-like." Having acquired a respectable reputation in New York drawing rooms and being touted by those "in the know" as a "comer," I was mortified to find that the tunes, which delighted Gershwin ("I Like the Likes of You" was his favorite, and, jokingly claiming that I invented the "*luft*-pause" style of jazz-playing, he was fond of imitating my manner of playing that song), were now in daily danger of being thrown out of the score. A battalion of ambitious songwriters was dogging Lee Shubert's steps, and I had somber visions of other people's hits blossoming on the dead carcass of my discarded music. To this day, should a musical show open in the provinces and get doubtful notices, a round half-dozen song merchants will be on the next train. One would think their pretentions futile and scoff at the little fellow slouched modestly in the back row of the orchestra, a squashed hat over his eyes; don't sell him short because, lo and behold, the little fellow is rehearsing an unfamiliar-sounding song with three comedians and a girl tap dancer mumbling unfamiliar lyrics, typewritten copies in hand. You then raise hell with the producer, who is all righteous innocence: never heard of the little fellow, nor his little song. The next evening you attend the show's performance and, just as you're busy counting the house, the conductor strikes up a new-sounding introduction and the little fellow's song raises its ugly (or pretty) head, catching you unawares. This may never have happened to Gershwin or Rodgers or Porter, but it happened to me — many a time.

No sooner did we arrive in Washington than Harburg, who had been singing "What Is There to Say?" with infectious ardor, if not in tune (he would start the chorus near the piano in the right key, then gradually progress to the opposite end of the room, getting away not only from the piano but from the tune as well as he progressed, waving his arms expansively and crouching bear-fashion at the climaxes), descended on me in another fit of rage. In a torrent of ill-punctuated words, he abused me for producing decadent, "unmanly," affected music instead of the good, simple, American tunes expected by the people. My settings of his lyrics were about to disappear from the score, he continued, and it was my own fault, as I wouldn't listen, etc. The gist of all this ranting was that I had better write *new* tunes — yes, three new tunes to replace the defective originals. This was too much and I, with equal heat, refused point-blank to cut "not only my own throat, but also the score's."

The next day as I walked down the corridor on my floor of the old Willard Hotel I heard sounds of a piano emanating from one of the rooms, and a man's voice singing a song, the lyrics of which sounded oddly familiar. On tiptoe, I walked to the door and listened; there was no mistake — what I heard was a brand-new version of "I Like the Likes of You," in no way resembling mine. "Ah-ha!" I muttered, teeth on edge, and walked on. It can't be — Oh, yes it was! — an entirely fresh and barely detectable "What Is There to Say" emerging from another room on the same floor, this time warbled with feeling by a tremulous girl's voice. My fists now clenched, I proceeded on my Sherlock Holmesian promenade, and hadn't walked two steps before finding myself face to face with one of the minor Harms benchwarmers, who gave me a furtive look and pretended not to recognize me. I found Lee Shubert and told him of the coincidence of three newly arrived tunesmiths *all* writing new tunes to the lyrics of *my* songs and *all* living and creating on my floor, which was entirely too much for human endurance; told him further that I was leaving immediately for New York, at my own expense, and that I didn't care whether my name was taken off the program, my royalties cut altogether, my small reputation ruined — in short, that I had had enough. Mr. Lee was kind and understanding and said something about "things arranging themselves" and "not to worry," but he didn't attempt to stop me from taking the train back to New York, which I did, a delicious sense of release enveloping my whole being.

On returning home, I plunged into "serious" pursuits, such as the first draft of the *End of St. Petersburg,* a cantata for three soloists, mixed chorus and orchestra, that I was writing in snatches between auditions, rehearsals and voyages. The "Epitaph" was a failure, but it had given me a taste for choral writing; I find the singing of a large choral group a greater musical thrill than the most ear-catching orchestral virtuoso display. The subject I chose for my cantata has been a constant challenge to me — and I was determined to find suitable sounds for it. In the words of Hugh Ross, who conducted it five years later: "In his choice of St. Petersburg, Dukelsky has a specially interesting subject, partly because of the curious artificiality of that city which Peter the Great built for Russia, a window opening upon the Western World; and also because St. Petersburg has both lived and died in the sense that it has now lost not only its name, but its position as Capital city of Russia." To every Russian, the sound of the words St. Petersburg instantly spells a strange enchantment. In a sense, we all are fetishists in regard to Petersburg, the city, and Pushkin, its poet. This adoration reached its zenith in 1937, which marked the centenary of Pushkin's death. That anniversary was celebrated, not only in Soviet Russia (with unprecedented pomp and circumstance), but in every last refuge of Russia's scattered refugees, with something akin to mass hysteria.

True, the city is now renamed Leningrad (unthinkable sacrilege) and is no longer the capital of Russia, but merely a gigantic museum within the gates of a Soviet port; and the old name St. Petersburg has a dangerously reactionary ring to the present keepers of the city's keys. No matter. It will live forever in the music of Pushkin's poetry, which needs no official endorsement.

In spite of the rich literary heritage dealing with our former capital, few musicians have seized upon it for inspiration; Glinka, Dargomijsky, Balakirev, Borodin and other renowned Petersburg composers chose a variety of exotic subjects for their operas and symphonic poems — but they shied away from the drab reality of the Petersburg streets. Nor were Mussorgsky and Rimsky-Korsakov inspired by the city — unless one considers the fairly unimportant, unfinished comic opera *The Marriage* (to Gogol's text), by the former. The honor of translating Petersburg magic in musical terms belongs to Tchaikovsky (*Pique Dame*) and Stravinsky (*Petrouchka* — or, in a much lesser degree, *Mavra*). But neither of these great musicians ever thought of erecting a "musical monument" to St. Petersburg (in the manner of Vaughan Williams's *London* Symphony, Delius's tone-poem "Paris," or Charpentier's opera *Louise*, another Paris hymn); and that was exactly the perhaps overambitious task that I had set myself.

My first and only trip to St. Petersburg (in 1914) left a lasting imprint on my memory, but it was not until 1928, when I saw the Soviet film *The End of St. Petersburg* in Berlin, that I was spurred on to a decision to compose a tribute to that vanishing city. In an effort to portray the spirit of St. Petersburg, I did not employ the text of any one man, but chose the works of nine poets, past and contemporary, who sang their town's changing glories. The eighth episode was a rather singular one. The poem, by Alexander Blok, deals with the futility of existence in a dead city. While the male chorus recites the eight-line poem in strict rhythm, the women wail *bouche fermée* in counterpoint, against the soprano solo, who reprises the sad street song of the opening measures of the work. A figure, reminiscent of the *ostinato* used by Tchaikovsky in the bedchamber scene of *Pique Dame* is employed in the orchestration to intensify the feeling of impending doom. The ninth movement, in which both the soloists and chorus participate, entitled "My May," is the workmen's proclamation of victory, the triumphant hymn of the new order, which brought the city's poetic history to a close, did away with its time-honored proud name and stripped it of its former supremacy as Capital of all Russias.

It's a far cry from Peter the Great's folly to the Follies of Ziegfeld, but my life was full of such abrupt transitions and I gradually became so used to them that proceeding in a straight line to a well-defined goal would have been a hindrance rather than a blessing; so I received only a minor shock when a telegram from John Murray Anderson interrupted my work on the St. Petersburg cantata. The telegram was to the effect that the Shuberts had asked Murray (whom I hadn't seen since Bob Chanler's golden period and who, as it turned out, didn't remember me) to restage the ailing revue and "bring it in" after as many additional weeks on the road as he, Murray, might deem necessary. According to Anderson, the only three things he liked about the show were the three Duke-Harburg songs, and would I come and see him as these songs *alone* might induce him to take over the job. Encouraged and gratified by thus becoming the main pivot in an important theatrical decision, I hastened to Anderson's Murray Hill flat. The producer, who was rather terrifying in his early days, received me with every evidence of benevolent consideration and flattering interest. English-Canadian by birth, Murray was agreeably placid and unhurried in manner, wore well-cut tweeds and a perpetually amused expression; his humor was of the outrageous-nonsense-Grandville-*cum*-Edward Lear sort — he gave his co-workers absurd names and delighted in making them do absurb things. His Englishness was so innate and untransplantable I had an odd notion that, were he induced to visit a speakeasy (Murray was a teetotaler), he would order a tankard of bitter and start a game of darts. The flat was cozily reminiscent of Cheyne Walk interiors, a huge gray cat was asleep in an armchair, and cucumber and watercress sandwiches were served with tea; Broadway seemed thousands of miles away. In a few minutes Murray was calling me The Grand Duke. "I don't know you," he said, his small lake-blue eyes twinkling shrewdly, "but I like your songs very much. They were, as I said in the telegram, the only good things in that *wretched* show. Play them for me." The piano, pretty to look at, had an odd hollow sound, and the pedals seemed to be out of order; nevertheless, I played my three numbers, "*luft*-pauses" and all, while Murray sang his own, highly individual, versions of them in a surprisingly resonant baritone. "You must come and help me if I agree to take over the *Follies,* O, Grand Duke," Anderson said, the musical interlude over. I plunged into an impassioned recital of my Washington woes, but Murray interrupted me. "I know all about *that.* You see, these things *will* happen in the theater; they are all part of the game and they are supremely unimportant. Don't be rash, and don't stay away from the theater. Your tunes are essential to the show and we all know it," the producer went on; and no sooner did I nod agreement, than he rose and said loudly: "By the way, there's someone in the next room who wants to shake hands with you." A few minutes later I found myself shaking hands with Harburg; work was resumed, and, thanks entirely to John Murray Anderson, the *Follies* saved.

This unforeseen resumption of my Broadway activities caused an abrupt change in my plans. I had corresponded all summer with Prokofiev in regard to a Paris *première* of *The End of St. Petersburg,* having found a prospective backer, a social-registered Philadelphian who offered to defray all expenses for the venture. Serge contacted Marcel de Valmalete, the Paris concert manager, and asked him for a detailed estimate; Valmalete agreed to provide a conductor, a well-trained chorus and either the Lamoureux or the Pasdeloup orchestra, and the entire cost of the proposed performance, including three rehearsals, was to be in the neighborhood of eight hundred dollars. Nevertheless, Prokofiev thought it unwise to enter into "marriage by correspondence," as he called it, and suggested that I come to Paris a month or two ahead of the *première* and attend to matters *sur place.* "Otherwise," he wrote, "the project may well cost you 100 per cent more." In another letter — of August 14, 1933 — Prokofiev told me of his own plans — breath-taking, and, geographically speaking, a good sample of his yearly peregrinations. "I sent Lina Ivanovna to Geneva for a rest, Grandmother and children to the Riviera, and stayed on in Paris (alone) for three weeks to catch up with my work," wrote Serge. "At the end of August I'll drive to Geneva to fetch my wife and together we'll go down to the Mediterranean to do a little swimming. Back to Paris around September 20th; in early October I'll go first to Riga and Warsaw, then to U.S.S.R. until December; thence to Italy. I'm writing you all this, so that you don't count on my being in Paris should you descend on that city again. U.S.S.R. was very interesting (as usual), not only Moscow and Leningrad, but also Caucasus, up to the Ararat mountains, at the foot of which I gave a concert — in Erivan. I want to take along some of your music in October to place it in the Composers' Alliance Library in Moscow. Do you remember our talks in New York, when you spoke of your correspondence with a modern music society in Mexico, while I told you of my project of cultural exchanges with Soviet musicians? The idea occurred to me of 'reciprocal' performances of Mexican music in U.S.S.R. and Russian music in Mexico. I succeeded in bringing about such an 'interchange' between Moscow and several capitals of Europe, and the 'interchange' livened things up considerably. [I wrote Chavez and Revueltas forwarding Prokofiev's suggestion.] Did I tell you that Fitelberg wrote me: Dukelsky's symphony had a good success and good notices? I'm shaking your hand, write me in Russian. You are not Markevitch, who cannot manage two words in his native tongue without stammering." In yet another letter, Serge told me of his "placing" my Second Symphony with Count Sammartino, then presiding over the Augusteo symphonic season in Rome; Molinari was to conduct my work, but somehow never got around to it. Lina Ivanovna, as I learned from the same letter, sang my Bogdanovitch songs at the American Club in Paris. Nothing stimulated me more than Prokofiev's unceasing efforts on my music's behalf; invariably, on receiving a letter signed "SPrkfv" I rushed to the writing table to prove to myself that I was still Dukelsky, composer, not Duke, tunesmith. But there was no denying that my dichotomy, unnatural and irritating (because nonclassifiable) to my contemporaries, had now become an all-enveloping characteristic of my musical self-expression; in other words, it seemed impossible for me to stick to one kind of music, without an occasional welcome excursion into the other field.

My music-loving Philadelphian soon vanished, having decided to put his money in a theatrical venture; putting aside *St Petersburg* for the nonce, I journeyed to a far less poetic place — Newark, N.J., where the *Follies,* revamped, redesigned, rewritten and, in part, recast, opened at the Shubert Theatre. Showmanship and taste, previously absent from the production, were now in abundant evidence, and it was fascinating to watch a singing and dancing Phoenix emerging from the ashes. Murray restaged "What Is There to Say?" unrecognizably and brought genuine poetry to "Water Under a Bridge," a weird "mood" song Harburg and I wrote for Everett Marshall to sing and Patricia Bowman to dance. This was, probably, the first of the "out of this world" (not heavenly, just plain uncommercial) tunes for which I achieved considerable notoriety; I don't want to call myself a prophet, but the odd harmonic structure of the piece, written in 1933, has all the earmarks of postwar "bop" conceptions and would provide the few remaining champions of that new *"frisson"* in jazz with a satisfactorily "crazy" vehicle. Although it was successful in the theater, the Harms sages refused point-blank to publish so outlandish a composition. "Duke, who are you writing for?" said Spitzer, shaking his head wearily. "If you yourself cannot sing it (it was true, I couldn't, although I tried) how do you expect us to sell copies?" The song remained unpublished and to "get even" with Spitzer, I recorded it for Liberty in 1934 (my first recording anywhere), with Bonnie Lake, Ann Sothern's vivacious sister, on the vocal and Ralph McLane, now Philadelphia Symphony's first clarinet, playing unearthly "subtone" variations around the melody. The record ("I'm Mad About a Man About Town", with lyrics by myself, is on the reverse) is now a collector's item, and I'd love the name and address of the "collector" who stole my copy.

As if by magic, the Newark critics, who evidently hadn't read their Philadelphia and Washington confreres, thought well of the revue. The sour adjectives gave way to nice, heart-warming bromides about a "gay and lively frolic . . . full of color and merriment," and "just the kind of show to provide relaxation in the holiday season."

We missed the holiday season by a few days — Murray was too much of a professional to risk another ragged opening — but finally "made" the Winter Garden on January 4, 1934. This time we were on sure ground and the "seven sages" of New York saluted "a smash hit." Louis Sobol summed up the Anderson miracle of resurrection when he admitted that "never had there been such sorrowful, undercurrent advance notices. As a result it was a listless audience prepared for the worst, but the snap and pep and the beauty of the opera sat us up in our seats." Only a professional can truly appreciate the immense relief brought by so complete an about-face; only a professional can know the dreaded, deadly agony of the much more common phenomenon: an eager, gaily expectant audience, told by "infallible" word-of-mouth, that they're about to witness a world-beating smash, wilting all at once after the first ten minutes of the show, aware, without a trace of doubt, that the "world beater" is a monumental fiasco.

Not this item. We were "in" and the critics were good enough to say so. They all put their seal of approval on Winter Garden's new tenant. Thanks to Murray, I was vindicated and my three candidates for a Washington heave-ho were singled out by the reviewers as the best of the score. There was now no denying the fact that I had clicked emphatically, and I could say together with Whitney Bolton that "I liked the likes of the *Follies*" — and the Follies liked the likes of me, for I was later signed to compose the second Shubert edition, with Ira Gershwin.

With the show a pronounced success, my telephone began to ring incessantly; Park Avenue hostesses came to the happy realization that I might not be a bad drawing card for their drawing rooms. I have already said that the *genus* composer was seldom encountered there, but a *performing* composer — ah, that's a different story. You were welcome on condition that you "performed"; when not performing, the correct demeanor was to be pleasantly unobtrusive, laugh at the host's jokes, smoke his cigars and join in the very general conversation, consisting entirely of a lively discussion of the comings and goings of the host's intimate friends. Dinner conversation of the "brilliant" variety, as we knew it in Paris or London, was not only unknown here, but definitely taboo. I once sat next to a ravishing young matron at a great Newport dinner where most of the guests had "horsy" inclinations, and since it was, visually, almost a replica of a Christabel McLaran or Mrs. Guinness party, asked my delectable neighbor what she thought of Proust. "What race is he in?" was the innocent rejoinder. Mrs. Clare Boothe Luce — then Brokaw — of whom I was rather afraid because, on meeting her at Constantine Alajalov's, she, having been told that I composed *Walk a Little Faster,* said with an icy smile: "Not very amusing, was it?" — the divine Clare had very pertinent things to say about "American Society and Near-Society," in an article of that name published in 1932. On dissecting a typical "smart" hostess of the period, Clare pointed out that: "She [the hostess] may, from time to time, entertain celebrities, but will never, never, under any circumstances, allow the talk at her table to deteriorate into conversation. She will have only the faintest idea of what is meant by the word 'salon,' and even if she cherished such continental ambitions, would find them impossible to satisfy, in an American milieu where politicians, artists, actors, authors, idlers, playwrights and, with a few exceptions, musicians are considered beyond the social pale. When such suspicious characters appear in American homes, it is usually as paid entertainers, or court jesters; seldom as friends and equals of their hostess." Correction please: entertainers and jesters, yes, but paid ones — hardly, unless you played for dancing or were hired to sing at the piano while the guests guffawed at each other's anecdotes; and there *were* a few *near salons* in the twenties, thanks to the industry of Paul and Zosia Kochanski, Artur Rubinstein and their friends. The celebrities could always be encountered en masse at Condé Nast's, Elsa Maxwell's or Jules Glaenzer's; pretty showgirls and mannequins congregated at Sherman Fairchild's or Everett Jacobs's, but those who thought themselves the *élite réelle* stuck to the old-fashioned — *i.e.* incurably provincial — social amenities. And why not? It's quite a jump from Main Street to Main Bocher.

A possible winner in the musical-show sweepstakes, thirty years old and, as I smugly pointed out before, reasonably presentable, I was "taken up" by the ever-watchful Elsa Maxwell, although I never became one of the regular performing lions at her shindigs. I don't think I ever did perform, just strutted about taking down telephone numbers and carrying on like the seasoned extra man I was fast becoming. So many of Elsa's soirees did I go to that a "return compliment" seemed in order; a friend of mine had just started a night spot named Caveau Basque in West Fifty-seventh, and was prepared to pay for a big initial "splash." I communicated the thought to mercurial Jules Glaenzer (Elsa's only rival in the fine art of party-giving, according to Maury Paul) and Jules was all for it. We joined forces and gave a "monster gala" cocktail party for Elsa on the eve of her departure for Palm Beach, which — again according to Maury — turned out to be the "jolliest, 'mixed' party of the season."

Things were looking up on the ballet front in Europe, and from ball to ballet was to be my next transition. René Blum and the oddly named Colonel Wassili de Basil (Wassili being Russian for Basil, he should really have been named Basil de Basil — his real name was Voskresensky) organized the Ballet Russe de Monte Carlo in 1932 and George Balanchine was his first choreographer. For de Basil, who was vaguely reported to have been a Cossack officer (while his enemies insisted he was an ex-policeman) George created *Le Bourgeois Gentilhomme, La Concurrence* (an amusing tale of two tailors, with George Auric's music) and *Cotillon* — probably Balanchine's all-time masterpiece. To a scenario provided by infallible Boris Kochno and with Bérard's top-drawer scenery and costumes, Balanchine created in *Cotillon* a divertissement which succeeded in being witty and wistful at the same time; the music consisted of a series of Chabrier's best piano pieces, astutely chosen and handsomely orchestrated. Notwithstanding so promising a start, the colonel and Balanchine came to an abrupt parting of the ways after a year's collaboration. Massine then was placed in full charge of choreography for the de Basil company, whereas George organized his own Les Ballets 1933 (in Paris and London) — which was discarded at the end of that year. The exciting news was that both Massine (in command of the colonel's forces) and Balanchine (accepting Lincoln Kirstein's and Edward M. M. Warburg's invitation to create a "School of American Ballet") were heading for these shores at approximately the same time — although certainly not together.

It was wonderful to see George again — he was a little thinner, a bit paler, but still unruffled, unspoiled, supremely unconcerned with worldly success, merely intent on doing a good job. His humor was as special, as wildly untranslatable, as before — he was still the Tiflis pixie and now delighted in improvising nonsensical verse — the sillier the better — in which game I joined readily. We threw meaningless quatrains at each other and laughed delightedly as the rhymes grew more and more outlandish. Balanchine played me a pretty waltz he composed, while I retaliated with excerpts from *Mistress into Maid* and the three "big" songs from the *Follies.* "They all sound the same to me," George said sniffing, but not disdainfully — it was an old habit of his. George, after divorcing Tamara Geva, married and was quickly divorced from Danilova — and was now a slightly bewildered bachelor again — a state that never really agreed with him. I expressed a fervent hope to collaborate on a ballet — a collaboration we had planned as long ago as 1927, in Florence, and wanted to know what sort of people Warburg and Kirstein were. George described them as enthusiastic, intelligent and rich — an unbeatable combination — and I, not wanting to burden my friend with the role of a go-between, decided to offer the young men my slightly soiled lyre, thinking that now that they had secured the services of one Diaghilevite, they might, conceivably, use those of another. I was received by young Warburg and told that their venture was, for the time being, on "educational" lines and that no new productions were contemplated. In a short while, however, new productions were in fact put in work, with scores by a wide variety of composers, ranging from Kay Swift to Benjamin Godard, but none by either Duke or Dukelsky. I don't believe my Russian birth had any bearing on my rigorous exclusions from the American Ballet programs as Soudeikine was entrusted with the sets of one of George's first works for the young company, and Tamara Geva engaged as guest artist.

Unwanted by Messrs. Warburg and Kirstein (I don't think I ever exchanged two words with the latter), I was grateful for a telephone call from Leonide Massine, then training his brilliant young company at the St. James Theatre. We met for lunch and I listened to Leonide's soberly worded recital of his tribulations following Diaghilev's death, his "drudgery" at the Roxy Theatre and the opportunity provided by de Basil, who, "while no Diaghilev, was, at least, trying to follow in his footsteps by hiring good artists and good dancers." Christian Bérard and André Dérain were the artists, George Auric and Emmanuel Chabrier (no longer living, but more alive by far than most twentieth-century men), the composers, and in addition to some ex-Diaghilevites, there were David Lichine, Nina Verchinina and the three "baby ballerinas" — Toumanova, Baronova and Riaboushinska. Massine introduced me to the colonel, a man devoid of social graces, clumsy in a room, clever in business and with the sketchiest-imaginable knowledge of the arts, especially music. His redeeming features were a strongly developed sense of humor and a certain, rather winning, easy bonhomie — of the "I'm a good simple guy, trying hard, take me as I am" kind — which he used with good effect in his business transactions. It was easy to see that Massine was the artistic dictator of the company, Grigoriev (formerly Diaghilev's aide-de-camp) its exacting drillmaster, but de Basil, who styled himself "Director General" (not General Director) was just that, when it came to paying bills and salaries and sharing profits, if any; I once told him, since he boasted of being the most truthful man living, that he should stick to his own rank and have the billing altered to read "Director Colonel." He pretended not to understand.

On reading Gide's *Counterfeiters,* I was struck by the profound poetry of the page wherein human life is likened to a day in a public park, and thought it the perfect *point de départ* for an imaginative ballet. I communicated the idea to Massine, who thought it fascinating. I don't remember how Jean Lurçat, better known for his tapestries than his paintings, became part of the project. André Gide was approached in Paris, and shown a photograph of me taken nine years earlier; Gide, liking it, expressed a desire to meet me, seemed disappointed when told that I was 3000 miles away and gave his permission to use his text as a "peg" for the ballet. (This was reported to me by Paitchadze, my Paris publisher.) I next went to see the colonel, and gave him an impassioned sales talk. "Wonderful, Dimotchka," de Basil cooed, smiling half benignly, half satanically. "You get the money, I'll put it on." Decidedly, the Diaghilev era was a thing of the past. In de Basil's defense, it must be stated that he, anything but a *grand seigneur,* had not the social or artistic contacts of his great predecessor. He was totally unknown in the U. S. and utterly ignored by "Tout Paris." I knew a few rich people in and around New York, but this was 1934 and the ballet renaissance was yet to come. I consulted Gershwin, who knew everybody and never lacked in backers, but the best George could do was suggest that I go see Max Dreyfus. "Why Dreyfus, George?" I asked incredulously. "He has little use for me; in fact, I don't know why he keeps renewing my contract. What would he want with a ballet?" "He wants *you* — otherwise he wouldn't re-sign you," George answered. "What would your ballet cost to produce?" "Oh, about three thousand dollars," I said — the figure (incredible today) having been supplied by Massine. "Well, he's advancing you more than that a year, isn't he? Tell him to add the three thousand to your advance — he'll get it back." This sounded fairly feasible, and having received George's assurance that he'd talk to Max about the ballet plan, I arranged with the publisher's secretary to visit him in Brewster, N. Y., where Dreyfus was recuperating from an illness. I remember being kept waiting, being offered a drink and being told with great deliberation that "serious" and "light" music didn't mix, that being successful in one field excluded the chance of success in the other, that there was no future in that sort of thing — all leading up to a flat "no."

A few days later I got the money through the good offices of beautiful and gifted Estrella Elizaga, one of the most popular figures in what's known as the "international set." Estrella played piano, composed songs, was equally at home at bullfights and the ballet, spoke French like a native and had the most tremendous chic, envied by women and admired by men. I adored Estrella and, understandably, my adoration rose to new heights when she told me with great simplicity and kindness, that she'd got the money for *Jardin Public* — the title Massine and I had chosen for our second joint venture.

The de Basil ballet went on tour after an artistically successful but financially unsatisfactory New York showing, and I followed them on to Boston, half the ballet composed. I felt Diaghilev's absence most keenly when I played the music to Massine and the colonel; De Basil's comment was worth quoting: "I don't understand you, Dimotchka, my dear," he said, after I finished playing. "Everyone told me that melody was your forte — didn't you write the follies of Mr. Ziegfeld? And here, the moment you start a tune and I say to myself — *'Khorosho, otchen Khorosho!'* [good, very good!] — you go 'off' completely, as though you were ashamed of yourself. Then it's all — drann, brann, whatever my left foot desires [Russian saying, signifying a maximum of disorganization]. Then I feel like howling like a dog — I grit my teeth and I suffer. But maybe I'm not qualified to judge — what do you think, Leonide Fedorovitch?" Massine said nothing, his dark, habitually tragic face an impenetrable mask. When he broke his silence, he gave me a heavy, perplexed look and said gruffly: "I won't know until I start working. Some of it is good — the dance of the Poor Lovers, especially. Let Dima finish it." That was all. Massine had no musical intuition; he didn't know or feel why a certain passage was right, another wrong. He never guided me the way Diaghilev did, by talking, or the Balanchine way, by sitting down at the piano and improvising the sort of music he needed.

There were a few rehearsals between performances, a detailed synopsis was worked out; the company then left Boston for the next town on their schedule, whereas I returned to New York. Massine and de Basil made the decision to open *Jardin Public* at the huge Chicago Auditorium and to attend to the staging while touring — not a good way to put on a new ballet, but they had no choice in the matter.

Early in May I was summoned by Lawrence Langner and asked to work with him and Armina Marshall, his wife, on a project of a musical play named *America Dances*. I read the first act, thought it interesting, although a bit sententious in spots, and agreed to write the music for it; Langner pointed out that this was a big and exacting job, as music was needed throughout — not merely songs and dances, but musicalized dialogue as well. He suggested that I go to Westport, Connecticut, for the summer to be near him, which would enable us to collaborate more closely. I didn't drive and the plan thus presented a problem, since New York suburbia is unthinkable without a car, yet I decided to give it a try. I found a minuscule hut, more like a picturesque outhouse, on Wright Street, just off the Boston Post Road and within walking distance of shops and buses. There was just enough room for an upright piano, and the bathtub wasn't much larger than a bidet, only it was shaped more like a kettledrum than a cello — but grass and trees were all around the hut and I immediately "took" to Westport. I sent Mother off to Staten Island, where White Russians had quite a colony, so I knew she wouldn't be alone, and moved my summer lares and penates to the little hut in Connecticut.

It took me a few days to organize my life there and, a strict working schedule blocked out satisfactorily, I plunged into the simple pastoral joys: swimming at the unluxurious Compo Beach, achieving a spectacular sunburn and drinking quantities of bad applejack with the natives — the glossy advertising-executives station-wagon set not having as yet discovered Connecticut. I wrote page after page of music in the morning — dance music for Charles Weidman and Doris Humphrey and a few songs to lyrics provided by the Langners. In the evening, I'd leave a quart of applejack for the ever-thirsty natives on my tiny terrace, and go off to dinner with friends, of whom I found not a few — Mario Braggiotti, Harry Kaufmann, the brilliant and sensitive pianist, courageous and kindly Cobina Wright, with Cobina, Jr., then a long-legged precocious child, and quantities of scientifically tanned summer sirens, languidly secure in the knowledge of their perhaps too uniformly good looks.

Having completed the first act of *America Dances* — some eighty pages of continuous music — I gave a preview of it at Langner's farm; the authors-producers found it very much to their liking and suggested that the dance portions be put in rehearsal immediately. Arrangements were made for me to work with Weidman and Humphrey — two of the most genuinely gifted yet insufficiently celebrated workers in their field — at their Greenwich Village studio. In contrast with Massine, Charles and Doris and their spectacular costar, José Limon, were endlessly inventive with the music at their disposal, and I found the three or four "workouts" we had together very stimulating. On my return to Westport I had difficulty in contacting Langner, busy with a new play's tryout; when I finally caught up with him, he said quite calmly that he didn't believe our musical would go "in its present shape," and that he had regretfully decided to postpone its presentation. It is now twenty years since America danced (in the Weidman-Humphrey studio) and, although the Theatre Guild got rich with America singing — thanks to Rodgers and Hammerstein — I don't think they'll ever get around to making it dance in our 1934 manner.

My Westport sojourn was not entirely a mistake, however. The bottom having fallen out of the Langner project, I was seized with a longing to be back in New York, where things were always happening — particularly in late summer, producers' offices all a-buzz with new productions and orchestra conductors returning from their European jaunts with novelties hot off composers' griddles. It was easy enough to board a train and reach Manhattan in a little over an hour, but with Mother on Staten Island and Alex in Cincinnati on an architectural job, what would I come back to? My Westport rent was paid for another three weeks and there I was, stuck with eighty pages of unwanted music, the summer sirens and the applejack; so I sat down "and then I wrote" (as the vaudeville-appearing songwriters used to announce) a paean to Manhattan — words and music both — as a "pendant" to "April in Paris" — the new one called "Autumn in New York." Both the long "conversational" verse and the constantly modulating refrain contained not a particle of what the Harms moguls called "popular appeal"; the song was a genuine emotional outburst and, possibly, this genuineness accounted for its subsequent "standard" status. I played it at one or two Westport get-togethers, and found the listeners retreating to the bar in the middle of the verse.

New York looked good to me when I finally returned there. The *Follies* were still "packin' 'em in" at the Winter Garden; Vassar and Sarah Lawrence girls were still requesting "Suddenly," "What Is There to Say," and "I Like the Likes of You" at the Stork or the El Morocco; and clever little Alex Gard began pondering the advisability of executing a caricature of me to adorn the walls of Mr. Sardi's establishment. Two producers announced my musical version of *Serena Blandish;* one of them was Robert Milton.

I was brought together with Lurçat, an intense, energetic Frenchman with a finely chiseled profile accentuated by a pipe and rust-brown tweeds, but a somewhat "arty-crafty" approach to the theater. With the return of de Basil's company, daily huddles with Massine were resumed; the "word of mouth" had it that in the Poor Lovers' *pas de deux,* Leonide surpassed himself both as dancer and choreographer. I was shown this and other disjointed episodes from *Jardin Public,* and marveled at the dark, lissome beauty of youthful Tamara Toumanova and the impudent, brazen slapstick quality of Genia Delarova, Massine's dancer wife. We racked our brains for a suitable number for her, and decided on a chair vendor's dance to the discordant strains of a decrepit military band in the park — which would have been happier in a musical comedy than a Gide hallucination.

Before journeying to Chicago, I heard from John Murray Anderson, who was putting together an Eddie Dowling revue titled *Thumbs Up,* for which my old friends Clark and McCullough were hired, as well as a trio of Southern lasses named the Pickens Sisters, Ray Dooley and Sheila Barrett, and two hopeful hoofers named Hal Le Roy and Paul Draper. It appeared that the producer needed a nostalgic evocation of Manhattan in the fall, red leaves falling in Central Park, young people coming home from vacations — in short, he needed "Autumn in New York." "Murray, I may have what you want," I said hesitantly, "only it's a crazy song; moves from key to key and that makes it hard on a singer." "Whose lyric?" "Mine." "What do you call it?" " 'Autumn in New York.' " Murray let out a refined whoop. "Get into a cab, you unfortunate Grand Duke; don't talk any more. Hurry!" In ten minutes I was at 15 Park Avenue, in twenty minutes the song was interpolated into the Jimmy Hanley and Henry Sullivan score; it was I who was now appearing in the role of the little guy in a battered hat encountered earlier.

Ruth Page, whom I knew in the pre-Diaghilev days, was doing pioneer work in the Native Ballet field in Chicago. I had seen her for a few fleeting moments in Monte Carlo in the late twenties, when she combined her honeymoon with a little postgraduate work in Diaghilev's corps de ballet. Through Ruth and her bosom friend, alert and articulate Betty Field, Lurçat and I were invited to put up at the Clows' residence in Chicago; Baby Clow, whom I subsequently introduced to her future husband, Mario Braggiotti, was a superb amazon of a girl and a dabbler in the arts, including that of the dance. I'll never forget my arrival at the Clow mansion. It was late at night, and as the Clows were out for the evening I was greeted by a faultlessly schooled butler and placed in the care of an affable, automatonlike Filipino, who ushered me into my room — as sumptuous as it was violently modern. The place was all intricate "functional" gadgets, an armchair — scary-looking but comfortable — and an oddly shaped bed that seemed small but was, in reality, large enough to accommodate a half-dozen orgiastic lovers. I was offered a choice of four or five magnificent dressing gowns, selected a black-and-red number and was led to an awe-inspiring bathroom (my host, as I found out, was a Bathroom King). The extra-low built-in tub was surrounded by a great many faucets. On leaning down, I discovered that one was marked "Guerlain," another "Coty," a third "Lelong," and so on; on turning the faucet a pungent stream of perfume would come out. I was impressed, but it was with some difficulty that I found a faucet with the legend "WATER." A few minutes later, smelling like a Grasse factory, I emerged from the tub, accepted a pair of pajamas that would not have been disdained by Sardanapalus, and slid into the luxurious bed. I instantly recalled the wisdom of Balanchine's maxim: "There's nothing like a dab of perfume to make you feel rich."

In the morning I was offered breakfast in bed, but disliking food in sleeping quarters, I was silently offered yet another choice of dressing gowns by the Filipino; this time I picked an apple green and orange creation, and descended to the dining room. I was told by the butler that Mr. Clow "will be down presently," and braced myself for an American Robert de Montesquiou, at the very least. Instead, in walked a tall, bespectacled man in his fifties, attired in the most colorful robe in his entire collection; shaking me athletically by the hand, he boomed: "Put it there, pardner, put it there."

Chicago was pretty wonderful in the thirties; it was out to beat New York, and nearly did, artistically speaking. Lurçat and I did a lot of sight-seeing when not rehearsing, ate great food at Ernie Byfield's home atop one of the Ambassador Hotels, marveled at the luxury of Lake Shore Drive rubbing shoulders with the worst and most odoriferous slums known to man, took in the ribald doings at Club 606, a close rival of Mexico's Teatro Garibaldi, saw a colored man shot at a North Side dive at 4 A.M. and stood in wonder before an electric sign reading "Chez Paree." "What language is that?" Lurçat, the Parisian, wished to know.

I gave out a lengthy interview, in which I tried to account for my dichotomy, to the eager young woman who wanted "the truth." "How do you go about writing two different kinds of music almost simultaneously?" she asked. "The two idioms in which I write are as different as work and play. Serious music is hard work; jazz is easy for me — that is, just recreation for which I happen to get paid," was my reply. To a more insipid, but inevitable, question about my "inspiration," I replied truthfully that nothing could inspire me more than a $5000 check.

According to my observant interviewer, I was "a tall, black-haired, handsome young man with very pink cheeks and an appearance of healthy, plump youth which he loathes. He wants to seem 40 and have a gray hair and a look of having done something spectacular in the way of suffering or accomplishment." Strange and a little terrifying. Twenty years later, I *still* want to seem forty — now that I do have *many* a gray hair and that my age is fifty. Chicago liked the *Follies,* then playing at the Grand Opera House. With that show on the boards and *Public Gardens* in active preparation, I was again in the limelight. After a round of dances and dinner parties, I was summoned to Philadelphia by Anderson to help with *Thumbs Up,* breaking in at the Forrest; on arriving at the station, I found a brace of Mallard ducks in my compartment, with Mr. William Clow, Jr.'s compliments.

I found Philadelphia pretty drab after Chicago's splendors. The town was full of conventions and no hotel space was available anywhere; I was finally given a hideous double room that had originally housed the hotel's laundry, as I was informed by the bellboy. It had no closets and smelled depressingly of yellow soap, making me long for the Clow bathroom; but, since most of my time was to be spent at the theater, anyway, I decided to make the best of it and signed the register.

For *Thumbs Up* I wrote a tango for J. Harold Murray to sing and a dance tune for Hal Le Roy to tap to, but both numbers were dropped from the score in Philadelphia, only "Autumn in New York" remaining as *finale ultimo.* At an audition I heard another "intruder" demonstrate a song intended for the revue; the song struck me as uncannily beautiful and I fought for it with the producers as though it were my own. The song's name was "Time and Tide," its composer Alec Wilder; what particularly touched me was a totally blind young man with a face like Shelley's who sang the song to Wilder's accompaniment. "Time and Tide" was essayed in Philadelphia and also dropped before the revue reached New York.

Shortly before returning to the Big Town, I received a thrilling visit from the girl I thought myself in love with — there was always one in those days — a tall, dark young woman with the face of a Sienese *quattrocento* madonna and a body glorified by Lucien Lelong whom I shall call Pamela. Southampton, L. I., and fifteenth-century Siena are an irresistible combination, and so I gave up resistance; we danced cheek to cheek at Condé's or Elsa's parties, and "I Get a Kick Out of You" (Cole Porter's most potent musical aphrodisiac) was our favorite dance tune. I hoped that Philadelphia would be the setting of our first night of love; we danced after the show, which had all the earmarks of a hit, then betook ourselves to my impossible hotel. Although the ex-laundry in which I resided was filled with dark red roses (Pamela's favorite flower), the girl went pale on entering it, took a whiff of the antiseptic air and exclaimed: "Goodness, these roses smell of soap. How sordid!" Romance was difficult after such an opener; I bowed to fate and took Pamela home, to the Bellevue-Stratford. Once again, love flew out of my window.

I spent Christmas in New York *en famille* in East Fiftieth Street, where we had moved from the Village, went back to Chicago for two days of rehearsals of *Jardin,* which was to open in March during the ballet's return engagement, and somehow managed to attend the New York opening of *Thumbs Up* on December 27th. The show turned out to be a decent, average revue and received decent, average notices.

Shortly after the holidays I received the following letter, dated January 12, 1935, from André Gide: "I'm happy to learn that you have not abandoned your beautiful project. To help its success, I gladly agree to forego my 'royalties' for the ballet's performances in America. The title that I already indicated to you, 'Jardin Public,' seems excellent to me and I hope you won't hesitate to use it. It would be best to indicate: 'after a page from André Gide's novel, 'The Counterfeiters,' and to reproduce said page 'in extenso' in the program, which would serve to explain the ballet."

Following my tiff with the Koussevitzkys as a result of the abortive Westchester festival, I picked another — this time with my easygoing Paris publisher, Gabriel Paitchadze, their appointee. The pace at which my "respectable" music was being published was positively lethargic and I was never noted for my patience. I sat down and wrote the man a series of blistering letters, demanding "action," suggesting, in parenthesis, that we — the Edition Russe de Musique and I — part company, unless such action be forthcoming. Paitchadze, finding the wording of one of these letters objectionable, took me at my word and gave me back all unpublished music I had sent him. This created an unforeseen complication with *Jardin's* score, as, no longer empowered to have my music copied, I handed it to Colonel de Basil, who assured me that he'd "take care of it."

In common with most Russians, the colonel was a great believer in letting things slide until the very last moment, and so, at 9 A.M. on the day before the Chicago *première* of my ballet, the score and parts reached New York after an exchange of frantic cables with the colonel's Paris copyist. At four-thirty in the afternoon the material had been delivered in Chicago by airplane. At five o'clock the orchestra started on its first and only rehearsal, under the direction of Antal Dorati, who shared with Efrem Kurtz the conducting duties of the organization. As a not unreasonable consequence the performance started something more than twenty minutes after the announced hour. The parts were, not unnaturally, crawling with mistakes, and my music, fairly dissonant in the first place, sounded like Schönberg married to Varèse and caused me to run out of the theater — then to return, panting and wishing I had stayed away. There were two or three highspots, applauded to the echo, but the total effect was one of a hopeless mess, although the *N.Y. Times* correspondent reported an "enthusiastic reception." An amusing and pertinent typographical error crept into his notice, which read: "Described as the last word in modernism. . . . The production was *resented* at the opening of a return visit of the Ballet Russe de Monte Carlo." That about summed it up.

There were two supper parties after the ballet. The Goodspeeds had one for Leonide Massine, his pretty wife and Vera Zorina, then very young and fabulously lovely; notwithstanding her youth and beauty, she was cast as the senile wife in the "Old Lovers" episode. "Seated with the Goodspeeds were Miss Gertrude Stein and Miss Alice B. Toklas, whose appearance has lost none of the glamour for their public," wrote the Hearst society columnist. "Again they were surrounded with people who made remarks about Miss Stein's famous little velvet hat and Miss Toklas's moleskin coat." I remember being introduced to Miss Stein by Alan Tanner, who had forsaken Paris for his native Chicago and was no longer rooming with Tchelitchev, but I don't, for the life of me, recall whether she said, "a hit is a hit is a hit," or, "a flop is a flop is a flop." The other party — Ruth (Page) and Tom Fisher's — was, in the words of the reporter, who taxied from one to the other, "very gay, amusing and mixed. White flowers, champagne and toasts to Lurçat and Dukelsky." At the Fisher party, Paul Dupont was overheard to say that "maybe Dukelsky's score and parts should never have reached the Chicago airport."

Two weeks later *Jardin,* brought to Broadway's Majestic Theatre, was again spottily performed and spottily received, although the music sounded better. S. Hurok, the impresario, stood at the back of the orchestra and glared at me during the more dissonant passages. When I complained about the wrong notes played by the musicians, he snapped: "It is *I* who should complain about the wrong notes you have written!" and walked away in anger. De Basil kept shaking his head mournfully: "Dimotchka, you assassinated melody and the critics assassinated me. Every time those trumpets go . . . trr, trr . . . I get a splitting headache." Most of my friends didn't care for the ballet, either, and I was getting tired of ducking the generous backers.

I decided to "get away from it all" and become "a certain Dukelsky, otherwise unknown to fame," in the happy phrase of Chicago's Mr. Dunn. The place I chose for my hideout was Harrisburg, Pennsylvania, and I couldn't have picked a better. An erratic and unpredictable young friend of mine named Mitchell Hodges, whose strange and fascinating adventures would make up a livelier volume than the present one, was doing WPA administration work in the colorful Dutch town and had attractive quarters on Front Street, where I joined him. We went on a splendid hike in the surrounding hills, lost our way after walking for miles, and finally alighted at a pretty establishment named the Crystal Lake Inn. After a hearty supper, we were asked by the landlady whether there was *anything else* we desired, and answered that sleep, lots of sleep, would do us fine. The woman gave us a strange look and told the chambermaid to get the Pink Room ready. The Pink Room sounded peculiar, but we were too tired to care. On entering the room we saw, to our consternation, that not only was the large and distinctly girlish bed of a luscious pinkness, but there were also a profusion of large pink dolls, a pink rug, pink towels, and mirrors, mirrors everywhere. Only one bed was visible — and I never could sleep with another human in the same bed, be it a man or a woman — but we both slept soundly that night. Early in the morning Mitchell and I were awakened by what sounded like a dozen beds squeaking rhythmically on all sides of us, which brought back vivid recollections of my first Monaco hotel. We went down to breakfast, which was succulent and plentiful, and asked the sullen waitress for the bill. "That'll be three-eighty for the both of ya," the girl said challengingly. Considering that we ate a large supper and a larger breakfast and slumbered in the fancy Pink Room, the figure seemed unusually low and I inquired whether there wasn't some mistake. "You two comin' here sure was a mistake," the waitress went on, with a dirty look. "Now beat it and don't come back; we don't want yer kind here."

The de Basil company, meanwhile, sailed back to Europe and an extended ballet season at London's Covent Garden, with *Jardin Public,* for which Massine and the colonel still entertained some hopes, among the season's novelties. It was with a sigh of relief that I returned to "Dukal" activities; in that less-exalted sphere, things soon began happening. Harburg received an offer to create a screenplay for Universal with *April in Paris* as the title and the song as theme. The Shuberts, encouraged by the success of their first *Follies* were busily preparing a second. Ira Gershwin was available for the lyric-writing job as George was working on *Porgy and Bess* with DuBose Heyward. When asked whom he would like for his music man, Ira suggested me — and Lee Shubert, not having done badly with me a year before, readily agreed.

The contracts signed, it was decided that George, Ira and Lee, Moss Hart and I take a house in Ocean Beach, Fire Island — an island discovered for jaded New Yorkers by none other than Fanny Brice. She raved about the place, which had a troubling, unsafe sound (it isn't too safe, actually, as old islanders who have weathered a hurricane or two would testify) but proved an enchanting and (in 1935) barely civilized hideaway. Wonderful swimming, boating, fishing, clamming, crabbing or just plain loafing, the absence of motorcars and telephones — all of these were features of Fire Island, then but sparsely populated, today uncomfortably crowded with just the people you want to stay away from.

Ocean Beach natives — simple, God-fearing folk, a good many of them of Irish descent — couldn't believe their eyes when they witnessed that summer's "foreign" invasion. Both Bea Lillie and Fanny Brice — inseparable friends — had big houses on the bay side, Herman Shumlin and Arthur Kober moved into the inner regions of the village (perhaps to be near Wolcott Gibbs, one of the island's first settlers), and the Gershwin-Hart-Duke quintet took up residence on the ocean side, in what I believe was the largest house on the place at the time (since demolished by the 1938 hurricane). George was seldom around, as he was always joining DuBose Heyward in some remote spot. Moss, too, had pressing business to attend to elsewhere

— so Ira and I were left alone with our songwriting in the daytime and Brice-Lillie-Kober-partying at night.

The reader will recall the "Khaki" incident in Monte Carlo; I met Joan, with whom I came closest to marriage later, in almost identical circumstances. I first saw the small, lithe figure, sturdily yet delicately molded, poised for an expert dive on the diving board. Joan, who looked like an adolescent Vivian Leigh, had an impudently upturned freckled nose and eyes of a purplish shade of blue, the shade of Russian cornflowers. Her strong, nut-brown body against the gleaming white of the bathing suit, a size too small for her, was an irresistible sight. Joan noticed my prolonged stare and asked: "What's your name?" in a surprisingly small, melodious voice. I told her. "Oh, you wrote my favorite song! It's . . . tell you later." And with that she dived into the water. "I learned to swim for Khaki," I said to myself, "but I'm damned if I'll learn to dive for this one." Joan soon emerged from the water and stood in front of me, rubbing herself with a big, rough towel. "What are you doing on the island?" the girl asked. I told her about the new *Follies,* the Gershwins and my looking forward to a summer of hard work. "I know the house where you live," Joan said reflectively. "I'm staying with early settlers — *real* island folks, not the likes of you. It's too bad that you fancy theatrical people should have discovered *our* island — you're going to spoil it." Little Joan turned out to be a real prophet, but I didn't like her remark and said morosely something about her being a "fresh kid." "I'm not a kid, although I may look like one," Joan protested peevishly. "As a matter of fact, I was raped by a lifeguard last summer on the beach. So there." She broke into gay laughter and rushed off, wrapped in her big towel. I suspect the lifeguard "rape" thing was invented by Joan to impress me with her maturity and sophistication. Following our bay-side meeting, I rowed her to dinner at a place called Maguire's, where teen-age boys in blue jeans brought their similarly blue-jeaned dates, and Joan behaved with exaggerated decorum, no doubt to forestall any amorous advances on my part. Another night we dined at the "Gershwin castle," and I was the recipient of so many good-natured cracks on the subject of cradle robbing that Joan and I decided not to see too much of each other on the island, in view of the staggering difference in our ages.

The new *Follies* were in active preparation. Lee Shubert was joined in the venture by an enterprising ticket broker named Harry Kaufman, a rotund busybody who affected "Man of Distinction" clothes and manner and had some excellent notions about improving the quality of Shubert extravaganzas. When I helped J. J. Shubert with an abortive revival of Sam Pokrass's *Cyrano de Bergerac* (musical version), some of the costumes bore a startling resemblance to the *Student Prince* uniforms, while the scenery was strangely redolent of *Countess Maritza.* No such money-saving boners for Harry the Purist, who insisted on the "best and most expensive," and generally got it. For a while there was some talk of entrusting Cecil Beaton with scenery and costumes; Cecil was anxious to design a big Broadway musical and wrote me repeatedly from London, offering his services. "The tunes that you have written for the Ziegfeld show are so splendid that, of course, it will be a knockout hit," Cecil said in one of his letters. "The number I would adore most is the Martinique Rumba." (This later became "An Island in the West Indies," which Ira still insists on singing at parties). "As for the money arrangement with the Shuberts, I am sure it could be arranged to both our advantages as they are so rich and I so poor. . . . As for 'Serena Blandish,' this sounds heavenly and I would be mad keen to do it." Cecil was mad keen and very gifted, but he didn't get either job. (When *Serena,* who is a pretty old lady by now, finally appears on the musical stage, it won't be my job, either). Harry Kaufman for some time had his eye on young Vincente Minnelli, one of the most inventive and resourceful all-around talents in the theater — and now the films — then just off to a skyrocketing start. After dressing Marshall Field's windows in Chicago at sixteen, he was snatched by Messrs. Balaban and Katz to design scenery and costumes for their stage presentations. He was sent by them to New York's Paramount Theatre late in 1929 — about the time when I appeared on the local scene — then began freelancing as designer and director. His scenery and costumes for the last Earl Carroll *Vanities* and for *DuBarry Was a Lady* were of such eye-filling splendor that Radio City made Vincente its art director in 1933. Then in came Harry with his gospel of "good, expensive shows," and hired Minnelli to direct and design *At Home Abroad,* to be followed by others, including the *Show Is On* (1936), in which I was also to have a hand. Anderson was already hired for the producing job on the *Follies,* so Vincente agreed to sandwich in a designing chore on our show between directorial commitments.

For some time now I'd been blowing Balanchine's horn as the greatest of all choreographers, and therefore indispensable to what was planned as the greatest of all revues. I wanted in the worst way to work with George and, having been turned down by Warburg and Kirstein for an American Ballet assignment, was determined to secure George for Shubert and Kaufman and the *Follies*. Balanchine was agented by that Bulwark of Broadway, the irrepressible "Doc" Bender — Larry Hart's aide-de-camp, troubleshooter and father confessor — a pushy and fast-talking character; his salesmanship was worthy of respect, because he only sold things he honestly and passionately believed in. He didn't have to sell Larry Hart, who was the best of all lyricists (not excluding Gilbert, in my opinion), but when he screamed at the top of his lungs that Balanchine was a god among choreographers, that Vivian Segal was without a rival in her line, or that I was the best white composer to write a Negro show, he was only voicing his inner beliefs and, being fanatically sincere, was undeniably convincing.

I never knew how he got George away from his American Ballet workshop, but, after concerted screaming by Bender and myself, the choreographer was signed to create the ballets for the *Follies.* The show was to have a spectacular cast — in addition to Fanny Brice and Gertrude Niesen, the songstress, Kaufman signed a hopeful young comic named Bob Hope and a genuine Paris importation, Mlle. Josephine Baker, originally of Harlem. La Baker, with a French count in tow, two beautifully groomed dogs of exotic appearance and a large assortment of the best Vuitton luggage, received us majestically in her hotel suite. It is not generally known that, in addition to the well-publicized flair for rotating her *derrière,* Mlle. Baker was also the possessor of a small but quite exquisite coloratura soprano. Ira and I wrote her two highly spiced tropical arias — "5 A.M." and "Maharanee" — with *fioriture* that would scare Lily Pons out of her wits; Josephine mastered the acrobatic intervals and larynx-defying trills like a trouper, although she was seldom audible. Miss Niesen, on the other hand, was very audible indeed, and found fault with everybody and everything. Bob Hope I thought a most engaging young man, with a freshly scrubbed, balcony-nosed face, rather self-effacing compared with our trio of female prima donnas and always worried about his waistline (so was I). We used to repair to Reilly's gym in Radio City and play paddle-ball, attired in gray, perspiration-producing woolies which made us look like a pair of cheerful Sing Sing inmates.

Summer came to a close and we, the Fire Islanders, ferried back to prosaic Bayshore, L. I., from the quaint little Ocean Beach harbor, a place resembling harbors in the British West Indies. Joan went to Scarsdale to graduate from high school, Ira and Lee to their new duplex on East Seventy-second Street and I to a new studio on West Fifty-seventh Street, Mother and Alex occupying a comfortable flat across the court from me. George Gershwin went back to *Porgy and Bess* and his studies with Joseph Schillinger, the man who revolutionized the art of composition teaching, and especially the study of orchestration. Gershwin did not go to Schillinger for the purpose of getting him to help with *Porgy*. He met the Soviet expatriate musician through Joseph Achron, the late composer and violinist, and apparently what he was seeking were fresh technical vistas, which would enable him to write fresher songs. On visiting George, I found his piano and writing table cluttered up with exercises dictated by Schillinger. George, who always took a childish delight in the simplest pleasures and discoveries, now had found a toy that was real fun and would also yield great dividends, an unheard-of combination.

I was pretty skeptical at first when confronted with pitch scales, units, etc. These terms had an antimusical sound and meant nothing to my unmathematical ear. George was indignant at my skepticism. "You just don't understand," said he. "I used to do all kinds of things — harmony and counterpoint, I mean — but I never knew why I was doing them — I thought they were just parlor tricks. They always went great at parties. Now they'll go right into my music." One day he played the ingenious "crap game" fugue from *Porgy*, his face beaming. "Get this — Gershwin writing fugues! What will the boys say now?"

I went to Boston with George for the tryout. At the orchestra rehearsal he grinned with delight at the well-organized sounds that emerged from the pit. I was sitting quietly in a seat in the last row of the orchestra when George startled me by suddenly appearing from the back and grabbing me by the shoulder. "Hey, Dukie!" he whispered fiercely. "Just listen to those overtones!" Yes, there they were. The Schillinger "slavery" brought an unexpected freedom to George's musical utterances. The tunes we all listened to around George's piano — "Summertime," "It Ain't Necessarily So," "I Got Plenty of Nothin' " — were now clothed in appropriate orchestral garb and shone with a new and dazzling brilliance.

Irving Berlin once told me that if he should study music he'd lose his natural knack for writing popular hits. Doubtless Berlin knows his limitations and is probably very wise, but the current prevalence of musically uneducated show and film writers is not born out of any historical precedent. From Offenbach on to Lehar, Oskar Straus, Messager, Reynaldo Hahn, Sullivan, and Victor Herbert, the kings of the operetta were solid craftsmen one and all, and orchestrated their own music. The real reason for the nonorchestrating composer, outside of his often self-confessed incompetence, is the lack of time, because of the rush invariably connected with the writing and subsequent production of a contemporary musical play.

After completing the score of the Second Violin Concerto in Baku in August, Prokofiev wrote me, on September 29th: "It was very pleasant to get your letter with colorful and accurate observations and to learn all about your activities, on the musical front, as well as in the whoring division. Unfortunately, I haven't heard your 'Jardin,' but 'Dedicaces' [a species of piano concerto with soprano obbligato I was then working on] interests me greatly — it's a rather unusual conception. I thought of going to the States this winter, but, since Bruno Walter failed to sign his contract, the New York engagement was cancelled. Outside of that, the four-act ballet [*Romeo and Juliet*] which I just finished composing and am now orchestrating will be staged at both the Bolshoy [Moscow] Theatre and the Marinsky [Leningrad]; a long absence at such a moment is not a good idea. I'm spending the summer in Bolshoy Theatre's estate near Serpukhov. It's a lovely spot, a bit noisy when 3/4 of the theatre's personnel arrive for a 'cure,' but I find those arrivals quite gay; especially, since I have a separate minuscule house with a Bluthner piano, and a terrace opening on the river Oka, with all the peace I need for productive work. Lina Ivanovna and the children are here also; everybody makes a great fuss over the boys and spoils them dreadfully. Now the opera and ballet artists have vanished and I spend *eight* hours a day scoring. I also wrote the Second Violin Concerto, two symphonic suites, two piano cycles and an album of children's pieces. Gania [Prokofiev's nickname for Paitchadze] is in no great hurry, but he's printing my music. I plan to be in Paris in a month for the Concerto's *première;* in December I go to Africa. Shostakovitch is talented but somehow 'unprincipled' and — like certain friends of ours — bereft of melodic invention; he is made too much of here. Kabalevsky and Jelobinsky *'sont des zero-virgule-zero.'* [French in the original.] I am flattered that you find certain works of mine 'timeless.' It's possible that therein lies the reason why men who are *too much of our time* often fail to understand my language. Rumors of my friendship with Poulenc and Igor [Stravinsky] are vastly exaggerated; as for half-Igor [Markevitch], I support him with difficulty. I embrace you; don't deprive me of your bounty and — should you get something printed not in the tra-la-la repertory, send it on." The phrase about men "who are too much of our time" was the first indication of an already-existing, ideological friction between the composer and the Soviet music authorities. It is interesting to note that Prokofiev, who had taken out a Soviet passport a short time previously, was permitted to travel continuously and extensively, and have his music published by the capitalist-refugee conductor Koussevitzky; present-day Soviet composers would languish in Siberia or be declared "enemies of the working class" and shot for such acts.

Late that summer, at a party in New York, I met an astonishing youth named John Treville Latouche, of Richmond, Virginia, of French descent and of unquenchable but ill-defined ambition. He was very small, dark and stocky, with the face of a precocious infant. Johnny's mind was ever alert, his wit ever sharp and often merciless; but the boy's essential goodness and kindness shone through his eyes. Extremely erratic by nature, Latouche worked spasmodically and swiftly on his poetry; short periods of work to be followed by long days and nights of blissful laziness and idle gallivanting. I met him through Elsa Beamish, a Harrisburg belle who shared a Park Avenue flat with another girl. Both girls were under Latouche's spell and invited me over for an exhibition of his talents. Johnny dusted off a few hot epigrams, then sat down at the piano and accompanied himself in a bouquet of night club-type songs — subsequently used by Spivy and others — containing references to the phenomena of the day. He sang and played atrociously, but the songs themselves, while of the self-consciously "smart" variety, were often amusing and effective.

Since Johnny was very poor in those days, I promptly began selling Moss Hart on the idea of hiring him as secretary — a crazier notion cannot be imagined. Moss, whose amiability, while occasionally strained, is admired by all, gave Latouche an "interview" and found him very nice, full of talent, but hardly secretary material.

The second Shubert *Follies* was a better show than the first, thanks to Minnelli, Balanchine and Anderson. Ira and I worked hard, writing and discarding dozens of songs, but somehow, perhaps owing to the performers, the score didn't come off too impressively in the theater. Ira's writing methods were slow and soothing and very restful after Harburg's strident screams and wild pacing of the floor. Our work sessions usually began with a family dinner with Ira and Leonore, joined by Fanny Brice or Ellen Berlin. After a long and copious meal, the company would repair to the drawing room, which housed the piano, and hectic conversation would ensue; I, on tenterhooks, would be dying to get to the piano and persuade Leonore and her guests to go elsewhere for their energetic gossip. I would shoot expressive glances at ever-placid Ira, who affected not to catch their meaning and willingly joined in the conversation. After an hour or so of this, I, totally exasperated, would invade the piano determinedly and strike a few challenging chords. This time Ira would heed my desperate call, stretch himself, emit a series of protracted sighs, say something to the effect that "one had to work *so-o-o* hard for a living" and more in that vein, then interrupt himself to intone the magic word: "However . . ." This "however" meant that the eleventh hour had struck and the period of delicious procrastination was over. Ira, sighing pathetically, would then produce a small bridge table, various writing and erasing gadgets, a typewriter and four or five books, which he seldom consulted — Roget's *Thesaurus,* Webster's dictionary, rhyming dictionary and the like — wipe and adjust his glasses, all these preparations at a *molto adagio* pace, and finally say in a resigned voice: "O.K., Dukie . . . play that chorus you had last night." After wrestling with last night's chorus for a half hour, Ira would embark on an ice-box-raiding expedition, with me, fearful of too long an interruption, in pursuit. There we'd stand in the kitchen, munching cheese and pickles, Ira obviously delighted with this escapist stratagem, I dutifully pretending to enjoy it too. Another sigh, another "however," then back to the piano. At 2 or 3 A.M. Ira would put away his working utensils and victoriously announce to Lee that he had completed four lines for the new chorus.

A fresh and novel "Ballad of Baby Face McGinty," imaginatively staged by Balanchine, was inexplicably dropped in Boston. George wound up with three choreographic contributions — "Words Without Music" (subtitled "A Surrealist Ballet"), sung by Gertrude Niesen and danced by Harriet Hoctor; "Night Flight," a solo for Hoctor; and Josephine Baker's "5 A.M.," an Aubrey Beardsleyish pipe dream.

Fanny was great in "Modernistic Moe" — a satire on "modern" dancing, "The Sweepstakes Ticket" — David Freedman's hilarious sketch, and especially his immortal "Baby Snooks Goes Hollywood" and in the "super-special musical photoplay" finale entitled "The Gazooka," in which Fanny appeared as "Ruby Blondell" and Bob Hope as "Bing Powell." Dave and Ira (who created this chef-d'oeuvre) proved a regular pair of Nostradamuses in this opus as the "Gazooka" — a parody on the "Carioca," the "Continental" and other fancy screen-created dance crazes — was announced as done "in Techniquecolor" on the "Widescope Screen." Hollywood producers kindly note that we were eighteen years ahead of time.

Notwithstanding all these delights, as well as "I Can't Get Started," expertly delineated by Hope and Eve Arden, and Eve's "Economic Situation," to a clever Gershwin lyric, the New York opening night was chiefly marked by Josephine Baker's unprecedented but, I fear, not unprefabricated triumph. The entire balcony was filled with her friends and admirers, and they made such a din at their idol's merest apparition, that no one, not even the audience-proof Fanny, could follow amidst the frenzied cheering accorded La Baker. In reality, that woman of indefinable talents — she's no trained dancer, an inaudible singer and certainly no comedienne in the American sense — failed completely in the *Follies,* as the critics were quick to point out the next morning. Neither did they care too much for Niesen, an exciting and original singer; Brooks Atkinson said she had "a cloudy voice suggesting an oboe with a cold." All he said about my tunes was that they were "probably all right." Percy Hammond said that "music seems to be lacking," and Richard Lockridge that "Mr. Duke's music isn't, to be sure, anything in particular, except a lot of horns." But, thank goodness, others dissented in my favor — among them John Anderson, Gil Gabriel, Bob Garland, John Mason Brown, Bob Coleman and, best of all, Broadway's own bible, *Variety*. "Ibee" of that esteemed sheet must be credited with being the real discoverer of "I Can't Get Started With You." "Show's melody hit song is spotted rather late," he said, "Bob Hope getting it across on the lyric end. Even so the tune was quickly recognized as the standout. Ditty is 'Can't Get Started' warbled to Eve Arden, who plays hard to get." The *Time* magazine man, too, singled out the song and even quoted part of the lyric for a, perhaps, transparent reason: "The Himalaya Mountains I climb, I'm written up in 'Fortune' and 'Time,' I'm asked to every State Ball, but I'm just behind the eight-ball with you." Of the daily critics, only John Anderson mentioned the song at all.

CHAPTER XV

IN MY THIRTIES IN THE THIRTIES

I HAVE been faithful to thee, Serena! In my fashion," is the way I could justifiably paraphrase Ernest Dowson. In 1936 I was still passionately in love with Miss Bagnold's and Mr. Behrman's *Serena Blandish.* As early as October 1935, Dwight Deere Wiman wired me: "Asked Howard Lindsay to lunch with me on Wednesday the twenty-third. Can you join us?" I readily forgave Dwight his role in my replacement by Cole Porter in *The Gay Divorcee* — one doesn't quarrel with a hit, particularly when it's studded with Cole's best songs — and we foregathered at Tony Soma's — "April in Paris's" birthplace. The lunch and drinks were good but Lindsay was not keen on tackling *Serena.* On December 19th Dwight wrote me: "I thought you were so busy with the Follies it might not be just the right time to talk. I have not been exactly idle on the Serena business. The first difficulty as we both know is in finding the ideal person to do something about the book." I must explain that Berry himself, who *would* have been ideal, didn't go beyond a promise to "come in" on the book when it had achieved the "rough draft" stage. "We would be quite unwise to bring the play in this year," Wiman went on. "I think if we can agree on the right sort of man to handle the book and if we could let him work on it during the late winter and spring to be ready for the fall, it would be much smarter showmanship. I will get in touch with you as soon as the Follies open." Moss Hart was approached next and declined the offer with his customary amiability.

Immediately upon the completion of the *Follies* score, I began the job of revamping and reorchestrating *Jardin.* While rusticating in Fire Island, I kept in close touch with Massine and the colonel, who were touring Europe and testing my ballet before Monte Carlo and Barcelona audiences, getting it in shape for the all-important Covent

Garden showing. What happened when my work was therein exhibited defies description. From the letters I gathered that *Jardin* got an "unusually noisy" reception, the noise being of the far from flattering sort. The critics really tore into me, Ernest Newman leading the pack with habitual thoroughness: "The music is like a belated ghost from the generation 1920–1930. . . . One feels, indeed, that it is just the sort of thing Diaghilev would have imagined to be truly representative of modern music in his last days." Why, thanks Mr. Newman, I said to myself, then read on: "Dukelsky, apparently, still thinks we are likely to be impressed by a profusion of discords without any distinction or continuity of idea to justify them." Constant Lambert, the orange-shirted "Kid" of my Diaghilev days, thought *Jardin* "a bit of a mess . . . the process of artistic digestion, so to speak, is incomplete. And small wonder when so much of the material is half-baked." After panning Lurçat's scenery and costumes unmercifully, Constant went to work on me: "Dukelsky's score is a disappointment after his earlier theatre work. 'Zephyr and Flora,' in spite of its rather costive harmonic and orchestral style, was one of the most attractive of the neo-classical Diaghilev ballets and had an agreeable melodic freshness. This and the jazz music he has written under the name of Vernon Duke suggest that his talent is 'au fond' simple and spontaneous. His new score, however, is very self-conscious." Only Francis Toye gave me a pat on the back: "Dukelsky's music possesses the great merit as ballet music of being extremely vivid and strongly contrasted if at times harsh and strident."

Massine and de Basil urged me to take out the "harsh and strident" sounds and butter the music with lush tunes — although the "Poor Lovers" already had one, and a good one, too. With all its faults, *Jardin* was orchestrated more dexterously than the Diaghilev *Zephyr,* but the orchestration failed to adequately underline and intensify the musical thought. I compared notes with Gershwin, who suggested consulting Schillinger without delay. When told that his help was needed because both the revamped ballet and *St. Petersburg* were to be performed, Schillinger proved most sympathetic and we went to work at once. Schillinger's workroom was full of his beloved "new age" instruments, such as a Hammond organ, a Novachord, and a Solovox, in addition to the "obsolete" piano. Our sessions — for they could hardly be called lessons — consisted of going over the two works page by page. A given page was subjected to the most minute analysis, both in its orchestral and purely musical aspects. Schillinger sought to determine, first of all, whether the musical thought was "orchestrable"; the next step was to hear a passage on the piano, and ascertain that the orchestration interpreted the music properly, that the shifting of sonorities was gradual if the music warranted it, or sudden when dynamic penetration was necessary. I was also shown the various Schillinger-invented "special effects"; those that had their origin in overtones and other acoustic phenomena were the most fascinating. Both works were given a new orchestral dress, not for the sake of greater superficial effect but because it was organically right for the correct projection of the music. Were it not for Joseph Schillinger, I would still be faced with: "What happened to your music? It sounded so well on the piano!"

While thus endeavoring to keep myself busy on both musical fronts, I went to the usual number of not overly amusing parties and saw a great many people who were uniformly friendly and just as uniformly indifferent to me as I was to them. Whenever there was a lull in my activities, I'd kill an hour or two by having drinks with easygoing chance companions or going through the motions of passion with "yes women." The resulting emptiness was often unendurable, and marriage seemed to be the only possible remedy. Mother's exemplary, though mercilessly short, married life was certainly a potent argument in favor of matrimony, even for so lighthearted a young man as myself. At thirty-two, it wasn't a moment too soon to think of marriage, and I spent the next six years (until Mother's death in 1942) experimenting with the idea. Karen and Bunny were my first, perhaps pardonable, missteps in that direction; with Joan I very nearly reached success. I knew full well after three or four romantic outings on Fire Island that the girl was too young for me — that her father, a conservative businessman and an old-time Republican, insisted on four years of college education for his daughter — and I discovered shortly that Joan's mother was a manic-depressive in a fairly advanced stage. I couldn't get the girl out of my mind and found wonderful solace in her childish frankness, in her lack of social or artistic pretensions and in the effortless, slightly seedy comfort of her parents' home in the suburbs. After too much studied badinage with well-advertised Park Avenue "lovelies," or the snappy "tough talk" of Tin Pan Alley, being asked to deliver a lecture "on modern music" at Joan's high school was pleasantly American and purifying. God alone knows what I talked about to eager-eyed besweatered coeds, who seemed quite nonplused by their "continental" lecturer with an odd voice and a foreign manner; but they absolutely ate it up and bombarded me with unexpectedly intelligent questions. I was driven back to Joan's house to partake of tea and crumpets, to sign several autograph books, and best of all, to receive a grateful kiss from Joan, who was proud as Punch at having "put me over" with her high-school contemporaries. It was after my "lecture" that I began to think seriously of marrying Joan.

Three good things happened around Christmas time. The "new" score of *Jardin* was read by de Basil's orchestra under Antal Dorati in Indianapolis and, apparently, voted a distinct improvement over the old one; Leopold Stokowski wrote to say that he'd be "most interested" in seeing the score of *St. Petersburg;* and Dwight Wiman, in his untiring search for the right adaptor for *Serena,* seemed to have finally found one in Arthur Macrae, the promising young English playwright and actor. Johnny Latouche was having a series of annoying illnesses and wrote me amusingly from St. Luke's Hospital to ask me to burn a candle for him, "at St. Vitus, please." Also that he had completed a libretto and two ballets. Since Johnny was in financial difficulties at the time, I got the bright idea of palming him off on the good colonel as a fifth press agent, on his release from the hospital. The colonel was astonished and irritated by the boy's extreme youth — he immediately voiced grave doubts as to his eligibility as "public relations man" in the loudest Russian. "What did he say?" Johnny queried nervously. "He wants to know whether you can read and write," I translated more or less accurately. I then explained to de Basil that Latouche was a great genius and could make the ballet palatable to cowboys or dockyard workers. This proved the real clincher, and Latouche was hired on the spot, although we had some difficulty in securing a much-needed twenty-dollar advance for him.

In Philadelphia Latouche was spotted in a fashionable bar buying drinks for a bevy of ballerinas; that evening I saw him backstage discussing the vagaries of the Russian soul with Irina Baronova. The colonel attempted to listen for a while, then asked me worriedly: "What is he saying?" — Latouche's English being as baffling to de Basil as de Basil's Russian was to Johnny. The colonel spoke French with a strong Kursk or Orel accent, whereas Latouche's French had distinctly Southern intonations — not the Midi of France but the Midi of Richmond, Virginia. They pretended to be unable to understand one another and rightly suspected me of being an inaccurate and dishonest translator; I couldn't very well tell one man what the other thought of him. "Ach, Dimotchka, Dimotchka," de Basil whined, "if only your little Babouche would write instead of talking to my ballerinas, we'd get somewhere." The next morning Latouche, having spent his entire advance on "high life," came to my hotel to join me for breakfast. Two weeks later he and de Basil parted company.

Gradually, an influential group of ballet enthusiasts was formed around the Monte Carlo Ballet, and, since they were Americans, the question of an all-American ballet arose. The only American work in the colonel's repertoire was the intermittently exciting *Union Pacific* by Archibald MacLeish and Nabokov — therefore only half "made in the U.S.A." This work, imaginatively choreographed by Massine, won a sizable success and made the colonel receptive to further essays in Americana. I suggested Paul Bowles and Carlos Chavez, excellent theatrical composers both and representatives of two widely divergent but equally authentic aspects of the new American musical thought. I always had the warmest admiration for Bowles, who used to come to my Village gatherings and whose music immediately appealed to me by virtue of its clearly personal "presence." His crystalline and strangely equivocal songs, the many apt and evocative "background" scores for Broadway plays he'd written and some equally remarkable piano pieces were all indicative of a potentially important ballet composer. Chavez already had several ballets in his portfolio, including *H.P.* and the more recent *Quatro Solis* — the last named as yet unproduced. The question of backers arose again, and of the two proposed works, the Mexican project had readier takers, as the Chavez score was already "on paper," whereas Paul's was barely begun.

Alice Halicka's *capitonnages* (she had replaced Lurçat), my "sweetened" music and the revamped choreography combined to make a slightly better ballet than *Jardin's* first version, but I doubt that Gide had any real cause for rejoicing. The "improved" version was presented at the N.Y. Metropolitan Opera House in April 1936; Estrella Boissevain and George Gershwin sat in my box and there was a lot of seemingly spontaneous applause. Robert Simon in the *New Yorker* said: "A practical, kaleidoscopic scenario, shrewdly choreographed by Mr. Massine, and goodlooking scenery and costumes. The score is sound ballet composition, and there are attractive melodies in it. The audience made a handsome fuss over 'Jardin,' which is to have further showings." Further *shovings* would have been more correct because, as Lincoln Kirstein gleefully recorded in his "Blast at Ballet" pamphlet: "Dukelsky's (Vernon Duke's) fatuous score for 'Jardin Publi*que*' [he might have brushed up on his French] received two complete extremely expensive decoratings and costumings in two seasons, was a failure in both, and junked in a third."

In the course of 1935 I saw a good deal of Pavlik Tchelitchev, who now shared a flat with Charles Henri Ford, a young avant-garde poet and magazine publisher. Pavlik had become extremely nervous and irritable, but he painted magnificently and was as friendly as ever with me. Ruth Ford, Charles's actress sister, a dark Southern beauty, was then eager to break into the musical-show game — and both Tchelitchev and his friend Cecil Beaton urged me repeatedly to "get her on Broadway." In this I failed; but I did give Ruth a setting of her brother's "Song of the Muse" to sing, which she did deliciously. Chick Austin and other Hartford, Connecticut, aesthetes ("Friends and Enemies of Modern Music," as they styled themselves) were staging a sumptuous "Paper" Ball in Hartford, and various *art moderne* personalities were asked to prepare "entrances." At the ball, Ruth Ford, extravagantly dressed by Tchelitchev, sang my "Song of the Muse" on the backs of four splendidly gilded but otherwise reasonably naked youths. The ball itself was a success; I attempted a flirtation with beauteous Mimi Soby, but she was snatched from me by Charlie Ford, who offered to teach her the "blackbottom" surrealist style.

Tchelitchev, in Harold Acton's words, "wished, above all, to be stronger than he was and his efforts led to strain." This was a new Tchelitchev, not the life-loving, insouciant youth I knew in Boulevard Montparnasse. Again according to Acton: "One could not speak of Bérard to Tchelitchev without an eruption. 'Bébé' Bérard was attacked as a plagiarist, a cad, a snob, a 'mondain.' " I remembered Bérard as a beardless weak-faced young man with high color and a passionate love for American jazz, especially as played by Gene

McCown, a blues-addicted Paris expatriate. I once dined with Bérard in 1928 in his parents' gloomy old house, which had a long, winding staircase and a profusion of darkly powerful portraits on the walls. I was astounded to learn that they were all painted by the weak-faced cherub who was my host that evening. "Yes, I painted these portraits," Bébé sighed unhappily. "It doesn't do me any good with Diaghilev — he just doesn't believe I can paint." I then recalled seeing Bérard often backstage at the ballet, chatting animatedly with the dancers but never with Sergei Pavlovitch. Being discovered by Diaghilev would have precipitated Bérard's success. That success, to hear Tchelitchev rant, was now an accomplished fact.

In the spring (1936), I sailed for Europe with de Basil, Massine and the entire Monte Carlo company on the S.S. *Paris*. The purpose of my voyage was twofold: to assist with "final" changes on *Jardin*, which was announced in Barcelona and London, and to meet and work with Arthur Macrae, who had accepted Dwight Wiman's *Serena* offer and was luxuriating on the Riviera prior to going back into the theatrical harness. I didn't see much of Massine, who was having marital difficulties, or the colonel, plotting dark plots with his "associates." Squiring seductive Vera Zorina and jasmin-faced, sinuous Sono Osato, or playing ping-pong with their dancing cavaliers, was more to my taste. On arrival, I was handed a cable which read: "Follies established hit but overhead so tremendous will be forced to close show unless authors agree 50% cut royalties. Ira already accepted. Will you follow suit. Cable acceptance. Harry Kaufman." This was a bit thick — 5 and 10 per cent cuts were not rare, but having one's income from a hit show cut in half was a near catastrophe. "However . . ." I said to myself, using Ira's favorite opener, "Ira is older and far more celebrated than I and he accepted — who am I to squabble?" With regrettable lack of business acumen, I cabled Kaufman authorizing the cut, and, on having dispatched the message suddenly realized that I should have checked with Ira first. I was right; I soon received a letter from Ira, who asked me why I agreed to so unprecedented a reduction in royalties. Apparently, Kaufman sent Ira an identical telegram, concomitantly with mine, but claiming that "Vernon already accepted, etc." Thus Ira and I were deprived of several thousand dollars, as the *Follies* had a long and prosperous run.

Macrae wrote, suggesting a Paris meeting. I looked forward to working on my favorite play in my favorite town. Prokofiev was in Russia. I dined with Paitchadze, a friend still though my publisher no longer. Neither the Parfenovs nor the Samoilenkos were in town. De Basil moved in with Dr. Zalevsky, the great Polish diet, or rather antidiet, specialist. The bulk of Zalevsky's patients consisted of women suffering from pernicious anemia and other serious ailments, resulting from overly zealous "slimming." One internationally known "society beauty," after living for a year on black coffee and orange juice, collapsed and was put in Zalevsky's care; she was slowly restored to life. Anna Pavlova was a patient of Zalevsky's, as were many film and Broadway stars. On the second floor of his spacious house were lodged various animals, all of them living on scientific diets: an overweight cocker spaniel barked at an emaciated goat and obese parrots cackled contemptuously at a starved eagle. Zalevsky invented Padinox, a miraculous "slenderizer" in suppository form, which was just beginning to catch on internationally when premature death put an end to the brilliant doctor's career.

Arthur Macrae, a self-effacing and attractive young Englishman, arrived in Paris; we lunched together, compared notes on *Serena* and planned a series of further meetings. The next morning I received a cable from Dwight Wiman telling me that "previous commitments" prevented him from producing *Serena Blandish* after all and wishing me luck with "another" producer, name unspecified. This, after carefully outlining my "way of life" and working schedule and paying Macrae in advance! Being enraged by producers was fast becoming an unhealthy habit with me. I summoned Macrae, who had received a similar cable, and who too was raging, in a discreet, more subdued manner, as befitted a Britisher. I obviously couldn't ask the young author, a total stranger to me, to work on speculation; we had a farewell drink together and he departed, his faith in Broadway magnates irreparably shaken. I wrote Dwight a long and nasty letter.

The trip to Spain with de Basil and Sevastianov, his secretary, was a refreshing change after the Kaufman and Wiman setbacks. With fellow Russians the colonel could be good company, if you were prepared to dispense with subtlety and wit, but then, Russian gaiety is neither witty nor subtle. I liked Barcelona, although it's probably the least Spanish of all Spanish cities. I was surprised to see de Basil, whom I had always considered a dyed-in-the-wool monarchist, on the best of terms with highly placed Catalonian politicians of extremely "progressive" tendencies. Massine, his dog Smoke and I were photographed on the theater's roof between rehearsals by the *Musical America* photographer. David Lichine, Riabouchinska and some of the more adventurous girl dancers dined nightly on suckling pig and heady Spanish red wine at the Caracoles just off the Ramblas. Forgetting Zalevsky's diet advice, I joined them enthusiastically — there's nothing like young pig meat grilled on a spit — and began gaining weight again at tremendous speed. By the time we returned to Paris, I had acquired a triple chin. I don't remember anything about *Jardin's* reception in Barcelona, except that half the orchestra made a wrong entrance in the middle of the Rhumba and no one, including the dancers, knew the difference.

Zalevsky took one look at me at the railroad station in Paris, where he awaited our arrival with an armful of roses for his favorite ballerinas, and let out a howl. "You must have gained forty pounds," he exclaimed jovially. "What a perfect guinea pig for my research work!" The "pig" reference was a little too close to home and I frowned; but the good Zalevsky embraced me paternally and assured me that he'd whip me into shape in no time. "It'll cost you nothing," the doctor assured me. "All I want you to do is to accept my humble hospitality and lodge with me for the next three weeks; I'm not doing you any favors — you'll be favoring me by letting me use you as my guinea . . . well, you know the animal I mean." I consulted a mirror, hated what I saw and readily accepted Zalevsky's generous offer.

On the first morning of my "cure" I was served a breakfast consisting of cereal, three fried eggs, quantities of butter, my beloved *croissants* and coffee with thick cream. Being hungry I swallowed everything and my admiration for Zalevsky grew. "This food must have been de-calorized or seasoned with thyroid," I thought. "No matter, it tasted fine." I did some composing that morning — or, rather, arranging, as I had sold de Basil an idea of adapting John Field's (1782–1837) enchanting piano pieces; Field was Chopin's model, the true inventor of the nocturne and a great glutton and drunkard. I called my balletization of his music *Field Day,* a rather pretty title, I still think. At one o'clock Zalevsky took me to lunch at Lapérouse, one of Paris's most famous restaurants; the menu — which I refuse to reproduce, as it might tempt me to cook a similar meal — was extraordinarily copious and studded with calories. A great deal of wine was also consumed. At five — tea with more *croissants,* butter and raspberry tarts. For dinner we visited Kornilov's and partook of vodka, *blini,* borsht, *pirojki,* Tzar's cutlets (stuffed with *foie gras,* truffles and melted butter), rum cake and coffee accompanied by liqueurs. That day I gained two more pounds. I didn't dare open my mouth for fear that another morsel of food would be put there by the diabolical Pole. The next day — the same overly gorgeous gorging; another pound and a half gained. On the morning of the next day I couldn't get into my trousers and decided to flee from Zalevsky's gastronomic trap, wrapped in a bed sheet if need be. Before I could execute my plan, the maid entered, carrying a tray; on it were lemon juice, half a grapefruit and black, unsweetened coffee. Lunch consisted of carrots, watercress, lettuce and a slice of pineapple; for dinner a huge steak, a raw tomato and tea with lemon. I was so delighted with the abrupt cessation of culinary excesses, I could hardly finish the steak. Two more days of the hunger diet — then a day of reckless stuffing (this time I gained only half a pound) — then back to the fasting. I also had to drink various liquids (no alcohol except on the "banquet days") and use Padinox every night. In three weeks I shed well over twenty pounds, could again wear my clothes "with an air," and thanked Zalevsky by dedicating *Field Day* to him.

London was next on de Basil's schedule (the ballet gave no performances in Paris). On arriving I was given a small room in the colonel's flat in Shepherd's Market. An acute feeling of hollowness was the effect London had on me after my seven years' absence. Most clichés are based on truth; I'm not sure that the one about the Englishman — "once a friend, always a friend" — is. I was certainly not lacking in friends in London during my four years' sojourn there; yet the only two people who seemed genuinely glad to see me back were Ewart Garland (by then happily married to his long-time love, Rosalind) and my old lyrical collaborator Desmond Carter (who also had a beautiful wife, Betty — as redheaded as Rosalind was blond). Desmond and I promptly collaborated on two songs.

Staying with the colonel was not a good idea — not by London standards. De Basil, utterly devoid of Diaghilev's magnetic charm and profound culture, made no effort to gain an entree into English (and, even less, into French) society and was at all times regarded as a dull and socially unacceptable executive. His aide-de-camp, "Gerry" Sevastianov was, on the contrary, a personable and ingratiating young man, who, although lacking in Boris Kochno's feline polish and dexterity, did what he could to give de Basil a little "salon veneer."

The London season was at its height; it would be an exaggeration to say that all doors were closed to me, but I frankly didn't bother to knock. After all, people knew (or did they?) that I was in town and there was always the telephone — which rang very seldom. I went to cocktails at Cecil Beaton's and saw a few "bright young" faces, relatively unchanged. There was a lot of hectic talk about people and things that must have appeared on the social horizon during my absence, for they all sounded unfamiliar. I telephoned Willie Walton, who, I was told, was in town, but there was no answer. He never made the slightest effort to reach me.

I ran into one of the "bright young things" of the Elizabeth Ponsonby circa 1926 entourage — not so young any more, but brighter than ever. I took her to lunch and no sooner were we ushered to our table than I spotted Constant Lambert lunching alone in a corner; he had grown very fat and his face was exceedingly red. He, too, recognized me and, in lieu of greeting, glared ferociously. I waved at him airily, which probably enraged him all the more.

Jardin had a gala "reopening" at the Covent Garden late in June. I took the ex-"bright young thing" and an old Russian friend, Prince "Vava" Golitzine, whose small country place in Chessington near London was the meeting place of the "nicer" White Russians in the twenties; Vava owned an antique shop in Berkeley Square and was still the gracious *grand seigneur* — a race now practically extinct; its representatives are easily spotted, since their graciousness increases as their fortunes dwindle — a difficult feat for the more numerous not-so-*grands seigneurs*. It was nice to see white ties and tiaras in the audience; the proceedings on the stage were less encouraging, but I couldn't really tell with the usual exhibitionist ovations and the bows Massine, Toumanova and I took together.

During the intermission, I did a little reconnoitering in the foyer, and, although I didn't hear much beyond the usual "divine," "unspeakably dreary," "absolute heaven" and "frightful bore," the spectacle that greeted my eyes was most arresting. The resplendent parade of homosexuals, shy and blatant, simpering and booming, dressed with the unmasculine exaggeration of every caprice of fashion so typical of their ilk, was something to see; the "boys" were on the town and Covent Garden was their citadel. Ten years later Cecil Gray summed it up fearlessly in *Contingencies:* "Ballet, in fact, is the homosexual art form *par excellence* . . . and at performances of the Russian Ballet the character of the audience was frequently such as to render one's presence in the midst of it — if one happened to be comparatively normal — so acutely distasteful that one preferred to stay away altogether. Whatever the future of art may be after the war, we can at least be fairly sure that it will not take the form of a continuation of this *danse macabre.*" The spectacle before me was indeed macabre, but the wildly chattering "gay" boys (according to Gray "those who share homosexual propensities refer to themselves and each other as being 'queer.'" Horrors! "Gay" is the word.) seemed affable enough and quite a few of them waved at me with Hellenic grace. I spotted a divinely tailored and discreetly rouged exquisite, an Honorable something-or-other whose face had the unmistakable stamp of the twenties, chatting with a busty, rather "countryish" debutante. A pretty shepherdess surrounded by effeminate fauns was an incongruous sight and I decided to come to her rescue. "Ah, Dukelsky," her escort intoned, "would you be an absolute angel and introduce me to Z [a good-looking male dancer]?" I thought it over quickly and made a counterproposal. "With pleasure — if you, in turn, introduce me to your absolutely angelic companion" — this with a significant leer in the girl's direction. She turned out to be the Honorable's cousin and her name, which I didn't quite catch, sounded like Penelope Bumpety-Bump. We shook hands with, perhaps, exaggerated warmth — the girl sensing my lack of "gaiety" — and her cousin permitted himself a disgruntled yawn. "I didn't know you were one of *those,*" he said. "How odd — I didn't know *you* were," I retorted and made arrangements to take Miss Bumpety-Bump to the Savoy after the ballet.

At supper, my debutante expressed her delight at meeting a male at last, although a rather out-of-the-way specimen. "You are most terribly bogus, you know," said Penelope with an arch look. "When I first saw you I thought you were an American, but I no longer think you are. What are you?" I meekly informed her that I was *Jardin's* composer.

If I couldn't tell the effect my refurbished ballet produced, the critics next morning could and did. "It is difficult to understand why Massine should have been at pains to revise his 'Jardin Public' . . . for it is the least successful of his productions" went the *Times.* "The music of M. Dukelsky is vulgar without being funny," declared Philip Page, *Referee's* dramatic critic: "also an authority on music," according to the editor, "writing in place of Constant Lambert, who will be back from his holiday next week." All at once, I found myself actively longing for Constant's return. "Pointless cacophony is intolerable, even in the wildest developments of modern ballet," Mr. Page added.

De Basil walked in and interrupted my reading. "You see, Dimotchka," he began, his big ears shining menacingly in the midday sun. "I told you to give me a little melody, but you put it all in the follies of Mr. Ziegfeld. How many times—" "Oh, leave me and the follies of Mr. Ziegfeld alone, you Cossack bully!" I screamed in the manner of Noel Coward's heroes. With that I ran out of de Basil's flat and headed, for obscure reasons, in the direction of Hyde Park. I felt wildly, epically miserable, hating the colonel, the ballet and its devotees, my absent friends, the mean critics, Harry Kaufman, and the whole not-so-wide world in general. I sat down on a park bench, the summer laziness of Hyde Park all around me. There was a fine smell of grass mingling with that of the ginger beer being consumed by a Cockney family sprawled out under a shade tree. Shopgirls and typists lay on the grass giggling gaily. Lovers were everywhere, embracing furtively and clumsily but with every sign of erotic enjoyment. Here was life, crude and unambitious, unseeing, unthinking, life savored for itself by little people whose very littleness was so obviously stronger and wiser than all my savage striving for success. And now that I was bogged down by failure, the unknown and unsung practitioners of the art of living on all sides of me seemed to be triumphantly successful precisely because they did nothing to attain their triumph.

Staying with de Basil, in view of the fierce critical drubbing I received, became unendurable, so I took a little "service flat" in Dover Street and spent evenings in the company of Penelope the debutante, who thought me less and less "bogus" with each succeeding meeting. Just as I began to forget faithless *Serena,* Milton Shubert turned up and displayed interest in the project, thinking it a good vehicle for Yvonne Printemps and Pierre Fresnay. We set up a meeting with the pair in Paris and my spirits rose again. I couldn't leave London quickly enough, although the colonel went on programing *Jardin*, which somehow rather interested the public and was a minor *succès de scandale*. Ever the opportunist, de Basil, who was all for "going American" in the States, approved of my *Field Day* as a proper appeaser for chauvinistic Britons. I had no time to orchestrate the Field music — things were brewing in New York, where Minnelli was assembling a new Bea Lillie-Bert Lahr revue — so I was entrusted with hiring a suitable orchestrator in Paris.

Paris soon cured me of my many-hued blues. I took a suite in a small hotel just off the Champs Elysées, guzzled *champagne nature* (the only kind of champagne I like and the one that doesn't "travel") and was given a prodigious meal at the Caneton by Zalevsky, who was delighted with my unchanged "silhouette" — it isn't difficult to diet in London — and thought I deserved a gastronomic prize. The *Serena* audition with Printemps and Fresnay went off well; it was hard to resist Printemps's magnetism, her youth, which was neither preserved nor restored, but which simply wouldn't desert its owner, or Pierre Fresnay's perfect manners and perfect English. I played several songs, mostly with lyrics of my own, like "Sailing at Midnight," and the couple seemed delighted.

Boris Kochno, now sharing Bébé Bérard's quarters, reappeared, polished and handsome as of yore — although his hair was fast receding and he had a jaded air, rather like a *petit poète* of eighteenth-century Paris salons, with only the snuffbox missing. He told me that jazz-record collecting was his new hobby and that several records of my songs were among his favorites. Having once helped launch me as Dukelsky in Paris, he was now — eleven years later — ready to put Vernon Duke on the city's musico-social map. "Play me some jazz, *du vrai* jazz," Boris implored me dreamily. I complied and, although no jazz "purist" would give me even a passing mark, Boris was electrified. He went to the telephone and in ten minutes I had three dinner invitations and one to the opera where Lifar announced the "creation" of *Le Roi Nu,* a ballet based on Hans Christian Andersen's tale, with music by Jean Françaix. Outside of the opera, ballet was dead in Paris and Diaghilev's imperial mantle was taken out of mothballs and undeservedly donned by Serge Lifar — a poor fit.

My new Paris success was small beer compared with the Diaghilev debut, but it had the effect of healing balsam on my London-inflicted wounds. I got a taste of Gershwin's salon pianistics — marquises and countesses sharing the piano stool with me and listening to my constipated roulades (they insisted on my "singing" the lyrics) with every evidence of rapture. My social sponsors, outside of Boris, were Marie-Blanche de Polignac, Denise Bourdet, the witty and observant journalist widow of the playwright, and Natasha Wilson, one of the most ethereally lovely creatures I have ever beheld. "Sailing at Midnight" — for which Howard Dietz later wrote a new lyric and I a new tune — was an "upsetting emotional experience" in the words of a titled *ravissante;* upsetting emotional experiences don't grow on trees and I rapidly became a veritable *coqueluche des salons.*

Marie-Blanche, who played the role of Lady Blessington to mine of Nat Parker Willis, couldn't get enough of my *Serena* tunes, and we saw each other almost nightly. Marie-Laure de Noailles, the rich and eccentric muse of so many Paris musicians and painters, was never altogether "sold" on me. For the *première* of *Le Roi Nu* Marie-Blanche was my hostess; in the intermission as we were chatting about the ballet, which no one seemed to like, Mme. de Polignac was effusively greeted by Tchelitchev and Charlie Ford, who were in Marie-Laure's party. I had no idea that Pavlik was in Paris and ran up to him impulsively to tell him of my joy at seeing him at the scene of my Diaghilev youth; I asked Tchelitchev to lunch with me in the Montparnasse quarter, as a sort of pilgrimage to the familiar phantoms of our past. The painter looked at me with obvious displeasure, asked about the date of my departure for the States and said that he was entirely "too busy" for sentimental outings. This was the coldest of showers, as cold as it was undeserved and inexplicable. I learned later that Tchelitchev was reported enraged by my social "triumphs," a report I thought hardly credible until I read in Acton's *Memoirs of an Aesthete:* "Though Tchelitchev pretended to have a horror of fashion, he could not help courting it. It was Bérard's success as an innovator of fashion that rankled most." Understandably, no Paris soiree was possible without Bébe Bérard, now bearded and sporting food-stained and paint-spotted tight little suits, but always radiantly gay and childishly entertaining; he was universally adored. The next day I saw Tchelitchev at Halicka's and told him of my resentment at the uncalled-for snub he administered to me at the opera; my frankness was, in turn, immediately and violently resented by Pavlik, who never forgave me — although, in all fairness, it was *he* who should have craved my forgiveness. He later told John Murray Anderson that I "bespitted" him.

I took Denise Bourdet and Natasha Wilson to supper at one of the large Russian night clubs where fading gentlewomen sang gypsy songs of questionable authenticity and violins shed their syrupy tears right into your borsht. We were joined by Lifar, his face an odd red-brown, mouth chronically half-opened, as if in delirious abandon. Lifar embraced me tenderly and wanted to know what I had done with *Mistress into Maid,* which Diaghilev never got to hear. He was planning a "Pushkin Gala" for the one hundredth anniversary of the poet's death and expressed a burning desire to hear the score of my two-act opera. Encouraged by Serge's interest, I told him of *St. Petersburg,* which contained a long aria with a Pushkin text ("I love thee, oh work of Peter"); this so transported the dancer that he nearly broke a violin bow that suddenly appeared under his nose. "Dima, what luck us meeting again!" he exclaimed, downing a glass of vodka. "Don't let's lose sight of one another. We met through Diaghilev — we meet again under Pushkin's Northern Star." We arranged to foregather at Paitchadze's music shop in rue d'Anjou the next afternoon. I brought both scores along and could hardly wade through them, so incessant were Lifar's ecstatic exclamations and other appreciative noises. It was decided that both works would be performed at the "Pushkin Gala" and that *Mistress into Maid* should be copied for his, Lifar's, use, at his expense. A few months later, my opera was duly copied, setting me back $410, and sent to Lifar, to the Paris opera; I never received the slightest acknowledgment of receipt, let alone a check. The Pushkinists managed to meet under their idol's Northern Star without my help. The task of orchestrating *Field Day* was entrusted to Tibor Harsanyi, excellent Neo-Parisian musician of Hungarian birth; not only was it left unproduced by de Basil but he managed to lose the orchestra and piano scores of that work together with the full score of *Jardin Public.*

Shortly before my return to the States, I sought out poor Uncle Iliko (Ilya), now employed as night watchman for a Russian antique store in rue St. Honoré. I could hardly recognize in the old, bent, shabbily clothed man, his head shaking owing to a chronic nervous affliction, the once spruce and lady-killing colonel of the gendarme corps. I met Iliko (to whom I'd been sending money the past two years) in his patron's shop, after hours; he was sweeping the floor and put the broom aside guiltily as I entered. I bought my uncle a good meal and great quantities of cigarettes, the smoking of which was his only remaining vice, as he meekly confessed. Iliko was not very old; but his life was behind him in Russia and he was now obediently and uncomplainingly going through the motions still expected of him. He died six years later in Nice, at the asylum for the aged. My encounter with Aunt Genia, Uncle Nicholas Kopylov's divorced wife, wasn't much gayer; continually sick herself, she was employed as a nurse and led a hopelessly gray life, the insufficient purpose of which was to keep Death from releasing her from her misery. Iliko and Genia were not on good terms before their exodus from Russia; having lost their relatives and friends one by one, they now saw each other often and clung together, old age and the starless night around the corner their only bond.

Diaghilev's "fourth son," pencil-slim, black-haired Igor Markevitch, born in Kiev but brought to France at an early age (hence his poor Russian, deplored by Prokofiev), was the composer *en vogue* in 1936 Paris. His early works, such as *Rebus* (introduced in the States by Koussevitzky) and *Icare,* were really remarkable and had a "new sound" years before the "new look" was invented. Listening to his music was exhilarating, but on closer inspection it appeared oddly devoid of substance — though there was never any question of the young man's genius for orchestration. Stories of Marie-Laure's deification of the slightly diabolical-looking, youthful *maître* (who was later to become one of Europe's ablest conductors) were running the salons. I went to Nadia Boulanger's lecture on the forthcoming *Paradis Perdu,* a huge oratorio Markevitch had just completed, and, to my astonishment, heard that worthy woman assure her elegant listeners that while "they were not privileged to attend Christ's birth, they will be accorded the supreme honor of attending the birth of Markevitch's *Paradise Lost.* Alas, the Paradise proved a total loss and half the audience left long before it was over; the work was interminable, unwieldy and monotonously, obstinately cacophonous. I liked Arthur Lourié's *Concerto Spirituale* (conducted by Charles Munch at another concert) infinitely better; that work, heavy with music and replete with religious fervor, deserves a speedy revival.

A few days before boarding the *Normandie,* New York-bound, I received the following cable from Chauncey Stillman, whom Mexico-loving Estrella Elizaga had sold on the Chavez ballet for de Basil: "Have succeeded in raising thirty-five hundred dollars including my own contribution for the *Quatro Solis* and have exhausted all efforts." The colonel and I had been writing Chavez (who had expressed his readiness to cooperate in New York) the past three months without ever receiving a reply. I sent Chavez an urgent cable plus a detailed letter outlining de Basil's plans for his work, and having thus also "exhausted all efforts" on behalf of a fellow composer, went back to my hotel to pack.

There has never been a ship like the late lamented S.S. *Normandie* of the French line; my only complaint was that the vessel was so huge and the sailing so smooth and rapid that one never quite felt that one was aboard ship, and the trip was over far too quickly. I spent most of the time in Jack and Natasha Wilson's luxurious cabin, which had a private deck where we sat lazily for hours, sipping long drinks and exchanging Paris gossip.

"Vernon Duke, back this week from Europe, will write some additional numbers for the returning 'Follies' and at least two numbers and two ballets for the Beatrice Lillie-Bert Lahr show. Somewhere in his portfolio, too, is the score of the musical version of 'Serena Blandish,' for which Pierre Fresnay and Yvonne Printemps are now being mentioned. Nothing much will be done about this, however, until a producer is found, Dwight Deere Wiman presumably having lost interest in the project," the *New York Times* chronicler reported on July 17th. Milton Shubert evidently got lost too, because to this day I haven't heard from him regarding *Serena*.

Crafty Harry Kaufman, not content with doing me and Ira out of half of our royalties, had been busily peppering the *Follies* (which had had to close suddenly in the summer owing to Fanny Brice's illness) with interpolated songs, notwithstanding my agent's strenuous protests. He had a good argument: none of my tunes had become popular, none were on the Hit Parade, none were even "plugged" by Max Dreyfus's underlings. In vain did Robert Benchley call my score "real music, which is something"—I had a "dead" score in a show that was very much alive. For two years I had begged Henry Spitzer to release me from my contract; he adamantly refused, claiming that I was "way in the red." "How can I be in the black when you refuse to work on my songs?" I protested. A shrug of the shoulders. "Go talk to Max," Henry suggested wearily. Since it was pleasanter to stay in the red than talk to Max, I shrugged the suggestion off in turn and we were just where we started — nowhere. On detecting Kaufman's newest machinations, though, I became grandly indignant (my capacity for indignation is the bane of my existence) and demanded an explanation from the professional manager, a tough Damon Runyon character who talked as if he had a pound of popcorn in his mouth. The man, who hated me violently, dragged me to Dreyfus's office for a showdown. "It's either me or Voinon Duke in this foim, Mr. Mex!" he shouted dramatically. "I'd be delighted to leave, Mr. Dreyfus," I chimed in quickly. "But how about a few plugs before I go?" Dreyfus smiled thinly through his thick cigar and dismissed us both. I stayed on — so did the professional manager.

Meanwhile Vincente Minnelli was putting *The Show Is On* together. A new era was upon Broadway and top craftsmen "took themselves to newer and smarter fields — the intimate sophistication of smart musicals," as one observant reporter had it. "Even the Messrs. Shubert, conservative gentlemen who still believe in Santa Claus, are brightening up their alley, sweeping out the tinsel and bringing in such clever lyricists for their musicals as Mr. Ira Gershwin and Mr. Ogden Gnash (as the Shuberts spell him; he's only a year behind with his copy). Pat to this point about the new smartness and almost girl-less musicals, and hearable this evening, is Ira Gershwin's opening number of these same Shuberts' 'Ziegfeld Follies' at the Winter Garden:

Gone is the day of the show girl
  Whose charms captivate the Don Juan;
This year we cater to no girl;
  Time marches on.
Beauty is fleeting and flimsy
  Tho' she has the neck of a swan;
This year we're featuring whimsy;
  Time marches on.

"So it goes. Thighs are a dime a dozen pairs now and the spectacular 'man on the flying trapeze' but an outmoded song even drunks have forgotten to mumble."

Ted Fetter, a baby-faced, ever-cheerful young man (he was in the *Garrick Gaieties* cast in 1930), Cole Porter's cousin and the son of a Princeton professor, was engaged by Minnelli and Kaufman to write most of the lyrics, I, most of the music. This was again to be an "assembled" score and my job was approximately similar to the one I performed for Billy Rose on my return from Mexico, except that Minnelli meant business and had an opening date. A strong and silent man named Gordon Jenkins, hitherto unknown on Broadway, was hired by Minnelli as conductor and orchestrator. Besides Fetter's and my contributions, the score boasted entries by the Gershwins, Harburg and Arlen, Rodgers and Hart, Hoagy Carmichael, Herman Hupfeld and two friends of mine, Norman Zeno and Will Irwin, a team that should have gotten places but somehow didn't.

I don't think there has ever been a greater disciplinarian or a more exacting perfectionist in the musical theater than Vincente Minnelli. He is now the top director in the musical film division and so formidable a tower of strength at M-G-M that Broadway producers have despaired of ever getting him back on the Great White Way. Where other directors wasted a lot of valuable time wrangling with costume designers, arguing with overpaid stars or kidding around with chorus girls, with Vincente — once the rehearsals started — it was all work and no play. We all felt like cogs in Minnelli's magical wheel and kept ourselves well oiled. Most revues, as I mentioned before, were not routined until dress-rehearsal time, and the routines kept being changed nightly out of town; not with Vincente. Once the material was decided upon and whipped into shape, it was blocked out and put together like pieces in a solved jigsaw puzzle; very little of the running order was changed for the New York opening.

Besides writing "Now," a flowing ballad well sung by Gracie Barrie, and "What Has He Got?" a Fred Astaireish "jingle," I was entrusted with the "Casanova" song and ballet, excitingly danced by Paul Haakon, and a curious bit of Americana named the "Tragedian" (subtitled "A Ballet of the Barnstormers"), the music of which, in view of its complexity and comparative daring, was signed Vladimir Dukelsky. Ironically, the one Dukelsky interpolation was bounced out of the show. Another casualty, a tragic one, was the failure of the late Bunny Berrigan (to whom I owe the ultimate success of "I Can't Get Started") to put his "Jam Session" finale across. It just didn't work in the theater.

After two postponements, necessitated by last-minute changes, *The Show Is On* opened and rocked Boston. "Casanova," a choreographic study of sex was received with startled "Oh's" and "Ah's" but furiously applauded.

It might have been a delayed reaction from my London shock, but I failed to be elated by so fine a debut. I made sincere and valuable friends in Boston in the persons of Robert and Dorothy Hillyer; I admired Robert's poetry, having set nine of his poems to music, and I loved Dorothy's *joie de vivre* and rare knack of turning the stuffiest Bostonian into a frolicking Pan. All civilized gaiety in Boston, not the gayest of cities, was organized by Dorothy and amiable Nat Saltonstall, the head of the Boston's Institute of Modern Art; the parties they gave were patterned after the London *conversazioni,* not the mournful Long Island merrymaking usually designed to provide the "younger marrieds" with a little extramarital titillation. Dorothy and Nat did everything to cheer me up; one evening I was pleasantly surprised to find Noel Coward, dashing as ever, in the Hillyer drawing room, spouting pithy sayings and running through a few new songs. Noel had sent me a most cordial wire for the revue's opening, for which I thanked him warmly; he then asked me to "do" some of the show's tunes. We ended by playing "Now" piano-duet fashion. These diversions were well enough in their way, but they didn't atone for the persistent, gnawing loneliness, the likes of which I had not experienced before.

Boston is a strange place. It welcomes visitors provided they remain "on the outside, looking in"; the Bostonians firmly believe in staying "inside, looking out" — for trouble. I was Trouble, having developed a persistent penchant for Boston's girls. On closer inspection I discovered that nearly every Back Bay virgin had something of a Salem witch in her — but then I would see another prim little head, a face like a plain field flower, with almost no make-up, hear the discreetly musical voice uttering neatly chosen words, scorning the brassy slang of Manhattan — and fall again, hard. I would have gladly given my all for *one* "Slender Naiad of Stone" (the phrase is Robert Hillyer's), provided she'd give me the nod.

The "Slender Naiad" came to my rescue momentarily the night before the Minnelli show concluded its Boston run and moved on to Philadelphia. The scene was a small supper party to wish me God speed and an eventual happy landing on Broadway. The livelier the party grew, the more down in the mouth I felt. The door opened, the captain bowed and admitted a bridal party consisting of youthful bride and groom (Milton, Massachusetts, written all over them), four bridesmaids and as many young men, presumably ushers. One of the bridesmaids, in a white tulle dress with a huge bouffant skirt, dark brown bangs over a radiant young face, put an end to my melancholy and turned a *miserabilis homuncio* into a Scott Fitzgerald youth, love-stricken at the sight of a starry-eyed divinity attending her first prom. I was unable to take my eyes off the Naiad, confessed my elated state to Mrs. Hillyer and asked her whether she could think of a way to effect an introduction; no one at our table knew either the bride or the groom or the members of their retinue — an unusual state of affairs for Bostonians, the most clannish people in the world. A Harvard boy in our party came to my rescue with a device as workmanlike as it was simple: he would "cut in" on one of the "Harvards" (so known to Damon Runyon) in the Naiad's party and I would in turn cut in on him.

In a few minutes I had my arm around the Naiad's waist; as though mutually hypnotized, we stared at each other and were unable to dance for quite a spell. "You may think this very strange, but I wanted terribly to know you, so I cut in on my young friend. You don't mind, do you?" "I don't mind at all," the Naiad said in clear Bostonian tones. "I like people who know their mind and speak it." At this point we were dancing or rather undulating slowly without the slightest regard for the music. "You are much too wonderful to be real. Who are you?" I asked. "I'm Polly Turnbull. And you?" I told her. "Oh, Broadway; Bea Lillie and all that . . ." she intoned disinterestedly. I hastened to assure the girl that distinctly un-Broadwayish activities were included in "all that." "Whatever I am, whatever you are, I must see you." "I must see you, too." "Could we leave this place and go somewhere together?" "How can I? I'm a guest of the Smiths'," she pointed to the young married couple. "We are going on somewhere after this." "But I'm leaving for Philadelphia tomorrow — please try." The Naiad hesitated, then gave me an even starrier look and smiled with sudden softness. "I know I'm horrible, and the Smiths will never forgive me," Miss Turnbull whispered, "but somehow I can't help myself. Go back to your table and I'll see what I can do. Ask me to dance again." I kissed her hand, a disgracefully un-Bostonian feat, and returned to my table, grinning idiotically.

On my return I was greeted with the customary joshing and facetious cracks, but my happiness was such that I didn't even bother to crack back. "The girl is a Bostonian, remember," Dorothy said. "Don't rush things, or you'll get nowhere. If you're capable of a true New England courtship, my blessings are with you, lad." A few minutes later I was dancing with Polly again. "The Smiths think me a lunatic," the Naiad confessed. "When I explained that I just had to go off with you, that you were leaving town, they said they understood perfectly. I'm sure they don't understand at all, and neither do I, but I'm coming with you." "Let's go then." "Where to?" "I want to take you to Bea Lillie's last-minute rehearsal after the show — it's now almost one A.M., but I know they're still at the theater, trying to lick the thing. This will only take a few minutes — then we'll go and sup somewhere — anywhere." "All right," Polly said resignedly, and went off in search of her cloak. She had her car outside the club and drove me to the Shubert. Tired chorus girls in practice clothes, stretching sleepily in orchestra seats, eyed the untheatrical new female curiously and a shade patronizingly — theater folks are snobs too. Polly, in turn, cringed at the sight of so many bare legs and probably speculated on their owners' morals. My Naiad was thrilled at meeting Bea Lillie, who is definitely a bacchante — and bacchantes are unknown in Boston.

It was so late by the time we left the theater that all restaurants were closed. I suggested that we try the Ritz, where I was staying. It was one-thirty; no service in the dining room — only room service. I must have been wonderfully persuasive that night, because, as if in a trance, Polly followed me into the elevator, startling the wise little boy in charge, who could tell that the Naiad was strictly Junior League stuff. In my room on the sixth floor I was more persuasive still; but the reader grunting "uh-huh" delightedly in anticipation of salacious descriptions, will be woefully disappointed. I never touched the girl, I merely touched her heart; I pleaded my love in accents un-Bostonian, but with such cataclysmic sincerity, that she was clearly fascinated and — for a brief moment — forgave me my regrettable birth in Old Russia instead of New England, the only acceptable birthplace for gentlemen. I told her that her entering the restaurant had changed my entire life and that all I wanted was for her to enter that life — and stay in it forever. Over supper and wine, served by a sleepy waiter, I vowed to make all necessary arrangements and promised not to "rush things"; Polly, most unexpectedly, told me of seeing *Jardin Public* in London the summer before and being "tremendously moved" by it.

My Naiad then vanished into the night. After the next evening's performance, I journeyed to Philadelphia with *The Show Is On* company, determined to make tons of money, kidnap Polly if necessary, and head for Paris on a honeymoon.

On walking down Broad Street, I stopped to read an eye-catching poster announcing our show and crediting the score to mostly Duke and Fetter, Rodgers and Hart, Dietz and Schwartz, the Gershwins, etc., all in the same size small print. This was clearly a violation of my contract, and made no sense, besides, as the reader could only deduct that the music and lyrics were "mostly by everybody." I descended on Harry Kaufman, who was busy arguing with the box-office manager, and demanded to know the reason for the offending posters. Harry, who had no use for me and could never understand why Minnelli picked me to do the bulk of the score, tore his hair and was about to start tearing mine, but then thought better of it (I was taller and had more hair), so compromised on shrieking in strident falsetto: "Making trouble again, Duke, eh? Why don't you write me a song hit instead? Can't you see I'm busy trying to put this show in shape for Broadway? Who cares about the goldarned posters? Go on and call your lawyer." With that he slammed the door in my face. Two hours later, the lawyer, a seasoned veteran of many theatrical disputes, arrived at the Forrest Theatre; Kaufman refused to see him. An hour later a half-dozen sturdy lads were observed in Philadelphia streets tearing down the posters, while two muscular members of the musicians' union took possession of the orchestra pit and began taking out the arrangements of everything signed by Duke and Fetter. This time Kaufman, tipped off by his henchmen, literally flew into the theater and nearly yelled his lungs out. The union brothers paid him no heed and calmly went on with their work; a heated exchange with my lawyer and Harry admitted defeat. He shook a plump fist at me, but the posters were changed and the Duke and Fetter items restored to the musicians' stands. But little peccadillos like that couldn't stop the progress of *The Show Is On,* which was emphatically a winner.

I had written Polly a ten-page love letter immediately upon arrival in Philadelphia, and here it was two weeks and not a word in reply. A short, yet not altogether discouraging, answer finally reached me in Washington; apparently, on returning home after our one momentous meeting, Polly found her father sitting on the doorstep, anxious and angry at her prolonged absence. The members of the wedding party had informed him of Polly's inexplicable exit with a "Broadway character," and such conduct was simply "not Boston." The girl gave her father a frank account of the events and stressed the correctness of my behavior, but was rigidly forbidden to see, write, or otherwise communicate with me. I did well to be patient for two weeks, as Polly's curiosity about so nonconformist a suitor as myself was naturally whetted by her father's hostility. In conclusion, Polly wanted to know whether I couldn't see her again — in Boston.

Couldn't I! Used to shuttling between London and Paris, I now began shuttling between Boston and New York. I was doing well, with *The Show Is On* clicking at the Winter Garden. I began to spend a goodly share of my royalties on weekly trips to Boston and wooed Polly with dogged determination, though little real encouragement. Due to the Turnbulls' point-blank refusal to have anything to do with me (Polly gradually overruled their veto on our "romance" — she was 23, after all, and had her share of Boston spunk), we usually met at the Ritz — Polly "sensibly," yet unbecomingly dressed (her white tulle evening frock was the only good dress I'd seen her wear), looking as though she hated herself for showing up; I trying every possible approach and not finding the right one.

After two or three inconclusive rendezvous, in the course of which Polly chided me for my dandified airs and my preoccupation with "flashy" theatricals and I, naturally nettled, criticized her overly conservative outlook and her hostility to everything outside her orbit, we had words and they were not pretty words. I packed hastily and was about to catch the next train to New York when the telephone rang; it was a Boston matron who knew the Turnbulls and didn't disapprove of me. "What have you been doing to Polly?" she demanded sternly. "The poor girl came to see me after you left her and was in an awful state. She said you had a fight with her and that all was lost, unless I got you to make up with her." True or false, I couldn't refuse so real a chance to win Polly and hastened to my kind intermediary's house. That afternoon I reached the pinnacle of my imaginary happiness; I sat in an armchair chatting with my hostess, while Polly, on the floor at my feet, gazed up at me lovingly. I could hardly believe it possible, but Polly took my hand impulsively and kissed it; it was the only kiss she ever gave me.

Late in February Prokofiev cabled from Paris: "First Symphony Lamoureux March 14th Second Symphony Pasdeloup March 20th regards." This meant that Serge, who always found time to worry about my music while immersed in his own multifarious activities, had arranged for my two orchestral works to be played in Paris. The orchestra parts of the First Symphony were still in New York, where they were used by Barzin in 1935, and I had to act fast to provide the Lamoureux organization with the material in time for the concert. Although sent with the utmost dispatch, the parts didn't arrive in time and the First Symphony was canceled. Astrov, Prokofiev's assistant, wrote from Paris to tell me that not only did Prokofiev "place" the two symphonies, but also made tentative arrangements with Charles Munch for a Paris *première* of *The End of St. Petersburg*. The figures arrived at by Munch and Astrov are worth quoting in 1954, as they demonstrate the catastrophic devaluation of the French franc and the huge increase in music-making costs which would make such an undertaking a total impossibility today. The chorus of sixty singers (male and female), twelve choral rehearsals and three rehearsals with the orchestra would have cost 21,000 francs, including the performance, plus 1000 francs for the choral coach. The sixty-five-piece orchestra wanted from 12 to 15,000 francs for three rehearsals plus the performance. Total costs — about 37,000 francs, plus 1000 (!) for the rent of the concert hall. Were I to pay in American currency at the present (official) rate of exchange, I could have "swung the deal" for a little over $100!

A few weeks later, Prokofiev himself arrived in the States, radiating good health and a kind of bombastic optimism. He told me that he owed his sound physical condition to dancing lessons he'd been taking in Kislovodsk, a Caucasian health resort. "Dancing lessons? You mean the polka, the mazurka, the Viennese waltz, the *pas d'espagne* — all those antiquated 'Russian' ballroom dances?" I asked in astonishment. "No, indeed, you idiot," Serge exclaimed with a wide grin. "The Russians are jazz crazy; all they dance is the fox-trot and the Boston waltz, not the Viennese kind. Watch!" Prokofiev executed a *pas seul* that would have been approved by an Arthur Murray instructor. "Speaking of Boston," he continued. "How are you and *Starik*" (Serge always referred to Koussevitzky as *Starik* — "the old man") "getting along? Still feuding?" I confessed that matters had not been patched up as yet, but that I had written a species of a piano concerto ("Dedicaces"), to which Prokofiev referred in an already-quoted letter, and thought it would be a possibility for Sanroma and the Boston forces. Serge demanded to see it. He read the difficult piano part with great flourish, then jumped up jerkily. "I'm going to Boston tomorrow and will stay with the Koussevitzkys. Why don't you come with me? I know they'll be happy to see you again and *Starik* is sure to like our 'Dedicaces' — it's a really good piece. What do you say?" What *could* I say, except, "Great"?

I took Serge to see Mother, who worshipped him. "Sergei Sergeivitch, do you mean to tell me that the Communists let you out — just like that?" she asked incredulously. "Just like that, Anna Alexevna," Prokofiev assured her, slapping his thighs — a favorite mannerism with him. "Here I am all in one piece, as you see." "And Lina Ivanovna?" Mother persisted. "She will come back to the States with me in October — I have enough engagements to warrant a speedy return." "What about your boys?" At this, Prokofiev changed the subject abruptly. I later learned that the Soviet authorities would not let them travel with their parents; in other words, that they were forcibly left behind in Russia, as hostages.

At dinner — Mother having discreetly refused to join us as we had "so much" to talk about — I asked Serge a difficult question, then uppermost in my mind. I wanted to know how he could live and work in the atmosphere of Soviet totalitarianism. Serge was silent for a moment, then said quietly and seriously: "Here is how I feel about it: I care nothing for politics — I'm a composer first and last. Any government that lets me write my music in peace, publishes everything I compose before the ink is dry, and performs every note that comes from my pen is all right with me. In Europe we all have to fish for performances, cajole conductors and theater directors; in Russia they come to *me* — I can hardly keep up with the demand. What's more,

I have a comfortable flat in Moscow, a delightful *datcha* in the country and a brand-new car. My boys go to a fine English school in Moscow. It's true, Lina Ivanovna whimpers now and then — but you know her. Being a composer's wife isn't easy." It was my turn to become quiet and serious. "Serge, what would you say if I told you that I plan to marry?" I asked my friend. "You? Marriage?" Serge cried out. "I've heard that once too often. Who is the new one?" The recital of my weird New England courtship over, Serge shook his head dubiously. "She sounds like a dull and priggish girl to me. I don't think you need a wife, but if you must have one, pick a rich middle-aged oil heiress. You can then give up your 'whoring' and stick to good music." This was sound advice, but I was in love, and advising lovers is a waste of time.

Prokofiev did me a great service by taking me along to the Koussevitzkys, as I had genuinely missed them and we now made peace in noisy osculatory style. At lunch, Natalya Konstantinovna, beaming grandly, asked me whether my forthcoming marriage was really forthcoming. "It won't be," Prokofiev answered for me, "until I look the girl over and bestow my blessings." "Why not bring her to the concert?" Tante Natalie wanted to know. "We could then all look at her and tell you what we think." I telephoned Polly, inviting her to the symphony concert at which Serge was to play his Third Concerto.

Serge's appearance was scheduled for the afternoon concert and Polly and I arranged to meet him at the Ritz before going to Symphony Hall. Regrettably, she wore a really impossible dress — a crumpled red-cotton number totally unsuitable for the occasion — but even the bad dress couldn't altogether mar her fresh good looks. I was amused by the bold way in which Prokofiev scrutinized my Naiad; far from being displeased, Polly, who like all Bostonians admired frankness, stared back at Serge with complete *sang-froid*. "I must say, I don't see what Dima sees in you," Prokofiev suddenly blurted out, to my horror. I needn't have worried, as Polly was not at all horrified. "I admire you for saying what you think, Mr. Prokofiev," she said with disarming directness. "Now, why don't you talk to me like that, Vernon? All you do is cover me with compliments." She gave Serge her most irresistible smile. After the concert, at which Prokofiev got a thunderous ovation and was recalled so many times that he "got tired of walking," as he later confessed to Sergei Alexandrovitch, I produced Polly for the Koussevitzkys in the conductor's dressing room. Natalya Konstantinovna thought her pretty in an uninteresting, outdoorsy sort of way, but deplored her gauche manner and wrong clothes. "Not for you" was the consensus, to which I, of course, paid no heed. Prokofiev and I were then taken to the Turnbulls' — pleasant, old-fashioned people who never let on that they knew of my persistent attentions to their daughter and asked Prokofiev "safe" questions about his composing habits — never a word about Russia. On the way back to the Koussevitzkys, Prokofiev asserted: "This will never come to anything. It's a nice, Victorian family — the whole of Boston is Victorian. Did you see the women who came to gush over me in *Starik's* room? Polly will be like them when she grows old. Peace and comfort and rusty old traditions — something to cling to — that's their way of life. You're restless and adventurous. It won't work." How right he was! A week later, in New York, I received the habitual matter-of-fact scribble from Polly, all about her exams and some tepid skiing experiences — "hope to see you soon. Fondly" — this in answer to my umpteenth passionate paean. I knew then — all at once — that I had to put a quick end to my unproductive and evidently futureless courtship. I summoned Mitchell Hodges, my Harrisburg walking companion, and persuaded him to go on a driving trip — anywhere except Boston — to get away from my writing table and telephone, from my grotesquely blown-up and one-sided love, even from my music.

On returning to New York after our trip — during which we spent every night under a different roof, ate heavy food (scorned lovers are notoriously heavy eaters) and read light fiction — I sought refuge in writing articles and raising hell 1926 London style. The *Stage* published an anti-prima donna outburst of mine titled "Musical Antics and Antiques," in which I claimed that "the modern American composer is a sacrifice on the altar of ancestor worship," that "the public is not only antic-minded (when it comes to conductors) but also antique-minded as to composers; to lure it to the annual premiere at the Metropolitan, the League (of Composers) had to bill the star conductor in letters three times as large as those that spelled out the name of the insignificant composer," and that, speaking of the small number of living composers accorded performances, in comparison with the dead, "were we to exclude from this number the works of the three big S's of new music (Sibelius, Strauss, Stravinsky), whose reputations were made from twenty to thirty years ago and who belong to another generation along with such men as Ravel, Rachmaninov and Roussel (all in their sixties), how many young or youngish men, men presumably representative of our up-and-coming age, will you find among the chosen few? A mere handful, and that does not necessarily mean that they were hand-picked." I was immediately sat upon by several indignant objectors, chief among them Mr. Samuel Chotzinoff, who didn't like my calling Toscanini "a notoriously bad program maker."

The Bachelor, a lively and provocative magazine for males which had quite a vogue in the thirties and then died a premature death, printed a tidbit from my pen — the confessions of a composer who reveals his likes and dislikes about New York. The town's credits (to this one man's way of thinking) were on the left of the page, the debits on the right. Among the credits were: "the teeth, feet and hands of the New York woman — the best in the world, cherrystone clams, sunset in Washington Square, in contrast to all popular beliefs the extreme friendliness and hospitality of the New Yorker, Murray Hill, the excitement of a first night (backstage and out front), Robert Benchley, Ira Gershwin and Dr. Leo Michel (Broadway's best-beloved medico), *all* the Gershwins, the navels of the showgirls at the Paradise and Hollywood, the curious dialects of Balanchine, Sam Lyons and Cecil Beaton, the singing voices of all colored performers, the poetry of a Liggett's Drugstore. Among the debits: "the fact that you cannot make love in a New York taxi, owing to the absence of the 1907 Daimler of London and its old-fashioned comforts ["Mr. Duke has either had bad luck in cabs, or with his companions," a columnist riposted.], Broadway and Sixth Avenue by daylight, the price of a plain omelet at Twenty-One, the Hudson River, which should be where the East River is and vice versa, the New York woman's emphasis on glamour to the almost total exclusion of charm, Central Park, which is one of the dreariest spots in New York, the decline and pseudo-sophistication of burlesque and its exponents, the difficulty of going between the East Side and the West Side when one is in a hurry, the neverending glorification in New York of foreign impostors in all fields and the inadvisability of flaunting one's masculinity in any salon with 'arty' inclinations." Most of these still hold after seventeen years.

I was interviewed by Alfred Hart of the *N.Y. World Telegram* and called "probably New York's most versatile musician." The headline was "Garret to Seller"; the subtitle, "ambidextrous Vernon Duke writes jazz as well as concertos because he likes caviar." At a Boston Symphony concert (I was back in Koussevitzky's *Wunderkinder* Garden) I ran into Carlos Chavez and asked him why, in view of my securing the backing for his *Quatro Solis,* he didn't choose to answer my letters. "You work for a White Russian policeman!" Chavez shouted, white with fury. "Not I." He disappeared before I had a chance to remind him that Archibald MacLeish and other eminent citizens were not above working for the White Russian policeman. In Koussevitzky's box, when I returned there, I found Chavez and Copland exchanging pleasantries, Copland giggling in his shrill E♭ clarinetlike falsetto. I quickly resorted to the Russian tearoom and had a dish of White Russian caviar on the sly.

My Second Symphony, conducted by Albert Wolff in Paris, received very poor notices. Shortly afterwards I wrote Prokofiev in Moscow to report on the unsatisfactory reception, on my break with Polly and on the reorchestrated *St. Petersburg,* a score of which I sent him. On June 10th he answered:

> Dear friend,
>
> Thank you for your letter of April 20th which gave me great pleasure. It's a month since I've received it — I purposely delayed answering, awaiting the promised score of the Oratorio; it has not arrived as yet. Everything is going well and I just completed the sketches for a Cantata, commemorating the 20th anniversary of U.S.S.R. — a huge machine for orchestra, two choirs, military band, a percussion "choir" and an orchestra of garmoshkis [slang for accordions]. When I think of the number of notes that I'll have to put on paper to orchestrate all this, I become seized with terror! The first "Romeo and Juliet" suite is being engraved. The car has arrived and, with a good chauffeur, it makes life much easier, especially come Spring, when one feels like an outing "ins grüne" [Prokofiev's favorite German expression]. The radio works marvellously — that is, the phonograph part, as I haven't as yet arranged to establish the antenna on our roof to take advantage of the radio reception. All our furniture arrived from Paris and I found, in my library, the manuscripts of your two songs. I'll have them copied and will send you the copy. So — it's good bye, Miss Polly? To the intense joy

of my friend C. [a girl we both liked] and the "nurse" [another?]. [The next sentence was unprintable.] Did they give your Oratorio in Paris? Have you any firm prospects with the Boston Symphony? You know probably that the performance of my "Russian Overture" was buried in Boston last April, as friend Gabriel [Paitchadze] failed to deliver the material in time. Yesterday I was visited by Burgin [Richard Burgin, the concertmaster of the Boston Symphony] who assured me that my engagement in Boston this coming winter is still "on." Burgin is here for a short stay, acquainting himself with Soviet works for possible Boston performances. Eh bien, cher ami, don't forget to drop me a line from time to time. I preserve "un souvenir très sympatique" of our "passe-temps" in New York. Regards from the family. I looked over Hindemith's flute sonata — it's very good, especially is the ending well "ausgedacht."

Bien à toi,
Serge

While Prokofiev communed with Shakespeare and Hindemith, I toiled for Vincent Astor and Hildegarde. The first-named was inaugurating the sumptuous Iridium Room at the St. Regis Hotel and had engaged his friend "Sunny" Forbes to sing at the opening — he wanted two new songs for her and hired Ted Fetter and myself to write them. The money was good and Mr. Astor insisted only on the word "iridium" being included in one of the two lyrics — a tough word to find a rhyme for; we didn't think "presidium" especially singable — but Ted proudly stuck iridium into the verse and made everybody happy. One of the songs was called "New York After Dark" and ended with the line "New York after dark is ours"; the *New Yorker* reported a drunk in the bar after the opening, singing dejectedly, "New York after hours is dark." Hildegarde first crossed my path in *Walk a Little Faster* days, when she, a tantalizing wholesome Milwaukee "bachfisch" was part of the Gus Edwards troupe and was brought to audition for Courtney Burr. Hildy, or rather her manager, wanted too much money and the thing came to nought. Now an established star, she and her enterprising sponsor, Anna Sosenko, thought of making an album of my songs, with me and Leo Kahn, Hildegarde's pianist at that time, playing two-piano accompaniments. It turned out a good album (Decca) — Dave Kapp supervising shrewdly, Hildegarde singing continentally and Leo and I playing "a lot of piano"; the album was well thought of and got an accolade from the future bard of Rodgers and Hammerstein — Deems Taylor.

The Gershwins and I had the same agents then — A. & S. Lyons, Arthur handling the picture deals, brother Sam attending to Broadway business. In October 1936, I wrote Ira: "I am delighted beyond words with the success you two (or rather three — for I hear Lee is the uncrowned queen of local intelligentsia) are making in Hollywood . . . am somewhat skeptical about my own clicking there, as my Dukal antics may prove too much or not enough in the land of levity and Levants. Am hard at work polishing up the 'End of St. Petersburg' for a Paris showing in the Spring." There was no Paris showing of *Petersburg* or anything else from my pen that spring, and on April 20th I again wrote Ira: "New York is getting insufferable as the females still insist on dieting; the great song hits are still written by everybody in the world except yours truly; Sam Behrman still breaks appointments; and I still don't know whether it will be Hollywood or Europe next." Well, Hollywood *was* next, but I would never have gotten there had it not been for the tragedy that rocked the entire world of music.

On Saturday, July 10th, Walter Winchell told his startled radio listeners that George Gershwin was critically ill in California. "He never learned that he had just been elected an honorary member of the Academy of Santa Cecilia, Rome, Italy's highest award to foreign composers," Ira wrote for Merle Armitage's 1938 Gershwin book. "We didn't bother him with correspondence although two days before the operation we were still discussing songs. He died Sunday morning, July 11, 1937, in Los Angeles at the age of 38."

Death can be kind and it can be just; but it had no business taking our George, who was in full flower of his fine youth and who was unquestionably doing his best work: *Porgy and Bess,* the first and so far the only good American opera (Gian-Carlo Menotti, although living and working in the U.S., is an Italian citizen), and the wonderful 1936–1937 songs — songs like "A Foggy Day," "You Can't Take That Away From Me," "Love Walked In" and "Love Is Here To Stay."

There have been so many incorrect and distorted versions of George's last days that I deem it a duty and an honor to give here a short and accurate account of what really happened, for which I'm indebted to Lee Gershwin. A little over three weeks before his death, George awakened Lee on a Sunday morning to complain of a violent headache. Dr. Siegel (Greta Garbo's doctor) was called and, basing his findings on George's symptoms, tested for a brain tumor, which caused Lee and George to laugh. "There's nothing wrong with me," George said. "I'm just overworked, exhausted." (In addition to his film assignments, George had an extensive concert tour that winter.) Siegel then called in a neurologist and eye specialist, who, too, suspected a tumor. Because of George's feeling that his headaches were caused by a nervous collapse due to overwork, and since he had had a year's analysis with the famous Dr. Zilboorg in New York, incomplete due to his moving West, it was deemed wise to bring in Dr. Simmel, a distinguished disciple of Freud's and head of the Freudian clinic in Berlin. Simmel, a doctor of the old German school, insisted on a complete physical check-up; George went to the Cedars of Lebanon for three days and all tests proved negative; he refused to take a spinal tap (usually resulting in severe headaches) as his headaches were already too violent without further aggravation.

On Gershwin's return from the hospital, Simmel went to see him every day, after comparing notes with Zilboorg on George's emotional background; he also provided a nurse trained for psychiatric work. Thus George was under constant observation, the three doctors visiting him daily. He was now sleeping more, had fewer headaches, abandoned work. About a week later, Dr. Simmel suggested moving George to a quieter house with no telephone or other disturbances. George spent the next two weeks in the smaller house, sleeping almost continually, with no awareness of the time's passing; doctors tested his reflexes, peered into his eyes, always on the lookout for the tumor. It was in the smaller house that Balanchine, engaged by Sam Goldwyn for the *Goldwyn Follies,* saw George in bed in a dark room, talking with difficulty in a strange faraway voice, intelligible but barely audible.

On Friday, July 9th, Dr. Simmel, who was with George all afternoon, asked him to play the *Rhapsody* for him — but the composer's coordination was gone. Dr. Simmel then knew the disease was organic; Ira and Lee were called to George's house to decide on the action to be taken. Lee remembers seeing six doctors testing George's reflexes as she entered the bedroom. George was half asleep, half awake, terribly sweet to everybody; they wrapped a bathrobe about him, called an ambulance, and took him back to the Cedars. It was then that Lee (*not Ira*) was told that George was suffering from a brain tumor. Lee immediately thought of Dr. Harvey Cushing, the celebrated brain specialist; the doctors suggested Dr. Dandy, a disciple of Cushing's, who was vacationing in Chesapeake Bay, on the governor's yacht. It was found impossible to establish contact with him. George Pallay, an old friend of the Gershwins, then called the White House, which succeeded in contacting the governor's yacht; but it was too late, although an open wire was kept for Dr. Dandy so that he could follow the progress of the operation, which was performed on Saturday night. In the course of the operation it was discovered that George had a cystic degeneration of the tumor. The cyst, which the doctor had hoped was the cause of George's illness, was in reality a growth on the tumor. The operation lasted all night, Lee and Ira leaving at daybreak. George didn't die until 11 A.M., and it was another George — Jessel — who was the first to call the hospital and be told of Gershwin's death. What followed was a kaleidoscope of nightmares: George's body in a hermetically sealed casket arriving in New York; Ira, white as a sheet, stepping from the plane, groggy after an overdose of sleeping pills; the overly elaborate funeral, at which I was one of the pallbearers; the hollow-sounding "eulogies." The terrible truth was that George was *dead* and posthumously eulogizing a career barely begun, seemed an ill-timed and premature postlude — for George was American youth itself, and his music was the voice of Young America, now inexplicably silenced. Most people while mourning the death of a friend will say, "Poor fellow, he died," and resume their everyday toil with renewed zeal, a nasty little voice within them adding, "Yeah, but I'm alive — see?" I don't think any of Gershwin's friends who are still living have ever gotten used to the idea of his not being among them. Time has a funny habit of marching on when it really should stop for a while to honor the prematurely dead, if only for manners' sake.

The work on the *Goldwyn Follies* was resumed and Ira was asked whom he would like as his brother's successor. Arthur Lyons suggested me, Ira agreed and Mr. Goldwyn asked me to come out to the Coast to complete the job on his film.

Joan, back in the States after two years of Europe and India, was getting ready for a college career; and I, having lost Polly and unable to latch on to Joan, somehow got myself engaged to a rich German girl, who was in love with me, for a change. George's death was the greatest loss I had sustained since my father died in 1913 and there was a welcome semblance of security in daily receiving love letters from Lili, the German girl, who was Europe-bound, while I, Goldwyn contract calling for $1000 a week in my pocket, made hasty preparations for my first Hollywood trip. Lee Shubert had picked up *Serena* after his nephew Milton "lost interest," and was trying to get Clifton Webb to play Lord Ivor Cream — a superb job of casting, but I was already on my way, and read about it on the Chief. "Clifton won't do it," I said to myself on reading the item. He didn't.

I am now a confirmed Californian, and wouldn't live anywhere else, but I still cling to the idea that, in direct contrast with New York, California "is a good place to live, but not to visit." A short stay in the L.A. area won't yield much to an observant visitor. The place looks like a watered-down Riviera on a large scale, the gas stations are more impressive than the palms and the natives are very clean and big-framed and look as if they spent their entire lives eating health foods, drinking fruit juices and getting a tan by speeding in shiny convertibles with the tops down. The weather is so uniformly good that it deprives people of their main topic of conversation; the distances are so great that no one in L.A. has ever been known to "drop in" on a friend, who usually lives ten miles away; the nightlife is of no particular distinction or variety and offers nothing that hasn't been seen already in New York or Chicago with fancier trimmings; most disappointing of all, people who are busy with studio or office work go to bed at 10 P.M. and get up at 6:30 or 7 A.M. A stranger with a car has little to do after ten but go boozing or take in a film. A stranger without a car is a dead duck! However, to know the place is to love it, as I discovered fourteen years later.

I put up at the Beverly-Wilshire Hotel, which in 1937 was uninvitingly dark and had no dining terrace or swimming pool. Since I couldn't drive, I rented a large black Packard chauffeured by a tall, handsome Canadian ex-officer, who wore a well-cut Edwardian uniform but knew little about Los Angeles and its complicated network of streets; as a result I never got anywhere on time, since my Canadian couldn't move for five blocks without asking for directions.

I was met by Freddie Kohlmar, then Goldwyn's assistant, and installed in a fine office with a grand piano and an anteroom presided over by an equally grand secretary. The theatrical columns were full of flattering references to the "successor to Gershwin" — and since news travels faster in Hollywood than anywhere in the world, my salary (not enormous, but respectable for those days) must have become common knowledge, because the first telephone call I received was from a fiddler I once met in New York, who wanted to borrow twenty dollars.

On my first afternoon at United Artists, a tall, meaty blonde gained admission to my "inner sanctum" by some tricky ruse, leaving her papa outside. After announcing herself she proceeded to sing in a loud and unusually disagreeable voice; I listened to eight unaccompanied bars and then interrupted her politely to point out that I was not the casting director. At this, she became furious and demanded in piercing tones that I take my hands (which were edging closer to the telephone) off her and how dare I take liberties with her and that for five cents she'd call her father, unless, etc. I beat her to the punch by calling Freddie Kohlmar, who arrived posthaste and threw the pair out.

I was disappointed at not being welcomed by my new boss, Mr. Goldwyn, whom I was not to meet until three days later. Freddie took me to a rehearsal hall where Balanchine was putting his dancers, notably Zorina, whom he was courting at the time, through their paces. George was too busy untwisting two young dancers who had got themselves entangled in a choreographic double nelson; he just winked at me and bade me wait. Zorina received me with open arms; I had played a not unimportant part in her early career, when, dissatisfied with her treatment at de Basil's hands, she had asked me for a Broadway entree. I took her to Louis Shurr, always referred to as "the doctor," the most romantic of Broadway agents, whose taste in white ermine and ermined blondes is justly celebrated; the doctor wanted a "new face" for Tamara Geva's role in *On Your Toes,* for the London production. One look at Zorina and his heart, under the exquisitely tailored lapel, stood still. Having made a big hit in London, Vera, on the strength of Shurr's transatlantic sales talk, was "sold" to Goldwyn for his *Follies* without the customary test. She told me of her happiness at having a leading part in the picture and at working with "Chorche" (that's how she pronounced it) on the ballet version of "American in Paris" he was staging.

I spent the next two days dictating personal letters to all my friends to kill time; sitting at a big glass-topped desk in a swivel chair, dictating to a neat sweater-and-skirted female made me feel like an executive — a sensation I hadn't experienced before. I rather liked it. On the third day, Freddie Kohlmar walked in and told me solemnly that Mr. Goldwyn was now ready to receive me; I braced myself for the big moment and followed Freddie to the second floor, where the great man had his quarters. We went through a long corridor, past innumerable cubbyholes where tidy, efficient girls sat typing tidy, efficient letters; an extra-tidy girl emerged from the last cubbyhole and, smilingly blindingly, ushered me into Mr. Goldwyn's office. It was a large room and one had to cover a lot of ground before reaching the massive desk at the other end, where my employer sat. The lengthy walk from the door to the desk gave Goldwyn an opportunity to scrutinize every new arrival, so that, by the time he or she reached the desk, he'd already formed an opinion of the visitor.

"Sit down, Duke," Goldwyn said, dispensing with the "Mr." His voice was high-pitched, clear and firm and had no trace of the accent I was led to expect. For two or three minutes I was treated to a helpful, if conventional, lecture on the task before me, the tremendous responsibility, the honor of working on the greatest musical film of all time. I listened, grunting understandingly at the proper moments, and wondered whether this was really the Goldwyn of popular legend, until the producer asked me abruptly: "What songs did you write?" I told him. "Oh, yes, the song about April," Goldwyn said. "That's good, but you won't get a firm footwork on the film industry until you've worked for me. Good-by, Duke." I then shook the hand of the man I *knew* was Goldwyn, and was dismissed.

I noticed, in the course of the interview, that Goldwyn's left arm was in a sling; upon questioning his satellites, I was told he had injured it while bawling out his technical staff, banging on the table the while. That afternoon I received an interoffice memo requesting my presence on Stage 2 to view Balanchine's version of "American in Paris." When I arrived, Goldwyn was seated in the director's chair, surrounded by Freddie Kohlmar, Alfred Newman, his musical director, the Ritz Brothers and Adolphe Menjou, all of whom had roles in the *Follies*. My old friend and landlord Kopeikine was at the piano; Balanchine, in shirt sleeves, hovered over a large ballet corps, members of which were all over the place in small groups of three or four, in immobile Balanchinesque poses. Having arranged the groups to his satisfaction, Balanchine walked over to Goldwyn and began explaining the first full-length ballet created expressly for the screen. The music started. Goldwyn, pointing to his injured arm, said that he'd like to watch the dancing from his directorial chair, but George wouldn't let him. In an English slightly better than his 1926 London brand but not much, he insisted that Goldwyn follow him and watch the various episodes as performed by the separate little groups, which necessitated Goldwyn's walking from place to place. Not at all happy about so unorthodox an audition, Goldwyn gave in, nevertheless, and it was a rare sight to see the man piloted by George, made to crouch and squat, the better to view a couple wriggling on the floor or peer straight into a dancer's navel — "that's where camerra vill be shott!" George would exclaim triumphantly. With every succeeding episode, Goldwyn's face got redder and angrier; he complained loudly about his arm hurting after so much crouching and squatting, and refused to peer into any more navels. "Bott I have more, Mr. Goldveen!" George exclaimed, aghast. "That's all right, George, I get the idea," the producer said. "When you get through, come to my office; I want to talk to you." With that he exited, followed by his co-workers.

I wasn't present at George's meeting with Goldwyn, but I saw my friend an hour later in his apartment, shaking with anger and packing hurriedly. "What on earth is the matter?" I asked nervously. "I'm going back to New York, that's what's the matter. Goldwyn told me that my ballet was very beautiful and 'artistic' but that the miners in Harrisburg wouldn't understand it. 'Mr. Goldwyn!' I replied, 'I'm not President Roosevelt — what do I care about the miners in Harrisburg?' Then I thought quickly and added: 'Besides, there are no miners in Harrisburg; I know, because I've been there!' Do you think *that* stopped him? Not at all — he just laughed and said that he was very sorry, but that the 'American in Paris' — my three weeks' work — was out. O.K., so I'm out, too; Doc Bender has a New York show for me." This looked serious, so I telephoned Freddie Kohlmar, whose diplomatic know-how I had soon learned to appreciate; Freddie arrived, gave George a fast convincer, and the choreographer, muttering something that even I couldn't grasp (it was probably Tiflis slang), began unpacking.

I found working on a musical picture easier and more rewarding than "tuning up" a legitimate show. There are fewer songs in a picture score to begin with — usually four to eight or nine, whereas a Broadway musical has at least twelve musical numbers, and twenty is not unusual. Now consider the financial end of it. Once signed to supply a "legitimate" score, the composer gets $500 (very seldom $1000) down from the producers, and perhaps $1000 from the publishers — on account of royalties on box-office and music sales. It takes from four to six months to write the score, during which time you get no additional pay; then figure on three to six months for the "backers' auditions" (these became the fashion in the forties). Assuming that the money has been raised, the show opens out of town, and if it does well, you may be in the black by the time it hits Broadway. If the show flops — either on the road or in New York (I have had both kinds), you not only don't make another cent, but it's highly advisable to leave town and stay away until people forget the flop and your connection with it. My advice is: if you get one flop — stay away for six months; another — vanish for a year; a third — leave the country; a fourth — open a grocery store or a gas station. I had six or seven in a row, left the country four times, and here I am back in show business and no one (well, practically no one) seems to mind.

On the other hand, should you get a Hollywood assignment with a major studio — you're in the chips before you write a note of music. You get so much per picture ($20,000 to $50,000 — I'm not naming Irving Berlin's or Cole Porter's figures, which are positively astronomic), get your money every week, never bother about backers or backers' auditions, and — better yet — don't care whether the picture is a hit or a miss. By the time it's released, you're working on another picture job, or a Broadway chore, or you can always lose your money in Las Vegas or Cannes, if you feel like it. You miss the strange fascination of feverish, nerve-racking rehearsals — granted; the overtouted excitement of an opening night — granted; the smells, sounds, hates and loves of the theater — also granted. But you do get much more dough in the pictures and you keep your health, if not always your self-respect. So when you contemplate your next bout with Broadway, close your eyes, stick your fingers in your ears, shake your head and ask yourself: "Is it worth it?" I'm afraid the answer is, "Yes."

For the *Goldwyn Follies* I wrote two songs ("Spring Again," sung by Kenny Baker, and "I'm Not Complaining," subsequently deleted) and two ballets — "Romeo and Juliet" and "Waternymph"; I also supplied the verses for the three Gershwin songs, anonymously of course. All that could be found of "Love Is Here to Stay" was a twenty-bar incompleted lead sheet; fortunately, Oscar Levant remembered the harmonies from George's frequent piano performances of the song and I was able faithfully to reconstruct it. Of the two ballets, "Romeo and Juliet" showed less respect for Shakespeare than either the new Prokofiev conception or the old Constant Lambert one; in the Balanchine scenario, the Montagues were represented as jazz addicts, the Capulets as "longhairs." Thus Romeo was what you would call today a "hepcat" whereas Juliet was distinctly on the "square" side; quite logically, I wrote Duke music for Romeo, Dukelsky music for Juliet. Goldwyn wasn't overly fond of our approach to Shakespeare and cut the ballet so drastically that it's point was almost entirely lost. The "Waternymph," with wonderful sets by Richard Day and Zorina's superhuman beauty, not to forget the pretty music, was a 100 per cent success, and is still shown Goldwyn's guests at dinner parties. The sixty-piece orchestra, admirably conducted by Alfred Newman, was a help, too.

Lovely Andrea Leeds and pert, diminutive Ella Logan were also in the *Follies*. I swapped London stories with Ella and talked *Serena Blandish* to serenely demure Andrea. "If Samuel Goldwyn is as smart as people generally think he is," a New York scribe ventured, "he will set about right away lining up Andrea Leeds to play in *Serena Blandish,* particularly because he happens also to have Vernon Duke in tow. No recent feminine discovery would be more suited to that particular part in the quaintly sexological story, once dramatized, and now to be made into a musical stage offering." In between these occupations, I corresponded with Stokowski and Hugh Ross, the director of the New York Schola Cantorum, regarding *St. Petersburg;* talked music with Oscar Levant, who was yet to make his Information, Please splash and was defiantly writing "longhair" music, some of it quite good; brought hopeful young actresses to Arthur Kober's for dinner; and tried to bring a bit of my own rather special and not always endurable brand of cheer into the lives of Lee and Ira, still dazed by the enormity of their cruel loss. Except for our work at the studio, I saw little of Balanchine, reported engaged to Zorina. With Oscar I visited my old flame Ginger Rogers, living in a typical Hollywood "dream house," and beat her at ping-pong. I also had a sentimental reunion with the one and only Eddie Goulding.

About the time I returned to Manhattan, Lili came back from Germany, full of nationalist slogans and greatly impressed by what she had seen; we had a series of unpleasant tiffs and soon came to a painless parting of the ways, which, I'm certain, was a relief to both of us. Thus, "disengaged" I returned to my first love — *Serena*.

Vincente Minnelli, also back from Hollywood, after a Paramount assignment, had made plans to do a musical *Serena* as his first production the next fall. "It is to be an independent venture, with music by Vernon Duke, whose idea it is," said the *N.Y. Times*. We "plotted" for a week or so with Fetter as lyricist, then Vincente left town and was not heard from for two weeks. On his return, Minnelli informed me that Sam Harris was going to co-produce with him, that S. J. Perelman would write the book of a "colored" version (which alone could give *Serena* the desired fillip, Vincente thought), that Maxine Sullivan would appear as Serena, Ethel Waters as the countess and Cab Calloway or Bubbles (of Buck and Bubbles) as Lord Ivor Cream, and also that Sam Harris insisted on Cole Porter writing the score. Completely stunned, I left in a huff and abandoned the wench *Serena*, to whom I was faithful in so unrewarding a fashion for so many years; the "colored" Minnelli-Harris-Porter version never went past the talking stage either.

Thanks to Goldwyn I was richer by some $9000, and so hit on the idea of letting the fairly solvent Duke pay for Dukelsky, the pauper; I decided to put some of my Goldwyn eggs in the *St. Petersburg* basket. Stokowski, judging from his letters, seemed to like the work, but his plans for its performance were extremely vague; Hugh Ross, on the other hand, liked *St. Petersburg* enough to offer to program it — but there was a serious catch. The Schola Cantorum's finances did not permit that organization to engage an orchestra. "May we give your work with piano accompaniment?" Ross wanted to know. This appeared unthinkable, as the cantata was constructed on massive lines, and an orchestra was essential to balance the opulent sound of a large chorus. Rather than refuse the rare miracle of a performance, I thanked the conductor for his interest in my music and told him not to worry about the lack of funds for an orchestra — that I'd gladly provide them out of my Hollywood earnings. My proposition gratefully accepted, I promptly produced a check for $1200, which was to pay for the services of the N.Y. Philharmonic for a solitary evening's performance plus two rehearsals. Since my cantata took but twenty-eight minutes of playing time, I asked Mr. Ross to add any well-known "classical" choral work of his choice, so as not to take away from the interest of the novelty. With this he readily concurred; Mrs. Elaine de Sincay Ross, the conductor's wife, was entrusted with the English translation, and a long series of choral rehearsals were planned for the autumn months.

Slonimsky wrote me: "While I'm always glad to read in Winchell's column that you are quite the dandy, and that you refused to attend Lindy's because they had no special rack for your special cane, and whereas I am delighted to watch your triumphant progress along the combined Broadway and Hollywood boulevard[s], I feel that your primary importance lies in what, for lack of a better term, is called serious music. So I am looking forward to the promised performance of your post-impressionistic (?) song-ballade (??) or whatever it is that our mutual friend Koussevitzky is going to enbaton. Sanroma tells me that Koussevitzky is indeed exultant over your piece ["Dedicaces"]. . . . Hoping that you did not dissipate your masculine strength unduly among the motion picture stars, and that you will arrive in Boston in a sufficiently moral state to suit the Back Bay standards, I remain, etc."

A few days later I received a letter from Koussevitzky (who seldom wrote): "I am overjoyed at the news of your success — musical, moral and material — in Hollywood. I intend to perform your 'Dedicaces' and am awaiting that promised score. As for performing 'St. Petersburg,' that would be utterly impossible in the coming season as I cannot include two works by the same composer in our 24 programs." This I didn't believe, as a fellow named Beethoven got as many as ten works played in the course of the same season — but, then, he was dead. The truth of the matter was that Koussevitzky, to my great chagrin, didn't care for my *St. Petersburg*.

There is an unwritten law in show business by virtue of which the composer of a Broadway hit automatically becomes a hot ticket in Hollywood — the reverse, perhaps because of the theater's defense mechanism and sense of superiority, does not work that way. In other words, a man importantly connected with a Class A musical picture does not gain in stature in the "legit" field. This I didn't know on my return from California, but in actual fact, outside of working on Ray Bolger's ballet in *Keep Off the Grass* (1939) I was among Broadway's unemployed until the 1940 advent of *Cabin in the Sky*. That didn't bother me unduly in the winter of 1937; I had two forthcoming "serious" *premières* — *St. Petersburg* and "Dedicaces" — and, meanwhile, went on partying with renewed energy.

The identity of the "classical" composer elected by Hugh Ross to share the Schola Cantorum program, made possible by my Hollywood earnings, was a dark secret — until the day when, chancing upon a choral rehearsal, I discovered to my dismay that it was to be Delius. Worse still, the Delius work selected by Mr. Ross was the heretofore unperformed in New York *Mass of Life*. This selection, I realized in a flash, would not only outweigh my entry by some forty minutes of playing time, but would also detract from the *première* excitement of *St. Petersburg*. The conductor, an urbane and learned man, assured me that there was no possibility of a "clash," as Delius was dead, his work already a classic in England, and written in a style that couldn't fail to put the modernity of my idiom in better relief — which arguments led me to agree reluctantly to the dangerous *voisinage*. The agreement was purely academic, in any case, since the Delius work was already rehearsed and carefully prepared for performance. An interesting touch: Delius was so greatly esteemed by the people of New York that a society bearing his name was in existence. This society was not heard from while the *Mass of Life* was in preparation, no support was offered by it and I had to pay not only for the performance of my music but also for that of my dead colleague. Delius, furthermore, received better "billing," in Broadway parlance (that is, his name appeared in larger type on the posters) — perhaps because his work was forty minutes longer than mine.

After two rehearsals the orchestra was so ragged that a third rehearsal became imperative. Koussevitzky attended the second one, manifested his displeasure and told me that I "couldn't afford" so chaotic a reading; what he didn't know was that I could and did afford the entire venture. I conferred with the secretary of the Schola, whose sponsorship committee boasts the names of some of our most affluent citizens, and suggested that since I was already $1200 out of pocket, I would deem it desirable and proper to have the costs of an extra rehearsal defrayed by the committee members. The answer was an emphatic "No!" — and out came my Hollywood fountain pen and two hundred and fifty more Hollywood dollars.

After a choral "preview" at the St. Regis, arranged by that capable impresario of social activities, the affable Prince Serge Obolensky, whose musical tastes lean more toward the Viennese waltz, and another — more intimate — one held at the George Waller Blow's house, the concert took place on January 12, 1938; my music got a good audience reception and the traditional "mixed" notices. Most gratifying of all was Elliott Carter, the gifted young composer, who wrote in the League of Composers' *Modern Music* magazine: "Dukelsky's popular songs have absolutely no connection with his original and imaginative serious music in either style or content. In this he is linear and dissonant and frequently violently rhythmic, fond of a dry, unresonant orchestration somewhat like that of the 'Symphonie de Psaumes' [Stravinsky]. The 'End of St. Petersburg' contains some of the best music by this composer since he wrote his exquisite 'Zephyr and Flora' for Diaghilev." It is well to note that all the reviewers who did not like my work complained that such an unworthy concoction should share the bill with Delius's "masterpiece." Little did they know that they wouldn't have had the opportunity to hear the masterpiece were it not for the offending concocter. As a final touch, I received no performance fee.

I was depressed by the absence of Prokofiev, who thought highly of *St. Petersburg* and, having smuggled it into Russia, exhibited the score to Miaskovsky and Khachaturian (in whose talent he had great faith), as well as to Boris Assafiev (Igor Glebov): Miaskovsky, the dean of Moscow composers, liked the cantata and *Zephyr,* played for him by Serge, enough to write Prokofiev a four-page letter containing a minute critical analysis (a flattering one) of both works. On January 14th Prokofiev (it was impossible to keep up with the man) wrote me from Paris: "Forgive me for not writing. I received your extremely interesting letter in September in Caucasus — and was overjoyed by your success, although it's in the domain of prostitution. Today Lina Ivanovna and I rolled into Paris, for two days only, alas: Prague and London follow then, on 29th, the 'Normandie' to the USA, where we hope to fall into your tender embrace on February 3rd, 'natürlich' if you will be in New York at the time. Your 'Leningrad' [the "Sovietized" title of my cantata] is, regrettably, nonperformable in the USSR for the time being; wrong timing; classics only are being played, while the only contemporaries included in the programs are Soviet ones. Miaskovsky saw the score and praised it. Will be tremendously happy to see you again." Serge's letter reached me in Palm Beach, where I was luxuriating during my first winter stay in Florida. I was a member of Mary Lee Huntington Hartford's (now Mrs. Douglas Fairbanks, Jr.,) house party, and there was a strange similarity between Prokofiev's terpsichorean pursuits in Kislovodsk, a Russian "luxury" resort, and mine in Palm Beach, an American ditto. No sooner did I arrive at Mary Lee's beautifully appointed little house than I was whisked away to Arthur Murray's for a rhumba lesson. The year 1938 marked the beginning of the rhumba craze in the States, and not to be able to dance Cuban style was equivalent to being tagged a social leper.

I thought Palm Beach something of a cross between Cannes and Beverly Hills; however, the commercialism so heavily present in those two places was conspicuously absent here. The difference lay in the fact that everyone I met in Florida was born rich and — barring the crash — would die rich; whereas Cannes and Beverly Hills are peopled with folk who have made money and are still busy making more. Being born and dying rich is seldom synonymous with leading a rich life, and most of my friends were engaged in the hollow game of killing time, for which game they were ceaselessly devising new and, at least momentarily, fascinating techniques.

The "younger group" — of which I became a parasitic member — swam, played tennis or golf, drank cocktails at the Alibi or the Taboo, took in a heavy massage or a little light fornication in the afternoon, followed by a scented bath, dressed quietly and leisurely for dining at small tables under outsize lanterns, the air balmy with cloying magnolias and the powdered shoulders of young girls, then went dancing at the Everglades (in the grand manner) or the Patio, where manners were not essential. You can scoff all you want, but unless you've danced at the Everglades with a wide-eyed, slim-hipped divinity in a dress weighing a mere ten ounces, with no discernible underthings, you haven't lived — and you can quote me.

Pretty and good-natured Mary Lee Hartford, my hostess, took me to an evening of films at Charlie Munn's, the attendance of which was a sure sign of "belonging." Munn himself, with whom I dined in Antibes only last summer (1953) and who looked younger and handsomer than ever, was a perfect host and did everything with an unobtrusive, indefinable flair, which made his status as the colony's uncrowned king understandable. Whatever Beau Nash did for Bath I'm sure was not comparable with the beneficial effects of Beau Munn's reign in Palm Beach, Florida.

After missing *St. Petersburg,* Prokofiev, with too many concert engagements to fill, had to miss my "Dedicaces," now postponed by Koussevitzky until late the next fall. We had a wonderful get-together on my return from Florida, although Lina Ivanovna, magnificent in sables and covered with glittering jewels, burst into tears at the sight of me, which so infuriated her husband that he insisted on my "parking" her at Mother's; once together, the two women, who scarcely knew each other, began sobbing in concert, Russian style, while Prokofiev and I journeyed to the nearest bar and talked music for hours. This time "America welcomed Prokofiev as an old friend and gave him a most cordial reception," testified Israel V. Nestyev, whose biography of Prokofiev, an able job on the whole, appeared in 1946 and got him into hot water with Soviet authorities, as Nestyev "sold himself out to American Capitalists" and allowed his book to appear in an English translation in New York (Knopf) *prior* to the publication of the original in Russia. After our lengthy session at the bar, we went back to Mother's flat to collect Lina Ivanovna. We found the two women chatting animatedly, having dried each other's tears, and exchanging dressmakers' notions. Women will be women, even in the land of the Soviets. Serge then departed on an extended tour, while in Los Angeles visiting Hollywood, "where he made a detailed study of the technical methods used for the musical backgrounds of American sound films," and was pleasantly surprised — his surprise unrecorded by Nestyev for obvious reasons — by the "superior" quality of my music, Eddie Powell's scoring and Alfred Newman's recording of the two ballets in *Goldwyn Follies.*

Having made a number of rich and music-conscious friends in Palm Beach, I thought of putting some of their money to good use; namely, to help the cause of new music. I mobilized Paul Bowles, Elliott Carter and S. F. M. Barlow, whose lovely house in Gramercy Park was the scene of so many "offbeat" musicales, and outlined my plan to them. They readily fell in with it; a week later the Newport, Southampton and Palm Beach residents were startled by a handsome blue-and-red circular which somehow found its way into their mailboxes. The circular read:

> You have received Picassos for Christmas, you have called in Bérard to do portraits of your pet Siamese, there is a head of your offspring by Epstein in the corner. But how many serenades

has Stravinsky been commissioned to write for your birthdays? Has Hindemith done your portrait in music? How many pieces by Markevitch bear your name in their dedications? You will talk race horses, clothes horses, British actors or psychoanalysts until you are blue in the face, but you become strangely silent at the mention of a modern composer. Perhaps you think that modern music is cacophonous or just plain dull. We intend to show you that it isn't. We intend also to show you that new music is a form of entertainment, and as such is a useful commodity obtainable at reasonable prices. Come to our concerts — hear our music — and should your grandfather want a cantata for his golden wedding day, your debutante daughter a set of variations on the Big Apple [the 1938 dance craze] or your favorite enemy a funeral dirge, we are the people to consult. Come to the first three High-Low Concerts to be given in the course of the present season. They will consist of 1. A signature similar to a radio theme-song, commissioned from Aaron Copland, played at the beginning of each concert, to fade into 2. A short and we hope amusing talk by one of the founders giving you a pretty precise idea of what is to happen, then 3. The concert itself, which will consist of the more palatable offerings in the realm of new music, as well as our added feature, three swing soloists: Miss Maxine Sullivan and Messrs. Duke Ellington and Benny Goodman — not in their usual repertoire which you can hear when you are in a dancing mood, but works either specially written for our concerts or not heard previously. The concerts are being given for the benefit of the composers' fund of the League of Composers.

It took quite a bit of doing to persuade the venerable League to cooperate with so frivolous a venture — although their entire cooperation consisted of accepting seventy dollars from me, our "profits" after the second and last concert — the Benny Goodman one never taking place. In 1938, Copland was already the ringleader of native composers and, although we were never close friends, he readily accepted my offer of fifteen dollars (all the High-Low Concerts, Inc., could afford) for a "fanfare," or rather, a "signature." He wrote a very good one and it was performed with excellent effect at both concerts. Some years later at a performance of Copland's "Outdoor

Overture," I nearly fell out of my seat on hearing our High-Low signature — in its entirety — as the overture's opening; this was all the more astonishing as our concerts were distinctly an indoor undertaking. Copland never informed me of the strange use to which he put our frivolous fanfare; but the original forms part of my collection of Musical Curiosa, and the Dukelsky Foundation will eventually inherit it, should I get rich enough to start one.

The first concert, with a foreword by Hugh Ross, and consisting, in addition to Duke Ellington and ensemble, of works by Popoff (a septet, loaned by Prokofiev), Theodore Chanler, Charles Ives, F. Jacobi, Marc Blitzstein, Robert McBride, Paul Bowles, Henri Sauguet and myself, was a "wow," according to *Cue* magazine, and a complete sellout. Emboldened by our spectacular debut, we thought of yet another moneymaking "gimmick," and asked our subscribers:

> How would you like to have your portrait done in music? We charge $100 for a faithful musical likeness of you, and will quote you a special price for a family group. You may hear samples of the portraits at the second High-Low Concert to take place on April 10th at the St. Regis. As our models, we have chosen Mrs. Muriel Draper, Prince Serge Obolensky and the Marx Brothers.

We had no trouble with Serge Obolensky or the Marx Brothers as sitters — none of them really "sat" for their portraits — but Muriel Draper was highly indignant at being chosen as a "model" and, for some reason, blamed me, not Elliott Carter, the "tonal" painter, for the effrontery. She wrote me a letter of protest, but the portrait was "unveiled" nevertheless. Mr. Kirstein, in the "Blast at Ballet" pamphlet already cited, took another blast at me: "Mr. Dukelsky, in his dapper personality as 'Vernon Duke' the Broadway songster, organized his High-Low Concerts, a tasty series at the St. Regis roof, which Muriel Draper promptly named the NEW LOW (in vulgarity). Duke attempted to veneer the younger American musicians with enough social glitter to make them passable to the international set by having 'portraits' of well known people set to a piano and oboe, or hiring a blues-singer to 'swing' a few eighteenth century songs. There is a special kind of Russian hors d'oeuvre which they make out of how-you-say? Indian sweet-corn and sour cream. It must be about the only Russian hors d'oeuvre that isn't absolutely divine." That's how *you* say, Mr. Kirstein; there is *no* such hors d'oeuvre in Russia. If what you're hinting at is a Russo-American appetizer, and "Indian sweet-corn" is meant to represent bad jazz (ours was excellent, by the way), I'll take sour cream, thank you. I've been allergic to corn all my life.

Honesty compels me to admit that, in spite of such blandishments as a solo on a double tin whistle played by the resourceful Henry Brant, who painted the Marx Brothers in music, or the genteel, ear-soothing likeness of Serge Obolensky provided by Sam Barlow, no one commissioned a portrait.

Prokofiev returned from his trans-American wanderings just in time to lift my spirits again. A few days prior to his arrival, I received an offer for his services (from my Hollywood agent), made by one of the major studios, at $2500 a week. I showed Serge the telegram exultantly; there was a flicker of interest for a mere instant, then, his face set, his oversize lips petulant, he said gruffly: "That's nice bait, but I won't swallow it. I've got to go back to Moscow, to my music and my children. And now that that's settled, will you come to Macy's with me? I've got to buy a whole roomful of things you can't get in Russia — just look at Lina's list." The list was imposing, and we went to Macy's department store, another sample of capitalistic bait designed by the lackeys of Wall Street to be swallowed by oppressed workers. Although he wouldn't admit it, Serge enjoyed himself hugely in the store — he loved gadgets and trinkets of every description. Suddenly he turned to me, his eyes peculiarly moist, his voice even gruffer than usual: "You know, Dima, it occurred to me that I may not be back for quite some time. . . . I don't suppose it would be wise for you to come to Russia, would it?" "No, I don't suppose it would," I answered, smiling bravely, my happiness abruptly gone. I never saw Prokofiev again.

Thus, in the course of one fleeting year, I lost my two best friends in music: George Gershwin, Duke's creator, and Serge Prokofiev, Dukelsky's protector.

CHAPTER XVI

THE FIERY FORTIES—PART ONE

I WAS now on my own. Still described as a "young" composer (the adjective "promising" having vanished a few years earlier), I had made a better than fair mark in both fields; what remained was the decisive "strike," or rather two strikes, simultaneously, if possible, that would bring me eminence and financial security by the time I reached forty. I had joined the American Society of Composers, Authors and Publishers in 1934, and my income from that excellent organization was mounting gradually, due to more and more frequent performances of my songs. *The Show Is On,* while a hit, was hardly a personal triumph for me, as I was merely a part composer of the score. The *Goldwyn Follies* was Gershwin's swan song and, although my contributions were considerable and well thought of, I had no intention of capitalizing on this "labor of love" chore. *St. Petersburg* was a near miss, in spite of all the publicity; what I needed badly were a symphonic success to justify my "serious" claims and a "book" show of both artistic and commercial value to silence my detractors from Lindy's, Sardi's and "21," the three strongholds of Broadway opinion.

Both Balanchine and I read and liked Robert Nathan's early short novel *The Orchid* and thought it would make a fresh and interesting musical — so did Ted Fetter. I met Nathan at one of Blanche Knopf's literary gatherings and began "selling" the writer on the idea. Nathan, not a man given to easy enthusiasm was sufficiently responsive to agree to meet with Balanchine and myself for further talks. Fetter brought the Krimsky brothers into the project and they agreed to pay Nathan an advance and put him to work on a "musicalization" of his own novel. Nathan was going to Truro, on Cape Cod, for the summer, which suited me, as I was planning to visit with my kin, the Paul Chavchavadzes, who owned a cottage nearby.

Balanchine was full of plans. He dreamed of an 1820 Russian romantic ballet with a Pushkinesque theme — and we started working on *Entr'acte,* a "ballet within a ballet," to George's imaginative scenario; this has proven another *Serena* so far, as here it is 1954 and it remains unproduced. Through his association with Rodgers and Hart and George Abbott, George had become a Broadway figure and, incidentally, the first choreographer to incorporate real ballet into a musical show's fabric, just as, with our "Waternymph" in the *Goldwyn Follies,* he brought genuine ballet to the screen. That summer our little group, consisting of Balanchine, Larry Hart, the irrepressible "Doc" Bender and myself, spent most of the week ends on Cape Cod. We were a strange quartet: George, the "Doc" and I wore berets (Bender in a beret was as incongruous a sight as, say, Malenkov in tails), whereas gnomelike Larry secured, God knows where, a bona-fide admiral's cap and wore it at a "salty" angle. We traveled about in Larry's big black limousine, and its owner's habitual luggage consisted of a pigskin week-end bag stuffed with fifths and quarts of every alcoholic classic, plus one diminutive toothbrush.

After a session with Nathan, we'd dine in Provincetown, that American Montparnasse-by-the-sea, a colorful *olla podrida* of bad paintings, good-looking painters, vividly garbed Lesbians, decent folk from Boston on an excursion, and a variety of smells — bracing sea air mingling with the fetid aroma of frying fish and popcorn. Even the much-advertised sunsets looked like an execrably executed landscape, but you couldn't help feeling brazen and silly and ready for anything in Provincetown.

Larry and I wrote a song during one of our gay outings, but the title — "Who the Hell Are You?" — made it ineligible for radio usage, so he tore up the lyric. The week end over, we would stop at Joan's; she was back from her first college year, pretty and impudent and full of sorority slang. George, Larry and Doc would then go on home, while I remained for an unhurried repast at one of the neighboring inns and, if Joan was in a receptive mood, a little love-making.

The papers soon came out with announcements of *"Carousel,* a musical play fashioned by Robert Nathan from his novel *The Orchid,* to be presented by John and Jerrold Krimsky." Besides Ted Fetter and myself on the score, and Balanchine on the dances, Elsie Janis, Militza Korjus, Armand Tokatian, Alfred Drake and Duke McHale — a weird mixture of names — were "mentioned" for the cast. All these fine people never went past an honorable mention; the book didn't pan out and the would-be "backers" backed out. By the time the successful Rodgers and Hammerstein *Carousel* hit the boards, no one remembered our abortive one.

The 1938–1939 season marked the fifteenth anniversary of Koussevitzky's leadership of the Boston forces. "Beethoven will be the predominating composer," read a specially issued leaflet, heralding the orchestra's 58th season. "Sanroma will play the piano part in the new concerto by Dukelsky." I was on surer ground in Boston than anywhere else in the States; although, romantically speaking, a failure in America's Athens, I was rated a musician of enviable notoriety and my name was definitely "news." Also, Boston critics were more *en rapport* with my muse than were their Manhattan colleagues: the three concertos ("Dedicaces," the violin concerto and the one for cello) had, on the whole, a very good press in Boston and a poor one in New York. For the record, Koussevitzky, whose custom it was to treat New York to only the "cream" of the crop of novelties, never displayed my wares there until "Dedicaces"; neither the *Zephyr and Flora* suite nor the two symphonies were brought to the Big Town by the Boston orchestra. I was astonished at the new ease and facility with which I tackled the orchestration of "Dedicaces" — the result of the Schillinger "consultations." The third movement sounded so well at the first Boston rehearsal that Sergei Alexandrovitch stopped the orchestra twice to express his surprise to me. He cringed a bit at one overtone-spiced passage, had it repeated, and then smiled, saying, "It does come off, after all, doesn't it?"

I made a wonderful new friend in Boston, Mrs. Florence Wessell, a woman of already advanced years, but briskly youthful, and infatuated with music — she was a great authority on voice. "Signora" Wessell was the mother of Mrs. Dudley Pickman, one of Boston's musical hostesses, who entertained Gershwin and Prokofiev with equal delight and had three handsome daughters. On Signora's piano I saw newly published songs by Theodore Chanler, whom I had met vaguely in my Montparnasse days — music of poignant lyricism and a clearly individual stamp. Mrs. Wessell told me that Teddy lived in the country nearby with his wife; we met and made music together. Every note I heard of Chanler's — he is rather like Fauré in that they both stick to chamber music — was of sterling quality and, in my honest opinion, which I have had no reason to change through the years, the man should occupy a place far above his better-advertised and more agile fellow composers.

"Dukelsky is a curious figure on the American musical landscape," the *Transcript* trumpeted. "He would seem sufficiently exotic if he were judged upon the single score of his serious music. Such a work as his 'Dedicaces' which Dr. Koussevitzky will introduce at the week-end symphony concerts, would alone be reason to seek the varied and conflicting sources of so ingenious and odd a creative intellect. But Mr. Dukelsky does not feed upon bread alone; he sweetens it well with the rich flavors of the musical comedy stage." Marguerite Porter, an excellent soprano, was picked by Koussevitzky to sing the difficult vocal "epigraph" of Guillaume Apollinaire's, and Jesús María Sanroma mastered the uncomfortable piano part with his habitual "brio."

The first of that week's pair of concerts was greeted with cheers, but it was Sibelius that the Bostonians cheered, not Dukelsky. I had good cause to echo Diaghilev's feelings about "Dehlius and Sibelius" — the first named eclipsed me at the Schola Cantorum concert, the second robbed me of a Boston triumph. I received no cheers, but had otherwise no cause for complaint — my "Dedicaces" met with every evidence of approval and I made three comfortable and unhurried trips to the stage to acknowledge the applause. Koussevitzky was elated over my success; when I went to see him in his dressing room, he, dripping with perspiration caused by the Sibelius climaxes and changing his shirt, exclaimed somewhat theatrically: "Next stop — New York!" This was gratifying to hear after four Boston tries (*Zephyr*, two symphonies and the ill-fated "Epitaph") and none in New York, but next morning brought an even greater thrill. Alexander Williams, whom I had seen at the Pickmans a few times, and who had replaced Philip Hale as the *Boston Herald's* music critic, opened his article with the kind of words that warm a composer's heart: "Mr. Dukelsky's 'Dedications' is the most impressive novelty that we have so far been offered this season. Provided that a pianist such as Mr. Sanroma can be had to play the difficult piano part — for it is not what is known as grateful music for the soloist — the work should stay in the repertoire for some time to come. It is a brilliant work and does not deserve the fate of so much new music, that of enjoying a solitary performance and a *succès d'estime*. [Well, it did a little better — got three performances and a *succès d'estime*.] The 'Sea' movement is music of amazing power and variety. Mr. Dukelsky has not once been tedious, he never goes on talking after he has ceased to have anything to say. If one heard this work in the distant future, doubtless one could place it historically as to its style. At the moment it sounds both original and interesting." Who could ask for anything more? But Warren Storey Smith proved a better prophet than the well-meaning Alec Williams: "Dukelsky, alias Duke, is an enormously clever young man, who can write effectively in any of the current styles. Whether Dukelsky of the Concert Hall or Duke of the lighter musical theatre and the films will predominate remains to be seen; but one or the other must do so eventually. God and Mammon cannot both be served for long." Sixteen years later, Duke and, I suppose, Mammon are predominating, whatever that may prove.

Balanchine got himself another picture job and wrote me from Hollywood: "The fate of our 'Carousel' is sealed, I'm afraid, Messrs. Monks and Finkelhoffe having refused to work on it. They don't know how to approach such a task, as the entire psychology of the play is foreign to them." Ira, also in Hollywood, wrote in answer to my inquiry about his eternal "previous commitments" which prevented us from resuming our collaboration: "No, it wasn't to Kern at the time (that I was committed). It was to Metro, Warners', Goldwyn, Twentieth Century, Grand National, Major, Republic and Little Productions, Inc. Not a studio in town but was after me for the life of George. First one, then the other, but at no time none. At Metro contracts were being prepared, money no object, when the war scare jumbled things up and suddenly the studios went cautious and presto! musicals disappeared from the face of the earth. So here I was stuck with a two year lease in this artificial, paper-moonish spot, of which, by the way, I'm very fond."

On March 7th, I became an American citizen and Vernon Duke became my legal name.

Balanchine's second picture didn't materialize and he was back in New York around Christmas. Still a bachelor, he joined thirteen others (myself included) to "make a barge captain's daughter a glamorous deb," as *Life* magazine headlined it. *Life* continued: "To lampoon debutantism and the Brenda Frazier type of debut, 14 of New York's gayest prince charmings gave a dignified coming-out party for an unknown Cinderella on December 22nd. The girl they chose was Wilhelmina Van Den Baard, a model who lives near the

Jamaica, L.I., racetrack with her father, a barge captain. Her unconventional debut was held at Chez Firehouse [the Brothers Krimsky's headquarters]. There she was introduced to celebrities by the 14 bachelors who called themselves her "uncles." Her only complaint (like Brenda Frazier's): 'My feet hurt.' Her attitude: 'I think most debutantes are dopes.' " "The whole affair was on a grand scale of burlesque," commented Lucius Beebe, "with a full length receiving line in opera length gloves, elaborated corsages, with fountains of champagne and all the most eligible young men in the town congregated at the bar. It received vast newspaper lineage and poked a well justified finger of scorn at the professional debutantes, face-cream indorsers, publicity pigs and third-rate socialites." Two days later Balanchine married Vera Zorina, after a long and persistent courtship; while I, inspired by George's marital victory, proposed to Joan (now back in college and voted the "prettiest girl of her class") and was conditionally accepted, the condition being that I'd wait until she got through college.

I lived unthinkingly "between the ascetic rocks and the sensual whirlpools," in George Meredith's phrase; but Mother, haunted by a fear of having outlived her usefulness to Alex and me and by yet another fear of her sons becoming "lone wolves," implored me to settle down and taste a happiness like the one she knew with my father. She disapproved of Joan, whom she thought too young and emotionally unstable; Mother was actually afraid of Joan's mother, a small, wiry woman who only visited her when in a state of extreme elation, threw herself on the floor and made interminable and incomprehensible speeches about Art and Mankind. I protested hotly that I was thirty-five and in love with Joan, that marriage would change us both and that her mother was really very kind and quite harmless. These discussions got us nowhere and I dreaded them, reluctantly sensing the truth of Mother's reasonings.

One afternoon I strolled through Central Park on my way to a typically meaningless cocktail party — the kind one professes to avoid and somehow always attends — and saw a middle-aged woman alone on a park bench feeding the pigeons. I am very short-sighted and had to come much closer before realizing that the pigeon-feeding woman was Mother. Her face was kindness and sadness itself. "Hello, *Moorashka*" (her special nickname for me, meaning "little ant"), she said softly, an overweight pigeon gurgling contentedly on her arm. "What are you doing in the park alone? Come and sit next to your old *mamasha.*" I did as I was bid and asked her in turn, "Why are you here, alone, Mother?" Mother smiled a pitiful smile. "I am almost *always* alone, *Moorashka,*" she said quietly. "I can't say that I like it — always — but I'm used to it. Besides, I'm not really alone; look at my pigeons — they know me and they trust me. I'm here nearly every day to feed them." I felt miserably ashamed, cursed myself for a heartless wastrel, and took Mother to tea at Schrafft's, ducking the cocktail party, where, I'm sure, I was not missed. There, in the genteel twilight of America's most respectable teatime institution, we sat for an hour, Mother and I, talking Russian and calmly happy together. For two or three years Mother's vacations had been spent in a peaceful colony of theosophists and occultists of all hues run by a saintly Englishwoman known to them as Sister Francis; the colony was called Joy Farm and was located in Cornwall Bridge, Connecticut, near the pretty village of Kent. Mother hoped that I'd "find time" to come and spend a few days with her there come spring — "if you can tear yourself away from your important business," she added meekly. This made me feel guiltier still and I fervently promised Mother to spend the entire summer at Joy Farm with her. I did go there in late spring for three whole days.

Having despaired of getting our *Carousel* on the stage, Balanchine and I toyed with the idea of a "musical to end all musicals," with book, sets, costumes, posters and program notes by . . . Salvador Dali. I'm sure Dali wouldn't have minded appearing in the leading role could he but sing and dance. All that remains of that project is a nine-page rough draft (very rough indeed), the title page reading: "Synops [*sic*] for a play by SALVADOR DALI — music by V. Duke, dialogues by J. Latouche [Johnny was back in the fold again], choreografy [*sic*] by George Balanchine. Working title — Les Nuées. Tentative titles — Clouds, the Enclouded, Men in Clouds, Clouds and men, For crying out Cloud."

On January 7, 1939, I had my Boston Symphony debut in Carnegie Hall with "Dedicaces." A day before the concert, Koussevitsky somewhat mysteriously told me that he was going to rehearse my piece in Brooklyn's Academy of Music and that he didn't want me to attend as he had a "thrilling surprise" in store for me. The thrilling surprise, as I discovered in his box at the performance, consisted of so submerging the all-important piano part that it became barely audible in "f" and "ff" passages. Already nervous and restless during the first movement, with Sanroma snowed under the thundering orchestra, I was ready to flee when, "upon its conclusion, the staid audience was startled by an energetic hiss from one of the boxes," as the *Times* described it on the following morning. However, I stuck it out and calmed down a bit, for there were no further disturbances, in fact "there was prolonged applause after the splendid presentation of the work, and the composer was forced to come on stage to take his bow." (Noel Straus, *N.Y. Times*) "Forced" was a little strong; "easily persuaded" would have been more like it.

But there was no Alec Williams in New York to lend me a hand. Most of the critical boys were frankly baffled by my piece and admitted it. "The poem itself is strangely conceived and the music founded on it proved even stranger and decidedly more cryptic, if it had anything definite at all to impart" — this from Mr. Straus. "Although the composition did not seem destined for posterity, it displayed Mr. Dukelsky's sure command of orchestral writing and his considerable, if misdirected, talents as a creator." True to form, Samuel Chotzinoff suggested that "perhaps the whole thing was meant as a joke and we shall find the new piece in the role of a 'number' in Mr. Dukelsky's next musical show. For Mr. Dukelsky, under the name of Vernon Duke, is one of our best composers of musical comedy scores." Only Bob Simon in the *New Yorker* appeared to like my "sort of piano concerto" and thought it "clever music by an unusually gifted composer."

In April my brother Alexis married Mona Burns, a Wisconsin girl of great charm, kindness and wisdom. The marriage, which proved one of durable and well-earned happiness, brought an end to his "life with Mother" phase and brought Mother face to face with a "living alone and liking it" mode of existence. She never got to like it and spent the last three years of her life visiting her sons, trying to make new friends and retreating to her beloved Joy Farm. She underwent an operation, not a serious one, and was constantly bothered with asthma, which showed no signs of abating in spite of prolonged treatments.

Nat Saltonstall, whose annual balls in conjunction with the Boston Institute of Modern Art were justly famous, hit on the bright idea of giving a surrealist ball at the old Somerset Hotel in Boston — a more piquant juxtaposition cannot be imagined. He asked me to suggest a surrealist "patron saint" for the ball, someone importantly connected with the movement. Several local names were brought up and dropped because of insufficient news value, when I suddenly thought of Dali, the Little Father of Surrealism, and a man not exactly averse to publicity. "The very man!" Nat exclaimed joyously. "But can we get him? Where is he?" Dali was at the Hotel St. Regis in New York and I felt sure that he could be had, as he was fond of lecturing and there is no better place for a lecture than easily shockable Boston; we all knew of Salvador's famous London lecture, when he arrived attired in a diver's suit and collapsed for lack of air on his way to the stage. I was entrusted with the task of bringing him and his wife, Gala, to Boston, to head one of the surrealist processions and, at a later date, to deliver a lecture under the Modern Art Institute's auspices.

As I predicted, Salvador took to the idea immediately. *"Ah, j'ai toujourrs voulu choquer Bostonne,"* he cried in his ruggedly Spanish French. At first he thought of taking a *girafe explosive* to Boston, a favorite fixation of his; a notion that was simplicity itself — all you had to do was to let the giraffe swallow a little dynamite, which would cause the animal to explode with great éclat, providing the ball with a tumultuous climax. This was thought a little dated and cumbersome, so Dali compromised by inventing authentic surrealist garb for the three of us. In twenty-four hours the costumes were ready; Salvador would appear in severely correct tails, his head encased in a huge shark's jaw with two full sets of teeth, which looked more like a prehistoric monster's, each tooth being the size of a cigar; Gala secured a Schiaparelli dress made up entirely of gilded safety pins, and I, a surrealist of doubtful authenticity, was provided with a human hand made of plaster, the kind you find in sculptors' supplies stores, which I was ordered to wear like a decoration, dangling on a black velvet ribbon tied around my neck. To further enhance the effect of the third hand, which appeared to be clutching my midriff, Dali suggested wearing my Barcelona-tailored crimson-red linen jacket; the effect was striking all right.

Nat wired me advising us to take the one o'clock train to Boston, as we were to attend a dinner party before the ball. "Someone will meet you Back Bay station," he added; but Dali was being interviewed at noon, so we caught the next train, a slower one, and wired Saltonstall to inform him of this slight change of plans. No one met us at the station, except an English-looking art critic from the *Transcript,* who pounced on Dali (ever receptive to the press) and wouldn't let go. It was half past seven when we reached the Somerset, and what with the persistent *Transcript* man firing questions at Dali in stilted French and Saltonstall telephoning frantically to make sure that we had arrived, we wasted another quarter of an hour. I, strangely impressive in the blood-red jacket with the large plaster hand dangling from my neck, begged the Dalis to start dressing, and they complied at last: Gala's dress, being all-metal, was very heavy, but she finally poured herself into it and looked magnificent, while Salvador, having forgotten to bring a wing collar, was busily cutting up one of Somerset's 1880 lampshades, to replace the missing article. In a few minutes a young man stormed into our suite, dressed as a Fokine Pierrot in white with shining black buttons, and implored us to hurry, as our hosts were awaiting us with impatience. *"Mais pourrquoi ounn Pierrrot?"* Dali demanded suspiciously, and inferred that our guest must have been a fugitive from a local carnival. Not at all — when we arrived, the host and hostess, as well as most of their guests, were sporting Pierrot costumes, looking exactly like a concert party at an English pier in summer. *"Ça doit etrre la mode surréaliste de Bostonne!"* Dali concluded philosophically, and dug into his soup, which was as cold as the smiles of our hosts, very much put out by our being so late.

At the ball we were greeted by Nat, beautifully turned out as — you guessed it — a Pierrot. He led us to his box, reserving the place of honor for Dali, happy as a child again, the shark's teeth like a monstrous necklace around his head. The "surrealist" parade was just starting, with mostly Boston art students participating; several of the entries were directly inspired by Dali's better-known paintings, which greatly pleased the artist. Nat was no longer in the box, but told Dali before departing that he, Dali, would be called upon for a public appearance just before his group's entree. Salvador, excited and anxious not to miss his cue, kept asking all and sundry at each new group's apparition — *"Moi? C'est moi?"* — but apparently his turn was yet to come. Some thirty or forty *défilés* paraded before the assembled Pierrots and non-Pierrots, some thirty or forty *"Moi's?"* from Dali — when Lo! the final fanfare sounded and the parade was over. The surrealists had forgotten all about their Patron Saint in the shuffle. The Dalis took it good-naturedly and departed on the morning train. Whenever I met Salvador following the surrealist ball, he'd say: *"Ah, Bostonne,"* and snarl satanically.

That spring I came close to writing a score for George Abbott, who thought of turning Shakespeare's *Much Ado About Nothing* into a musical — no doubt encouraged by the success of *The Boys from Syracuse,* which Balanchine had choreographed; the *pas de trois* from that show was certainly one of George's happiest inventions. Abbott wanted Marcy Wescott and Alfred Drake for the show. I met Drake, at the house of Clytie Mundy, the English vocal teacher and mother of Meg, who achieved fame overnight several years later in *The Respectful Prostitute.* Alfred sang beautifully and with rare intelligence; he knew how to project the words so as to make every one of them understandable without ever sacrificing the purity of the melodic line. Singing actors of Drake's caliber are almost nonexistent; small wonder that he became America's Number One musical-comedy man — his performances in *Oklahoma* and *Kiss Me Kate* were of unsurpassed brilliance. Yet he has told me many a time that he'd rather act than sing.

Mrs. Mundy's flat was the scene of many pleasant musical evenings, at which Alfred and Meg sang duets, and Alfred's brother, another good singer, often joined them in operatic excerpts. There was a pre-Raphaelite quality about Meg's beauty, an unstudied wistfulness and remoteness that rather put off the impressionable young men who flocked about her. The remoteness did not faze my enterprising friend Mitchell Hodges, who had met Meg at a WPA concert at the public library (where my music shared the bill with Rebecca Clarke's); I had accompanied Meg in the Robert Hillyer songs and together we had scored a tidy little success. Mitchell, then utterly broke — his last exploit was to bicycle all over the country to "find out how people felt about the coming war" and sell his findings to the *Saturday Evening Post,* which had refused to buy — had insisted on an introduction to Meg, which I provided. Following the introduction, they were constantly together, although Mrs. Mundy complained irately about Mitchell's deplorable failure to appreciate, or even tolerate, serious music. The romance progressed by leaps and bounds and I was soon favored by a visit from Mitchell, who begged me to intervene and assure Mrs. Mundy that he was really a most deserving young man and a not undesirable suitor. "Yes, but what will you live on, Mitchell?" I queried."You wouldn't want to live off Meg's earnings, surely," I persisted. It must be explained that I, struck by Meg's tragic beauty, had taken her to Alex Liberman, the artistic director of *Vogue*; she became their best model and got paid handsomely for her services. Mitchell grinned. "Not at all; I'm going to be rich by a new method. Take a gander at this!" He produced a newspaper clipping which read: "DON'T WORRY: let a professional worrier worry for you; all worrying done on the premises, attractive rates, etc." "That *is* a new method. Any replies?" I wanted to know. "Oh, yes . . . I've had six replies so far; strangely enough, they are all from tailors' wives. Look, here's one: 'Dear Mr. I don't know whether you may be kidding but I'll try anything. I'm so desperate. Jake is worried something terrible,' and so on."

I had a slight cause for worry myself, as I was suddenly stricken with appendicitis and taken to an Episcopalian hospital in Brooklyn (that's where my doctor, an Episcopalian, lived). The operation proved fairly painless and I actually enjoyed myself in the hospital, with its relaxingly monotonous daily routine, quantities of reading material brought by friends and freshly starched nunlike nurses. My convalescence was speedy and I was much touched when Meg telephoned and, with her habitual endearing shyness, insisted on taking me home in her little car, bought out of her *Vogue* earnings. She came with Mitchell, who disapproved of such excessive solicitude, and, while driving Meg's car, kept looking back to make sure that Meg and I weren't holding hands. Meg and Mitchell were married shortly afterwards; their marriage lasted six months — too much worrying, obviously.

With the stitches still in my belly, I was rushed to Boston to write a ballet for Ray Bolger, who was opening in *Keep Off the Grass,* another Shubert revue that proved short-lived, perhaps for lack of Minnelli magic. The music was by Jimmy McHugh, a good songwriter but not noted for ballet composition; so Bolger had Balanchine choreograph a ballet version of "Raffles," the society bandit, for him. I wrote the ballet, which was industrious Gwen Bolger's idea, in a few days, with Balanchine dancing out whole hunks of it, humming to himself, throwing himself on the floor and saying at intervals: "Here I want about a minute of music for the guests . . . tra-ta-ta . . . tra-la-la-lee . . . something like that; now . . ." as he ran to the other end of the room. "That's where Bolger comes in, like this . . ." — a hop and a couple of turns — "about twelve bars. You see?" I saw — and wrote the thing in three days, a nurse in constant attendance. When I got a little stronger, I walked over to Slonimsky's on Hemenway Street, behind the old Opera House, for some music gossip and a perusal of a sonata whose sole virtue was that its composer dwelt in Guatemala or Iceland and was, by that fact, "Slonimsky material."

"Raffles" turned out pretty well and was generally considered the revue's highlight. "Mr. Bolger performs his astonishing footwork with the usual gangling precision, and is at his best in a 'Raffles' number, with music by Vernon Duke," opined John Anderson. But the real highlight of 1939, as far as I was concerned, was my final exit from Dreyfus's kingdom to cast my lot with that erratic, unpredictable, almost too colorful, but withal lovable leprechaun of popular music — Jack Robbins. He first came in contact with me back in 1936 when he wrote to tell me of his admiration for "I Can't Get Started" and of the great things he could do with that tune were it in his catalogue. My weekly stipend from Dreyfus was reduced in 1938 — which was paradoxical in view of the increase in my performances and another ASCAP promotion; this, coupled with Spitzer's dramatic exit from Chappell, was a good pretext for asking and — after eight years — obtaining a release. Robbins was a complete antithesis to enigmatic, slow-spoken Max Dreyfus; my new publisher, a red-faced, choleric, compact little man, was a past master of the art of unstudied insult and torrential, crushing invective. I firmly believe that Jack abused people and made them fighting mad with his taunts in order to hide the — to him — shameful fact that he was basically a "good guy." Two of the mildest terms he habitually applied to his acquaintances were "self-appointed genius" and "mixed-up sonofabitch." He was especially fond of insulting people on the telephone and the procedure was fascinating to watch: Jack would first sit quietly and listen with deceptive patience to the man at the other end of the wire, then — unable to endure the heresies he had to listen to — would leap to his full height (about five feet six inches), his face a bluish-red, and go to work on the heretic. His secretary, a serene, inhumanly patient little blonde, would flee in terror as Jack flayed his listener with every known and unknown, printable and unprintable, noun and adjective. Then he'd stop, emit a few hoarse "hellos," look at the silent telephone questioningly (as district attorneys do in Class B movies) and slam the receiver down, roaring: "The sonofabitch hung up on me; talk about manners!"

His partner in the "Big Three" (Robbins, Feist, & Miller) and editor-in-chief was bland-faced, rotund, bespatted Domenico Savino, a skilled musician with a "classical" background and a flair for Italianate, extravagantly colored "lush" orchestration. Jack doted on Savino, but abused him continually, which the diplomatic Italian took in his stride, refusing to take "the boss" seriously. Jack and Savino talked a lot about "real" American music, which to them consisted of Gershwinesque piano pieces by Ferde Grofé, Dana Suesse, Lou Alter, Peter de Rose and others, later blown up to orchestral proportions by Savino and Grofé and originally selected for "big melodic strains" (to be converted into solid hits, like "Deep Purple") and Rhapsody-in-Blueish harmonic devices.

One chord in particular, mildly dissonant, and used by Gershwin with great effect in the *Rhapsody,* as a climax preceding a long piano solo, was a sure earmark of "authentic Americana" to Jack and absolutely *de rigueur* in a "modern" piano piece, Jack's modernism being more like a streamlined racing car than the lucubrations of an Anton von Webern. He'd listen to a new piece of music, then suddenly interrupt the performer: "Why the hell don't you stick *my* chord in there — you know, the *dyspeptic* chord; here, play it for him, Mimi [Savino's nickname]!" Savino would oblige and Jack, on hearing the *dyspeptic* chord, would exclaim, his face shining: "That's it! *That's* America!"

Another time, while abusing an erring song-plugger to his heart's content on the telephone, Robbins jumped up, while Savino and I nudged each other wearily as if to say: "Here it comes," screamed into the phone: "You know something? You're the kind of a guy that would steal a nickel off his dying mother's breast. *Good*-by!" and sat down with a smug look. "For heaven's sake, Jack," I ventured. "What's all this about his dying mother's breast?" "You pretentious, mixed-up White Russian!" Jack snarled. "Tell him, Mimi, about what you Italians do to your dead." Savino sighed with a bored air. "You got it all wrong, Jacques," he said reprovingly. "You must be referring to the old custom of placing a coin under a deceased's eyelid." "That's just what I said," Jack concluded curtly, and dismissed his two editors.

For that's what I was in Robbins's music organization — an editor. Every morning I'd go through a batch of songs or instrumentals, analyze them thoroughly and dictate a series of brief memos to Jack: "Front strain O.K., release poor, lyric unacceptable"; "Nothing"; "This may happen"; "A dog"; and the like. On reading the memos,

Jack would destroy all but the favorable ones (of which there weren't many) and send for me. He usually had a visitor in his office, not at all pleased by my intrusion, but Jack had a one-track mind, so he'd interrupt his caller to yell: "What do you mean by okaying this lousy so-and-so thing, you miserable snob? See what I have to go through?" — this plaintively to the visitor, inviting sympathy. Before the visitor had a chance to open his mouth, I'd chime in with, "Jack, I think you're wrong, this piece has a certain *'entrain,'* " because Robbins loved words that were new to him and had a grudging respect for their user. "What's that? How do you spell it?" he'd ask, suddenly interested. "That's a good word — must remember it. Hey, look what I picked up last night at the China Doll! " The China Doll was a retreat for rhumba, samba and mambo addicts, of which fraternity Jack was an honorary member; most of his fraternity brothers were well-heeled middle-aged businessmen, whose only recreation was to take daily rhumba lessons from professional Cubans or Puerto Ricans and then show off the new steps to other members of the cult. Robbins now executed an extremely fancy pivot, closed his eyes in ecstasy and mamboed back to his desk. "Not bad, eh? Ha — ha — ha. Can George Abbott do that?" Abbott, although hardly the type, was another addict, with years of energetic ballroom experience behind him.

Besides editing, I was also doing some composing for Robbins. Early in 1940 I wrote some songs for the Seymour Felix-staged *Midnight Frolics,* with lyrics by Harold Adamson. I also embarked on a geographical series glorifying American cities, at Jack's insistence. The series consisted of fruity piano pieces (filled with dyspeptic chords), styled "Lake Shore Drive" (Chicago), "Nob Hill" (San Francisco), "Back Bay" (Boston), "Rittenhouse Square" (Philadelphia), "Beverly Hills," and so on. The best of them was "New York Nocturne," which fast became Charlie Barnet's theme song. For Helena Rubinstein I wrote the "Apple Blossom Waltz," which earned me a round trip to Palm Beach and a two weeks' stay at its Whitehall Hotel, where the new cologne and the new waltz were launched.

All of this was mere preluding for 1940's main event, and the all-time high in my Broadway career — *Cabin in the Sky.* Originally titled *Little Joe,* it started as that unheard-of thing — a completed libretto (dialogue and all) ready for the musical setting. Its author was Lynn Root, a Minnesota boy and Hollywood scriptwriter; he met

Teddy Hart, the comedian and Larry's brother, at a Hollywood party, and handed him the script for Larry to read. Larry read it and, liking it, gave it to Doc Bender, who, liking it, passed it on to George Balanchine, who, liking it but not understanding it too well, asked me to decipher it. On reading the script, my first impulse was to turn it down because much as I admired the Negro race and its musical gifts, I didn't think myself sufficiently attuned to Negro folklore. Yet, I loved Lynn Root's book and couldn't tear myself away from it. I had a maid called Florence, a tall, loose-limbed octoroon, still young and fun-loving, who spent her evenings jitterbugging at the Savoy. "Florence," I asked her at breakfast. "Do you think I could write a colored show?" "You sure could, Mist' Duke," she declared solemnly. "Why, you is the music-writingest gemmun I ever see." This sounded encouraging; I tinkered with a few tunes and then tried Robbins. Jack became highly indignant. "See what I have to go through?" he asked Savino with stagy pathos. "I don't need you for colored shows — I already have Duke Ellington. Why don't you write me some modern-American instrumentals that the schools would go for? Vernon, Vernon, when will you learn?" Ten minutes later I called Doc Bender and told him that I'd write the music for *Little Joe*.

Getting a suitable lyricist was the next step. Ira Gershwin was my first choice, and also that of Balanchine, who was in Hollywood staging a new Zorina picture and gave Ira the book. On February 26th Ira wrote: "Saw Balanchine and read 'Little Joe.' I like it and think it has a very good chance, but I'm afraid that lyrically, I am already bespoken. On New Year's Day Moss Hart called me and asked me would I do a show with him and Kurt Weill if I liked the idea he had. Naturally I said 'yes' and last week when Moss, who was out here for 'Man Who Came To Dinner,' told me the notion, I agreed to work with them. Either Mercer [Johnny Mercer] or Yip [Harburg] would be excellent for 'Little Joe.' Lots of luck on it." I then tackled Harburg, who was in New York, played a few strains and showed him the book; the book was turned down for lack of significance, social or otherwise. It may be pertinent to note that in 1943, when the M-G-M film version of *Cabin in the Sky* was produced, with Minnelli directing, Harburg thought the venture significant enough to interpolate two songs into it, with Harold Arlen supplying the music (I, being in the armed forces, was unavailable).

Johnny Latouche, with my help, succeeded in selling his "Ballad for Americans," an effective "cantata" with Earl Robinson's music, to Robbins, and it occurred to me that Johnny, being a native of Richmond, Virginia, might be the man for *Cabin.* I tried the notion on Larry, Doc and Balanchine, my co-conspirators in the venture, and they all thought it a good gamble; Johnny himself was willing, nay, enthusiastic. Bender brought Albert Lewis, the producer, into the project and, leaving our sponsors to the sordid business of raising money, Latouche and I journeyed to Virginia Beach to imbibe the "atmosphere," although there wasn't much to imbibe in Virginia Beach except highballs.

Thoroughly saturated with southern talk and Negro spirituals, we decided to stay away from pedantic authenticity and write our own kind of "colored" songs. Latouche was erratic as ever; would work hard one day and loaf even harder the next — but we returned to New York full of fried chicken, Smithfield ham and with a rough draft of the score.

Money for *Cabin* wasn't easy to get, although the affluent and well-liked Vinton Freedley joined Al Lewis with a view of presenting the colored musical in the fall. While awaiting developments, I wrote a little serious music and spent all my week ends with Joan. We were still "more or less" engaged; Joan wore an antique bracelet I gave her in lieu of an engagement ring, but I couldn't make head or tail of our relationship. A typical incident occurred one evening when, after a harrowing New York day running in all directions and getting no place, I arrived at the station hot, exhausted and pretty despondent. Joan, fresh as an unripe peach, was at the wheel of her car. "Why are you late, stupe?" she demanded. I told her in Wertherian tones of my struggles and disappointments and thanked Fate for providing me with someone "to come home to." "That's great," Joan said placidly, chewing gum the while. "Only right now I could do with someone a little livelier." This so incensed me that I hopped into a cab and demanded to be taken back to Manhattan, money no object. Joan soon overtook the cab and got me back into her car by force, apologizing abjectly, but the evening was ruined.

On April 5th, Prokofiev wrote from Moscow: *"Mon cher ami* — it's a century since I've heard from you. I thought of coming to America in February, but there's fighting in Europe — and I had to postpone that pleasure. Just read in the 'Musical Courier' that you were present at a reception, which means that all's well with you and I'm happy to know it. *Alors, vieux bonhomme*, what's new? What did you write 1) by way of music, 2) by way of tra-la-la? Does the tra-la-la still pay off? Are you married or still at the mercy of *'petites demoiselles'?* This past summer I wrote a 5-act opera based on a rather lively novel by Kataiev, entitled 'I am the Son of Working People.' I am looking for another title. It's being rehearsed in Moscow at present and the opening will take place in two to three weeks. My ballet 'Romeo and Juliet' was 'created' by the Leningrad Opera in January with great pomp and our best dancers. The last named were rather defiant at first, but after 15 recalls on the evening of the performance, decided that new forms may prove acceptable after all. I wrote a fat sonata for piano (25 minutes) which I will send you as soon as it's published. *Alors,* I embrace you, *mon vieux. Drop me a line* [English in the original; the remainder of the letter was in French]. Always yours, S.P." and a P.S. in the left-hand corner: "Best greetings. Duckie, dear. L.P." (Lina Prokofieva).

While Serge was creating ballets and fat sonatas, I created — you'll never guess — a prize-winning hat for a *petite demoiselle.* Together with six other "representative gentlemen" — a painter, a writer, an actor, a magician, a "socialite" and a "man in the street" — I was invited to participate in an amusing contest, with a prize for the male amateur who turned out the best hat. The contest was a feature of Walter Florell's hat-fashion charity show at the Ritz-Carlton; the Japanese Gardens were packed with professional and society matrons and seven well-publicized debutantes were our models. "From a large wheel barrow of the most preposterous millinery 'props' ever gathered together, each man drew for himself the material and basic foundation feature with which to go ahead," wrote Antoinette Donnelly in the *Daily News.* "Magician Paul Duke used a straw frame on which to arrange some of his playing cards. Otto Soglow, the artist, built his 'masterpiece' with the aid of two enormous purple wings, long ribbon streamers and a huge bunch of carrots for the one-eyed coquettish effect. The prize winner, composer Vernon Duke, chose a flat, small tin plate upon which he arranged a bunch of scallions and pink carnations." We were given exactly ten minutes in which to "create" the hats, and the feat of standing on a runway, like so many burlesque strippers, fooling with bobby pins, hundreds of shrewd feminine eyes scrutinizing us gleefully, was no picnic. My model had a smile so disarmingly roguish that I became determined to win — and did —

in four short minutes, well ahead of my flustered competitors, including such practiced hands as Ludwig Bemelmans and Serge Obolensky.

Such is the singularity of my defense mechanism that whenever things aren't going right, my immediate impulse is to indulge in the most childish frivolity; most men become frivolous and start "painting the town" *after* achieving success — I want my fun *before* achieving it. I was unhappy about Joan, who wrote me a letter in which she said that she would marry me if I thought she should, but that she knew she would not be the right wife for me. I showed the letter to Mother, who said that it confirmed her worst fears and begged me not to go through with the marriage in the autumn as planned. I decided to wait and see; what I had seen so far was not encouraging.

Enlisting Balanchine's help (his wife was on the road with *Louisiana Purchase*) I invented sillier and sillier distractions. One of them was a party given by Mr. Vernon Duke to meet Mr. Vladimir Dukelsky. My pride was hurt when most of my guests wanted to know who in hell Dukelsky was; two or three of the Dukelskyites present professed complete ignorance of Duke's identity, but they were in a distinct minority and, after listening to some blatant boogiewoogie, caught on fast and left in a hurry. On meeting a Viennese refugee tailor de luxe, Balanchine and I lent an ear to his tales of woe; he had money, an elegant establishment on Fifth Avenue, featuring a huge *panneau* by Giorgio di Chirico depicting a gent in tails gazing at an enormous white horse, but no customers. "That's simple," George and I said. "Make us a suit apiece for free and we'll get you all the customers you can handle." "For free?" the tailor remonstrated in alarm. "My suits *start* at two hundred and forty dollars." "That's O.K.," George said, his face a mask. "No free suits, no customers." The poor Viennese was in even greater alarm at such ruthlessness; we finally won out and, to compensate the tailor, volunteered to "model" our free suits at a cocktail party to be given at his shop. He was to pay the expenses for the party in addition to giving us the clothes, whereas our job was to parade in his creations before an assorted group of New York's most recherché dandies. The party took place, our free suits were universally admired and the tailor got himself some paying customers — everybody was happy.

All these recreations were, no doubt, absurd, but they were certainly harmless. It was far more alarming, in the course of an afternoon at somebody's house, to come face to face with a hatchet-faced lady novelist or a lobster-eyed lawyer and listen to violent denunciations of the country of my adoption, as opposed to the Russian paradise on earth, snide little asides about those who saw no crime in Americanism (synonymous with Fascism to "fellow travelers"), the barbs delivered in a nauseating mixture of brittle New Yorkese and Communist-*Gemütlichkeit* clichés. One met such characters more and more frequently at opening nights, literary teas and avant-garde concerts and exhibits — "they always kibitz at exhibits" as my friends Nat and Max Lief, lyricists and boulevardiers, said. I was once taken to a T.A.C. "political cabaret" performance, listened for an hour to anti-Churchill and Daladier harangues and cute songs about every American's right to overthrow his government, as well as nursery rhymes in which Abe Lincoln was extolled as a forerunner and spiritual brother of Karl Marx, and left in a state of cold rage. This business sounded frighteningly familiar; I recalled the hysterical, wild-eyed orators in 1917 Russia, shouting defiance and demanding an immediate cessation of the German war and death to the traitors of the working class. The parallel was vivid and brutally realistic — the hatchet-faced and lobster-eyed sympathizers, who sympathized with everything except their country, were soon among those marching and shouting, "The Yanks are not coming," in unison.

My "on again, off again" romance with Joan did not terminate in marriage, just as the girl predicted. Her mother was taken violently ill and died without regaining consciousness; I was summoned a few days before her death in a neighboring hospital, but found my role extremely trying. Father and daughter seemed to want to be alone with their grief and, on returning from frequent visits to the hospital, would go into long huddles behind closed doors. Joan's father, while he didn't exactly resent my presence, didn't appear to find any solace in it either — although I tried to help in every way possible — and, worst of all, neither did Joan. Their tragedy was too personal, too intimate to allow it to be shared by onlookers, however well-meaning; and I felt keenly my unenviable role of such an onlooker. My leaving before her mother's death, although caused by my inability to be of real service, was resented by Joan, who wrote me in a spirit of reproach. Her mother's death didn't bring us closer together — it merely precipitated the final break. A few months later, Joan married a bright young lawyer.

That summer it was Westport again for me. There is something about that overgrown Connecticut village with its poor beach and crowded traffic that puts me in a working mood. It may be the attractive people who live there, or the fact that it's really a pocket edition of New England within every New Yorker's reach, or because of the two or three delightful inns it boasts — but I never went to Westport without pleasurable anticipations, never left it without regret. The "house" I found in the summer of 1940 was almost as small as the Wright Street one, but there were no applejack-swilling neighbors. Here I resumed my work, with Latouche on the songs for *Cabin,* and on the ballets with Balanchine, a frequent visitor. "Many New Yorkers appear to believe strongly in 'Cabin in the Sky,' " Ward Morehouse wrote in the *Sun.* "Certainly it isn't every show that can claim a financial support of such a quartet as Martin Beck, Gilbert Miller, Sam. H. Harris and young Harris Schmidlapp." Thanks to the machinations of Al Lewis, Vinton Freedley, Dick Krakeur and the formidable Doc Bender, money was found, little by little; it's not the amount an illustrious "angel" invests, it's *who* the angel is that counts on Broadway. Should one noted angel put a few dollars in a show, all the other, less noted, angels flock to it together, ready to singe their wings.

With 60 per cent of the score written, Lewis, Bender, Latouche and I descended on Ethel Waters, fresh from her *Mamba's Daughters* triumph, and, not without difficulty, sold that wonderful woman on our play. Todd Duncan, Rex Ingram and the then comparatively unknown Katherine Dunham followed suit. Meanwhile, Jack Robbins, still frowning on my Ellingtonian escapade ("The wrong Duke," he kept shouting), busied himself with Sonja Henie's "It Happens on Ice," the first (if I mistake not) "Icetravaganza" to be produced at the Rockefeller Center Theatre. For the purposes of this ice opera, he teamed me with Al Stillman, Radio City's staff lyricist, and we turned out a fairly hummable score in little over a week. Something went awry, however, and other writers, including the late Fred E. Ahlert, soon "horned" in; in the end, only two of my numbers remained — "Long Ago" and "Don't Blow That Horn, Gabriel" (with Stillman and Will Hudson) — for which I received a flat weekly salary.

Rehearsals for *Cabin in the Sky* started in late September at the

Martin Beck Theatre. These were really something, what with three Russians — Balanchine, Boris Aronson, who did the sets and costumes, and myself — pitted against the prodigiously gifted and eager, but bewildered, Negro members of the cast. I must emphatically state that for all-around musical and dancing ability in the theater, Negroes are immeasurably superior to their white counterparts; they catch on more quickly, are born actors and throw themselves into their work with extraordinary relish — I've never yet seen a *bored* Negro chorus girl. Ethel Waters was known far and wide as an extremely difficult woman to work with, but I won her over by a time-tested device — I hereby recommend it to composers wishing to please their leading ladies. I kissed her hand in lieu of "good morning" and "be seein' you."

George Ross, an articulate word-slinger, described our rehearsals in the *Telegram:* "Pit a threesome of turbulent Russians against a tempestuous cast of Negro players from Harlem and what have you got? Well, in this instance the result is a lingual ruckus approaching bedlam. At least half a dozen times at each rehearsal of 'Cabin in the Sky,' Ethel Waters, Todd Duncan, Rex Ingram, J. Rosamund Johnson, Katherine Dunham and her dancers have paused in puzzlement while the argumentative trio of Muscovites disputed a difference of opinion in their native tongue. The Russian vowels and consonants fly as thick as borsht. After ten minutes of such alien harangue and retort, Miss Waters asks what it is all about. 'George,' Duke generally interprets, 'just said the answer is "yes!" ' and then rehearsals are resumed under a flag of truce until the next vocal flare-up. So, yesterday, one of the 'Cabin in the Sky' players with a gag mind went out and had one of those phony headlines made up which he posted near the stage door. The streamer-type screams 'DUKE DENIES KNOWING BALANCHINE. NEVER HEARD OF BORIS EITHER.' " Certain members of the cast were so alarmed by listening to our outlandish gibberish that they thought seriously about taking Russian lessons to get in on the arguments. In his turn, "Balanchine, whose own Russian accent is unmistakable, soon became somewhat of an authority on Negro dialect and inflection," Ross continued. "Although the voluble Russians are keeping their fingers crossed, the Negro cast of 'Cabin in the Sky' was assured of success the other day by a happy omen. In one of the scenes, the script requires Miss

Waters to roll the dice and turn up a 7–11 in succession. Miss Waters obeyed orders and so did the dice — a legitimate pair — with two straight passes. Yeah, Man!"

There were strange goings-on backstage that the observant Ross was not privileged to see. Vinton Freedley and, especially, Martin Beck were alarmed by the sinuous, sex-laden writhing of the Dunham troupe and by Balanchine's novel approach to the Negro dancing. Negroes were noted for their show-stopping hoofing and tapping (Bill Robinson or Nicholas Bros. style); putting them through the motions of a highly stylized ballet seemed pretty iconoclastic to the producers. They begged George to let the Dunhamites do a little hoofing — no dice. Finally, Beck decided on a showdown, the purpose of which was to oust Balanchine and replace him with a tap-routine specialist. Aronson and I tagged along; George knew which way the wind blew and was fit to be tied. The meeting opened with an address by Vinton, who acted as arbitrator, but, apparently, his tone was too mild and conciliatory for Beck, who banged the table with his fist and interrupted Freedley to thunder: "To make it short, Mr. Ball-an'-chain [that's how he pronounced George's name], you either fix these silly dances of yours, or get out of my theater!" "No!" George shouted, poker-faced no longer. "It's *my* theater — I am director! You get out!" The tableau that ensued resembled the Moscow Art staging of the final scene of Gogol's *Inspector General;* the producers opened their mouths, but words refused to come out, and we, the three mad Russians, walked out dramatically, heads high and nostrils flaring. Work was resumed with no tap or hoofing to mar our art.

The other episode concerns itself with *Cabin's* score. Our show, originally scheduled to open at Boston's Colonial Theatre, was forced to forego a road tour entirely as our finances did not permit so big a gamble — a show usually loses money on an out-of-town tryout — and give three or four pre-opening benefits right in New York; these were, in reality, dress rehearsals. We had "first-act trouble," as the finale was inconclusive and a letdown; a "warm" touch was needed just before the curtain fell. Vinton, an astute showman, was responsible for the idea of ending the act with Joe and Petunia alone on the stage, the wayward little man ready to turn over a new leaf. But this improvement, charmingly "dialogued" by Lynn Root, wasn't made until after the first two previews, which in spite of the many highlights, were so dismal that Max Gordon suggested that Lewis close the show *before* opening it and cut the losses. We needed a heart-warming song to put the first act over and underline the "turning a new leaf" notion. The song Latouche and I had originally written was a plaintive and rather "offbeat" lullaby, pretty enough but carrying no "sock"; it was in six-eight time, and few hits in the annals of our theater were ever written in that meter. Miss Waters didn't care for the "lullaby" and wanted some "meat and potatoes" instead. I reached for the trunk — three days before the opening — and stumbled on "Fooling Around With Love," a song Ted Fetter and I had written for the unproduced Abbott show. I tried it on Latouche; he fell for the tune but thought the title not sufficiently "on the nose" for the dramatic situation. An afternoon's work, with an assist from Fetter, followed, and what emerged was "Taking a Chance on Love," one of my better-known songs, an immediate hit and a solid standard today.

I took Ethel to the downstairs lounge at the Martin Beck, in-between rehearsals, to play her the song, and she stopped me after the first eight bars with: "Mister, our troubles are over. That's it!" Vinton ran in to hear the next eight bars, tweaked my cheek affectionately, exclaimed: "That's my favorite composah!" and was off, quick as lightning. Johnny wrote four more choruses for the song, and he could easily have written another half dozen — ask anyone who was present at *Cabin's* opening, on October 26, 1940. If ever a song stopped the show, but cold, it was "Taking a Chance on Love." Ethel kept coming back, again and again, tears of happiness in her eyes, singing chorus after chorus; five reappearances — no more choruses. To the best of my recollection, she had to sing the last available one *thrice*.

Cabin's opening night was one of those gladsome, shining things we always pray for, but so seldom get. Following those first disastrous previews the word of mouth along the street was very bad: the best thing that can happen to a show, provided it's a good one. At the *première*, after the first gloomy ten minutes, Joe's death, Petunia's despair and religious fervor, the entrances of the Lord's General (Todd Duncan) and Lucifer, Jr. (Rex Ingram), came the songs — "Cabin in the Sky," sung by Ethel and Rosamund Johnson's wonderful choir with affecting lyricism, Katherine Dunham's teasing "Love Me Tomorrow," Ethel's "Taking a Chance on Love," which really wrapped it up — and we were in, in, IN!!!

In later years, when flops came in fast and furious, there was no place I dreaded more than the theater's lobby at intermission time. Any author or composer who hasn't been mortified, petrified and crucified during those heavy-as-lead fifteen minutes, hasn't lived . . . beg pardon, hasn't died a thousand ingenious deaths. You spend this dreaded period ducking friends and enemies alike, rightly fearing the solicitous commiseration of the first, the cutting, gloating politeness of the second. Those in between — casual observers — do one of two things. If they're not sure about your show, they'll buttonhole you and screech: "Why, hello, Jack! Have a nice summer?" — then you know you still have a chance. But if they peer at you sadistically and say quietly and without a trace of emotion, "Jack — what do *you* think of the show?" — Brother, get the hearse ready — you're *dead*. Neither happened that night. Friends, enemies and casual bystanders told *you* — and what they said was good to hear. After the opening, having kissed every member of the cast, cried with Ethel and slapped Max Meth, the frenzied conductor, on the back a dozen times, Balanchine, Zorina and I repaired to "21" and sat in a happy haze, drinking Pommery Greno of the right year, to be joined at 2:30 A.M. by Vinton, his eyes shining, who waved the ecstatic Brooks Atkinson's review and then read it to us in a quivering, happy voice. Here, in part is what he read: "Perhaps 'Cabin in the Sky' could be better than it is, but this correspondent cannot imagine how. For the musical fantasy is original and joyous in an imaginative vein that suits the theatre's special genius. Lynn Root began it by writing an extraordinarily fresh book about heaven, hell and the common earth where black people work out their destiny. By great good fortune everyone associated with him has met him on equal terms. For it would be difficult to prove that the book is happier in style than George Balanchine's lyrical direction or the excellent performance by a singularly well-chosen Negro cast. Ethel Waters has been essential to happiness in the theatre for some time. But she has never given a performance as rich as this before. At the present moment, this theatre-goer imagines that he has never heard a song better sung than 'Taking a Chance on Love' . . . She stood that song on its head last evening and ought to receive a Congressional medal by way of reward. . . . Since Dooley Wilson plays the part of 'Little Joe' with a kind of discouraged bewilderment and since Katherine Dunham plays the baggage at a blistering temperature, the triangular frolic is comic, disarming and incendiary by turns and 'Cabin in the Sky' ranks with the best work on the American musical stage. . . . George Balanchine is artist enough to appreciate the gusto of the people he is working with in this performance. Musical shows seldom acquire dancing such as he has directed here — motion in many lines set on fire with excitement . . . he has released them [the dances] from the bondage of hack dancing and ugliness. As a matter of fact, the joy of creative work shines out of all the corners of Mr. Root's fantastic cabin. Vernon Duke has written racy music in several veins from song-hits to boogie-woogie orgies. Mr. Latouche has composed crisp and jaunty lyrics. Boris Aronson has done his finest work. Put 'Cabin in the Sky' down as a labor of love by a group of theatre people who have enjoyed working on something that is bursting with life. Mr. Beck will need plenty of fire insurance as long as 'Cabin in the Sky' remains at his theatre."

We all slept soundly that night. I don't think anyone connected with the show got up before noon the next day, and by that time all the other papers were in — all the reviews were favorable except John Anderson's in the *Journal* and John Mason Brown's in the *Post*. There were some reservations about the book — I only hope to get that good a book again! — but everyone, including Brown and Anderson, liked the dancing and the score. Richard Watts, Jr., thought " 'Taking a Chance on Love,' as brilliantly presented by Miss Waters, so gay and charming that one hates to think how the radio is certain to go to work on it from now on." Alas, the radio bigwigs wouldn't meet the songwriters' just demands, and the entire ASCAP catalogue soon went off the air in toto, *Cabin* included, leaving the innocent listeners to be saturated with "Jeanie With the Light Brown Hair," and other such public-domain fare. Nevertheless, the songs being authentic, immediate hits — something that never happened to me before or since *Cabin* — they were accepted as such by the "trade" and played all over the country.

The day after the opening I charged into Jack Robbins's office, swinging an ivory-topped walking stick. "Well, what do you say now, Jack?" I asked challengingly. Robbins rose to the occasion — he had a way of sidestepping defeat that was the envy of his ever-loving associates. "Showing off already, eh?" he countered, scowling unconvincingly. "There'll be no talking to you now that you have a half-baked hit. Why don't you dust off the monocle, too?" I told Jack that I couldn't help feeling exhilarated. "Exhilarated?" he intoned pensively, the scowl gone. "Say, I like that word — remind me to use it." He grabbed Henrietta, the frail blond secretary, and executed a new China Doll mambo step. "Not bad, eh? Can Ethel Waters do that?" I exited rapidly and ducked into the stock room to find out whether orders for my songs were coming in: they were. Robbins, not having any faith in *Cabin's* future, placed the score with the smallest of his three firms — Miller Music — but that didn't stop it. When the M-G-M film of *Cabin* was made, my songs were switched to the next biggest firm, Feist, Inc., went back on the air with a vengeance, and became hits all over again.

CHAPTER XVII

THE FIERY FORTIES—PART TWO

EXHAUSTED by overwork and overanxiety, Balanchine and I went to Cuba to recuperate. Jack Robbins had a local branch of his music firm in Havana and we were royally entertained by his Cuban staff. I wrote, at Jack's instigation, a *bolero-canción* called "Rio Cristal" to Spanish words, subsequently published, and extensively played by Latin American orchestras. We drank *jugo del piña* (Cuban pineapple juice, not equaled elsewhere), swam in the too-blue transparent water at La Playa, watched *jai-alai* games and spoke in Balanchine-invented Spanish, which we tried on puzzled natives. "Why bother learning Spanish?" George reasoned. "All you have to do is add 'ados' to any English word — and the Cubans will understand. If you want a match — say 'matchados'; a glass of milk will be 'milcados,' a steak 'steakados,' and so on. Watch me." He summoned a waiter and pompously addressed him in Balanchine Spanish; the Cuban caught on immediately and brought the desired article. I was impressed, until I learned that the waiter had gone to high school in South Orange, New Jersey.

The weather was ideal, but during our return trip aboard a small United Fruit steamer, it blew up a bit. Balanchine met a Russian psychoanalyst aboard ship; they became very cozy and George spent the rest of the voyage in the psychoanalyst's cabin, pouring out his heart to the man. An unusual feature of these confessions was that both the psychoanalyst and his patient were continually seasick, thus creating a new, non-Freudian idea in analysis — where both parties lie down. Why not?

On our return George and I played two pianos for Zorina and Anton Dolin (whom I hadn't seen since he danced the role of Zephyr in my ballet) in a *pas de deux* I wrote and Balanchine choreographed for the British War Relief Society's gala at the Winter Garden. *Cabin* was playing to standees and "It Happened On Ice" was a hit, in its way, too.

Latouche and I were now in great demand as a team. Johnny married Theodora Griffis, Stanton's daughter, and went off on a Mexico honeymoon. Snapping their fingers at ASCAP's ban from the airwaves, the recording companies brought out *Cabin in the Sky* records with lightning speed; this was still the era when good music supplied by "name" writers commanded respect in recording circles and wasn't side-stepped in favor of horrendous "novelties" and pseudo hillbillies manufactured by fast-buck hunters from Nashville, Tennessee. Liberty brought out the show album with Miss Waters singing — alone — practically the entire score, and record reviewers swooned in print; Benny Goodman, Artie Shaw and Ella Fitzgerald helped, too.

It looked as though Duke and Latouche could now write their own tickets. We wrote two of them, which was a mistake — although the first of the two was very nearly a winner. Writing two scores at the same time is a perilous procedure and we should have known better; but the producers of the two shows were so persuasive that it became difficult not to give in. Besides, the producer of the first of the two — a musical version of *Three Men On a Horse,* with Eddie Cantor — was kindly, stooping Al Lewis, one of the three men on *Cabin,* and turning down his offer would have been something like ingratitude. The other project began as a Dennis King extravaganza, earlier identified as *She Had to Say Yes,* which flopped resoundingly on the road and was picked up by Georgie Hale, dance director and a friend of ours. Stewart Chaney's scenery was to be retained and a new book and score written around it — a rather novel notion. Oscar Hammerstein, good sport that he is, once took out an impressive *Variety* ad in which — having clicked with *Oklahoma* — he listed his six or seven flops in a row. I am not Hammerstein, but I resemble him closely in this respect; I, too, had six or seven flops in a row, beginning with Georgie Hale's *The Lady Comes Across.* The signal difference lies in the fact that Oscar's flops were vindicated by as many (or more) colossal, epic hits, while I am still waiting for one medium-sized success to make up for the failures. Luckily, I had successes in other fields in the 1942–1952 decade, and thus could thank my stars for having created a two-headed monster — with a two-track music mind.

Outside of writing the scores of two new shows and a full-size violin concerto, the year 1941 was not particularly memorable for me. I made some new friends, including the quick-witted Benjamin Welles, Sumner's son, then fresh out of Harvard and on his first *N.Y. Times* assignment. He came to see me in the capacity of an interviewer a few days after my return from Cuba — a tall, faun-faced, prematurely worldly wise youth, and already a capable journalist. I'm well aware that this book is often sweetened by flattering descriptions of myself, culled from contemporary journals, but I think I've been just as liberal with excerpts from my detractors; so I'm going to quote from Benny Welles's interview, if only because it contains my last prewar pen-portrait. Following Mother's death and the war, I lost much of my notorious foppishness and acquired a fine, healthy layer of extra-thick skin, which in view of subsequent vicissitudes, was a good thing to have. "Vernon Duke has often been called the 'caviar' composer," Benny wrote. "Duke's sleek black hair and expressive Russian eyes, his continental urbanity and American love of mischief, and his theatrical addiction to brilliant color in his clothes have served to stamp him as a cocktail-party character — but this, in essence, he is not. Vernon Duke is the suave front for a hard-working and highly accomplished musical creature, born thirty-seven years ago and christened Vladimir Dukelsky. Duke's flamboyant tendencies have been checked in recent years, but his attire for a matutinal interview recently included a brilliant blue robe with salmon-colored pajamas, topped off by a healthy sunburn acquired in Havana. . . . The recurrent theme of Gershwin in the symphony of Duke's life has often been commented on and draws a shrewd appraisal from Duke himself. 'George was my earliest musical idol,' he says reflectively, caressing an expensive Havana cigar and gazing from his window into memory. 'When I met him, he was leading the American popular composers away from the light operatic genre of Offenbach, Sullivan, Herbert and Kern into a field accentuated by new rhythms. He was also discrediting the old theory that a score should contain two hits and so much incidental music. George lavished care on everything he wrote.'" Avoiding the sickening "What comes first — words or music" query, Benny asked the second stock question fired at every tunesmith: *"How* and *where* do you write your music?" That's a tough one, but, on going through my "catalogue," I realized that few of my better songs were written at the piano or the writing table. "He seldom uses a piano to compose, but develops a melody in his head," Benny reported, on my say-so. "He writes on trains, on boats, on trams and cars, on anything that moves. The sway and roll and rock and rhythm is his inspiration." That may sound a little phony — it is, nevertheless, true. Two of my recent songs were written in places hardly conducive to creative effort — one on the Super Chief, the other in a San Francisco cable car.

The idea for writing a violin concerto originated with "Mr. Violin" himself — the peerless and Olympian Jascha Heifetz. We met at a party where we both essayed some jazz — Heifetz plays it on the piano, not on his violin, and plays it very well; in between choruses, he asked me: "Why don't you write a violin concerto? I'll play it if it turns out well." This was not a commission, not the kind Willie Walton and Louis Gruenberg obtained; they got paid and they got played. But then I never expected a commission, since I was universally thought a rich and successful composer and it would have been bad business to deny it. I am also that rare bird — a non-prize-winning composer; I owe nothing to Messrs. Pulitzer or Guggenheim, to Mesdames Elizabeth Sprague Coolidge or Alice Ditson, or the Critics' Circle. Broadway and Hollywood have fed and clothed me since 1930, and such questionable sponsors have probably made me ineligible for the higher awards. The only two commissioned works I can boast of are the cello concerto written for Piatigorsky in 1942 and the harpsichord sonata composed for Fernando Valenti in 1949 — paid for but, as yet, unperformed.

Anyway, I tackled the violin concerto with great zeal and spent a lot of time studying that instrument's literature. *Cabin,* while not breaking records, was doing fine at the Martin Beck and neither Mother nor I had to worry about the next meal. Unshaven and pajama-clad, I spent long hours taming the violin, an instrument that doesn't lend itself to imaginative experiments. Halfway through the first movement, I was interrupted by a Western Union messenger, who handed me a telegram reading: "Your *Cabin in the Sky* most enchanting play in town. Congratulations. Mary Lee and Douglas Fairbanks, Jr." Great! Now, if only Heifetz would wire to tell me that my concerto is the most enchanting work in that idiom, I thought. This is what the violinist wrote me eight months later: "I have just recently had a chance to play the work through, and I am very sorry to say that it does not appeal to me to my *entire satisfaction.*" The unwieldy phrase irked me considerably at the time; I wasn't writing the concerto for his or anybody else's "entire" satisfaction. Just a little satisfaction would have done nicely.

The piece, turned down by Heifetz, was soon picked up by Richard Burgin's handsome wife, Ruth Posselt, one of the few really good violinists of her sex, and played by her with the Boston Symphony two years later. Putting the concerto aside for a spell, I went back to Washington Irving's "little world of traps and trickery" — the theater.

There was plenty to do and not much time to do it in. There were meetings with Joe Quillan and Izzy Ellinson, who were adapting *Three Men On a Horse,* at Eddie Cantor's suite in the Essex House, followed by meetings with Dawn Powell and Fred Thompson, teamed up by Georgie Hale for the former *She Had to Say Yes* — the new titles for which were successively *Listen Lady, Nice Dreaming* and, finally, *The Lady Comes Across*. There was a song to write for Fefe Ferry's Monte Carlo, where John Buckmaster was scheduled to appear in a witty "lecture in three parts" written by Johnny Latouche; the subject of the lecture was Lady Birds — the Ritzicum Floosibus, or Yellow-crested Cinch (whose cry is "Yo'all, yo'all, yo'all") and the Tomatokins Lushivus, or Night Flyer (this bird, whose cry is "Wow!" may be mistaken for the Carotus Phonius, which is an out-and-out canard). The lecture was delivered by Buckmaster as Major Gristle-Griswold, a blustering, hearty, roast-beef type of Englishman with a monocle. The three ladybirds stripped down to essentials, while chanting our lascivious roundelay, "Sisters Under the Skin." This "show" proved so successful that it achieved a seventeen weeks' stay at the Monte Carlo.

Having run out of "inspiring" locales in my geographical series, I wrote an "American Arabesque" for Meredith Wilson's Decca album and helped Duke Ellington, one of the greatest charmers among musical folk, put together an "American Lullaby" for the same enterprise. With Balanchine and Latouche, I wrote a song poem entitled "Fog" for Zorina to dance at the Carnival for Britain, as well as a musical setting for a monologue delivered by Gertie Lawrence on the Friendship Bridge radio program, sponsored by the British American Ambulance Corps. Meanwhile, *Cabin in the Sky,* only a modest success in New York in spite of all the raves and the fact that it was voted the Best Musical Show of the 1940–1941 theatrical year by George Jean Nathan, who also rated my "Taking a Chance on Love" the best show tune of the year, took to the road and played to standing-room-only business everywhere. After a good look at the box-office statements, Latouche and his shy young bride deserted the metropolis for Stanton Griffis's Connecticut *"bicoque"* and I developed a taste for hired limousines and luncheons at "21."

The big news on the Georgie Hale front was the signing of Jessie Matthews, the English musical-comedy star whose eloquent legs had captivated Londoners in the late twenties; she was to be teamed with Ray Bolger, who, dissatisfied with the script, withdrew at the last minute. Joe E. Lewis and Mischa Auer were signed, following Ray's departure. Nearly everybody else available was being signed for *Banjo Eyes* (the new title for *Three Men On a Horse*). While getting ready for *Lady's* rehearsals, Balanchine purchased a home out at Fort Salonga, near Northport, L.I., and had the house re-done entirely to suit his own architectural ideas. He spent hours designing and arguing with the architects; they tried to insist on usual specifications, but George won out and the house was built in Balanchine baroque. It was a fine house and would have startled Le Corbusier; in his anxiety to put his ideas over, George forgot all about the front door.

Doc Bender and I were worried about Latouche's chronic nonattendance of the Essex House powwows; rumors of his life of rural splendor were all over town and the producers began shaking their heads portentously. We borrowed Larry Hart's car and chauffeur and motored to New Canaan to track down the recalcitrant lyricist. The massive gates leading to the Griffis estate, smartly liveried servants everywhere and the immaculately kept grounds were certainly impressive. After questioning the major-domo, the butler and several fleet-footed footmen, we were escorted to an attractive formal garden. A group of earnest-looking German and Viennese refugees in summer garb were reclining on the grass listening with rapt attention to Latouche, their host, striking in baby-blue jeans, a white bandanna tied around his head, reading poems obviously not meant for either *Banjo Eyes* or *Lady Comes Across*. There was prolonged applause after the offering and the German-accented voice of a countess was heard to exclaim: "Zere iss only one Tchann Cocteau in France, only one Tchonnee Latouche in America!" Doc and I, not daring to interrupt the proceedings, joined the poetry lovers on the grass. The seance over, Latouche greeted us effusively and volunteered the information that grouse and Romanee-Conti would be featured at dinner, also requested that one of the footmen show us to our rooms. The rooms were splendid, the dinner even better, but our every effort to divulge the reason for our mission to the host fell on a deaf ear. I was ready to admit defeat when the ever-resourceful Bender muttered significantly: "Don't you worry — I'll get the guy in line if it's the last thing I do!" After breakfast the next morning, Doc went in search of Latouche, found him, pushed him next to the piano, where I was sitting, a prop smile on my lips, and said resoundingly: "There — now get to work, you two, or there'll be nothing but trouble." Johnny, pouting disagreeably, produced a pad and a pencil and we began wrestling with a rhumba Cantor intended to sing to one of the race horses in the play. I played a chorus; Johnny made a face. I tried another; he shook his head disdainfully. "All right, listen to this — it's the best of the lot," I said, ductile to a degree, and played yet a third rhumba. "Good heavens, Vernon!" Johnny shrieked in disgust. "If you only had a little less agility, and a little more ability!" A frightful fracas ensued, Bender and the butler participating energetically. Somehow, peace was restored and we all went back to New York with a fourth and final rhumba for Eddie Cantor's horse.

Banjo Eyes opened in New Haven on November 7th and made history in that on opening night the final curtain didn't go down until 12:45 A.M. — with practically no one except the chorus girls' mothers, the backers and their families remaining in their seats for the finale. Eddie Cantor's idea was to get twice too many scenes, gags and songs into the show for the opening, and then, guided by the audience's reactions, to get rid of the dross and retain only the high spots. At least four of our songs were yanked out after the opening, for lack of room, and scene after scene followed the discarded songs into the producer's wastebasket. Nevertheless, the "stuff that hits are made of" seemed to be there, and the Yale men shouted themselves hoarse welcoming the little comedian's return to the stage after eleven years' absence. It's true that you never can tell from a New Haven break-in — as Broadway wiseacres will concede. Shows usually play only three performances there (Friday and twice on Saturday), the houses are sold out to theater-loving undergraduates and swarms of Broadwayites, who storm New Haven on such occasions, murder in their eyes, and return in a body on the same train Friday after the performance, murder on their tongues.

Boston is another story. Traditionally the best show town outside of New York, with Philadelphia a close contender, it can also be uncomfortably independent (as it is in all other fields) and give many a "sure" hit a nasty jolt. Boston adored *Cabin in the Sky,* which did turnaway business there after the N.Y. run, and I felt idiotically confident that it would take *Banjo Eyes* to its heart, too. It didn't, though the critics hailed it as a genuine smash "still in need of pruning." I suspect that Bostonians' esteem and affection for Cantor had a lot to do with the surprisingly good notices the show received. Fortunately for *Banjo Eyes,* Cantor and Lewis weren't fooled; on the second night, in Row D sat Max Gordon, Moss Hart and George S. Kaufman and they were placed there by Al Lewis to make a diagnosis. I never did learn what the three would-be doctors said to Al and Eddie — theatrical doctors seldom mince words on such occasions — but I finally cornered Moss, who informed me with his traditional amiability that he didn't care for the score. The next day Johnny and I, heretofore extolled to the skies as honest-to-goodness supermen, were told by Lewis that the score had no hits in it and by Cantor that it contained no Cantor songs. Latouche was now the archvillain; he and Hazzard Short, our director, didn't see eye to eye, Short dismissing every new lyric with a deprecating, "If it's by Latouche it can't be good." Eddie had taken to waking me about 3 A.M. and demanding my presence in his suite; I'd get into a dressing gown, feeling sleepy and desperate, and ride in the elevator to Cantor's floor, the elevator boy staring at me commiseratively — the Ritz's elevator boys always know everything that goes on in the hotel. On entering Cantor's suite, I'd see the banjo-eyed comedian playing cards with assorted Ritz Brothers in various stages of undress. "Yes, Eddie?" I'd ask ingratiatingly. "I must get a real Eddie Cantor song, Kid," the comedian would pipe in his oddly high-pitched voice. "Play me that last one you wrote." I'd obediently go through the chorus, the Ritzes bidding and passing unconcernedly. Chorus over. "It's not Cantor, Kid, it's not Cantor. Go to bed now and write me an 'If You Knew Susie' tomorrow. Good night." Having written a round dozen of would-be Susies with Latouche, I knew I was fast getting sterile. In a few days, following a tempestuous scene John was ousted and replaced by Harold Adamson, a quiet and philosophical chap with many "commercial" achievements behind him; together we wrote "We're Having a Baby," full of obstetrical innuendo, and Cantor promptly stopped the show with it, while Latouche went back to New York to help put the English *Lady* across.

Jessie Matthews arrived from London suffering from bomb shock; her singing and dancing were decidedly rusty, but it would be uncharitable to dwell on the misfortunes and tribulations that led to her mysterious disappearance three days before the New York opening, and replacement at zero hour by her courageous understudy — Evelyn Wyckoff. *Lady Comes Across* was full of good things: Balanchine's glowing choreography, especially in a wacky "Tango" and a wackier "Polka"; young Gower Champion and his partner Jeanne in "Lady," a melancholy waltz with a fine lyric, danced languidly and slickly and self-interrupted with snatches of romantic dialogue — a trick successfully used by Champion in later years; at least three songs equal to anything in *Cabin* — "You Took Me By Surprise," "Summer Is A Comin' In" (probably Latouche's top achievement to date, interpolated into the MacMillan and Ratcliffe 1953 revival of *Cabin* with Juanita Hall) and "This Is Where I Came In," sung by siren-voiced, callipygous Wynne Murray; it also had the Four Martins, led by Hugh Martin and Ralph Blane, who later did all right for themselves as a songwriting team and who stopped our show with the pre-Chaucerian "summer" number; such dancers as Genia Delarova, Massine's ex-wife, Lubov Rostova and Marc Platt; but one thing it didn't have — an intelligible book. It was a rehash of something left over from the original production and was now being rehashed nightly in a frantic effort to give the show a unifying thread. The show started weakly enough in New Haven, went downhill in Boston and expired in New York after a three days' run. *Banjo Eyes,* having started shakily, was rapidly shaping into a four-star hit and played to tremendous grosses in Philadelphia.

The Cantor show opened at the Hollywood Theatre, New York, on December 25th. *Lady Comes Across* started its three-day career at the 44th Street Theatre on January 9th. The first got a 100 per cent critical accolade (according to *Billboard's* statistics it drew a "yes" from every critic) and was an immediate sellout; the second got a universal panning and a bum's rush to Caine's warehouse. Most of the love songs were deleted from *Banjo Eyes* with the exit of Sara Ann McCabe, who left the show after its Boston engagement, and I shuddered at the thought of what the critical boys would do to my practically balladless score (the nearest thing to a ballad was "Not a Nickel to My Name," expertly danced by the De Marcos); my fears proved unfounded, as Brooks Atkinson spoke of a "vibrant score of metallic music with John Latouche's witty handsprings for lyrics" and Richard Watts, Jr., thought well of "We're Having a Baby," a showstopper almost of "Taking a Chance on Love" caliber, but a radio impossibility on "moral" grounds. *Banjo Eyes* played to big business for six months, then abruptly ended its run when Cantor had to undergo a serious operation. After the opening of *Lady Comes Across,* Balanchine and I took a bevy of dancing beauties to a Russian night club and proceeded to drown our fears in quantities of vodka, accompanied by caviar, knife-throwing Caucasian sexagenarians, and a faded blonde in a *kokoshnik,* left over from the *Chauve Souris,* who sang chorus after chorus of *"Kirpitchiki,"* the saddest post-Revolution Russian song written. I heartily recommend it to those who cry with difficulty; this song is a powerful tear-jerker. George and I wept on each other's shoulders between encores.

This, our first real flop, caused us to plot a speedy getaway — any town looks dismal the morning after a fiasco, but New York is truly the "City of the Dreadful Opening Night," to make free with James Thomson. Though Russians, George and I are no melodramatic masochists, and we'd seen enough films to know the virtue of that great Hollywood adage: "Let's get outa here"; Doc Bender, who was always a ready hand at borrowing other people's cars and chauffeurs, produced both again and, before any Broadway sleuths could get at us, we were on our way to Sarasota, Florida, stoically refusing to read the evening papers. George had a contract with John Ringling North to stage the ballets for that year's circus, under the supervision of John Murray Anderson. This was the edition that had as many dissenters as it had admirers, owing to the revolutionary ideas of Norman Bel Geddes (I remember the sand in the circus arena being of a powder-blue shade), the hiring of Vera Zorina, who headed the elephants' procession riding on the head of the tribe's leader, and the commissioning of a polka for the selfsame elephants from none other than Igor Fedorovitch Stravinsky. The polka, a strangely undanceable little piece costing North a young fortune, was played reluctantly by the Ringling Bros. band, and I can testify to the fact that the big beasts disliked their new music actively, refusing to dance to it and emitting ear-splitting roars. Like all new music by Stravinsky, the polka featured the "truncated line" — probably to glorify the elephants' trunks — but the animals would have none of it.

Leaving George and the Doc to continue with their circus exploits, I went on to Palm Beach for what proved my last holiday before donning a uniform. On arriving at the Surfside Hotel, I was handed a huge, heavy package by the clerk; thinking it a crate of fruit, I opened it with pleasurable anticipation and found that it contained 5000 copies of "We're Having a Baby," my radio-banned showstopper from *Banjo Eyes*. An unprintable message from lovable Jack Robbins was enclosed. That same evening Jack telephoned me from Grossinger's in Miami, and after a lot of verbal abuse invited me to an all-night saturnale, with a grand tour of Miami's hotspots. "Come on, lover, don't be difficult," he coaxed. "It's all on Metro." A footnote for the unenlightened: Jack and M-G-M had parted company some years back when the publisher, on his own admission, was thrown off the lot for "constant and damaging interference." Jack's two methods of revenge consisted of writing an epic entitled "Heels I've Met in Hollywood" (I believe he's still writing it) and taking out clients and friends on costly binges, charging the bills to Metro as "professional expenses." It was hard to be really angry with Robbins and I needed a little merry mayhem to sweeten up my Broadway blues; so I went to Miami and spent an extra-wild night in the company of Jack, who needed no benzedrine to outplay and outdance his younger contemporaries, and an outlandish assortment of "real hep" guys and dolls, led by the Great Nemo, songwriter and, according to Nemo, inventor of double talk. I slept off the effects of the "evening on Metro" in Palm Beach and on awakening was pleasantly surprised by a letter from George Abbott with words of warm praise for the score of *Lady Comes Across*. George is like that; a man of somewhat forbidding, glacial mien, he knows what he likes (and dislikes) and is not afraid to be kind to a flop, or to deride a hit.

Life in Palm Beach was pleasantly uneventful and, outside of an ever-increasing number of charity balls and war benefits, there wasn't much war talk; a number of "eligible" young men appeared in spiffy uniforms at dinner parties and civilians began wearing an apologetic look, especially if they were of draft age. I wrote Mother, telling her of Florida's salubrious climate and of my plan to set her up in a small house near Sarasota, where the air, I thought, would be beneficial to her asthma. Mother answered typically, suggesting that there was no sense worrying about her, that she was fine and happily settled in a small apartment she had found in the East Thirties, that the Florida house sounded lovely, but that I had better straighten out my military status first. The "straightening out" came from Uncle Sam himself; before long I, thirty-eight at the time, received the President's greetings and was requested to appear before my draft board in New York.

On January 12, 1942, Natalya Konstantinovna Koussevitzky died in Brookline, Massachusetts, the news reaching me in Palm Beach. She was sixty-one, six years younger than her husband. I was genuinely saddened by Tante Natalie's passing, because I knew that, in spite of our one serious estrangement, set right by Prokofiev, she was fond of me in her own despotic and Old-Russian way.

A few whirls at the Everglades — and I was back in Manhattan, slightly overweight again, but otherwise fit as a fiddle. I had a frightful shock on seeing Mother, who came to meet my train; she had always looked younger than her years, had a healthy color and a sturdy frame. I now beheld a gray-haired, emaciated woman, unmistakably sixty, her wonderfully kind eyes burning feverishly in the pale, haggard face. I couldn't help expressing the sudden terror that flared up within me: "Mother, what's wrong? Are you ill? You must have lost twenty pounds!" Mother smiled bravely, with a heroic attempt at light-heartedness. "It's nothing, *Moorashka*. . . . I had a common cold . . . haven't gotten rid of it yet; this silly asthma of mine doesn't help, you know. . . ." There was no use asking Mother why she didn't go to a doctor; she had no faith in doctors and rather prided herself on possessing an organism which presented a constant puzzle to them. "They never know what's wrong with me and it's just as well; it's better not to know," she was in the habit of saying, half-jokingly. I didn't have to look at Mother again to know that her illness was no joke this time.

Mother led me to my new flat, rented for me by Alex in the same rather too rigidly "functional" apartment house in which he lived with Mona on East Thirty-fifth Street; Mother's apartment was three blocks away. After showing me the place, which was half furnished and looked depressing, Mother gasped for breath, smiled with visible effort again and said: "I had better sit down. . . . I don't feel very strong today." In real alarm, I decided to force the issue of medical help and demanded that she see the doctor without delay. "There I was in Palm Beach, lolling in the sun and eating far too much, and you never even wrote me to tell me of your poor health. Why, Mother, why?" Mother became silent and thoughtful for a moment. "Ach, Dima. What would have been the sense of worrying you? As if you didn't have enough trouble with Mr. Cantor's horses and the bomb-shocked English star." There was no use arguing with her, so I took her by the hand and off we went to see the doctor. On reaching his office, Mother begged me to leave her there and not to wait — to get a good night's sleep and telephone her in the morning. I did as I was told.

In the morning I found Mother in tears, which she no longer attempted to hide. "The wretched doctor wants me to go to the hospital for a thorough checkup," she said. "I'll go, of course, but I know I'll never leave the place once I get there. A checkup indeed!" She then asked me what I thought of her new flat. Faded photographs of Father, and of Alex and myself as children graced the walls along with signed portraits of Krishnamurti (whose camp Mother had visited) and Annie Besant; there was peace in Mother's little place and an indescribable modest comfort, which was her very special gift. "Must I leave all this? I like it here and it's so near you boys," Mother said, and then stood up straight. "I must pull myself together. Do you know, I'm all packed and ready to go?" I assured Mother that she was doing the right thing and would be back in her new quarters after the checkup; she seemed encouraged by my optimism and, after a long and nerve-racking taxi ride, we reached the hospital, located in a wide, tree-lined street near Columbia University. She died there less than two weeks later, although two days before her death the doctor telephoned to pronounce her "out of danger."

Every decent man loves his mother and thinks her superior to other people's mothers; I don't know, nor care, about how my mother stacked up against others — she was everything I had in this world and if my feeling is what smart alecks call "mother fixation," so be it. Her memory will sing in my heart as long as it beats. And it's the small, everyday things I'll always remember — the way she started every sentence when speaking English with "so that," for which Alex and I chided her unmercifully, her artless admonitions to "listen to me while I'm still here," her refusal to indulge in even the smallest luxuries, her selfless and unreasoning love for her sons and her intense suffering at our slightest setbacks — these are the things that tug at my throat and will never leave me.

Koussevitzky, who liked Mother and was admired by her, sent me a touching letter of condolence and invited me to Brookline for a week end "to take your mind off your cruel loss." Mother died in April, Natalya Konstantinovna only three months earlier; they were about the same age. "I know exactly how you feel," the conductor said at dinner after my arrival. "When Natasha died, only one part of me went on living — the music in me." The next day an agile, good-looking and immensely self-assured young man called Leonard Bernstein joined us for lunch. He had singular and uncompromising views and was fond of airing them in ringing tones, punctuating his statements with a triumphant smile; Sergei Alexandrovitch thrived on that kind of talk from young people and was, in spite of his reputation for a colossal ego, a very good listener. "Noo, noo, go on. . . ." He'd nudge Bernstein with a wink at me, and Lennie would plunge into *boutade* after *boutade*. He reminded me uncomfortably of myself in my twenties, for that was exactly how I had comported myself and how Koussevitzky had reacted to my youthful "showing off" some twelve years earlier. Prokofiev and I were the official "amusers" then and no meal with Koussevitzky was complete without us sailing into some heavy favorite of the conductor's and pulling him to shreds, egged on by delighted "noo, noo's" of the host. So Bernstein was the new "amuser"; this rather nettled me and I began contradicting him. My irritation was shrugged off by the new favorite, who obviously regarded his paradoxes as unshakable axioms. On getting to know Lennie I developed a real fondness for him and a sincere admiration for his gifts, but he is a narcissist and so was I in my youth, and two self-lovers seldom get along on first acquaintance. During the conversation I learned that Bernstein was under contract to Harms — just as I had been some years back; knowing that Lennie was Koussevitzky's pupil in conducting and reputed to be a Boston highbrow, I asked him incredulously whether he wrote songs. "Oh, jazz and I are on excellent terms," was the typical answer.

I appeared before my draft board and was pronounced 1-A after a rigid examination. Alex was judged unfit, his eyesight not meeting the required specifications. Not content with becoming a buck private at thirty-eight, I tried for a commission and made several unsuccessful trips to Washington, where I had "connections"; remembering Uncle Gigisha, who was Admiral Makaroff's aide, and my narrowly missing the St. Petersburg Naval Academy, I tried the Navy, but was rejected for defective vision. A retired colonel I knew in New York had Coast Guard contacts, and thought he could get me a chief bandmaster's rate. I didn't "make" chief, but was given, for no particular reason, the "seagoing" rate of a coxswain, or petty officer third class. The only seagoing experience I had had previously had consisted of trips to Europe aboard transatlantic steamers, some swimming and a good deal of rowing. Soon enough I found myself in boot camp — on Ellis Island.

The "manual of arms" was a tough nut to crack, and I bribed an Armenian boatswain's mate who wore impressive hash stripes to help me on the shooting range; I had a nasty habit of closing both eyes when shooting a Smithfield rifle, and he cursed me in Armenian until I learned to shut only one eye, leaving the other half opened. Making up my bunk according to the rigid rules of the Bluejacket's Manual, eating ice cream and pork chops off the same plate and tying knots were other problems; as were saluting with the proper dash, squashing one's G.I.-issue hat until it assumed the devil-may-care "salty" look, putting on "leggin's" and switching from dress to undress uniform in two minutes' time. The enlisted men were youths in their teens and early twenties, and I didn't mind being called "Pop" and actually enjoyed leading a "boot's" life; the strenuousness of my new duties was a good antidote for the gnawing despair caused by Mother's passing. I obeyed the rules, "rose and shone," caught the drift of sailor talk, the one recognizable feature of which was interpolating a certain four-letter word as frequently as possible, and even became popular with my "shipmates" (I never saw a ship in my two and one half years in the Coast Guard, except at a distance), who thought me a "character" but "pretty regular" withal. I, in turn, liked the rough kids, who scoffed at anything except "liberty," drinking and picking up "dames" — which was a transparent cover-up, for few of them were stupid — but they had healthy faith in a "square deal" and in an American way of life. Some of their habits seemed regrettable to me: their passion for fried food — they even wanted their steaks fried — and their insistence on dividing all females into two classes — "dogs," or desirable damsels, and "pigs," or duds. Sample of typical dialogue between two sailors back from a forty-eight-hour liberty: "Hey, Pete, who was the pig you was with Sattiday?" "That was no pig, it was a dog." "The hell you say."

I tasted the joys of my first liberty with unexpected relish; it was thrilling to take a pine-scented hot bath, don civilian pajamas and crawl into a triple-size bed in East Thirty-fifth Street again, after climbing exhausted into an upper berth in disinfectant-reeking barracks on Ellis Island and listening to a concert of snoring G.I.'s. I went to the Hollywood Theatre, where Cantor was still drawing full houses, and bumped into Cole Porter, who surveyed me in my tight dress blues from head to foot and whined: "Vernon, my boy — what did they do to you?" At a party after the theater, I saw Howard Dietz with his pretty wife, née Tanis Guinness, whom I knew in London in the twenties, and played some new tunes for him; Howard, one of the brightest and keenest men in the game, lent a willing ear, picked the best of the lot and volunteered to write it up. "I have a book for a musical you may like," he said. "I'll send it on to you."

Back in the barracks I read *Dancing in the Streets,* the book, by John Cecil Holm (who authored *Three Men On a Horse*) and Matt Taylor, given me by Dietz, and thought it amusing. Howard and I decided on a collaboration, my Coast Guard duties permitting. Following the Ellis Island boot training, I was "shipped" across the Hudson to the Barge Office at the Battery and given the humiliating job of pushing little flags across a large wall map of New York, which had to do with the movements of Coast Guardsmen assigned to pier duty. I soon got sick of that — and asked for a transfer; they transferred me downstairs in the same building, where I tasted "eight on — eight off" type of duty as signal receiver. This meant sitting for hours with a pair of earphones and getting fire signals in one ear and ship signals in the other; the din was at all times terrible and completely antimusical. Worst of all, my "detail" meant sitting up all night and sleeping in the daytime, a thing I abhor. I beefed again and got "transferred" to pier duty, which was more fun; together with a lively chief, a quick-thinking Jewish boy, we inspected cargo carriers and transports, mostly those flying foreign flags (Russian included) for inflammatory stuffs, the list of which I learned by heart. After two transfers, the gold braid, notoriously suspicious of artists in uniform, especially musicians, decided that I was too restless for my own good and shipped me to Peekskill for some "advanced" training. If they thought it a punitive measure, the officers were greatly mistaken; it was a rough deal but I took to it at once. My new ambition was to shed fifteen pounds and return to the svelte proportions of my youth; marching, giving men calisthenics (I was a petty officer, remember?), firing away at the shooting range, crawling on my belly under barbed wire was great for the figure, and I astonished everybody by my zeal. "Aw, take it easy, willya, Pop?" a nineteen-year-old apprentice seaman would wail disgustedly. "Where's the fire?" My energy didn't disguise my utter ignorance of the Bluejacket's Manual, and the hundreds of everyday practices known to the regulars, who never let me forget that I was "reserve," a guy with pull, a goldbrick. "How did you get that rate?" my shipmates would inquire, eyeing my modest solitary red stripe. "You sure must of known somebody. Some guys have all the luck." Although elected to lead the "B" army at maneuvers, of which fact I was inordinately proud, I was no good at strategy and soon got my entire "army" captured by the enemy, for which I caught hell from the tough lieutenant, j.g., in charge.

As a result of the Peekskill "advanced training," I slimmed down to the desired weight, acquired bulging muscles and was ready to punch anybody who dared call me a "boot." Since the Coast Guard medicos pronounced me unfit for active duty and I narrowly escaped boarding an 83-footer shuttling between the Port of New York and Alaska, the "gold," disregarding my angling for a bandmaster's post, ordered me to report to Brooklyn Barracks, at the foot of Columbia Street. This was a dismal spot, lacking in vegetation of any sort and smelling evilly, owing to the proximity of a glue factory; yet it was better than donning deafening earphones, or bobbing up and down freezing in a sailor's pea jacket aboard an 83-footer. I don't remember the nature of my duties in the Brooklyn Barracks encampment, but I'm sure they were of the sort that any able-bodied Spar could have performed with equal efficiency; after three days of whatever I was made to do, I went to see the C.O., a jovial ex-football star, and asked him whether I could form a dance band. The C.O. roared with laughter and asked me whether I could play the "swinette," an instrument unknown to me; then, growing serious, he said that he had no objection to my starting a band on my "liberty time" but that it would have to be "unauthorized," as the Brooklyn Barracks didn't rate an authorized band.

I went back to my quarters to tell my new friends that Lieutenant Brodil (the C.O.) had authorized me to form an "unauthorized" band, which announcement was greeted with rude noises. I found four or five seamen who half-heartedly admitted to playing a musical instrument, but were unenthusiastic about it, as, to their knowledge, all musicians were regarded as "sissies" and "goldbricks" by the enlisted men. "Why don't you get Caesar? He can sure play the sax," one of my prospects volunteered. I was then led to Caesar's bunk and shook hands with a big, hulking lad of nineteen, who wore a sour expression on his not unhandsome face and whose brown hair was uncombed. This was Sid Caesar, seaman second class, of Yonkers, New York. At hearing my name, his face brightened up. "You Vernon Duke?" he asked incredulously. "The guy who wrote all those songs?" "I am." "Say, what are you doin' in this outfit? How come you're not an officer?" My truthful answer to that was that I had no college degree and had only been a citizen for four years, instead of the required ten. Caesar became friendly. "No kiddin'? Well, welcome to Brooklyn Barracks, fellah. Say, do you know Ibert's concertino for the saxophone?" I knew the piece but was startled that Caesar, who looked and talked like a neighborhood tough guy, should be familiar with such highbrow fare. In a few minutes we were talking music over a beer; Sid confessed to having played tenor sax with Shep Fields's orchestra and agreed to help me form a small dance band in Brooklyn Barracks.

Sid and I rounded up all available talent and discovered that while there were a few sax and clarinet players, a drummer or two, a guitar and a bass, the only brass obtainable consisted of buglers, who could execute a pretty bugle call but had no affinity with jazz whatsoever. *Faute de mieux* we padded our B.B.B. (Brooklyn Barracks' Band) with more and more saxophones, until we had nine of them, which afforded the possibility of big, luscious harmonic progressions in Robbins's best "American modern" style; the dyspeptic chord was by then distinctly old hat. It was pure luck finding one of Benny Goodman's arrangers in camp; we put him to work on the "jump" tunes, whereas I stuck to ballads. Caesar not only played a good sax but was also of great help to me with inventing figures, runs, licks and the like. Broadway publishers, flabbergasted at my sailor suit and the absence of a walking stick, gave me tons of band material, including so-called "stock" orchestrations and even special arrangements, which Sid and I would rearrange for our rapidly growing "combo."

The enlisted men, at first contemptuous and given to interrupting our rehearsals with derisive noises, gradually got to liking the idea of their own dance band, and our "debut" at a servicemen's dance in the barracks was a distinct click. Soon the Friday-night dances with the B.B.B. officiating became a popular feature and did much to relieve the monotony of our daily grind, which caused several enterprising souls to apply for sea duty, although the Coast Guard reserve had a not wholly unearned reputation for being confirmed "landlubbers." Another feature of the Friday dances were truckfuls of Brooklyn YWCA inmates and the telephone company's employees, mobilized for those occasions. I was a poor conductor and a merely acceptable dance pianist, used as I was to solo playing, but managed to "front" the band passably.

Lieutenant Brodil asked me to provide entertainment for one especially "dressy" occasion, which officers from other stations were invited to attend. I found a juggler, an impersonator and a "hoofer," but was stuck for a comedian; so I consulted Sid Caesar, who hesitantly ventured to oblige with a few "bits" — monologues and such. His repertoire included impressions of an Italian eating spaghetti, an excitable Frenchman spouting Caesar-invented French, a German beer-drinker and, to top it all, the inimitable "airplane pictures" satire. Sid rattled off the lot with a "you asked for it" look and registered surprise when I told him that he had the makings of a top-notch comedian. "Comedian nothing," he remonstrated sourly. "I'm a musician — period!"

That Friday Caesar appeared at the barracks' dance as an entertainer and flopped — his shipmates failing to get the hang of his humor and almost forcing the youth off the floor; all they cared about was jitterbugging, anyway, and went on cruelly interrupting Sid with "Play sax, sailor!" Furious, the big boy swore he'd stick to music from there on, but, after a persuasive pep talk from me, essayed his stint a few weeks later at a YWCA canteen dance and raised the roof with it. The climax was reached at the Waldorf Astoria Servicemen's ball, with over a thousand enlisted men and women attending; the B.B.B., now tricked out with fancy specially painted stands glorifying Brooklyn, represented the U. S. Coast Guard, and the ham in me had good cause for rejoicing — the boys and girls loved us. Then Caesar went on, did the "airplane pictures" bit and caused a stampede. The whistling and cheering disconcerted the seasoned and well-publicized "headliner" who was scheduled to follow him and couldn't.

A new deal was made possible for me through the good offices of Lieutenant Brodil, who got me the coveted O.K. for working on *Dancing in the Streets* with Dietz. The lyricist and M-G-M vice-president had a house on lower Fifth Avenue and a luxurious summer place in Port Washington, L.I., complete with swimming pool. My "detail" in Brooklyn allowed me most of Saturday and the entire Sunday off, and week ends at the Dietzes' became a regular feature of my life and something to look forward to. Dietz was a gob himself in World War I; he was now everything and anything he wanted to be. Howard shone at everything he undertook; he never "dabbled" in a new hobby, but applied himself to it with ferocious energy. He tackled bridge, golf, tennis, croquet and swimming fairly late in life and was soon outplaying and outswimming his younger companions, trained for such pursuits in childhood. A brilliant executive — generally considered the best publicist in the film industry — he was also an inventive and facile lyric writer. Together with Arthur Schwartz he fashioned some of America's smartest show scores, with *Band Wagon* an all-time high. We should have been a great team, for we had many traits in common, such as facility, adaptability and a "sophisticated" outlook; but we just didn't "pan out" as a combination, probably because we had too much in common. No two people were less alike than Richard Rodgers and Lorenz Hart, than George and Ira Gershwin, than (the classic example) Gilbert and Sullivan; yet they complemented each other, the qualities lacking in one were abundantly present in the other and vice versa — therein lay the reason for the success of their teamwork.

Chatting with Greer Garson or Sylvia Ashley or Tanis Dietz by a swimming pool and partaking of subtly spiced viands — after standing in chow line to "Come and get it" (the "it" usually being fried pork chops or hot dogs, garnished with vanilla ice cream) — was very good for the morale, and the stomach as well. *Dancing in the Streets,* a gay tale of wartime Washington, was "writing itself"; we'd dash off a song in the afternoon and exhibit it to the Dietzes' guests in the evening. Then back to the barracks I'd go, to my lowly duties in the daytime, canteen and service dances at night — two or three of these a week, as a rule. As my shipmates insisted, I had me a "good racket."

Case histories of hits are of interest to the reading public and of help to professionals; everybody hopes to come up with an *Oklahoma,* a *Kiss Me Kate* or a *Guys and Dolls.* Nobody cares about *why* a flop was a flop — and frankly, neither do I, once the flop is behind me. My shows between 1930 and 1942 turned out successful, for the most part, and that is why I permitted myself to dwell on them in considerable detail. Were I to do this about my failures (1942–1946), I'd be instantly accused of "passing the buck" or "stepping on people's toes." Some of my fellow sufferers have gone on to big gilt-edged successes and I am happy in that knowledge; I will therefore refrain from too many of the tales of horror that invariably accompany a flop on its downhill course.

The reader will wonder why I, a man of solid and many-sided experience, should have allowed myself to be connected with unsound and obviously defective ventures. Ah, that's just where the rub comes in: the defects are seldom obvious in the initial stage. A book may appear fascinating when read, but prove untheatrical and next to unperformable (*Sweet Bye and Bye*); a score may go great at cocktails and get a "so what?" from the critics (*Jackpot*); a producer may seem the salt of the earth and a theatrical colossus at backers' auditions and prove an utter jerk or (worse still) a crook after the dress rehearsal; a highly touted director may also be an alcoholic and have just enough strength left to direct himself to the nearest bar; a star may be great on the screen and less than great on the stage — and so on, ad infinitum. Every show reaching production stage — whether a hit or a flop eventually — follows more or less the same pattern in the beginning, that is, *after* all the money has been raised, which is almost as difficult as to make money on Broadway (*Oklahoma* and *Kiss Me Kate* had a record number of "money" auditions and their fates hung in the balance for months).

Everybody loves everybody when the rehearsals start. The actors nudge each other at the book's first reading, smiling knowingly as if to say: "It's in the bag, Kid"; the chorus girls make eyes at the composer and lyricist when first treated to the show's score and whisper dreamily: "Gee, that thing sends me. . . . Watch it climb on the Hit Parade"; the backers sneak into the theater to take a gander at their favorite's backside rotating rhythmically to the rehearsal pianist's beat, and bark: "Can't miss," at the producer. The second week things seem to be progressing smoothly, when all at once the entire structure begins creaking, holes and dull stretches are discovered in the book, the prima donna acquires psoriasis, the dance director fires the backer's favorite, the songs don't sing any longer and the actors start acting up — but not on the stage. You open out of town and the papers pan you unanimously; the producer puts up a fine front and appears unconcerned: "It's a New York show, boys. Wait till Atkinson gives it the once-over." Atkinson gives it the once-over and thinks it terrible; the show flops. Should your show please the out-of-town customers and even break records everywhere, the producer becomes overconfident and allows the performance to deteriorate, makes last-minute replacements and illogical changes, or, more dangerous still, "freezes" his show, that is refuses to make any corrections at all, even if absolutely necessary, on the grounds that the "show is a smash. Are you gonna argue with a hit?"

With clever Harold Rome, a corporal stationed in Brooklyn, but nowhere near Columbia Street, I tinkered with yet another play, called *Nantucket,* written by the late Samuel Hoffenstein and Gottfried Reinhardt, Max's son. Gottfried was then a sergeant in the Army's Special Services and had a hand in various documentary films.

March 1943 was a big month for me, as I had three "world *premières*" following on each other's heels. On the 11th M-G-M's *Cabin in the Sky* with Ethel Waters; Lena Horne (replacing Katherine Dunham), Rochester (replacing Dooley Wilson) and Duke Ellington and his orchestra were added to the cast. This was Vincente Minnelli's first musical for Metro, with Arthur Freed producing. On the 19th and 20th Ruth Posselt gave the first hearings of my Violin Concerto, under her husband's baton, in Boston; and the 22nd marked the opening of *Dancing in the Streets,* starring Mary Martin, produced by Vinton Freedley, at the Shubert Theatre, Boston. Such exaggerated nonmilitary activity on the part of a mere enlisted man was frowned upon in the Third Naval District, and I had some trouble explaining that *Cabin* was written in 1940, the Violin Concerto in 1941 and *Dancing in the Streets* on my liberty time; in other words, that the writing did not interfere with my duties. Of the three, the filmed *Cabin* was an immediate success, the concerto was splendidly received both at Sanders Theatre, Cambridge, and Symphony Hall, Boston — Ruth Posselt's virtuoso performance helped a lot — and *Dancing in the Streets* got lukewarm notices and an SRO sign nightly through its Boston engagement. There was a musical play entitled *Away We Go* trying to make a go of it at the Colonial and playing to mediocre business, although receiving a good press; this was soon to be renamed *Oklahoma*. Our business at the Shubert was so great that I, on leave from Brooklyn Barracks, had to stand in the back of the orchestra to see the show and, at another performance, share the piano stool with the pit pianist. Mary Martin was delicious as the heroine, Bob Alton's dances were fresh and energetic, and I still think "Indefinable Charm," set to a remarkably unhackneyed lyric of Howard's, one of my best ballads. Why, then, did *Dancing in the Streets* fail? Strange to relate, it didn't. It was "yanked off for repairs" — in Broadwayese: the three all-important male comedy parts had been entrusted to three excellent "straight" actors who, by no stretch of the imagination, could be called comedians — Dudley Digges, Ernest Cossart and Jack Smart. All three were miscast and all three had "run of the play" contracts; since the show was doing smash business in Boston, they saw no reason for resigning, which is what the management wanted them to do. Thus, three weeks later, I was awakened from uneasy slumber in Brooklyn Barracks by Max Meth, the conductor, to be told that Vinton had closed the show, unable to make the necessary replacements. He wanted the book rewritten, the tempo speeded up, and then to reopen in the early fall. Mary Martin, surely the most enchanting of those responsible for enchanted evenings in the theater, and her clever husband, Dick Halliday, were so "sold" on *Dancing in the Streets* that they considered taking it over from Freedley, who showed no signs of progress after the show's unexpected closing, which stunned the whole of Broadway. Unfortunately for our side, S. J. Perelman and Ogden Nash (my future collaborator and closest friend) began to wave the completed script and score — with stylish and perversely Mittel-

European tunes by the late Kurt Weill — of *One Touch of Venus* in the star's face — until she was duly touched by these attentions and succumbed to the lure of becoming Broadway's most seductive goddess.

I found quite a few changes being made in the Brooklyn Barracks on my return. Sid Caesar married a pretty brunette from his home town and I officiated as best man. A few hours before the ceremony, which took place in a small Jewish temple on Second Avenue, I was given full instructions as to my conduct while the rabbi officiated, caught on with some difficulty, and then did everything wrong, to the intense amusement of the guests. The genial Lieutenant Brodil got transferred to Jersey City and was replaced by an ex-lawyer, now a lieutenant, j.g., reported engaged to one of the *Banjo Eyes* chorines. He disliked me on sight, probably thinking my noisy publicity out of order for a petty officer third class. I was shipped to Rahway, New Jersey, an unpopular spot with the G.I.'s, as it was rumored to be a commando-training unit. My sleeping quarters were in the gunner's shack, which was also the arsenal, and the crafty "regular" gunner's mate and I, the sole occupants of the shack, had chronic insomnia, owing to our fear of being blown to pieces at any moment. I am sure that my military duties at Rahway did even less for the war effort than those I performed in Brooklyn. The new C.O. saw to it that I wouldn't resume any musical "nonsense," although Rahway was crawling with buglers who were not averse to tackling a hot trumpet on the sly. Whatever I was doing in New Jersey, it didn't agree with me, for I soon contracted something called "sinusitis" and my frequent visits to sick bay, where I was fed enormous white pills, Coast Guard's standard all-healing drug, failing to restore my health, I was finally sent to a marine hospital nearby for "observation" and tests.

Prior to my illness I managed to sneak away to Port Washington for huddles with Dietz on a Coast Guard revue we were assembling. Two enterprising chiefs from 42 Broadway, where the Coast Guard had its public relations unit, plotted to start a traveling troupe made up of enlisted personnel, to help sell war bonds and also to sell the citizens the fact that our branch of the service tasted gunpowder along with the rest of the armed forces. To that end Dietz and I wrote "The Silver Shield," a stirring march on the theme of Coast Guard invaders overseas, which subsequently became the outfit's official marching song. Howard's versatility and past experience in the Navy served him in good stead, and about the time I entered the marine hospital, we had a round dozen of numbers suitable for a seagoing answer to Irving Berlin's *This Is the Army*.

After three days in the hospital, I was told by the doctor that I should apply for a medical discharge and that I had an excellent chance of getting it. Having spent some eighteen months in the Coast Guard without contributing in any great degree to that service's record, the thought of donning "civvies" again was mighty attractive. I went to the medical authorities at 42 Broadway following my hospital checkup and duly obtained the discharge. On returning home, I heard the telephone ringing — it was the Coast Guard headquarters in Washington requesting my presence the next morning. My assertion that I was no longer in uniform didn't cut any ice with the yeoman at the other end of the wire, so I flew to Washington after a blissful night in my own bed. On arriving I was taken to Captain Ellis Reed-Hill, the head of U.S.C.G. Public Relations, who was somewhat startled to see me in a gray flannel suit. "In a hurry, aren't you, Duke?" said the captain with a wink at his yeoman. "Sorry, sir, but I have my discharge," I retorted, and was about to produce the certificate. Reed-Hill waved it aside and continued: "I know all about that and I know, too, that you have served without your talents being put to any use. I'm sorry about that, Mr. Duke [that "Mr." certainly sounded good coming from a commissioned officer], but we need you now, badly. I hear you've written a revue with Howard Dietz?" I began to see the captain's drift of thought. It was his intention to produce a recruiting revue for the purpose of getting more Spars into service as more and more men were being shipped overseas and office personnel were needed behind the lines. As Captain Reed-Hill outlined his project to me, I assured him that both Dietz and I would be glad to help put such a show on, but the kindly captain said the show wouldn't carry the same weight with a pair of civilians writing it; he wanted me back in the service in the Temporary Reserve, which is a Coast Guard term for limited duty. "What would you say to a commission?" said the captain. To an enlisted man, even with a medical discharge in his pocket, a commission sounds as if he were suddenly elected President of the United States. "Did you say a commission?" I stammered. "Yes, how about my turning you into a lieutenant, j.g., overnight?" This made me bold to the point of daring. "I'm afraid I'm too old for a lieutenant, j.g.," I told the captain sanguinely. "Better make it lieutenant commander." Reed-Hill roared with laughter and said, rubbing his hands with glee: "Tell you what we'll do — we'll settle for a full lieutenant. How's that?" It sounded pretty staggering; the captain dismissed me, assuring me that he'd take up the matter with Admiral Waesche, the Coast Guard's commandant, and let me know the next day whether the suggested metamorphosis could take place.

The commandant saw no objection to the plan and I was asked to stay on in Washington for a few days to discuss the format, casting and dates for the projected revue. I had always liked Washington, a small Paris with a Southern accent, and then especially so, because Alex and Mona lived in Silver Spring nearby, my brother being employed by the Federal Public Housing Authority to design houses for war workers.

Captain Reed-Hill asked me to go through the complete lists of Coast Guard enlisted personnel and make up a tentative cast for *Tars and Spars* (Howard Dietz's title for the revue); he said I'd be given carte blanche in casting and could get any suitable ex-performers "on orders," provided they were not on active duty. Gower Champion, stationed at Catalina Island, California, and George Bauer, a yeoman in Maryland and one of the more talented pianists of the younger generation, were available. Victor Mature, just back from convoy duty, was a chief and, apparently, could be had. I brought up the name of Sid Caesar, a nonentity at the time, and told the captain that several items in our revue were written around his personality and that, to my way of thinking, Sid was definitely a "comer" among comics and that his "airplane pictures" skit would stop any show. Captain Reed-Hill promised to look into it and get Caesar "on orders" if need be.

Meanwhile, I was put to work on *Battle Stations,* a two-reel short extolling the Coast Guard's exploits on the high seas; this was directed by Garson Kanin, borrowed from the Army, who had seen *Dancing in the Streets* in Boston and liked the score. *Jackpot,* bearing no resemblance to *Dancing* and starring gifted Nanette Fabray, velvet-voiced Alan Jones and droll Jerry Lester, was trying out in the provinces, and in spite of a machine-made book and a hastily contrived score (my poorest to date), was clicking resoundingly.

By Christmas I was back in New York, having completed the background music for *Battle Stations* on Alex's upright in Silver Spring and handed it to Clare Grundman, a rising young orchestrator and a fellow Coast Guardsman from Minnesota, to score for military band. On January 5th, I received an alarming telephone call from Alex in Washington, telling me that he had just seen *Jackpot* and didn't care for it; neither did Jay Carmody in the *Washington Star,* although the other papers "ate it up." January 5, 1944, was a bad day for me, because that same evening my Violin Concerto, picked up by Artur Rodzinski, failed to repeat its Boston success at a N. Y. Philharmonic concert in Carnegie Hall, despite the efforts of Ruth Posselt, its creator, and the thorough and incisive preparation given my piece by Lennie Bernstein, then the Philharmonic's assistant conductor. Unimpressed with the work at first, Lennie came up to me at the last rehearsal beaming and said: "Vladie, I didn't 'get' your piece when I read it; now that I know it, I like it very much and only hope that I'll be given a chance to conduct it." The concerto was rehearsed by Bernstein because of Rodzinski's illness. Not two hours before the concert, Rodzinski suddenly recovered and conducted the work, with which he was not overly familiar; a pity because all the fine polishing and adjusting made by Lennie went for nought. The orchestral accompaniment was understandably insecure, the tempi erratic, the public reception on the cool side.

I was again — temporarily — a civilian, being investigated and "screened" prior to receiving a Temporary Reserve commission as a full lieutenant. Quite unexpectedly, Alex descended on me from Washington with sketches of sets and costumes for an "imaginary musical comedy," which he asked me to show to Howard Dietz. I took the sketches to Howard, who was so impressed that he telephoned Cedric Gibbons, the head of M-G-M's art department in Culver City, and had my brother practically hired on the spot. While negotiations were in progress, Alex, electrified by the success of his mission, went back to Washington to wind up his affairs there before coming back to New York to await Metro's final directives. I, meanwhile, went on with my own investigating of theater-minded tars and spars in the Third Naval District, and even journeyed to my former "base" — the Brooklyn Barracks — where the B.B.B. was still actively functioning, with Sid Caesar "fronting" the orchestra.

I told Sid of my Washington mission and the Coast Guard revue that would make him a star overnight; the Yonkers lad was lukewarm about the plan. He had a good deal in Brooklyn, he opined; the C.O. thought highly of his work and needed him as a morale builder. He would never let him go, Sid felt, and should he apply for a transfer, the C.O. would deem it the basest ingratitude and "ship him for sure" — which in view of his happy marriage would result in a catastrophe for everybody concerned. I said that if his C.O. wouldn't let him go to Palm Beach, where *Tars and Spars* was scheduled to open, I'd get him transferred to Florida "on orders" from Washington.

I was greatly helped in my G.I.-talent scouting by Dorothy Gillam, an ex-actress and a lieutenant in the Women's Reserve. Miss Gillam had appeared in supporting roles with Katherine Hepburn, wrote intelligently about the theater and was a selfless and fanatical worker; she proved a splendid organizer and I shudder to think of what *Tars and Spars* might have become without Captain Reed-Hill and Dorothy Gillam.

While awaiting the *Jackpot* opening, Howard and I toiled on the musical version of *Rain,* which A. P. Waxman, former press agent, had acquired from Maugham, John Colton and Clemence Randolph (the last two having authored the play). This was looming as an important project, what with Paramount reported putting up $75,000, Rouben Mamoulian set to co-write the book with Dietz and direct the movie, Boris Aronson to design the scenery and every actress in the land hankering for the role of Sadie, the immortal floozie. Marlene Dietrich, Ginger Rogers, Celeste Holm, Libby Holman, Gertrude Niesen, Ann Sheridan and Bernice Claire were among the candidates; I well remember Marlene, looking as young and provocative as she did in the *Blue Angel* days, listening to our songs in my East Thirty-fifth Street flat, smoking a cigarette and dangling her smoothly silk-stockinged, history-making legs, an oddly winning yet disdainful I've-no-use-for-men-but-look-at-me-if-you-must kind of smile on her lips. It was Ethel Merman who eventually got the part — only to relinquish it after a week's rehearsals; I still believe she would have been the perfect musical Sadie.

Everyone around Sardi's thought *Jackpot* a cinch after its provincial showings and a big New York advance reported by the box office. Exuding confidence, I took Sally Horan, one of the town's better-looking career girls, and Iva Patcevitch, the president of the Condé Nast magazine empire, to the Alvin opening on January 13th. After the first ten minutes, my guests began to wilt along with the rest of the audience — ten more minutes and I began wishing I were dead; the jokes that made out-of-town customers cry with laughter were falling flat with a dull, sickening thud, until the actors were playing to masses of raised eyebrows and no applause. Even sadder than the already described deadly intermission after an unpromising first act is the customary party for those concerned with the show after a doubtful opening night. I don't know what's harder to take — the heroically smiling Park Avenue hostess determined to make *her* party a success, even though *your* show is a flop, the overworked actresses, hugging each other with exaggerated affection, probably thinking the while, "Just wait till you see the notices, my lass," the shouts of the bibulous guests demanding a performance of "Tea for Two" when the show's hit is called "Coffee for Three," or the unfathomable, elaborately aloof countenance of Mr. George Jean Nathan, which was invariably the first thing I saw upon arriving at each of my after-flop parties, and there were several.

I was really crushed by the notices, especially in view of the forthcoming *Tars and Spars;* such a press couldn't do much to enhance the prestige of the commissioned officer I was soon to become. Armed with Captain Reed-Hill's carte blanche, I approached Max Liebman, the director, about staging *Tars and Spars,* and intimated that it might be a good way for him, a civilian, to help the war effort. Max, whom I had met in 1939 at Camp Tamiment, where he discovered and nurtured Danny Kaye, seemed very much interested, and I arranged a meeting between him, Dorothy Gillam and Captain Reed-Hill, which resulted in his being hired for the job. I told Liebman that he'd find working on *Tars and Spars* rewarding, if only because of Seaman Second Class Sidney Caesar's presence in the cast. "And who may that be?" Liebman inquired somewhat skeptically. "Another Danny Kaye," I assured him. "Too many of those around," Liebman sighed. "Let's hope he'll be the one and only Sid Caesar."

This time I had no Balanchine or Doc Bender for traveling companion; I made the trip to Palm Beach with Tommy Dowling, a seaman second class, many-time ballroom-contest winner and a great rhumba specialist, whose "transfer" was our revue's gain and Brooklyn Barracks' loss, in an elegant Lincoln Continental convertible. The first sight that greeted my eyes on arriving at the resort was Caesar and Bert Kempe, clarinet-playing young Swede from Chicago, being propelled about in a luxurious sedan chair by an elderly white-clad Negro; they were smoking dollar cigars with a "tomorrow we die" look. That evening I delivered a preliminary "pep talk" to some three hundred Spars at the Biltmore Hotel and, with Lieutenant Gillam's help, began "recruiting" the revue's chorus. I rather enjoyed my role as a Coast Guard Earl Carroll, which consisted of visiting the Spars' "restricted" beach and "taking in" a few dozen of the prospects' legs, now that their owners, having shed their Molyneux-designed uniforms, looked like any other female beachcombers. Selecting the chorus was a tough job, as some of the prettier candidates were allergic to stage appearances, some of the hopelessly unattractive ones were, on the contrary, dying to get into the show. Max Liebman arrived and began a series of huddles with Caesar to determine whether the boy was all he was cracked up to be; doubtful at first, Liebman soon took Sid in hand and began coaching him and strengthening his material, including the "airplane pictures" skit. Gower Champion found a delectable young partner in the person of Coralee Burson (a California girl, who had had her innings at the Pasadena Playhouse) and was inventing new routines to George Bauer's accompaniments; Ted Gary started putting the finally selected chorus through their paces; Harry Blumenthal, an original member of the Borah Minnevitch gang, nearly swallowed his harmonica; Marc Ballero, a seasoned vaudeville impersonator, played practical jokes on gullible Gillam; the Coast Guard Invaders orchestra, which had seen action in both the Sicilian and African invasions aboard the U.S.S. *Samuel Chase,* invaded the snooty Patio for their rehearsals; Victor Mature, the Tarzan Tar, wore a splendid assortment of tailored uniforms, and signed countless autograph books; and Alajalov, the *New Yorker* cartoonist, painted scenery. It was a funny way to fight a war, but most of the people in *Tars and Spars* were professional theater folk — not professional soldiers.

Came the fateful day and I was sworn in in Miami, returning to Palm Beach in natty officer's grays, the entire cast of *Tars and Spars* saluting like mad, their mouths open in amazement. "Say, that isn't you, Duke?" Caesar gulped, and added quickly, "Beg pardon, sir." Everybody laughed, but I had the last laugh: "I can now tell your

Brooklyn C.O. where he gets off," I said. "I outrank him by a half stripe."

I mobilized all my "posh" Palm Beach friends and the Tars and Spars were entertained extensively. We did a lot of resounding drumbeating in the plushier villas and got pages of "free" newspaper space after suitable appeals to the editors' patriotism. The show opened at the Paramount Theatre, Palm Beach, on March 29th and was an instantaneous hit, Sid Caesar laying them in the aisles and grabbing the notices. Tom Dowling, originally a Walter Winchell discovery, shared dancing honors with Gower Champion and his Coralee and Bill Skipper. The house was packed and the proceeds went to the Coast Guard Welfare fund.

Dietz and I wrote some good things for *Tars and Spars* — "Arm in Arm," "You Gotta Have a Reason to Be a Civilian" and "Palm Beach" among them. After a successful Miami showing, I returned to New York and the Old Guard of Carnegie and Broadway, a Coast Guard success behind me. The felicitations of Admiral Waesche and Captain Reed-Hill on helping the men's "morale" did much to build up my own, sadly shaken by "civilian" failures.

There was a lot going on in New York. Daniel Saidenberg conducted my reorchestrated "Ballade" (now scored for piano solo, strings and timpani) with faithful Nicolas Kopeikine attending to the pianistics; Koussevitzky's twentieth year as conductor of the Boston Symphony was to be celebrated by a group of American composers with a testimonial dinner at the Hotel Plaza on May 16th; Stokowski again displayed keen interest in the *End of St. Petersburg* and offered to perform it at the New York City Center; Herman Levin wanted me for a musical version of *Berkeley Square* (another worthwhile idea that never materialized); and *Sadie Thompson* (formerly *Rain*) was in active preparation. Aaron Copland had made rapid strides as composer and organizer; there was no musical or musico-theatrical enterprise of which he wasn't president, vice president or, at least, chairman. He was, naturally, "in the chair" for the Koussevitzky dinner and helped arrange the musical program, gotten up by the entire Koussevitzky *"Wunderkindergarten."*

Stokowski went over *St. Petersburg* with me in great detail and asked me to suggest a good choral conductor. I thought of young Robert Shaw, whose Collegiate Chorale was making quite a splash and who had helped me with a patriotic chorus of mine, titled bombastically "Rhapsody in Red, White and Blue," in my "enlisted" days. I arranged a meeting between Stokowski and Shaw; a few days later the young man asked me to play the cantata for him. He sat in stern silence throughout my very unsatisfactory performance (I have difficulty with a vocal projection of a 32-bar refrain; here I had to be an orchestra, three soloists and a mixed chorus all at once) and left abruptly, "Kinda hard, isn't it?" his only comment. I haven't heard from either Shaw or Stokowski since this audition; the posters which formerly announced my *St. Petersburg* (renamed *Leningrad* to appease our new allies), heralded Robert Shaw in charge of the choral forces at the Center. My cantata was quietly shelved.

Those were the days of the Stalingrad struggle, and all Russians — ex-Russians like myself included — hoped for German defeat; the ex-Russians also hoping against hope that Hitler's destruction would in some miraculous way bring about the destruction of the other tyrant — Joseph Stalin. Most of us, especially those with some post-Revolutionary experience, knew how Utopian such wishful thinking was, but there existed another possibility, stemming from the new Russo-American friendship, which was based, of course, on our "all-out" help, without which the land of my birth would undeniably have been crushed. We all felt that with a closer *rapprochement* between the two countries, the Russians would eventually regain their freedom and a few of the civil liberties unheard of alike in Soviet Fairyland and Hitler's Aryan Playground. There were hopeful signs all over the country; Russo-American societies — cultural, literary and musical — sprang up overnight, and the "sympathizers" who had formerly sneered at anything made in U.S.A. found themselves riding high on what they imagined to be the Stalin-Roosevelt ticket. To stop my leftist detractors here and now, let me remind them that I was actively for Roosevelt myself — minus Stalin, whom the "liberals" pictured as a fellow Democrat. I was for Roosevelt because, with all his mistakes, I saw in him a great American and a great human being, who did more for our country's prestige in the Old World than any other public figure within memory.

Most of my evenings were spent with Dietz and Mamoulian; *Sadie Thompson* was entering rehearsal stage. Ethel Merman, who seemed to like the songs, was mastering them in her Central Park duplex, with Lew Kessler, her accompanist. Mamoulian, a fine director, had a rather pontifically highbrow, Moscow Arty approach to Maugham's immortal strumpet which I thought somewhat misplaced; also, he insisted on Reverend Davidson singing "opera style" à la Chaliapin, with which I disagreed, thinking that the hypocritical cleric would be best characterized as "songless," like the villainous whites in *Porgy and Bess*. Rouben, a determined, dark Armenian, was rated "tops" on Broadway, after *Oklahoma,* and I gave in, against my better judgment; as a result, Davidson's "arias," entrusted to big-voiced Lansing Hatfield, were synthetic as music and theatrically incongruous.

I wrote the rest of the score in Ocean Beach, Fire Island, where my "temporary reserve" status permitted me to don civvies — or, rather, swimming trunks again. Together with my monumental boxer, Petrushka, remarkable for his size and stupidity alike, I rented a "Westport-size" hut on the bay side; the little place had all the comforts, except a piano. While searching for one, I ran into Wolcott Gibbs; "Ma" Pastorfield, one of the island's original settlers, had told me on the sly that Mr. Gibbs had a piano which no one had been known to play and which was dodecaphonically out of tune — but an honest-to-goodness piano, notwithstanding. Without further ado I asked the morose critic whether he would please rent his instrument to me. "I *might* do that for you," Gibbs drawled pensively, "but then suppose I didn't like your score — I wouldn't be able to rap it since you wrote it on my piano. Perhaps I had better not." I eventually found a decent little upright rusting away in the back of the firehouse.

I spent a month on the island, composing in the morning, feeding Petrushka five or six times a day, and clamming and crabbing. Back in New York there were complications; La Merman didn't see eye-to-eye with Dietz on the lyrics, which were chic while she wanted them "sock." Each stood his ground; Ethel was finally ordered to sing the lyrics "as is" (she had them rewritten by anonymous helpers but, not permitted to use the new versions in the theater, would say "number over" rather than sing the original lyrics) and, refusing to do so, quit after a week. She was replaced by June Havoc, an excellent actress, but hardly a singer. "I have four notes to my voice, all of them bad," she was fond of saying. Three of Merman's numbers had to be dropped as they were way out of June's range. Eddie Caton, hired to stage the dances after we had viewed and liked his *Sebastian* ballet, to a pretty score by Gian-Carlo Menotti, had his troubles, too; the son of Czar Nicholas II's favorite jockey, he was the only native-born American I ever met who spoke English with a strong Russian accent and started every sentence with, "Noo, noo, boys . . ." His ballet people were supposed to represent South Sea Islanders and many of them were beefing about jumping around in the nude in the cold theater.

We opened in Philadelphia and it was hard to say whether the show was "in," or "nowhere." I would say it was dangling perilously over a precipice; the book was excellent, the staging uneven to a degree, the casting ditto and the music, bereft of the Merman bombshell specials, good in spots and much too heavy in others. We did good business the first week at the Forrest, and took quite a dive the second, yet succeeded in bringing a pretty respectable *Sadie* into the Alvin. The comments in the intermission were mostly of the "Had a nice summer, kid?" persuasion, so it looked as if we had a fair chance. There was a party at Gypsy Rose Lee's after the opening, at which I promptly fainted from exhaustion and was taken home by two Polynesians from Canarsie. At nine the next morning I was awakened by a girl I then liked (who was responsible for Petrushka's death, having "borrowed" the dog and taken him to Mexico, where he was run over by a car), and she proceeded to read the *Tribune* notice — which was good — over the telephone. A half hour later she telephoned again to read the *Times's,* which was bad. "Thank you. Now leave me alone, please," I mumbled, the reading over, and had my first taste of a minor nervous breakdown. This calamity lasted three or four days and the doctor wouldn't let me read the notices, which I found, on my recovery, to be mixed, with a capital "M." The show could be diagnosed as a mild success or a flop *d'estime;* it turned out to be the latter.

Thanks to Sid Kornheiser, the head of Paramount Music, which published the score, "The Love I Long For" got recorded by Henry James and promptly shot up to No. 2 on the record bestsellers' list, where it remained for several months, making me $9000 richer.

My destitute alter ego, Dukelsky, came in mighty handy at times. Sick of my theatrical ups and downs I persuaded mellow-voiced Rose Dirman, whom I had heard in Benjamin Britten's "Illuminations" at the Saidenberg concert, where my "Ballade" was played, to give two concerts of Unfamiliar Music — my old obsession, which found its ultimate fruition in the Society for Forgotten Music I founded in Paris three years later. Miss Dirman, one of our best oratorio singers, was agreeable and after two months' research we announced two really corking programs. The concerts were given at the tiny Times Hall, next to Sardi's, boasted several "first performances" of seventeenth- and eighteenth-century music, drew small crowds and very good notices by all the first-string men, including Olin Downes and Oscar Thompson, who had never set foot in the "out of the way" Times Hall before. We financed the two recitals ourselves and lost every penny—but it was money well lost.

Around Christmas *Tars and Spars,* a popular success everywhere, was sold to Columbia Pictures for $50,000, with the help of Milton Bren, Hollywood producer and lieutenant commander in the Los Angeles Public Relations Division, USCG.

My last chore for the U.S. Coast Guard was a trip to Hollywood in the early spring of 1945, at so much per diem; I was to keep an eye on the filming of *Tars and Spars.* But whether I kept an open ear too was supremely unimportant to the enterprising Mr. Bren, who had Sammy Cahn and Julie Stein, then just starting to make a noise on the West Coast, to write a brand new score. The picture turned out to be a Class C musical, chiefly notable for misusing Alfred Drake's great talents and relying on Sid's venerable "airplane pictures" bit for the grand climax. There was no connection whatever between our fresh and uninhibited little revue and Bren's flat-footed essay in musical flagwaving.

There were several compensations in California. I rejoiced in a reunion with Alex and his Mona, happily established in a small Neutra house in Westwood—just two houses above my present dwelling. I argued with swarthy Gottfried Reinhardt, his pixieish Sylvia and genial Sam Hoffenstein over their *Nantucket* book and the score, with Rome's wisecracking lyrics, I had brought along. There were merry outings in the Hollywood Hills with Moka, the Reinhardt's black poodle, dinners with Ira and Lee Gershwin and drinks with Herb Spencer and Eddie Powell, Goldwyn alumni both, now toiling for Twentieth Century-Fox. Whatever this, my last Coast Guard mission accomplished, I was promoted to lieutenant commander and "mustered out" shortly afterwards.

CHAPTER XVIII

PARIS INTERLUDE

THIS is getting to be a big book. Whatever it's worth, the reader could never say: "No man went down to posterity with a smaller volume under his arm," which is what Dickens said of Thomas Gray. Come to think of it, I have never been ambitious enough to write or compose for "posterity" — judging from the gigantic mass of forgotten worthwhile music and literature I have studied, the less you depend on your survivors or their descendants, the better off you are. No, writing music for the man who is still walking this earth is enough for a task for me. There is a righteous, hats-off-don't-you-know-who-I-am quality about composers' autobiographies (Stravinsky's, for one) that glosses over or skips ingenuously all that was not sublime, not godlike, in their lives. I have not hidden my frivolity, my ephemeral anecdotes — hardly germane to the lofty subject of my Musical Self — my preoccupation with *flânerie,* food or clothes. The world may find me, under my own hand, "a weaker man than perhaps I may have passed for, even among my enemies." Thus Colley Cibber in his endearing and unpretentious *Apology*. "With all my heart! My enemies will then read me with pleasure, and you, perhaps with envy, when you find that follies, without the reproach of guilt upon them, are not inconsistent with happiness. But why make my follies publick? Why not? I have passed my time very pleasantly with them, and I don't recollect that they have ever been hurtful to any other man living." Amen.

The past ten years of my life — since my "demobilization" — can be roughly divided into three distinct phases: a) the New York post-bellum phase (1945–1947); b) the European reinvasion (1947–1949), during which I made three trips to Europe — mostly Paris, remaining there nearly the whole of 1947; and c) "Farewell to New York" (the title of a song I wrote on the Super Chief) and settling in West Los Angeles, where I am now making my new and, I hope, my last home (from 1951 on).

On my return from Hollywood, I resumed scoring the cello concerto for Piatigorsky (the work itself was begun in 1942). We played the concerto for Koussevitzky, who immediately called it the "best contemporary concerto" for the instrument — Sergei Alexandrovitch often lavished adjectives like "best" or "greatest" on a new work, but his enthusiasms were not always of the enduring kind — and accepted it for performances in both Boston and New York in the 1945–1946 season. "My dear Dima," he added, affection and sadness in his voice, "you must write a symphony to Natasha's memory; she loved you and fought for you — and now that we have the Koussevitzky Foundation, what could be more fitting than your composing your third symphony for us? Eh, Grischa?" The good Grischa nodded emphatically and, deeply grateful to both men, I resolved to surpass myself in the new work. That spring Dorothy Kirsten recorded both "April in Paris" and "The Love I Long For" for Victor. Carl Van Vechten asked for a manuscript from my pen for the George Gershwin Memorial Collection at Fisk University — Carl was among *Cabin's* biggest boosters. Harold Rome and I put the finishing touches on *Nantucket.* However, when the final version of the Gottfried Reinhardt book arrived in New York, we both thought it overwritten and heavy-handed; Gottfried, in turn, disapproved of some of the songs, and this disagreement, coupled with an ill-fated production of a monstrosity regrettably styled *The Girl from Nantucket,* brought about the last "finishing touch" — the project was abandoned by mutual consent.

In the early summer I met Ogden Nash, whom I had seen briefly in 1935, at the time he wrote a sketch for the *Follies* and came to Philadelphia from Baltimore where he lived, shy and bewildered and immediately endearing. We've been friends and collaborators (with very little encouragement from Lady Luck) for ten years now and I still think Ogden the finest human being I was ever privileged to know and the freshest lyrical talent in this country since the death of the one-and-only Lorenz Hart. An old hand at the Gentle Art of Making Enemies, I can only marvel at the fact that Ogden hasn't a single enemy in the world; there *are* a good many people *he* doesn't like but I've never met a man who doesn't like *him.*

I have a few treasured Ogden Nash items in my library, which, while not rich in first editions (I love the contents of a book, not the date of its publication), is filled with out-of-the-way volumes — French romantics illustrated by Grandville, Gavarni, Daumier and Tony Johannot, obscure poetic anthologies and books on music and the theater that are not easy to find. I wouldn't part with my Nash items for any sum, because they are all "association" and inscribed copies — and the inscriptions are mostly in verse not included in the Bard's collected works. The future Nash bibliographer will thank me for reprinting these inscriptions here, a joy I am unable to resist. The first, on a copy of *The Face Is Familiar* is:

> Like Kostelanetz
>   and lesser planets
> I am learnon
>   fast from Vernon.

This was written in the summer of 1945, after the get-together, which resulted in "Born Too Late," the first song we wrote together (still unused). At the end of the summer, Ogden inscribed his *Many Long Years Ago* optimistically and much too flatteringly:

> *So it goes, or, All for the Best*
>
> Christ got a gospel by St. Luke
> I got a score by Vernon Duke.

In view of subsequent unhappy events, a score by Duke proved more of a curse than a blessing, but we were neither of us prophets — and a year later, Ogden took a nice, clean copy of the 1936 *The Bad Parents' Garden of Verse* from his mildewed shelves, and wrote on its flyleaf:

> For Vernon — The most valuable tome in his
>   bookish garrison!
> It makes the rest of his tomes look so good
>   by comparison.

This was signed: "Ogden A.D. 1946, A.S.B. and B.2." For the uninitiated — the latter meant Anno *Sweet Bye and Bye* 2, as our first show was still unproduced; true, it should never have been produced, but we could hope, couldn't we? Three years later came the telltale post-mortem — in view of the sadness of the occasion, poetry was dispensed with: "To Vernon — in deep appreciation of his interludes of patience during our three years of pushing water up hill. Ogden 2/23/49." All I can say, to return the compliment, is:

I hope that soon the fashian
Will be for lyrics Ogden Nashian.

That summer of 1945, having put my Coast Guard uniform in mothballs, I betook myself to Nantucket, which is not unlike Fire Island, except that it has a history, a lot more trees and plenty of atmosphere. The only atmosphere I ever detected in Ocean Beach, Fire Island, was that provided by Polly Adler, who descended on the place one fine morning in search of a Home that was Not a House. The score I wrote with Harold Rome was put together *before* my visit to Nantucket, but I was soon able to ascertain that Harold wrote about the place as if he were born there — the dunes and the whalers' ghosts were there intact, just as we had rhapsodized them in our songs. With my old talent for discovering homes that resembled not so much houses as outhouses, I found a three-room job with an ancient fireplace, a bed that might have been large enough for a whaler's apprentice but that accommodated me with some difficulty — thus condemning me to chastity, as it was decidedly impractical as a *champ de bataille* — and, best of all, a small, private beach. Ogden took his family, consisting of his beautiful wife, Frances, a Baltimore belle with all the magic of a Scott Fitzgerald heroine as well as far too much intelligence for one so lovely, and two leggy daughters of the extra-awkward age, given to shrieks, whisperings and incessant beach outings. Linel, the older, was the more sedate of the two, married very young and soon made Ogden the happiest of grandfathers; Isabel, an elfin, unpredictable girl, inherited her father's poetic gifts; some of her poems, which Ogden was dishonest enough to steal and read to me, were really very good. She easily outdid papa in the realm of imagination: when *Mademoiselle* printed one of her earlier efforts, Isabel calmly informed the editor that she was born in Paris. When Ogden took her to task, asking her sternly: "Why did you say that, when you know perfectly well you were born right here in Baltimore?" Isabel replied, unabashed: "That's what you say, Father. I may very well have been born in Paris, for all we know."

We were working on *Sweet Bye and Bye,* which had a cockeyed and wildly phantasmagorial libretto by my erstwhile collaborator S. J. Perelman and his new writing partner, the bearded and amiable Al Hirshfeld, previously known principally as an observant and sharp-witted caricaturist. I promised earlier not to dwell on what makes a flop a flop, so I'll give this one — the noisiest and floppiest of them all — the lightest possible treatment, which is easy to do after nine years, "S. B. and B." having been produced late in 1946. In all fairness to my collaborators, their book seemed excruciatingly funny when read — particularly when read by that master of deadpan nonsense, S.J. himself. Transplanted to the theater, all the fun evaporated mysteriously, perhaps because the book dealt with the Time Capsule, lowered into the Long Island ground at the World's Fair and, owing to a catastrophic flood, floating back to the surface two hundred years later, or much too soon for our descendants' comfort. Following the horrors of the war and the atomic bomb nobody was in the mood to look ahead, the prospects being as bleak as they were — and are. The postwar audiences were like so many ostriches, burying their heads in the fine sand of everyday domesticity regained once more — and this all-too-obvious psychological reaction on the part of people returned to peace we neglected entirely — with disastrous results.

Once the money ($200,000) had been painfully assembled, we began auditioning producers, which had the charm of novelty after the tedium of backers' auditions and wasn't as heartbreaking as auditioning actors. The man we entrusted with our show was Nat Karson, better known as set designer than producer. The cast was headed by Dolores Gray, one of the most gifted young women on the musical stage, who went straight into the English production of *Annie Get Your Gun* after our turkey and covered herself with glory.

While "S. B. and B." was in "active preparation," I gave the balance of my energy to completing the symphony and making last-minute changes in the Cello Concerto, which Piatigorsky was scheduled to play in Boston under Koussevitzky's baton on January 4 and 5, 1946. This concerto proved somewhat more accessible to the public than the first two and got many more performances. Its Boston *première* was, again, auspicious and reasonably successful; the New York performance, typically, less so, although the work had a better reception there than had the Violin Concerto under Rodzinski.

Piatigorsky liked my piece well enough to take it to Montreal, where the orchestra was temporarily presided over by Vladimir Golschmann of Paris and St. Louis. Grischa had a resounding success with the concerto in Montreal, but I suspect that he would have created an even greater sensation had he played a set of virtuoso variations on "Chopsticks"; the representative music lovers of the town, whom I met at supper afterwards, were all politely noncommittal about my work. The critics the next morning, while praising Grischa to the skies, tore me to bits.

In the early spring I wrote Koussevitzky, advising him of the completion of the Third Symphony and my desire to play it for him — as it was *his* piece, written in Natalya Konstantinovna's memory at *his* instigation. The Koussevitzky household, now in Brookline, was run by Olga Naumoff, his late wife's niece, a pale, ascetic-looking girl, whose tact and *savoir-faire* were of great help to the conductor; Olga had been his secretary for many years, and we composers were in the habit of arranging for appointments and auditions through the sweet-voiced, self-effacing *"secretarotchka,"* as I called her. The name stuck, and many of Miss Naumoff's letters to me were signed with it. The other new member of the widower's ménage was Mme. Henrietta Hirschman, who once kept a celebrated "salon" in Moscow, was noted for her great beauty and painted by the better *portraitistes* of her day. After the war, my friendship with Olga cooled perceptibly, perhaps owing to my loud denunciations of some of the members of the All-American *Wunderkindergarten* (they were *Kinder* no longer), whom the *"secretarotchka"* favored. But I was not prepared for the marked coldness with which I was greeted on my arrival in Brookline with talented young Lukas Foss, who had kindly offered to help "project" my symphony piano-duet fashion. Miss Naumoff bid us enter, and vanished almost immediately, leaving us in the drawing room with Mme. Hirschman. Sergei Alexandrovitch soon appeared, looking tired and cross, and said quickly: "This is a bad time to play new music for me, Dima; the season is almost over and I am very tired. Besides, I must tell you at once, that I will be unable to conduct your symphony, even should I like it, next season. 'We' already have Arosha's (Aaron Copland) Third, which 'we' commissioned." I was completely taken aback. "But I thought mine too was commissioned, Sergei Alexandrovitch," I said in astonishment. Koussevitzky gave an impatient shrug. "I don't know what made you think that. *You* offered to write a symphony dedicated to Natasha's memory — but it was *not* a commission; commissions are decided upon by our board. However — now that you're here — play the symphony for me. I warn you, I'm not in a receptive mood today." Never before had I played for Koussevitzky in so unpromising an *ambiance*; but I had made my Boston trip for the sole purpose of delivering what I thought a commissioned work, and was determined to accomplish my mission. After the first movement, the conductor's face was a mask; he warmed up somewhat after the second and actually permitted himself a flicker of a smile after the finale. "I don't understand the first movement at all," Koussevitzky said. "There are some good things in the funeral march blended with the scherzo in the second — and the *coda* of the finale is the best music in the symphony. Believe me, I appreciate the allusion to dear Natasha [there was a hymnlike, religious resignation in the apotheosis] and I want to thank you for the dedication. Come here." To my surprise, Koussevitzky embraced me, kissed me on the forehead and shed a tear. "But I cannot perform your score. . . . Maybe later," he concluded uncertainly.

On March 15th I received a cable from Moscow reading: "Thanks for very interesting letters stop please send scores letter follows greetings. Prokofiev." I sent Serge the two concertos and an orchestra score of *Entr'acte,* the receipt of which he acknowledged in a strange letter written in three languages — French, English and German words artfully mixed, so as to baffle the censor, most likely. This significant document was displayed to a group of musical friends in New York, after which it mysteriously vanished; I only hope it didn't fall into the hands of Prokofiev's all-powerful enemies, who were already at work, busily undermining the composer — Assafiev and Khrennikov (whose symphony was introduced by Stokowski in this country) chief among them. I never heard from Serge again.

Sweet Bye and Bye opened in New Haven on October 10th and played the usual crowded three days, bedlam reigning on both sides of the orchestra pit. Our leading man, Gene Sheldon, a renowned vaudeville mimic, was utterly lost in the wilderness of the musical-comedy stage and had to be replaced after the New Haven engagement. Dolores Gray was a tower of strength and stopped the proceedings with "Roundabout" and "Just Like a Man," transplanted into Bette Davis's *Two's Company* six years later. But even valiant Dolores couldn't carry the whole show on her back, especially a show as incurably sick as ours was. The real nightmare began in Philadelphia, our next stop. Will I ever forget the ten mad hours in Sid Perelman's suite at the Warwick, in the course of which we telephoned every available and unavailable juvenile in New York, Hollywood and, if I remember right, Australia? Sheldon was eventually replaced by Eric Rhodes, a capable character actor, but hardly a musical-comedy lead. The entire structure began crumbling with the dress rehearsal at the Forrest, to which the critics had to be invited as our opening coincided with the *première* of an important straight play. It was strongly rumored that the local orchestra contractor, who angled for the job in New York and didn't get it, incited the pit musicians to revolt; in spite of the conductor's frantic admonitions, the "boys" drowned out the singers, played "clinkers" continually and ended each number with an ear-splitting discord. For the second week of its "engagement" our show was moved to the Erlanger, probably the most sinister theater in the world, situated in a street chiefly noted for cheap furniture stores. The inside of the Erlanger looked like a furniture store too — I never saw so many empty chairs in my life.

This was my fifth failure in a row and I began thinking seriously of branching out as teacher, gave two lectures on orchestration at Juilliard and even took on three composition pupils; I soon found that I had no pedagogical ability in my make-up. The Cello Concerto was behind me, the new symphony orchestrated and about to be delivered to Koussevitzky, who was in no hurry. "Where do we go from here, little man?" I asked myself. The answer came from the most unexpected quarter. A few months before the *Sweet Bye and Bye* disaster, I had had the unforeseen thrill of piloting Boris Kochno and Christian Bérard through Manhattan; they had come to the States as semiofficial cultural ambassadors with France's "Théâtre de la Mode," a lush exhibit of French fashion and theater, the first of that country's artistic manifestations since the Liberation. I took

Boris and Bébé to all the shows, introduced them to the *cuisine régionale,* with strange dishes like oyster stew and fried chicken, and even gave them a taste of Harlem, a place long past its Golden Era. Boris was back in the ballet fold, having just started Les Ballets des Champs Elysées with youthful and precocious Roland Petit; he had also retained his early love for American jazz. He listened to some of mine, his eyes shining, then got up abruptly. "Dima, it's over twenty years since Diaghilev gave you your start in Paris," he said. "I may be able to give you a fresh start today — now that Paris is herself again. I want a new ballet score from you." I was about to sail into my 1938 *Entr'acte* and suggest that Balanchine create the choreography, when Boris stopped me with an indulgent smile. "No, that's not what I want; I need a jazz ballet — one by Duke, not Dukelsky," he explained. "In fact, I already have the scenario — all you have to do is set it to music. The story is very simple: it concerns a street musician who passes a laundry, playing a clarinet. He is followed by a young errand boy, who forgets all about his errands while listening to the clarinet player. The washerwomen, also entranced by the music, abandon their work. They become sentimental and imagine themselves in love with the errand boy, but he spurns them all — except one, and she joins him in a dance. Finally, the washerwomen surround the couple and improvise their own Washerwomen's Ball. That's all there is to it." I liked the typically Kochnoesque "argument" and set to work with joy: *Le Bal des Blanchisseuses,* certainly the most successful of my three stage ballets, was completed in three weeks.

The piano score was dispatched to Boris in Paris at about the time when we were still auditioning producers for *Sweet Bye and Bye.* I soon received ecstatic cables from Kochno and Roland Petit, who were very happy with the music. *The Washerwomen's Ball* was produced, staged, costumed, and rehearsed without its composer's assistance — and yet clicked everywhere; I began to think that maybe I had better stay away from my shows too and they would then have a bigger chance of success.

On November 18th Lennie Bernstein conducted my "Ode to the Milky Way" at the New York City Center; the first half of the concert was an all-American program of music composed by "veterans" of World War II, and included works by Samuel Barber, Alex North and John Lessard. My "Ode" had existed in a piano sketch for about three years and was orchestrated shortly after my discharge from the Coast Guard. I had this to say for the program notes: "The Ode can perhaps be described as a kind of musical monologue — the unspoken thoughts and yearnings of a man stretched out on the deck of a transport and looking up at the Milky Way." The "transport" I referred to was, in reality, the United Fruit Line passenger ship on which I cruised the West Indies — but this was a "veterans'" concert and the transport sounded more "apropos." I was always partial to my "Ode," which has a truly "celestial," Hayden Planetarium kind of sound, but I didn't think the public would like it; wrapped in most uncelestial gloom, following the *Sweet Bye and Bye* catastrophe, I sat through my piece, admirably conducted by Lennie, expecting nothing, when at its conclusion applause came thick and fast, sounding sweet to my unbelieving ears. The critics, instead of administering the customary shellacking, sang soothing choruses of praise and thought it "the best, by far, of the new works on the program."

I had dedicated my "Ode" to Olga Naumoff, in view of her habitual kindness to me in former years and, perhaps, to regain her friendship; I was hurt by her disappearance at the time of the unproductive Boston audition of the symphony. Two days after the Bernstein concert I wrote Koussevitzky: "Lennie introduced my 'Ode to the Milky Way' at City Center. This is the piece dedicated to Olga and which I hope she will be interested in hearing one day. . . . I am elated at the emphatic success this music has scored. My third symphony, which you heard last spring in a piano duet version, is now ready. You were very hesitant about performing the work this year, owing to so many previous commitments; do you want me to send you the score, or would you rather wait until next spring, when you'll have more time on your hands?" On December 7th Koussevitzky wired me: "Many thanks for your letter delighted to hear from you and of your Ode success. Hoping to see you before long." I never had the slightest acknowledgment of the dedication from Olga — it was later hinted by a mutual friend that I should, perhaps, have asked the lady for a *permission* to dedicate the work to her, rather in the fashion of Sir Arthur Sullivan securing such a permission from Queen Victoria prior to dedicating his *Ivanhoe* to her. It was not until much later that I learned that Sergei Alexandrovitch and Olga were *present* at Lennie's concert but for reasons best known to themselves (probably disliking the work and being too polite to admit it) failed to give me a sign of life; which would have been easy to do, since I spent fully ten minutes in Lennie's dressing room. My star, after the "best contemporary cello concerto," was evidently in decline again with Koussevitzky.

The pleasant reception of the ten-minute "Ode" was not enough to atone for the severe shock caused by the *Sweet Bye and Bye* calamity. New York is but a small town, compared to Paris or London, where theatrical or musical activities are spread out over a vast area; there's a lot of music going on in Chelsea, and in Bloomsbury, that Albert Hall never hears; there are good shows being tried out in Montparnasse that will never see the boulevards — and there is a public for them all. Not so in New York: if you're a musician, better display your prowess in Carnegie or Town Hall, if a Broadway composer or playwright, where can you function except in Times Square and its immediate vicinity? The gathering places of creative folk are all located in a small area between West Forty-second and West Fifty-seventh Streets. You can, of course, hide in Park Avenue or Greenwich Village, but the first is dull and the second mad; what's more, they too live by the Broadway barometer and the inhabitants rate you accordingly.

I took a few tentative steps to rehabilitate myself, such as playing the Third Symphony for Fritz Reiner, Pierre Monteux, Stokowski and Golschmann; sent it to Rodzinski, Defauw, Mitropoulos and Ormandy. The first three promised performances; these promises are yet to be fulfilled. Rodzinski and Defauw wrote, promising nothing; Mitropoulos and Ormandy didn't write. Golschmann conducted the "Ode to the Milky Way" in St. Louis at Christmas, and the notices were even better than the New York ones. The "break" came with a letter from Boris Kochno, in which he said: "Read and rejoice! On December 19th we gave the *première* of your ballet at the Théâtre des Champs Elysées. The success was *enormous,* the audience brilliant, the press rapturous. It is a spectacle of rare beauty and, notwithstanding its novelty and a certain strangeness — friends and non-friends both adore our 'Bal.' During the last performances we were *forced* to repeat the *coda* of the Finale. This may give you a vague idea of the noise made by the Paris public. I spoke of you and your music often on the radio. To sum up — 'Le Bal des Blanchisseuses' is a theatrical event of first magnitude. You can imagine how happy it all makes me; I'm happy for you and happy for myself, as we were not lacking in 'doubting Thomases' before the opening. George Auric sends you his congratulations."

This hide-saving letter was handed me by Vertès, the fashionable painter, at a New Year's party given by Tatiana and Alex Liberman for their *Vogue* associates and *Vogue*-sponsored friends. Vertès had arrived from Paris by plane that afternoon and his entrance with the Stanislao Lepri decorated program of my *Blanchisseuses* in hand sent my stock up at once, and even Salvador Dali's blacker than ever mustache began to bristle in honor of my success 3000 miles away. Vertès reported in *Vogue:* "The newest ballet hit is 'Les Blanchisseuses,' a bubbling affair. Against Lepri's fresh clothesline décor of patches, of chalk white and deep green with the sharp twist of Lautrec, Roland Petit gives one of his best performances to the lovely, careless, beaten jazz lilt of Vernon Duke's music." "Home is where the hit is," I thought. Paris to the rescue again — was my New Year's resolution.

In an effort to clear up the status of my symphony, which I still hoped would achieve the "commissioned" rank (like its composer in his Coast Guard days), I wrote Koussevitzky, whose last wire, already cited, had a friendly ring to it. His answer hurt me to the quick and precipitated my European trip: "It's rather difficult to answer your letter," he wrote, "as the basic principle of the Koussevitzky Music Foundation is, obviously, not clear to you. This fund was formed on a purely artistic basis, not on family — or friendly considerations; to encourage beginners and young composers in need of moral and material support, also to bestow prizes on *recognized masters* and *composers of renown.* Decisions are made at special meetings by our five directors. A commission to this or that composer is arrived at by mutual agreement. Your dedication of the symphony to Natalya Konstantinovna's memory was very touching — but it was *your own* initiative and the expression of your own personal feeling; our Fund did *not* commission your piece and, consequently, it is not on our list. From that list you can judge, that the majority of the composers did not know Natalya Konstantinovna, while a close friend, such as [Arthur] Lourié, is not included." In going over the foundation's list I found that the first four men given grants were Samuel Barber, Nicolai Berezowsky, Benjamin Britten and Bohuslav Martinu; the first two were hardly in need of "material" support, and none, with the possible exception of Martinu, could exactly qualify as "recognized masters" in 1942, when the awards were made. To the growing list of "commissioned" composers six former Russian nationals were gradually added: Stravinsky, Lopatnikov, Haieff, Nabokov, Arthur Lourié and Alexander Tcherepnin — one "recognized master," four men older than myself and one "beginner," Haieff. No further elucidations were necessary.

This time I was stopped on all fronts and I knew it. There was no use "plugging" my unwanted symphony turned down by the man who had asked me to write it, and who had been my benefactor for twenty years. There was no use angling for another Broadway show — it would take producers many months to forget the last, the only redeeming feature of which was that it never got to Broadway. Ogden and I wrote and published a quasi-children's book called *Musical Zoo* — it didn't sell, perhaps because children are smart and have little use for anything "quasi." Yet, on the other side of the Atlantic, there was a composer "people talked about" in all three *Vogues;* a composer whose music French papers called "scintillating," "full of verve and *entrain,*" "diabolically entrancing," "laden with dynamite," "chockful of melody — melancholy and humorous by turn," and "extraordinarily attractive"; a composer who was a lion in the salons — an invisible lion, it's true. Rapidly ascertaining the state of my finances and finding it fairly satisfactory, thanks to ASCAP and an ever-growing batch of recordings, I booked passage on the S.S. *America* and secured a fine green traveling passport — my first American passport to Paris. Ogden Nash's bon voyage wire read: "Ah, April in Paris! Not my kingdom for a horse but my dukedom for a horse chestnut."

I stayed at a well-run, fairly expensive establishment in Place François Ier; one look at the mustachioed concierge and the slow-moving, old-fashioned *ascenseur* — which is *not* our American elevator, nor yet the English lift, but which serves the same purpose — and I felt thoroughly at home and younger by fifteen years. I ordered a *quart de Vichy,* exchanged Parisian pleasantries with the waiter, took a bath in the yellowish oddly shaped tub, wrapped myself in the rough white bathrobe French hotels supply their guests with instead of a bath towel, sniffed the Paris air — there it was, lilacs and gasoline, same as ever — and began telephoning all my friends — twenty or thirty of them. Most of them still had the same telephone numbers, lived in the same flats, and seemed to think it perfectly natural that I should be in Paris after so many American years. *"Dima, quel bonheur,"* I heard Poulenc's nasal and attractively lazy voice. "Aren't you happy to be in Paris again — in *our* Paris?" *"Mon cher Dukelsky,* what a delicious surprise," murmured Henri Sauguet and sang a passage from *Blanchisseuses* into the telephone. *"C'est bien beau."* "Ah, Verr-non!" exclaimed angelic Claude Alphand, with whom I had made music in New York, and without whose guitar and wistful voice no party was complete in that city, where she sang at the Blue Angel. "How lucky that you should be telephoning me; I've asked a few friends to supper — do come, it will be so good to see you." Decidedly, these geographical changes of scene were as beneficial to me as musical ones; I was alive and gay again just because I heard friendly welcoming voices, because I had a successful ballet on the boards, because I was *in* Paris and *of* Paris once more. On the way to the Alphands (her husband, Hervé, the ambassador, courageously broke with the Vichy regime while in Washington in wartime, was deprived of his "terres" by Pétain, and flew to join de Gaulle in London) I watched the Paris street scene as if in a happy dream: the blue-clad working man downing *une limonade panachée* (a strange blend of beer and lemonade) at the corner bar; the sallow-faced little brunette pedaling energetically on her bicycle, a *sac* of groceries, including a gray-colored loaf of bread — white bread was still unobtainable in 1947 — and a bouquet of wild flowers strapped on to the vehicle; the wildly swerving, rickety taxicabs; newsboys screaming: "Demandez le *Paris Soir!";* and groups of excitedly chattering *petites mains* crossing the street expertly to catch the Métro home to partake of the family soup. I entered a *bistro du quartier* and ordered coffee. *"Du national?"* the *garçon* asked with a peculiar inflexion, after a good look at my "foreign" clothes. I didn't know what "national" coffee was until it was brought to my table, the fumes nearly choking me. It tasted like indelible ink flavored with kerosene. I counteracted its effects with a double "calvados" and hurried to the rue du Faubourg St. Honoré, where the Alphands lived.

I was late at the Alphands' and entered on tiptoe, for music was being played. It's pleasant to walk into a drawing room and see a duchess playing Poulenc instead of canasta. Claude, looking like an Andrea del Sarto *religieuse* modernized by Christian Dior sang "Les

Filles de St. Malo," an old Breton song I have always loved. I saw Lady Diana Manners in the corner listening rapturously; Elizabeth Chavchavadze, George's wife, of epic proportions and one of the new Tout Paris hostesses; Madame Renaud, Claude's devoted mother, whom I always called *"chère femme compositeur"* (her songs, tender and sensitive, were published at the break of the century) while she addressed me as *"mon génie";* Hervé, who, were he not one of France's better diplomats, could make a fortune as the world's greatest and cruelest impersonator; Francis Poulenc, grown handsomer with the years; and Marie-Blanche de Polignac, her hair snow white, her face still young and haughtily lovely. I ran up to embrace Claude, who was catching her breath before tackling the ever-delicious "Nous avons fait un beau voyage," from Reynaldo Hahn's *Ciboulette,* a duet, in which La Belle Alphand was expertly seconded by her mother's energetic baritone. I was received with "oh's," "ah's" and kisses on all sides, some comments on my excessive girth (I was off my diet again and ready to plunge into gastronomic excesses, without which there is no sense in returning to Paris) and my first postwar snub, which came, inexplicably, from Marie-Blanche. As I bowed to kiss her hand, and uttered warm words to express my delight at seeing my 1936 *protectrice* again, the priestess of the Nadia Boulanger and Lanvin cults gave me a lemon-freeze look, and when I asked whether she remembered the music we had made together, replied: "Peut-être . . ." in a faraway voice. I heard later that Sauguet had seen an opened piano score of my *Blanchisseuses* on Marie-Blanche's piano; it must have been sneaked in while Nadia wasn't looking.

The next day I walked all the way to Avenue Emile Deschanel, where Fatima-Hanoum Samoilenko still lived. Paris was mercifully spared by the bombs and looked completely unchanged; once again, I was the Dukelsky of Diaghilev days. Facts and dates were of no consequence; death itself might have been a man-invented farce, "voluntary" imprisonment in Soviet Russia an implausible phantasy. I had an odd feeling that both Serges — Diaghilev and Prokofiev — were here in Paris, as immortal, as real as the city herself. There were a few slight changes in the place, mostly for the better: the girls were better-looking and had sturdier, shapelier legs — a result of the new vogue for *les sports* and bicycling during the occupation; the *"flics"* were all young, slim and athletically built, most of them youths with fine Résistance records; Paris was even more virtuous than before with the closing of the brothels; the concierges seemed friendlier and the taxi drivers cleaner, although they still shook their heads disdainfully if your place of destination was not in the direction of their home or their *bistro.* The book hunting was still in full flower on the *quais,* the fishermen still fished for nonexistent fish, and the Paris dogs still made with the charm and seldom talked back to their owners, although they didn't always agree with them. On the way to Fatima-Hanoum's, I saw an old *bourgeoise* walking an ugly fat mongrel on a leash; the animal, under the influence of the fine spring day, made passes at every dog he met en route. The *bourgeoise,* bored by her pet's excessive amorousness, gave his leash a powerful yank and addressed him in a loud voice: "Had enough, *hein?* Are you going to walk on, like a good boy, or are you still tormented with sex?"

My heart beat loudly as I approached the *carrefour,* after walking the entire length of Avenue Rapp; the *tabac du coin* was still there and this . . . this must be Fatima's own little garden, her prize possession. In a minute we were clinging to each other wildly, laughing and crying at intervals; Fatima-Hanoum led me into her once-celebrated salon, which, like all other similar historical landmarks, was left untouched after Boris Samoilenko's death. The dining room had become Fatima-Hanoum's workshop, where she created the loveliest hats in Paris; besides the hats, finished and unfinished, luxurious and modest, but all imbued with that special "made in Paris" magic, the workshop was inhabited by a large charcoal-gray Persian cat — the famous Babass, a personage of primary importance. As well as winning Fatima's approbation, every visitor had to meet Babass's rigid standards before becoming a Samoilenko habitué. "Come, Dook, come," said Fatima, after introducing me to Babass — she never called me anything but Dook. "Do you remember this room?" Did I! Every armchair, every ashtray were familiar to me and unchanged since 1929, when I had last sat in Fatima's salon prior to returning to the States. Here were the photographs: Prokofiev in a characteristic pose, lips bulging impudently; there another, taken of a bust of Gleb Derujinsky, the Russian sculptor; a faded one of Boris Samoilenko himself, smiling jovially; there the famous portrait of Fatima-Hanoum by Shukhaiev, one of the former Samoilenko "regulars"; some orange-brown crayon sketches by Jacovlev, another "regular." I felt absurdly, defiantly young in Fatima-Hanoum's salon that afternoon — perhaps by contrast with the "vanished pomps of yesterday" that surrounded me. It was essential not to give in to the bittersweet all-pervading nostalgia of the place, and so, to counteract its effects, I produced my humble presents; the treasured "international" coffee (not the "national" Laval poison), tinned edibles, stockings and such. Since my last meal with Mother and my last outing to Macy's with Prokofiev, I have not had so rich, so humanly warm, a day in my life.

There were other joyous reunions that week: with Pierre Souvtchinsky, whose curiosity about my new music and excitement at the prospect of hearing it were a fine tonic after the Koussevitzky letdown; with Robert Pikelny, my old painter friend, a kindly cynic and irrepressible bohemian — he lived in unspeakable squalor with a lady ex-lion tamer of impressive height and weight, who could easily lift her little lover with one hand, but who, having decided that their liaison was, indeed, *le grand amour,* catered to his every whim; with the Parfenovs, as courtly and hospitable as in the twenties; with Poulenc and Sauguet, who played me their latest works and listened to mine, just as they had done in the old days. I lunched at George Auric's, a few blocks away from the Alphands'. George had become France's most successful and prolific film-music composer and Nora, a frail and modish beauty, had made a name for herself as portrait painter. I dined at the Gabriel Paitchadzes, and played chess with the host who, having checkmated me in ten moves, sighed and declared that I was a better composer than chess player. This was a cue for some gossip about the absent chess-playing composer, Prokofiev, who had not been heard from in several months and whose silence worried us.

A few months before arriving in Paris I had composed a score to Albert Willemetz's French lyrics for a Francis de Croisset libretto. Willemetz, a crafty and rich old songsmith and theater owner, saw the *Blanchisseuses* opening and declared himself delighted with both my ballet and my settings of his words for the de Croisset operetta. As usual, the book needed work and the producer needed money, which was just as difficult to get in liberated France as it is in the free United States, except that *les théâtres lyriques* are, for the most part, state supported, on condition that the authors and composers be French citizens. I, an American national, began to receive gentle hints to the effect that living in the richest country in the world, I could perhaps interest some of the 140,000,000 millionaires that make up its population (every American being a millionaire according to the unshakable French maxim) in helping to finance the show. This sounded like a French *Sweet Bye and Bye,* and I hastily assured my new collaborators that Broadway was bankrupt and that no money would be forthcoming from that source.

Mr. Virgil Thomson, the critic of the *Herald Tribune,* attended the Paris scene in 1947, and made this interesting comment on one of Balanchine's new ballets: " 'Serenade,' a ballet by Balanchine to the music of Tchaikovsky's Trio, orchestrated anonymously, is a light fantasy rather long for its substance . . . ." This was too much, and I pointed out in a letter to the Paris *Tribune* that *Serenade* was Tchaikovsky's well-known Serenade for Strings, and that the orchestration, far from being anonymous, was by Peter Ilyitch himself! In retrospect, this amuses me the more upon reading the pundit's comment in his Sunday article of February 21, 1954, in which he sententiously points out: "Another common fault of the reviewer, and one which causes the greatest bitterness among artists, is carelessness of statement." Just a small matter of whose ox is gored, one deduces.

I went to see Paul Gilson, the poet, whom I had met in New York at the beginning of the war; he had worked for the French radio at the time of the German occupation and had gotten me to do some clandestine broadcasting (with musical interludes) to his enslaved countrymen at that time. Gilson had been a handsome, excessively shy man with a flair for American jazz. In the years that had elapsed, Paul had gotten promotion after promotion, and, at the time of our reunion, was director of programs for the entire Radio Diffusion Française. He was hard to recognize; the diffident, easily flushing creature of 1942 had become an imperious, irritable boss, ordering his employees about sternly and barking into the telephone between nervous pulls at his cigarette. "We'll put you to work at once," Gilson said with amiable gruffness. "How about a weekly broadcast? We're too poor to pay you what you deserve, but you'll get the regular *cachet*. What do you say?" I said, "Fine," and we began arguing about the format of my proposed broadcasts. The American "society singer" Anne Francine, a Philadelphian of Hecate-like beauty, was staying at my hotel and singing in better Paris *boîtes;* I hit on the idea of a bilingual piano and voice fifteen-minute-weekly broadcast, with Claude Alphand and Anne Francine the vocalists. They were to express the French and American feminine viewpoints on Paris, men, love, food, clothes, sports and other pleasurable pastimes — both in dialogue and song. With the help of Jean Calvel, a local radio scribbler, the Broadway-Champs Elysées series was written, composed and quickly launched.

Paris is, I daresay, the one town in the world where "April in Paris" is not a success; the two French versions of the lyric are of deplorable banality, which may have been the reason for its not "catching on," but I suspect that the tune itself is too special and fancy for the French, who lean more towards the *ginguette* style in their popular music. Claude, however, sang my "April" charmingly — and so did Anne; their impassioned versions of my standby influenced me to write a new Paris song (in French, this time) every week — Paris being the one subject I can go on musicalizing until doomsday. The idea appealed to Claude, as consummate a Parisienne as any drawn by Constantin Guys, and all I needed was a poet whose verse would sing Paris along with my music. I found such a poet in Francis Carco, and asked him whether he'd write some poems about Paris I could set to music. "Write them? I've already written them — in *La Bohême et Mon Coeur;* I wish I could give you a copy, but I don't have an extra one." This provided me with an additional opportunity for bookhunting along the *quais.* I must have bought forty dusty volumes before I unearthed a soiled copy of Carco's evocative *recueil* — a 1939 reprint — in wrappers. The earliest verses from *La Bohême et Mon Coeur* date from 1904 — a year after I was born — the last were written in 1937; all are almost painfully redolent of Paris, all seemed to beg for a musical accompaniment — I couldn't put down the shabby little book. With potent incentives like Carco's book and the voices of my two coworkers the songs came fast and furious; I wrote them all for Claude, whose range is limited — and the broadcasts attracted considerable attention.

I finally caught up with my *Bal des Blanchisseuses,* when Kochno's and Petit's ballets reappeared at the Théâtre des Champs Elysées in June. Roland, an unusually tall (for a dancer and a Frenchman) youth, displayed great enthusiasm at meeting me and covered me with praise for *Le Bal* and *Un Petit Coin aux Cieux* — the French version of M-G-M's *Cabin in the Sky* — then playing in a Champs

Elysées cinema and the subject of a long laudatory article by Paul Gilson. I saw my ballet, somewhat startlingly choreographed by Roland (apart from Daniele Darmance's acrobatics, the French laundresses seemed to ignore the very spirit of jazz), and was greeted effusively by many of the new Tout Paris stalwarts.

Gilson, encouraged by the success of our Broadway-Champs Elysées broadcasts, manifested a desire to collaborate on a Paris cantata with me. At the word "Paris" I again pricked up my ears; a tribute to the city that made me and was remaking me so generously — what assignment could be more proper and fitting? The idea for the cantata came easily: a man and a maid come to Paris to breathe its magic and to find romance; they see each other while exploring the Eiffel Tower; it's love — heady and sudden — at first sight; they think of a dozen ways of effecting a meeting, are too young and timid to take the all-important first step; sing an impassioned duet, staring at each other rapturously, but not daring to come closer; and part in despair, having failed to seize the golden opportunity — the chorus chiming in with an apotheosis to express the hope that they will finally meet, "in another song." I introduced a children's chorus — the French children, having picked up "pop" strains from the G.I. liberators, punctuating the lovers' plight with ragtime-accented nursery rhymes. I submitted the notion to Gilson, who wrote it up in imaginative verse, and *Paris Aller et Retour* was swiftly born. Summer vacation time came upon us, the broadcasts were temporarily halted, to be resumed in the fall — and I invited Pikelny, my circus-loving painter friend, to join me in a Riviera holiday; I relished the thought of completing my Paris cantata on the spot where *Zephyr* was created.

Pikelny and I took the morning train to *La Côte* and alighted at Nice, where Vera Dityatin, Mother's friend of the Kiev period, awaited me. A fine-looking old woman, she lived at the Asylum for the Aged, where Uncle Iliko had died during the occupation. Madame Dityatin's son Andrew had married the daughter of a Nice innkeeper and practiced the profession of house painter. He was still young and looked like a blond *jeune premier* in a Moscow film. We sat down to a fine, pungent *Niçois* meal, the four Russians chattering excitedly about pre-Revolutionary Kiev while Andrew's sloe-eyed Latin wife listened sympathetically and filled our glasses.

I needed secluded, roomy quarters for my work on *Paris Aller et*

Retour, and they were hard to find in Nice, crawling with tourists and vacationing government employees. Andrew suggested Beaulieu, chiefly noted for La Réserve, a haunt of the rich, and wholesome boredom. The place sounded just right for my purpose and there I secured a five-room apartment for 11,000f. a month — about forty dollars — with a maid "thrown in." We spent a productive month there, I getting my cantata in shape, Pikelny painting "Horse Carriages at the Cannes Railroad Station." There were no horse carriages in Beaulieu, but Cannes was only a few miles away. However, he was too lazy for a daily trip to Cannes, and there was nothing worth painting in Beaulieu, where the landscapes were entirely too "landscapy" and lush; so he settled for an "evocation" of a memorable scene.

We took a few melancholy trips — to Monte Carlo, unspeakably depressing and decadent, the Casino, the Hôtel de Paris and the café across the square all looking as if they had gout and didn't care who knew it: "Only Swiss and Belgian tourists these days," said a dead-faced waiter at the hotel, "and they don't tip"; to Cannes, as pretty and well-scrubbed as ever, fried-chicken-colored *vedettes* in white Bikinis sprawling on the beach while even-darker-skinned playboys paraded their impressive sexual equipment, alluringly accentuated by what the French naïvely term *"un slip."* I never cared for the Croisette, Paradise of the Cosmopolitan Phony, but know of few places lovelier than Cannes Harbor — proud fishermen's boats rubbing shoulders with millionaires' yachts, the swarthy townfolk returning from picnics, their small children walking docilely hand-in-hand, Les Freddie's Boys playing bad jazz on a café terrace, sun-baked port characters engrossed in their beloved game of *boule,* the sea air a head-turning blend of watermelon, seaweed and fresh cucumbers (here's rich, beautiful prose for you, but sniff the air in Cannes Harbor and see who has the last laugh).

Anne Francine took a fine villa overlooking Grasse, and there I met Edmond Colomb de Daunant, a Nîmes landowner of old Huguenot Protestant ancestry, an agreeably placid young man and, in Nat Parker Willis's words, a "here-and-thereian," like myself. He and I went to Venice, a city I had always longed to see. We put up at Countess Cavalieri's, to whose small "house" we were taken in a gondola. The trip defied description, and so did Venice, a place too beautiful for any mortal's comfort. Avid to absorb as much of this beauty, in the short space of ten days, as I possibly could, I walked and walked, often skipping meals, accompanied by equally impressionable Edmond or, on rarer occasions, the venerable countess, a Russian *grande dame* and a widow for many years, with her four large unkempt poodles. We had tea at Elizabeth Chavchavadze's *palazzo,* swam at the Lido with her daughter, went to Shostakovitch's *Lady Macbeth of Mzensk* — energetically booed by the Venetians — at the Teatro Fenice, and plotted a pilgrimage to Diaghilev's tomb on the island of San Michele. The countess had known Sergei Pavlovitch and had seen him often on his annual visits to Venice. Somehow we never journeyed to San Michele, preferring to keep Diaghilev's spirit alive by affectionate remembrance, rather than by honoring meaningless death.

Paris was abuzz with activity on our return; to stay away from it was as unthinkable for a "professional" as it would have been to stay away from New York. I had my share of the preseason fever: meetings with Henry Barraud, one of France's best musicians, a man hard to know, but eminently worth knowing if he can find time for you, with Desormière, with Souvtchinsky, with Gilson. I planned a series of Franco-American exchanges with Barraud and enlisted the help of capable little Anita Lauve of our Embassy to that end; Desormière coached Irene Joachim and Raymond Amade in my *Paris Aller et Retour,* a piece he took to immediately; Souvtchinsky and I made daily "rediscoveries" for the Society for Forgotten Music we had organized, taken under the French radio's wing, thanks to Barraud; and Gilson wanted a replacement for Anne Francine, who went back to the States unexpectedly, having received a Broadway offer. I spent a gay week end at Les Moulins, the Alphands' exquisitely appointed country place near Chartres, and played the Willemetz songs for Claude, who promptly fell in love with *"En Valsant,"* the best of the lot, and sang it all over Paris. For recreation and for "the soul" there were interminable affectionate arguments with Fatima-Hanoum in her miniature garden near the Eiffel Tower and leisurely strolls with André Beucler, Leon-Paul Fargue's biographer, the most Parisian of literary *flâneurs* and half Russian, his father, a French teacher in Tzarskoe Sielo, having married a Russian girl.

With the help of a débrouillarde bilingual secretary, I finally landed a fairly comfortable four-room flat in the Avenue Emile Zola

— a most unchic neighborhood, inhabited chiefly by workingmen's families. The apartment house was comparatively new and boasted some of the elementary comforts, such as a bathroom *with* a bathtub. The proprietor was a foxy little man in his late forties, a cripple; on learning from my passport that I was born in Russia, he smiled with sudden warmth and disclosed that he was married to a Russian. "Why did you become an American?" he asked suspiciously. I was rather taken aback by this and said something to the effect that I liked the place, the people and the freedom. "Freedom? *Tiens* . . . You're not a Negro, I see." The man chuckled sarcastically and changed the subject. The price he asked was somewhat high but I was tired of ringing bells and exchanging time-consuming *politesses,* and I could have the Emile Zola flat by the month. So a satisfactory deal was concluded and I moved in the next morning.

I couldn't find a suitable replacement for Anne Francine, and my broadcasts were abandoned — which was just as well, in view of new excitements crowding my schedule. I had sent a score of the Third Symphony to Paul Collaer, the Belgian musicologist, conductor and head of the Radio Diffusion Belge, at Henry Barraud's suggestion. The answer contained a flattering estimate of my work, a decision to include it in the season's programs and a long list of available conductors. Some big European names were on the list and I could hardly believe my eyes when I read: "Kindly indicate which of these conductors you would like to entrust with the *première* of your symphony." I settled, at Collaer's suggestion, for Dann Sternefeld, a young Antwerp conductor especially attuned to contemporary music. Collaer programed my piece for early October.

Gilson's and my *Paris Aller et Retour* was announced for February. For contractual reasons, we couldn't get the French radio's best orchestra, the National (which toured the States in 1948 under Charles Munch), and had to content ourselves with N2 — the Radio-Symphonique. This also meant my losing Roger Desormière, the National's conductor; my cantata was handed to Jean Clergue, an able technician. On September 14th Maurice Bialkin, talented young cellist, who later became my devoted collaborator in the Society for Forgotten Music, played my Cello Concerto with the CBS Symphony under Bernard Herrmann at the League of Composers' Twenty-fifth Anniversary. It had taken me seventeen years to get a *repeat* engagement with the choosy League.

Early in October I went on to Brussels for the *première* of my symphony. I didn't know a soul in Belgium except an amusing friend of Claude Alphand's, a witty and worldly divorcee, who took me to dinner at the Argentine Ambassador's and held my hand while Sternefeld rehearsed my music. The orchestra was fine and the young conductor was obviously intent on doing a good job. Paul Collaer was unfortunately out of town, and I didn't meet any of the local musicians; I was flattered when one of the first violinists produced a copy of my Violin Concerto and asked me to inscribe it. People often ask Duke to autograph his songs or records; they seldom bother Dukelsky with such requests. Brussels rather reminded me of Montreal, and I thought the Belgian accent just as singular as the Canadian one; some of the food was good — especially *matelotte d'anguille* (an eel stew) and the *fondue* (a cheese concoction) — but terribly heavy and rich. My symphony shared the bill with Beethoven, Arthur de Greef (a Flemish composer) and Benjamin Britten; it was a stimulating program and I was happy about the way my music sounded, but there was no audience except Claude's friend and Sternefeld's wife — it being a nonpublic broadcast — and there were no newspaper echoes; a relief, in a way.

I went for Christmas to Edmond Colomb's fine seventeenth-century house in Nîmes; it had a good library, beautifully kept grounds and the kind of subdued yet faultless taste well-bred Frenchmen impart to their living quarters. Like all small towns with a glamorous past, Nîmes was replete with well-bred nostalgia, but you could hardly call the place stimulating. My only memory of that 1947 Christmas is a "reveillon" with the delightful Godebskys (of Ravel and Sert fame), their relatives arriving from all corners of France; the almost Dingley Dellish, Pickwickian atmosphere and the atrocious wailing of the choristers at Midnight Mass — they not only sang out of tune, but persistently two bars behind the organist. At the party I met a cousin of Edmond's who owned a Texas-style ranch on Camargue, near the far-famed Saintes Maries de la Mer, where the gypsies come once a year to burn candles to Sarah of Egypt and Marie-Salomé.

Mr. Perrin, my Communistic landlord in Paris, had a fine home-coming surprise in store for me; I found a caricature of General Eisenhower on my pillow, with an even ruder caption than the one that graced Senator Taft's distorted likeness some time before. I had three more weeks to go on our arrangement, but the place was not the same and the onslaught on the general, whom I had always admired, was the last straw. I was so annoyed that I packed that afternoon and went to the expensive and well-run Hotel Bellmann (ex-Metropole) in the rue Marboeuf. Money from home having arrived on my return from Cannes, I decided to splurge and invested in a particularly fancy room; having transformed my dollars into a thick wad of crisp 5000-franc banknotes, I treated myself to a splendid repast at the Grand Vefour. The next morning I was awakened by the excited cries of newsvendors in the street, extra-loud and disturbing but unintelligible. I sent for the waiter and ordered *Le Figaro* with my coffee; the headline ran: 5000 FRANC NOTES DECLARED INVALID. Invalid! My entire three months' ASCAP "remittance" was in 5000-franc notes. Dressing hastily, I consulted the cashier, who, after much philosophical shrugging and grimacing, suggested that I "await developments" and that meanwhile the hotel would advance me a few thousand francs for "necessities." That was kind of him, but what do I do about food? I wanted to know. Another shrug followed by an accommodating smile: *"Monsieur's* credit is good in our *maison; monsieur* will do us the honor of taking his meals at the hotel and paying his bill when convenient. Our cuisine is highly thought of, if I may say so." It was, indeed, since the Bellmann was another Tour d'Argent-operated inn. But the prices! Fancy taking three meals a day at the Tour d'Argent; you'd have to have the bankroll of another Duke — the one named Doris. However, I knew no other way out, so I wangled as many dinner invitations as I could — the measure was directed chiefly against blackmarketing foreigners, and few French were affected by the decree — and lunched meagerly, but elegantly, at the astronomically priced Bellmann. In two or three weeks I managed to exchange my "illegal" notes for respectable 1000-franc bills, losing quite a considerable sum on this transaction; my "distinguished" Bellmann food came to nearly $400 in that period.

Both the symphony and *Paris Aller et Retour* were broadcast in February; both were well received by the listeners, although these not being public performances I had few newspaper comments.

Henri Sauguet, whose ballet *Les Forains* (Boris Kochno-Christian Bérard-Roland Petit) is a minor masterpiece, a work of *déchirant* lyrical impact, wrote about my symphony: "A work of remarkable quality . . . . Dukelsky is also Duke, the generously applauded author of 'Le Bal des Blanchisseuses,' one of the successes of the Ballets des Champs Elysées — a composer of many gifts and varying talents. His Symphony displays nervous and vigorous writing, brilliant and powerful orchestration. It's a strong work, a work of lyrical beauty." The cantata came in for its share of praise, too, and was so highly thought of by Desormière that he gave a public performance of it a year later — again with the ravishing Irene Joachim — with France's best orchestra, the National. The *Blanchisseuses* were garnering fresh triumphs all over Europe, including England, some of whose critics, probably not realizing that Duke was also Dukelsky, whose *Jardin Public* they had crucified, actually liked my lighthearted score.

Encouraged by these victories, I returned to New York, not dreaming that I'd be back in Paris in three months. My name having appeared in various international social columns, two or three business magnates with an eye on the French market helped by the Marshall Plan hit on the bright idea of availing themselves of my services in Paris, as a sort of well-connected "front man."

The magnates and I sailed on the S.S. *Nieuw Amsterdam* in May. In between the two European trips I founded the New York chapter of the Society for Forgotten Music, with the generous help of Sydney Beck of the N.Y. Public Library's Music Division, Yves Tinayre, Leon Barzin and Gustave Reese, the musicologist and chief editor for Carl Fischer, Inc. Yvonne de Casa Fuerte, the founder of the Parisian *Serenade,* one of the very few truly idealistic music lovers left in the world, Benny Herrmann, Arthur Lourié, Slonimsky, Rieti, Riegger and other well-known musical figures were also on the board. With scouts in Paris, London, Vienna and Milan, we gained access to countless neglected treasures — such as Arriaga's quartets, Mendelssohn's unpublished quartet, Dussek's astonishingly "modern" and Brahmsian Sonata in F-sharp Minor, written in 1810, Spohr's Nonet, Hummel's Piano Quintet, Valentini's superb Concerto Grosso and many others. In the course of two seasons, the society acquired 250 paying members, gave 15 concerts, two radio series — and wound up *in the black* — an unheard-of phenomenon.

The 1948 Paris escapade needn't detain us long. With the help of Colomb de Daunant and Pierre Guerin, a "social" and art-conscious journalist, I introduced my magnates to everybody worth contacting in their respective fields, with I know not what results. I stayed at the Ritz, played the salon game with renewed ardor, and even gave an eminently successful ball, the expenses of which were footed by my new associates. With my *"Bal de la Péniche"* I started the rage for other similar entertainments, a fact duly chronicled by the Paris *Vogue;* for the purposes of our party, Edmond, Guerin and I rented Consuelo de Saint-Exupéry's barge stationed near the Alexander III bridge on the Seine. The barge was charmingly decorated by Rina Rosselli; a French band played American dance tunes and the champagne was plentiful; I stood on the bridge and "received" some 250 Tout Paris guests, most of whom, as I subsequently learned, were convinced that I had inherited a huge fortune.

With the help of Barraud and Gilson, the proposed exhibit of worthwhile American music, *without* insistence on the inclusion of two or three names that invariably appear on such programs, was finally realized. My original plan called for two symphony concerts, but we were lucky to manage *one* with the little encouragement the plan received. The works were selected on the basis of their value, without sticking to the "correct" American Party line in music. The program arrived at did not contain a bar of my music, in accordance with my express wishes. I trust I have proven my bona-fide Americanism in my Broadway output, yet I do not consider myself "a typical American composer" in the "serious" field, although I'm as proud as the next fellow of my American citizenship. Also, I had a successful ballet on the boards and decided to step aside in favor of my colleagues.

Accordingly, the following list was made up: Walter Piston's Second Symphony, Wallingford Riegger's Canon and Fugue, David Diamond's "Rounds," Morton Gould's "Pavane," Charles Ives's "In the Night" and Edward MacDowell's D-minor Piano Concerto, with the gifted Vera Franceschi as soloist. An eclectic list, as you see, yet it had these virtues: (1) all the music was of good quality; (2) it had decided audience appeal; and (3) it paid no respects to our Tammany Music Hall. The concert took place on July 2nd, a few days after I had returned to the States, was conducted by Jean

Giardino (no American conductors being available at the time) and scored a pronounced success.

The French radio's representative in New York had a terrible time for nearly six months trying to get the music from the composers or their publishers. Most of them were dubious of the whole enterprise, wanted substantial remuneration, the biography of the conductor, etc. As it turned out, *all* of the orchestral parts for the concert were obtained *in Paris,* thanks to the valiant efforts of Anita Lauve of the Cultural Division of the American Embassy, and the well-stocked musical library of the Paris Information Center. In exchange, I obtained scores by Elsa Barraine, Claude Delvincourt and Henry Barraud which were subsequently performed with success by Leon Barzin and Dean Dixon in New York. I was also entrusted with several novelties by my friends Henri Sauguet and Daniel Lesur and took them straight to that ultra-rugged individualist Bernard Herrmann. I don't know of a single individual in the entire United States who did as much, with as little personal gain, for forgotten old and neglected new music as Benny at CBS; also, without the slightest allegiance to the Tammany Music Hall — brave man!

CHAPTER XIX

CALIFORNIAN CODA

IN THINKING of my two best and most cherished friends in music, Serge Prokofiev and George Gershwin, I am struck by a perhaps not too farfetched analogy in their musical fate. Both were endowed with exceptional pianistic gifts; both were blessed with a great gift of melody, the essential trademark of every first-rate composer; both appealed strongly to the people's imagination; both had pronounced nationalistic traits without a trace of chauvinism (one can discount the government-dictated "occasion" pieces of Prokofiev's, none of them successful). Gershwin was as genuinely American (although of Russian antecedents) as Prokofiev was profoundly Russian; neither practiced the synthetic art of pastiche; neither rationalized, preached or issued grandiloquent advance notices of their own work; both were wonderfully generous with their contemporaries and readily embraced music of a cast entirely foreign to their nature, provided it was recognizable as the work of an authentic musician. Both composers are looked down upon by the fashionable "terrorists" of dodecaphonic persuasion, such as the loudly trumpeted and importantly supported Pierre Boulez. Souvtchinsky took me to hear the young man's music in Paris in 1953 and, instead of being shocked, I was reduced to a state of abject boredom. True revolutionaries in music, who enraged their contemporaries with the daring of their utterances, may have provoked hostility and hate — but they were never, never *dull.*

The cleavage between the composer and the listener, already considerable in the beginning of the century, has now been leveled to the status of a complete divorce. Young men writing music today are given the choice of only two ideologically correct styles — dodecaphonic (post-Schoenbergian) or pseudoclassical (neodiatonic, as opposed to the twelve-tone dicta — in other words, Stravinskian). The first style dominates present-day musical Europe, the second (with an admixture of Coplandesque "basic," barren and tortured Americanism) prevails on our shores. The two manners have one thing in common — they provoke the audience's apathy. I, for one, cannot imagine whom the followers of Schoenberg and Stravinsky are writing for, unless for fellow followers. The old bromide about misunderstood genius is based mostly on wishful thinking; contrary to the commercial laments of the fictionizing biographer, few great composers of the past had any legitimate complaints about audience indifference.

Chopin and Liszt managed to be good composers and good drawing cards in the concert hall and no one tried to minimize their importance because of their popular appeal, as so many do when talking down Prokofiev, or Gershwin. Closer to our own time, Scriabin and Rachmaninov may not have been men of Chopin's or Liszt's stature, but they too wrote quite a few pages of musicianly as well as exciting stuff. All these men kept in close touch with their audience and their audience returned the compliment by begging for more. You can't get away from the fact that unless your music does something for the people, the people won't do anything for your music. In this respect it is significant that none of the contemporary works which have attained genuine popularity owe much — in most instances, nothing — to either Schoenberg or Stravinsky. One need only name Villa-Lobos's "Chôros," Martinu's Concerto Grosso, Gian-Carlo Menotti's operas, Bartók's Violin Concerto, Poulenc's "Figure Humaine," Hindemith's *Mathis der Maler,* Honegger's *Jeanne d'Arc au Bûcher* or Liturgic Symphony, Kurt Weill's *Three-penny Opera,* Henri Sauguet's "Les Forains" or Shostakovitch's Piano Quintet.

Every dogma has its day; but good music lives forever. In the last twenty years, this country's composers can boast a record of achievement that compares favorably with Europe's output for the same period. At the top of the list I must place Walter Piston's Fourth Symphony, a truly first-rate work employing distinguished material masterfully organized and incomparably orchestrated. Israel Citkovitz's String Quartet, impressively lyrical and flawlessly written for the instruments, can hold its own in any company; Leonard Bernstein's *Fancy Free,* full of glowing vitality and high spirits, is a model ballet score; Theodore Chanler's poignantly human songs should find a place on singers' programs the world over; Paul Bowles is a Daedalean theater composer; Lukas Foss has enriched the choral literature and can be expected to produce a monumental piece in that idiom at any moment; Bernard Herrmann and Alex North have taken film-background music out of the ready-cliché morass and imbued their every new score with imagery and topnotch workmanship; and George Gershwin's *Porgy and Bess* is still the best all-around opera written since 1930. No Stravinsky or Schoenberg influence in any of these, either.

To emphasize my point, let me cite a striking exhibit from each school, the unpopular or snob-supported and the popular or snob-rejected. (The snobs I allude to in this instance are of the domestic variety.) Exhibit A is Stravinsky's *Rake's Progress,* hailed by the snobs as a rare masterpiece. *Time* observed that it has cost the Met $60,000 to mount. When "revived" for the sixth time in two years: "the opera suffered the worst fiasco that we have seen occur at the Metropolitan in 30 years of attendance there," reported Olin Downes, a critic not noted for bias. "By the end of the second act people were leaving in scores. . . . It is clear that the public has tired of this opera and by no means without justification, in view of its immense stretches of empty and artificial music." Exhibit B is Gershwin's *Porgy and Bess,* once defined by that champion of things Gallic, Virgil Thomson, as "music of not very good society." Yet it has had hundreds of performances the world over and is an artistic and commercial triumph everywhere. Far from being tired of *this* opera, the Parisians, careful spenders as a rule, mobbed the Théâtre des Champs Elysées when *Porgy* played there, and have clamored for a return engagement ever since. Let me assure the caste-conscious Mr. Thomson that the very best society took Gershwin's opera to its collective heart.

Yet Mr. Thomson asserted in 1935 (in *Modern Music*): " 'Green Pastures,' the last act of 'Run Little Chillun,' 'Four Saints in Three Acts' [Mr. Thomson's entry, which Prokofiev called "Four *Notes* in Three Acts"] and 'Porgy' are little eminences on the flat horizon of American opera. . . . Two of these are straight folklore. The third [Mr. T's entry] is straight opera. 'Porgy and Bess' is the least interesting of the four, because it is not straight anything." A straight flush perhaps?

At no time have I been prouder of my American citizenship than in 1948. While in Paris, I read with horror the notorious Pravda editorial of February 10th, subtitled "Decree by the Central Committee of the Russian Communist Party," reprinted in the Soviet *Literary Gazette*. Under the pretext of condemning a minor work (the opera *Great Friendship* by V. Muradeli) the Politburo dictators lashed out at "neuropathic formalists," "anti-Soviet musical wreckers" and "degenerate lovers of bourgeois culture"—Comrades Shostakovitch, Prokofiev, Khachaturian, Shebalin, Popov and Miaskovsky. All six were instantly removed from the Politburo's favor, four of the men from public office; Prokofiev, who held no official post, was the real culprit in the eyes of Assafiev, Khrennikov and Koval, Soviet bureaucrats, parasites and informers first and composers last. As reported by Nabokov (in a Virgil Thomson translation) Sergei Sergeivitch's name was "linked with such 'servile and corrupt musical businessmen' as Stravinsky, such 'degenerate, blackguard, anti-Russian lackeys of the Western bourgeoisie' as Diaghilev." According to rumor, Prokofiev was banished to a small provincial town and denied the right of residence in Moscow, his music removed from concert and theater programs. Little did *October* cantatas, birthday odes to Soviet potentates and a marriage to Lazar Kaganovitch's niece help my friend, thus buried alive in the Free Republic of the Peoples of Russia; Shostakovitch "sang" in the proper Communist key, was soon exonerated and added to the delegation of Soviet "intellectuals" sent to the U.S. on their famous Waldorf Astoria "Peace" mission. I thought of unyielding, undiplomatic Prokofiev, peacefully sweating it out in his "socialistic" promised land, and my heart bled for him. Last year I heard of the plight of a young, Russian-born *Time* magazine reporter who didn't like his assignment of following Shostakovitch around at the time of his "Peace Congress" sojourn in New York; vividly recalling Mme. Kasenkina's "jumping to freedom" from the Soviet Consulate's window, he asked his co-workers ruefully: "It's all very well to shadow 'Dimitri,' but suppose he jumps too?"

My Paris mission behind me, Ogden Nash and I were inveigled into a new Broadway project—a revue this time. Its creator, Ken Englund, the Hollywood screenwriter, long obsessed with the eternal and insoluble battle of the sexes, wrote some sketches depicting the laughable pitfalls for American men and women unable to work out a realistic design for living. Originally called *Neuroses of 1948,* the Englund revue soon became *He and She.*

Englund was a persuasive salesman; Ogden and I, still licking our *Sweet Bye and Bye* wounds, were anxious to vindicate ourselves and lent willing ears. Ken and I spent the rest of the summer in the last and smallest of my series of summer cages — the 1948 one was located immediately behind an Italian seafood restaurant in Little Boar's Head, New Hampshire. Ogden took a largish house a few miles away from us and lived in Nashian comfort, getting painfully pink in the hot sun on the beach and then splashing about in the ice-cold water, which so paralyzed me that I was unable to swim or even float. Ken and I played ping-pong, argued and went on bookhunting expeditions in Newburyport and other neighboring towns. The summer over, it was a case of "mixture as before" — some seventy or eighty backing auditions; lunches with actors, directors and choreographers, all of whom had a great feeling for the show, according to ever-optimistic Englund and all of whom went off to other lunches with other authors and producers; "slumming" Park Avenue potentates minus their checkbooks all over again; battles with Jack Robbins, who would praise our score one day and throw it back in our faces the next; fine, impressive announcements in Zolotov's and Bert McCord's columns, resulting in hectic phone calls from half of Broadway; no announcements for the next two weeks, resulting in equally hectic inquiries as to "what goes with your revue?"; letters from girls who needed jobs; letters to stars who declined the jobs with thanks; meetings with three agents allegedly representing one actor; meetings with three actors all "up for the part," represented by one agent . . . but why go on? It's crazy enough when the show gets produced, but *He and She* didn't. Englund, a changeable sort of lad, given to mysterious disappearances at audition time and barricading his hotel room with telephone books, joined forces with Stewart Chaney, the scenic designer, who, to hear Ken tell, too had "a great feeling for the show." Ogden and I soon had a great feeling that our producers weren't hitting it off and that the show was falling apart — it did.

In between auditions and lunches, I officiated as lecturer, accompanist and program-note writer at the Society for Forgotten Music concerts, broadcasts and so-called "workshop tryouts"; these consisted of sight-reading of forgotten chamber works by our musicians, mostly from Benny Herrmann's CBS symphony. The readings were followed by lively discussions of the works just read and the desirability of according them a public or radio performance. The "workshop tryouts" were very popular and we found it hard to accommodate all the members and their friends who wished to attend. There was some internal friction within our organization's ranks — musicologists, like composers, being notoriously uncooperative — but on the whole we felt we had a worthwhile aim and were doing courageous work. Marc Pincherle, the distinguished Paris critic and the greatest authority on Vivaldi, was elected president of the Paris "mother society," which was kept going by our members' dollars.

In the spring of 1949 I received a cabled invitation to compose the music for the Paul Gilson-Nino Frank French romantic musical, based on the 1830 story of "Milord l'Arsouille," who was, in reality, Charles La Battut, bastard son of an English peer and a French mother, Lord Seymour's unsuccessful rival for the affections of the Parisian people. The legend had it that the poor folk of Paris received untold bounty — money, food and wine — at Carnival Time from an anonymous benefactor whom they firmly believed was Lord Seymour, the eccentric president of the ultra-fashionable Jockey Club. The real benefactor was La Battut, who was denied recognition for his generous spending; the more he gave, the louder the populace cheered Seymour. Unable to convince his fellow Parisians that it was he, La Battut, who befriended them, ruined by his unappreciated extravagance, the poor publicity seeker (he was credited with inventing the Can Can, an outgrowth of Musard's "diabolical *galop*") ended his life by his own hand. So much for the story, based on actual fact, not fiction; but when you add to it the enchantment of the period — the heyday of Balzac, de Musset, de Vigny, George Sand, Sainte-Beuve, Théophile Gautier, Delacroix, young Victor Hugo, Eugène Sue, Dumas *fils* and so many others — the period immortalized by artists like Grandville, Gavarni and Daumier, one begins to wonder why it has never been put on the musical stage. Pictorially speaking, can you think of prettier clothes than those worn in the day of the Good King Louis Philippe? As for men's fashions, they have not been equaled since that true era of dandies, of the czar's brilliant court with Natalie Pushkin its bright shining star, and her husband, Alexander, Russia's greatest poet, its tragic victim. Having paid obeisance to the Romantic *floraison* of the first half of the nineteenth century in my first stage work, *Zephyr and Flora* (strictly an 1830 conceit), having written the

Pushkinesque *Entr'acte* for Balanchine, how could I refuse to help transplant my favorite period to the contemporary musical theater?

The third of my postwar European voyages resulted in what I and my listeners firmly believe is my best musical-comedy score, and a sentimental setback of major proportions. Since, however, I wrote well because I loved well, I can now — after six years — put the trip down as a success. Oddly enough, I musicalized my emotional fiasco *before* it happened — in a musical setting of Walter Benton's best seller *This Is My Beloved,* a rather florid and stylistically questionable record of a tragic love affair.

Simon Copans, the head of the Voice of America in Paris, scheduled a radio recital of my music and wanted an American singer for the Carco songs, the ones I wrote for Claude Alphand. Souvtchinsky recommended a French vocal teacher who had several promising American pupils, and Estelle was one of them. The girl was blond and pretty in a Campus Queen way, complete with sweater and skirt, socks and sneakers; probably a throwback in my mind to Joan, who was the classical American college belle.

I was lucky to find a spacious studio in rue Lauriston (not far from where the German Gestapo was located during the Occupation), thanks to Fatima-Hanoum, my Paris guardian angel. There is nothing easier than to fall in love in the very special Paris June, when the whole city aches with romantic longing; all you need is a girl. Estelle didn't look like the right girl to me, but no matter. She had a voice of seductive, velvety quality and fairly well trained, but she sang without a trace of feeling or style; she did well enough for my purposes, as the Carco songs were easy, and I was convinced that with a little coaching she would do them justice. The "little coaching" became a daily occurrence; after three visits to rue Lauriston, Estelle told me of her ambition to become the greatest opera singer in Europe, two more visits and I offered to write an opera for her. She didn't show up the next day — perhaps frightened by the prospect —, and I was lost in despair; that night I knew that I was in love, and that life without Estelle wasn't worth living. The next day I proposed to the girl — who, understandably, appeared startled and asked for the usual "thinking it over" privileges. Two days later she reappeared with a huge bouquet of roses (bought with her rent money, she proudly explained) to tell me that she would accept my proposal — on two conditions; one, *no* full-scale love-making prior to marriage, owing to her previous experiences with ardent lovers who had disappeared after a few nights of bliss, and, two, that I give her the chance of going to Italy, where she had won a vocal scholarship, for the rest of the summer, *alone*. Somewhat taken aback, I agreed to both conditions, which pleased Estelle so much that she promptly asked, "Now, may I write Mummy all about our engagement? It's on the level, isn't it?" I assured her that it was and we agreed on an October marriage date in New York.

The rest of that rosy-hued June I lived in a self-invented crazy Paradise. With Francis Claude, a witty and prodigiously gifted Basque, I wrote song after song, one better than the other, in a creative frenzy the like of which I had never experienced. Evenings were spent with Estelle, who sang my songs charmingly and, best of all, talked of her love for me incessantly. At first I found it difficult to restrain my passion, but, having given my word to the girl, stuck to our bargain.

All that existed of the "Milord" book was the first scene — very promising — the rest was being written by the two librettists, supposedly around a synopsis Claude and I had read and approved. We soon perceived that the authors were getting away from the original simple tale and imbuing their "book" with a nightmarish "existentialist" overtone not at all in keeping with the romantic bravado and amorous songfulness of our contributions. Being in love and writing reams of a lover's music, I refused to take this fatal discrepancy seriously and went right on composing and loving — the whole vast world around me merely a setting for my happiness.

Soon came the "temporary" and tearful parting, I running beside the departing bus with no realization that I'd never see my fiancée again. The night before, the girl had slept in rue Lauriston, on a couch in the studio where I did my composing; we were late returning from the country, where we had gamboled with friends, and she had injured her knee while leaping over a fence. I, intent on being a gentleman to the bitter end, never touched the girl that night, which might well have been a cardinal mistake.

Estelle, who was part Irish, wanted an Irish engagement ring, the kind that represents lovers' hands clasping — I believe it's known as a "friendship" ring in Ireland. I, therefore, planned on going to Dublin, a town I had always wanted to see after reading Joyce's *Dubliners* and *Ulysses* and viewing *The Informer*. Benjamin Welles was doing his *New York Times* reporting in London, so I stopped off in that town on the way to the Emerald Isle. After sending me a daily post card and telephoning twice from Mentone, Estelle suddenly stopped writing and my worry and loneliness increased daily. I even had Benny Welles "trace" my fiancée through his Rome newspaper connections, her silence ruining my London trip.

In 1949 London had had about as much "austerity" as it could swallow, and even the heroic Cockney, who assuredly deserved three square meals a day and a little comfort after weathering the "blitzes," grumbled at having to tighten his belt still further — there being no more notches left in the belt. Benny Welles and his handsome Scots wife lived in an attractive house near Sloane Square. When we went to lunch at Claridge's, the *plat du jour,* of which the fancily tailored *maître d'hôtel* seemed to be excessively proud, was an ungodly concoction of canned corn and tinned lobster served *au gratin* in a massive silver chafing dish; we washed down the mess with minuscule dry Martinis, made, so far as I could judge, of French vermouth and water. I sent my fiancée a cable to Rome, urging her to at least tell me whether she had arrived safely, and went out for a long walk. People in the street, especially women, were pathetically shabby; the men, though obviously owning but one decent suit, were traditionally spruced up; that is, their bowlers and Homburgs were still the right shape and make, the collars were as stiff as their owners' upper lips, and the umbrellas as eel-like, as in 1936, but their crisply pressed trousers shone with a telltale brilliance and the cuffs of the once-perfect shirts were frayed. Night was descending on London and the city's illumination too, seemed meager and austere. I had the strange impulse to walk down King's Road to Church Street, the scene of so many candlelit dinners and "love" trysts in the twenties; Chelsea looked woebegone and pitifully down-at-the-heel, but the old familiar landmarks were all there intact. Church Street at last. I hurried on, past dirty little urchins playing hop scotch without enthusiasm; a few more blocks — here, to the left, would be my 1928 dwelling. My heart, literally, stood still — what was once a small Jacobean house had become a vacant lot — neat and clean but thoroughly empty, except for an emaciated cat who gave me a disdainful look and turned away. "My" house, in all likelihood destroyed by a German bomb, was no more; this I immediately interpreted as a foreboding of disaster.

The next morning a typical London bellboy, the kind that owns a light soprano voice and a fallen cherub's face, handed me a cable from Rome. It read: "Am well don't worry send New York address" — which was odd, as Estelle could still airmail a letter to my boat, which was sailing from Cobh, Ireland, in five days; but a cable, however unsatisfactory, was better than nothing, and I cheered up considerably, such being the way of lovers at the slightest glimmer of light.

Arriving in Dublin, I didn't see much of the town, spending a bare forty hours there, but was disappointed in what I saw. Dublin can easily lay claim to being the cleanest city in Europe and, at first glance, is utterly devoid of the traditional squalor with all manner of danger lurking in its disreputable, scum-infested taverns — the picture I was led to expect by the reading matter I had absorbed. Try as I would, I couldn't find a single dirty pub — all such establishments being finely scrubbed, run by polite, gentlemanly barkeeps and frequented by well-behaved solid citizens. Irish cops, in particular, were things of fragile beauty, wore dazzlingly clean white gloves and, when signaling, used their arms with a grace that would have been envied by a Mitropoulos.

Two things one saw everywhere in Dublin were bicycles — with people young and old on them — and so-called "choc parlors," or ice-cream dispensaries, often as many as two or three to a block. Girls, always in pairs, moderately comely and without a trace of make-up, walked the streets eating ice cream, when not bicycling. I bought just the ring Estelle wanted in an old silversmith's shop — an exquisitely made golden ring with a barely visible inscription: "From John to Peggy with love 1838." "May I advise you not to send it by post, sir," the courtly whitehaired shopkeeper said, after I had given him six guineas for the ring. "Precious metals are not to be taken out of Ireland, according to the law. Do not place it in your luggage, either, as the customs people may confiscate the ring, but keep it on your person — in your coat pocket — where it will be quite safe. You can then post it from the States to your fiancée, sir." I assured the old man that I would follow his advice.

My next stop was Cork, an attractive, prettily situated town; it was there that transatlantic voyagers took the small suburban train to Cobh, where the United States Lines ships docked. I had but two handbags, and carried them myself, no porter being visible, the precious engagement ring in my pocket. I bought my railroad ticket to Cobh, and walked on leisurely to the toylike, apple-green train standing in the station. Suddenly, one of the bags was snatched out of my hand by an odd-looking dark male, wearing no necktie but adorned with a gigantic single earring: a gypsy, judging from his appearance. Before I had a chance to open my mouth in protest, the enterprising gypsy pushed me into a vacant compartment, jostling me slightly in the process. He then placed my bags carefully on the baggage rack and smiled in lieu of explanation; I judged him to be in his early thirties, yet there was not a tooth in his mouth.

We were alone in the dark compartment and I felt oddly uneasy with my strange vis-à-vis. "Why did you do that?" I asked him, pointing to the bag he carried for me. Another toothless smile; the gypsy's face would have been quite handsome, had it not been for that horrible gaping cavern of a mouth. "Beggin' your pardon, sarr . . ." the man said soothingly, in an oddly melodious voice, "I'm an employee of the United States Lines in a mannarr of speakin', sarr. Do you see those shillelaghs up there, sarr?" He pointed to a stack of cudgels, Ireland's specialty, up on the rack. "I sell them to boat passengers — I take it you are one, sarr." This sounded plausible and I thanked him for the courtesy. The little train started. The car we were traveling in was empty, except for the shillelagh-vendor and myself. We struck up a conversation. "Do you know much about Irish customs and legends?" I asked. "I do indeed, sarr. What do you wish to know?" "Well, I just bought an old ring for my fiancée; I'd like to know its origin and its significance." An odd gleam appeared in the gypsy's eye. "May I see the ring, sarr?" "Certainly," said I and put my hand in my coat pocket — the ring was gone.

I knew at once that, while jostling me, the gypsy had quickly dived into my pocket and appropriated the ring — an antiquated pickpocket's device, straight out of *Oliver Twist*. "You haven't *lost* the ring, sarr, have you? . . . That would be badd luck, I'm afraid, sarr," the villain said, obviously enjoying himself. His fiendish remark gave me another jolt. "The creature is right," I thought. "First the Chelsea house where I lived — gone; now the ring — gone, too. Estelle is next on the list."

Estelle's mother and sister came to see me on my return and assured me that my fears were groundless. "My daughter is young and inconsiderate, but she is a good girl and she loves you," the mother said. "I am so happy for you both. Estelle needs someone older, like you, to guide her; just think of how much you two could do together in music — you will write it and she will sing it." In a few days a letter came; a childish letter full of schoolroom gossip and the beauty of Rome — the only explanation for the delay being that the sender was "way behind" in her studies and, having to catch up with other scholarship winners, had no time for correspondence. I went to Third Avenue antique shops in search of another Irish ring and, after hours of unproductive rummaging, found an almost exact replica of the stolen one. Letters from Italy began to arrive fairly regularly; not very satisfactory letters they were — but containing references to love, living arrangements, getting a wedding dress that had been in the family for 15 years altered, and other such encouraging trivia. We were to be married in the Russian church on East 123rd Street sometime in October, and I even went best-man and apartment hunting; my quarters on East 35th Street being of the *garçonnière* variety.

Two months later, a week before Estelle's scheduled departure from Genoa, two letters from her were placed on my breakfast table by Florence, my jitterbug-addicted maid. The first expressed my fiancée's burning desire to be "back in my arms again"; the second, written ten hours later, began: "I know that I'm hurting you terribly, but it will be best for both of us," and announced the breaking of our engagement. Reasons given: the difference in our ages, and music being her only *real* love; Estelle had sold her steamship ticket; deciding to remain in Rome and dedicate herself to her "God-given voice — her life, her child, her everything." A year later she returned to New York and married a sculptor she had met in Rome. She instantly gave up singing and presented the sculptor with a set of twins.

It took me about a year to recover from this upset. At forty-five, adjusting one's entire world to the idea of marital existence is not simple; having effected such an adjustment — *before* entering into marriage — it's doubly difficult to readjust oneself to the "confirmed bachelor" status. Some of my friends insisted that it was not I but merely my pride that was hurt; they were right to some extent, as Estelle calmly wrote her mother that she had never loved me and had accepted my marriage proposal only because she was afraid her father would cut off her allowance, thus making it impossible for her to go on with her singing lessons. She therefore considered breaking with me a *noble* gesture, as she felt her innate honesty prevented her from "using" me. Nevertheless, pride played but a small part in my emotional downfall; by falling in love with Estelle, absurd though my love may have been, I got away from my own self and learned to like this selfless state. With Estelle abruptly stepping out of my life, I was left free to face myself again, and self-contemplation is hardly a substitute for love.

Music came to my rescue, as it had so often in the past. There was the Yaddo Festival, at which Nancy Chase sang and Dean Dixon conducted my six songs from Housman's *The Shropshire Lad,* and the performance of my Violin Sonata by John Creighton Murray, to my accompaniment, in Carnegie Hall — both works, especially the sonata, receiving good notices. The sonata, originally written for Roman Totenberg, had already been played by Maurice Wilk in Paris — on the same Voice of America broadcast in the course of which Estelle sang two of my Carco songs. I had a record taken off the air at the time, and it was strange and rather horrible to put it on now that Estelle was no more than an empty sound; to hear myself playing the short piano introduction and then my ex-love's clear, limpid voice intoning my melody to Carco's half-tender, half-wanton verses — without much feeling, but with laudable concentration on getting the French words right.

> *Il pleut. C'est merveilleux — je t'aime.*
> *Nous resterons à la maison . . .*

she sang. No, this was still remembered, so I sought refuge in Forgotten Music to help me forget.

Dean Dixon, one of our most authentic musical talents, needed a fresh start desperately that fall, having lost the children's concerts of the New York Philharmonic, some of which he had conducted, as well as his position as leader of the Juilliard training orchestra. A Negro "fronting" a dance or recording band is an established tradition in this country, but a Negro conducting a full-size symphony orchestra is something else again; after giving concerts with hastily assembled groups, borrowing money right and left to pay the musicians and getting few, very few, jobs like the Yaddo one, Dixon came to the tragic conclusion that all doors were closed to him in the States. Having read about my project of Franco-American musical exchanges, he wanted to know whether something could be done about a Paris debut for him. I wrote Barraud, who replied punctually to the effect that he'd be glad to give Dixon one or two radio dates, but suggested his hiring a hall — Salle Pleyel or the Théâtre des Champs Elysées — so that he would have at least one public appearance and get the press to come.

Dean was broke but, happily, I had a brainstorm which presented a workmanlike solution. There are many talented young Americans who dream of playing with European orchestras, getting an impressive set of notices and cashing in on such a showing in the States. Why not get three such soloists, make them contribute five hundred dollars each to the expenses of the concert, and have them all appear under Dixon's baton in Paris? "Sounds good," Dean said, "but where do we get solvent soloists?" How we got them is unimportant, but we did get them: Maurice Bialkin, my cello-playing Forgotten Music champion; Mildred Waldman, the capable Chicago pianist; and Charles Holland, a Negro tenor with a voice of rare beauty. The four musicians sailed together, having obtained two symphonic "dates" from Barraud — a concert of Forgotten Music under the two joint societies' auspices, and an American Embassy recital.

This time I was not as unselfish as with the 1948 All-American Paris venture. My altruism not only hadn't paid off, but I was even accused by one of the composers represented of being "patronizing." Following the break with Estelle, Duke stepped aside in favor of Dukelsky, who, in addition to *The Shropshire Lad* and the Violin Sonata, had his "Ode to the Milky Way" played by the CBS Symphony under Herrmann on October 2nd, *Le Bal des Blanchisseuses* reprised in Paris on November 13th, *Paris Aller et Retour* accorded a public performance at the Théâtre des Champs Elysées, the Cello Concerto *premièred* by Bialkin under Dixon at the Salle Erard on December 5th, and the Third Symphony conducted by Dixon at the Salle Pleyel on December 13th. Three performances of a symphony by as many conductors in the course of two years was a new high for me.

Dean Dixon scored a tremendous success, with the Parisians flocking to see a Negro conduct white orchestras in programs judiciously mixing Brahms with Gershwin and other Americans. Any work of Gershwin's spells *box office* in Paris, and Dean conducts George's music especially well, endowing it with extraordinary intensity and whipping foreign orchestras, ill-suited to the "relaxed" playing essential in jazz, into a state of ritualistic frenzy. Dean is now one of Europe's busiest conductors, and I'm proud of the role I played in his progress.

Another conductor, Leopold Stokowski, having had good reports on both my latest symphony and the "Ode to the Milky Way," wrote me a series of courteous and encouraging letters (ten of them) concerning both works and his plans for their performance. As early as October, 1948, Mr. Stokowski began looking for a good "place for the symphony" on his programs; in March, 1949, he worked on "reconsidering" the programs and wanted to know the playing time of my symphony, also displaying lively interest in my "rediscovery" of neglected works. "Things Are Looking Up"—I hummed the Gershwin song of that name to myself. But in August of the same year Mr. Stokowski, although admitting that he enjoyed "studying the symphony very much," confessed his utter inability to find the coveted "good place" for it, not realizing that I would have been happy with a not-so-good one; he promised to listen to the "Ode" as performed by Benny Herrmann. In December, having heard the performance, the conductor thought it "very well done" and asked for a list of my "symphonic compositions." Two weeks later he thanked me for the list I forwarded and requested the score of *Midwinter Night's Dream,* a ballet announced but not completed; in June, 1950, I was startled to receive another letter, wherein the industrious Mr. Stokowski informed me of resuming his search for a "good place on one of his programs" for . . . the long-suffering Third Symphony. "In case we broadcast it, is the duration twenty-two minutes or twenty-six?" he wished to know. I told him. In July the conductor expressed a desire for a record of the said symphony made by the French Radio. Owing to technical difficulties, this record was not made available to me, which fact I reported to my correspondent. In August he wrote offering to study the work by the piano-duet arrangement. In September the get-together took place and Mr. Stokowski wrote to tell me of his enjoyment of what he heard, adding that he would send me Apel's *Harvard Dictionary of Music,* which he thought "absolutely first class of its kind." Thus, our lengthy correspondence produced a beautifully inscribed copy of the dictionary (which, unlike Becky Sharp, I did *not* throw away), but no performance of the symphony.

To the unperformed (in America) symphony should be added yet another unproduced Broadway show, a merry spoof on fashion magazines and the folk employed by them titled *Wedding Day,* book by Leonard Gershe, lyrics by Ogden Nash. The show's opening number, called "I Hitched My Wagon to Harper's Bazaar," so delighted the editorial staff of that periodical that they reprinted a whole page of the song in a montage with a suitably arresting caption. The non-production of *Wedding Day* proved embarrassing to me, as the magazine's readers began telephoning and writing for first-night seats in advance, and were understandably vexed when the first night was postponed "indefinitely." I was fast acquiring an unenviable reputation as Broadway's No. 1 Composer of Unproduced Shows, a reputation justly earned.

Somewhat wearied by all this unproductive activity, I went to Fire Island to recuperate; but the place was not the same. Ocean Beach had become all the rage, and New Yorkers were fighting for living accommodations, money no object. The rents shot up prodigiously and the real-estate people, taking advantage of the boom, were asking $3000 for a barely livable five-room cottage for the "season" — and getting it. The natives didn't think much of the garish exhibitionists who had invaded their homes, but the money was good, so they bore their grudges in silence and grew rich on the fat of the mainland.

The great social pastime in postwar Ocean Beach was that decadent capitalistic invention — the Cocktail Party. Domestic help was scarce and uncooperative in the evening, which they preferred to reserve for their own party-going; consequently dinners in private homes became anachronistic, as they rapidly got to be in New York too. After intensive sun-bathing and wrestling with the treacherous undertow, it was pleasant to don slacks and journey to the nearest cocktail-giving household to compare your tan with that of your closest competitor and to flirt with pale new arrivals from Manhattan. In 1950 the island was chiefly inhabited by psychoanalysts, Broadway press agents, militantly self-assertive homosexuals, progressives — so-called because of their steady progress in the direction of Moscow — and liberals — whose claim to that much-abused term lay in the fact that they were liberally sprinkled with Stalinism. Socially insignificant people achieved social significance overnight merely by preaching Stalinism. The island's hostesses, laudably impartial and devoid of social or sexual prejudice, invited anybody who was at all presentable and, when pressed for extra men, quite a few who were not; after all, they couldn't very well tell a man's politics or sexual quirks underneath the fine tan and the loud-striped madras trunks he wore.

One of the island's busier hostesses asked me to come to a big shindig at her beach house. On appearing at the appointed time, I pushed my way through a mass of summering matrons and reached the well-stocked bar with some difficulty. Scotch-and-soda in hand, I turned around to espy an elegantly undressed middle-aged woman whose "permanent" had a time-defying Rock-of-Ages look, and whose face was not unfamiliar, without my quite being able to place it — a Cocktail Party face. "Oh-h, Mr. Duke! Fancy seeing *you* here," the female cooed. "Where is *our* Millie? You're a member of the Millie Cult, *of course?"* I regretfully confessed to knowing no Millie, adding that the only woman I cultivated was Euterpe; but that proved the wrong answer. The woman's face stiffened, to match her rocklike permanent, the welcoming smile was gone; she barked, "Fascist!" and, shaking a magnificently manicured Lenin-red fingernail at me, lost herself in the crowd.

I got the uneasy feeling of being in the wrong place, and, on spotting the belligerent face of a well-known "progressive" lawyer, knew that it was time to push on. One of the women present brought her twelve-year-old son with her and, as I made my way to the door, I overheard the boy asking his mother in a high-pitched whine, "Mummy are the Hollywood Ten a good band — *better* than Tommy Dorsey?"

I didn't care for the "new look" of Fire Island, but I cannot say I liked the look of the *new* New York much better. The city's fathers were doing unattractive things to Washington Square, removing my beloved Murray Hill hotel, but inexplicably leaving the horrors of West Forty-second Street and Broadway alone. I found it increasingly difficult to compose in my East Thirty-fifth Street flat, with the dental-drill-like riveting on all sides giving me goose pimples. Agents and actors resumed their embarrassing telephoning to ascertain the truth of Mr. Zolotow's or Mr. McCord's statements; these hardworking men were themselves bewildered by the ever-increasing number of "promised and hoped-for" products of my working table. Park Avenue friends preceded telephone invitations to drinks with, "By the way, Vernon, that show of yours . . . it *is* going on, isn't it?" A celebrated Manhattan party-giver made a special trip from Newport to secure a list of promising young entertainers she could spring on her party guests from me; I gave her six or seven names of the faithful "kids" from our audition "token casts." At the end of the year they all called to thank me for the "opportunity" and to express their surprise at my not having been among those present. Broadway boulevardiers, on bumping into me at Sardi's or "21," would gaze at me silently and sorrowfully, as if to say, "You were good once — wouldn't you be better off dead?" The Roland Petit second season on Broadway (he made a big hit the year before) brought the not unreasonable guess that Broadway had become allergic to my talents and would have none of them; my *Bal des Blanchisseuses,* after a long and honorable career in Europe and South America, was finally to be shown in this country. The posters announced it snappily and the ballet chroniclers gave it plenty of space; some thirty friends of mine bought tickets for the opening. At 3:00 P.M. on the day of the *première* I was notified by one of the Shubert underlings of my ballet's cancellation. "Technical reasons" was the only explanation given.

Howard Hoyt, who was then my agent, asked me whether I would consider writing the score to *Casey Jones,* a book Richard Flournoy had based on the hero of the railroad saga, to lyrics by Sammy Cahn. "What, another show?" I exclaimed in anguish. "I couldn't tackle another show score, Howard; it wouldn't be fair to the producers. In the last few years I have collected at least six advances *against* royalties — only there were no royalties, because the shows never 'happened'! It's a living, if you will, but there must be other ways of making a buck." Howard assured me that *Casey Jones* was one show that was *certain* to go on (it didn't) and that Sammy Cahn, anxious to secure me for a collaborator, was ready to take a plane to New York, should I say yes. "Sammy and Jule Styne came to a parting of the ways," my agent explained. "They were only the most successful songwriting team on the Coast. You wouldn't say 'no' to replacing Jule, would you?" That was powerful arguing and I said that I'd be delighted to meet successful Sammy and take a gander at a six-page synopsis of *Casey Jones,* which I thought, on examining it, not devoid of promise.

Sammy Cahn soon arrived, a small, fidgety man with a black mustache and a supercharged personality. He expressed his joy at meeting me, "a man he always admired from afar," as he put it; the adjective he used continually in connection with my person and gifts was "great," which was a nice adjective after reading so many less nice ones used to describe my music. I will always be grateful to Sammy for having engineered my exodus to the West, and I know that whatever happened to *Casey* was no fault of his. The man was a capable and immensely industrious worker, and had enough humility and capacity for self-criticism not to be content with everything he wrote — a rare quality, not always characteristic of *my* methods. "We already *have* that," Sammy would say, having just finished what I thought a good lyric to a serviceable tune. "Now let's try another tack." And thus we'd write several variations on the same theme, in no way resembling one another.

After completing a half-dozen songs for *Casey* and assuring me that I was doing "great," Sammy offered to take me to the Coast, there to meet and work with Dick Flournoy and, perhaps, get a picture job with him as my team-mate. It was my turn to say, "Great!" because I was sick of New York, which was seemingly as sick of me, and because I wanted to be with my "new" family — Alex, Mona and Natasha, their daughter — again, after five years.

My brother was still at Metro, doing well and highly rated by his associates and superiors. He now owned a house on Shelby Drive, not far from Culver City, where he had to report every morning; it was a small and unremarkable house which, because of his unfailing architectural skill, he had turned into a fine modern residence. I stayed with the Dukelskys in the beginning, then — when the "breaks" came — moved to a small Neutra-built house in Westwood, where I live today.

Spurred on by Sammy Cahn's enthusiasm and by my brother's tranquil family life, I rapidly became a California "convert." Although the musical "climate" of Los Angeles is hardly comparable with that of other big cities, the place must have a real attraction for composers — as both Schoenberg and Stravinsky settled there permanently. The habitual maligning of Los Angeles, especially Hollywood, by those who describe it as half hothouse, half whorehouse, inhabited by hams, punks and quacks, a place where flowers have no fragrance, fruit has no taste, and women have no brains, worst of all a place where a year has no seasons, only a continuous synthetic summer, occasionally enlivened by floods and earthquakes and something called "smog" — is not based on fact. The legend of Hollow Hollywood can be laid squarely at the door of Eastern writers who come to the Coast on a ten-week assignment, meet a few "dollaristocrats," collect their checks and go back home, spouting with rage.

I'm not much good at coining words, which was a specialty of my favorite forgotten author, Nathaniel P. Willis, who wrote for the New York *Mirror* one hundred and twenty years ago, and is the trademark of the present word-wizardry titleholder Walter Winchell. But "dollaristocrat," whether I coined the word or not (I believe I did), is an apt, succinct term for the species of Hollywoodian, that, owing to the present precarious state of the film industry, may soon become extinct. There aren't many dollaristocrats among the actual makers of movies, creative men and women who seem to be nice, everyday folks, good to talk to and fun to be with. A dollaristocrat may be an agent, a music publisher or a "business manager" (without whom no self-respecting Hollywoodian would be able to arrange his affairs, pay his taxes and keep out of trouble) — but you can tell him a mile away, and if you can't, he'll tell *you*. "Whaddya notice when you first meet a guy, kid?" a member of the clan once asked me. "Why, his eyes, I suppose," I ventured mildly. "Gee, you're green, fella," the dollaristocrat snorted. "Ya look at his shoes. I don't care what else you wear — but get yasself a paira custom-mades, and whaddya get? Ya get *respect.*" Anxious to succeed I made a mental note to get the handmade article. "When ya go to a guy's house, whaddya notice first?" my advisor went on in stentorian tones. This required some concentration. "Would it be architecture?" I hazarded. "Na-aw!" the man retorted in disgust. "The doors, stupid; thass wot ya notice, see? Go to a good hardware store and they'll fix you up with nothin' but the best. Then, whaddya get?" "I know, respect." "Right!" the dollaristocrat gave me full marks on that one; lesson over.

The fact that they don't speak the King's English — nor, certainly, the President's — matters not at all; the dollaristocratic language consists almost entirely of snappy sayings like: "I got news for ya";

"She fractured me"; "Get this *bit*" (with a sneer); "This is the greatest"; and so on. A dollaristocrat is always busy cutting an impressive figure, when not cutting a competitor's throat. Absolute musts are Kalifornia Kut Klothes and a Klassy Kadillac Kar, preferably of this year's make; last year's car is looked upon with suspicion by other dollaristocrats — could it be that the guy is slipping? The accepted thing then is to make some discreet inquiries and start "moving in" on the outgoing rival.

One of the tribe once took me in hand and, after watching me closely for a week, came out with firm orders to "stop being a foreign snob." This, after twenty years in the States, was a bit thick and I asked my mentor, with some heat, just how this accursed foreign snobbishness of mine manifested itself. "I got news for ya," said the mentor. "Nobody likes ya, because ya wear them funny coats with extra pockets and slits on the sides." (He was referring to the single-breasted "hacking coat" model I had copied from my English tailor's original, subsequently adopted by every ready-made clothes dealer in the States.) "And say, where d'ya get the nerve to kiss the broads' hands? The husbands don't like it — better cut it out."

One must not be too unkind to Hollywood "operators" — after all, they have such a heavy double cross to bear. Extra pockets and handkissing notwithstanding, I made several good new friends in Los Angeles and I hope to keep them; now that I'm a fairly expert driver, visiting friends is no problem. In between song and other music writing, I hop into my car and descend on Vincente Minnelli (when he is not toiling arduously at Metro), Ira and Lee Gershwin (still the best party-givers in Beverly Hills), on John Houseman, the brilliant director, and his beautiful wife, on the Tony Duquettes, whose house is a miracle of taste and ingenuity, or on Edwin Lester, the boss of the L.A. Civic Light Opera, who just bought a third option on my 1949 Paris-made "Milord." Lester has two rare advantages over all other musical producers — he is an excellent musician himself (having started in life as accompanist to opera singers) and *he never holds backers' auditions;* the money is supplied by Lester's guarantors the moment a new production is decided upon.

Ira Gershwin who has ducked writing my lyrics since 1937 for geographical and other valid reasons, is noted for sports and recreations of his own highly individualistic designing. Not overly fond of large gatherings, the lovable versifier prefers inviting five or six people known for their love of argument, and letting them loose in his drawing room; the feathers fly while Ira grunts contentedly, puffing on an aromatic Montecristo (special selection). The other night while Oscar Levant and I screamed at each other at the tops of our lungs, worried Leonore about to send for help, Ira beamed delightedly, took the Montecristo out of his mouth, and said with a purr: "Now, isn't that better than a stupid big party, where nobody knows anybody?"

My career began in Hollywood quite auspiciously with two Warner musicals, *She's Working Her Way Through College,* a poor remake of the *Male Animal* which made money, and *April in Paris,* with Doris Day, Ray Bolger and Claude Dauphin, quite a pleasant film, which was voted the "best American musical of the year" by the English equivalent of the Hollywood "Academy." The lyrics for both pictures — except for *April's* title song — were by Sammy Cahn. It was at Cahn's grandly appointed Holmby Hills house that we held audition after audition for *Casey Jones.* Dick Krakeur, Vinton Freedley's associate on several musical successes and producer of Celeste Holm's *Affairs of State,* "bought" the show after hearing five songs and reading ten pages of the book. Mike Connelly and other Hollywood columnists praised our score immoderately in the trade papers and George Abbott joined Krakeur in the venture — as coproducer and coauthor. He disapproved of the original book and insisted on a new librettist — Arthur Carter by name. Sammy and I went to New York to play some more auditions — which was no trouble at all, because Cahn is about the greatest demonstrator of songs, without possessing either a matinee idol's physique or a voice; Carter came through with a corking first act, money began pouring in, Capitol paid an unheard-of sum for the preproduction rights to the show's album and we returned to the Coast, proud of a job well done.

Then came the earthquake, only it didn't occur in California but back East in Abbott's office. While Cahn and I were discussing the part of Casey with Eddie Albert (who would have been perfect for it), in walked Dick Krakeur with a somnambulist's gait, his eyes wide and uncomprehending. In his hand he held a telegram from George Abbott, which he wouldn't let us read until Albert was out of the place. The earth-rocking message contained in the telegram was to the effect that Archie (Carter) hadn't come through with a suitable second act, that he, Abbott, didn't see his way clear to getting a new one and that the only course open to him as producer, author and investor was to step out — regrets, regrets, regrets.

Krakeur attempted to continue with the project on his own but soon gave up, and *Casey* went back to Paramount, which had owned the property in the first place, there to repose until someone starts a Society for Forgotten Musical Comedies.

While in New York I contracted to write the music for a revue starring Bette Davis, with lyrics by Ogden Nash and three additional ones by Sammy Cahn, who was the first to be approached about the project, and then turned it over to me and Ogden when Warner's offered him a producer's berth. *Two's Company,* Bette's revue, ended tragically because of the star's illness, and I have no intention of further aggravating matters by giving a detailed account of the show's misfortunes. These would easily fill a fascinating second volume, which I do not propose to write. I thought *Two's Company,* saved by a last-minute assist from John Murray Anderson, whose recent death was a cruel blow to all of us who loved and admired him, a spirited, vastly entertaining and often beautiful revue which, after pronouncedly "mixed" notices, played to three months of capacity business; all the New York columnists, including Winchell, Morehouse, Sobol, Lyons, Sullivan and Walker, agreed with this estimate, and so did the audience at the Alvin Theatre. As for Bette Davis, I will say only that she did the best she could in an unfamiliar idiom, and that her best was often very good indeed. Nora Kaye's work in *Two's Company* was superb (her first appearance on the Broadway stage), and so was that of Jerry Robbins, one of the more gifted and original choreographers, with whom I did *not* have the privilege of working.

Robbins came to the office of Russo and Ellis, our producers, listened to some numbers Ogden and I had written and appeared to be anxious to work on a revue, as he rightly believed that form to be more pliable for ballet purposes than the form of a book show, wherein a choreographer is always weighted down with the handicap of a plot. I, in my turn, was overjoyed at the prospect of working with Robbins; I well remembered his virtuoso display pieces, such as *Fancy Free, Billion Dollar Baby* (otherwise a poorish show) and the Mack Sennett ballet in *High Button Shoes.* A collaboration with Jerry Robbins on three solid ballets — what an opportunity for a composer! Yes, but for another composer, as it turned out; prior to signing with Russo and Ellis, Jerry made it a condition to be allowed to pick his own musical collaborator on the ballets. I was informed two weeks later by the producers that Jerry's choice was Geneviève Pitot, a resourceful musician and a nice woman; but to be thus side-tracked after having amassed several respectable "credits" as ballet composer, after having worked successfully with Balanchine, Massine and Roland Petit, was an undeserved slight. Mellowed by the California sun and Warner Bros. dollars, I made up my mind to be tractable and diplomatic, and acted as though Mme. Pitot's imaginative but more than free versions of my tunes were exactly what I wanted them to be. I was not only not consulted about these versions, through no fault of Mme. Pitot's, but asked specifically to stay away from Robbins's rehearsals, although at recess time Jerry and I were on the friendliest terms.

At orchestra rehearsals, Jerry's methods appeared more singular still; sitting immediately behind the conductor, Milton Rosenstock, he would exchange ideas with him, punctuating his remarks (inaudible to me) with, "Take out the clarinets," or, "Give this to the trombone." I sat in the back of the orchestra, radiating patience and good will; when I disagreed with a particularly startling change, I voiced a polite protest, but received such a ferocious scowl from the choreographer that shutting up seemed to be the only course to take. Two of my numbers with Nash — "Purple Rose," a spoof on hillbillies, and "Roll Along, Sadie," the Bette Davis-Sadie Thompson finale — were completely reworked and rearranged by Rosenstock, and placed in rehearsal without anyone bothering to consult us as to the desirability of the changes made.

Ogden found himself in the strange position of having to rewrite his lyrics daily to make them suit the choreography (in my experience, choreographers have staged their dances to express the lyrics); whole verses and second choruses were dropped, although containing some of Nash's best lines. "Roundabout," our strongest song in the score, originally sung by Dolores Gray in *Sweet Bye and Bye* — as was "Just Like a Man" — got an entirely new verse "explaining" the ballet that followed; the ballet was brilliantly staged and magnificently danced by Nora Kaye — but not to my music. The end justifies the means, I'll allow, and Jerome Robbins's choreography was probably the best feature of the show; I was man enough to watch the dancing calmly and try not to listen to the mutilated score. Ogden planned to publish an unexpurgated edition of the Robbins-dropped lyrics.

Two's Company, in spite of all its vicissitudes, began shaping up like a hit and I returned to the Coast in time for Christmas. Sammy Cahn, having become a producer at Warner's, had his hands full, and I welcomed the opportunity to do a little California loafing. Late in February I was on my way to Europe again, having received Uncle Alexis's urgent request to visit him in Ljubljana, Yugoslavia, now that Tito was on our side. Uncle Alexis, seventy-seven years of age, was in good health but wanted to make some arrangements about his estate — "what there was of it" as he put it. Besides, Balanchine was going to Milan to stage Stravinsky's *Baiser de la Fée* at La Scala, and we thought of resuming activities on behalf of the 1938 *Entr'acte.*

While aboard the S.S. *Saturnia,* I learned of the death of Stalin, and a few days later was shocked by the news of Prokofiev's death. Through Paris friends I had known long before of the two strokes Serge had suffered, following his political downfall, and of his being partially paralyzed. The ship's orchestra went on playing "La Golondrina" and "The Isle of Capri" for the bored passengers, to whom the name of Serge Prokofiev meant nothing whatever. On arrival in Naples I bought an American newspaper published in Rome; the headline read: "Bette Davis Ill, Her Show Closes."

My first impulse was to fly home to the States, but a telegram from Uncle Alexis, in which he expressed his pleasure at the prospect of our reunion, was awaiting me at my hotel, and after two days' brooding in Naples, I went on to Rome and thence to Milan. Balanchine was already there, working hard with the Italian company, which was unused to George's choreographic language. At the Yugoslav border I was made to pay twenty-one dollars' duty for three pairs of nylon stockings and two kilos of coffee, articles which I had bought for my aunt and uncle at the suggestion of the Yugoslav consul in San Francisco. The customs officials wore Moscow-styled uniforms and spoke a language that sounded like Russian read backwards, but were otherwise very polite. I found my aunt and uncle relatively unchanged since our brief meeting in Constantinople; Ljubljana, a pretty Austrian-style town, was clean and poor, although rich in music. Uncle Alexis, intensely interested in my composer's career, proudly displayed me to the leading musicians of his town and made me play my music for them; they returned the compliment by treating me to a recital of recordings by the local composers, many of them genuinely talented. I saw two tolerably well-produced and sung operas at the small Ljubljana opera house — Dvořák's *Russalka,* a full-blooded, lyrical folk legend which would do well at the City Center, and Britten's rehash of the *Beggar's Opera* (why, after the fine Dr. Pepusch original and the Kurt Weill masterpiece?), an ill-considered pastiche, incomprehensible in a composer of Britten's stature. There are ten or twelve symphony orchestras in Yugoslavia (I heard the Ljubljana Philharmonic, a good, thoroughly professional orchestra; the horns were especially fine) and as many opera houses.

The rest of my European trip was fairly routine, and traveling from country to country actually depressed me this time; I never stopped thinking of Prokofiev's dying in Russia, away from his friends, who loved and missed him always. I spent three months in Paris, where the Marquis de Cuevas accepted my *Entr'acte* for production (with Balanchine agreeing to stage it), only to give it up in favor of his Biarritz party. It rained continually in Paris that summer and I went to London to catch up with the sun, two days after the Coronation; found London surprisingly gayer than Paris, almost as gay as in the Diaghilev era; did some motoring and partying with Tony Lindsay-Hogg; dined with Dean Dixon in Copenhagen and rejoiced in his great success at the Tivoli; returned to Paris only to miss Stravinsky's *Rake's Progress,* which was not the hit *Porgy and Bess* was, the Gershwin opera breaking all records at the Théâtre des Champs Elysées; went on to Antibes for a short stay with Rina Rosselli, the Florentine painter; and sailed for home on the S.S. *Vulcania* in August, 1953, from Cannes.

America looked good to me on my return — and I "got lucky" again. I was taken to see a fine revival of *Cabin in the Sky* in Sea Cliff, Long Island — produced by two young men, Ratcliffe and MacMillan, and brightly directed by Herbert Machiz, with Juanita Hall, Josephine Premice and "Nipsy" Russell in the cast. The audience adored it, and I adored them for making the principals sing reprise after reprise of the old favorites, as well as two cannily injected "novelties" — "Summer Is Icumen In" (from *Lady Comes*

Across) and "Not a Care in the World" (late of *Banjo Eyes*). I recorded an album of sixteen songs with the modest title "Vernon Duke plays Vernon Duke" on Johnny Latouche's Bechstein-Moore, a piano with an extra keyboard (never before used for recording purposes), for Atlantic Records. Gala Ebin, an ambitious young producer with an ANTA and Theatre Guild background, asked me to write the music for *Miss Dilly Says No,* an entrancing novel by Theodore Pratt — and I joined forces with my new friends and partners Bob Lee and Jerry Lawrence — two of the brightest new talents in the game — to work on the assignment.

When Ogden Nash appeared on the Man of the Year telecast in December of 1953, he also served as lyricist for the song of that name written by Vladimir Selinsky, the program's musical director. The song was attractive, and Ogden, as always, inimitable; so I sent him a telegram reading: "Loved you and the show and the song but who is the new Vladimir thought you had enough trouble with old one." On December 14th Ogden appeared as "narrator" with Thomas Sherman's Little Orchestra, reciting his verses for Saint-Saëns "The Carnival of Animals." Two days later I received an envelope containing flattering reviews of the momentous occasion and a "memo" from the "narrator": "Dear Vernon — Now I too am a Vladimir!"

On perusing these pages, I am struck by the unprecedented number of "names" — big and small — that adorn them. "What a name dropper that man is!" the patient reader will conclude. I hereby plead guilty to this practice, for I'm dropping the name of Vladimir Dukelsky and henceforth will sign all music that may still flow from my pen — regardless of its nature — as Vernon Duke. And, having once obtained a passport to the Champs Elysées of Paris as Dukelsky, Russian, I shall humbly aspire to the more permanent Elysian Fields, the Elysium of the Ancient Greeks — "The place where the good dwelt after death, located in the Western Ocean . . ." according to *Webster's Dictionary* — as Duke, American and Westerner.

INDEX

Los Angeles Poems

Translated by Boris Dralyuk

Los Angeles

I.

INTRODUCTION

O city whose praises have yet to be sung,
whose image is stained by your filmmaking neighbors—
you're but an amusing chimera to some:
that con artist, Hollywood, did you no favors.

No poets have dared to embrace our fair town—
they find tabloid glory too chintzy to chase.
Alas, poor L.A., you are simply too young . . .
No picturesque ruins . . . Your past leaves no trace . . .

Since I, quite by accident, turned Angeleno,
my smooth-sailing ship ran aground, as it were:
I don't yearn to see the Tyrrhenian Sea, no—
not even Sonoma, not crisp Mendocino,
not beautiful Napa, Carmel, or Big Sur.

For here are my curtains, my backdrop, my stage,
my footlights and spotlights—dramatic illusion . . .
I'm comfortable here in my green Palisades,
where I hobnob with mountains and clouds and the ocean.

II.

SANTA MONICA BEACH

How nice to bask upon the beach;
the water is so clear, so light.
On one side is a swan-white chest,
and all around are meaty thighs.

Awakened by a gentle breeze,
I'll sidle up, lean on your shoulder,
while a slim boy dives in the waves,
as does—his aunt? Plumper and older.

The dogs have fun digging up sand
and barking loud without their muzzles.
A mother feeds her newborn son
while bodybuilders flex their muscles.

Sailing near shore, a merry boat
pierces our ears with its sharp whistle.
Schoolboys and schoolgirls take no note—
pour Coca-Cola down their throats
to wash down undigested lessons.

A lady quite advanced in age
eclipses, even blinds the young—
her skin puts all their tans to shame:
a scintillating scarlet-brown.

Bustling about are rowdy crews
of poets, acrobats, and swimmers.
The damsels' swimsuits are the hues
of sunset, rich in reds and blues.
It's sunset? Off for home and dinner.

III.

FISH PIER, SANTA MONICA

Look—Santa Monica,
so much like Italy.
Old friend, remember when
you and I lived down here?
See all those fish shops?
Here, come this way.
A huge orange lobster
squats on display,
beside two poor oysters
soldered together.
Fleet-footed seagulls
squawk in displeasure.
Plump as a cuttlefish,
a sailboat glides past.
A dripping-wet beauty
cries out for her dress.
Mischievous schoolgirls
glitter like caviar
and put me in mind of
how spry we once were . . .
A new crowd is forming,
in search of a prize—
cheap phony rifles
aim at bull's-eyes.
Waves, wild and fizzy,
tumble ashore.
A bug-eyed cod slumbers
forevermore.
Lovers lie dozing
between the pilings—
kissing, embracing,

now silent, now sighing . . .
There's Mrs. Hammersley,
still playing cards . . .
Ah, that harmonica!
Oh, that sweet piccolo!
Sing, Santa Monica—
let music flow . . .

IV.

BEATNIK (VENICE, CALIF.)

His ears stick out through stringy,
uneven, greasy hair.
Bedraggled with insomnia,
he hasn't bathed all year.
His long arms dangle loosely
as through a toothless scowl
he wheezes out the blues or
simply emits a howl.
Pity virtue's defender,
helpless and innocent;
the beatnik's heart is tender,
his head, hidden in sand.
Upon a scuffed old drumhead
he rattles a tattoo
to drown out inner torment
and summon his own dormant
nirvana, pure and true.
"Remember?" No . . . he doesn't . . .
He's happy in his cell:
the vague eternal "present."
Tomorrow is unpleasant:
a gaping door to hell.
His eyes are both concealed by
his bangs—a tangled knot . . .
Still, maybe he can see what
the rest of us cannot.

V.

HOLLYWOOD BOULEVARD

"This wind's too much! I nearly stumbled
and barely made it to this stop,"
a young Black woman coyly grumbles,
trembling in her Italian top.
With nature's ire drawing nearer,
a Chinese fellow and his wife
escape into a heated theater,
where one buck buys the easy life.
Soap-scented chewing gum helps scatter
thoughts of foul weather, mundane woes—
just for a while it doesn't matter
that he's a cook and she cleans clothes.

VI.

SUNSET STRIP

Poor lady is in tatters,
disheveled and distressed—
a star of yesterday.

Abandoned by the cameras,
no wonder she's depressed:
her heart is drained away.

Look all you like, no matter—
won't guess how old she is . . .
Her dress is dull and gray:

despite her stately manners,
she can't keep up appearances
without her former pay.

Her days drag on, relentless,
her eyes look tired and lifeless,
her furs are worn and frayed . . .

O Hollywood, how horrid . . .
Lord, work your little wonders:
restore her faded fame.

VII.

BEVERLY HILLS

A chauffeur lazily maneuvers
an elephantine Cadillac—
his insolence meets with approval
from the grande dame who sits in back.
The car is crawling, barely inching
beside a shop's gilded display.
The mannequins are all bewitching;
the lady scans them with a sigh.
"What foolish dresses—simply funny.
I see the skirts are long this year . . ."
This woman won't spend any money
but she will have something to share
with her dear friend, who follows fashion,
over the evening's game of bridge,
once she returns to her big mansion—
well built, and colder than a fridge.

VIII.

VENICE, CALIF.

Here lived a wealthy eccentric with a passion for Venice.
He couldn't make money abroad, so he had to come back.
California again? What a bore! What a shameful misfortune . . .
Never mind. He would build his own Venice, fortune be damned.
His workers began by destroying the small shacks and houses.
Marble and granite? Imported—together with old gondolas.
"I swear, he's gone crazy," the neighbors complained to each other,
so he bought out the neighbors and found them new lots.
They burned off the weeds and the bushes, dug crooked canals,
raised bridges across them—a poor imitation, it's true . . .
Exactly like Venice, he thought. But the snide locals shrugged:
"You called us all fools, but it seems that the real fool is you.
You lay out a cheap little square and you call it 'San Marco'?
You dress up as a Doge, pointlessly getting your fur up?
This gondolier—Joe? Drop the act. The man is a cowpoke.
It's 'America First'—we don't need to impersonate Europe."
But our captain of industry, brave Abbot Kinney, persisted.
He set up a glorious theater and gave it a gift.
His god was the dollar, but he knew that a goddess was called for—
his Olympus of drama would need the Divine Sarah B.
He shelled out some gold, since actresses tend to like gold,
and Bernhardt arrived . . . But nobody came to her play.
Not a soul in the seats. You could hear the rats squeak, gnawing holes.
Outside, a dog barked. Farther off, a lone donkey brayed.

....

That premiere is forgotten. The canals have mostly dried up.
The best of the bridges is crumbling, covered with burdock.
Venice is nothing like Venice. It's full of loud drunks.
And San Marco, alas, is the playground of indigent urchins.

IX.

MALIBU

The fireflies of countless cars
sparkle and die out in a flash;
exhausted fishermen have cleared
the ocean of its final fish.
Now Malibu is humid, fragrant—
a plated slice of cantaloupe.
The night encloses in its coffin
the living corpse of daytime hope.
There's precious little left for mortals:
white snow over a mug of beer,
a curious, peculiar torpor,
and waves, monotonous and drear.
Two at the bar—amid the hubbub,
they chat as if alone tonight;
Their trousers are as tight as rubber;
their shirts are neat and gleaming white.
One's past his prime—passed it by plenty.
He's rich, if looks do not deceive.
The other's huge, and maybe twenty.
Wrestler, perhaps? Soldier on leave?
The younger one is downing whiskey;
the older sips Crème de Banane.
The Californian fog, all frisky,
tickles the eyes as it creeps in.
"How's tricks, my boy?" "Oh, I've been better.
There isn't any work these days."
"Yes, so I've read. Good luck, dear fellow."
A second round. "Oh, by the way . . .
You got a fiver you can spare?
Landlady's after me for rent . . .
I'm waiting on a package there . . ."

The old man's eyes turn sharp, like flint:
"Five dollars isn't nothing, friend."
He pays the bill. "Let's get some air.
It's awful stuffy in this bar."
Then, slowly and without a care,
they make their exit, arm in arm.

X.

FARMERS MARKET

Plump little clouds, like rolls of bread,
lie on the sky's blue tablecloth.
The sun is orange marmalade
scooped generously from the jar.
Breakfast is ready, it would seem,
but we will never reach that high—
besides, our time has not yet come:
we're plenty happy where we are.
Just show us to the Farmers Market,
that citadel of gluttony,
lavish abode fit for Lucullus,
where fruits and vegetables and flowers
arch like a rainbow over earth
and dazzle countless looky-loos.
The meat upon a nearby tray
is ruddy with ferocious health—
at any moment it might leap
right down and turn into a calf.
A fresh-caught fish puffs out its cheeks
and gives a crab a flirty wink;
its scales still drip with salty water,
all iridescent, nacre-like.
Bronze-colored coffee from Brazil
does battle with the sea's strong smell,
but both are in the end defeated
by the aroma of the dill,
the savory odor of Dutch cheese,
the serenade of gorgonzola.
To right and left are restaurants,
and also strangers, apparitions—
but not the type you find in Blok,

just average girls, everyday women.
Beautiful Ladies don't abound.
Some are in trousers, some in skirts.
No mysteries—it's clear as day:
teeth gleaming, bosoms ample, fragrant—
all attributes are on display,
and there's no need to get acquainted.
Let's sit down at the nearest table,
and I will go and fetch—your choice!—
Mexican rice flavored with saffron,
a salmon of the palest pink,
a lobster with two piercing whiskers,
sweet buttered cobs of golden corn . . .
Perhaps Italian minestrone?
Or a gray soup of swallow's nests,
prepared, of course, a la Chinoise?
There is no perfume, no thick fog—
all is so obvious, so plain,
and tuneful without any music:
a purely thoughtless tenderness,
uncomplicated happiness—
and that, my dear, will do for us.

January 1, 1962

Nature Morte

Is this Crimea? Is it the Pacific?
Same salty water, same sweet sun, same view:
a picture-postcard seaside panorama
beneath the same clear sky, same shade of blue.
The water has the smell of fresh cucumbers.
A jellyfish coils like a blown-glass snake.
Rising behind him with its snowy lining,
a wave's thick shirt descends to overtake
and drape a swimmer. On the shore, a crab
offers his well-worn communistic greeting
and millions of fish with crimson gills
commence their International's big meeting.
Yet in Alupka I was but a boy,
while Santa Monica's my denouement . . .
The smoke of time swirls like a curly cloud
above the figure of a tanned old man,
who lies with fingers laced behind his head.
He smiles, recalling his unlikely story.
America, Crimea—does it matter
where I cross over into Purgatory?

June 1963

Letter to My Wife

What shall I wish for you, dear Kay?
October's scent is in the air
and we're still here, a happy pair,
four years after our wedding day.
Scenes from our courtship seem to grow
ever more vivid—I recall
first seeing you: a chorus girl
in Lotte Lehmann's *Figaro.*
Beneath the light layer of cosmetics
I saw your features, your pure face—
felt young, ridiculous, romantic—
such silliness, so out of place . . .
After the curtain, idle banter,
a smile, a nod, an argument.
"The girl is Scottish, from Montana,"
said the conductor with a wink.
"A lovely voice, quite musical . . .
And look at her . . . she's a Renoir."
My tartan girl, dressed for the ball,
came up to us. "How young you are!"
slipped from my lips, a careless comment,
and then another compliment.
Nothing unique. Not for a moment
did I believe that we were meant
to be together. We were colleagues.
Why hope in vain, why self-deceive?

Another old, used-up Onegin
with sweet Tatiana—so naive . . .
Again the calls, again the meetings,
the midday laughs, the midnight sobs . . .
I felt I'd paid fat Cupid plenty—

he'd get no more, the little slob . . .
Alas, I felt from you a gentle
calm, childlike warmth: it seemed to me
that I could talk, or even prattle,
and all I said—you would believe.
That gullibility was touching.
I understood I couldn't lie
to you, Madonna of Montana—
so it was best to sneak away,
make of my serenade a scherzo,
for peace and freedom lay ahead.
But suddenly my heart awakened
and whispered, "No you don't—not yet . . ."
Weeks passed. The town of Santa Barbara,
where you then lived, became to me
the safest of all earthly harbors,
a source of electricity.
I was so grateful for those journeys,
my newfound ardor. With a grin,
I mocked himself: "You dirty scoundrel—
how dare you fall in love again?"
In truth, my dear, you were my *first* love.
I hadn't known true love at all.
Love is a peaceful force of nature,
not a destructive sudden squall
that sweeps you up and sends you soaring,
only to throw you back on shore.
No, honest lovers do not hurry
and do not tease those they adore.
You had a roommate, a young woman,
but I, the former anchorite,
wanted a duo, not a trio,
when visiting your home at night.
In cramped conditions we would feed on

delightful music, without fail.
You would sing Schubert's finest Lieder,
my Caledonian nightingale.
Your piano was beat-up, a goner—
at times it mewled, at times it squeaked.
Nor did I help things with my tenor
(admittedly a little weak).
We'd laugh, and swim, and kiss, and after . . .
No sense in sharing details here . . .
There was no talk of wedding altars:
such furniture can kill careers.
Yet I had hopes I could not bury,
which lent a sadness to our trysts—
for you had never wished to marry
and I would never dare insist.
Then I grew ill—with pills and pillows,
bandages, doctors, fever dreams . . .
Verdi inverted: you—Alfredo,
and I—the fallen girl, it seems . . .
One of those days you came to see me,
tears welling up in you big eyes,
and said, "I know now." Was I dreaming?
Oh, what a fabulous surprise!
The weeks that followed were a whirlwind—
and then: your stunning turquoise dress,
my wan "best man," your girlfriend singing
(alas, I wasn't too impressed),
the pulpit looking like a scaffold,
the organ's sticky marmalade,
you walking up, so shy and careful,
and I still nervous, still afraid . . .
But all the nerves quickly departed—
we took our vows, exchanged our rings,
made our way home after the party,

and felt, in autumn, warmest spring.
Since then, of all the things I'm sure of,
this one remains most firmly true:
though I may fall at any moment,
I pledge my love and life to you.
And when it comes, that fateful day
when I break off my earthly tune,
remind me please, my darling Kay,
of our enchanted honeymoon.

Autumn 1961

Two Dollars

In all the dizzying pre-wedding turmoil
(like Gogol's hero, I had awful jitters),
running around to get champagne and flowers
(they didn't smell like flowers from Crimea)
and every other necessary trifle,
I nearly didn't make it to the office,
my darling Kay, where newlyweds, by law,
have to obtain a proper marriage license.
I found you waiting there, impatiently,
casting quick glances at your bracelet watch
(my Scottish heather brought up in Montana).
Then, holding hands, like children off to school,
we rushed up to the counter, panting wildly,
and I declared, "Here are the documents,"
as I threw down the papers with great pride.
"Two dollars," grunted the unfeeling clerk,
who looked to me just like a sunburnt cactus.
In desperation, I took out my wallet
and found no money. I had spent it all
on things we needed for the celebration
(an L.A. wedding is a big production).
But, hastily, you drew from your own wallet
a crumpled, crinkly pair of greenish bills,
resembling two squirmy little lizards,
and slipped them to the clerk—"Two dollars, is it?"—
then, with a faint smile, added shyly, "Thank you."
Pursing his lips, the gruff clerk merely grunted,
and we raced off towards the church, like mad.
Along the way, you whispered to me, "Honey,
always remember who paid for the wedding."
And I'll remember, always, darling Kay
(my Scottish heather brought up in Montana).

* * *

Then came the hour of our first real parting—
of that sweet sorrow, as the Bard described it.
I had to travel to New York, for reasons
I've long forgotten. At the sooty station,
we kissed each other sadly and embraced,
reluctant to let go. True newlyweds.
"I'll have to eat all by myself tonight,"
you said so sweetly, with a little sigh,
then rummaged in your wallet. "I'm afraid
I have no money." I pulled out two dollars.
"All right," you said. I stepped aboard the train.
The smoke of it smelled strange, rather disturbing.
A little later, in the Pullman car,
where it was cool, I wore my blue pajamas
and thought of you. I drifted off, and dreamt
of Scottish heather growing in Montana . . .
Then came a vision of my own finale
(I hope it, too, will come with some delay):
Bottles of medicine. Half-darkness. By my bed,
you, darling Kay—clenched tightly in your hand
a crumpled, crinkly pair of greenish bills,
resembling two squirmy little lizards.
Brimming with love and fear, you say to me,
"Here, honey . . . Don't forget the telegram . . .
Send it as soon as you arrive . . . It won't be easy
for me to stay here, all alone, on earth . . ."
As difficult as it may be, God willing,
I'll still discern your words, with gratitude,
but I'll no longer need to take your money.

* * *

Friend, you and I have two of everything.
Two homelands—your America, my Russia
(a Scottish heather and a Slavic birch).
A pair of dogs. And a duet for piano.
Two dollars. And two lives. Until the end.

June 1963

Christmas in Santa Monica

Heat in December—not the frost
that pokes us with its unseen pins.
The mouths of tykes emit no steam
and paper Christmas trees look out
onto the merry, decked-out scene.
Instead of snow—fluff, cotton wool,
and a glass floor posing as ice.
People gaze up and feast their eyes,
for free, as a fake angel flies
amid the strings of ersatz pearls.
The traffic lights, like cigarettes,
flicker in rhythm down the street,
while a supposed Santa Claus,
sweating right through his fur-trimmed coat,
explains, in tones so rich and sweet,
the charms of winter at the Pole.
On TV youngsters smile profusely,
sing carols, then, in swimming trunks,
race one another to the waves
(without the beach, we can't have music).
And farther down, beside the bridge,
on fragrant eucalyptus trees,
a triptych of bright lanterns swings
to glorify the newborn King.
The night descends. A star's suspended
between the palms; this strange and shoddy
mirage of Yuletide makes no sense.
Still—Merry Christmas, my dear friend!
You'll give it all, love everybody.

January 1965

Whisky a Go Go

They don't have anything to say,
nor are they listening to me,
these juveniles under the sway
of tireless Terpsichore.
Most fellows have long manes, bare faces—
it is as if they've traded places
with all their dates, who wear not skirts
but trousers with tight buttoned shirts.
The Twist, Watusi, other crazes—
they're up to date . . . And who is that
insensate, zealous acrobat?
Lady? No, bearded. With loose knees.
Around him—hives devoid of bees
and stuffed instead with girlish heads.
Their eyes lined thick, their bodies bony,
these lasses tower over lads.
They really should come with a warning,
our sirens out of California . . .
They toss back liquor from their flasks
and, like cows busy at their task,
chomp, chomp, and chomp on their sweet gum.
The guitar quacks. A writhing brute
growls nasally, "Hey, Johnny's cute."
A dancer twirls her scrawny rear . . .
I'm standing close and clearly hear
the jangling tambourine, the drum . . .
I'm old enough to be their father—
but kids like these? I wouldn't bother.

February 1965

Heat Wave

Today the sun is unrelenting,
its rays refusing to recede,
pouring their oil upon the wilted
salad of houses in the street.

The evening couldn't get much warmer.
While sails hang limp and seamen mope,
a lazy cop sulks on the corner
and nurses an illicit hope:

a glass, a juicy, springy olive,
a whispering ambrosial stream
in a secluded bar—the call of
some tinkling voice . . . A man can dream . . .

August 1966

Arizona

Are you gaga over ozone?
Does it simply make you swoon?
Come on down to Arizona,
as befits a proper loon.
Cowboys with their copper faces,
Gary Cooperish attire,
loaf around, twanging like oboes,
wet with sweat, smelling of mire.
With their legs encased in leather
boots of an enormous size,
they appear as Gullivers
to our Lilliputian eyes.
They make money in fake gunfights
staged for television screens,
but when those long shoots are ended,
Arizona's where they spend it—
the calm desert is their scene.
Rich old ladies much admire
all these cowboys, tall and plain—
they expect erotic fire,
but they wait for it in vain.
The main city here is Phoenix—
rather sleepy, rather dull,
all the buildings single-storied,
nondescript . . . "Oh, what a cynic,"
I can hear my readers drawl.
In the evenings, out of bars,
comes the strumming of guitars.
In the mornings, after golf,
stingy gentlemen ride off
in Mercedes, Jaguars . . .
And at middays, with a groan,

everyone, in unison,
cools off with a bit of gin.
Come to Arizona, campers,
where the palm trees reek of camphor!

June 1963

Request

Our world is one of suffering and toil,
yet this spring is the sweetest spring of all—
so sweet that grief itself might crack a smile—
and I'll be turning sixty come next fall.

O ripe old age, I won't try to evade
your blows: my sunken cheeks are at your service.
But please don't rush—you know my bills are paid
and there are pianos waiting to be played . . .
O horses, please don't make the coachman nervous . . .

1963

In Memory of Boris Poplavsky

I knew him in Constantinople,
the Russian Lighthouse, Rue de Brousse,
where, in a worn toupée, a singer
received the refugees' applause,
where ladies, elegantly grazing,
hand fed their erstwhile millionaires,
where, my composer's lyre abandoned,
I dabbled in a stream of verse.
From time to time, for our enjoyment,
the ones in charge would throw a ball,
where, squinting raffishly, Vertinksy,
intoned "Your Fingers Smell of Incense,"
and faeries fluttered through the crowd,
enraptured by the fluty waltzes,
cooling their pallid little foreheads
with rapid flicks of homemade fans.
Through this American-built dwelling
scurried a hungry profiteer:
"Hold on a minute, Mr. Jackson—
five-carat diamond—make a deal?"
There, cast adrift by Reds advancing,
a portly journalist would wail—
this former henchman of Denikin
was craven, voluble, depraved.
A priest, a kindergarten, high school,
the Boy Scouts' Motto: be prepared . . .
for inactivity, monotony—
the fate of children and old men.
Once, in the main room, in the evening,
I saw a youth, his shoulders broad,
off in a corner, leaning slightly—
an athlete, maybe, or a clerk.

Hair parted. Jacket and a bowtie.
I thought, "Some model . . . Drop the pose.
You might be dressed like a romantic,
but you've an onion for a nose."
At sixteen, we're all prone to envy . . .
That jacket's what I hankered for—
unthinkably extravagant;
and yet my dandy was quite poor.
Failing to track down a librarian,
he said: "Poplavsky. Got Renan?"
But he would surely have preferred
a baker with a warm croissant.
We were both young. We got to talking—
a lot of nonsense, truth be known.
But then he read his sweet-stringed poems,
in a peculiar nasal tone.
His lines were awkward and uneven—
strange poison seemed to ooze from them;
the verse of helpless love, it sounded
like sinful cherubs at their song.
Yet they were wonderful, these poems—
yes, they gave off a magic smell.
Each one to me seemed like a window
swung open to an unknown realm.
It was divine—a transformation—
to me his jacket now appeared
to be the toga of young Horace:
from hell to heaven! Then a bar,
where we lapped up the local ouzo
(a blend of anise and wild flames);
poetry's captivating music
flowed in and filled me up again.
. . .

Wore a beret. And slouched a little.
Wasn't a looker, but quite strong.
Adored Rimbaud, the streets, and football.
Was quick to fall in love—headlong.
Even back then, he'd raise a scandal
to ruffle up a boring scene.
Never would he salute a general.
Galata's crooks ate from his hand.
His strange grandiloquence would leave
people bewildered, at a loss,
and yet this Russian Don Quixote
would blush before a buxom lass.
Beneath the careful decoration
and the romantic suit of mail,
there lurked a pitiful, befuddled
hero of unheroic scale.
What bound us to each other? Europe?
No—we took off for different lands.
But there, in gold Constantinople,
we swore we'd stay eternal friends.

1961

Vernon Duke, accomplished composer of modern classical music and important contributor to the Great American Songbook ("April in Paris," "Autumn in New York," "I Can't Get Started," etc.), was born in 1903 in the former Russian Empire as Vladimir Dukelsky and fled war-torn Ukraine with his family in 1919. A friend and collaborator of, on the one hand, George and Ira Gershwin, and, on the other, Sergei Prokofiev and George Balanchine, Duke had a front-row seat to musical history in Paris, London, and New York. Among his major accomplishments was the score to *Cabin in the Sky* (1940), a Broadway musical with an all-black cast. He served in the US Coast Guard during World War II, where he discovered Sid Caesar, then a saxophonist for the Coast Guard Band. In the 1950s he settled in Southern California, where he married the singer Kay McCracken and lived happily until his death in 1969.

Boris Dralyuk is the author of *My Hollywood and Other Poems* (Paul Dry, 2022), editor of *1917: Stories and Poems from the Russian Revolution* (2016), co-editor of *The Penguin Book of Russian Poetry* (2015), and translator of volumes by Isaac Babel, Andrey Kurkov, Leo Tolstoy, and other authors. His poems have appeared in *The New York Review of Books*, *The Hudson Review*, *Raritan Quarterly*, *Best American Poetry 2023*, and elsewhere, and his criticism and translations have appeared in the *Times Literary Supplement*, *London Review of Books*, and *The New Yorker*, among other venues. Formerly editor-in-chief of the *Los Angeles Review of Books*, he is currently a Tulsa Artist Fellow, editor-in-chief of *Nimrod*, and professor of English and Creative Writing at the University of Tulsa.